INVITATION TO World
Religions

INVITATION TO World Religions

SECOND EDITION

JEFFREY BRODD
California State University, Sacramento

LAYNE LITTLE
University of California, Berkeley

BRADLEY NYSTROM
California State University, Sacramento

ROBERT PLATZNER
California State University, Sacramento

RICHARD SHEK
California State University, Sacramento

ERIN STILES
University of Nevada, Reno

Oxford   New York
Oxford University Press

Oxford University Press is a department of the University of Oxford.
It furthers the University's objective of excellence in research,
scholarship, and education by publishing worldwide.

Oxford   New York
Auckland   Cape Town   Dar es Salaam   Hong Kong   Karachi
Kuala Lumpur   Madrid   Melbourne   Mexico City   Nairobi
New Delhi   Shanghai   Taipei   Toronto

With offices in
Argentina   Austria   Brazil   Chile   Czech Republic   France   Greece
Guatemala   Hungary   Italy   Japan   Poland   Portugal   Singapore
South Korea   Switzerland   Thailand   Turkey   Ukraine   Vietnam

Published by Oxford University Press
198 Madison Avenue, New York, New York 10016
http://www.oup.com

Library of Congress Cataloging-in-Publication Data
Brodd, Jeffrey.
   Invitation to world religions / Jeffrey Brodd, California State University,
Sacramento [and 5 others]. -- Second edition.
      pages cm
   ISBN 978-0-19-937836-4
   1. Religions. I. Title.
   BL80.3.B754 2013
   200--dc23

                                                            2015004579

Printing number: 9 8 7 6 5 4 3 2 1

Printed in the United States of America
on acid-free paper

BRIEF CONTENTS

CONTENTS

PREFACE

THE WORLD'S RELIGIOUS TRADITIONS have offered answers to the weightiest questions of human existence, contributed to the formation of political and social institutions, inspired masterpieces of art and literature, and provided many of the cultural values and ideals on which entire civilizations have been based. Today, religions continue to play a powerful role in shaping the ways in which people understand themselves, the world they live in, and how they should live.

Invitation to World Religions, Second Edition, welcomes all students who may come to this course with concerns such as these. In these pages, we open the doors and invite the reader to explore with wonder and respect. We describe the essential features of the world's great religions and show how they have responded to basic human needs and to the cultural settings in which they developed. We also compare the answers religions have offered us regarding some of the most essential human questions—Why are we here? What is the nature of the universe? How should we live? Our aim has been to balance concision and substance in an introductory text that is accessible, as well as challenging.

A team of authors cooperated in writing this book, each one of us bringing our particular scholarly expertise—as well as years of teaching experience—to our respective chapters. We wrote with important learning goals in mind. We want students to gain an objective understanding of the beliefs and practices associated with the world's religions, but we also encourage an empathetic appreciation of what their beliefs and actions actually *mean* to adherents. By emphasizing the connections between religious traditions and their cultural contexts, we seek to heighten awareness of the extent to which religions have influenced, and been influenced by, politics and society, literature, the arts, and philosophy. We also examine the role of religions in our contemporary world, particularly the frequently uneasy boundaries between religion and science, urbanization, and globalization. A thoughtful reading of this book will provide a clear understanding of the characteristics that are unique to individual religions and highlight many of their shared qualities and concerns. Finally, we trust that every reader will find here a means of making sense of other ways of believing and living and of finding a solid basis for the tolerance and respect that are so critically important in times like ours.

Religions are multidimensional. Accordingly, all but the first and last chapters examine three primary aspects of each religion: **teachings**, **historical development**, and **way of life** (practices and experiences). In the second edition, these three aspects are presented in the same order in every chapter in which they appear. Although they appear in the same order, however, we do not strive to devote equal attention to each category. To do so would be to ignore the varying nature of the religious traditions. Judaism, for example, naturally calls for extensive attention to historical development; Jainism, for which an early historical record barely exists, does not. In each case, we shape our coverage in the way that seems most natural given the characteristics of the tradition under discussion.

Teachings. Commonly found in scriptures, myths, creeds, and ethical codes, the basic teachings of a religious tradition convey its answers to fundamental questions, such as: What is the human condition? How can the human condition be improved or transcended? What is the nature of the world? What is ultimate reality, and how is it revealed? The authority on which a religion answers questions such as these is also important. Are its truths revealed? Are they the products of intellectual effort? Are they insights gained in moments of profound psychological experience? Or are they simply traditional ways of looking at reality and our place within it that have been passed down from generation to generation?

Historical Development. Every religious tradition has a history that reveals how and why it developed its distinctive features, including its system of beliefs, leadership and governance structures, social institutions, and forms of artistic expression. Sometimes the forces that generate change arise largely from within a tradition, as in the case of conflict between opposing sects or schools of thought. At other times they operate from the outside, as with the influence exerted by Western powers on foreign colonies and spheres of influence or through the expansion of a tradition into a new cultural milieu. A religion's history also functions to unite the individual with others in a shared memory of the past that helps to explain the present.

Way of Life. By way of life we mean practices—the things people *do* in making practical application of their beliefs, such as engaging in prayer, meditation, communal worship, or various other forms of ritual. Closely related to practices are modes of experience, the ways in which a religion's adherents actually experience the consequences of applying its teachings. These might include a sense of inner peace, a more acute sense of community with others, a greater awareness of the divine, or a state of profound enlightenment.

ORGANIZATION

Our survey begins with an introductory essay on the academic study of religions found in Chapter 1. After considering what religion *is*, Chapter 1 identifies some of the other important questions scholars ask: What do religions do? What issues of universal concern do they address? What do scholars mean when they speak of mystical experience or of transcendence? What are the constituent parts of religious traditions? How are religions today being affected by the forces of modernization, urbanization, globalization, and science? Finally, the chapter explains why a multidisciplinary approach is necessary in any serious attempt to understand the world's religions.

Chapter 1 is followed by two chapters on indigenous traditions. The book concludes with a chapter on new religions. The ten chapters in the middle are organized according to geographical and (roughly) chronological order, as follows: first, the religions of South Asian origin (Hinduism, Buddhism, Jainism, Sikhism); next, those of East Asian origin (Chinese religions, Japanese religions); and, finally, those of West Asian (or Middle Eastern) origin (Zoroastrianism, Judaism, Christianity, Islam). By studying the indigenous traditions first, students will gain an appreciation not only for the many living traditions that continue to thrive but also for certain ways of being religious (such as emphasis on oral transference of myths and other sacred lore) that at one time were predominant in most of today's major world religions. By studying new religions last, students will likewise gain appreciation for living traditions, along with glimpsing the sorts of innovations that occur within the old traditions, too, as religions respond to the cultural, technological, social, and cultural changes and challenges of the world around them.

NEW TO THE SECOND EDITION

- **Modified chapter structure:** We have altered the three-part structure of each chapter, moving the history module earlier, thus allowing a closer alignment of teachings and history. All chapters share a parallel structure: Teachings, History, and Way of Life.
- **Chapter 10, Zoroastrianism:** In response to suggestions from teachers and reviewers, the second edition of *Invitation to World Religions* now includes a full chapter on Zoroastrianism. Dynamically illustrated with images of contemporary practitioners, this new chapter provides students with a compelling opportunity to explore the ancient beliefs that resonate in more familiar religions.
- **Expanded Chapter 14, New Religious Movements:** Chapter 14 now includes new sections on Rastafarianism, Theosophy, and Unitarian Universalism.
- **Comparative questions:** These questions, which appear in the margins of each of the three main sections of Chapters 2 through 13, encourage critical and comparative thinking. As the semester progresses and students increase their knowledge of different religions, these questions provide opportunities for discussion, review, research, and reflection.
- **Enhanced coverage of women in religion:** Although the three-part chapter structure of *Invitation to World Religions* allows integrated coverage of the roles of women in the history, teachings, and practices of each religion, the second edition expands on that coverage with a specific discussion in each chapter of the contributions women make—and the challenges they sometimes face—within each religion.

- **Expanded map program:** To help students better appreciate the geopolitical contexts for religions in our globalized society, many chapters now include maps showing the populations of different religions around the world.

In addition, the chapters on Hinduism and Buddhism have been extensively revised to be more accessible to today's learners.

FEATURES AND PEDAGOGY

Because the concepts and contexts of the world's religions are immeasurably complex, we have worked to present a clear and accessible introductory text. Our tone throughout, while deeply informed by scholarship, is both accessible and appropriate for a wide range of undergraduate students. Consistent chapter structure also helps students to focus on *content* rather than trying to renavigate each chapter anew. With the exception of Chapters 1 and 14, every chapter in the book includes **three core modules: the teachings of the religion, the history of the religion, and the religion as a way of life**. This modular and predictable structure is also highly flexible, allowing instructors to easily create a syllabus that best reflects their own scholarly interests, as well as their students' learning needs.

The study of religions can be daunting to newcomers, who must plunge into a sea of unfamiliar words, concepts, and cultures. For this reason, we have provided a variety of ways for students to engage with important ideas, personalities, and visuals, such as:

- Voices: In personal, candid interviews, a diverse array of people share the ways they live their faith.
- Visual Guide: A key to important religious symbols, provided in an easy-to-read table for quick reference and comparison, is included in each "Way of Life" section.
- Maps and Timelines: Each chapter begins with a map to provide geographical context for a religion's development. Key features and places mentioned in the chapter are called out on the map. A Timeline at the beginning of each chapter provides social and political context to help students situate each religion and trace its development. Finally, a comprehensive Timeline of all the main religions covered in the book now appears on the inside front and back covers.
- Seeking Answers: After each chapter's Conclusion, we revisit three essential questions that religions strive to answer. This feature helps students to review the chapter's key concepts and informs their ability to *compare* constructively the ways in which different religions address the same fundamental human questions:

    1. What is ultimate reality?
    2. How should we live in this world?
    3. What is our ultimate purpose?

Other elements that facilitate teaching and learning include:

- Glossary: Important terms are printed in **bold type** at their first occurrence and are explained in the **Glossary** that follows each chapter. In addition, a glossary at the back of the book includes all of the key terms from the entire text.
- End-of-Chapter Questions: Each chapter concludes with two sets of questions to help students review, retain, and reflect upon chapter content. For Review questions prompt students to recall and rehearse key chapter concepts; For Further Reflection questions require students to think critically about the chapter's nuances and encourage both discussion and personal response by inviting students to engage in a more penetrating analysis of a tradition or taking a comparative approach.
- Suggestions for Further Reading: These annotated lists of some of the best and most recent works on each tradition, as well as online resources, encourage students to pursue their exploration of the world's religions.
- Rich, robust, and relevant visuals: Finally, we have filled the pages of *Invitation to World Religions* with an abundance of color photographs and illustrations that add visual experience to our verbal descriptions of sacred objects, buildings, art, and other material aspects of religious life.

SUPPLEMENTS

A rich set of supplemental resources is available to support teaching and learning in this course. These supplements include an Instructor's Manual, Computerized Test Bank, PowerPoint lecture outlines, and PowerPoint art database on the Oxford University Press **Ancillary Resource Center (ARC)**; a **DVD of CNN Videos** to accompany World Religions courses; Student Resources on a **Companion Website**; integrated and automatically graded Student Resources on **Dashboard** by Oxford University Press; and **Learning Management System** Cartridges with Instructor and Student Resources.

The Oxford University Press **Ancillary Resource Center (ARC)** at oup-arc.com houses the following Instructor's Resources:
- A Computerized Test Bank, including
  - 40 multiple-choice questions per chapter
  - 30 true/false questions per chapter
  - 30 fill-in-the-blank questions per chapter
  - 10 essay/discussion questions per chapter
- An Instructor's Manual, including
  - A "pencil and paper" version of the Computerized Test Bank
  - Chapter Summaries
  - Chapter Learning Objectives
  - Suggested Weblinks and other Media Resources
  - Weblinks to Sacred Texts, accompanied by brief descriptions of their content
  - Lists of Key Terms and their definitions, from the text

- Customizable PowerPoint Lecture Outlines
- A customizable PowerPoint Art Database with images from the text

The **CNN Video DVD with Instructor's Video Guide** offers 15 recent clips on significant beliefs, practices, and places related to a variety of traditions covered in *Invitation to World Religions*. Each clip is approximately five to ten minutes in length and accompanied by a summary and series of discussion and multiple-choice questions. For a sample, please visit the Instructor's Resources page on the Companion Website at www.oup.com/us/brodd. To obtain the complete DVD, available to adopters of any OUP World Religions textbook, please contact your OUP representative or call 1-800-280-0280.

The **Companion Website** at www.oup.com/us/brodd houses links to the Instructor's Resources, as well as the following Student Resources:

- Level-one and level-two Student Quizzes taken from the Test Bank, including
  - 20 multiple-choice questions per chapter
  - 16 true/false questions per chapter
  - 16 fill-in-the-blank questions per chapter
  - 6 essay/discussion questions per chapter
- Chapter Learning Objectives
- Suggested Weblinks and other Media Resources
- Weblinks to Sacred Texts, accompanied by brief descriptions of their content
- Flashcards of Key Terms from the text
- An interactive map showing distributions of religions throughout the world

Student Resources are also available on **Dashboard**, by Oxford University Press. Dashboard delivers a wealth of activities and assessments for *Invitation to World Religions* in an intuitive, text-specific, integrated learning system. The *Invitation to World Religions* Dashboard site houses the following resources:

- Automatically graded level-one and level-two Student Quizzes from the Companion Website, with each question linked to a Chapter Learning Objective for instructor analysis of students' specific strengths and struggles
- Flashcards of Key Terms from the text
- A complete Glossary of Key Terms from the text
- An interactive map showing distributions of religions throughout the world

Access to Dashboard can be packaged with the text at a discount, stocked separately by your college bookstore, or purchased directly at www.oup.com/us/dashboard. For details, please contact your OUP representative or call 1-800-280-0280.

Learning Management System Cartridges are also available for *Invitation to World Religions,* and include the Instructor's Manual, the Computerized Test Bank, and all the Student Resources from the Companion Website. For more information on this, please contact your OUP representative or call 1-800-280-0280.

ACKNOWLEDGMENTS

This book has been a long time in the making. Along the way, family members, friends, and colleagues have supported us with love, patience, insights, and suggestions. We also are grateful to the people who kindly granted us interviews. Although there is no way we can adequately thank them here, we can at least acknowledge them: Edward Allen, Dr. Onkar Bindra, Rabbi Brad Bloom, Jill Brodd, Jon Brodd, Rev. Lucy Bunch, Mary Chapman, Tunay Durmaz, Lin Estes, Rev. Dr. Christopher Flesoras, Rustom Ghadiali, George and Kausalya Hart, Kathleen Kelly, Hari Krishnan, Sammy Letoole, Ray and Marilyn Little, Terrie McGraw, Watanabe Minoru, Annie Nystrom, Festus Ogunbitan, Mia Sasaki, Katherine Sei, Girish Shah, Kitty Shek, Davesh Soneji, Jason Ch'ui-hsiao Tseng, Archana Venkatesan, Krishna and Jayashree Venkatesan, and Fr. Art Wehr, S. J.

We have also benefited immensely from the hard work and good suggestions of colleagues across the country. In particular, we would like to thank:

Kenneth Atkinson, University of Northern Iowa

Robert E. Brown, James Madison University

David Bush, Shasta College

John L. Crow, Florida State University

James Ford, Rogers State University

Matthew Hallgarth, Tarleton State University

Jon Inglett, Oklahoma City Community College

Maria Jaoudi, California State University–Sacramento

Kate S. Kelley, University of Missouri–Columbia

Mirna Lattouf, Arizona State University

Iain S. MacLean, James Madison University

Benjamin Murphy, Florida State University–Panama City

Arlette Poland, College of the Desert

Marialuce Ronconi, Marist College

John Sanders, Hendrix College

Paul G. Schneider, University of South Florida

Joshua Shelly, University of Illinois—Urbana-Champaign

Glenn Snyder, Indiana University–Purdue University Indianapolis

Phillip Spivey, University of Central Arkansas

Dennis P. Tishken, Eastern Florida State College

James A. Zeller, San Joaquin Delta College

We extend our special thanks to Ravi Gupta of Utah State University who responded so very helpfully to our request for expert advice.

We would also like to acknowledge the suggestions of reviewers for the first edition, which continued to inform our work on this new edition:

Asad Q. Ahmed, Washington University in St. Louis

John Baumann, University of Oregon

Todd M. Brenneman, University of Central Florida

Dexter E. Callender, Jr., University of Miami

Philip R. Drey, Kirkwood Community College–Cedar Rapids

James Ford, Rogers State University

Kathleen Hladky, Florida State University

Jeffrey Kaplan, University of Wisconsin–Oshkosh

Brad Karelius, Saddleback College

Erik Larson, Florida International University

Peter David Lee, Columbia College

Wade Maki, University of Toledo

Isabel Mukonyora, Western Kentucky University

Samuel Murrell, University of North Carolina, Wilmington

Tom Norris, Florida International University

Robert Y. Owusu, Clark Atlanta University

Claudia Schippert, University of Central Florida

Theresa S. Smith, Indiana University of Pennsylvania

Hugh B. Urban, Ohio State University

James W. Ward, James Madison University

Keith Welsh, Webster University

Mlen-Too Wesley, Pennsylvania State University–Altoona

David Wisdo, Columbus State University

Finally, we owe a debt of gratitude to the editorial staff at Oxford University Press. Our thanks go to Executive Editor Robert Miller, who originally invited us to publish with Oxford and continues to oversee the project. Robert has put us in the excellent care of Senior Development Editor Meg Botteon, whose professionalism and skill have been an essential guiding force. Editorial Assistant Kaitlin Coats helpfully managed reviews and other editorial tasks, including work with art and images and with the development and production of supplements for the book. Our thanks also go to Senior Production Editors Jane Lee and Theresa Stockton for managing the final stages of the book's production.

INVITATION TO # World Religions

An INVITATION to the STUDY of WORLD RELIGIONS

ON AMERICAN COLLEGE CAMPUSES, indications of the world's religions are readily observable. Bulletin boards bear fliers announcing upcoming events pertaining to Buddhist meditation or Hindu sacred art or the Islamic observance of Ramadan. Campus religious groups engage in outreach activities at tables alongside walkways or in student unions, oftentimes with posters quoting scripture or displaying religious icons. Some icons even commonly adorn the students themselves—a cross necklace, for example, or a tattoo of the *yin/yang* symbol.

To study the world's religions is to progress from mere observation of things to understanding their meaning and relevance. Anyone who observes the *yin/yang* symbol can appreciate the beauty of its spiraling, interweaving symmetry, but studying Chinese religion reveals a much more complex meaning. Mysterious in their origins, *yin* and *yang* are complementary primal energies that give rise to all creation. For the human being, to maintain a perfect balance of *yin* and *yang* is to live an ideal life. The nearly ubiquitous symbol of the cross similarly takes on new depths and complexities of meaning, even for many who identify themselves as Christian, when approached through the study of world religions. To Christians, God, the creator of all things, having taken on human form in the person of Jesus Christ, willingly suffered the painful death of crucifixion on the cross to save humanity from the power of sin.

On many campuses, people of different religious perspectives gather for candlelight vigils to observe times of sorrow as well as celebration.

We can expand on our understanding of the meaning and cultural relevance of these two icons through a brief comparative study. Chinese religion, with its belief in the creative, complementary energies of *yin* and *yang*, has neither need nor room for a creator such as the Christian God. The Christian concept of sin and the corresponding need for salvation are alien to the Chinese quest for balance of *yin* and *yang*. These two icons, in other words, signify profoundly different cultural orientations.

To study the world's religions is to enhance one's understanding and appreciation of the rich variety of cultures around the globe. This chapter introduces this field of study by exploring the significance, examining the foundational concepts, and describing appropriate strategies for the academic exploration of religion. ☀

APPROACHING THE STUDY OF WORLD RELIGIONS

In order to be an educated person today, one must have an awareness of world religions. To learn about this subject matter is to increase one's cultural literacy—the objective that lies at the heart of this study. The religious traditions examined in this book are foundational aspects of cultures around the globe. Religion plays a crucial role in molding, transforming, and transmitting cultures. Interacting and intermeshing with other cultural aspects—politics, economics, aesthetics—religion is arguably a culture's most potent force, in ways both constructive and destructive. When people believe they are acting in a manner that is condoned by a transcendent power or is in keeping with timeless tradition, they tend to act more fervently and with greater potency. In other words, religions are powerful, sometimes even dangerous. Knowing about them is crucial for negotiating our richly complex world.

"World Religions" has been a prominent course of study in American colleges and universities for nearly a century. Recently, the category has come under scrutiny by some scholars, as has the so-called "world religions discourse" that often accompanies it.[1] Although such scrutiny sometimes tends to lose sight of the obvious—that "world religions" as an academic category, whatever its origins, is here to stay and that learning about its subject matter is vitally important—critics are correct to demand sound academic approaches to the study. A primary concern involves the fact that the study of world religions, and indeed the entire enterprise of the academic study of religion, arose within the nominally Christian European intellectual culture that tended to take for granted that Christianity was a model of what a religion ought to be and, commonly, that it was the only *true* religion. Until the late decades of the nineteenth century, theorists applied the term "world religion" (in the singular) only to Christianity. Eventually Buddhism, Judaism, and occasionally Islam were grouped with Christianity as "world religions" (or "the world's religions"). By the 1930s the list had grown to include the ten to twelve religions that still today are normally categorized as world religions.

And so, to the basic need for knowing about the world religions (however they came to be categorized), we can add another vital need: that we go about studying them appropriately through awareness of what we might call the "do's and don'ts" of religious studies, which this chapter explores in some detail. We can begin by noting that an appropriate study of world religions does not privilege any religion as being somehow exemplary or the model with which others are to be compared. On a related note, we need to avoid terms and categories that are rooted in such privileging. For example, "faith" is a natural term to use when studying Christianity, but it can hardly be applied to the study of Confucianism or Shinto. Other important issues involve underlying motives or assumptions that can too easily creep in. A common one is this: All religions ultimately say the same thing. This is an intriguing possibility, but in fact, it is impossible to prove by way of a sound academic approach—that is, well-reasoned theorizing based on careful analysis of the evidence.

The challenge of mastering the "do's" and avoiding the "don'ts" only enriches our study. We begin by considering the rise of the modern academic field of religious studies.

Religion as a Subject of Academic Inquiry

The academic study of religion, commonly known as "religious studies" (or sometimes as "comparative religion" or "history of religions") is a relatively recent development. Prior to the European Enlightenment of the eighteenth century, it rarely occurred to anyone to think of a religion as an entity that could be separated from other aspects of culture, and therefore as something that could be defined as a distinct category and studied as such. Enlightenment thinkers, most influentially the German philosopher Immanuel Kant (1724–1804), conceived of religion as something separate from the various phenomena the human mind is capable of perceiving.[2] This impulse toward categorically separating religion, coupled with European exploration of distant lands and their unfamiliar "religions," launched efforts to understand religion that have continued to the present day. This shift means that we modern observers need to be cautious when appraising the religious aspects of other cultures, lest we make the error of assuming that all peoples have recognized religion as a distinctive category. Most cultures throughout history have had neither the conceptual category nor a term meaning "religion."

The academic study of religion is generally distinct from theology, the field of inquiry that focuses on considering the nature of the divine. Unlike religious studies, theology is an important example of *doing* and *being* religious, which naturally invites consideration of the supernatural and of the "truth" of religious claims. Religious studies, like most other academic pursuits, is to a large extent based in an approach to knowledge that depends on analysis of empirical data. The discourse and actions of human beings can be observed and studied through normal means of academic inquiry; empirical evidence can be gathered, and through rational argumentation hypotheses can be formulated and supported. Supernatural beings and events normally are held to be beyond the reach of academic inquiry. The academic study of religion, as understood by the authors of this book, is therefore not theology, however much we

William James defined religion as "the feelings, acts and experiences of individual men in their solitude. . . ." Caspar David Friedrich depicted the solitary, contemplative individual in his 1818 painting, *Wanderer Above a Sea of Fog*.

World religions today.

might admire theologians and enjoy studying their work, which is itself an important human enterprise and a major component of religion.

The Definitional Challenge

A natural outcome of the Enlightenment impulse toward categorically separating religion from other aspects of culture has been to produce a universal definition of the term. Scholars from various academic disciplines have struggled with this challenge without having produced a single definition that pleases everyone. Many theorists today dismiss the challenge as futile, and some even go so far as to argue that use of the term "religion" in academic study should be abandoned altogether because of its ambiguity and misleading inferences. Most scholars involved in religious studies, however, agree that they are studying basically the same subject, and for lack of a better term most are content with calling it "religion."

The relevance of defining "religion" can be understood through an analogy that compares religions to houses. Embarking on a study of religions without concern over *what*, exactly, we are studying would be akin to setting off for foreign places to explore the nature of houses without first agreeing on what counts as a house. Would we include apartments? Vacation cabins? Palaces? Defining terms helps us draw clear boundaries around the subject of study. Another challenge involves our preconceived notions of things. We might assume that everyone shares a common idea of a typical "house" (like the kind we learned to draw in grade school), but such an assumption is mainly the result of preconceptions based on our own culture's norms. People from other cultures might dwell in structures that have little in common with our standard notion of a house.

Let's consider some notable attempts at conceptualizing "religion" while keeping in mind our "house" analogy. In fact, when exploring the more specific category "world religion," it will be useful to think of a similarly more specific category of house: a mansion, and more specifically, an old mansion that has undergone a long process of refurbishing. Although certainly considered a type of house, a mansion has many rooms that serve a wide variety of functions and styles. Imagine an old mansion that has kept the same foundation and basic structure over the years, but to which various inhabitants have made changes that have enabled the structure to survive into modern times. Our study of the world's religions is an invitation to explore several extraordinary "old mansions." Our tools of study—beginning with considerations of definition—are designed to help us make the most of our explorations, to take in fully the teachings, the histories, and the practices of the world's religions.

Three Classic Definitions

The history of the attempt to formulate suitable definitions of "religion" is intriguing. In many instances, definitions reveal as much about the historical era and about the intentions of the individual theorist as they do about the nature of religion.

The following well-known definitions of "religion" were set forth by notable theorists in different fields:

A religion is a unified system of beliefs and practices relative to sacred things, that is to say, things set apart and forbidden—beliefs and practices which unite into one single moral community called a Church, all those who adhere to them.[3]

—Émile Durkheim

[Religion is] . . . the feelings, acts and experiences of individual men in their solitude, so far as they apprehend themselves to stand in relation to whatever they may consider the divine.[4]

—William James

[T]he religious aspect points to that which is ultimate, infinite, unconditional in man's spiritual life. Religion, in the largest and most basic sense of the word, is ultimate concern.[5]

—Paul Tillich

French sociologist Émile Durkheim (1858–1917), a founding figure of the sociological study of religion, emphasizes in his definition the *social* nature of religion. He insists on the unification brought about by "beliefs and practices," culminating in a "moral community called a Church." Durkheim surely hits on some central functions of religion, but most scholars contend that he overemphasizes this social orientation. On the other hand, American psychologist William James (1842–1910) emphasizes the *individual* nature of religion. Although this aspect is also clearly important, his definition omits any mention of religion's social nature. The definitions put forth by Durkheim and James, although provocative, are therefore problematically limiting.

Paul Tillich (1886–1965), a Protestant theologian, naturally connects religion to a focus on "man's spiritual life." His notion of religion as "ultimate concern" has been quite influential over the past several decades, probably in part because many find it true to their own experiences. But the definition is very broad, and it says nothing regarding the specific content of religious traditions. In emphasizing the existential concerns of religion, it neglects the social and institutional components of the traditions. People commonly claim to be "spiritual" while also denying that they belong to a religion. A sound definition needs to accommodate this distinction or else avoid this ambiguity altogether.

Two Prominent Definitions Let us now consider two definitions of religion that currently enjoy wide favor and that avoid these sorts of shortcomings. The *HarperCollins Dictionary of Religion*, a popular reference work, states: "One may clarify the term religion by defining it as a system of beliefs and practices that are relative to superhuman beings."[6] This definition encompasses a wide array of cultural phenomena, while at the same time restricting the category, most especially with the concept "superhuman beings."

Bruce Lincoln (b. 1948), one of the most prominent contemporary theorists of religion, asserts in his definition that a religion always consists of four "domains"—discourse, practice, community, and institution:

1. A discourse whose concerns transcend the human, temporal, and contingent, and that claims for itself a similarly transcendent status . . .
2. A set of practices whose purpose is to produce a proper world and/or proper human subjects, as defined by a religious discourse to which these practices are connected . . .
3. A community whose members construct their identity with reference to a religious discourse and its attendant practices . . .
4. An institution that regulates religious discourse, practices, and community, reproducing them over time and modifying them as necessary, while asserting their eternal validity and transcendent value.[7]

Lincoln's definition, although considerably lengthier than the *Dictionary*'s, is impressively precise. It also is helpfully inclusive. By basing religion on the notion of the "transcendent" rather than on "supernatural beings" or the like, Lincoln's definition encompasses Confucianism and forms of Buddhism, including Theravada, that do not focus on belief in supernatural beings. (Chapters 5 and 8 explore in more detail the categorization of Buddhism and Confucianism, respectively, as religions rather than "philosophies".) The religions featured in this textbook conform to Lincoln's definition. This is not to say that Lincoln, or for that matter any other theorist, has determined what religion "truly" is. In the words of sociologist Peter Berger (b. 1929), commenting on the challenge of defining religion, "a definition is not more or less true, only more or less useful."[8] For purposes of our study, Lincoln's definition provides a useful means of categorizing the subject matter. It clarifies why the traditions featured in this book qualify as religions while also, especially with its insistence that a religion involves an "institution," establishing helpful limits. The general category "spirituality," for example, would not necessarily qualify as religion based on Lincoln's definition.

We now shift our focus from what religions *are* to consider what religions *do*. In the next section, we analyze various functions of religion, concentrating especially on the fundamental questions to which religious traditions provide answers.

WHAT RELIGIONS DO

Whatever one thinks a religion *is*, this much remains certain: a religion *does*. This fact is closely related to the challenge of defining religion. Some theorists have emphasized this functional side of religion in their explanations. Underlying Durkheim's definition, for example, is a theory that reduces religion to being an effect of societal forces. Religion, in turn, serves to promote social unity. Here is a clear case in point that definitions reveal as much about the intentions of the theorist as they do about the nature of religion. As we have already noted, Durkheim is regarded as a founder of sociology;

it is not surprising that he emphasizes the social aspects of religion. Consider also this assertion from psychologist Sigmund Freud (1856–1939):

> Religion would thus be the universal obsessional neurosis of humanity; like the obsessional neurosis of children, it arose out of the Oedipus complex, out of the relation to the father.[9]

Freud was an atheist whose psychological theory held religion to be undesirable. Political philosopher Karl Marx (1818–1883), likewise an atheist, offers a similarly negative assessment, which is even more antagonistic toward religion:

> *Man makes religion*, religion does not make man. In other words, religion is the self-consciousness and self-feeling of man who has either not yet found himself or has already lost himself again. But *man* is no abstract being squatting outside the world. Man is the *world of man*, the state, society. . . . Religion is the sigh of the oppressed creature, the heart of a heartless world, just as it is the spirit of a spiritless situation. It is the *opium* of the people.[10]

At sites like this Confucian temple in Beijing, China, Confucius (Master K'ung) is honored for his enduring contributions to Chinese culture. Sound definitions of "religion" are flexible enough to include Confucianism as a religious tradition.

Marx, strongly affected by what he perceived as the economic disparities of the Industrial Revolution, was a thoroughgoing materialist who dismissed all forms of ideology as being abstractions and, to some extent, obstacles to the pursuit of true well-being. Freud similarly regarded religion as an effect of other forces, viewing it as a by-product of psychological forces. According to Freud, religion functions as an unhealthy but soothing buffer against the inner terrors of the psyche. For Marx, religion functions in a similarly unhealthy manner, as an opiate that deters the suffering individual from attending to the true cause of affliction.

These functionalist explanations, although provocative and at least somewhat insightful, are largely regarded now by scholars as being severely limited in their perspectives. Perhaps religions *do* function in these ways at certain times in certain situations; but surely religions do much more. In fact, neither Freud nor Marx ever actually tried to define religion; rather, they tried to explain it away. This does not diminish, however, the enduring relevance of these theorists for purposes of striving to understand the "big picture" of the role religion plays in the lives of individuals and in societies.

We can widen our vantage point on the functions of religion and produce a fairer and more accurate depiction by considering the variety of life's challenges that these traditions help people to face and to overcome.

Religious Questions and Challenges

It might seem disrespectful or even blasphemous to ask, Why do religions exist? But in fact this is a perfectly legitimate and instructive question. As human enterprises, religions naturally respond to human needs and readily acknowledge reasons for their doctrines and rituals. A typical reason has to do with some kind of perceived separation from the sacred or estrangement from a state of perfection or fulfillment. The human condition, as ordinarily experienced, is regarded as being disconnected from the fulfillment that lies at the end of a spiritual path. Various related questions and challenges are addressed by religions, with these three prominent questions recurring in some form in nearly every system:

1. What is ultimate reality?
2. How should we live in this world?
3. What is our ultimate purpose?

The rest of this book's chapters explore the ways major religions answer these questions. For now, let's consider these questions more broadly.

What Is Ultimate Reality?   It is difficult to imagine a religion that has nothing to say about ultimate reality—even if this involves asserting that "ultimate" reality consists of no more than the natural world and we human beings who inhabit it. Religions typically assert that ultimate reality is somehow divine, and explanation of the nature and role of the divine takes center stage in a religion's belief system. But the "divine" is not necessarily thought of as God or gods. When it is, we refer to that religion as a **theistic** (from Greek *theos*, or god) belief system. When it is not, the religion is said to be **nontheistic**. Some forms of Buddhism, such as Zen, are clearly nontheistic. A helpful middle ground descriptive term is **transtheistic**, acknowledging the existence of gods—but of gods that are not vital with regard to the most crucial religious issues, such as the quest for enlightenment or salvation.[11]

Theistic religions can be further categorized. **Polytheism** (from Greek *polys*, or many) is the belief in many gods ("gods" is considered a gender-neutral term and can—and often does—include goddesses). **Monotheism** (from Greek *monos*, or only one) is the belief in only one god (and hence the term is normally capitalized—God—a proper noun referring to a specific being). Here, a kind of middle ground comes in the form of **henotheism** (from Greek *hen*, the number one), which acknowledges a plurality of gods but elevates one of them to special status. Some forms of Hindu devotion to a particular god such as Vishnu or Shiva are henotheistic.

Pantheism (from Greek *pan*, or all) is the belief that the divine is identical to nature or the material world. Although not one of the world's living religions, the ancient Greek and Roman religious philosophy known as Stoicism is an example. It is important to bear in mind, too, that the world's religions often feature entities that are supernatural and yet are not necessarily gods. These quasi-divine figures, such as angels, demons, and the monstrous characters that feature prominently in myths, are typically difficult to categorize but are important elements of religion nonetheless. To complicate matters further, scholars of non-Western religions have commonly used the term "god" to refer to supernatural beings that are more similar to angels, or even to the saints of Catholic tradition. The *theos* in the "polytheism" of such non-Western religions therefore often refers to a very different type of being than does the *theos* in "monotheism." Simplistic application of such terms is misleading.

Nontheistic belief systems include those that uphold **atheism**, which in modern parlance is a perspective that denies the existence of God or gods. In ancient times, a person could be labeled an atheist for denying the significance of deities, even while believing that they exist. Among the ancient Greeks and Romans, for example, Epicureans were considered to be atheists. Even according to the modern meaning of atheism, some atheists nevertheless could be regarded as religious—depending on how one defines "religion." The *HarperCollins Dictionary of Religion* definition, with its basis in "supernatural beings," likely would not leave room for atheism, whereas Bruce Lincoln's definition could. (The issue of atheism as religious or not is taken up in "The New Atheism" section of Chapter 14.)

This painting, produced in 1810, depicts the Hindu deities Shiva and Parvati with their children, Ganesha and Kartikeya. Hindus believe in many gods and goddesses, these four—and especially Shiva—being among the most popular.

Nontheistic religions (and here the term is on surer footing) also include those that conceive of the divine as an impersonal force or substratum of existence. Some nontheistic religions, such as various forms of Buddhism (Chapter 5) and Hinduism (Chapter 4), even assume the existence of divine beings while rejecting the notion that such beings can truly help humans find spiritual fulfillment. Some Hindus, for example, while believing in many gods and goddesses, hold that Brahman, impersonal and ultimately indescribable, is the essence of all. Those Hindus therefore embrace **monism** because of this primary belief that all reality is ultimately one. Monism is also described as nondualistic, because there is no distinction between the divine reality on one hand and the rest of reality, including human individuals, on the other.

Such a categorizing scheme admits to some complications. Some Hindus are monistic because they understand all reality ultimately to be one thing: Brahman. But some of those same monistic Hindus also pay homage to a variety of supernatural and divine beings, and thus might also be described as polytheists.

Along with asserting the existence of ultimate reality, religions describe how this reality is revealed to human beings. The foundational moments of **revelation** are frequently recorded in sacred texts, or scriptures. In the case of theistic religions, scriptures set forth narratives describing the role of God or the gods in history and also include pronouncements directly attributed to the divine. In the Jewish and Christian Bible, for example, God's will regarding ethical behavior is expressed directly in the Ten Commandments. The giving of the Ten Commandments is described in the long narrative about the Exodus of the Israelites from Egypt, in which God is said to have played a central role.

Among nontheistic religions in particular—but also among the mystical traditions that form part of every religious tradition—revelation usually combines textual transmission with a direct experience of revelation. Revelation is usually experienced by a founding figure of the religion, whose experiences are later written about; subsequent believers can then experience similar types of revelation, which requires their own participation. Buddhists, for example, have scriptural records that describe the Buddha's experience of "unbinding" or release, as well as pronouncements by various deities praising the ultimate value of that experience. Followers must then connect to such revelation through practices such as meditation.

Another helpful way of thinking about revelation is offered by historian of religions Mircea Eliade (1907–1986), who makes much descriptive use of the phenomenon he calls "hierophany," or "the *act of manifestation* of the sacred," which helps a people to establish its cosmology, or religious understanding, of the order of the world.[12] Eliade emphasizes how this concept applies to indigenous or small-scale traditions (those of "archaic man" in Eliade's terminology). But the phenomenon of the hierophany is readily apparent within the world's major religions, often, but not always, as a theophany, a manifestation of God or of gods. The role of hierophanies in establishing places of special significance can be observed in many of the sites related to the founding figures and events of the major religions: Christianity's Church of the Nativity (and other sacred sites related to the life of Christ); Islam's sacred city of Mecca; Buddhism's Bodh Gaya, site of Gautama's foundational experience of Enlightenment; and so on. Sacred moments establish sacred spatial monuments, thus establishing a sense of centrality and spatial order.

Along with often referring to other worlds, religions have much to say about *this* world. Human beings have always asked searching questions about the origin and status of our planet and of the universe. Typically these two issues—origin and status—are intertwined. If our world was intentionally fashioned by a creator god, for instance, then it bears the stamp of divine affirmation. Thus the early chapters of the Book of Genesis in the Hebrew Bible (the Christian Old Testament) describe the measured, creative activity of God, including the creation of humankind. In contrast, the creation stories of some religious traditions deemphasize the role of the divine will in bringing about the world, sometimes (as in the religion of the ancient Greeks) describing the advent of the principal deities *after* the universe itself has been created. The gods, like humans, come into a world that is already established; gods and humans are depicted as sharing the world, which naturally affects the relationship between human and divine. In other religions,

Ka'ba, Mecca.

notably those same South Asian traditions that embrace liberation as the ultimate religious objective, this world is depicted as a kind of illusion, somehow not altogether real or permanently abiding. It is thus not so surprising that liberation involves being completely freed from the confines of this world.

These are but a few examples of religious understanding of the nature of the world, a general category known as **cosmology** (from *kosmos*, the Greek term for world or universe). Along with clarifying the origin and sacred status of the world, cosmology also explains how the world is ordered. Many traditions attribute the order of the universe to the doings of divine being(s) or forces. Yet in certain respects modern scientific explanations set forth cosmologies that are intriguingly similar to some religious cosmologies taught by religious personages of the distant past,

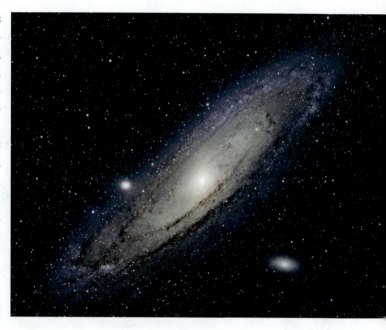

The Andromeda Galaxy.

such as Gautama the Buddha or Epicurus, a Greek philosopher who espoused a theory of atomism, arguing that reality is composed entirely of a very large number of very small particles. (Recall that the Epicureans were labeled "atheists" because they denied the significance of the gods.)

Of course, a particular religion's cosmology strongly influences the degree to which its adherents are involved in caring for the world. Religions that are indifferent or hostile toward the natural world are not apt to encourage anything akin to environmentalism. On the other hand, a religion that teaches that the world is inherently sacred naturally encourages a sense of stewardship toward the natural world. Native American traditions, for example, are notably environmentally oriented.

How Should We Live in This World? Many religions have much to say about God or other superhuman beings and phenomena, and yet all religions are human enterprises. Their teachings are communicated in human languages, their rituals are practiced by human participants, and their histories are entwined with the development of human societies and cultures. Religions also explain what it is to be a human being.

Explanations regarding what it is to be human also figure largely into ethical or moral considerations. Are we by nature good, evil, or somewhere in between? Religions tend to recognize that human beings do not always do the right thing, and they commonly offer teachings and disciplines directed toward moral or ethical improvement. To say that we are by nature good, and at the same time to recognize moral failings, is to infer that some cause external to our nature is causing the shortcoming. If we are by nature evil, on the other hand, or at least naturally prone to doing

Sixteenth-century triptych (altar painting) depicting the creation of Eve (center), the eating of the forbidden fruit (left), and the expulsion from the Garden of Eden (right). This story of humankind's first sin sets forth basic biblical perspectives on the human condition.

wrong, then the moral challenge lies within and the means of improvement would need to be directed inwardly.

Religions typically prescribe what is right behavior and what is wrong, based on a set of ethical tenets, such as the Jewish and Christian Ten Commandments. In fact, the very prospects of improving upon the human condition and of faring well in an afterlife quite commonly are deemed to depend in some way upon right ethical behavior. The ethical teachings of many religions are notably similar. The so-called Golden Rule ("Do unto others what you would have them do unto you"[13]) set forth in the Christian New Testament is pronounced in similar forms in the scriptures of virtually all of the world's major traditions.

The religions differ, however, over the issue of the source of ethical truth. Some emphasize **revealed ethics**, asserting that God, or some other supernatural force such as Hindu *dharma* (ethical duty), has established what constitutes right behavior and has in some manner revealed this to human beings. The divine will might be conceived of as God (or gods), or it might take the form of an impersonal principle, such as *dharma*. Another common approach, in some forms of Buddhism, for example, emphasizes the role of conscience in the moral deliberations of each individual. These two emphases are not necessarily mutually exclusive. Some religions, Christianity among them, teach that both revealed ethics and individual conscience work together as means of distinguishing right from wrong.

What Is Our Ultimate Purpose?

The challenge of mortality—the fact that we are destined to die—is sometimes cited as the primary motivating force behind religion. And although it is true that all religions have at least something to say about death, the wide diversity of perspectives is quite astounding. For example, whereas Christianity, with its focus on the resurrection of Christ and the hope of eternal life, can be said to make mortality a central concern, Zen Buddhism, drawing inspiration from the classic Daoist texts, refuses to make much at all of death beyond acknowledging its natural place in the order of things.

Both the challenge of mortality and the issue of our moral nature relate to questions regarding the human condition—and what can be done about it. In many faiths, how we conduct ourselves in this world will determine our fates after we die. Most religions readily acknowledge that human beings are destined to die (although some, such as Daoism, have at times aspired to discover means of inducing physical immortality). As we have noted, some religions have little to say about the prospects of life beyond death. But most religions do provide explanations regarding the fate of the individual after death, and their explanations vary widely.

Hinduism, Buddhism, Jainism, and Sikhism all maintain belief in *samsara*, the "wheel of life" that implies a series of lives, deaths, and rebirths for every individual. The ultimate aim of each of these religions is liberation from *samsara*. Buddhist nirvana is one such form of liberation. But most of the adherents of Buddhism and these other religions anticipate that death will lead to rebirth into another life form (not necessarily human), one in a long series of rebirths. Furthermore, the reborn are destined for any one of multiple realms, including a variety of hells and heavens.

Other religions, notably Christianity and Islam, teach that individuals are destined for some sort of afterlife, usually a version of heaven or of hell. Sometimes the teachings are more complicated. The traditional Catholic doctrine of purgatory, for example, anticipates an intermediary destiny somewhere between the perfect bliss of heaven and the horrible agony of hell, where an individual can gradually be purified from sin, ultimately achieving salvation and entry to heaven.

Given what a religion says about the human condition, what ultimate purpose is the religious life intended to achieve? Is there a state of existence to which the religious person can hope to aspire that perfectly completes or even transcends the human condition, overcoming entirely its cares and shortcomings?

One such state of existence is the **numinous experience**, as described by Rudolf Otto in his classic work *The Idea of the Holy* (1923). Otto (1869–1937), a Protestant theologian and a philosopher of religion, describes the encounter with "the Holy" as "numinous," a term he coined from the Latin *numen*, meaning spirit or divinity (plural, *numina*). A genuine numinous experience, Otto asserts, is characterized by two powerful and contending forces: **mysterium tremendum** and **fascinans**. *Mysterium tremendum*, which in Latin means "awe-inspiring mystery," is the feeling of awe that overwhelms a person who experiences the majestic presence of the "wholly other."[14] *Fascinans* (Latin, "fascinating"), is the contrasting feeling of overwhelming attraction. The encounter with the Holy is thus alluring (*fascinans*) even as it is frightening on account of the awe-inspiring mystery (*mysterium tremendum*). The biblical phenomenon of the "fear of God" fits this description, as the God who is being feared is at the same time recognized as the source of life and the hope for salvation.

Otto's insightful analysis of the numinous experience suffers from a significant limitation: based in his Protestant Christian outlook, it may ring true to a Protestant; from a global perspective, however, the analysis is rather limiting. For example, Otto discounts the **mystical experience**, a category that includes such phenomena as Buddhist nirvana, the complete dissolution of an individual's sense of selfhood said

Moses and the Burning Bush (1990), charcoal and pastel on paper by Hans Feibusch. In the drawing, God reveals himself to Moses in a bush that is on fire but not consumed by the flames. The event is described in Exodus, the second book of the Hebrew Bible (Old Testament).

by Buddhists to be a state of perfect bliss and ultimate fulfillment. According to Otto, nirvana involves too much *fascinans* without enough *mysterium tremendum*.

Recall that Bruce Lincoln's definition of religion is based on the notion of the transcendent. Both the numinous experience and nirvana are examples of transcendent states of existence. For Otto, the numinous experience depends on the existence of "the Holy," or God. For many Buddhists, the experience of nirvana does not depend whatsoever on belief in God or gods. Most world religions, whether they embrace belief in a supernatural being or not, assert the possibility of such a transcendent state of existence, an ultimate objective of the religious life that brings complete fulfillment of all spiritual longings. For a Buddhist who has experienced nirvana, for example, there is, paradoxically, no longer a need for Buddhism. The religious life has been lived to its fullest extent, and the ultimate objective has been reached. Because nirvana involves the complete extinction of individual existence, it is truly transcendent of the human condition. Other religions, in widely varying ways, also set forth ultimate objectives, whether or not they imply the complete transcendence of the human condition. In some cases spiritual fulfillment can be said to consist of living in harmony with nature. Others readily acknowledge the supernatural—usually God (or gods)—and the need for human beings to live in perfect relationship with it. Christianity, for example, offers salvation from the effects of sin, which otherwise estrange the individual from God. Sometimes spiritual fulfillment is thought to be achievable in this lifetime; other times it is projected into the distant future, after many lifetimes of striving and development.

Of course, improving upon the human condition does not have to involve complete transcendence or anything close to it. Day to day the world over, religious people improve upon the human condition in all sorts of ways. Belief in a loving God gives hope and fortitude in the face of life's uncertainties. Meditation and prayer bring an enhanced sense of tranquility. Religious motivations often lie behind charitable acts. Belonging to a religious group offers social benefits that can be deeply fulfilling. Even for individuals who do not participate directly in a religious tradition, sacred art, architecture, and music can bring joy to life.

DIMENSIONS OF RELIGIONS

Sound definitions strive to be universal in scope. Along with a sound definition, a means of categorizing the common, though not necessarily universal, components of a subject of study can often prove beneficial. We now explore possibilities for identifying religious phenomena, in part to bring home the important point that there is no "right" or "wrong" way to go about categorizing them. Instead, we seek the most useful means given the task at hand. This will lead naturally to clarifying how this book goes about organizing its presentation of material.

Some scholarly approaches to the world's religions feature specific categories of phenomena as the primary means of organizing information. Religious scholar Ninian Smart's (1927–2001) "dimensional" scheme, for example, divides the various aspects of religious traditions into seven dimensions:

- The mythic (or sacred narrative)
- The doctrinal (or philosophical)
- The ethical (or legal)
- The ritual (or practical)
- The experiential (or emotional)
- The social
- The material[15]

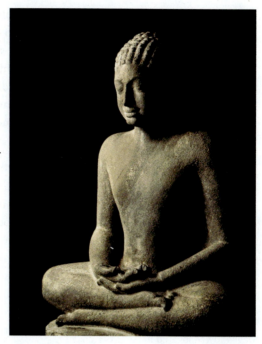

Meditating Buddha, sixth century C.E. (Thai). Sculptures of the Buddha typically depict the serene calm of the enlightened state.

Such an approach to the content of religious traditions is very useful, especially if one focuses on a comparative analysis that emphasizes particular motifs (that is, "dimensions" or aspects thereof).

In this book, we organize things into three main categories: teachings, historical development, and way of life. Although each chapter of this book is organized around these three main categories, we do not strive in all chapters to devote equal attention to each category. To do so would be to ignore the varying nature of the religious traditions and to force an inappropriately rigid structure. Judaism, for example, calls for extensive attention to historical development in order to best understand the context of its teachings and practices; Jainism, for which an early historical record barely exists, does not.

Teachings

Obviously, religions tend to involve beliefs. But as long as they remain private to the individual, beliefs are problematic for the student of religion. As public elements of a religion's teachings, however, beliefs can be observed and interpreted. Such public beliefs are manifested as doctrines or creeds—sets of concepts that are *believed in*. (The term "creed" derives from the Latin verb *credo*, or "I believe.") Among the world's major religions, Christianity most emphasizes doctrines. Most Christians, for example, regularly acknowledge belief in the statements of the Nicene Creed.

Religious teachings include another significant category, often referred to as **myth** (as noted in Smart's "mythic" dimension). Quite in contrast to the modern connotation of myth as a falsehood, myth as understood by the academic field of religious studies is a powerful source of sacred truth. Set forth in narrative form and originally conveyed orally, myths do not depend on empirical verifiability or rational coherence for their power. They are simply accepted by believers as true accounts, often involving events of primordial time that describe the origin of things.

As we have noted previously, religions typically include ethical instructions, whether doctrinal or mythic, among their teachings. And as Smart readily acknowledges, the various dimensions are closely interrelated; the ethical dimension, for example, extends into the doctrinal and the mythic, and so forth.

Historical Development

It almost goes without saying that the world's major religions—all of which are many centuries, even millennia, old—have long and intricate histories. Thus the historical development of religious traditions incorporates a vast sweep of social, artistic, and other cultural phenomena.

The wide array of artistic, architectural, and other aspects of material culture generated within religious traditions is of course obvious to anyone who has studied art history. The ornate Hindu temple sculptures, the majestic statues of Jain *tirthankaras*, the mathematically ordered architectural features of Islamic arabesque décor—these, among countless other examples, attest to the extensive role of religion in the nurturing of material culture. Other forms of artistic creation, most prominently music and theater, also are common and significant features of religions. And, as Smart helpfully clarifies when discussing the material dimension of religion, natural entities (mountains, rivers, wooded groves) are designated as sacred by some traditions.

Devils Tower, located in northeastern Wyoming, is regarded as a sacred place by many Native Americans.

Social institutions and phenomena of various sorts—economic activities, politics, social class structures and hierarchies—have typically played highly influential roles in the historical development of religious traditions. As we have observed, Marx and Durkheim went as far as to reduce religion to being entirely the effect of economic and societal forces, respectively. Even for theorists who opt not to go nearly as far as this, the relevance of such phenomena is obvious.

Way of Life

This main category tends to feature two general types of religious phenomena: practices and modes of experience. Recall that Smart includes the ritual (or practical) and the experiential (or emotional) among his seven dimensions of religion. Some such elements are tangible and readily observable and describable, such as a **ritual** like the exchange of marriage vows or the procession of pilgrims to a shrine. Others are highly personal and therefore hidden from the outsider's view. One of the great challenges of studying religions rests precisely in this personal, private quality. Modes of experience such as Buddhist nirvana are by definition beyond the reach of empirical observation and of description. Rudolf Otto, throughout his analysis, emphasizes the impossibility of describing the "numinous" experience fully. Even common practices such as prayer and meditation tend to involve an inner aspect that is highly personal and quite inaccessible to anyone who is not sharing the experience. A book such as this one can do its best to illustrate and to explain these experiential phenomena but cannot be expected to provide a full disclosure at certain points. Such is the nature of religion.

RELIGIONS IN THE MODERN WORLD

A sound analysis of the world's religions must pay heed to the rapid changes that characterize the modern world. Historical transformations, accelerated during the past several centuries by such diverse and powerful factors as colonialism, the scientific revolution, and economic globalization, have reshaped religious traditions. This book takes into account such factors whenever appropriate. Here we introduce four specific phenomena that will reappear frequently in the pages that follow: modernization, urbanization, globalization, and multiculturalism. We give special attention to two features of modernization that are especially noteworthy for our study: the increasingly visible place of women within religious traditions and the encounter of religion and science.

Modernization and Related Phenomena

Modernization is the general process through which societies transform economically, socially, and culturally to keep pace with an increasingly competitive global marketplace. Its net effects include increased literacy, improved education, enhanced technologies, self-sustaining economies, the increased roles of women in various aspects of society, and the greater involvement of the general populace in government (as in democracies). All these effects involve corresponding changes within religious traditions.

Higher literacy rates and improved education, for example, facilitate increased access to religious texts that previously were controlled by and confined to the religious elite. Technological advances, strengthened economies, and increased participation in government all nurture greater equality for and empowerment of the common people. A general feature of modernity, moreover, is its tendency to deny the authority of tradition and the past. Traditional patriarchal modes, for example, have tended over time to be diminished. Around the globe, we are witnessing a general erosion of long-standing power structures within religions. Obviously this is not the case in all circumstances; changes have tended to occur in different societies at different times, and some religious institutions are better equipped to ward off change. But over the long haul, modernization clearly has influenced the reshaping of religious traditions.

Urbanization   A significant demographic effect of modernization is **urbanization**, the shift of population centers from rural, agricultural settings to cities. A century ago, only about 10 percent of the global population lived in cities; today, more than half of us are urbanites. Many religious traditions developed within primarily rural settings, patterning their calendars of holy days and rituals around agricultural cycles. Such patterns have far less relevance today for most religious people.

Trinity Church, built in 1846, sits amidst the skyscrapers of Wall Street in New York City.

Globalization   **Globalization** is the linking and intermixing of cultures. It accelerated quickly during the centuries of exploration and colonization and has been nurtured considerably by the advanced technologies brought about by modernization. The extent of this linking and intermixing is evinced in the very term "World Wide Web," and the pronounced and rapidly evolving effects of the Internet and other technologies have been extraordinary. The almost instantaneous exchange of information that this technology allows is more or less paralleled by enhanced forms of affordable transportation. In sum, we now live in a global community that could hardly have been imagined a few decades ago.

Multiculturalism   The most pronounced religious effects of globalization pertain to the closely related phenomenon of **multiculturalism**, the coexistence of different peoples and their cultural ways in one time and place. Many people today live in religiously pluralistic societies, no longer sheltered from the presence of religions other than their own. This plurality increases the degree of influence exerted by one religion on another, making it difficult for many individuals to regard any one religious tradition as the *only* viable one. This circumstance, in turn, fosters general questioning and critical assessment of religion. To some extent, such questioning and critical assessment erodes the authority traditionally attributed to religion. Globalization, then, like modernization, has nurtured the notably modern process of **secularization**, the general turning away from traditional religious authority and institutions.

The Changing Roles of Women in Religions

One of the more pronounced effects of modernization on world religions has been the increased visibility and prominence of women within many traditions. To some extent this increase also has *caused* the furtherance of modernization. As women increasingly feel themselves empowered and are afforded opportunities to effect change, their momentum propels modernizing transformations. Traditional patriarchal modes have tended to give way to more egalitarian ones, and old assumptions have gradually receded. To cite just one example, the percentage of clergy in Protestant Christian churches who are women has recently risen quite dramatically. According to a 2009 survey, in 1999 5 percent of senior pastors were female; ten years later this had doubled to 10 percent.[16]

Corresponding to the increased visibility and prominence of women in many religions has been the dramatic development over the past five decades of feminist theory and its application to the study of religion. Sometimes referred to as women's studies or as gender studies, academic approaches based in feminist theory have revealed the strong historical tendency of religious traditions to subordinate women and to enforce the perpetuation of patriarchal systems. On the one hand, these studies have revealed contributions of women through the ages that have hitherto been largely ignored, while on the other hand they have prompted changes within some religions that have expanded the roles of women and have provided opportunities for higher degrees of prominence. In other words, studies based in feminist theory have to some extent *changed* the religions themselves, along with providing new and potent means of studying them.

The Encounter of Religion and Science

Perhaps no single feature of modernization has been more challenging to traditional religious ways—and more nurturing of secularization—than the encounter of religion with science. One need only think of the impact of Charles Darwin's *Origin of Species* (1859) and its theory of evolution to note the potential for conflict between scientific and traditional religious worldviews. The question of whether the biblical account of creation should be taught alongside the theory of evolution in schools is a divisive issue in some predominantly Christian societies today. In the domain of cosmology, too, science has tended to overwhelm traditional perspectives, such as the idea that the Earth is somehow the center of the cosmos, as implied in the Bible and in the creation myths of many traditions.

Many more examples could be drawn from the history of religions and the history of science to illustrate the ongoing potential for conflict between these two domains.

Of course, religions are not always hostile to science. In fact, as we have already noted, sometimes modern scientific theories seem almost to converge with ancient religious outlooks. Acquiring a more sophisticated perspective on the encounter of religion and science requires us to consider the underlying reasons for both conflict and convergence.

Fundamental to the scientific method is dependence on empirical data, the observable "facts" of any given situation. To a large extent, religions do not rely only on the observable as a source of determining truth. Religious belief is often characterized precisely by commitment to the *non*observable, such as a supernatural being. This very term, "supernatural," indicates another, related point of contention between religion and science. For whereas the latter takes for granted that the universe consistently obeys certain laws of nature, religions commonly embrace belief in beings and events that are not subject to these laws.

And yet, these issues of natural laws and of the observable versus the unobservable also lead to points of convergence between science and religion. Certain basic and extremely significant scientific questions remain unanswered. For example, what is the ground of consciousness? What causes gravity? What existed, if anything, prior to the Big Bang, and what caused *its* existence? Science and religion can perhaps generally agree over this: mystery abounds. Granted, the scientific response to a mystery is "let's solve it," whereas the religious response typically is, "this is a mystery and is meant to be." But in the meantime, mystery abides, allowing for a certain kind of convergence. It is probably no accident that the percentage of scientists in the United States who regularly attend religious services is almost the same as the percentage for the general population.[17]

AN ACADEMIC APPROACH TO THE STUDY OF RELIGIONS

Scholars approach the study of religion in a variety of ways. And although there is no such thing as *the* correct approach, it is helpful to keep some basic concepts in mind.

Balance and Empathy

One concept is the maintenance of a healthy balance between the perspective of an insider (one who practices a given religion) and the perspective of an outsider (one who studies the religion without practicing it). For, although an insider arguably has the best vantage point on the lived realities of the religion, presumably the insider is primarily concerned with *being* religious and not in explaining the religion in a manner most effective for those who hold other religious (or nonreligious) perspectives. It is quite natural for an insider to feel bias in favor of his or her own religion. The outsider, on the other hand, would have no reason to feel such bias. But the outsider would not have the benefit of experiencing the religion firsthand. It is analogous to trying to understand a goldfish in a pond. An outsider can describe the fish's color, its movements, its eating habits. But the outsider can say very little about what it is actually like to be a goldfish.[18]

The academic approach to the study of religions attempts to balance the perspectives of insider and outsider, thereby drawing upon the benefits of each. It is not an intentionally religious enterprise. As we have noted previously, it is not *doing* religion or *being* religious, unlike theology. Instead, it strives to analyze and describe religions in a way that is accurate and fair for all concerned—insiders and outsiders alike. An instructive parallel can be drawn from the discipline of political science. Rather than advocating a particular political point of view, and rather than *being* a politician, a political scientist strives to analyze and describe political viewpoints and phenomena in a fair, neutral manner. A good political scientist could, for instance, belong to the Democratic Party but still produce a fair article about a Republican politician—without ever betraying personal Democratic convictions. A good scholar of religion, of whatever religious (or nonreligious) persuasion, attends to religious matters with a similarly neutral stance.

Another basic concept for the academic approach to religion is **empathy**, the capacity for seeing things from another's perspective. Empathy works in tandem with the usual tools of scholarship—the observation and rational assessment of empirical data—to yield an effective academic approach to the study of religions. The sometimes cold, impersonal procedures of scholarship are enlivened by the personal insights afforded by empathy.

A miniature illustration from the "Automata of al-Jazari," a Muslim scholar, inventor, engineer, mathematician, and astronomer who lived from 1136 to 1206.

Comparative and Multidisciplinary Approaches

A sound study of the world's religions also features a comparative approach. The chief benefit of this was emphasized by the nineteenth-century scholar Friedrich Max Müller (1823–1900), who is generally regarded as the founder of the modern field of religious studies. He frequently asserted that to know just one religion is to know none. In other words, in order to understand the phenomena of any given tradition, it is necessary to study other traditions, observing such phenomena as they occur in a wide variety of situations. This naturally requires that the study of world religions be cross-cultural in scope. As we proceed from chapter to chapter, the usefulness of comparison will become more and more evident.

This is not to say that comparison should be undertaken haphazardly or with intention only to discover similarities while ignoring differences. Those critics mentioned earlier who deride the "world religions discourse" tend to be suspicious of attempts at comparison, claiming that too often similarities are indeed valued over differences and that the categories used to make comparisons tend to privilege Christianity over other traditions. Sometimes the results of the comparison of religion differentiate religions into groups that are too sweepingly general: for example, "Eastern" and "Western" religions. Still, the benefits of comparative analysis outweigh the risks, and the potential pitfalls that these critics appropriately warn against can indeed be avoided through a conscientious approach.

Along with being cross-cultural, religious studies is multidisciplinary, or poly-methodic, drawing on the contributions of anthropology, history, sociology, psychology, philosophy, feminist theory, and other disciplines and fields of study.

This chapter on many occasions has made use of the term *culture*, the study of which is the domain of anthropology. We have noted that religion plays a crucial role in molding, transforming, and transmitting cultures and that it interacts and inter-meshes with other cultural aspects. A sound study of the world's religions requires careful consideration of the interrelationship between religion and culture; in other words, it requires a healthy dose of cultural anthropology.

The need for involvement of the other disciplines should be likewise apparent. Given their historical and social aspects, the appropriateness of the disciplines of history and sociology for the study of religions is to be expected. And especially when trying to make sense of the modes of religious experience, psychology offers important inroads to understanding that the other disciplines are not equipped to provide. Along with Freud and James, whose definitions we have considered, Swiss psychologist Carl Jung (1875–1961) deserves mention for his vital contributions to the study of religious symbolism and of the general role of the unconscious mind in the religious life. The philosophy of religion, in certain respects the closest to actually *doing* religion (or theology), endeavors to assess critically the truth claims and arguments set forth by religions. Questions involving the existence of God, for example, are among those taken up by philosophers. Feminist theory, as noted previously, has contributed substantially toward advancing the study of world religions. Theories and methods of the natural sciences also have contributed substantially, at a pace that is accelerating rapidly. The widest array of innovations has come from cognitive science, which studies both the physical capacity for thinking (i.e., the "brain"—although this category can also include computers and other systems of artificial intelligence) and mental functions (i.e., the "mind"). Cognitive science is itself a multidisciplinary field with contributors who include neuroscientists, evolutionary biologists, and computer scientists, along with specialists from the social sciences.

Suffice it to say that the multidisciplinary nature of religious studies accounts for its very *existence* as an academic discipline. Without the involvement and contributions of its many subdisciplines, there could be no academic field of religious studies.

CONCLUSION

In this chapter, we have explored the nature of religion and how to study it from an academic perspective. The main objective is to prepare for the study that follows, a chapter-by-chapter examination of the major religions of the world. But the relatively theoretical and methodological content of this introductory chapter is relevant and challenging in its own right. Indeed, some readers might be surprised to learn that the search for an adequate definition has posed a daunting challenge or that the study of religion requires special means of approach. Hopefully these same readers have come to recognize the complexity of the ideas and the challenge of the task without feeling daunted about going forward with our study.

We have noted that the rest of this book's chapters feature a threefold organizational scheme consisting of teachings, historical development, and way of life. Although these chapters, with their focus on the religious traditions themselves, naturally are quite different from this introduction, it is worth noticing that in this chapter, too, we have featured historical development—of both the attempts to explain or define religion and the approaches to studying it—and teachings, most especially the theories of various notable contributors to religious studies. The "way of life" aspect perhaps has been less obvious, but in fact it is important and deserves consideration as we end the chapter. On more than one occasion we have drawn a distinction between the academic study of religion and *doing* religion or *being* religious. Where, then, does this leave the individual who wants to do (and be) both? Ultimately, this is a question to be left for the individual reader to ponder. But it might prove helpful to know that the degree of *being* religious among scholars of religion spans the spectrum of possibilities, from not religious at all to highly devout. Either way (or someplace in between), one thing is true for all who venture forth to study the world's religions: we are investigating important and enduring aspects of human cultures, down through the millennia and around the globe. Our understanding of things that matter is sure to be enriched.

REVIEW QUESTIONS

For Review

1. Who is Émile Durkheim, and what is notable about his definition of religion?
2. Bruce Lincoln, in his definition of religion, identifies four "domains." What are they?
3. What is "revelation," and how is it pertinent to the question: What is ultimate reality?
4. Identify and briefly describe Ninian Smart's seven "dimensions" of religion.
5. What is "empathy," and how is it relevant for the academic study of religion?

For Further Reflection

1. Sigmund Freud and Karl Marx, while tending to be dismissive of the enduring importance of religion, asserted explanations that continue to provoke and to enrich academic consideration of the role of religion. Based on their statements included in this chapter, how might their perspectives be provocative and enriching in this respect?
2. This chapter and book pose three prominent questions with regard to the challenges addressed by the world's religions: What is ultimate reality? How should we live in this world? What is our ultimate purpose? Drawing on examples and ideas presented in this chapter, discuss to what extent and in what ways these three questions are interrelated.
3. Explore the interrelationship of these features of religions in the modern world: globalization, secularization, and multiculturalism.

GLOSSARY

atheism Perspective that denies the existence of God or gods.

cosmology Understanding of the nature of the world that typically explains its origin and how it is ordered.

empathy The capacity for seeing things from another's perspective, and an important methodological approach for studying religions.

globalization The linking and intermixing of cultures.

henotheism The belief that acknowledges a plurality of gods but elevates one of them to special status.

modernization The general process through which societies transform economically, socially, and culturally to become more in keeping with the standards set by industrialized Europe.

monism The belief that all reality is ultimately one.

monotheism The belief in only one god.

multiculturalism The coexistence of different peoples and their cultural ways in one time and place.

mysterium tremendum and fascinans The contrasting feelings of awe-inspiring mystery and of overwhelming attraction that are said by Rudolf Otto to characterize the numinous experience.

mystical experience A general category of religious experience characterized in various ways, for example, as the uniting with the divine through inward contemplation or as the dissolution of the sense of individual selfhood.

myth A story or narrative, originally conveyed orally, that sets forth basic truths of a religious tradition; myths often involve events of primordial time that describe the origins of things.

nontheistic Term denoting a religion that does not maintain belief in God or gods.

numinous experience Rudolf Otto's term for describing an encounter with "the Holy"; it is characterized by two powerful and contending forces, *mysterium tremendum* and *fascinans*.

pantheism The belief that the divine reality is identical to nature or the material world.

polytheism The belief in many gods.

revealed ethics Truth regarding right behavior believed to be divinely established and intentionally made known to human beings.

revelation The expression of the divine will, commonly recorded in sacred texts.

ritual Formal worship practice.

secularization The general turning away from traditional religious authority and institutions.

Stoicism Ancient Greek and Roman pantheistic religious philosophy.

theistic Term denoting a religion that maintains belief in God or gods.

transtheistic Term denoting a theological perspective that acknowledges the existence of gods while denying that the gods are vital with regard to the most crucial religious issues, such as the quest for salvation.

urbanization The shift of population centers from rural, agricultural settings to cities.

SUGGESTIONS FOR FURTHER READING

Eliade, Mircea. *The Sacred and the Profane: The Nature of Religion*. Translated by Willard R. Trask. New York: Harper and Row, 1961. Eliade's most accessible work, offering a rich analysis of sacred space and time.

Hinnels, John, ed. *The Routledge Companion to the Study of Religion*. 2nd ed. Oxford: Routledge, 2010. Coverage of significant issues in religious studies by leading scholars.

(continued)

Masuzawa, Tomoko. *The Invention of World Religions: Or, How European Universalism Was Preserved in the Language of Pluralism*. Chicago: University of Chicago Press, 2005. Careful historical analysis of the term and category "world religions."

Pals, Daniel. *Eight Theories of Religion*. 3rd ed. New York: Oxford University Press, 2014. The best introduction to the history of religious studies as an academic field, including chapters on Karl Marx, William James, Sigmund Freud, Émile Durkheim, and Mircea Eliade.

Smart, Ninian. *Dimensions of the Sacred: An Anatomy of the World's Beliefs*. Berkeley and Los Angeles: University of California Press, 1996. An engaging presentation of Smart's "dimensions."

Smith, Jonathan Z. *Imagining Religion: From Babylon to Jonestown*. Chicago Studies in the History of Judaism. Chicago and London: University of Chicago Press, 1982. A collection of essays that exemplify Smith's impressively wide-ranging and astute approach to the study of religion.

Taylor, Mark C., ed. *Critical Terms for Religious Studies*. Chicago: University of Chicago Press, 1998. Articles on various central topics for the study of religions, written by leading scholars in the field.

ONLINE RESOURCES

American Academy of Religion
aarweb.org
The largest and most influential North American academic society for the study of religion.

Pew Research Religion and Public Life Project
pewforum.org
Excellent source of information on issues involving social and political aspects of religion.

The Pluralism Project at Harvard University
pluralism.org
Offers an impressive array of helpful resources, especially with regard to the world's religions in North America.

INDIGENOUS RELIGIONS of NORTH AMERICA

THE HOT AFTERNOON SUN beats down on the eighteen men and women who dance in patterned formation in the midst of a circular enclosure. Caleb, a twenty-six-year-old medical technician from Rapid City, South Dakota, is one of the Eagle Dancers. Caleb and the others dance to the rhythmic beating of a large drum, their faces turned upward to the eastern sky. This is the sixth time this day that the group has danced, each time for forty minutes, each time gradually shifting formation in order to face all four directions, honoring the spirit beings of the East, the South, the West, and the North. One more session of dancing, later this afternoon, will bring to an end this year's annual **Sun Dance**. The Sun Dance is a midsummer Native American ritual that spans nearly two weeks, culminating in four days of dancing. This Sun Dance, in the wilderness of the Pacific Northwest, is open to all participants—from all Native American nations and even non-Native Americans.

In the center of the circular enclosure stands a remarkable tree. Perhaps a hundred bundles of colorful cloth hang from its boughs. Its central limbs hold a branch of chokecherry, from which hang effigies of a buffalo and of a man. The cottonwood tree was carefully selected months in advance for this purpose, then ceremoniously felled the day before the dancing began and carried many miles to be positioned at the enclosure's center.

This photo from 1910 shows several Cheyenne people gathered in preparation for a Sun Dance ceremony.

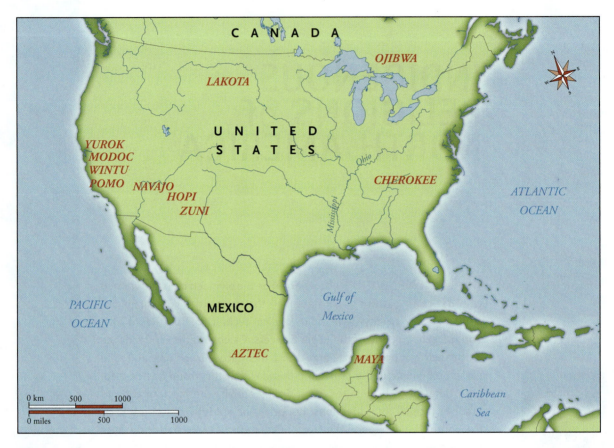

Indigenous peoples of North America that are discussed in this chapter.

The tree's significance for all those gathered at the Sun Dance can hardly be overstated. Due to the ritual of the dancing, the circle for these four days is sacred space. The tree stands at the center and marks the most sacred space of all. In fact, it is the tree that *establishes* the circle and defines the sacred space. Added to this is the significance of its verticality. By reaching upward, the tree is thought to be the point of contact with the spirit world that connects the sacred expanse of the sky to the sacred space of the circle and to Caleb and the dancers. In every respect, the cottonwood tree is a kind of **axis mundi** (Latin, "the center of the world"), a symbol that scholars of religious studies and mythology have recognized in cultures and traditions globally. Planted in the earth, reaching skyward, and establishing the sacred enclosure of the Sun Dance, the tree is perceived by the participants as being the center of the world—and of reality itself.

Caleb is a member of the Lakota Nation, a people of the Northern Plains. Caleb is a very special type of dancer known as an Eagle Dancer. He and the two other Eagle Dancers dance attached to ropes that are strung from the tree's trunk and looped around skewers that were pierced through the skin of their chests on the first day of dancing. At the end of the fourth day, they will fall back on their ropes, pulling the skewers free from their flesh. This act is considered a sacrifice to the Great Spirit, or God, a gift of the one thing that is truly one's own to give—one's being. The Eagle Dancers spend almost the entire four days in the midst of the sacred circle, enduring the days' heat and the nights' chill, and taking neither food nor drink. Though he is a young man, Caleb has spent several years preparing for this Sun Dance, the first summer of three in which he will be an Eagle Dancer. Training under the guidance of a Lakota healer, Caleb has practiced the difficult arts of fasting and enduring the heat.

As the temperature hovers near 100 degrees, the dancers gradually complete this round. The challenges of the fast and the hot sun are especially daunting for the three Eagle Dancers. As the youngest and least experienced of the Eagle dancers, Caleb has difficulty enduring the harsh conditions and the rigors of the dance. He nearly faints on several occasions.

The Sun Dance incorporates many ritual features: the sounds of the beating drum, often accompanied by chanting of sacred words; the sights of the tree and the dancers; the smell of cedar smoke used to ritually purify the grounds and participants; and, for the Eagle dancers, the experiences of fasting and the acts of sacrifice. The cumulative effects of these features are self-evident to Caleb and the others involved. The perception of sacred space, with the tree as *axis mundi*, is complemented and enhanced by the perception of sacred *time*. The usual partitioning of everyday life is superseded by the ritualized stages of the dancing and of the ceremony at large. For Native Americans like Caleb, these effects tend to induce a state of heightened awareness of the spirit world—and of the Great Spirit, or God.

TIMELINE
North American Religions

20,000 years ago Anthropologists believe humans migrated to the Americas from Asia.

300–900 C.E. The Mayan culture is flourishing; elements of *Popol Vuh* seen in hieroglyphic script.

700–1400 The city of Cahokia is inhabited in Illinois.

900–1519 The Mayan cities decline; major urban centers are deserted.

1050 The first pueblos are built in the American Southwest.

1100–1519 The Aztec civilization thrives.

1492 Columbus arrives in the Americas.

1513 The Spanish arrive in Florida.

1519 The Spanish arrive in Mexico; Hernan Cortes.

1540s The Spanish arrive in southwestern United States.

1550s First written copy of the *Popol Vuh*.

1565 The Spanish establish St. Augustine in Florida.

1560s First French colony in Florida.

1607 The English establish Jamestown.

1700s The *Popol Vuh* written in Quiché Mayan language in Roman script.

1857 The *Popol Vuh* published in Spanish language.

1819 The Civilization Fund Act is passed.

1870 The First Ghost Dance.

1889 Wovoka's vision.

1890 The Second Ghost Dance.

December 29, 1890 Tragic battle at Wounded Knee ends the Ghost Dance.

1904 The Sun Dance banned in the United States.

1918 The Native American Church is founded.

1978 The American Indian Religious Freedom Act is passed.

1995 The use of peyote is made legal for religious purposes.

The Sun Dance has been practiced for centuries by many Native American tribes of the Northern Plains. Details have varied, depending on particular tribal traditions. The Sun Dance retains its importance today and is becoming more popular as Native peoples strive to rediscover and to nurture traditions rooted in the past. No one ritual, however important or popular, can exemplify the religious practices of all

Native Americans. Still, the Sun Dance features certain elements—such as the *axis mundi*, the perception of sacred space and sacred time, and the communing with the spirit world—that are quite common to the religions of North America. ☀

In this chapter, we will explore indigenous religions of North America. Because these religions are so numerous, we will not attempt to discuss them all but rather will select examples from a few. It is important to observe that these religions are not relics of the past. Although they are practiced on a smaller scale, they are not simpler or more basic than large religions like Christianity, Buddhism, or Islam. Therefore, they should not be considered evidence of a "primitive" or less developed religious mentality. Rather, Native American religions are highly complex belief systems, with sophisticated cosmologies and firm ethical principles. Although followers, like Caleb, certainly inherit ideas and practices from their ancestors, the religions are not simply copies of ancient religions. They have changed—and continue to change—in response to interaction with other belief systems, other cultures, and technological advances.

Although we explore these religions together in a single chapter, it is important to note that there is much diversity in the indigenous religions of North America. Today, more than 700 tribal nations are recognized in the United States alone. In the past, there were many more. The human landscape of North America changed dramatically with the arrival of Europeans. Prior to European contact, the population of the Americas as a whole was estimated to be as high as 100 million. However, due to disease and conquest, the Native population throughout the Americas was decimated, and it is likely that some religious traditions were lost forever.

There is much diversity in Native American religious traditions, but there are also some common patterns in Native American religious practice, teachings, and historical development. Ritual practices like the Sun Dance are found in many Native American religions. Also, many religions share the belief that the sacred coexists with and infuses everyday life. Similarly, many share a belief in the interconnectedness of all things in the natural world and thus emphasize the importance of reciprocal relationships between humans and other elements of the natural world. Also, although these religions each have individual histories, they have faced similar issues and events in modern times, particularly with the European conquest of the Americas.

THE TEACHINGS OF NATIVE AMERICAN INDIGENOUS RELIGIONS

We will begin our exploration of Native American religions by looking at the belief systems and teachings of some of these religions. Because they are complex and varied, we will focus our attention primarily on elements of belief that are common in many Native religions. We will look particularly closely at beliefs about creation and human origins, the interrelationship of humanity and other elements of the world, and the nature of sacred language.

Most Native American religions do not have a specific creed or statement of belief. Rather, essential teachings are revealed in mythic narratives and shared and enacted through religious practice. As we learned in Chapter 1, all religions have a mythic component. The religions of North America have especially rich and detailed sacred narratives. Myths contain sacred knowledge about the world, humanity, and the meaning of existence. It is through hearing and retelling myths that people commit this knowledge to heart and pass it on to the next generation. In most Native religions, knowledge is highly valued, and those people who have it are greatly respected. With their intriguing characters and compelling stories, myths are a powerful way for people everywhere to learn about their origins, the supernatural, and ethics and morality. As in other religions, the myths of Native American religions also provide guidelines for human behavior, relationships, and ritual practice.

Creation and Origins

Creation stories abound in the myths of native North America, and there is a remarkable variety in types of creation narratives. Some myths focus on the creation of the earth and the origins of humans in general, and others simply account for the origins of one particular people. Some myths tell of people coming to the surface of the earth from deep underground, and others tell of humans being fashioned from corn by creator gods. Despite this diversity, most Native American mythologies regard the Americas as the original ancestral home.

The Creators and Sacred Power In Native American myths, acts of creation are most often attributed to superhuman beings, often referred to simply as "creators." Because of the vast differences between Native religions, it is difficult to make generalizations about Native conceptions of superhuman beings. Some Native religions, like those of the Great Plains tribes, hold a belief in a Supreme Being, sometimes known as the Great Spirit. Such religions, like the religion of the Lakota, may also teach that all elements of creation, both animate and inanimate, contain the spiritual essence of the Great Spirit. Sometimes, the Supreme Being is thought to be somewhat removed from the day-to-day lives of human beings. Spirits or lesser deities, however, may be more active in everyday human affairs.

Many Native American religions also share a belief in a supreme force or sacred power. This sacred power may be manifest in different ways. It may be inherent in parts of the natural world or may be an important quality of gods or other supernatural beings. The Navajo of the southwestern United States teach of a **Holy Wind**, which is a spiritual force that inhabits every element of creation. The Holy Wind enters living beings through their own breath and directs their actions and thoughts. In this way, the Holy Wind connects all living things.

The Aztecs of central Mexico recognized a sacred power that infused elements of everyday life and supernatural beings. Aztecs also recognized many different deities, who possessed different aspects of sacred power. Some deities were associated with the power of creation and fertility, and others with the sun. The god **Quetzalcoatl**, who is often depicted as a feathered serpent, was thought to possess the sacred power of creation. Many mythic narratives surround Quetzalcoatl. One myth teaches that he assisted with creation by providing food and nourishment for the Aztec people. As a result, he is regarded as an important cultural hero in Mexico.[1]

Human Origins and Human Ancestors   The creation narratives of indigenous North American religions differ significantly from each other in their accounts of the origin of humans. Some myths describe how humans were created, and others focus on how they came to live in a particular geographic locale. Despite such differences, however, North American Native myths often teach that human beings and human ancestors originated in the Americas. This belief contradicts anthropological theories that the Americas were settled by people from Asia tens of thousands of years ago.

The Mayan people of Central America have very complex creation narratives. Mayan cultural roots go back thousands of years. Although most myths of the Americas have been transmitted orally, the Maya have an ancient written language and texts that contain their mythic heritage. The Quiché Maya, one of several Mayan ethnic groups, are from the highlands of Guatemala. The Quiché creation epic, known as the *Popol Vuh*, contains stories about creation, the exploits of the gods, and the first humans. The written text of *Popol Vuh* in the Quiché language dates back several centuries.

The *Popol Vuh* contains a dramatic account of the creation of the first humans. The creator gods attempted to make humans several times but failed in their first three attempts. The first time, the gods succeeded in creating animals, but they could only squawk and chatter—they could not speak. This disappointed the gods, who wanted humans to be able to worship them with spoken language. The second time, the creators made humans out of mud, but the clumsy figures just melted away. The third time, the gods fashioned wooden manikins. The manikins looked human and could talk, but they were cruel and heartless. The *Popol Vuh* tells that these manikins became the first monkeys. Finally, the creators mixed cornmeal with water to fashion human beings. This attempt was successful, and the humans could talk, think, and worship the gods.[2]

Think about the nature of sacred narratives, or myths, in Native American and other religious traditions. Do myths play a similar or different role across religions? How so?

Other Native American myths do not describe the creation of humans, but instead account for their emergence on the surface of the earth. The Zuni live in the southwestern United States. In Zuni mythology, a god called Awonawilona created the world from his own breath and body. At the time of creation, the ancestors of the Zuni lived underground in dark and unpleasant conditions. Eventually, two warrior gods were created. They led the ancestors out from under the earth to live on its surface in the sun. Zuni mythology teaches that the Zuni were the first people on the surface of the earth, but every few years the earth would open again and another people would emerge. The Zuni regard the other Southwest peoples who followed them, like the Navajo and the Hopi, as their younger siblings.[3]

Navajo creation myths similarly describe the ancestors of humans, sometimes known as **Holy People**, emerging from under the surface of the earth. The myths tell that ancestors of the Navajo lived a stressful and conflict-ridden life underground. This unpleasantness was due to the inherent chaos of their environment—there was neither order nor purpose to life under the earth, and people behaved badly toward one another. To escape the turmoil, the ancestors traveled through many subterranean worlds in search of one in which order would prevail. They finally emerged on the surface of the earth. First Man and First Woman were born, and it was their responsibility to help create this world.

This seventh- or eighth-century vase from Guatemala depicts scenes from the *Popol Vuh*.

The ancestors prepared the world for humans through specific rituals using special objects. The rituals established order and served as the foundation for Navajo religious practice, even as practiced today. In one ritual, the ancestors created a painting on the ground, in which they depicted all that was going to exist in the world. Then, through prayer and song, the real world came to be from this wonderful painting. In stark contrast to the chaos underground, the world was perfectly balanced and ordered. Eventually, an important figure known as **Changing Woman** was born. She gave birth to heroic twins, who prepared the way for humanity by vanquishing monsters that roamed the earth. Then, Changing Woman created the first Navajo people from her own body.[4]

In some religions, ancestors are the spiritual representations of what humans can hope to become. The Pueblo peoples are cultures of the Four Corners region of the American Southwest that include the Hopi and the Zuni. Among the Pueblo peoples, ancestral spirits are known as **kachinas**. Kachinas, which may take the form of animals, plants, or humans, represent the spiritually perfect beings that humans become after they die. The Hopi believe that in this life, humans are spiritually imperfect. But in the afterlife, the Hopi leave their human nature behind and become unsullied spirits. Humanity's spiritual imperfection is represented in public dances and ceremonies by clowns. This is because, in Hopi mythology, a clown led human beings as they emerged from the ground. In some of these ceremonies, masked dancers portraying the kachina spirits tell the clowns to mend their imperfect ways and strive to be better human beings. When the dancers don the masks, the kachina spirits inhabit and inspire them.[5]

Life Lessons in Myths

Native American mythologies contain teachings about how to live properly in the world. From myths, people learn to live respectfully with others in society, to make a living off of the land, and to understand the meaning of life. In many Native myths, these lessons are taught through the exploits of a character known as a **trickster**. The trickster figure is often an animal who has adventures and engages in all manner of mischief. In many myths, the trickster suffers repercussions because of his failure to follow established rules about social behavior. Because of this, those hearing the myth are warned about the importance of proper behavior.

One trickster tale featuring Coyote comes from the Pima of Arizona. In the past, Bluebird was an unattractive color. The bird decided to bathe in a special blue lake every morning for four days. After the fourth dip in the lake, the bird grew beautiful blue feathers. Coyote, who was green at the time, saw the beautiful color and asked Bluebird how he could become beautiful, too. The bird explained his method, and Coyote turned a beautiful blue. Coyote was very proud, and he looked around arrogantly as he walked to make sure he was being admired. But he did not watch where he was going, and he tripped and fell in the dirt. When he got up, he was the color of dirt, and now all coyotes are dirt-colored.[6] This short tale teaches an important lesson about the dangers of arrogance.

Myths of North America may also account for the origins of subsistence activities, such as hunting and farming. Often, the subsistence practices of a people are said to have been determined by the gods. This divine origin of daily activity casts everyday life and everyday activities, such as planting crops or preparing food, in a sacred dimension.[7]

Consider, for example, the many diverse myths about the origins of corn. Corn, or maize, has been a staple crop of great importance throughout North America. Some myths explain that human beings have a special duty to raise corn. Myths may tell of a particular god who is responsible for providing the crop or for protecting the fertility of the earth. The Cherokee, historically of the southeastern United States, tell a myth in which the goddess Corn Woman produced corn through the treachery of her son and his playmate. In the myth, Corn Woman rubbed her body to produce food. One day, the two boys saw her doing this. They thought she was practicing witchcraft and so decided to kill her. After they attacked her, she instructed the boys to drag her injured body over the ground. Wherever her blood fell, corn grew. This myth teaches about the relationship between life and death: the blood that causes death can also produce life.[8]

Many other myths teach about life and death. The following passage from the *Popol Vuh* is a moving speech made by the heroic twin gods to the maiden Blood Moon. At this point in the myth, the lords of the underworld have defeated the twins. The severed head of one of the twins has been placed in a tree, and his skull impregnates the maiden with his spittle when she holds out her hand. Blood Moon will eventually bear the next generation of hero twins who avenge their fathers' deaths and prepare the world for the arrival of humans. In the twins' poignant speech to the maiden, we learn something about the Mayan view of the meaning of life: even after death, we live on in our children.

And then the bone spit out its saliva, which landed squarely in the hand of the maiden. . . .

"It's just a sign I have given you, my saliva, my spittle. This, my head, has nothing on it—just bone, nothing of meat. It's just the same with the head of a great lord: It's just the flesh that makes his face look good. And when he dies, people get frightened by his bones. After that, his son is like his saliva, his spittle, in his being whether it be the son of a lord or the son of a craftsman, an orator. The father does not disappear, but goes on being fulfilled. Neither dimmed nor destroyed is the face of a lord, a warrior, a craftsman, orator. Rather, he will leave his daughters and sons. So it is that I have done likewise through you. Now go up there on the face of the earth; you will not die. Keep the word. So be it."[9]

Stories of heroic twins are also common in other indigenous American mythologies. This shows an important degree of continuity between traditions throughout regions of North America. As you recall, Navajo mythology includes a similar tale of heroic twins preparing the world for humanity. The Apache, also of the southwestern United States, share a similar tale.

The Importance of Balance: Humanity and the Natural World

Many indigenous North American religions emphasize the interrelationship of all things. As we saw earlier, the elements of creation, humans included, are often thought to share a common spiritual energy or sacred power. This may be understood as a life force or as the presence of the Supreme Being. This idea is beautifully captured by the words of **Black Elk** (1863–1950), a famous Lakota religious leader. In a book titled *Black Elk Speaks* (1972), he tells of his life and of a great vision. He opens by saying: "It is the story of all life that is holy and is good to tell, and of us two-leggeds sharing in it with the four-leggeds and the wings of the air and all green things; for these are the children of one mother and their father is one spirit."[10]

This interconnectedness often extends to humanity's relationship with animals. In some teachings, humanity is created as the companion of other creatures—not as their master. In other traditions, humans are thought to be descended from animal or animal-like ancestors. A myth of the Modoc of Northern California tells of the special relationship between humans and grizzly bears. The Sky God created all creatures and also created Mt. Shasta, a 14,000-foot volcanic peak, which served as the home for the Sky God's family. One day, his daughter

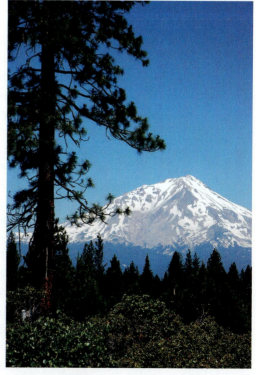

Mt. Shasta, in northern California, is regarded as sacred by many tribes in the region.

fell to earth from the top of the mountain. She was adopted and raised by a family of grizzly bears, who could talk and walk on two feet. Eventually, she married one of the bears, and from this union were born the first people. When the Sky God eventually found his daughter, he was angry that a new race was born that he had not created. He then cursed the grizzly bears to forever go about on all fours.[11]

As a result of this interconnectedness, many Native American religions emphasize the importance of maintaining balance among all things. Often, this is viewed as the primary responsibility of humanity. A critical part of religious practice is therefore focused on developing and preserving harmonious relationships between humans and other elements of the world. As we have learned, Navajo myths tell that the ancestors learned to maintain this balance as an example to later generations. The myths of the Yurok of Northern California similarly describe a time when the Immortals inhabited the earth. The Immortals knew how to maintain balance, but humans did not. Thus, the Immortals taught the Yurok people ceremonies that they could use to restore the balance of the earth.[12]

Sacred Places and Spaces   The focus on balance extends to the physical landscape. According to Native American religious traditions, humanity is often thought to live in a reciprocal relationship with the land: each relies on and must care for the other, and all are part of a sacred whole. Certain geographical features, like rivers, mountains, and rocks, may be permeated with sacred power. Such places often feature prominently in mythology and are infused with power because of what happened there in the mythic past. One such place is Mt. Shasta. Many tribes of the region regard the mountain as sacred because of its importance in mythology. Myths tell that the Creator made the mountain so he could reach the earth from the heavens. (As we saw in the Modoc myth, the Creator resided in the mountain with his family.) Because of its sacred history, areas of Mt. Shasta are powerful places where Native religious experts can make contact with the spirit world. To this day, leaders from several tribes use the area for religious ceremonies.

Among the White Mountain Apache of Arizona, the significance of certain places comes alive in the stories people tell about them. Tales about the local landscape are an important part of Apache cultural and religious knowledge, and they convey important moral teachings. The landscape is thus imbued with life lessons. An Apache woman named Annie Peaches told the anthropologist Keith Basso (b. 1940–2013) about a place called "Big Cottonwood Trees Stand Here and There." In the tale, the Apaches and the neighboring Pima were fighting at the place of the big cottonwood trees. The fighting awakened a sleeping old woman, but she thought the noise was simply her son-in-law cursing her daughter. She yelled at him and told him to stop picking on the young woman. The Pima heard her, rushed in, and killed her. The tale illustrates the danger of disregarding appropriate behavior: in Apache culture, a woman should not criticize her son-in-law unless her daughter asks her to intervene. The old woman suffered dire consequences from interfering, and when Apache people pass the place known as Big Cottonwood Trees Stand Here and There, they are reminded of this social rule.[13]

Myths that cast the land in a sacred light may also teach people how to build their communities. Thus, even architecture has a sacred dimension. Among the Navajo, the guidelines for building the sacred dwelling known as a ***hogan*** are found in myth. The Holy People taught that a *hogan* should be built as representation of Navajo lands and the cosmos. Four posts, which represent four sacred mountains that surround the Navajo homeland, support the *hogan*. The roof represents Father Sky, and the floor is Mother Earth. The ***tipi***, a typical structure of the tribes of the Great Plains, has a similar sacred blueprint. Each *tipi* is an image of the universe. The perimeter of the *tipi* is the edge of the universe, and the lit fire in the center represents the center of all existence. Joseph Epes Brown, a scholar of Native religions, writes that the smoke from the fire, which escapes the *tipi* through a hole in the ceiling, can carry messages to the spirit world.[14] The *tipi* is thus another *axis mundi*, connecting different planes of existence.

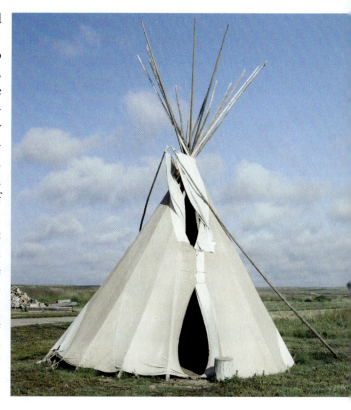

The *tipi*, a typical structure of the tribes of the Great Plains, has a sacred blueprint. Each *tipi* can be understood as an image of the universe.

Sacred Language and Sacred Time

In many Native American cultures, time is regarded as circular, not linear. Thus, events that happened at one point on the circle of time are not simply past; they will be experienced again. Beliefs about death further illustrate this concept. In many Native American religions, death is considered to be an important spiritual transition. During old age, death may be welcomed and prepared for, and funeral rituals ease the transition of the deceased into the next stage in the afterlife. In many cultures, the transition of a person from birth to death is thought to be comparable to the cyclical nature of the seasons of the year.[15] Thus, just as winter precedes spring, human death is connected to the reemergence of life. Recall the Cherokee myth about the origins of corn, which emphasizes the necessity of death to produce life. As you read the next passage, think about cyclical time and the nature of death. Joseph Epes Brown tells us how Black Elk explained this to him:

> This cyclical reality was beautifully expressed . . . when I noticed how the dignified old Lakota man Black Elk would relate to little children. He would get down on his hands and knees and pretend he was a horse, and the children would squeal with joy. . . . There obviously was no generation gap; he fully connected with children. I once asked him

Navajo *hogans* are built to represent the Navajo lands and the cosmos.

how it was that he could so relate to the children, and he replied "I who am an old man am about to return to the Great Mysterious and a young child is a being who has just come from the Great Mysterious, so it is that we are very close together."[16]

The words of Black Elk illustrate the important relationship between the elderly and the very young. In many Native religions, elders teach youngsters about their religious heritage through myths. Often, the telling of myths is regarded as sacred speech. Because of the cyclical nature of time, the events related in myths are not thought to be a part of a distant and irrecoverable past but rather are representative of another place on the circle of time. Recounting a myth re-creates the events of the myth, transporting listeners into mythic time.[17]

Earlier in this chapter, we learned how the ancestors of the Navajo sang and painted the world into existence. Thus words and language were the building blocks of creation. The rituals of the ancestors provide the foundation for Navajo ceremonial practice, which is focused on maintaining order in the world. This is primarily done through practices known as **chantways**. Chantways involve ritualized singing and chants and may take place over several days. The songs and chants retell the stories of creation and thus, through language, bring the power of the time of creation into the present. Chantways are used in many contexts, such as marriages, births, and puberty rites, and are thought to have the power to bring great benefit. The chantways are used for healing by aiming to bring afflicted individuals into harmony with their surroundings. Normally, the ceremonies take place in *hogans*.

VOICES: An Interview with Lin Estes

Lin Estes is a woman of Shawnee, Choctaw, and Welsh descent. She is a student who is pursuing a degree in American Indian Studies at Black Hills State University.

What is your religious background?

I grew up in an atmosphere where religion was not forced on me. This was a good thing because I never bought the concept that sitting in a building one day a week made me a good person. I preferred to be outside absorbing the world.

In your view, what is the nature of the world? What is humanity's place in it?

I think that we are all connected. I believe that there is a Creator and that we have many paths to the Creator. I believe that people share a desire to be content, safe, and have food, shelter, and comfort for their families. Our core beliefs allow us to function and to find meaning when unfortunate events impact our lives. There are always some people who, through ignorance, greed, or fear, will cause unrest. It is then that we either reach inside for an answer or accept that matters are out of our control. We all want freedom from the oppression of our beliefs. In the United States, many policies have been enacted to keep Natives from expressing their spirituality.

Lin Estes

Could you describe your religious practice and your personal spirituality?

Even though I did not have a structured religious upbringing, I knew from a young age that I was part of something greater. I knew Connection of Spirit early on. I believe that we are a part of Mother Earth—we are connected to every living thing. In my thirties, some of my uncles, who were Episcopalian ministers, told me that I was like my great grandmother Eudora. She had been called Prophetess by her community, and her "ways" were not Christian. They advised me that I had gifts of insight that she had. However, they thought that I should be more "Christian" and turn away from Eudora's ways. Because of assimilation, my uncles didn't consider themselves Native. Certain events during their military careers in the 1940s and 1950s led them to hide behind their lighter Shawnee complexions. They did not want to be Indian. But I knew who I was. I lived from the inside out instead of trying to be who others told me I should want to be or instead of practicing a religion that did not work for me. I live in Spirit, connected to the Native Spirit that is Creator. I have also embraced Buddhism because it has similar qualities.

What opportunities and challenges do you face as a member of a native community in the United States today?

I believe that the indigenous people of the United States have been and are still the targets of genocide. While some of the overt policies of the past are no longer in place, Native people still lack freedom to express spirituality. Bear Butte in South Dakota comes to mind. Bear Butte is a sacred place where Native peoples travel to pray, to prepare for Sun Dance, and to cleanse. One will find prayer ties and tobacco ties offered to Creator for the passing of a loved one. Just near Bear Butte there is a town called Sturgis, where roughly a half million people gather for a biker rally every August. Natives praying at the Butte are subjected to the stadium-type lights, loud music, and the nonsacred atmosphere of the many bars built to accommodate the bikers. Strip clubs, wet t-shirt contests, and drunkenness offend those who travel to the Butte for ceremony. The state of

South Dakota and Sturgis are more concerned with money than they are with "those Indians" on the Butte. Today, I think Native spiritual practice is still viewed as "primitive." I hope there will be a time when there is equality for Natives. I have been called a "witch," a "psychic," and also a "Lamanite" [*see Chapter 13*]. But I am a Native woman who has been blessed with the strength to know who I am. I am not troubled by those who call me anything else or tell me I can't practice the way that is right for me.

THE HISTORY OF NATIVE AMERICAN INDIGENOUS RELIGIONS

As we have seen thus far in this chapter, the beliefs and teachings of indigenous religions of North America are complex and multifaceted. Just like other major world religions, these traditions have developed historically and have both resisted and accommodated cultural changes. In this section of the chapter, we will look at how Native North American religions have responded to the social and political changes in the modern world. As you read this section, think about how indigenous American religions have adapted and endured despite colonialism, encroaching Christianity, and culture change.

Conquest, Colonization, and Christianity

The expansion of European imperialism from the sixteenth through the early twentieth century ravaged and radically influenced indigenous religious traditions in the Americas. Throughout North America, the effects of colonialism on indigenous peoples were disastrous: indigenous populations were devastated by disease and warfare, forced to move far away from their ancestral homelands, and sometimes enslaved or indentured to work for the colonists.

Spanish, British, and French colonial powers sent Christian missionaries to their imperial holdings (and beyond) in North and Central America with the aim of "saving" indigenous peoples from what were viewed as their pagan ways. As a result, many indigenous peoples converted (forcibly or by choice) to the Christianity of the colonizers. Some colonizers, such as the Spanish, also believed that they could bring about the second coming of Christ by completing the work of taking the gospel to the ends of the earth.

More recently, in the nineteenth and twentieth centuries, Native American children in the United States were forcibly removed from their homes and sent to boarding schools, where they were taught the "errors" of their cultural and religious ways. The 1819 Civilization Fund Act, which aimed to educate native children in an effort to "civilize" them, led to the development of many of these boarding schools. In the interview earlier in the chapter, recall that Lin's uncles were ashamed of their Indian heritage. As another example, in the southwestern United States, Navajo children were adopted by white families and raised in Mormon or other Christian traditions.

However, indigenous religious traditions were never entirely eradicated, even when Native peoples identified as Christians. When the Spanish conquistadors arrived in Mesoamerica, the indigenous religion of the Mayan peoples was banned, written versions of holy texts were burned, and the Maya were often forcibly converted to Roman Catholicism. Although many Mayan people today identify as Catholic, elements of indigenous religion remain. Catholic saints may be equated with Mayan gods, and some Maya have equated Jesus and Mary with the sun and the moon in Mayan cosmology. Today, many Mayan people may draw on both elements of Catholic and Mayan religion in their beliefs and practice.

In the United States today, many Native Americans identify as Catholics, Protestants, or nondenominational Christians. However, as with the Maya, this does not necessarily mean that the beliefs and practices of Native religions are no longer relevant. Furthermore, Christianity is sometimes understood as an indigenous American religion by Native Christians. Among the White Mountain Apache of Arizona, some religious leaders make the claim that they "have always had the Bible."[18] As with the Navajo, an important part of Apache girls' initiation is the assumption of the powers of Changing Woman. In Apache mythology, Changing Woman was distressed about the difficulty of life on earth and prayed to God to change it. God answered her prayers by impregnating her with the rays of the sun, and she gave birth to a heroic son, who made the earth safe for humans. Some Apache religious leaders interchange the names of Jesus and Mary for Changing Woman and her son. Furthermore, at the girls' puberty ceremony, participants draw parallels between other sacred Apache narratives and the stories of Genesis. It is in such contexts that practitioners argue that Christianity is indeed an indigenous American religion that predated colonization.[19] For other Apache Christians, however, traditional religion is viewed not as a complement to Christianity but as a relic of the past that good Christians should reject.

In Chichicastenango, Guatemala, Mayan men take part in a religious ceremony where saints are taken to the streets by members of religious brotherhoods.

Resistance Movements

Many resistance movements developed in Native communities in response to European-American encroachment throughout North America. Such movements often had an overtly religious dimension, and indigenous religious leaders were frequently at the forefront of resistance movements. Many movements had influence far and wide and can therefore be understood as pan-Indian religious movements.

One such movement was the **Ghost Dance**. In the mid-nineteenth century, a religious leader of the Northern Paiute claimed to have had a vision that taught him that the white occupiers would leave if the Indians performed a special dance described by the spirits. This event was called the Ghost Dance because of the belief that it would usher in the destruction and rebirth of the world and that dead ancestors would return. Versions of the dance spread rapidly throughout the western United States in 1870 because many Native people embraced the possibility that the dance not only could allow them to communicate with deceased ancestors but also could revive the Native cultures in the face of European domination.

In 1890, another Paiute man of Nevada named **Wovoka**, who had studied Paiute religion and participated in the first Ghost Dance, founded a second Ghost Dance. In 1889, Wovoka experienced a powerful vision in which the Creator told him the ancestors would rise up. If people demonstrated their belief through dances, human misery and death would come to an end. The dances spread quickly across the Great Basin and to the Sioux of the northern Midwest and other Plains peoples.

Regrettably, many white Americans feared the dances, and the U.S. government interpreted the widespread dances as an armed resistance movement. The Ghost Dance came to a tragic end on December 29, 1890, at Wounded Knee, South Dakota. American troops killed hundreds of Lakota people, including women and children, who had gathered for a dance. The Ghost Dance came at a critical time in the history of Native American peoples and was seen by many participants as a final attempt to revive the ways of the past. Although the second Ghost Dance ended in catastrophe, the movement brought together people of different Native backgrounds and contributed to creating a shared sense of identity, history, and purpose among peoples of diverse origins.

Although the massacre at Wounded Knee is perhaps the most well known of U.S. attempts to control Native religious practice, government suspicions of religious practice continued well into the twentieth century. In 1904, the Sun Dance was officially banned because it was considered chaotic and dangerous. And as we have learned, for much of the nineteenth and twentieth centuries, the U.S. government backed a program in which young Native American children were taken from their homes and relocated to specially built boarding schools, where they were forced to leave behind their religious beliefs, languages, and other cultural practices while adopting the ways of European-Americans.

The **Native American Church** can be considered another resistance movement. In the early twentieth century, followers of **peyote religion** formed this church to protect their religious practice. The hallucinogenic peyote cactus has been used for thousands of years in indigenous religions of northern Mexico. In the late nineteenth and early twentieth century, the use of the plant spread to Native communities in the United States, particularly in the Plains. Around 1890, a Comanche chief called **Quanah Parker** (1845–1911) spread the call for American Indians to embrace peyote religion. He had been introduced to peyote use in the 1890s when he was treated with peyote for an injury, and he became an important defender of the use of peyote against detractors. Peyote is not habit-forming and is primarily used for healing purposes and to encourage encounters with the spirit world. However, Christian missionaries and

As you read through this and the next chapter, do you see similarities in how indigenous peoples in Africa and the Americas responded to colonization and the efforts of missionaries?

other activists in the United States preached against peyote use, and federal and state governments eventually outlawed its use. (Centuries earlier, the Spanish colonizers had also prohibited the use of peyote in religious practice as a result of a decree of the Spanish Inquisition.) In 1918, followers of peyote religion incorporated as the Native American Church to request legal protection for practicing religion.

In 1978, the **American Indian Religious Freedom Act** was passed in an effort to give Native peoples the right to express and practice their beliefs, according to the First Amendment of the U.S. Constitution. However, Native peoples have not always been able to protect their rights to religious freedom by referencing the act. Some practices, like the use of peyote for religious purposes, continued to face challenges from the government for years. Since 1995, however, the use of peyote has been legally permissible.

Native Religions and Non-Native Practitioners

Despite the history of antagonism toward Native religions in North America, many non-Native Americans are interested in learning about Native religious traditions. Today, people in the United States and elsewhere are attracted to what they view as the nature-centered focus of Native religions. In recent decades, some non-Native Americans have started following religious practices, rituals, and beliefs of Native religions as an alternative to what they perceive as drawbacks of Western religious traditions like Christianity and Judaism.

A photograph of Wovoka (seated).

In the 1960s, many people, particularly those involved in the so-called counter-cultural movement, began to develop an interest in the teachings and practices of Native religions. Some were attracted to teachings about the interconnectedness of all things and found what they thought to be an appealing lack of materialism in Native religions. Others were particularly interested in practices that involved the use of hallucinogenic plants like peyote.

Some Native Americans appreciate the growing interest of non-Natives in indigenous religions. However, non-Native interest in Native religious practices has also been criticized by Native thinkers. Critics argue that selective adoption of certain practices, like peyote use, removes the activity from the cultural and historical context in which it developed. Sometimes, conflicts arise over the use of sacred places. In recent years, for example, non-Native Americans have felt the pull of Mt. Shasta. Their interest has not always been welcomed by American Indians—primarily because of a perception that non-Natives are appropriating Native spirituality without proper understanding or proper training. Among the Native people of the region, the springs and meadows of Mt. Shasta are treated with great reverence, and they believe a person should not approach these places without proper guidance from an expert or elder with great religious knowledge. Non-Native spiritual seekers, however, often bathe in sacred springs or play music in sacred groves and meadows without the advice or permission of religious leaders in the area, which offends some Native practitioners. Native views of the sacred nature of the land often conflict with the aims and goals of non-Native Americans, many of whom see the potential for development on the very lands that Indians consider sacred.[20]

NATIVE AMERICAN INDIGENOUS RELIGIONS AS A WAY OF LIFE

This section of the chapter examines the practices of Native American religions. Followers of Native American religions do not usually make stark distinctions between what is "religious" and what is "secular." As we have seen, myths instill everyday life with a sacred quality by providing explanations even for seemingly mundane activities such as planting or preparing food. Therefore, many actions have a religious dimension.

Healing

In Native American religions, healing the sick is often part of religious practice. Healers may use religious knowledge to cure physical and mental illnesses. In addition, healers are frequently well known for their understanding of local plant remedies. Because of this, the term "medicine man" has often been used for healers. Some healers undergo years of training to acquire great depths of religious knowledge. Others are considered specialists not because of particular training but because they have an inherent ability to interact with the spirit world or have been selected by a spirit to become a healer. In many Native traditions, healers are also religious leaders.

In addition to the Navajo chantways we learned about earlier in this chapter, Navajo healing ceremonies also use an art form known as **sand painting**. The Holy People gave the paintings to the Navajo people. As the name suggests, sand paintings are created using vivid colors of sand and other dry materials such as pollen. The paintings are created on the floors of *hogans* and treat illnesses by bringing individuals into alignment with nature. A healer, or singer, selects the subjects of the painting in consultation with the family of the person being treated; these may include animals, plants, and mythic figures.

During the ceremony, the afflicted person is seated in the center of the painting, which tells one of the creation stories. As sand is applied to his body, he identifies with the Holy People depicted in the painting. During the treatment, the painted figures are thought to come to life to aid in the healing of the patient. After the ceremony is complete, the painting is destroyed and the sand is removed. In the past, Navajo people never kept permanent copies of the paintings because it was thought that it would diminish their healing power. Today, small paintings are sometimes produced for sale, but ideally these permanent paintings should not represent or depict the important figures and symbols used in healing practice.

Medicine bundles may also be an important part of healing in Navajo communities. The bundles contain a variety of religiously significant objects, and some items may be very old. Navajo singers usually own their own bundles and use the powers of the items in the bundle in healing. Other Native communities also use similar bundles in healing.[21]

Women and Gender in Native American Religions

The roles of women and conceptions of gender vary across Native American religious traditions. As you have learned, the sacred narratives of Native American religions often include tales of important female spiritual beings, like Changing Woman. Furthermore, women have often had prominent roles in certain aspects of religious practice, such as healing, and many Native religions mark the transition from girlhood to womanhood in a profound manner. For example, as you will read in the next section, young Navajo girls embody Changing Woman during the ritual marking their transition to adulthood.

Among the Iroquois, balance and reciprocity have long been emphasized in the relations between men and women, and many scholars regard the historical Iroquois as a fine example of a gender-egalitarian society, in which neither men nor women dominated. This emphasis on balance has been reflected both in religious symbols and in religious practice. In the Iroquois Longhouse Religion, which is in practice today, the house of worship is divided into male and female spaces, and male and female religious leaders known as "faithkeepers" are of equal importance in spiritual matters.[22] The ceremonial year is very important in regulating ceremonies honoring Creator and spirits, and women have historically been in charge of ceremonies during half of the Iroquois year. Women's songs are sung to accompany the planting of corn to encourage fertility.[23]

In other Native religions, women have also often been highly regarded for their expertise in spiritual matters such as healing. A well-known twentieth-century spiritual healer was **Mabel McKay** (1907–1993), a Pomo woman of Northern California. As a young woman, Mabel was called to be a liaison between her people and the spirit world. Spirit guides told her that she would develop a special gift of healing. Here, Mabel McKay's close friend Greg Sarris describes how she was called by a spirit to be a healer.

> The spirit talked to her constantly now. . . . Sometimes it felt as if her own tongue were moving, shaping the words she was hearing. This happened when she sang the songs that came loud and clear. "Am I going crazy?" she asked once. . . . "No," the spirit said, "it's me. And what is happening is that you have an extra tongue. Your throat has been fixed for singing and sucking out the diseases I've been teaching

you about. It's talking. It's me in you." "Well, how am I to suck?" Mabel asked. "You'll know when you get to that point. You will have a basket to spit out the disease. All your baskets will come from me. Like I told you. Watch how things turn out."[24]

Two-Spirit Many Native North American cultures have historically recognized the existence of a third gender—people who are regarded as being neither male nor female. A **two-spirit** person might be biologically male but adopt the dress, occupations, and behaviors of a woman. Collectively, such individuals are called "two-spirit" people, as they are regarded as having the spirits of both men and women. Historically, two-spirit persons were treated with respect and were regarded as having special spiritual abilities, and many took on a special religious role in the community. With the arrival and domination of Europeans, however, the role of the two-spirit people was suppressed. European understandings of gender did not acknowledge third or fourth genders, and two-spirit people were often regarded as deviant rather than occupying a special social role.

Rites of Passage

Like other religions around the world, Native American traditions use rituals to recognize important changes in a person's social status. Such rituals are known as **rites of passage**. Often, rites of passage mark the transition from childhood to adulthood. Many Native cultures have elaborate rites marking this transition for young women and men. In this section, we will examine two rites of passage. First, we will look at

Navajo man preparing a sand painting.

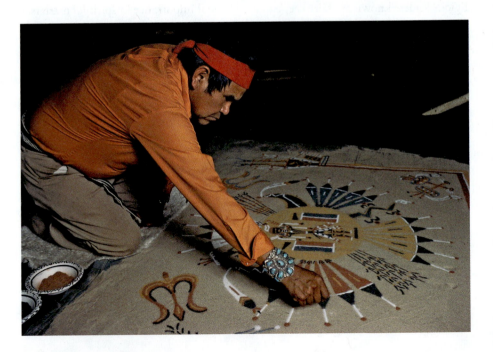

the ***Kinaalda***, which marks a Navajo girl's transition to adulthood. Then we will examine a spiritual rite of passage known as a **vision quest**.

The Kinaalda The Navajo puberty rite for girls is known as the *Kinaalda*. It takes
place soon after a girl begins menstruating. Each girl undergoing *Kinaalda* has a sponsor. This is an older woman who serves as a guide and role model and teaches her about
the expectations of her as a Navajo woman. The ceremonial activities last several days
and are part of the chantways. Thus the ritual has its foundation in mythology.
Changing Woman experienced the first *Kinaalda*, which is the model ritual for all
girls. Indeed, girls are believed to take on the identity and spiritual qualities of Changing Woman during the ritual. Because she takes on the identity of Changing Woman,
a girl going through the rites is thought to have special healing powers. People may
visit her to request healing for their ailments.

One important *Kinaalda* activity is baking a giant cake of cornmeal. The initiate
prepares the cake with the assistance of her family. She grinds the corn and prepares
the batter carefully, since it is believed that if a cake turns out well, she will have a full
and productive life. A poorly made cake bodes ill for her future.

The Vision Quest A rite of passage common to many North American religions is
the vision quest. This is the attempt by an individual to communicate with the
spirit world. It is especially well known among peoples of the Great Plains and Great
Lakes regions, such as the Sioux and the Ojibwa. The quest may be undertaken by men
or women, depending on the culture, and may occur once or at several points in an
individual's life. In some cultures, the vision quest marks the transition from childhood to adulthood.

Usually, the goal of the vision quest is for an individual to make contact with the
spirit world. This is frequently accomplished through contact with a spirit guide.
Often, the spirit guide takes an animal form, which may be revealed during the quest.
Sometimes, individuals report that the spirit guide appeared to them directly. Others
learned the identity of the guide by spotting a particular animal during the quest. In
other vision quests, the focus is not on a spirit guide but rather on accessing a spiritual
power more generally.

In most quests, the initiate will remove himself from normal society by spending
several days alone in the wilderness. The vision quest can be both mentally and physically demanding, as it may require long periods of isolation and fasting. A vision quest
teaches a person about the importance of seeking and following guidance from the
spirit world and has the potential to cultivate a mental and physical hardiness that will
serve the individual throughout his or her life.[25] Among the Ojibwa, boys normally
undertook the vision quest at puberty. After a period of preparation, a boy was taken
deep in the woods where he would remain by himself, fasting, until he received a vision.
For many boys, visions were journeys into the spirit world, and spirit guides would

What rites of passage
are important in other
religious traditions? Do
they always mark the
transition to adulthood,
or can they mark other
transitions?

VISUAL GUIDE
North American Religions

Among Pueblo peoples such as the Hopi and Zuni, kachina dances are a type of renewal rite. When dancers wear the masks of the kachinas, they are thought to become imbued with the spirit of the kachinas. Kachinas have the power to bring rain and enhance fertility. This is a Hopi kachina doll, representing a kachina, from Arizona. The doll dates to before 1901, and is made of painted wood, feathers, and pine needles.

In North American religions from Mexico to Alaska, sweat lodge ceremonies ritually purify and cleanse the body. In these ceremonies, participants build an enclosed structure that is filled with heated stones.

The *tipi* is a typical structure of the tribes of the Great Plains that has religious significance. Each *tipi* is an image of the universe. The perimeter of the *tipi* is the edge of the universe, and the lit fire in the center represents the center of all existence.

help the boy figure out his life's path. Boys who were not able to endure the fast could try again at a later time.[26]

Rites of Renewal and Rites of Purification

As we learned earlier in this chapter, many Native American religions focus on humanity's important role in maintaining balance with other elements of creation. This goal forms the foundation of many kinds of ritual practice, specifically those ceremonies known as **rites of renewal**. Like the term suggests, rites of renewal seek to renew the sacred balance of all things. Such rites are often seasonal because they are designed to correspond with the cycle of planting and harvesting or moving herd animals for grazing. They may aim to enhance natural processes like rainfall or the growth of crops.

As you recall, the Yurok tell of the knowledge given to human beings by the Immortals, who lived on earth before humans. The Immortals taught human beings a ritual known as the **Jump Dance**, which restores the balance of the earth and renews the harmony that was present in the time of the Immortals. Along with a number of other rituals, the Jump Dance is performed during the World Renewal Ceremonial Cycle. This is a cycle of ceremonies that are performed by many Northern California Indians at various times of the year, and their purpose is to maintain the balance of all living things. In the Jump Dance, men march to a special place that has been sanctified by a priest, where they dance. By engaging in this religious practice, which imitates and repeats the words and actions that the Immortals taught humans, the mythic time is called into the present, and the earth is renewed. And because an entire community may participate in rites of renewal, they also enhance group solidarity.[27]

In North American religions from Mexico to Alaska, **sweat lodge** ceremonies are used to ritually purify and cleanse the body. They are rites of purification. In these ceremonies, participants build an enclosed structure that is filled with heated stones.

Pouring water over the stones generates steam. The steam has the power to cleanse the body and clear the mind of anything that might distract an individual from focusing on the divine. A sweat bath may be used to prepare for other ritual activities, such as the Sun Dance described in the opening part of this chapter. The ritual use of the sweat lodge encourages a bond between all those who bathe in it. And sometimes the cleansing power extends even beyond the inhabitants of the lodge to other elements of creation.[28] In this way, this rite of purification also serves as a rite of renewal. The ritual use of the sweat bath is such an important part of religious practice that some states have been ordered by federal judges to provide Native prisoners access to sweat lodges.[29]

Among Pueblo peoples such as the Hopi and Zuni, kachina dances are a type of renewal rite. As we discussed earlier in this chapter, when dancers wear the masks of the kachinas, they are thought to become imbued with the spirit of the kachina. Kachinas have the power to bring rain and enhance fertility. Among the Hopi, who recognize over 200 kachina spirits, several dances take place during the part of the year between the winter solstice and the summer solstice. The songs used with the dances often call for fertility of the land, for rainfall, and for the flourishing of crops. Rites of renewal also often have significance beyond these material aims. The Hopi dance for rain calls not just for nourishment of crops but also for nourishment of the cosmos. In the Hopi belief system, the spiritual qualities of rain underlie all of existence. Thus rain dances rejuvenate the entire cosmos, not just the crops in a particular locale.[30]

The kachina dances also teach young people about ethics and morality. Children are not allowed to see the dancers without their masks. This is so the children will have a strong association of the dancers with the kachinas and think of them only as representing the idealized qualities the kachinas possess. However, when they are old enough, children learn that their parents or other relatives are behind the masks. This disillusionment is part of their religious development, as children learn that the world is not always as it seems.[31]

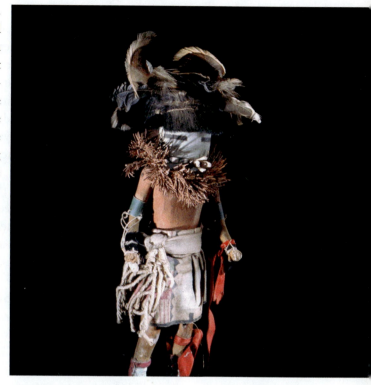

This Hopi kachina doll from the twentieth century might be used to remind children of the qualities the kachinas possess.

CONCLUSION

Native American religions are not relics of the past but are living traditions that continue to develop and change. One of the major challenges Native American religions have faced is the spread of Christianity, particularly through European colonialism. However, even in those areas that have seen widespread conversion to other religions, elements of indigenous religions have often been maintained and even incorporated into the practice of the colonizing religions. In North America, many non-Native peoples have found Native American religions attractive because they offer a compelling and seemingly earth-centered spiritual alternative to other religions. However, American Indians respond to such interest from non-Native spiritual explorers in different ways. Some welcome this interest, and others reject what they view as an inappropriate appropriation of Native religious ideas by non-Native peoples.

What does the future hold for the religions of Native North America? It is likely that Native and even non-Native peoples will continue to find great spiritual meaning and religious fulfillment in the teachings and practices of indigenous religions. Although many Native Americans are Christians today, as we have seen, Native religious ideas often coexist harmoniously with Christian teachings and practices. In many communities, Native Americans are advocating a resurgence of indigenous religious ways, and, as we saw with the Ghost Dance and the Native American Church, pan-Indian or intertribal interest in certain types of religious practice will likely continue. Although throughout this chapter we have emphasized the importance of recognizing the diversity of Native American religious traditions, it is also essential to acknowledge that pan-tribal movements and ceremonies can be an important means of fostering a collective Native American identity.

SEEKING ANSWERS

What Is Ultimate Reality?

Myths contain sacred knowledge about ultimate reality and the nature of the world. In Native American religions, the world is believed to have been created by creator deities. The entire world, and the many elements within it—including human beings—may be believed to be infused by the spiritual essence of a Supreme Being, or Great Spirit.

How Should We Live in This World?

In most Native American religions, myths provide the foundations for the way people should live their lives. Humans are one part of the general order of existence and live in a reciprocal relationship with the land, plants, and other animals. Myths teach that it is the responsibility of humans to maintain balance, order, and right relationships with other elements of creation.

(continued)

SEEKING ANSWERS (continued)

What Is Our Ultimate Purpose?

Native American religions differ in terms of humanity's ultimate purpose. Some religions focus on humanity's role in maintaining balance with the natural world, and certain religious practices, such as the Jump Dance, aim to do this. Maintaining this balance can improve the human condition, and upsetting the balance can have terrible consequences. Many Native American religions conceive of life and death as cyclical in nature. In Native religions, the transition of a person from birth to death is thought to be comparable to the cyclical nature of the seasons of the year. In some religions, the deceased transitions to the land of the dead, which may resemble this life.

REVIEW QUESTIONS

For Review

1. Why is it difficult to make generalizations about Native American religions?
2. Many Native American religions emphasize the interconnectedness of all things. How does this play out in religious practice?
3. What are some common themes in Native American mythology? What do these themes teach the listeners?
4. What was the significance of the Ghost Dance?

For Further Reflection

1. How do Native American traditions answer some of the Great Questions that many religions address? What is unique to Native traditions? What do they share with other traditions?
2. How are Native American religions tied to specific places and landscapes? Do you see this in other religions described in this book? Why do you think some religions emphasize ties to specific locales?

GLOSSARY

American Indian Religious Freedom Act 1978 U.S. law to guarantee freedom of religious practice for Native Americans.

axis mundi (ax-is mun-di; Latin) An academic term for the center of the world, which connects the earth with the heavens.

Black Elk Famous Lakota religious leader.

Changing Woman Mythic ancestor of the Navajo people who created the first humans.

chantway The basis of Navajo ceremonial practice; includes chants, prayers, songs, and other ritual practice.

Ghost Dance Religious resistance movements in 1870 and 1890 that originated in Nevada among Paiute peoples.

hogan (ho-gan; Pueblo) A sacred structure of Pueblo peoples.

(continued)

GLOSSARY *(continued)*

Holy People Ancestors to the Navajo people, described in mythic narratives.

Holy Wind Navajo conception of a spiritual force that inhabits every element of creation.

Jump Dance Renewal dance of Yurok people.

kachina (ka-chee-na; Hopi) Pueblo spiritual beings.

Kinaalda (kee-nal-dah) Rite of passage for young Navajo women.

McKay, Mabel A Pomo woman who was well known as healer and basket weaver.

Native American Church A church founded in early twentieth century based on peyote religion.

peyote Hallucinogenic cactus used in many Native American religions.

Popol Vuh (po-pol voo; Quiché Mayan, "council book") The Quiché Mayan book of creation.

Quanah Parker Comanche man who called for embrace of peyote religion.

Quetzalcoatl (ket-zal-ko-at'-l; Aztec) Aztec God and important culture hero in Mexico.

rites of passage Rituals that mark the transition from one social stage to another.

rites of renewal Rituals that seek to enhance natural processes, like rain or fertility, or enhance the solidarity of a group.

sand painting A painting made with sand used by Navajo healers to treat ailments.

Sun Dance Midsummer ritual common to many Native American religions; details vary across cultures.

sweat lodge A structure built for ritually cleansing and purifying the body.

tipi A typical conical structure of the tribes of the Great Plains which is often constructed with a sacred blueprint.

two spirit An additional gender identity in many Native North American cultures; often thought to have special spiritual powers.

trickster A common figure in North American mythologies; trickster tales often teach important moral lessons.

vision quest A ritual attempt by an individual to communicate with the spirit world.

Wovoka A Paiute man whose visions started the Ghost Dance of 1890.

SUGGESTIONS FOR FURTHER READING

Brown, Joseph Epes. *Teaching Spirits: Understanding Native American Religious Tradition*. New York: Oxford University Press, 2001. A comprehensive look at Native American religions including topics like geography, creativity, and ritual.

DeLoria, Vine, Jr. *God Is Red: A Native View of Religion*. New York: Dell Publishing Company, 2003. A seminal work on Native American spirituality from a Native perspective.

Gill, Sam. *Native American Religions: An Introduction*. Boston: Thomson Wadsworth, 2005.

Hirschfelder, Arlene, and Paulette Molin. *An Encyclopedia of Native American Religions*. New York: Facts on File, 1992. A useful encyclopedia with detailed entries on many aspects of Native American religious belief and practice.

Kehoe, Alice Beck. *The Ghost Dance: Ethnohistory and Revitalization*. Long Grove, IL: Waveland Press, 2006. A detailed look at the Ghost Dance in its cultural and historical context.

Neihardt, John G., and Black Elk. *Black Elk Speaks: Being the Life Story of a Holy Man of the Oglala Sioux*. Omaha: University of Nebraska Press, 1961. An intimate account of the religious visions and worldview of the Lakota religious leader Black Elk.

ONLINE RESOURCES

National Museum of the American Indian
nmai.si.edu
This museum, part of the Smithsonian Institution, has many materials about the research collection online.

National Archives
archives.gov/research/alic/reference/native-americans.html
This portal page at the website of the National Archives leads to the Archives' research materials on federally recognized tribes.

INDIGENOUS RELIGIONS of AFRICA

TEPILIT OLE SAITOTI is a Maasai man from Tanzania, a country in East Africa. The Maasai are a cattle-herding people, most of whom live in Kenya and Tanzania. As a promising young student, Tepilit eventually studied in the United States and Europe. In 1988, he published his autobiography, *The Worlds of a Maasai Warrior*. In the book, he describes the initiation ceremony that transformed him from a young boy into a warrior.

When Maasai boys reach adolescence, they are circumcised in a public ritual to mark their transition to the status of warriors. Different ceremonies mark the transition of Maasai girls into womanhood. In the Maasai culture, warriors are known as **moran**. The *moran* are a special group of young men who have particular responsibilities. They are usually between the ages of fifteen and thirty-five and are traditionally responsible for protecting the community and for herding the cattle and other animals. Boys who become *moran* together form a special bond that continues throughout their lives. But first, a young man must survive his circumcision. For Tepilit, undergoing the circumcision ceremony was an intense and transformational experience:

> Three days before the ceremony my head was shaved and I discarded all of my belongings such as my necklaces, garments, spear, and sword. I even had to shave my pubic hair.

Competitive jumping can be part of the young Maasai warriors' rite of passage ceremonies.

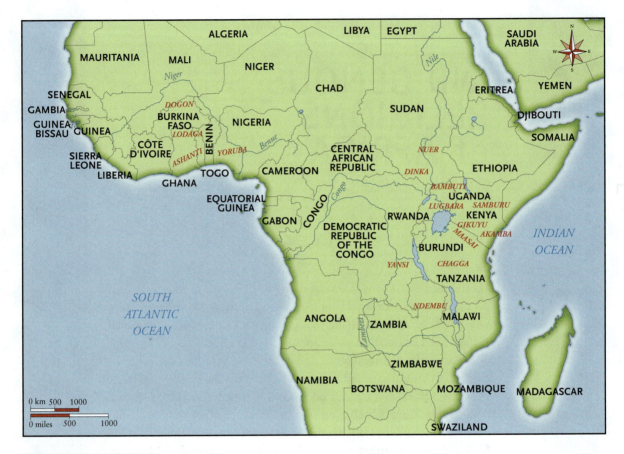

African peoples and cultures that are discussed in this chapter.

Circumcision in many ways is similar to Christian baptism. You must put all the sins you have committed during childhood behind and embark as a new person with a different outlook on life.[1]

Tepilit describes the apprehension he felt as the day approached. The circumcision was important not just for Tepilit but for his entire family. His father and brothers warned him that he must not cry, scream, or kick the knife away when the circumciser removed his foreskin because that would embarrass his family. It could even jeopardize his future. Bravery is highly valued in the Maasai culture, and people would lose respect for Tepilit if he showed himself to be a coward. He would never be considered for a position of leadership if he became known as a "knife-kicker."

The circumciser appeared, his knives at the ready. He spread my legs and said "One cut," a pronouncement necessary to prevent an initiate from claiming that he had been taken by surprise. He splashed a white liquid, a ceremonial paint called *enturoto*, across my face. Almost immediately I felt a spark of pain under my belly as the knife cut through my penis' foreskin.[2]

Tepilit made it through the ceremony bravely, and his friends and family congratulated him. His head was shaved to mark his new status as a man and a warrior.

> As long as I live, I will never forget the day my head was shaved and I emerged a man, a Maasai warrior. I felt a sense of control over my destiny so great that no words can accurately describe it.[3]

Like the Maasai, most African cultures (and cultures everywhere) have rituals that mark the transition of young people into adulthood. Although details of the ceremonies vary from culture to culture, they share the public recognition that a young person has entered a new phase of life. Often, this new phase of life is understood through a religious worldview. In African religions, other phases of life are also marked through specific ceremonies. For example, birth marks the journey of an individual soul from the spirit world to the human world, and death is the transition back to the spirit world.

In this chapter, we will explore the indigenous, small-scale religious traditions of Africa today and in recent history. Although many Africans are Muslims, Christians, or followers of other large-scale religions with roots elsewhere, we will concern ourselves here with religions that originated in Africa. Because North Africa (Egypt, Libya, Algeria, Morocco, Tunisia) has been predominantly Muslim for about 1,000 years, this chapter explores Africa south of the Sahara, where indigenous religions have remained more prominent until the present.

Today, about 1 billion people live on the African continent. There are thousands of different African cultural, ethnic, and linguistic groups. This cultural diversity is reflected in the religious diversity of the continent. There is not one single "African culture" or "African religion." Because African religions are so numerous, we will not attempt to discuss them all in this chapter. Instead, we will explore examples from a few religions that reflect African cultural and geographic diversity. And although we address them together in a single chapter, it is important to remember that all African religions are not the same. Because of this diversity, it is not easy to generalize about them in a textbook chapter.

TIMELINE
African Religions

300s C.E.　King of Axum (Ethiopia) converts to Christianity.

700s　Arab Muslims extend control across North Africa.

1000s　Islam begins to spread throughout West Africa and coastal East Africa.

600–1100　The empire of Ghana rises.

800–1400　The rise of great cities and empires of Mali.

1500–1800s　Muslim Swahili city-states thrive on the East African coast.

1500s–1800s　Atlantic slave trade; African religions begin to spread to the Americas.

1884　Berlin Conference; European colonial powers divide Africa.

1800–1900s　European colonization and Christian missionary work in Africa.

1804–1809　Usman dan Fodio leads campaigns in northern Nigeria to rid Islamic practice of indigenous religious elements.

1905　Kinjiketele organizes Maji Maji revolt against German colonizers in Tanganyika (today's Tanzania).

Early 1900s　Several new African Christian churches are founded.

1920s　Josiah Oshitelu founds an independent Yoruba Christian church, known as the Aladura church.

1950s–1990s　Decolonization: sub-Saharan African countries gain independence.

1962–1965　Vatican II permits local church leaders around the world to be more accepting of local practice.

African indigenous
beliefs today.

And yet, despite this diversity, it is possible to identify some common characteristics in the realms of practice, teaching and beliefs, and historical development. The story of Tepilit's initiation explores one of these characteristics: many African religions have specific ceremonies that mark the transition from one social state of being to another. Many African religions also share some elements of belief and worldview. For example, many share the belief in a supreme deity, or creator God. Also, many African religions are primarily concerned with life in the here and now, rather than with what comes after death.

African religions also share a great deal in terms of historical development. Most African religions originated in small-scale communities and thus may be connected intimately with a particular culture in a particular place. And although some followers of African religions live in small-scale societies today, many more have been incorporated into large political systems and market economies in the modern, global era. Furthermore, in the nineteenth and twentieth centuries, African religions faced the reality of widespread European colonialism on the continent. In addition, the influence of African religions has spread far beyond their places of origin. This was primarily a result of the Atlantic slave trade, which lasted from the 1500s to the 1800s. As we will learn in this chapter, certain religions of the Americas, such as **Vodou** and **Santeria**, were derived from and share a great deal with African religions.

THE TEACHINGS OF INDIGENOUS AFRICAN RELIGIONS

For followers of indigenous African religions, "religion" is not considered to be separate from everyday existence. Religious practice is not relegated to particular times, places, or spaces. Instead, religious beliefs and practices infuse and inform daily life and everyday concerns. We will begin our discussion of African religions by considering their beliefs and teachings. Although the religions of Africa differ significantly, certain ideas about the supernatural, the natural world, and humanity's place within it are common to many of the continent's religions.

Myths

We find the beliefs of African religions primarily in mythic narratives, which contain essential teachings. All religions, as we learned in Chapter 1, have a mythic component. African religions are no exception, and most have a very rich mythic heritage. Myths are not falsehoods; rather, they are narratives that we humans tell about our origins and ourselves. In religions the world over, myths relate compelling stories about gods, spirits, heroic figures, or human ancestors. Because of these intriguing narratives, myths have the ability to teach the listener about the origins of humanity, about supernatural beings, and about morality and ethics in a powerful and memorable way.

In most African religions, myths have been part of an oral tradition and have been passed from one generation to the next through the spoken word. Today, however, many myths also exist in written form. In many African cultures, elders or religious leaders are responsible for maintaining and disseminating the teachings of myths to others. Although all members of a culture may be familiar with basic mythic narratives, elders and religious specialists often know more details and deeper meanings.

The myths of many African religions are most often concerned with this world—the world of humanity—rather than the greater universe. Myths most often tell stories about the origins of the earth and of human beings and about human social life and social organization. Myths often convey moral lessons. When African myths contain stories of gods and other supernatural beings, the stories frequently focus on the way in which these beings interact with or relate to humanity.

Among the Dogon people of Mali and Burkina Faso, in West Africa, myth has been part of the oral tradition for generations. The Dogon are primarily farmers, and although some Dogon are Christians or Muslims, most still follow Dogon religion. Dogon religious experts know far more about myths than the average person and are therefore responsible for preserving, understanding, and passing on the myths. Dogon mythology is intimately related to religious and social life. It involves complex explanations of the origins of the world and human beings and the way in which human beings should live on the earth, such as explanations for farming practices. Throughout this section of the chapter, we will consider various myths from different African religions, including the Dogon, as we learn about beliefs and teachings of African religions.

Supernatural Beings: Gods and Spirits

Many African religions teach that everyday human life is influenced or even controlled by gods or other supernatural beings. African religions are therefore *theistic*, a term you will recall from Chapter 1. Most also share the belief in a supreme deity, or High God. African religions normally believe that the High God is all knowing, all powerful, and the creator of the world and of humanity. This supreme deity is often associated with the sky and may be more specifically connected to the sun or the rain because both of these have life-giving powers. Most African religions regard the High God as eternal. And although the High God is generally not thought to be human-like, the supreme deity may be described as having human-like attributes, such as mercy, goodness, and a concern for justice.

Many African religions consider the High God to be transcendent and removed from the lives of humans. As a result, there are rarely temples, churches, or shrines devoted to the High God. Because the High God is removed from everyday life, most religious practice focuses on communicating with spirits or lesser gods. In the religion of the Dogon, the High God **Amma** is an example of a deity who is distant from the lives of ordinary humans. The Dogon creation myth tells that Amma made the earth out of mud and clay. Although he was active in creation, Amma eventually retired from the earth and left lesser deities to manage earthly affairs and attend to human interests. Other African mythologies explain the transcendence of the High God as the result of a transgression committed by humans or animals that upset the High God, who then left this world for a supernatural realm. We will examine some of these myths later in this chapter.

In some African religions, the High God is associated with the qualities of both a father and a mother. In others, the High God has no gender. The Samburu people of Kenya believe that God, known as Nkai, is flexible in gender and in form. In the Samburu language, the word "Nkai" is feminine. God is associated with procreation and is considered to have many female characteristics. Interestingly, some Samburu people who claim to have been taken to the divine home of Nkai have reported that the deity is not one individual at all but is actually a family group.[4]

VOICES: Interviews with Sammy Letoole and Festus Ogunbitan

Sammy Letoole, a young Samburu man from Kenya, is a student at Friends Theological College in Kaimosi, Kenya. Although he is studying Christianity, he was raised in the Samburu religion and finds that it does not conflict with his Christian faith. The Samburu people live in northern Kenya, and Samburu culture and religion share some elements with Maasai culture and religion. Festus Ogunbitan is a scholar of religion from Nigeria whose ancestry is Yoruban. Festus was raised in a Christian home, but he explored his ancestral religion as he matured. An author, he has written several books on Yoruba religion.

What is your religious background?

Sammy: My religious background is Samburu and now I am a Christian. I was raised in a pure Samburu family who believed in traditional Samburu religion. Every day, my father woke up very early in the morning to go out and pray for everything—including the animals and the children. As a result, my faith in God became very strong because I saw my dad praying without stopping. And this makes my Christian foundation strong.

Sammy Letoole

Festus: I am from the Yoruba nation of the southwestern part of Nigeria. I was born into a Christian family who were biased about the values and virtues of their ancestors' culture. This happened to many Africans, since Christianity and Islam declared their religion as the universal religion. When I grew up, I started to read books about the religion of my ancestors, and I discovered that religion is a social process—it is like a plant growing up to bring forth fruits. Therefore, my Yoruba religion does not need to be suppressed by any foreign religion.

Sammy, you don't seem to see much conflict between Christianity and Samburu religion. Could you explain their similarities and differences? How does your religious practice draw on both traditions?

The Samburu religion and Christianity have a similar conception of God. In both traditions, God is a creator, provider, and protector and is caring and loving. The Samburu people believe that God is found in the mountains, so they name their gods after those big mountains. During the time of the Old Testament, Moses climbed Mt. Sinai to pray, and he was given the commandments; similarly, the Samburu pray to their God to give them direction.

There are many things that Samburu religion shares with the Bible, especially the Old Testament. During that time, the Israelites were not supposed to eat all grey animals without divided hooves and who did not chew the cud. Even now, the Samburu do not eat those animals. Also, the people in the time of the Old Testament offered sacrifices to their God; the Samburu also offer sacrifices to their God.

Festus, could you explain your view of the nature of the world and humanity's place in it and how this developed through learning about the religion of your ancestors?

I believe that the universe is created by God, and the universe is part of God through nature. I believe in the ancient Yoruban concept of God which says that nature is part of God—plants, animals, outer space, and human nature. As a result, they worship nature and human nature by reinforcing them with praise singing. I believe that nature is divine, and a sincere and ingenious person is divine, and we should respect them. If we treat nature and creativity in humans as divine, we shall be able to get lots of good things from them—such as the invention of products and services for the needs of mankind.

Could you both describe your worship and religious practice?

Sammy: My worshiping styles and praises are influenced by Samburu religion. Samburu prayers and Christian prayers differ because the Samburu believe that God is found in mountains, rivers, and good springs. Therefore, when performing prayers a person must face a certain mountain like Mt. Kenya or Mt. Nyiro. Christians forward their prayers to God through Jesus Christ, our savior. Although people pray to God in different ways, they all seek protection, guidance, love, and satisfaction.

Festus Ogunbitan

Festus: I am not a Christian, and I don't really practice Yoruba traditional religion in a shrine. But I have faith in the religion of my ancestors, most especially Ogun—the Yoruba god of Iron—which is half of the pronunciation of my last name. My last name, Ogunbitan, means "a child through whom Ogun the god of Iron shall create history." By writing a book called *Lyric Poems on Creation Story of the Yorubas*, I have fulfilled this promise.

In addition to the belief in a High God, most African religions also recognize other supernatural beings that are lower in status than the High God, but still powerful. As you learned in Chapter 1, a belief system in which many supernatural beings (including gods and spirits) are recognized but in which one of these beings is elevated to a higher status is known as henotheism. In African religions, gods or spirits interact with human beings and are sometimes thought to be mutually interdependent with humans. Because of this, much religious practice focuses on these beings. Therefore, unlike the High God, these lesser gods and spirits often have temples, shrines, and rituals devoted to them.

In many African religions, including the Dogon, the Ashanti, and the Igbo, the earth is an important female deity. She is often understood to be the consort or daughter of the High God, who is typically associated with the sky, the sun, or the heavens in general. In Dogon mythology, Amma created the earth and then forcibly took her as his mate. A jackal was born from this union. The Dogon consider the birth of the jackal to be unfavorable because it was a single birth, not a twin. In Dogon culture, twin birth is considered ideal. This misfortune of the jackal's birth is attributed to Amma's unjust rape of the earth.[5]

Dogon religion provides another example of lesser deities. Although the original union of Amma and the earth was problematic, Dogon myths tell of a second union.

This was favorable and produced twins—an ideal birth. The twins took the form of another supernatural being—a lesser god called the Nummo. The Nummo twins represent the balance of male and female elements. The Nummo plays an important role in Dogon myths about the origins of humans and the development of human social structure. The Nummo is active in the affairs of humans, while Amma is not.

Some African religions have large and complex **pantheons**, or groups of deities. One example of a pantheon is in the religion of the Yoruba people, a large ethnic group in West Africa. Although many Yoruba have converted to Islam and Christianity, indigenous beliefs are still prominent, even among the converts. In Yoruba religion, the High God, known as Olodumare, is accompanied by other categories of deities. One such category is the *Odu*, who were the original prophets gifted with the ability to look into the future. Another category is the *orisa*, who are believed to inhabit an otherworldly realm called *orun*. The *orisa* live in a hierarchical social order that closely reflects Yoruba social organization. Yoruba mythology teaches that the hundreds of *orisa* were the first inhabitants of the earth. The High God sent the *orisa* to earth to create land from the water and gave each a specific duty. Yoruba people believe that the High God ultimately determines their destiny, although they serve different *orisa* as their personal deities.

One of the foremost *orisa* is a goddess known as **Oshun**. Oshun is merciful, beautiful, and loving, and she is associated with fertility and the life-giving properties of water. Because of this, Yoruba people may call on her to help them with matters pertaining to childbirth and family. She is also known as the "hair-braider" or "hair-plaiter" and is powerful in this ability to make people beautiful. In Yoruba mythology, Oshun was present at the time of creation, but she was the only female, and the *Odu* ignored her. However, Olodumare reproached them and explained how important Oshun was. The following passage from a Yoruba myth relates how the *Odu* appealed to Oshun for forgiveness. In the myth, Oshun eventually bears a son who joins the other Odu.

> They returned to Oshun
> And addressed her: "Mother, the pre-eminent hair-plaiter with the
>   coral beaded comb.
> We have been to the Creator
> And it was discovered that all Odu were derived from you.
> And that our suffering in the world would continue
> If we failed to recognize and obey you."
> So, on their return to earth from the Creator,
> All the remaining Odu wanted to pacify and please Oshun.[6]

In some African religions, such as that of the Nuer people of Sudan, the High God may manifest as multiple deities. The anthropologist E. E. Evans-Pritchard (1902–1973) lived with the Nuer in the 1930s and made a detailed study of their religion.[7] He argued

This picture of a Nuer homestead was taken by anthropologist E. E. Evans-Pritchard in the 1930s.

that the Nuer belief system should be considered both monotheistic *and* polytheistic because the different deities recognized were simply reflections of the High God. Although many Nuer people are Christian today, some elements of Nuer religion remain important. The Ashanti people of West Africa similarly regard the many gods in their belief system as the way in which the High God manifests.

In African religions, spirits are often considered to be a part of God's creation, like humanity. Most often, spirits are thought to live alongside human beings in a shared world. As a result, in many African cultures, spirits are a part of normal daily life. Spirits are commonly believed to be immortal and invisible. Many African religions associate spirits with elements of the natural world, such as mountains and trees, and forces of the natural world, such as rain and lightning. However, they are able to interact with human beings in various ways. Like human beings, spirits are neither entirely good nor entirely evil. They are typically thought to be more powerful than human beings, but humans can learn to interact with and even manipulate them to some degree. Religious experts or leaders may even call upon the spirits to act as messengers between humans and God.

Spirits of the Dead   In many African religions, the spirits of deceased humans are very important. In fact, most African religions do not regard death as a final state of oblivion. Instead, death is a change to another spiritual state. As birth is believed to be a transition from the world of the spirits to the world of the living, death is a transition back to the spirit world. This belief often has a basis in mythology. In Dogon myths, the original human ancestors became spirits, who then paved the way for later generations to enter the spirit realm after their death. Although the spirits of the dead are sometimes called "ancestor spirits," scholars of African religions argue that this term is not very accurate. This is because the category includes the spirits of many people who have died—not just those who bore children and have living descendants to whom they are ancestors.[8] Therefore, children or people who died childless can also become spirits.

The spirits of the dead are often active in the lives of their relatives and descendants for several generations. These spirits may also be concerned with upholding cultural values and family unity from beyond the grave. They are also frequently believed to be the most effective intermediaries between the High God and humans. Because of this, living people engage in specific practices to maintain positive relations with these spirits. And the spirits depend to some extent on humans. The living may symbolically care for the spirits by offering food and drink or making sacrifices to them. Like other supernatural beings of African religions, ancestor spirits are not necessarily good or bad, and they can both help and hurt their living relatives. If spirits are neglected, they may become angry and cause problems for the living. It is therefore very important for the living to respect their elderly relatives, who are close to transitioning to the spirit world. It is also essential to remember to pay respect to the deceased.

The Gikuyu people of Kenya (also known as the Kikuyu) recognize several categories of spirits of the dead. One category consists of deceased members of the immediate family, and another category includes the deceased members of the extended family group, or clan. The former are active in the day-to-day life of the living immediate family, and the latter spirits maintain an interest in the welfare of the clan. Living people may consult with the spirits of the dead for advice or guidance in their own affairs.[9] Therefore, in African cultures such as the Gikuyu, a person's family is considered to include not just his living relatives but also those who have passed on. The Gikuyu believe that if the spirits of the dead are neglected, they can harm the living as a form of punishment for such bad behavior. They may cause illnesses or bring about other misfortunes on their negligent descendants. Usually, the living make an effort to care for the spirits of the dead until the last person who knew the deceased during his life has died. At this point, the deceased moves into a different spiritual category in which he will have less active involvement in the lives of the living, or none at all.[10]

Why is it difficult to describe some African religions as simply "monotheistic" or "polytheistic"? Do you see this in any other religions you have studied so far?

Humanity and the Human Condition

Most African religions are anthropocentric, which means that they recognize humanity as the center of the cosmos.[11] Because of this, African belief systems understand the cosmos and elements within it, like supernatural beings, in terms of their relationship to humanity. Unlike many other religions, most African religions do not teach about the possibility of salvation or punishment in an afterlife. Rather, teachings generally focus on the importance of the present world.

This anthropocentrism is reflected in the many African mythologies that begin with the creation of human beings instead of the creation of the world. As we have seen, a High God is often the creator of human beings. In many African myths, God creates humanity from clay or mud. The Dogon creation narrative tells that after the birth of the Nummo twins, Amma decided to create eight human beings from clay.

The Dogon recognize these eight beings as the original human ancestors. In myths from other African traditions, God brings forth humanity from beneath the earth or out of a rock or tree. In still others, human beings come to this world from another one. The myths of the Chagga people of Tanzania explain that humanity descended to earth from heaven by the gossamer thread of a spider's web.

In some creation narratives, lesser gods are responsible for creating human beings. In a Yoruba narrative, the deity Obatala, son of the High God, was assigned by his father to make human beings from clay. Once the beings were made, the High God breathed life into them. One version of the myth tells that Obatala got very thirsty during his work of making humans. To quench his thirst, he started to drink beer. He became so drunk that he fashioned some people who were missing limbs, had crooked backs, or had other physical problems. When he sobered up, Obatala was so distraught at what he had done that he vowed to watch over the disabled people he had made. This myth accounts for people who are born with disabilities and for Obatala's special concern for them.

Many African religions teach that humans were created in a male-female pair as either husband and wife or (less often) as brother and sister. Dogon myths explain that the first eight humans each had a dual soul—they were both male and female. As a result, all humans are born with a dual soul. Circumcision reduces this dual soul to one soul—male or female. Other African cultures also regard humans as having a dual nature. Sometimes this is understood to be a physical body and an immaterial essence, like a spirit. The Lugbara people of Uganda believe that human beings have multiple souls. Each soul is associated with a different part of the body, like the heart or the lungs.

As we discussed earlier in this chapter, African religions often teach that the High God is removed from everyday human life. However, many teach that the High God was not always distant but originally lived with humans in a time of complete happiness, when God provided people with all they needed. However, God and humanity became separated. In some religions, this separation from God introduced death and toil into the lives of humans. These religions tend to emphasize the past—when humans coexisted with God—as an ideal, paradise-like existence.

In myths, the separation from the High God often was the result of humans breaking one of God's rules. In a myth of the Dinka people, who are cattle herders in southern Sudan, death is explained as the result of the anger of the first woman. In the beginning, the High God gave one grain of millet to the first woman and her husband. The woman was greedy and decided to plant more than a single grain. In her eagerness to plant, she hit God with her hoe. God was so angry that he withdrew from humanity and severed the rope that connected heaven and earth. Because of this, the Dinka believe that humans are doomed to work hard throughout life and then die. The myth also teaches an important moral lesson: humans should avoid being prideful and greedy.

Sometimes, human mortality results from the actions of animals who deliberately or unintentionally betrayed humans. The religion of the Nuer people teaches that a rope originally connected earth to heaven; this is similar to the Dinka myth. If someone climbed the rope to heaven, Kwoth, the High God, would make that person young again. One day, a hyena and a bird climbed the rope. Kwoth said they were not allowed to return to earth because they would cause trouble there. However, they escaped and returned to earth. Then the hyena cut the rope. Because of this, humans could no longer get to heaven, and now they grow old and die.

Many African religions also teach that the High God created human social organization, customs, and rules of conduct. Ethical and moral teachings often focus on the importance of maintaining agreeable relationships within human society and the spirit world. Sometimes, this extends to the proper relationship between humanity and the earth. Dogon mythology teaches that after they were created, the Nummo twins taught human beings how to farm. In many African cultures, farming is an important activity not only for subsistence but also in terms of religion. As we read, Dogon myths explain that the first child of the unfortunate union between Amma and the earth was a jackal. The jackal defiled its mother, the earth, by attempting to rape her. Humans, however, have the ability to correct this defilement and purify the earth through farming.

THE HISTORY OF INDIGENOUS AFRICAN RELIGIONS

Just like large-scale world religions, African religions have developed historically and accommodated cultural changes. Individual African religious traditions have unique histories that would be impossible to explore fully in a single chapter. Furthermore, the task is made more difficult because there are few surviving written records documenting the histories of these religions before the modern period. However, African religions have faced some common challenges and concerns in modern history that we can address together. We can also examine how indigenous African religions and their adherents have responded to the increasing influence of large-scale world religions, colonialism, and globalization.

The Spread of Islam

Large-scale world religions, especially Christianity and Islam, have been prevalent in Africa for centuries. More Africans convert to Islam and Christianity every day. However, even when people become Christians or Muslims, the influence of indigenous religious traditions remains and has shaped the form that these world religions take in Africa. In much of Africa, indigenous religious ideas, narratives, and practice coexist with Christianity and Islam. Africans often combine elements of many religions in their own worldviews and practice.

Islam has been present in Africa since the seventh century c.e. By the eighth century, Arab Muslims controlled North Africa from Egypt to Morocco, and Islam has been the dominant religion in North Africa for several centuries. Islam spread more slowly throughout sub-Saharan Africa. The number of Muslims in sub-Saharan Africa increased as Islam spread throughout West Africa and along the East African coast from the eleventh century until the present. Today, in addition to North Africa, the populations of much of West Africa, Northeast Africa, and the East African coast are predominantly Muslim.

In most cases, Islam spread through trade and through the teachings of traveling scholars. Often, elite Africans adopted Islam as a means to facilitate trade connections, because Muslim traders from North Africa were more likely to trade with other Muslims than with non-Muslims. As Africans became Muslims, they often retained elements of indigenous religious practice. For example, in Northeast and East Africa, the spirits known as *zar* are part of the religious worldview and practice of Muslims and Christians, as well as followers of indigenous religions. This is similar to the persistent belief in *bori* spirits in West Africa among Muslims and non-Muslims alike. The belief in possession by *zar* and *bori* spirits preexisted the arrival of Islam and has been incorporated into the religious practice of African Muslims. We will discussion possession in more detail later in the chapter.

Christianity and Colonialism

Christianity has also been present in Africa for centuries and is very widespread in Africa today. The Ethiopian Coptic church is an indigenous African church that dates to the fourth century C.E. However, Christianity did not become widespread outside of North and Northeast Africa until much more recently. In fact, much of African Christianity today is the result of missionary efforts and European imperialism in the nineteenth and twentieth centuries. Missionary movements and proselytizing often went hand in hand with imperialism, and almost all of Africa was colonized by European powers—primarily Britain, France, and Portugal. Ethiopia is a notable exception.

The colonial powers sent missionaries to convert Africans to Christianity, and the Christian Bible was translated into numerous African languages. Often, the process of converting Africans included cultural indoctrination. African people were taught not only that their indigenous religions were false but also that their cultures were inferior to Western ways of life. Therefore, when Africans became Christians, they sometimes left behind their own cultural practices and cultural identities. Often, the new Christians were incorporated in the colonial bureaucracies as government officials. African Christians were also sometimes put in charge of missions and were charged with furthering European aims by converting their own people.[12]

Reform and Resistance

Both today and in the past, African Muslim and Christian communities have debated whether practices derived from indigenous religions are an appropriate or authentic part of Muslim or Christian religious practice. In some cases, disapproval of indigenous practices and customs has led to major reform movements. Such criticisms of indigenous religions have largely been based on the idea that the beliefs, teachings, and practices of indigenous religions are at best "primitive" deviations from Christianity or Islam and at worst heretical and sinful.

Beginning in 1804, Usman dan Fodio (1754–1817), a West African Muslim reformer and religious leader, waged a campaign in northern Nigeria to rid Islamic practice of what he thought were inappropriate indigenous elements. One of the practices that he specifically criticized was spirit possession by the *bori* spirits, which was widespread at the time among both Muslims and non-Muslims. For over two decades, Usman dan Fodio and his followers tried to rid Muslim religious practice of what they viewed as inappropriate "African" elements such as this.

Similar campaigns have also been launched more recently. Christian and Muslim religious leaders have often targeted initiation rites such as those discussed earlier in this chapter. The rites have sometimes been described as "backward," "un-Christian," and "un-Islamic" or have simply been condemned as relics of a past best left behind. In some cases, Muslims and Christians have been receptive to the criticism and have stopped performing initiation rites or have replaced them with ceremonies that are deemed more appropriate by Muslim and Christian religious leaders. However, elsewhere, Muslims and Christians have continued to participate in the rites, despite the condemnation. Advocates argue that the rites are important means of achieving adulthood and are not in conflict with Christianity or Islam. Later in the chapter, we'll explore such rites of passage in more detail.

Occasionally, religious leaders who criticized the rites in the past have changed their approach. For example, at one time the Catholic Church in Zambia strongly restricted female initiation rites in some Zambian cultures. However, in the 1960s, Vatican II (a meeting of Roman Catholic Church leaders to address issues facing the church at the time) permitted church leaders to be more accepting of local practices. As a result, Zambian Catholic leaders changed their point of view. They argued that the initiation rites could be used to instill Catholic teachings about marriage and family in young women.[13]

In the first decades of the twentieth century, African Christian leaders began to develop new Christian churches that spun off from the long-established mission churches, like the Anglican and Catholic churches. African Christian leaders were often frustrated with their inferior status in the mission churches. Their new churches aimed to make Christianity more accessible and appropriate in African cultural contexts. The new independent churches became very popular, and today there are thousands of independent churches in Africa.[14]

In the 1920s, a man called Josiah Oshitelu (1902–1966) founded an independent Yoruba Christian church known as the Aladura church. As a young man, he thought witches plagued him. However, a Christian healer explained that it was God testing him and that if he prayed, he could chase away the evil. Oshitelu began praying. He received visions, and he tried to convince others that the old African religions were

How do debates in Africa about the authenticity or appropriateness of religious practice compare with other religions discussed in this book?

disappearing and that they should all become Christians. His teachings focused on the power of prayer and fasting to influence the will of God. Interestingly, many indigenous Yoruba religious beliefs and practices still held relevance for Aladura Christians. For example, most of the practitioners maintained beliefs in witchcraft and powerful spirits. The emphasis on prayer is also reminiscent of Yoruba ideas of harnessing spiritual power. Furthermore, the Aladura church focused on improving life in this world in much the same way as Yoruba religion.[15]

The Maji Maji Revolt Throughout Africa, religious groups spearheaded anticolonial movements, and indigenous religious leaders were at the forefront of some of the most important of these. In 1905, a religious leader called **Kinjiketele** organized a rebellion against the German colonizers in Tanganyika (later called Tanzania). The revolt was known as the **Maji Maji** (Water Water) rebellion. Kinjiketele, a diviner, was believed to receive communications from the spirit world. One well-known story about him reports that a spirit took him into a river pool. Later, he emerged completely dry and carried a message to his people that their dead ancestors would all come back. Many people came to see him and to take the sacred water, which they believed would make them impervious to the bullets of the Europeans.

Kinjiketele attracted a large multiethnic following that supported his call for rebellion against the German colonizers. His message was compelling because it drew on indigenous religious beliefs in the power of spirits and the power of sacred waters. (The revolt takes its name from this sacred water.) Eventually, a group of Kinjiketele's followers, impatient with waiting for him to signal the proper time, began the revolt against the Germans without him. The uprising lasted two years and was eventually defeated by the Germans.[16]

A Benzedeira, or Brazilian traditional healer, tends to an altar in the temple that is also her home.

African Religions in the Americas

The influence of African religions has spread far beyond the continent. In fact, many religious traditions of the Americas are derived from African religions. During the Atlantic slave trade, the religion of the Yoruba and other West African peoples such as the Dahome and the Fon spread far beyond the shores of their homelands. Most of the millions of African people who were enslaved and brought to the Americas followed indigenous religions. And although the religious traditions and practices of Africans were most often suppressed or even forbidden by white slave owners, indigenous beliefs often survived and sometimes flourished.

The worship of Yoruba *orisa* remains popular to this day in communities of African descent throughout the Americas. The religious tradition known as **Candomblé** owes much to the Yoruba slaves who were brought to South America; Candomblé has been particularly prominent in northeastern Brazil. African slaves managed to keep worshiping Yoruba deities in the face of conversion pressure from the European slave master by cloaking the *orisa* in the guise of Catholic saints. Many of the divination practices of *Ifa* have been incorporated within Candomblé. **Santeria** is a Cuban religion that bears similarity to Candomblé and also incorporates the *orisa*. The Cuban diaspora has spread the religion throughout the Caribbean region, including northern South America, and the United States. Today, it is likely that there are hundreds of thousands of practitioners of Santeria in the United States alone.

Another example from the Caribbean is the **Vodou** religion, which originated in Haiti and then spread elsewhere in the Caribbean and southern United States. Also known as *voodoo*, this religious tradition owes much to both Catholicism and religions of West Africa, especially the religions of the Yoruba, Fon, and Kongo peoples. The term "vodou" comes from the Fon word "vudon," which means spirit. Practitioners of vodou recognize many different spirits. The spirits are called *loa* and have origins in West Africa. As in Santeria, the spirits are also sometimes identified with Catholic saints. Today, the majority of Haitians claim vodou as their primary religious affiliation, although earlier in the twentieth century the Catholic Church denounced it as heretical.

INDIGENOUS AFRICAN RELIGIONS AS A WAY OF LIFE

For followers of African religions, religion is something that infuses everyday life. It is not reserved for just one day of the week or for certain times of the year. Instead, religious practice is a daily activity. As we have learned, most African religions do not focus on reward or punishment in the afterlife, so religious practice does not normally center on preparing for an afterlife. Instead, rituals and ceremonies focus on improving life in this world. Thus religious practice might address vital material needs, such as a good harvest, or social needs, such as a harmonious family life. Also, because the High God is often believed to be remote from day-to-day human life, most African religions do not emphasize worshipping a supreme deity. Instead, religious practice normally focuses on communication with other supernatural beings.

Communicating with the Spirit World

Many African religions believe that the world of the spirits and the world of humans are closely intertwined. Spirits live near human beings in the same communities and often exist in a reciprocal relationship with them. Because spirits can interact and interfere with the lives of humans, religious rituals and ceremonies often focus on communicating with spirits or accessing their power. People may ask spirits to intervene with God on their behalf or to assist with particular problems in family or work life. In this section, we will discuss three practices associated with communicating with the spirit world: sacrifice, divination, and spirit possession.

Sacrifice   In African religions, the primary way people communicate with supernatural beings is through sacrifice. In many religions the world over, the dedication of

VISUAL GUIDE
African Religions

Among the Dogon, the *dama* is a rite of passage for young men, which also helps the recently deceased enter the state of being ancestors. The rite happens only once every several years, and masked participants dance to usher the recently deceased into the world of the spirits. The masks prepared for the *dama* are elaborately carved and represent animals and the mythical ancestors.

This early twentieth-century wooden tray is used to determine future events with the Ifa divination system, a part of Yoruba religion.

These nineteenth-century Yoruba sculptures from Nigeria commemorate twins who died. Twins are of great significance in many African religions, as among the Dogon, discussed in this chapter.

something valuable to a spirit—a sacrifice—has the power to influence that spirit. A sacrifice can be relatively small, like a prayer or a portion of one's daily food or drink. In some religions, such as the Yoruba, individuals may have a special relationship with one or more spirits or gods, and they might make these small offerings every day to maintain their goodwill. Yoruba families often have household shrines at which they make similar offerings to the spirits of the dead.

In other African contexts, larger sacrifices, such as an animal, are necessary. In some religions, there has traditionally been a close relationship between practices of healing and sacrifice. Illnesses may be attributed to a spirit's punishment of a person's bad behavior. In such cases, an animal may be sacrificed as a form of repentance and as a request for forgiveness from the aggrieved spirit. The Nuer, for example, typically sacrificed animals as a substitute for the person who was afflicted with an illness. The animal was offered to the spirits in exchange for the health of the person. However, in recent years, as Nuer people have begun attributing illness to biological causes instead of angry spirits and as more have adopted Christianity, the use of animal sacrifice in healing has diminished.[17]

Divination In some African religions, people use a practice called **divination** to communicate with spirits. Divination is the attempt to predict the future through supernatural agents or powers. The Yoruba use a divination system called ***Ifa*** to communicate with the spirit world. A person called a diviner performs the divination. Yoruba religion teaches that *Ifa* was developed when the High God removed himself from the earthly world. His children remained behind, and he gave them a divinatory system to communicate with him. They shared this system with human beings. Through *Ifa*, humans are able to communicate with and make requests of the gods and the spirits of the dead.

Yoruba diviners also use *Ifa* to predict the destinies and future of individuals. The diviners use a special collection of poetic verses and palm nuts to foresee future events and converse with supernatural beings. Most of the verses are from sacred Yoruba texts, and they tell of the time of

Palm nuts with a blue cloth bag, used by the Yoruba people for divination.

the gods and ancestors. Diviners select specific verses because they contain the solution to problems that faced the ancestors and are thus helpful in solving current problems.

Spirit Possession Another way people communicate with the spirit world is through spirit possession. A belief in spirit possession is prevalent throughout Africa, and in many places this sort of interaction with spirits is a normal part of daily life. People communicate with spirits through a **medium**—an individual who has become possessed. Although women and men may both become possessed, in many cultures women are far more likely to become so. The possessed individual is called a medium because she *mediates* between the human world and the spirit world. The spirit takes over the medium's body, and the medium then acts according to the will of the spirit while she is possessed. Because spirit possession usually takes place in public, many people can witness the possession and interact with the spirit through the medium. When a spirit possesses a person, she enters a state of trance. Others may then talk to or make requests of the spirit through her.

Throughout Africa, people ascribe different meanings to possession. Some traditions view possession negatively. It might cause illness or cause the medium to harm others. In such cases, they may call on a spiritual healer to drive the spirit away. Elsewhere, people may encourage possession in order to communicate with the spirit world. Individuals may use special dancing, music, and drumming to entice a spirit. In such contexts, some people, such as women, may be more prone to spirit possession than others. Sometimes, people who have the ability to become possessed achieve a special religious status.

In West Africa, there is a widespread belief in spirits known as **bori** who have the power to possess people. There are many different *bori*, and they have individual personalities. Among the Mawri people of Niger, spirits such as Maria, a flirtatious young prostitute, regularly possess mediums.[18] In Northeast Africa, the **zar** spirits are similar to the *bori* and prominent throughout the region. Possession beliefs are also prevalent among Muslims and Christians in Africa. As these religions gained adherents in sub-Saharan Africa, many elements of preexisting religious practice remained. For example, Mawri people began converting to Islam in the mid-twentieth century, but the *bori* spirits remain. In Northeast Africa, the *zar* spirits possess both Muslims and Christians.

Two Orixás, or orisas, who possess the women, dance in their finery at a Candomblé festival in Brazil held in their honor.

How do people communicate with gods and spirits in other religious traditions? Are practices similar across religions or different?

Why do people become possessed? What does it mean for those who become possessed? Many scholars have tried to answer these questions. Some have argued that spirit possession is therapeutic for those who have mental or physical illness. Others suggest that spirit possession is a way for people to deal with rapid cultural change and the problems of modernity. For example, when the spirit Maria possesses Mawri women, they might be expressing an internal conflict between their desire to be traditional wives and mothers and the temptations of urban life and consumer culture, which Maria loves.[19]

Using Supernatural Powers

Practitioners of African religions believe that some people have the ability to manipulate the supernatural for their own ends. Western scholars have traditionally used the term **witchcraft** to explain the use of supernatural powers to cause illness or other misfortune. (It is important to note that in other religions, such as Wicca, the term "witchcraft" does not have negative connotations. For more on Wicca, see Chapter 14.) In African languages, many different terms are used to denote witchcraft, although the idea that one can use supernatural powers to cause harm is fairly widespread. Often, witchcraft pervades everyday life and is understood as a normal part of existence. However, the use of witchcraft is not always thought to be intentional. In fact, in some cultures, people may be "witches" without even knowing it. As a result, they may cause harm to others unintentionally.

One of the most well-known examples of witchcraft is from the Azande people, who live in Sudan and the Central African Republic. The Azande believe that witchcraft is a physical substance that is present in some people's bodies. Evans-Pritchard, who conducted research among the Azande in the 1930s, showed that witchcraft beliefs were part of the Azande theory of causation. Witchcraft is a way of explaining why certain things happen to certain people. For example, if a man happened to be killed because he was sitting under a granary when it collapsed, the Azande would attribute this to witchcraft. Even if the granary collapsed because termites had destroyed the supporting wooden posts, the question of *why* it collapsed when a particular individual was sitting underneath it remained. The Azande would argue that this was an instance of witchcraft: the termites explained how it collapsed, but this explanation did not answer the question of why it collapsed when it did and killed the man sitting under it. Only witchcraft could answer the "why" question.[20]

Sometimes, people use supernatural powers or call on supernatural beings to facilitate healing. Healers may use special divination methods to determine what has caused an illness. Although illness might be attributed to biomedical causes, a healer normally looks for an ultimate cause, which might be witchcraft or the malicious actions of spirits. Then the healer can take special ritual action to try to cure it. A cure may involve repairing damaged social relationships that have caused jealousy. Or a cure may involve a sacrifice to appease an angry spirit that caused the illness. Among the Ndembu of Zambia, some illnesses are believed to be caused by a particular spirit that is attracted to social conflicts. The spirit eats at the flesh of quarreling people with a sharp "tooth." To get rid of the spirit, Ndembu religious priests encourage the afflicted people to air their grievances against one another. During this discussion, the priest will use a special cup to extract the "tooth" that has been causing the illness.[21]

Life Cycle Rituals

Most African religions emphasize the life cycle. Celebrations and ceremonies that mark the transitions from one phase of existence to another are an important part of religious practice. These ceremonies define individuals as new members of the human community, as adults with full responsibilities and privileges of adulthood, or as having departed the living for the world of the spirits. African religions frequently believe that the life cycle begins before birth and continues after death. Rituals (Chapter 1) are formal religious practice. They are repetitive and rule-bound, and people often enact them with a specific goal in mind. The goal could be pleasing a deity, encouraging a good crop, or smoothing the transition between phases of the life cycle. As you learned in Chapter 2, rituals that facilitate this transition are called **rites of passage**. These rituals may be performed after a birth, during the transition from childhood to adult-hood, or at death, when the deceased moves to the world of the spirits.

Birth: The Transition to the Human World In many African religions, birth is the first important spiritual transition in a person's life. It is the moment a new individual enters the living community of humans. Preparing for a birth and welcoming a child is a process that often begins long before the child is born. Among the Bambuti people of the central African rainforest, a pregnant woman will offer food to a god as thanks for the pregnancy. In other African cultures, a pregnant woman is expected to observe certain rules and restrictions as a means of protecting herself and the child. For example, a woman may avoid certain foods or sexual relations with her husband while pregnant.

Practices surrounding the birth of a child vary tremendously from culture to culture in Africa. However, there are some common beliefs surrounding birth. One of these is the belief that birth marks the transition of the newborn from the world of spirits to the world of the living. Ceremonies after birth designate the child as belonging to the entire community, not just the mother. In many cultures, the placenta symbolizes the link between the child and its mother in its dependent state in the womb, and special care may be taken with its disposal after the child is born. The disposal of the placenta can symbolize the necessary separation of the child from its mother. The Yansi people

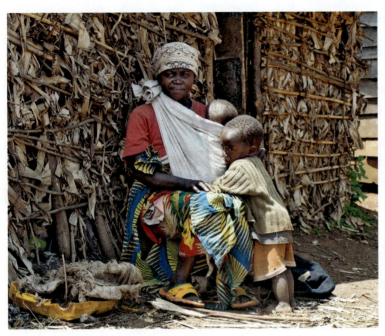

Bambuti woman and children in Uganda.

of the Democratic Republic of Congo throw the placenta into a river. This act symbolizes that the child no longer belongs only to his or her mother but now belongs to the entire community.[22] The Gikuyu of Kenya practice a rite with a similar meaning. After she has given birth, a mother's head is shaved. This represents the severing of the exclusive tie between her and the child and also represents renewal: the mother is now ready to bear another child. Like the Yansi, the Gikuyu then recognize the child as a member of the wider society.[23]

Many African cultures have special naming ceremonies for children to mark their transition from the spirit world to the human world. The Akamba people of Kenya name a child on the third day after he or she is born. The next day, the child's father presents him or her with a special necklace, and the parents have ritual intercourse. Together, these events mark the transition of the child from the spirit world to the world of living humans.[24] The Yoruba name their children after a special birth ritual called "stepping into the world." The ritual teaches parents how to raise their new child. At the request of the new parents, a diviner uses the *Ifa* divination system (discussed earlier in this chapter) to determine the baby's future. Using special tools, foods, and texts, the Yoruba diviner will try to determine the nature of the infant and will select a name based on what is found out. In one of the most important parts of the ritual, the diviner holds the baby's feet in the center of a special divination tray, which represents the entire world. This act places the baby symbolically in the center of the world and lets the diviner understand the baby's nature.[25]

Initiation Rites: The Transition to Adulthood Rites of passage marking the transition from childhood to adulthood are extremely important in African religious traditions. Although they differ significantly in the details, rites of passage focus on successfully initiating a young person into adulthood and setting him or her on the path to becoming a complete member of the community. The new adult will have new privileges and responsibilities and will be expected to behave with maturity and wisdom appropriate to this new status. Often, it is rites of passage at adolescence that create a fully gendered adult. In many cultures, young people are able to marry only if they have been initiated. Sometimes, young people acquire special religious knowledge during initiation. Rites of passage also form important bonds for young people who go through them together. Among the Ndembu people of Zambia, for example, boys going through initiation are secluded for circumcision rites. Their mothers bring them food, which all the boys share. The boys spend all their time together and develop close friendships, which are intended to last their entire lives.

Young Maasai men (like Tepilit, whose story begins this chapter) become warriors when they go through initiation. Much later, when men are in their thirties, they will be initiated as elders and be allowed to marry. Maasai girls are also circumcised when they reach adolescence. However, they do not transition into an intermediate warrior stage but become ready for marriage. Young women change the way they dress, and they spend much time preparing beautifully beaded necklaces and head ornaments to wear. Many of these young women marry soon after they are circumcised, and they most often move away from their homes to the villages of their husbands. As with the young men, girls become fully socially mature when they transition through these important rituals. For both, the coming of age rituals express important community values, such as strength, responsibility, and maturity.

Maasai women often wear intricately beaded necklaces.

Death: The Transition to the Spirit World Many African religions understand death not as an end to existence but as the transition to the spirit world. Funerals and other rituals surrounding death are important because they have the ability to ease the transition of the deceased from one state of being to another. In many cultures, the spirits of the dead cannot make the transition to the spirit world without the proper rituals. Normally, the living relatives of the deceased must facilitate the performance of these rituals. The LoDagaa people of Ghana hold complex funeral rites to facilitate this transition. The LoDagaa carve a special tree branch that represents the deceased. Ideally, a son cares for the branch as a representation of his late parent. While the symbolic branch is being cared for, the soul of the dead person is believed to travel to the world of the dead. The ritual is very important. If the living relatives do not perform it properly, then the soul of the deceased will be trapped in his or her village instead of moving to the realm of the dead.[26]

Among the Dogon, a rite of passage for young men also helps the recently deceased enter the state of being ancestors. This rite is known as the ***dama***, and the basis for it is laid out in myths. In the *dama*, which happens only once every several years, masked participants dance to usher the recently deceased into the world of the spirits. The masks prepared for the *dama* are elaborately carved and represent animals and the

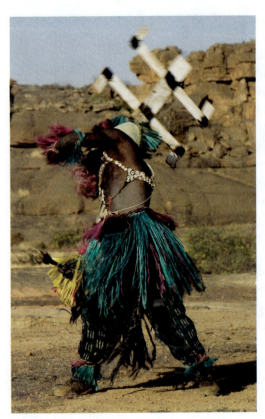

A Dogon masked dancer.

mythical ancestors. The *dama* is also important for the living. If the dead do not enter the world of the spirits, they can cause problems for the living. Therefore, a successful *dama* frees the living from misfortune caused by the spirits of the dead and restores the normal balance of life and death. Today, these masked dances not only are used for ritual purposes but are also performed to entertain tourists; versions of the masks are produced for the tourist trade.

The rituals surrounding death are not always sad, and they may even be joyful. Among the Yoruba, for example, if a person over forty years old dies of natural causes, then the death is regarded as an important and happy transition to the world of the spirits and gods. This world is called *orun*, and the spirit of the deceased person will remain there and be called upon to assist in the affairs of her living relatives. However, if someone is under age forty at the time of death or dies of unnatural causes, the Yoruba consider it to be a great tragedy. Their spirits cannot enter *orun* but are rather doomed to wander the earth unhappily forever.[27]

Women in Indigenous African Religions

As we have seen, women play many roles in African indigenous religions. The teachings of many African religions acknowledge and honor important female deities or spirits, and women are actively involved in many aspects of religious practice. Women have also been essential to the historical development of Christianity and Islam in Africa.

As noted earlier in this chapter, women often play a prominent role in possession cults and are more likely to become possessed than are men. When possessed, a woman becomes a powerful representative of the spirit world. Some scholars have argued that this allows women to achieve a temporarily high status in male-dominated societies and in religions in which men control mainstream religious practice.[28] However, women's spirit possession practices are frequently at the center of religious life, not relegated to the margins. In Nigeria, Edo women participate in the worship of the god Olokun, who is at the heart of Edo religion. In Edo cosmology, Olokun is a very important god who has authority over fertility and wealth. By participating in the possession cult, Edo women gain permanent high status in the community. And although women who serve Olokun as priestesses do not have political authority in the same way men do, they can exert a great deal of power by settling disputes and acting as medical advisors.[29]

Women have been important in the historical development of religion in Africa. Some scholars have argued that women's active role in spirit possession has led to their prominence in new religious movements. Because mission churches such as the Anglican and Catholic churches most often prohibited women from holding leadership roles, women were highly influential in the development of the African Independent Christian churches. Women founded new churches across Africa.[30] For example, a woman called Grace Tani founded the Church of the Twelve Apostles in Ghana in 1914. Tani was regarded as a prophet, and like many other influential women leaders, she incorporated many local traditions into her Christian practice.[31] Although many of these new churches are now headed by men, women have often maintained important roles in preaching, leadership, and healing in the churches. The Aladura Church, which we discussed earlier in this chapter, has separate male and female leadership structures.[32]

Women have also played active roles in African Islam. In early nineteenth-century West Africa, the teacher and scholar Nana Asma'u, a daughter of Usman dan Fodio, dedicated her career to encouraging the education of Muslim women. She taught that all women had a duty as Muslims to seek knowledge, and she is still a role model for Muslim women in Nigeria today.[33]

As you have read, some African religions emphasize the importance of male and female circumcision. In recent years, much controversy has surrounded female circumcision. It is often described as having a religious basis, sometimes to maintain the sexual purity of women, and it is not practiced solely within one religious community. In Africa, followers of many different religions practice female circumcision. This includes Christians and Muslims, in addition to followers of indigenous religions. Circumcision can take many forms. It can range from a simple incision on the clitoris to draw blood to what is known as infibulation. In infibulation, most of the external female genitalia are removed, and the incision is then sewn together. Because the more extensive types of circumcision, such as infibulation, can endanger the health of young girls, many people have called for an end to the practice. Some countries, such as Uganda, have banned it. However, reaction to these calls is mixed. Many women in Africa argue that circumcision is an essential part of their cultural identity.[34] They stress that a girl would never be considered a marriageable adult without undergoing the procedure during initiation. Others resent what they see as a movement led by Western activists, who remain silent about male circumcision because it is also prevalent in the West. Still others have succeeded in replacing circumcision with different kinds of rituals to mark the transition from girlhood to adulthood.

CONCLUSION

What does the future hold for the indigenous religions of Africa? Will these religious traditions maintain relevance in the face of ever-expanding world religions and in an increasingly globalized world?

The challenges of colonialism and growing world religions in the last few centuries have vastly increased the numbers of Africans following such large-scale religions as Islam and Christianity. Although the majority of Africans today profess one of these two faiths, their prevalence has certainly not eradicated indigenous African religions.

As we have seen in this chapter, people throughout Africa have incorporated beliefs and practices from indigenous religions into large-scale religions. As a result, Islam and Christianity have taken on distinctly African forms and have essentially *become* indigenous African religions. We have learned that African religions tend to focus on the present, and much African religious practice looks for ways to improve one's immediate circumstances. These concerns have remained meaningful to many people in Africa, even when they become followers of salvation-oriented religions such as Christianity and Islam.[35]

Furthermore, religions such as Santeria and Vodou, which are derived from African traditions, are flourishing in much of the Americas. Through increasing migration and mobility, practitioners of these religions make them significant and relevant in diverse cultural contexts and introduce others to their teachings and practices. Today, you can find practitioners of Santeria and Vodou who have no ancestral ties to Africa. As a result, these religions will likely continue to thrive and even grow in the Americas. And as more Africans move to parts of Europe and Asia for work or schooling, their religious practices will likely go with them and will adjust to new contexts.

In sum, we can assume that African religions will continue to change and adapt to wider social environments both in Africa and in the African diaspora. Although their forms and modes of practice will change from one generation to the next, this development only continues processes of change that are characteristic to all religions. African religions are not relics of the past; rather, they are meaningful living traditions that will continue to thrive in the future.

SEEKING ANSWERS

What Is the Nature of Ultimate Reality?

Most African traditions understand the world to have been created by a High God. The natural world, the supernatural world, and the social world of human beings are not separate and distinct realms but are often considered to be interlinked. Dogon creation narratives illustrate this idea. Most African religions are *anthropocentric*, or human-centered; they teach that God created humans and that creation and the universe revolve around humanity. Often, it is believed that humans and God once coexisted in an idealized past, but that something happened to separate humanity from God. African religions differ in terms of how ultimate reality is revealed to human beings: humans communicate with the divine through possession, sacrifice, and divination.

(continued)

What Is Our Ultimate Purpose?

African religions do not tend to focus on salvation or the goal of transcending the human condition but, rather, seek to emulate an idealized past in this life. However, many traditions hold that after death, people may transition to a spiritual state and may continue to interact with living humans. There are some exceptions to this. The Dogon and the Yoruba, for example, conceive of the possibility of a grand afterlife.

How Should We Live in This World?

Many African religions emphasize the importance of caring for and respecting the living and deceased members of one's family, the necessity of maintaining beneficial relationships with the beings of the spirit world, and the importance of harmony with the natural world. Because most African religions do not focus on reward or punishment in the afterlife, religious practice does not normally center on preparing for an afterlife. Instead, rituals and ceremonies focus on improving life in this world.

REVIEW QUESTIONS

For Review

1. What is the relationship between humanity and gods in African religions? Give specific examples from religions.
2. Describe the spirits of the dead. What role do they have in the lives of the living in particular religions? How are the beliefs about the dead reflected in religious practice?
3. What are the three main ways African religions communicate with the supernatural? Describe each.
4. What influence have African religions had on American religions? How did this happen?

For Further Reflection

1. Do you see any similarities between the religions of Africa and the religions of Native America? How do conceptions of the supernatural differ? Do they share similarities?
2. What parallels can you draw between Native American and African religious resistance movements? What motivated these movements, and how were they carried out?

GLOSSARY

Amma (ah-ma; Dogon) The High God of the Dogon people.

bori (boh-ree; various languages) A term for West African spirits.

Candomblé New World religion with roots in West Africa—particularly Yoruba culture—which is prominent in Brazil.

dama (dah-ma; Dogon) A Dogon rite of passage marking the transition to adulthood and to the afterlife.

divination The attempt to learn about events that will happen in the future through supernatural means.

Ifa (ee-fah; Yoruba) The divination system of the Yoruba religion, believed to be revealed to humanity by the gods.

Kinjiketele (kin-jee-ke-te-le) The leader of the Maji Maji rebellion in Tanganyika (today's Tanzania).

Maji Maji (mah-jee mah-jee; Swahili) A 1905 rebellion against German colonizers in Tanganyika (today's Tanzania).

medium A person who is possessed by a spirit and thus mediates between the human and spirit worlds.

moran (mor-an; Samburu and Maasai) A young man in Samburu or Maasai culture who has been circumcised and thus has special cultural and religious duties.

Odu (oh-doo; Yoruba) The original prophets in Yoruba religion.

orisa (oh-ree-sha; Yoruba) Term for lesser deities in Yoruba religion.

Oshun (oh-shoon; Yoruba) A Yoruba goddess.

pantheon A group of deities or spirits.

rites of passage Rituals that mark the transition from one life stage to another.

Santeria (san-teh-ree-a; Spanish) New World religion with roots in West Africa; prominent in Cuba.

Vodou (voo-doo; Fon and French) New World religion with roots in West Africa; prominent in Haiti and the Haitian diaspora.

witchcraft A term used by Western scholars to describe the use of supernatural powers to harm others.

zar (zahr; various languages) A term for spirits in East Africa.

SUGGESTIONS FOR FURTHER READING

Abimbola, Wande. *Ifa: An Exposition of Ifa Literary Corpus*. Ibadan, Nigeria: Oxford University Press, 1976. Scholarly look at Yoruba religious texts and beliefs.

Evans-Pritchard, Edward E. *Witchcraft, Oracles, and Magic Among the Azande*. New York: Oxford University Press, 1976. Classic anthropological account of beliefs about witchcraft and magic among the Azande people of southern Sudan.

Griaule, Marcel. *Conversations with Ogotemmeli*. London: Oxford University Press, 1965. A firsthand description of Dogon cosmology based on conversations with a Dogon elder.

Mbiti, John S. *African Religions and Philosophy*. New York: Praeger, 1969. Useful introduction to African belief systems and religions.

McCarthy Brown, Karen. *Mama Lola: A Vodou Priestess in Brooklyn*. Berkeley: University of California Press, 1998. Engrossing ethnographic account of a modern-day Vodou priestess.

Olupona, Jacob K. *African Traditional Religions in Contemporary Society*. St. Paul, MN: Paragon House, 1998. Useful look at African religions in the present day.

Ray, Benjamin C. *African Religions: Symbol, Ritual, and Community*. Upper Saddle River, NJ: Prentice Hall, 2000. Introduction to African religions aimed at students focusing on religious practice.

ONLINE RESOURCES

National Museum of African Art

africa.si.edu

The National Museum of African Art, part of the Smithsonian Institution, offers abundant useful resources for African religion and material culture.

African Voices

mnh.si.edu/africanvoices

The Smithsonian's "African Voices" site explores the diversity of African cultures and their connections to the global world.

HINDUISM

ON A SPRING MORNING in the Salt Lake Valley, Indra Neelameggham and her husband Neale join a gaily dressed crowd, many of whom clutch offerings of flowers, fresh fruits, and coconuts. Indra and Neale have watched friends and the community work to create a beautiful place for worship in this stark region of Utah.

This is the third of three days of rituals celebrating the temple's opening, during which nearly 1,000 people have passed the temple threshold, gathering to attend the intricate consecration ceremony.

A week ago a three-foot-tall icon of Ganesha had been moved from Indra's house, where she had hosted him as an honored guest for eight years while the temple was being constructed, to his new home in the temple.

With his elephant head and human body, Ganesha is one of Hinduism's most easily recognized deities. As the patron deity of arts and sciences and the god of wisdom, new beginnings, and commerce, he is especially venerated by students, writers, travelers, and businessmen. Ganesha is worshipped at the beginning of every new undertaking, and he is the first deity invoked in almost any Hindu ritual context. He is often depicted as carrying objects in his four arms (including an axe, a noose, and an elephant goad) that he uses to destroy, subdue, or control the obstacles of life. He also often holds a bowl of sweets, symbolizing his benevolent and loving nature.

Ganesha appears adorned for worship in the sanctum of the Sri Ganesha Hindu Temple of Utah. Because Hindu deities are often associated with the land in which they are worshipped, he is affectionately called "Uppu Vinayaka" or the "Salt" Ganesha, by some of the local devotees.

TIMELINE
Hinduism

2600–1700 B.C.E. Indus Valley Civilization.

2000–1300 B.C.E. Migration into Northwest India of Indo-Aryans.

c. 1200 B.C.E. *Rig Veda.*

c. 1200–900 B.C.E. Later *Vedas.*

c. 900–200 B.C.E. *Upanishads.*

400 B.C.E.–400 C.E. *Mahabharata.*

200 B.C.E.–200 C.E. *Ramayana.*

c. First century C.E. *Bhagavad Gita.*

100–500 C.E. Expansion of Hinduism into Southeast Asia.

c. 320–540 Gupta Dynasty; rise of Hindu temple culture.

300–500 Earliest *Puranas*; Hindu law books.

700 Flourishing of *bhakti* in the South.

999–1226 Mahmud of Ghazi; repeated raids of India.

Fifteenth century *Bhakti* movement begins in northern India.

c. 1398–1518 Kabir, *bhakti* poet

1526–1757 Mughal rule in India.

1651 The East India Company opens first factory on the Hugli River in Bengal.

1786 Sir William Jones lectures on the common ancestry of Sanskrit and many European languages.

1828 Brahmo Samaj founded by Ram Mohan Roy.

1834–1886 Sri Ramakrishna.

1869–1948 Mohandas (Mahatma) Gandhi.

1875 Arya Samaj founded by Swami Dayananda Saraswati.

1893 Swami Vivekananda at the World Parliament of Religions, Chicago.

1925 RSS (Rashtriya Swayamsevak Sangh) founded.

1947 India gains independence; partition with Pakistan (and Bangladesh).

1964 VHP (Vishwa Hindu Parishad) founded.

1992 Destruction of Babri Masjid and widespread riots.

2014 BJP (Bharatiya Janata Party) wins Indian elections by a landslide.

The previous day, at midnight, the statue of Ganesha had been permanently affixed to its base in the temple's innermost sanctum. Now, the priest conducts a ritual that invites the actual divine spirit into the icon, transforming a simple stone image into a deity. The final step of the ritual requires that the priest awaken the gaze of the deity. While the priest outlines the icon's eyes with a golden needle, a sculptor pierces the pupils with a diamond-tipped chisel. The deity is now awake, and Ganesha's initial powerful gaze must first fall on things that represent good fortune: a cow with its calf, young children, mounds of rice, and bountiful offerings of food that will be distributed to the devotees.

Like the other devotees at the temple, Neale and Indra are overcome by reverence and exuberance. They realize that they have helped to build not just a temple, but a community. And at the center of it all is their Ganesha of Salt Lake. They step forward to have **darshan**—that is, to see and to be seen by the divine—and feel the immense presence of a living being. ☼

Unlike many other religions discussed in this book, Hinduism has neither a single founder nor a single sacred book. There is no single historical event that marks its birth. The history of Hinduism embodies both continuity and change. Having never had a sole central authority, Hinduism's fluid character has always allowed it to adapt to a variety of social and cultural contexts. This diversity has led many scholars to argue that Hinduism is not one religion at all but a constellation of many religious sects that share some common aspects. Others see enough by way of common beliefs and practices to regard Hinduism as a single religious tradition. In this chapter, we will explore Hinduism's variety of sects, beliefs, and practices and seek to understand what unites a religious tradition capable of thriving as far away from its homeland of India as Salt Lake Valley.

THE TEACHINGS OF HINDUISM

Prior to the nineteenth century, the word "Hinduism" did not exist. Most Hindus identified themselves by their sectarian orientation and their communal or caste affiliations. The word *Hindu* was initially a term used by the ancient Persians to describe the people who lived beyond the Indus River in the northwestern corner of the Indian subcontinent. By 325 B.C.E., Alexander the Great had crossed the Indus; the Greek conquerors adopted the Persian convention of calling the river the "Indos" and the land beyond it "India." In the centuries that followed, the term "Indu" or "Hindu" became a territorial, as well as a racial, social, and cultural, designation for the people of India. After the sixteenth century C.E., the word appeared occasionally in Indian literature to distinguish "Hindus" from Muslims or other "foreigners." Although the "-ism" was added to "Hindu" in the early 1800s, only toward the end of the nineteenth century did the word "Hinduism" become widely used by Hindus themselves.

A photograph taken of a Hindu temple in Trinidad in 1931. The presence of Hindus in the Caribbean and South America can be traced back to the nineteenth century, when Hindus came as indentured workers on sugar cane plantations.

Some Hindus look to the authority of a group of texts known as the **Vedas** and may rely on **brahmin** priests to officiate at various rituals. Others reject the centrality of the *Vedas* and *brahmins*. Some Hindus join organizations built around saints or sages. Others seek solitude to practice contemplation, meditation, or yoga. Some Hindus believe that God is a divine person with identifiable attributes. Others say that divine reality is so expansive as to be beyond all description.

Despite Hinduism's diversity, it is possible to identify common core concepts in which most every Hindu believes. For instance, the law of **karma** determines the nature of one's incarnations in **samsara**, the continuing cycle of death and rebirth. At the end of this cycle is **moksha**, or liberation, the final release from the trials and tribulations of *samsara*.

For the sake of simplicity, in this chapter we have organized our investigation of Hindu teachings around four main topics. First, we examine beliefs about God or divine reality. Next, we explore Hinduism's key doctrines and social concepts. We then take up a discussion of Hinduism's foundational texts. We conclude with a brief survey of *Vedanta*, a philosophical school, and Hinduism's three major sects.

Hindu Beliefs about Divine Reality

In keeping with Hinduism's general diversity, Hindu beliefs about divine reality are wide ranging. Indeed, one of the most fundamental differences in Hinduism is the split between monistic and dualistic (or devotional) viewpoints. Monism, as explained in this book's introductory chapter, is the doctrine that all reality is ultimately one. It is nondualistic in that there is no distinction between the divine reality and the rest

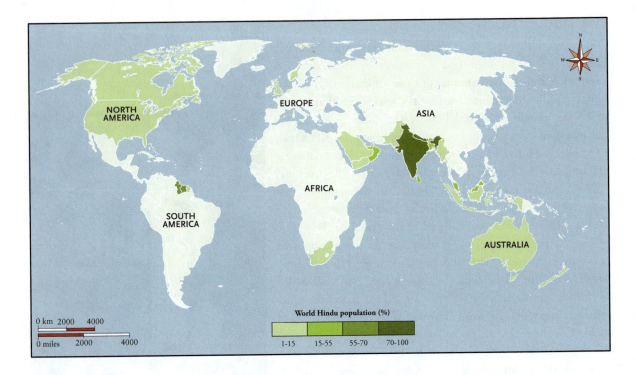

World Hindu population.

World Hindu population (%)

| 1-15 | 15-55 | 55-70 | 70-100 |

of reality. The Hindu dualistic viewpoint, on the other hand, understands divine reality as God, a personal being separate from the rest of reality. This means that God is separate from the individual, and therefore devotion to God is possible. Devotional practice of this sort is a primary religious activity of Hindus who hold this dualistic viewpoint. The majority of Hindus understand divine reality in this dualistic manner.

Names of the Divine Reality   Hindus refer to divine reality in a variety of ways. In this chapter, in order to maintain clarity between references to the monistic and the dualistic viewpoints, we use two distinct terms. When referencing monism, we use the term ***Brahman*** (lit. "expansive") to denote the divine reality, which monistic Hindus believe is the supreme, unitary reality that is the source of all being and all knowing. When referencing dualistic or devotional Hinduism, we use either "God" or the name of the specific deity under consideration.

In actual Hindu practice, conventions of naming the divine are often not so simple as our chapter's use of these two distinct terms might imply. Sometimes monistic Hindus, for example, refer to *Brahman* as "God." Many dualist Hindus use "God" to denote a universal being that encompasses all the various deities worshipped in Hinduism, and sometimes they use the term *Brahman*. When dualistic Hindus refer to a particular deity, they often use the specific name, such as Krishna, Rama, or Shiva. Devotees of the goddess traditions refer to God as *Mahadevi* ("Great Goddess") or *Mataji* ("mother"). Sometimes Hindus use Sanskrit terms such as *Bhagavan* (lit.

"Magnanimous One;" also an epithet for Vishnu) and *Svami* (or Swami, lit. "Master"; also denoting an initiate of a monastic order).

One Divine Reality, Many Gods The monistic viewpoint does not preclude belief in gods and goddesses. In a famous passage from the ***Upanishads*** (a collection of early philosophical texts), a sage is asked how many gods there are. Initially, he says there are "three hundred and three, and three thousand and three," but, upon reflection, he ultimately concludes that there is only one.[1] The sage explains that the various powers of the divine manifest as countless deities. In later times, the traditional number grew to 330 million. The passage from the *Upanishads* concludes with the sage giving the name of the one god: *Brahman*, which is the supreme, unitary reality, the ground of all Being.

Although *Brahman* is the true nature of all that exists, including ourselves, it is indescribable from the ordinary human perspective. *Brahman* can be described only by way of some general attributes: infinite being (*sat*), infinite awareness (*chit*), and infinite bliss (*ananda*). A passage from the *Upanishads* states that *Brahman* is *neti, neti*: "not this, not this."[2] When all of the identifiable particulars of the universe are subtracted away, what remains is *Brahman*, the essential substratum of all existence. This is monism, the belief that all reality is ultimately one.

These passages from the *Upanishads* influence how later monistic Hinduism forms its understanding of the mystery and majesty of Being. Many monistic Hindus believe that God is simultaneously one—as *Brahman*, the ground of all Being—and many. Given the worship of many deities, along with affirmation of the ultimate singularity of the divine, and indeed of *all* reality, this form of Hinduism can be described as both polytheistic and monistic. Unlike polytheistic religions that see the various gods as limited, Hinduism regards each god as a manifestation of *Brahman*.

Divine Reality as Sound The primordial sound **OM** (or, more literally, *AUM*), is constituted of three sounds of the Sanskrit language: *A, U,* and *M*—the first two, vowels, and the last, a consonant, respectively. *OM* therefore encompasses all words and all things they represent. *OM* is the sound through which the universe is manifested and thus is the very expression of *Brahman*. Some *Upanishads* also identify it with four states of consciousness: *A* is waking consciousness, *U* is dreaming consciousness, *M* is deep sleep without dreaming consciousness, and *AUM* in its entirety is the fourth and final state, oneness with *Brahman*. In later Hinduism, the sounds are identified with the gods Brahma, Vishnu, and Shiva and their functions of creating, preserving, and dissolving the universe.

God as Image Paradoxically, given the difficulty of comprehending the nature of divine reality, Hinduism is an intensely imagistic religious tradition. This is especially true of dualistic Hinduism, as imagistic representations of God are naturally well suited for devotional practices.

Ringed by cosmic time represented by a fiery ring, Shiva as Lord of the Dance (Nataraja) performs his Five Activities: creation (represented by the drum in his upper right hand), preservation (signified by the positions of his lower right and left hands), destruction (symbolized by the fire in his upraised left hand), illusion (personified by the tiny Demon of Forgetfulness crushed beneath his right leg), and liberation (offered by surrendering to his upraised left foot). Chola period, c. eleventh century. India, Tamil Nadu.

Images of supernatural beings and mythical beasts decorate Hindu temples, as well as Hindu homes. This love for the divine form emerges from Hindu notions of the simultaneous immanence and transcendence of God. An image of a deity is a symbolic representation meant to aid devotees in contemplating the deity's divine attributes, but the image is also believed to be suffused with divine presence, as we saw in the opening narrative about the Ganesha temple. Thus, Hindus believe that God becomes accessible to devotees through images. For Hindus, an image of a god *is* God.

Some images feature multiple limbs and faces that represent the deity's many aspects (such as compassion, serenity, or ferocity). The multiple hands of a deity depict gestures or hold objects that reveal his or her activities, such as providing protection, granting wishes, or holding a book of wisdom. Images can be richly adorned stationary icons enshrined in temples or beautifully crafted bronze icons carried in religious processions. Some images are quite large, such as the statue of Ganesha we encountered at the beginning of this chapter. Icons in personal shrines in Hindu homes tend to be small. Today, some Hindus revere print and online images of the divine. Because of the emphasis on divine images and their worship, Hindus sometimes have been falsely characterized as idolatrous. For Hindus, however, images of God are imbued with the divine essence. It is this essence that is worshiped and invoked through ritual action.

The Divine in Nature   If *Brahman* is everywhere and everything, it follows that the natural world is an expression of the divine. This belief is held by most Hindus, whether inclined toward the monistic or the dualistic viewpoint. The worship of such natural entities as rivers, the earth, mountains, and the sun, as well as a reverence for certain trees and animals, can be traced back to the roots of Hinduism.

Many sacred sites arose in conjunction with the worship of rivers and mountains. Rivers in particular are worshipped as embodying the creative energy that generates the universe, as well as being powerful places of crossing between the divine and terrestrial worlds. It is for all of these reasons that many Hindus bathe in rivers—of which the Ganges in India is the most important—believing that they wash away one's sins. The renowned classical Sanskrit writer Kalidasa (fifth century C.E.) described the Himalayas as a *devatatma,* a great spiritual presence. For centuries, the awe-inspiring peaks of the Himalayas have attracted monks, yogis, and pilgrims seeking an experience of the divine. Mount Kailasha, believed to be the home of the god Shiva, draws devotees who perform a ritual circumambulation of the mountain over the course of several days, reaching elevations of greater than 18,000 feet on the trek. Hindu mythology portrays the sun, planets, and other celestial bodies as gods.

For Hindus, all living things are sacred, and some especially so. For example, the Pipal (*ficus religiosa*), the type of fig tree under which Gautama the Buddha attained enlightenment (Chapter 5), is sacred to the god Vishnu. As is well known, a special place is given to the cow in Hindu society, a practice that has deep historical roots in the various pastoral, cattle-tending communities found throughout India. Because a child, once weaned from its mother's breast, is frequently given cow's milk, the cow is revered by Hindus as a second mother. Cows are worshipped on the first day of the important Hindu festival of *Diwali*, as well as on the first day of a harvest festival observed in southern India. For Hindus, the worship of cows is an expression of respect for creatures that help humanity.

Although Hinduism has a long history of reverence for natural entities, this has not always translated into ecological awareness and activism. The worship of rivers does not mean that India's sacred waterways are pristine. Because rivers are divine, they are said to be able to absorb the sins of worshippers and still remain unaffected. Thus, for many Hindus, rivers remain pure even if they are polluted by waste. In recent years, Hindu environmental activists have begun to challenge these assumptions by employing Hindu beliefs about the divinity of the natural world to promote more informed ecological awareness.

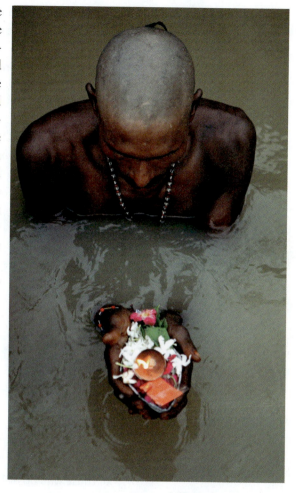

A Hindu devotee performs rituals dedicated to the Sun God as he takes a holy dip in Allahabad, India, at the confluence of the Ganges and Yamuna Rivers, one of Hinduism's important centers.

God Comes Down: Avatars Two of the most popular deities in Hinduism are Krishna and Rama. Each is an **avatar**, a "descent" (Sanskrit, *avatara*) of God to earth in a physical form with the specific goal of aiding the world. Like most avatars, they are manifestations of Vishnu, whose primary function is the preservation of order in the world. Vishnu is believed to have ten such forms, of which nine have already appeared. As noted, the most popular of the avatars are Rama, Vishnu's seventh form, and Krishna, his eighth. It is said that Vishnu's final avatar, Kalki, will arrive at the end of the present age to usher in an era of peace.

We have seen that Hindus often use the names of particular gods as a way of referring to divine reality. This is the case with avatars. For example, Hinduism's best-known sacred text, the *Bhagavad Gita* (*The Song of the Lord*), presents Krishna as a manifestation of the supreme Being.

In the *Bhagavad Gita*, Krishna asserts the principle that although God's essential nature is unchangeable, God chooses to descend into the world in the form of an avatar when intervention is necessary to reinstate peace and harmony. Krishna says:

> Although I am unborn,
> an imperishable self,
> and the Lord
> of all Beings,
> I govern my own
> earthly nature,
> and come into being
> by my own creative force.
> Son of Bharata,
> whenever there is
> a decline
> in *dharma*,
> and the absence
> of *dharma*
> increases,
> I create myself.
> I come into being
> from age to age
> with the purpose
> of fixing *dharma*—
> as a refuge for
> those who do good
> and as a doom
> for those who do evil.
> (*Bhagavad Gita*, 4:6–8)[3]

We will learn more about the *Bhagavad Gita* later in this chapter.

The Individual and the Quest for Liberation

Having explored Hindu perspectives on divine reality, we turn now to basic concepts that form the framework of the Hindu outlook on the individual and the quest for liberation. Some of these concepts, such as *samsara* and karma, are shared by other religions (Buddhism, Jainism, and Sikhism), although each treats these concepts in different ways.

Atman All Hindus believe in an undying soul or self, the **atman**, whose nature is neither limited by the physical body nor defined by its relationship to the world. It is the *atman* that moves from body to body through successive incarnations.

The task of recognizing the true nature of the essential self is understood to be arduous and rarely achieved. Most Hindus assume that this will require many lifetimes.

One's life ordinarily revolves around a sense of selfhood that is limited, constrained by desires and by ignorance of the true nature of *atman*. Life, therefore, ordinarily is lived by the egoistic "self" that is by nature (as the term suggests) selfish and stuck with the false identification of the self with the physical body. This leads to suffering, as the body undergoes painful changes brought on by disease, old age, and death.

Monistic Hinduism, true to its basic premise that all reality is ultimately one, teaches that the *atman is Brahman*. In a famous passage from the *Upanishads*, a young man named Svetaketu receives instruction from his father on the true nature of the *atman*. Using a number of analogies, the father explains that despite the appearance of multiplicity, all reality is one. The father emphatically declares: *Tat tvam asi svetakato iti* ("*You* are that, Svetaketu!").[4] *Atman* is *Brahman*.

Karma The course of the *atman* through successive incarnations is determined by karma. In its original, most basic sense, karma means "action," but for Hindus it means the consequences of action as well. Karma functions in accordance with the law of cause and effect: good actions produce good effects, bad actions produce bad effects. Karma encompasses all kinds of action, physical as well as mental. A person's situation in any given moment has been shaped by all previous actions. Consider, for example, being a college student. This situation is no accident, but rather the effect of certain kinds of thought and behavior during high school years that put the person on this course. Similarly, the karmic forces that we set in motion in our present lives will determine the nature of our future incarnations. To ensure that the future will be good, our actions now must be good—and that means living in conformity with *dharma*.

Dharma For Hinduism, the term ***dharma*** can mean law, duty, righteousness, or even "religion," all of which have to do with living in a way that upholds cosmic and social order. *Dharma* is traditionally believed to have been divinely revealed to the *rishis*, the poet-sages who composed the *Vedas*.

Through the centuries, Hindu texts have set forth ritual and social obligations that define a good life. The *Laws of Manu*, for example, a classic juridical text from the period 200 B.C.E. to 200 C.E., contains detailed prescriptions for correct behavior in all aspects of life. The two ancient and enormously influential Indian epic poems, the *Ramayana* and the *Mahabharata*, depict the simultaneous particularity and universality of *dharma*. As we will consider in more detail in a later section, both poems present epic heroes who must resolve conflicts between social or family obligations and their own personal sense of what duty demands from them.

Samsara Hindus use the term *samsara* in two closely related ways. *Samsara* is the continuing cycle of birth, death, and rebirth. *Samsara* is also the this-worldly realm in which birth, death, and rebirth recur. When the physical body dies, the eternal self or soul, the *atman*, moves on to another body. This process continues until the true nature of the *atman* is recognized. As noted previously, the nature of each rebirth is determined by karma. Virtuous acts of kindness and generosity over lifetimes ensure favorable rebirths, perhaps even in the blissful heavens of the gods. Selfish action and meanness lead to undesirable rebirths.

Hindus believe in a multitude of heavens and hells, as well as other regions in between. A rebirth in a heaven or hell could last for thousands of years but is still only temporary. The most desirable rebirth of all is as a human being in a situation that offers the greatest opportunity for realizing liberation from *samsara*; for example, as a sage or an ascetic.

The concept of *samsara* presents some basic questions. What gives rise to *samsara*? And why are human beings so prone to remain stuck in this *samsaric* realm? Through the ages, Hindus have offered various answers to these questions. Some of these answers have involved the concept **maya**, which in the *Vedas* refers to the magical power the gods used to create this world. Is the world an illusion, as is often the case with magic, or real? Hindus are divided on this issue. In either case, they agree that human beings are powerfully attracted to this world, with its many particulars—our egoistic selves, our relationships, our possessions, and the seemingly countless objects of our desires. Our attachment to such things in all that we think and do and the karma it generates steer us after each lifetime back into the *samsaric* realm of particulars.

All of this leads to another basic question: Why should anyone *want* to escape from *samsara*? After all, the prospect of a future filled with numerous lifetimes would seem to be appealing. Hinduism's answer is simple: beyond the *samsaric* realm lies something inexpressibly better.

A *sannyasi*, or Hindu ascetic. His sectarian affiliation is indicated by his forehead marking, which demonstrates that he is a worshipper of Vishnu.

Moksha Freedom from the bondage of *samsara* is achieved through *moksha*, "release" or "liberation." Having overcome attachments to this world, the *atman* realizes its true nature. For monistic Hindus, *moksha* is the union of the *atman* with *Brahman*, such that no sense of individuality any longer exists. For dualistic or devotional Hindus, for whom the divine reality is identified with their supreme God (be it Vishnu, Shiva, or another), *moksha* involves the eternal existence of the *atman* in the company of God. Hindus also have differing opinions on whether *moksha* can occur for a living person or whether it must await death of the physical body. For all Hindus, however, *moksha* marks the end of the *samsaric* cycle of rebirth and the end of the effects of karma. Like *Brahman*, *moksha* is virtually impossible to describe, beyond being characterized—also like *Brahman*—as infinite awareness and eternal bliss.

It almost goes without saying that the quest for *moksha*, for liberating oneself from *samsara* even while constrained to the limits of this world, is extremely challenging.

Hinduism offers three main paths to *moksha*, each one providing means of eradicating ignorance and egoistic attachment and thus freeing the *atman*.

Three Paths to Liberation

Typical of the diverse nature of Hinduism, there are a variety of approaches to the goal of liberation. Traditionally they have been categorized as three paths, or *margas* (also called *yogas*), each one featuring its own set of practices and being suited to certain personality traits and life situations. **Karma marga**, for those engaged in the activities of family and career, emphasizes ritual and ethical works. **Bhakti marga**, for the vast majority of Hindus who regularly worship in temples and in their homes, is devotion to a deity. **Jnana marga**, for those privileged to devote time and energy on study and contemplation, focuses on spiritual insight. The paths are by no means exclusive of one another: Hindus commonly engage in more than one. Almost all Hindus, for example, practice some form of *bhakti marga*, and *karma marga* is a natural way to approach life's everyday tasks. All three *margas* function to diminish the ignorance, attachment, and false identification of the self with the physical body that characterize life in the *samsaric* realm.

Typical of its synthesizing nature, the *Bhagavad Gita*, which was composed in about the first century of the Common Era, sets forth all three *margas*, explaining characteristics common to all three and making clear their mutual compatibility. Of fundamental concern is the need to eradicate the ignorance and attachment born of an egoistic sense of selfhood. One passage puts it this way: "He who abandons all desires and acts free from longing, without any sense of mineness or egotism—he attains to peace."[5]

Karma Marga As noted previously, all Hindus are required to act in conformity with *dharma*, the duty to live in a manner that upholds cosmic and social order. *Karma marga* combines focus on *dharma* with an attitude of detachment with regard to acting and to the results of action. In the words of the *Bhagavad Gita*:

> Relinquishing attachment,
> men of discipline perform action
> with body, mind, understanding, and senses
> for the purification of the self.
> Relinquishing the fruit of action
> the disciplined man attains perfect peace;
> the undisciplined man is in bondage,
> attached to the fruit of desire.[6]

When the self, or *atman*, is devoid of attachment to the results of action, the problems of egotism, and the suffering brought about by birth, disease, old age, and death, are resolved.

Bhakti Marga The path of devotion, *bhakti marga*, is the most widely practiced of the three paths to liberation. This chapter's survey of the history of Hinduism includes a section detailing the rise of the *bhakti* tradition. In an important manner, the tradition is grounded in the *Bhagavad Gita*, which, along with prescribing the other two *margas,* gives pride of place to *bhakti.* In the *Bhagavad Gita,* the featured deity is Krishna. *Bhakti,* however, can be directed toward whatever deity one chooses. Hindus typically worship more than one deity, depending on personal preference and on the occasion; for instance, during the festival in honor of Saraswati, goddess of education, Hindu schoolchildren offer devotion to her. There are numerous such festivals of the gods in the Hindu year.

In the *Bhagavad Gita,* Krishna makes clear to his devotee Arjuna the great benefits of *bhakti*:

> But men intent on me
> renounce all actions to me
> and worship me, meditating
> with singular discipline.
> When they entrust reason to me,
> Arjuna, I soon arise
> to rescue them from the ocean
> of death and rebirth.
> Focus your mind on me,
> let your understanding enter me;
> then you will dwell
> in me without doubt.[7]

Like *karma marga* and *jnana marga, bhakti marga* functions to eradicate egotism, ignorance, and attachment to the objects of desire. By devoting one's time and energy to a deity rather than to one's individualistic yearnings and concerns, the true nature of reality is realized, the effects of karma are neutralized, and liberation from *samsara* is achieved.

Jnana Marga   Generally agreed to be the steepest ascent to liberation, *jnana* ("knowledge") *marga* requires disciplined study of sacred texts and intensive contemplation, typically through the practice of meditation. This is the path of wisdom, the special pursuit of philosophers. The *Bhagavad Gita* says:

> There is nothing on earth equal in purity to wisdom. He who becomes perfected by *yoga* finds this of himself, in his self [*atman*] in course of time.
>
> He who has faith, who is absorbed in it [i.e., wisdom], and who has subdued his senses, gains wisdom, and having gained wisdom he attains quickly the supreme peace.[8]

The wisdom gained through *jnana marga* is spiritual knowledge or insight of a special kind. To attain this wisdom is to become aware of the true nature of *atman.* For monistic

Hindus, this is to become aware that the *atman* is none other than *Brahman*, the ultimate, unitary reality.

In a later section of this chapter we explore Yoga, one of the most important of Hinduism's six philosophical schools. The Yoga school teaches specific physical and mental exercises designed to promote *jnana*. It is this form of *jnana marga*, with its meditative practices often performed in the lotus position, that is commonly envisioned by non-Hindus when pondering the spiritual life of India.

Here, we turn our attention to *Vedanta*, the most influential of Hinduism's philosophical schools and a primary example of *jnana marga*.

Vedanta: The Predominant School of Hindu Philosophy

The philosophical system that emerged out of the *Upanishads* is called **Vedanta,** which in Sanskrit means "the end of the *Vedas*"—"end" not only as conclusion but also as culmination. The *Vedanta* school asserts that the *Upanishads* reveal the truth about the fundamental questions of existence. The *Upanishads* are both profound and challenging and are open to a variety of interpretations. Following the composition of the early *Upanishads,* philosophy became a very important part of Hinduism. Predictably, there even arose a number of different schools within *Vedanta*. Each school of *Vedanta* sought to understand the precise nature of the relationships between *Brahman, atman,* and the world.

The impact of *Vedanta* on the development of Hinduism cannot be overestimated. As different Hindu sects emerged, their distinctive understandings of *Vedanta* shaped their philosophical orientations. Of the many schools of *Vedanta*, the three most important are *Advaita, Vishishta-Advaita,* and *Dvaita*.

Advaita Vedanta Known as Hinduism's uncompromisingly monistic school of philosophy, *Advaita* ("Non-dualist") *Vedanta* teaches that the *atman* is identical to *Brahman* and denies any distinction whatsoever between *Brahman* and everything else. This school of thought grew directly out of the *Upanishads* but was further developed in the eighth century C.E. by Shankara, its most famous proponent. Shankara posited that the world is *maya,* "illusion." Earlier in this chapter we noted that the *Vedas* present *maya* as the magical power the gods used to create this world. For Shankara, *maya* veils the mind, such that it does not discern the true nature of the self (*atman*). According to Shankara, it is this lack of discernment, or ignorance, manifesting as attachment and desire, that keeps one bound to the cycle of death and rebirth (*samsara*). When one uses wisdom and discernment, one can cut through ignorance and recognize the inherent unity of all things, including the oneness of *Brahman* and *atman*. This in turn results in *moksha* and the complete dissolution of one's sense of individual selfhood.

Vishishta-Advaita Many of the sects that worship Vishnu differ on the subtler aspects of the relationship between *Brahman* and *atman*. For *Vaishnavas, Brahman* is identified with Vishnu. The school of *Vishishta-Advaita,* founded by the twelfth-century C.E.

philosopher Ramanuja, declared that all is *Brahman* and that the material world and individual souls also are real. The world is not illusion (*maya*); rather, it is the body of God. All beings are a part of God, eternally connected to Vishnu but not the same as him. We are more like cells in the divine body. Unlike Shankara, Ramanuja interpreted the ignorance that obscures true knowledge as forgetfulness—in particular, the devotee's forgetfulness of our eternal relationship with Vishnu. In this manner, Ramanuja's *Vedanta* marries philosophy to the devotional, sectarian traditions of Vaishnavism.

Dvaita Vedanta   The school of *Dvaita* ("Dualist") *Vedanta*, founded by the thirteenth-century theologian Madhva, advocates a complete distinction between *Brahman* and *atman*. It posits that there are five acknowledged aspects of complete separateness or difference: between the *atman* and *Brahman*, between *Brahman* and matter, between the various souls, between the souls and matter, and between various forms of matter. This philosophical strain, too, is associated with the worship of Vishnu, particularly in his avatar as Krishna.

The Individual and Society

The Hindu individual's quest for liberation is played out in a life situation that is defined to a large extent for that particular person depending on factors such as gender, caste status, and age. Like all aspects of the religion, the rules governing these factors admit to diversity even while conforming to basic patterns that have persisted through the centuries. Collectively, these rules are known as *varnashrama dharma*: the religious law regulating caste (*varna*) and stage of life (*ashrama*). Traditionally, all Hindus are required to comply with *varnashrama dharma*.

The Caste System   The Sanskrit term **varna** (literally, "color"), commonly translated as "caste," refers to a system of hierarchical social organization. A more accurate way of expressing the meaning of *varna* in this context is through the English term "class." There are four main classes in Hindu society: *brahmin*, the priestly class; **kshatriya**, the warrior and administrator class; **vaishya**, the producer class (farmers and merchants); and **shudra**, the servant class. *Varna* is determined by birth and is propagated through endogamy, or marriage only within a particular group. The caste system, and *varnashrama dharma* generally, has traditionally been most important for males of the three higher classes, the so-called "twice-born" castes.

We encounter the first mention of *varna* in a poem known as the *Purusha Sukta*, an early Sanskrit poem found in the tenth book of the *Rig Veda* (c. 1200 B.C.E.). The poem, which describes the primordial sacrifice of the cosmic man, ascribes a mythical origin to the *varna* system. From the various parts of the cosmic man emerge the component parts of the universe—the sun, the moon, the breath, and fire among them. At the very end, people emerge. From his mouth emerge the *brahmins*, from his arms the *kshatriyas*, from his thighs the *vaishyas*, and from his feet the *shudras*.

The *varnas* are organized along a continuum of purity and pollution. A person's state of purity or pollution is determined by the degree of contact with substances that are considered polluting (corpses, for example). Although it might appear from the *varna* system and from the *Purusha Sukta* that *brahmins* are at the top of the hierarchy, we know that from the earliest period *brahmins* and *kshatriyas* (and to some extent *vaishyas* as well) existed in close, mutually dependent relationships. The *brahmins*, with their ritual knowledge, gave legitimacy to kings and ambitious chieftains who might come to power. In turn, kings supported the priestly class with gifts of wealth and land, while merchants and landlords paid taxes and sponsored priestly activities.

A fifth group below the *shudras*, called the "untouchables" or "outcastes," was later added. Today, this lowest group constitutes nearly 20 percent of the population of India. During the Indian Independence movement of the early twentieth century, Mohandas (Mahatma) Gandhi (whom we will discuss later in the chapter) sought to uplift this class socially, referring to them as *Harijans*, "Children of God." Many people of this class now refer to themselves as **dalit**, a word that means "oppressed." In modern India, educational institutions and government jobs have been opened to the *dalits* and have helped many with social and economic mobility. Nevertheless, *dalits* continue to suffer terrible oppression, especially in rural communities in India.

The caste system is further classified through thousands of subcastes called *jatis*. **Jati** literally means "birth group." The term is often used to describe different orders of plants and animals, implying that the difference between human groups is similar to that between different species. Usually, a *jati* is composed of an endogamous group. One can marry within *jati* communities that are equal in social and ritual status, but not into a *jati* above or below one's own position. Marriage across *jatis* is usually undertaken to widen communal alliances. Over time, the *jati* system has made social hierarchy more fluid.

In modern times, the strictures of caste have broken down. Many Hindus have embraced a more utilitarian and even egalitarian outlook formulated by nineteenth-century Hindu reformers. These reformers regarded intercaste marriage as essential to bringing about social equality and the development of the Indian nation. In urban areas, caste status has often given way to a modern class-based system in which one's marriageability is based on education, current employment, and financial status, rather than solely on caste. But caste remains a challenging issue for many Hindus, particularly those living in rural settings.

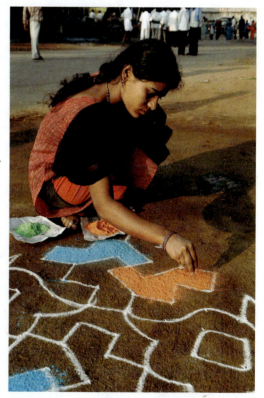

The Hampi Bazaar in Karnataka, India, a sacred town where doorsteps and houses are decorated by *rangoli* or *kolam* ritual protective drawings.

The Four Stages of Life   Another main aspect of the *varnashrama dharma* system involves the *ashrama*, or "stage of life." Traditional Hinduism describes four *ashramas*:

1. The student
2. The householder
3. The forest-dwelling hermit
4. The renouncer (the *sannyasi*)

As affirmed by the *Laws of Manu*, the repository of *dharma* discussed earlier, fulfilling the duties of these stages is said to repay three debts of life, which are:

1. To the ancient seers (by studying the revealed texts known as the *Vedas*)
2. To the gods (by making offerings as a householder)
3. To the ancestors (by having a son—again, as a householder—who will continue to perform ancestral rites)

The specific regulations pertaining to each stage of life are meticulously spelled out in Hindu texts. For example, the *Laws of Manu* prescribes the ritual of initiation for boys who are about to enter the student stage:

> In the eighth year after conception, one should perform the initiation (*upanāyana*) of a *brāhmin*, in the eleventh [year] after conception (that) of a *kṣatriya*, but in the twelfth that of a *vaiśya*.[9]

The student's main duty is to acquire a sufficient understanding of the *Vedas*. Upon getting married, he enters the stage of the householder, whose duties include supporting those in the other three stages of life. Hindus in the last two stages focus primarily on seeking *moksha* or liberation, first by detaching themselves from the worldly concerns of the householder and then, once this detachment has been achieved, by entering the fourth stage of the renouncer, or **sannyasi**.

Renunciation is understood to be the most effective life situation for working to achieve *moksha*. As we have seen, attachment to objects of desire binds one to *samsara*. Renouncing, or no longer clinging to, such objects is empowering. By not indulging one's desires for the impermanent things of this world, the true nature of the self (the *atman*) can be realized. Most renouncers are ascetics, celibate wanderers who engage in meditation and yoga. Some take formal vows and join a monastic order. Although estimates of the number of *sannyasis* vary, there may be as many as 15 million in India.

The four stages define the ideal life for men. Women participate primarily in vaguely defined supporting roles through the last three stages and thereby assist in repaying the three debts. Some Hindu texts, including the *Laws of Manu*, emphasize that women hold a place of honor because of these roles. In general, however, Hindu society has been highly patriarchal. (The place of women in Hinduism is explored in more detail a later section.)

The Four Aims of Life   Whereas the four stages of life describe an individual's social and familial responsibilities from birth to death, the four aims of life set forth Hinduism's primary spiritual purposes and goals. The four are: *dharma,* duty or righteousness; *kama,* sensual enjoyment; *artha,* material wealth and social prestige; and *moksha,* liberation. A Hindu is meant to diligently pursue all four of these goals.

As we have seen, *dharma* applies throughout life. Along with taking care to observe regulations governing everyday routines, some Hindus may take vows to practice nonviolence, perhaps maintaining a vegetarian diet as part of that goal. Others have strict rules for maintaining ritual purity or observe a complex ritual regimen each day to ensure the harmony and well-being of their household and family members.

The next two aims of life—*kama* and *artha*—apply especially to the second stage of life, that of the householder. *Kama* is directed at the fulfillment of desire. It encourages Hindus to enjoy the human experience and celebrate the sensual aspects of life. *Artha,* the pursuit of wealth and social prestige, is also encouraged. It is a Hindu's duty to provide security for loved ones but also to savor and share life's bounty. Of course, *kama* and *artha* must conform to *dharma.*

Moksha, the ultimate aim of human existence, is the special focus of the last two stages of life (the forest-dwelling hermit and the renouncer). Having fulfilled the duties and obligations of student and householder, one is ready to turn inward, to contemplate the nature of the *atman.*

The four stages and the four aims of life represent traditional ideals intended primarily for upper-caste men. We do not know the extent to which the prescriptions of the stages and aims have been followed in the long history of Hinduism. These ideals, while to some extent impractical in today's contemporary society, still inform the beliefs and practices of many Hindus.

VOICES: An Interview with Jayashree Venkatesan

Jayashree Venkatesan is a wife, a mother, and a retired accountant who lives in Chennai, India. She is a devotee of the goddess Sharada (a form of Saraswati, Goddess of Wisdom), whose most important temple is in the town of Shringeri, South India.

As a Hindu, what is the most important part of human existence? What should Hindus do or focus on in life?

As a Hindu, I believe that God is in all things, in every aspect of creation and in every aspect of life. Consequently, one must practice compassion and nonviolence towards all things. It is how we learn to see and experience the divine presence all around us. I also believe in the tenet that work is worship. It is an act of surrender. You don't shirk your responsibilities, whatever they may be—whether as a mother, a student, a professional—but do not cling to the fruits of work. As a Hindu I trust that when you surrender fully, God will provide you with the solution and guide you through both the happy and difficult moments of life.

What aspect of your day-to-day life as a Hindu would you characterize as being most spiritually gratifying?

Every morning and evening, I light an oil lamp in my puja room (home shrine) before the image of the Supreme Mother, Sharada Ambal. I see Sringeri Sharada Ambal as my mother, as one who takes care of everyone in this world. In these moments of quiet peace, I feel Her presence and Her guidance. I begin my day by surrendering myself into Her loving care.

What is your favorite Hindu holiday, and why?

I would not say I have a favorite Hindu festival. I like them all, as they are all so different. However, one of the most important festivals for me is Navaratri, which celebrates the Great Goddess. The festival falls sometime between September and October. We worship the goddess in Her three forms as Durga, Lakshmi, and Saraswati over nine nights and ten days. During this festival, I recite the *Lalita Sahasranama*, the one thousand names of Devi, several times a day. I do more elaborate puja (home rituals) to the goddess. Most importantly, it gives me the opportunity to invite several women of all ages to my home to feed them and give them clothes as I honor them as aspects of the Great Goddess.

Jayashree
Venkatesan

Hindu Sacred Texts

The great diversity within Hinduism is reflected in its astonishing array of texts, composed in many different languages over the course of centuries. Down to present times, Hindu texts have facilitated the asserting of new ideas, the overturning of old ones, and the reasserting of the dominance of fading traditions. In this next section, we undertake a brief survey of Hinduism's main texts and their continued relevance.

The *Vedas* The term *Veda* ("knowledge") is used in two ways when categorizing Hindu texts. In the broader sense, the *Vedas* refers to all of Vedic literature. These texts are regarded by most Hindus as revealed. That is, they are believed not to have been composed by man but rather "heard" by the *rishis*, the poet-sages of ancient times who were divinely inspired. Vedic literature thus belongs to the category of Hindu texts known as **shruti** ("that which is heard"), as opposed to the other category, **smriti** ("tradition").

In the more narrow sense of the term, *Vedas* refers to four collections (Sanskrit, *samhitas*) of texts. Composed in Sanskrit between 1200 and 900 B.C.E. and drawing on centuries of oral tradition, these are the earliest Hindu texts and are generally considered to be the world's oldest scriptures. The four *Vedas* are: the *Rig Veda*, a collection of hymns to the gods; the *Sama Veda*, melodic renditions of hymns from the *Rig Veda*; the *Yajur Veda*, ritual formulas; and the *Atharva Veda*, hymns, spells, and incantations.

Following upon the four *samhitas*, the *Brahmanas* set forth instructions for *brahmin* priests. The next collection of texts, the *Aranyakas* (or "forest treatises," so-named because they record esoteric teachings conveyed to students in secret), form a bridge from the *samhitas* to the *Upanishads* by exploring hidden meanings of rituals. The *Upanishads* are speculations with regard to the deeper truths of the *samhitas*, especially the *Rig Veda*.

The 1,028 hymns of the *Rig Veda*, the oldest and by far the most important of the *samhitas*, praise the gods and ask for their blessings. The gods include Indra, God of Rain and Thunder and King of the Gods; Agni, God of Fire and Messenger of the Gods; and Varuna, the God of Law and Order (who later becomes the God of the Sea). New deities emerged in the later portions of the *Rig Veda*. One that has enduring influence is the *Purusha* (literally, "Man"), who is praised and described in the famous Vedic hymn known as the *Purusha Sukta,* which was discussed earlier in connection to the caste system. This later Vedic hymn is also significant for the ways in which it asserts the centrality of sacrifice, and it continues to be recited in Hindu rituals even today. The *Purusha Sukta* describes the sacrifice of a primordial, cosmic man out of whose body the universe is created. As a creation myth, it has parallels in numerous Indo-European traditions. As we have seen, the *Purusha Sukta* not only details the first sacrifice but also delineates the structuring of society.

The *Upanishads* (900–200 B.C.E.)   The *Upanishads*, also known as *Vedanta* ("end of the *Vedas*"), are so distinctive from the earlier Vedic texts and so important as to deserve their own treatment here. The term *Upanishad* means "sitting down near [a teacher]." The term *Vedanta*, while identifying these texts as the concluding portion of Vedic

HINDU SACRED TEXTS

SHRUTI ("THAT WHICH IS HEARD")
Samhitas ("Collections")

Rig Veda
Yajur Veda
Sama Veda
Atharva Veda

Brahmanas
Aranyakas
Upanishads

SMRITI ("TRADITION")
Dharma Shastras (including *Laws of Manu*)
Epics and Puranas

Ramayana
Mahabharata
Bhagavata Purana
Markandeya Purana

Darshanas (treatises of the philosophical schools)
Tantras (scriptures of the various sects)
Writings of Hindu gurus

literature, implies for some Hindus—for example, followers of the *Vedanta* philosophical school—that the *Upanishads* contain the culmination of the wisdom of the *Vedas*.

Departing from the Vedic focus on ritual, and especially sacrifice, the *Upanishads* feature philosophical speculation on the nature of the divine, the self, the world, and the relationships between them. These texts signal a significant shift away from emphasis on the external performance of sacrifice characteristic of the Vedic era. The *Upanishads* also mark a new stage in the development of religious texts, having been composed in part by people of non-*brahmin* backgrounds. The newfound emphasis on philosophical speculation, no longer the sole domain of the *brahmin* class, had an enormous impact on the development of Hinduism. It propelled the development of the contemplative disciplines of yoga and meditation and influenced the philosophical concepts found later in the *Bhagavad Gita*.

The *Upanishads* are also significant for describing for the first time the concepts of karma, *samsara*, reincarnation of the soul, and the soul's immortality, which were initially closely guarded secrets. We had occasion earlier in the chapter, when discussing *Brahman* and the monistic concept that *atman* is *Brahman*, to draw from the *Brhadaranyaka* and *Chandogya Upanishads*. They are two among the thirteen so-called "principal *Upanishads*" (some scholars set this number at ten). Traditionally there are 108 *Upanishads*, although the term has been applied to some 200 texts, some of which were written in recent times.

What advantages and disadvantages can you think of when comparing the flexibility of Hindu beliefs with that of other religions?

Hindu priests perform *arati*, waving a lamp of burning camphor before an image of Hanuman (the monkey god of the *Ramayana*) at a temple in Kuala Lumpur, Malaysia, during the festival of Diwali.

Ramayana   For most Hindus, belief and practice are informed by and disseminated through storytelling traditions and narrative texts. Two of the most significant of these are the Sanskrit epics the *Ramayana* and the *Mahabharata*, both of which are categorized as *smriti* rather than *shruti*—although this in no way diminishes their relevance as Hindu sacred texts. Both epics are among the most important sources of Hindu notions of duty, or *dharma*.

The *Ramayana* ("The Journey of Rama"), composed between 200 B.C.E. and 200 C.E., is a compelling tale of political intrigue, romance, and philosophical speculation. It tells the story of a ten-headed demon King named Ravana, who was rewarded for his austerities with the granting of a wish by Brahma. Ravana asks for protection from gods, celestial beings, and other members of his own demon race. Protected in this way, he and his demon hordes dominate the earth and eventually even enslave the gods of heaven. But in his arrogance, Ravana neglects to ask for protection from humans and animals.

In the meantime, King Dasharatha of Ayodhya and his three queens, desiring an heir, perform a sacrifice in hopes that the gods will grant their wish. The king is blessed with four sons—Rama, Lakshmana, Bharata, and Shatrughna. Rama, as we have noted earlier (p. 95), is an avatar of Vishnu. Rama eventually marries a princess, Sita. As Rama is beloved by all for his righteousness and virtue, King Dasharatha, wishing to step down from the throne, announces that Rama's coronation will soon be held. Then Kaikeyi, Dasharatha's favorite wife, suddenly calls in two wishes that the king had once granted her. She demands that Rama be banished to the forest for fourteen years and that her own son, Bharata, ascend to the throne of Ayodhya instead. Distraught, King Dasharatha dutifully grants Kaikeyi's wish but dies of a broken heart.

Rama accepts his exile without protest and is accompanied by his brother Lakshmana and his wife Sita into the forest, where they spend many years, until one day Ravana kidnaps Sita and carries her off to his demon stronghold on the island of Lanka.

A despairing Rama and Lakshmana wander in search of Sita. They eventually meet Hanuman, a messenger from a kingdom of monkeys. Hanuman, along with the support of the kingdom of bears, helps to search for Sita. At the citadel of Ravana on Lanka, Hanuman finds Sita held prisoner in a garden. He tells her not to lose hope, promising that Rama will soon come to free her.

Upon hearing Hanuman's news, Rama and his army march to Lanka. During the fierce battle that ensues, Rama kills Ravana and is united with Sita. However, after spending a year in another man's house, Sita must publicly prove her chastity through a trial by fire. With the fire-god Agni as her witness, she passes through the flames and into Rama's embrace. Their exile concluded, Rama, Sita, and Lakshmana return to Ayodhya, where Rama is reinstated as the rightful king. All are happy for a time, but later, because of rumors circulating about Sita's chastity, Rama is compelled to abandon Sita in the forest. He doesn't know she is pregnant with their two sons, who are raised by the hermit Valmiki. Valmiki, who, while meditating, has seen all that has come to pass, composes the *Ramayana* and teaches it to the two boys, who eventually sing it before their father. Rama dies shortly thereafter, sadly pining for Sita.

For many Hindus, the characters in the *Ramayana* serve as exemplary social role models. Sita is the faithful wife, Rama is the ideal man and perfect king, Lakshmana is the loyal brother, and Hanuman is the selfless devotee. The text grapples with issues involving *dharma*, both in the public, political realm and in the private, familial realm. The characters of the *Ramayana,* however, are also understood to be divine. Thus the *Ramayana* is as much a text that imparts religious and ethical knowledge as one that reinforces Hindu beliefs about the accessibility and immanence of God.

Rama and Lakshmana, with their army of monkeys and bears, are camped outside the palace of the demon-king Ravana on the isle of Lanka, while the demons try to rouse Kumbhakarna, the giant brother of Ravana. India, Mughal period, c. 1595–1605.

Mahabharata   The other great Hindu epic, the *Mahabharata*, is composed of over 100,000 verses and is the longest epic poem in the world. Like the *Ramayana*, this work is deeply concerned with issues of *dharma*. The epic also introduces Krishna, the beloved avatar of Vishnu.

The main storyline of the *Mahabharata* concerns a dynastic conflict between two groups of royal cousins. These are the *Pandavas* (the five sons of King Pandu), the heroes of the epic who are all descendants of the gods, and their antagonists, the *Kauravas* (the hundred sons of the blind king, Dhritarashtra). Their dispute ultimately results in a terrible war that marks the end of an epoch for humanity.

On the eve of the great battle, as the two armies face each other across the battlefield, the great Pandava warrior Arjuna experiences crippling doubt. When Arjuna asks his charioteer, Krishna (an avatar of Vishnu), to pull the chariot into the middle of the battlefield, he sees his friends and relatives on both sides clamoring for war. He does not want to commit the sin of killing his kinsmen; and overcome with sorrow, he refuses to fight. It is at this key point in the story that the profound philosophical discourse known as the *Bhagavad Gita* ("Song of the Lord") begins. Many Hindus regard this conversation between Krishna and Arjuna as the most significant philosophical work in Hinduism.

Krishna, in the guise of Arjuna's charioteer, counsels the warrior on the verge of battle against his kinsmen. The battle scene in the Mahabharata is the setting of the *Bhagavad Gita.*

The *Bhagavad Gita* (The Song of the Lord)

The *Bhagavad Gita*, the conversation between Krishna and Arjuna, was probably composed around the first century C.E. The text, which seeks to reconcile the tension between renunciation and worldly life, also presents radical new ideas about the pursuit of *moksha*, including the three *margas* or paths to liberation that we explored in an earlier section.

The *Gita* begins with Arjuna refusing to act on his *dharma,* as is demanded of a member of the *kshatriya,* or warrior class, out of fear of the consequences of killing his kinsmen. Krishna responds to his dilemma by revealing that one does not need to give up action to achieve *moksha*. Rather, as we noted before, one gives up the *fruit* of action. That is, one cultivates "desireless action," or acting without attachment to the fruit or benefit of the action.

Arjuna must honor his *dharma* as a warrior and fight his own kinsmen. But he transcends the karmic repercussions of this act by relinquishing personal attachment and realizing that Krishna is the primary cause leading all the individual actors toward this inevitable outcome.

The *Gita* emphasizes the concept of *bhakti* (devotion), which later comes to dominate Hindu practice and belief. The *Gita* suggests that the path of *bhakti* is available to anyone, regardless of caste or gender, as its only requirement is devotion. By allowing people to live in this world, adhering to their *dharma*, *bhakti* offers an alternate course to *moksha*. The *Gita* teaches that it is possible to achieve *moksha* by being active in the world, provided that, through selfless devotion, one surrenders clinging to the expectation of any particular result. This contrasts with earlier philosophical systems that advocated complete detachment through renunciation as the primary means for escaping *samsara*.

The concept of *bhakti* influences the development of the dualistic or devotional Hindu traditions. *Bhakti* is intimately connected to the rise of Hinduism's various sectarian affiliations and the growth of temple cultures. *Bhakti* advocates a deep, abiding love for God and encourages the devotee to nurture an intimate and personal relationship with the divine. The devotee is free to choose a favored, personal deity, who is perceived as the supreme entity and toward whom devotion is directed. For many Hindus, *bhakti* is both a belief and a practice. That is, they cultivate *bhakti* as the most effective way out of *samsara*.

Puranas In addition to the rich storehouse of narrative material in the epics, there are equally important collections of mythic stories known as **Puranas** (Sanskrit *purana*, "ancient"). Like the epics, the *Puranas* existed in oral form before being committed to writing—in this case, between the fourth and sixteenth centuries. The *Puranas* contain useful historical data, such as the genealogies of regional kings, but they also reflect the rise of dualistic or devotional Hinduism. This is evident primarily in their narrations of the deeds of the great deities such as Shiva, Vishnu, and Devi. They also take great interest in the genealogies of gods, rules governing the proper worship of the gods, the construction of temples, the observance of festivals, the undertaking of pilgrimages, and similar topics.

There are eighteen major *Puranas*, two of the most influential of which are the *Bhagavata Purana* and the *Markandeya Purana*. The *Bhagavata Purana* focuses on Vishnu and his incarnations, most especially Krishna. It is one of the most widely recited, performed, and studied texts in contemporary Hinduism. The tenth book, which serves as the primary source for Krishna's life story, is particularly important. The *Markandeya Purana* includes within it the *Devi Mahatmya,* which is an important text of Shaktism, one among various Hindu sects that we explore in the next section.

The Sects of Hinduism

There are three primary sects in Hinduism. Each features veneration of one of the major deities at the center of Hindu cosmology. The devotees of these sects are called **Vaishnavas** (devotees of Vishnu and his avatars), **Shaivas** (devotees of Shiva), and **Shaktas** (devotees of the Great Goddess, Devi). Within each of these sects are numerous individual orders that differ in the sacred texts and saints they revere, their modes of worship, and their philosophical orientation.

Vaishnavism *Vaishnavas* worship Vishnu and his consort (wife) Lakshmi as supreme. Vishnu mercifully intervenes in the world through his avatars (such as Rama in

A contemporary painting of the inner sanctum of the famous temple at Sri Rangam. Sri Ranganatha ("Lord of the Stage") is a cosmic form of Vishnu lying on the serpent, Ananta ("Infinity"), as he floats on the Cosmic Sea of Milk. This signifies the place of primordial essence from whence he emanates all of the universe.

the *Ramayana* and Krishna in the *Mahabharata*) and is inseparable from his beloved Lakshmi, who is the goddess of auspiciousness and good fortune. For *Vaishnavas*, Vishnu is the source of all existence and, as his name denotes, "The All-Pervading One." These ideas about Vishnu's fundamental nature are expressed in myths and poems that invoke him as the lord who measured out the universe in a primordial act of creation.

Hindus worship Vishnu in a number of different forms. He is often depicted reclining with Lakshmi on a thousand-headed serpent that floats on the cosmic ocean. From his navel rises a lotus, upon which Brahma the Creator God is seated. Visually, this image asserts that the world is born from Vishnu and he is its sole originator and sustainer. Brahma, Vishnu, and Shiva constitute the so-called *trimurti*, a triad of gods whose roles are, respectively, to create, preserve, and dissolve the universe as it moves through epochal cycles. For *Vaishnavas*, Vishnu is not just the preserver but the supreme god who performs all three roles, thus incorporating the functions of the *trimurti* within his own being.

In Hindu sacred art, Vishnu typically is shown holding objects in his four hands that symbolize his powers and characteristics. In his upper right hand, he holds a flaming discus (symbolizing the sun and omniscience); his upper left hand bears a white conch shell (the moon and creativity). In his lower right hand, he holds a mace (power), and in his lower left hand, he holds a lotus (purity). Most *Vaishnavas* have special devotion for Vishnu's avatars, Rama and Krishna.

Shaivism   Shiva is the destroyer while at the same time a benefactor. He embodies both the ideal of ascetic renunciation and a full and sensual participation in the material world. Beyond being the god of spiritual insight and of yogis and ascetics, Shiva is also the god who destroys the universe at the end of time before a new cycle of creation can begin. Most *Shaivas* worship Shiva as a god with no beginning or end who transcends time but also presides over its endless cycles. Some *Shaivas* emphasize that Shiva is also a family man, to be venerated with his divine queen Parvati and their two sons, the divine princes Ganesha and Skanda.

Shiva is usually depicted sitting in deep meditation on Mount Kailasha in the Himalayas, with a tiger skin wrapped about his waist and wearing serpents for jewelry. His third eye is turned inward in meditative contemplation, and he wears the crescent moon and the holy river Ganges in his matted hair. A common symbol of Shiva is the *linga*, an abstract phallic symbol that represents his creative potential. His consort Parvati is also believed by *Shaivas* to represent the creative energy of the universe.

Shaktism The cults of the Great Goddess venerate her as the supreme cause and end of the universe. Although she has many names and many forms, the Great Goddess is most often referred to as Devi, Mahadevi, or Shakti. Devotees of the Goddess are referred to as *Shaktas*.

The primacy of Devi is definitively asserted in the fifth century c.e. Sanskrit text called the *Devi Mahatmya* (*The Greatness of Devi*) which, as noted previously, is part of the *Markandeya Purana*. The *Devi Mahatmya* posits that the supreme cause of the universe is feminine. The text argues for Devi's greatness through three main myths, the most important of which tells how she killed the buffalo-headed demon, Mahisha, who threatened the world and whom even the gods Vishnu and Shiva were not able to vanquish.

To *Shaktas* the Goddess is all-powerful and pervades the entire universe. She is the one who creates, preserves, and destroys the universe in harmony with the rhythms of cosmic time. The *Devi Mahatmya* teaches that the goddess is eternal and that she manifests herself over and over again in order to protect the universe as a mother would her child.

Shaivas and *Shaktas* have much in common, as Shiva and Devi (also called Parvati) are believed by both sects to be married. So the difference between Shaivism and Shaktism is a matter of emphasis regarding the importance of each of these two primal forces. For *Shaivas*, Shiva is pure consciousness that pervades all existence, and Devi is his creative (but subordinate) power. On the other hand, *Shaktas* believe that Shiva is entirely passive, and that Shakti is the creative energy that constitutes and governs the whole of existence. Thus the *Shaktas* say that "Shiva without Shakti is *shava*" (Sanskrit, "a corpse").

This idea, iconographically represented in the form of the goddess Kali dancing upon the inert body of Shiva, is a profound metaphor for the embodied soul. Shiva represents the pure consciousness in all beings that is transfixed by Kali, who is creative energy made manifest as all form, feeling, thought, and sensation. Kali's enrapturing dance makes one forget that one's true nature is Shiva/*Brahman*. But Kali also delights in granting *moksha* by letting believers awake to the true nature of her cosmic dance and the reality that *atman* is really *Brahman*.

Accompanied by a legion of other goddesses and fierce creatures and riding a lion, Devi, in the form of the goddess Durga, protects the world by battling the buffalo demon Mahishasura. (The buffalo is associated with Yama, the God of Death.) Pallava period, seventh century, Mahishasura Mardini Cave, Mamallapuram Tamil Nadu, India.

A modern painting of the goddess Kali, whose name means both "Black" and "Time," dancing on the body of Shiva. From the Indian state of Orissa.

Gurus, Saints, and Sages Entire sects of Hinduism are constantly forming around the veneration of gurus, saints, and ascetics. The fully enlightened are regarded as being one with God and therefore the most immediate means of accessing God directly, either for material and mundane blessings or to receive spiritual teaching to quicken one's own journey toward *moksha*. Some saints are venerated not as embodiments of God but for being humble and perfectly surrendered devotees. Some gurus are powerful religious authorities and preside over well-established institutions, in which the divine authority of a guru has been passed down to his senior disciple in an unbroken lineage for many generations. Certain important gurus and saints have been responsible for the formulation of the specific philosophical orientation of various sects and monastic orders, making interpretation of sacred texts and belief more systematic and consistent.

THE HISTORY OF HINDUISM

Hinduism is a vibrant tradition that has exhibited dynamic change and a willingness to embrace innovations in thought and practice. At the same time, Hinduism has preserved many of its most ancient elements to the present day, cherishing some traditions that go back more than 3,000 years.

The history of Hinduism can be traced back to the Indus Valley Civilization (c. 2600–1700 B.C.E.) and to the Indo-Aryan peoples who composed the *Vedas* (c. 1200–900 B.C.E.).

The Indus Valley Civilization

As its name suggests, the Indus Valley Civilization developed along the river Indus, which flows through modern Pakistan. It reached its developmental peak between 2300 and 2000 B.C.E., when its thriving cities, such as Harappa and Mohenjo-Daro, enjoyed a surprisingly high standard of living. Extensive archaeological excavations at Indus Valley sites have yielded evidence of trade with regions as far away as Mesopotamia and impressive skill in metallurgy, handicrafts, and urban planning. The archaeological finds include a vast number of stone seals that were perhaps used to stamp products for trade. These are decorated with depictions of animals and people and with a script that has not yet been deciphered.

Some scholars believe that in the Indus Valley seals we can detect very early elements of Hinduism. For example, the most famous seal has been called the Proto-Shiva seal because its central image may be an archaic form of Shiva. The male figure is seated in a yoga posture, wears a buffalo-horned headdress, is surrounded by

Significant sites in the history of Hinduism.

animals, and appears to have three faces. Later images of Shiva often show him in meditating in a yoga posture, being in the company of animals, and having three faces.

Of course, without a decipherment of the script it is difficult to understand fully this and other images depicted on the seals.

Archaeologists working in the Indus Valley have also discovered a number of terracotta figures depicting women. Some scholars have identified these as representations of a mother goddess. It may be that the widespread worship of goddesses in later Hinduism originated in the veneration of female deities in the ancient Indus Valley Civilization.

At some point early in the second millennium B.C.E. there was a sudden

The Proto-Shiva seal. The male figure, sometimes called the "Lord of the Animals," is surrounded by various totemic animals, such as an elephant, a tiger, a rhinoceros, a water buffalo, and two antelopes or deer.

The great bath can be seen amid the ruins of the ancient cityscape of Mohenjo-Daro, an important city of the Indus Valley Civilization. A towering granary can be viewed in the distance.

decline in the Indus Valley Civilization, which was to collapse by 1300 B.C.E. Although most scholars believe that the primary cause of the fall of the Indus Valley Civilization was climatic change that disrupted agriculture, it is possible that the migration of Aryans into the Indus Valley was a contributing factor.

Who Are the Aryans?

The brilliant English linguist Sir William "Oriental" Jones (1746–1794) described how Sanskrit, Latin, Greek, and several other ancient languages shared a common linguistic ancestor. These languages are referred to as "Indo-European" and probably stem from a lost language we call "Proto Indo-European." Jones's discoveries astounded Europeans, who soon learned that Sanskrit was closest to the original language spoken by the earliest Indo-Europeans.

The ancient speakers of Sanskrit who moved into the Indian subcontinent around 1500 B.C.E. referred to themselves as the *Arya*—that is, those who are "noble," "cultivated," and "civilized." Today, we call them Indo-Aryans or, more simply, Aryans. Skilled in handling the horse and chariot, the Aryans were a warlike and nomadic people who were well prepared to make themselves the dominant elite soon after they entered the Indian subcontinent.

Like other Indo-European peoples, the Aryans revered the horse, placed special importance on sacrifice, and organized their society into a three-part structure. For the Aryans, sacrifice was a means to maintain order in the universe. The priests (*brahmins*) who conducted sacrificial rituals occupied the top rung of the social order because of the religious power they wielded. The rulers and warriors (*kshatriyas*) were equally important. Last were the traders and farmers (*vaishyas*). As the Aryans did not place a great deal of emphasis on agriculture, one can see why the *vaishyas* would occupy a lower social position. This threefold social structure has remained fundamental to Indian society until today.

The Aryans, who eventually settled across northern India, have left us a body of texts composed in Sanskrit, of which the earliest example is the *Vedas*. It is to the era of these texts that we now turn.

The Vedic Period

Ritual was of ultimate importance in Vedic times, as rites of sacrifice were performed to sustain cosmic order and please the gods. Much of ritual sacrifice involved the pouring of offerings into a sacrificial fire as Vedic hymns were recited. Although the construction of their fire altars became quite elaborate, Indians of the Vedic period inherited from their nomadic ancestors a very "portable" religion with no fixed buildings or icons and with sacred knowledge maintained by priests.

In Vedic times, as today, fire was considered a god. Known as *Agni*, he was the mouth of the gods and the gateway to the celestial realms, so offerings were magically transported through Agni to whichever god was invoked.

In Vedic mythology it is Indra, god of thunder and lightning, and the virile god of fertility itself, who is the most powerful of the gods. More hymns in the *Vedas* are addressed to Indra than to any other god, but in later Hindu tradition and mythology he is somewhat comical: haughty, proud, and often drunk. Many of the Vedic gods continue to play a part in the later Hindu pantheon but endure only in a subordinate status.

A *yajna* or fire sacrifice, one of the most archaic of Hindu rites, is performed by priests before an image of Durga during the Durga Puja festival in Calcutta, India.

In the later Vedic period, philosophical innovations began to supplant the older Vedic emphasis on sacrifice. It is in hymns from the later period that Vedic religion begins to take a decisive turn, shifting away from an emphasis on myth, cosmology, and sacrifice to a keener interest in philosophy and introspection. In these hymns the perception of the nature of existence emerges as being more important than upholding the cosmic order through sacrifice. Late Vedic hymns mark a transition toward what would be the philosophical revolution of the speculative texts known as the *Upanishads*.

During the time of the *Upanishads* (c. 900–200 B.C.E.), contemplative and philosophical reflection became more widespread. Many philosophers moved from urban areas to the forest in order to lead simpler lives. Some lived as hermits, some lived in colonies of contemplatives, and others practiced strict ascetic disciplines in the solitude of the jungle. Still others became wanderers, going from town to town begging for food and engaging in lively philosophical debates.

The Age of the Guptas

Most scholars characterize the time of the Gupta Empire (c. 320 to 540 C.E.) as a period of remarkable creativity. The Guptas, who ruled much of northern India, patronized the arts, sciences, religion, and literature. Their reign was an era of relative peace and prosperity, often described as "the Golden Age of India." It was during this period that the epics took on their definitive forms and the first of the *Puranas* was compiled.

The Gupta rulers practiced religious tolerance and sponsored groups and institutions associated with Buddhism, Jainism, and other religions. The Guptas, who were themselves Hindus, promoted Hinduism and sought to organize society in accordance with Hindu beliefs. Thanks in part to Gupta patronage, the worship of Vishnu and Shiva became increasingly popular during this period, which also saw a shift from worship at open-air sacrificial altars to worship in temples. As temple institutions arose, so did special forms of temple art and architecture. These developments quickened the spread of *bhakti* and the emerging devotional sects.

A very significant religious development during the age of the Guptas was the rise of devotional Hinduism. The two great Sanskrit epics, the *Ramayana* and the *Mahabharata*, had been completed and were well established by this time. As we have seen, these epics are concerned with political problems, dynastic successions, duty, and obligations. But they also feature the exploits of the gods and have much to tell us about popular deities and avatars and forms of devotion to them. Composition of the *Puranas* commenced during this period, indicating the growing popularity of devotional Hinduism.

The Development of *Bhakti*

The devotional aspects of Hinduism became increasingly popular under the Guptas, but they took on new life in southern India between the sixth and ninth centuries c.e. in the form of the ecstatic movement of *bhakti*. This movement and ideology spread all over India, changing and adapting to new regional and linguistic circumstances. Like the radical innovations of the *Upanishads* and the *Bhagavad Gita*, *bhakti* changed the course of Hinduism, giving it an ecstatic dimension that expressed itself through poetry, art, architecture, and temple building. *Bhakti* was instrumental in the development of the various sectarian orientations of Hinduism and in its vibrant temple cultures. Closely linked to the most important dynasties of the time, *bhakti* was equally important for the challenge it issued to caste and gender hierarchies.

By the late fifth century c.e., Buddhism (Chapter 5) and Jainism (Chapter 6) were deeply entrenched in southern India. *Bhakti* arose as a challenge to these traditions. Over the next four centuries, wandering poets roamed the Tamil country and converted royalty and commoners alike to the devotional ethos of *bhakti*. Royal patronage for Jainism and Buddhism waned, and kings sought legitimacy through poets' songs that praised the kings as the representatives of the gods Shiva and Vishnu. The religious networks forged by the itinerant poets sometimes developed into political networks and strengthened alliances between religion and politics.

By the twelfth century, the *bhakti* movement had taken on a new role, becoming a weapon wielded against caste and gender prejudice. It often rejected ritual and temple-based worship, insisting that the body is itself a temple and that God dwells in every individual.

Caste and *Bhakti* Many scholars argue that the *bhakti* movement had such a far-reaching impact because it was egalitarian, revolutionary, and frequently anti-*brahmin*. *Bhakti* poet-saints represented a variety of caste backgrounds. Furthermore, rather than using Sanskrit, the language of the *Vedas* and of priestly authority, the *bhakti* poets used vernacular languages such as Tamil, Kannada, Marathi, and an early form of Hindi. The *bhakti* poets asserted that caste and other circumstances of one's birth did not determine one's access to God. Rather, it was the quality of one's surrender to God that mattered. Although a text such as the *Bhagavad Gita* espoused similar ideas, that text also simultaneously stressed the importance of one's duty according to caste. In defining one's sole duty as the practice of perfect surrender to God, the *bhakti* poets were revolutionary. Nonetheless, the radical ideas espoused by the poets were often blunted when absorbed into mainstream Hinduism.

How does the criticism of special knowledge and power wielded by *brahmins* compare to criticism of the power of priests and religious authorities in other religions?

Tantra

Bhakti was not the only revolutionary new idea to challenge the strictures of gender and caste. *Tantra*, another new system of thought and practice, emerged alongside it. Making use of symbols, rituals, yogic postures, breathing techniques, mantras, and other spiritual practices—sometimes in shocking or forbidden ways—*Tantra* offered the possibility of sudden liberation from *samsara*. By the seventh century it had come to influence not only Hinduism but Buddhism and Jainism as well.

Tantra (Sanskrit, "loom") assumes the interweaving and interconnectedness of all things. These include pure consciousness (identified with *Brahman* or Shiva) and material reality in its most basic state (*prakriti*, identified with Shakti), which are interwoven in a relationship of mutual interdependence and love. Similarly, *samsara* and *moksha* are not understood as two different things but as aspects of a single continuum of being. For practitioners of *Tantra*, the material world is a manifestation of the divine energy associated with pure consciousness (*Brahman*/Shiva). Their spiritual practices are said to give them the ability to manipulate or channel that energy in order to gain liberation. Unlike the ascetics who renounced the material world and its sensual pleasures as part of their spiritual quest, practitioners of *Tantra* made use of material things and the senses as means by which to transcend them. For them, *moksha* could be found in the midst of everyday experience.

Tantra likely arose among mystics in Kashmir, Nepal, and possibly Bengal and Assam. These Tantric sages and yogis asserted that the ritual transgression of social boundaries could create ideal conditions for transcending the egocentric self and achieving instantaneous *moksha*. Recognizing that people's egos are deeply embedded in caste identity and rooted in taboos regarding purity and pollution, practitioners of *Tantra* performed transgressive rituals in which they identified their bodies as deities, ritually consumed meat, fish, and wine, and engaged in ritual sex with low-caste partners. Such rituals were designed to break through the narrow confines of what one assumes the self to be.

As *Tantra* increased in popularity, it also became increasingly secretive. Many were attracted by its reputed ability to enable one to avoid the rigors of spiritual progress over the course of many lifetimes by using its rituals to achieve liberation in one's present life. But there were also allegations that some adherents exercised seductive magical powers, reports of others suffering mental breakdown, and disapproval of rituals that violated social conventions. For these reasons, much of *Tantra* remained hidden during its later development.

Early Hindu Encounters with Islam and Rule Under the Mughal Dynasty

One of the earliest sustained encounters between Hindus and Muslims in India was initiated by the raids of Mahmud of Ghazni (Afghanistan) early in the eleventh century. Attracted by India's immense wealth and motivated by religious zeal, Mahmud repeatedly raided the subcontinent, annexed states headed by Hindu, Buddhist, and Jain kings, and left them in charge as his vassals. His most famous incursion involved the looting and destruction of the great temple of Shiva in Somnath (1025). According to Muslim sources, more than 50,000 defenders of the temple were killed, and its immense wealth taken back to Ghazni. These Muslim accounts also speak of the forced conversions of Hindus to Islam. Contemporary Hindu nationalists often point to this early encounter with Islam as the beginning of centuries of oppression and persecution under Muslim rule.

By the time the Mughal Empire was established in India, Islam had established a strong foothold there, particularly in the northern regions. The Mughals were Muslim rulers of Turkic-Mongol origin. They ruled from 1526 until the mid-eighteenth century, after which their state continued to exist but with weakened rulers incapable of exercising control over it. Under the Mughals, a complex relationship existed between Hinduism and Islam. Some Mughal emperors were hostile to religions other than their own and to Hinduism and Jainism in particular. Others, such as Akbar (1542–1605), were open to them. Akbar encouraged dialogue with representatives of different religions at a weekly salon. He even invented his own religion, the "Divine Faith" (*Din-I-Ilahi*), which incorporated elements of various religious traditions including Hinduism, Islam, and Zoroastrianism. Akbar was a clever political strategist who understood non-Muslims as subjects rather than infidels, counted Hindu kings among his closest advisors, and married the daughters of Hindu kings to cement political alliances with them. Good relationships between Mughal emperors and high-ranking Hindus helped to produce a vibrant pluralistic culture.

Under the Mughals, the conversions of Hindus to Islam do not appear to have been forced. Instead, Hindus converted for a variety of reasons, the most common being improved economic and social standing and sincere belief in the teachings of Islam. There were also conversions of Muslims to Hinduism, especially when Muslims married into Hindu families.

Some of the greatest of Hindu thinkers, poets, and philosophers lived during the time of the Mughals. The influential poet-saint Tulsidas (1532–1623), a member of Akbar's court and a devotee of Rama, wrote the *Ramcharitmanas*, an epic retelling of the original Sanskrit *Ramayana* in Hindi. The Muslim weaver-mystic Kabir (c. 1440–1518) was inspired by a Hindu teacher and composed poetry that seamlessly combined Hindu and Islamic philosophical ideas while at the same time critiquing the social policies of Hindu and Muslim rulers.

Colonial Critique and the Hindu Reformers

When employees of the British East India Company established an imperial presence in India in the late eighteenth and early nineteenth centuries, they initially adapted themselves to local customs and practices. They learned regional languages, married into local families, and even embraced local religious beliefs. One particularly colorful example is that of an Irish general in the Bengal Army, Charles Stuart (1758–1828). Stuart was such an avid admirer of Hinduism that his colleagues nicknamed him "Hindoo Stuart." His book, *Vindication of the Hindoos* (1808), was intended to discourage the ever-growing support for British missionaries who sought to convert Hindus to Christianity. When these missionaries tried to embarrass Stuart by calling attention to aspects of Hindu mythology that seemed strange to Westerners, he eloquently wrote in response: "Whenever I look around me in the vast region of Hindoo Mythology, I discover piety in the garb of allegory: and I see Morality, at every turn, blended with every tale; and, as far as I can rely on my own judgment, it appears the most complete and ample system of Moral allegory that the world has ever produced."[10]

But not everyone involved with the British East India Company admired Hindu beliefs and customs. Many felt that the "primitive backwardness" of Hindu belief was enough to warrant colonial intervention. By the middle of the nineteenth century, and certainly after the 1857 Indian Uprising (referred to as the "Mutiny" by British chroniclers, but as the "First War of Independence" by many Indian historians), the attraction to Hinduism and Indian culture represented by figures such as "Hindoo" Stuart and the linguist William "Oriental" Jones began to fade. As the commercial and administrative presence of the British East India Company gave way to the colonial control of the British Crown, critiques of Hinduism became an increasingly important means of exerting political power over the subcontinent.

By the mid-nineteenth century, English-educated Hindus took up the work of reform as a response to colonial critiques of Hinduism. They, too, began deriding Hinduism's many gods, erotic symbolism, temple worship, and rituals as crass corruptions of the purity of the authentic Hinduism embodied in the *Vedas* and *Upanishads*. They sought to transform Hinduism from within.

One of these reformers was Ram Mohan Roy (1774–1833), a member of a wealthy Bengali *brahmin* community who established the Brahmo Samaj (Community of *Brahman* Worshippers) in 1828 as a neo-Hindu religious organization open to all, regardless of religious orientation. Believing that British rule offered India considerable opportunities for progress, Roy devoted his life to religious, social, and educational reform. He was particularly concerned with issues involving the protection of women, such as child marriage, polygamy, dowry, and the practice of *sati*. *Sati* was an upper-caste practice in which a widow immolated herself on her husband's funeral pyre. This ritual suicide was believed to bring great honor to the family and raise the status of the dead widow to that of a goddess. Roy campaigned for the abolition of *sati*, arguing that there was no scriptural basis in the *Vedas* for this practice. Finally, in 1829, *sati* was made illegal in Bengal. Roy was among the first members of the Indian upper

Temple volunteers unveil a statue of Swami Vivekananda at the Hindu Temple of Greater Chicago, Saturday, July 11, 1998, in Lemont, Illinois. The statue honors Vivekananda as "the first man to bring Hindu religion and the practice of yoga to America."

classes to visit Europe, traveling there in 1830 to ensure that the British would not overturn the *sati* law. He died in 1833 and was buried in Bristol.

Another influential reformer was Dayananda Saraswati (1824–1883). Having become a wandering monk early in life, Dayananda studied under a blind sage who urged him to campaign for a return to what he considered the pure and original Vedic religion. Following his advice, Dayananda rejected the epics and *Puranas* as departures from the purity of the *Vedas* and spoke out against all aspects of temple tradition, image worship, and pilgrimage. In 1875 he founded the Arya Samaj (the Noble Community) as a "Vedic" religious organization whose social reform platform condemned child marriage and untouchability while promoting the equality of women. He rejected social hierarchies in the form of *jati* and thought *varna* should be decided based on one's character, which the organization would determine in a public examination. Although Dayananda Saraswati, like Ram Mohan Roy, favored a return to Vedic religion, his Arya Samaj distinguished itself from Roy's Brahmo Samaj in its encouragement of Hindu nationalism, anticipating the more extreme Hindu nationalist groups that would appear in the early twentieth century.

Other figures, less influenced by colonial and Christian critiques of Hinduism, were not as concerned as Ram Mohan Roy and Dayananda Saraswati to reform Hinduism in ways that would appeal to the West. One was the enormously popular Bengali mystic, Ramakrishna (1836–1886). A devotee and temple priest of the goddess Kali, as a young man Ramakrishna prayed for and then experienced a vision of her as an ocean of blissful light. He then devoted himself to spiritual exercises drawn from different religious traditions, including Vaishnavism, Advaita Vedanta, Tantrism, and even Islamic Sufism and Roman Catholicism. These deepened his sense of identity with the divine and served as the basis for his teaching that all religions are directed toward the experience of a God who creates religions to suit the spiritual needs and tastes of different peoples. Seen in this way, Hinduism could claim the same legitimacy as any other religion.

Among Ramakrishna's disciples was Narendranath Datta (1863–1902), a former law student who took monastic vows during Ramakrishna's last days and was thereafter known as Swami Vivekananda, founder of the Ramakrishna Math, an order of monks devoted to the teachings of Ramakrishna. Swami Vivekananda had an enormous impact on the representation of Hinduism in the West, particularly in the United States. In 1893, he visited the United States to speak on behalf of Hinduism at the World Parliament of Religions in Chicago. Quoting from the *Bhagavad Gita*, he represented Hinduism as a tolerant and universal religion. Like his teacher, Ramakrishna, Vivekananda asserted that all religions are true. His stirring speech was a milestone in changing Western attitudes toward Hinduism. It also ensured his fame and popularity in America, and he went on to establish the Vedanta Society of New York. Today, Vedanta Societies throughout the world are dedicated to the study, practice, and promotion of Hinduism, emphasizing the philosophical tradition originating in the *Vedas* and *Upanishads*.

Gandhi and the Struggle for Indian Independence

Mohandas Karamchand Gandhi (1869–1948), a towering religious, political, and social reformer in India, recast many Hindu ideas in the service of the fight for Indian independence. Born into a middle-class family of merchants, Gandhi was an English-educated lawyer and a deeply religious man. As a law student in England, he had read the *Bhagavad Gita,* and it had a profound impact on him.

Gandhi's political career began in South Africa, where he worked as a lawyer. It was here, in a struggle against racial discrimination, that he began to develop his political philosophy of nonviolent resistance. He characterized nonviolent resistance as *satyagraha* (Sanskrit, "grasping the truth") and explained that its strength lay in converting wrongdoers to justice rather than striving to coerce them.

Gandhi returned to India in 1915 to join the fledgling Indian independence movement, which sought to free India from British colonial rule. Deeply influenced by the American writer Henry David Thoreau (1817 – 1862), especially his thoughts on civil disobedience, Gandhi established an *ashram* (a place of religious seclusion) to train freedom fighters. The *ashram* chose as its motto a statement from the *Upanishads*: *satyameva jayate*, "the truth alone will prevail." Like his Upanishadic forebears, Gandhi believed that truth could be sought only through selfless service and humility, which could in turn be achieved by disciplining the body through fasting and celibacy.

Gandhi did not hesitate to criticize certain Hindu beliefs and practices, particularly that of *varnashrama dharma*, the ancient system by which society was ordered into various classes or castes. He worked tirelessly to abolish untouchability, calling the untouchables *Harijans* ("Children of God"), thereby seeking to increase their respectability. Gandhi also strove to improve the status of women.

Gandhi's charisma and influence were so great that even in his lifetime he was revered as a saint or *Mahatma* (Sanskrit, "Great Soul"). A lifelong Hindu, Gandhi also advocated the universality and truth of all religions and sought throughout his life to reconcile Hinduism and Islam. Tragically, on January 30, 1948, he was assassinated by Nathuram Godse, a Hindu nationalist who thought Gandhi was too accommodating of Muslims. Godse was later executed for the crime despite the pleas of Gandhi's two sons and Jawaharlal Nehru (1889–1964), India's first prime minister, who believed that violence would dishonor everything Gandhi represented. After decades of struggle, Gandhi had lived to enjoy just five months of freedom after Great Britain had partitioned colonial India into the independent states of India and Pakistan in mid-1947.

Hindu Nationalism and *Hindutva*

Whereas reformers such as Ram Mohan Roy, Vivekananda, and Gandhi sought to build bridges with the West and other religions by calling attention to their commonalities with Hinduism, other figures, such as V. D. Savarkar (1883–1966), insisted on the distinctiveness of Hinduism. Savarkar called this concept **hindutva** (Sanskrit, "Hindu-ness"), a term he coined in a 1923 pamphlet. For Savarkar, *hindutva* was a force to unite Hindus in repelling all dangerous foreign influences. As president of the Hindu Mahasabha, a Hindu nationalist political party that embraced this concept, Savarkar argued that India was an exclusively "Hindu Nation."

In 1925, the Rashtriya Svayamsevak Sangh (RSS; National Volunteer Corps) was founded. Although it has presented itself as a Hindu cultural organization, its members have a long history of political actions that have intensified communal tensions, precipitated violence, and propagated religious intolerance. The founder of the RSS, K. B. Hedgewar (1889–1940), was himself inspired by V. D. Savarkar's concept of *hindutva*. The RSS was meant to be a training ground for the self-empowerment of Hindu youth who were committed to defending a Hindu nation from the perceived threat posed by the Muslim world. Gaining independence from oppressive foreign rule can often rob nationalist movements of their momentum, but this was not the case in India after 1947. Hindu nationalists continued to be a major force in that country. The political backlash following Gandhi's assassination led many Mahasabha members to leave the party and ally themselves instead with a new political organization called the Bharatiya Jana Sangh (Indian People's Alliance). Its founder, Syama Prasad Mookerjee (1901–1953), had been a member of both the Mahasabha and the RSS when he organized the Indian People's Alliance in 1951. This was a Hindu nationalist party specifically created to oppose the Indian National Congress, the more moderate party of Jawaharlal Nehru and Mahatma Gandhi. In 1981 the Indian People's Alliance became the Bharatiya Janata Party (BJP). Today, the BJP and the Indian National Congress are the two major parties in India's political system. In 2014, the BJP won a landslide victory in India's national election. Narendra Modi, India's new prime minister, has been one of the party's most visible leaders.

Today, organizations espousing Savarakar's *hindutva* ideology come under an umbrella group called the Sangh Parivar (Family of Associations). The RSS is the cultural wing, the BJP is the political wing, and the Vishwa Hindu Parishad (VHP; World Hindu Organization) is the religious wing of the Sangh Parivar. The RSS continues to attract mostly lower-middle-class male youth, who feel empowered by the strong sense of cultural identity that it advocates. The RSS has awakened a deep sense of cultural pride among Hindu youth, but some of its members have been leading participants in sectarian violence against Muslims in recent years.

In 1991 the BJP led a pilgrimage around India gathering bricks to build a temple to Rama in Ayodhya, India. This was to be no ordinary temple. The pilgrims claimed that a fifteenth-century C.E. Islamic mosque called the Babri Masjid had been erected over an older Hindu temple that marked the exact birthplace of Rama. Their purpose was to tear down the mosque and build a grand Rama temple in its place. Members of Sangh Parivar rallied around the cause, which culminated in more than 200,000 participants converging on Ayodhya and demolishing the mosque with their bare hands. RSS youth then targeted the local Muslim community, destroying other mosques, ransacking Muslim homes, raping Muslim women, and murdering Muslim men. The backlash of these events echoed throughout India and Bangladesh, resulting in more than a thousand incidents of riots and communal violence perpetrated by both Hindus and Muslims. By the time calm had been restored, more than 4,000 people had been injured and at least 1,100 had lost their lives.

The BJP has also employed less aggressive strategies in its campaign to create a thoroughly Hindu India. For example, in the 1980s and 1990s it attempted to rewrite Indian history by distributing new school textbooks throughout India. These textbooks reflected the BJP's vision of India as a Hindu nation and Hinduism as a unified, monolithic tradition. Most important, and dangerously, this historical revisionism minimized Muslim contributions to the development of India and described India's Muslim rulers as foreign invaders. The RSS also has a strong presence in the Hindu diaspora communities in Europe and North America. Many Hindu emigrants send their children to RSS youth camps to give them a sense of their Hindu identity and cultural pride.

The Future of Hinduism

Encouraged by nationalist groups and political parties in India, some of today's Hindus see Hinduism as monolithic, homogeneous, and impermeable, closed off from what they perceive as the corrupting influences of the West and foreign religions. At the same time, an emerging global movement is seeking to transcend traditional boundaries to better serve the needs of an increasingly diverse Hindu community. Hinduism has always displayed a unique ability in the face of changing conditions to sustain ancient traditions within new and ever-changing contexts. How this ability will manifest itself in the future remains to be seen, but it seems certain that the efforts of both Hindu traditionalists and progressives will ensure the continuing vibrancy of the world's oldest religions.

HINDUISM AS A WAY OF LIFE

Hindus often insist that Hinduism is more a "way of life" than a system of beliefs. Indeed, Hinduism does place greater emphasis on what one *does* rather than on what one *believes*. The emphasis on doing rather than believing might explain the disconnection

VISUAL GUIDE
Hinduism

In Hinduism, folding one's hands and offering salutations by saying *namaste* (nom-us-tay) is a simple way of giving a respectful greeting, as well as saying, "I bow to the divine in you."

OM or AUM is the most sacred syllable in Hinduism and may be traced back to the Vedas. It is regarded as the primordial sound through which the universe is manifested. It is considered sacred by Hindus, Jains, Buddhists, and Sikhs.

The word "swastika" (Sanskrit, *svastika*) is derived from the Sanskrit *su* (good) + *asti* (it is), and may be understood as "fortunate" or "auspicious." The swastika itself is an ancient solar symbol and denotes harmony, balance, and good fortune. It is venerated by Hindus, as well as Buddhists and Jains.

Hindu forehead markings: *bindi*, *tripundra*, and *namam. Bindi* (drop) is a decorative mark on the forehead signifying auspiciousness. An additional "dot" is often applied by married women to the top of the head where the hair is parted. The mark between the eyes is situated to signify the "third eye" (the faculty of perception beyond ordinary sight). Some forehead markings denote sectarian affiliation, such as the three horizontal lines of sacred

(continued)

between textual injunction and actual practice that one often encounters in Hinduism. Hindu texts provide many prescriptions for how to live (e.g., the aims of life and the *varnaashrama dharma* system), but these do not always translate into actual lived practice. In this section, we will explore Hinduism as a way of life.

Seeing the Divine Image: Temples and Icons

Hinduism encourages a sensory religious experience in its adherents. This experiential aspect is nowhere more evident than when a Hindu goes to a temple. As religion scholar Diana Eck observes, the devotee doesn't say, "I am going for worship." Rather, the devotee asserts, "I am going for *darshan*." The Sanskrit word *darshan* means "to see," but in the Hindu context it refers specifically to the interlocking gaze shared by the deity and the devotee. That is, *darshan* is the intimate act of both seeing the deity and being looked upon by the divine, an act which establishes a loving relationship between devotee and God.[11]

As we learned earlier in this chapter, the image of a god in a temple or a personal shrine at home is not just a representation of the deity; rather, it is imbued with the divine presence. Thus, devotees believe that to see an image of a deity is to see the deity itself. In turn, the gaze of the deity's image is believed to confer blessings on every person who comes into its presence. In many ways, the act of *darshan* is often the most meaningful experience for Hindus.

Today, most Hindus go to a local temple or on pilgrimage to a sacred site for *darshan*. For this reason, the temple is a central religious and cultural institution in Hindu religious practice.

Temples generally house two different kinds of icons. The first type is the main image (or images), which resides at the center of the temple. These images are generally made of stone and permanently fixed in the shrine. The second type of icon is the processional image, typically cast from an amalgam of five metals. Smaller and more mobile than fixed images, processional images are brought out of temples on special platforms or chariots for temple festivals and are usually adorned in elaborate costumes and jewels. Hindus gather for a *darshan* in the presence of the divine form these mobile images embody. Although both types of icons are made by human hands and are constituted of material substances, while the icon is being worshipped it is understood not to be *merely* stone or metal but the very body of God.

In temple rites, deities are treated as royal guests. Temple worship usually involves sixteen different offerings. Of these, the most significant is the eighth offering, which involves pouring various types of auspicious substances over the icon. These might include scented water, milk, and sandalwood paste. After the ritual, the deity is adorned in ornaments, textiles, and flowers. The temple rituals end with a waving of lamps before the image. For Hindus, this is the ideal moment for *darshan*.

Divine images can also directly convey religious teachings. For instance, Nataraja, Lord of the Dance, is one of the most iconic forms of Shiva. In his dance, Nataraja represents what *Shaivas* call the Five Activities of Shiva, which can also be understood as the five principal manifestations of divine energy: creation, preservation, destruction, illusion, and liberation.

Forms of Worship

The Sanskrit word ***puja*** is commonly used to describe worship in Hinduism. In its most simple form, *puja* involves making some offering to the deity (such as fruit, incense, or flowers). The deity is then believed to partake of the devotion inherent in the offering. The material aspect of the offerings left behind is thought to be infused with the deity's blessing.

Puja can be simple or elaborate. Along with material items, offerings can consist of such things as washing or clothing the image of the deity, greeting it, prostrating oneself before it, and similar gestures. *Puja* can be offered almost anywhere—before a home shrine, at a temple, at pilgrimage sites, by sacred trees or rivers, at roadside shrines, or within temporary structures specially made for a specific rite. Rituals may be carried out as an expression of love for the deity, in a rite of passage, in celebrating a holiday or festival, when asking for blessings, in order to create an atmosphere of

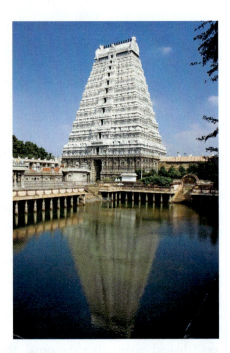

Clouds of incense billow from a terracotta censer as devotees pray before a multi-armed clay icon of Durga (upper center), Ganesha (lower left), and other deities. This is the final opportunity for *darshan,* as the icon is about to be dissolved by immersion into the Ganges River at the conclusion of the festival of Durga Puja. Kolkata, India.

The majestic gate of a Shiva temple in southern India is reflected in one of the two ritual bathing tanks found within its precincts. These towers are erected in the four directions and are often covered in sculptural imagery that refers to the sacred myths of the gods venerated within. Arunachaleswar Temple, Tiruvannamalai, India, eleventh century.

peace and harmony, or to propitiate the gods in times of trouble. Ritual occasions are ideal for maintaining and strengthening community ties, as we learned at the beginning of the chapter with the consecration of the Sri Ganesha Hindu Temple of Utah.

Certain particular forms of Hindu worship are so popular as to deserve our special attention. Here we describe three of them: *arati, mantras,* and sacrifice.

Arati As a form of *puja,* **arati** involves an offering of light. *Arati* is a very common practice; in fact, some Hindus use the term *arati* rather than *puja* to refer to worship generally. A lamp fueled with *ghee* (clarified butter) or camphor is lit and waved in a clockwise direction in front of the deity. The five flames used in *arati* symbolize the five elements (earth, water, fire, air, and ether), as well as the totality of the universe. This waving of the lamp is thought to remove evil influences and to return the object or recipient of the offering to an auspicious state, regardless of any negative thoughts or desires that might have been projected onto it. At the end of the ritual, participants wave their hands over the flame and touch them to their foreheads, taking the divine light of the deity into their innermost being.

Mantra Nearly all rituals in Hinduism are accompanied by the recitation of **mantras**. These are ritual formulas used to produce a spiritual effect. *Mantras* can be used for a variety of reasons: to heighten awareness of God, to enhance the efficacy of an offer-ing, to aid the practice of meditation, or to produce some magical effect. *Mantras* are usually—but not always—in Sanskrit.

The *mantra* that we have considered previously, *OM,* is prominent throughout Hinduism. The intonation of *OM,* the sound through which the universe is mani-fested, is thought to attune the mind to the essence of reality. Various Hindu sects use specific *mantras* especially suited to them. For example, the most important *mantra* for *Vaishnavas* is *Om Namo Narayanaya,* which means "obeisance to Narayana" (another name for Vishnu). For *Vaishnavas,* this *mantra* articulates the relationship between God and the devotee while also asserting the fullness and unity of Vishnu. Reciting and con-templating the *mantra* is an act of devotion that brings the devotee closer to Vishnu.

Sacrifice Fire sacrifice has been an essential component of Hinduism since the Vedic period. Sacrifice usually involves building an altar, kindling a fire, feeding it with *ghee,* and casting auspicious offerings (milk, cereals, fruits, flowers, etc.) into the fire while chanting *mantras.* Although fire sacrifice is usually performed by a *brahmin* priest, these rites can be performed by any married upper-caste man. A fire sacrifice is a cru-cial component of life cycle and temple rituals.

Although sacrifice has persisted as an important feature of Hindu worship through the centuries, perspectives on the relevance and meaning of sacrifice have varied. In the Vedic period, sacrifice was seen as essential to maintaining cosmic order. This is the reason that one of the most important Vedic myths describes the universe as being born from the sacrifice of the cosmic man. The *Upanishads,* how-ever, tend to diminish the relevance of sacrifice as an effective means of liberation from *samsara.* These texts argue that the true sacrifice takes place internally, with the breath itself fueling an inner sacrificial fire that awakens one to knowledge. The *Bhagavad Gita* follows in this line of interpretation, asserting that it is the surren-der of the fruit of action (through *bhakti*) that is the true meaning and purpose of sacrifice.

In the earliest period, the sacrifice of animals was an important aspect of Hindu ritual. However, over time (and particularly under the influence of Jainism and Buddhism), animal sacrifice ceased to play a role in upper-caste sacrificial rituals. In such sacrifices, coconuts and pumpkins came to act as substitutes for the animals. Animal sacrifice continues to play a significant role in folk Hinduism.

Yoga

Yoga in its most basic sense means a "yoking" or "uniting." In religious discourse, it refers to the uniting of the self with God. Yoga is sometimes used instead of *marga* (path) to designate any one of the three great paths one can take in the pursuit of *moksha*: *karma, jnana,* and *bhakti.* Yoga is also used more narrowly as the name of one of the six schools of philosophy and is one form of *jnana.* Understood in this way, yoga refers to the many systems of physical and mental exercise that have developed within

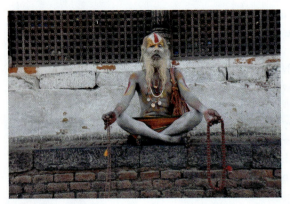

A Hindu ascetic sits in the lotus position, a prominent bodily posture for the practice of yoga.

the Hindu tradition. Most of us are familiar with *hatha* yoga, which makes use of physical exercises to promote the health of the body. But there are also forms of yoga, such as Raja ("Royal") Yoga, that employ both physical and mental techniques in order to make liberation from *samsara* possible. It is this form of yoga that most concerns us here.

The origins of yoga are obscure. Most scholars see elements of yoga in the *Vedas* and *Upanishads*. It is unmistakably present in the *Ramayana* and *Mahabharata*, whose heroes perform yogic exercises. By the fourth century C.E. the principles and techniques of yoga had been systematized in the *Yoga Sutras* of Patanjali.

The *Yoga Sutras* consist of 196 instructional sayings about the moral, physical, and mental conditions and techniques that can enable the individual to achieve *moksha*. These are evident in the eight steps through which practitioners move in their quest for liberation. The first two steps have to do with moral preparation. Prohibitions against harming other beings, lying, stealing, sexual irresponsibility, and greed must be observed. In addition, the five virtues of cleanliness, contentment, discipline, studiousness, and devotion to a god must be practiced. The next three steps involve preparation of the body. The practitioner learns postures (especially the lotus position) that promote comfort and alertness and how to breathe in rhythmic patterns that calm the body. Once these ends have been achieved, it becomes possible to withdraw the senses so that they no longer demand the mind's attention. The next two steps prepare the mind for liberation. By focusing its attention on a single thing, all other particulars fade away. All that remains is to gently remove this single object of attention from the field of the mind's awareness. This brings the practitioner to the eighth step, which is also the ultimate goal: *samadhi,* a state in which one's awareness is of the self as *Brahman.*

Rites of Passage

Hindu rites of passage are intended to invoke blessings and divine favor during important times of transition. In addition, they help socialize individuals, assisting them as they move into new roles and stages of life. Some rites of passage occur very early in life. These include the naming ceremony of a child, typically held on the tenth or twelfth day after birth; a child's first haircut, usually performed between the first and third years of life; and ear piercing, which is typically done for both boys and girls before age five. The following are also major rites of passage.

A Boy's Initiation   Historically, the *upanayana,* or sacred thread ceremony, was an initiatory rite for *brahmin, kshatriya,* and *vaishya* boys. (Recall the passage from *Laws of Manu,* p. 104) Today, it is performed almost exclusively for *brahmin* boys at about the age of eight, giving them permission to perform certain religious functions. Beginning with a fire sacrifice, the ritual culminates in the promotion of the initiate to the category of "twice-born." The initiate is given a sacred thread that symbolizes a kind of umbilical cord linking the boy to the sun, the source of all light and knowledge. The sacred thread lies across the chest, resting over the left shoulder and under the right arm, and consists of three cotton threads, each composed of three strands, that are joined together by a single knot. The sacred thread is a very visible sign of caste status. It is worn throughout one's life and is discarded only if a man renounces the world.

A Girl's First Menstrual Period   The onset of a girl's first menstrual period, which marks the transition from childhood to adulthood, is celebrated with rituals performed for girls from all castes. Sometimes these observances include spending the first three days of her first period secluded, although friends can visit. The young woman takes a ritual bath on the fourth day, and a feast is held in her honor. This transition is a public affair because it announces her availability for marriage. Often the young woman is taken to the local temple to receive a special blessing from an older married woman in her community, who will perform an *arati* ceremony to honor her new potential to bear children. Her life radically changes afterward and, for many communities, her freedom to have unsupervised interaction with boys may be greatly curtailed.

Marriage   Marriage is a very important rite of passage. It is through marriage that one enters the householder *ashrama* that provides the main support for society as a whole. Marriage was traditionally arranged by the parents between a bride and groom of the same *jati* after consulting an astrologer, who determined the couple's compatibility. In the last few decades, caste strictures have eased somewhat. As a result, marriages for love have become more commonplace.

The marriage ceremony is sanctified through a fire sacrifice in which the gods are asked for blessings and offerings are poured into the fire. A thread is tied around the bride's wrist, and she is asked to step three times on a grinding stone from the groom's family as a demonstration of her fidelity to the new household she is joining. At the high point of the rite, the bride and groom walk together seven times around the sacred fire. The bride's family then provides a sumptuous meal for all guests. After the last day of celebration, the bride goes to the home of her husband and begins her new life.

Death   Hindus often liken the cremation pyre to a fire sacrifice and speak of the funerary ritual, which usually involves cremation, as "the last sacrifice." Generally, cremation takes place on the same day as death. The body is washed, smeared with sandalwood paste, wrapped in a cloth, and then carried on a litter by male relatives, who chant a holy name or phrase as they bear the body to the cremation ground. It is usually the duty of the eldest son of the deceased to conduct the last rites and light the pyre. An ancient practice that is still often observed requires him to also crack the skull of the deceased in order to release the soul from the body, a daunting task for a son to perform.

Although cremation is the usual means of disposing of the body, there are exceptions. Earth burial is practiced for babies and among some low-caste communities. Saints, yogis, and ascetics are also buried. Their bodies are placed in special tombs, around which shrines are sometimes erected and worship performed.

Following the funeral ceremony, the family and home of the deceased are considered to be polluted for a period of about ten days. The bereaved are expected to keep to themselves until rites of ancestral offerings are completed. During this period, the deceased is offered balls of rice with which he or she is believed to construct a body in the spirit world or intermediate realm. This rite, which reflects the gestation of a human embryo for ten lunar months, may very well predate the formulation of a belief in reincarnation that was developed by the time of the *Upanishads*.

Pilgrimage

Hindu pilgrimage routes in India.

In Hinduism, sacred pilgrimage sites are believed to lie at the border between this world and that of the divine. Many of the earliest pilgrimage sites were located at sacred rivers and pools, and pilgrimage specifically involved ritual bathing as a means of purification. Some revered sites, marked by a shrine or temple, commemorate a sacred event or the life of a holy person. For pilgrims, these sites allow immediate, tangible access to the sacred.

One of the most important Hindu pilgrimage sites is the sacred city of Varanasi on the banks of the Ganges. Many Hindus believe that to die in Varanasi is to be immediately released from *samsara*. For this reason, many old and sick people travel to Varanasi to die. However, because the Ganges is held to be the most sacred river in India, people who are unable to go to Varanasi to die arrange to have their ashes scattered in the river. In this way, the sacred river is believed to carry the dead from this life into the divine realm.

The largest pilgrimage in India is to the sacred city of Prayag (Allahabad), where the Ganges and Yamuna Rivers (as well as the Sarasvati, a now-vanished river mentioned in sacred texts) come together. To bathe at the confluence of these three rivers is considered especially auspicious. Every twelve years, the *Kumbha Mela* festival takes place at Prayag. During the *Kumbha Mela*, the largest gathering of humans on earth takes place as pilgrims converge to bathe in the holy waters in the hope that all their sins will be washed away.

There are many other important pilgrimage sites in India. Some are dedicated to the goddess Devi and are referred to as *Shakti Peethas* ("Seats of Power"). Still others, like the city of Vrindavan in northern India, attract devotees of Krishna, who believe that it is not only the site of the god's birth and childhood but also the place where he continues to live.

How do Hindu pilgrimage practices compare to those of other religions, such as Buddhism, Islam, and Christianity? How do pilgrimage sites arise, and how do they serve the practical and spiritual needs of the visiting pilgrim?

Women in Hinduism

Hindu tradition has tended to be patriarchal, both subordinating and marginalizing women. Although there is some evidence in the Vedic literature that some women participated in early philosophical movements or dialogues, for the most part their public roles have been secondary to those of men. The role of Hindu women has been primarily domestic.

Classical Hindu texts generally give little attention to women, but there are exceptions. One example is the *Laws of Manu,* which, in the course of its extensive coverage of *varnashrama dharma*, includes some statements that confer upon women a relatively high place: "Where women are honoured, there the gods are pleased; but where they are not honoured, no sacred rite yields rewards."[12] At the same time, numerous passages subordinate and marginalize women, clearly asserting the predominance of father, husband, and even sons.

The *bhakti* movements enabled women to overturn social hierarchies. Women poets and saints such as Meera, who lived during the fifteenth century in Rajasthan, rejected marriage, devoted themselves to a spiritual life, and challenged the limits of gender, class, and caste. Today, Hindu women are increasingly assuming leadership roles in India and in the Indian diaspora. Women sometimes act as priests and are beginning to wield influence as spiritual teachers, monastics, and theologians. One of the most important contemporary female **gurus** is Mata Amritanandamayi Devi (b. 1953). Known to her followers as Ammachi ("Mother") and popularly referred to as "the hugging saint," she is believed by her devotees to be the embodiment of Devi, the divine mother.

In contemporary South Asian and Southeast Asian Hindu society, women are regarded as the custodians of traditional beliefs and ritual for the family. Generally, the social roles of men and women are expressed through clothing and other outward signs. While men wear contemporary slacks, dress shirts, and ties, women prefer traditional modes of dress. While many men eschew sectarian forehead markings except on ritual occasions, most Hindu women, especially those who are married, adorn their foreheads with the *bindi*. In addition to performing *puja* at the home shrine, observing festivals, and encouraging regular temple visits for the family, women also perform *pujas* and *vrata* for the spiritual welfare of their husbands and children on certain holidays.

Vrata A *vrata* is a vow of temporary self-denial usually undertaken by a woman. This generally involves a short period of fasting, but a *vrata* can also be a vow of silence or a short-term renunciation of anything to which one is attached. A woman usually undertakes a *vrata* for a specific purpose, such as to ensure the health and well-being of her husband and family. There are many special *vratas* observed at specific times throughout the calendar year. One of the most popular, observed by married women throughout southern India, always falls on a Friday in early August. This *vrata* involves a period of purification and fasting, after which the woman invites the goddess Lakshmi into her home. The hope is that Lakshmi, goddess of wealth and good fortune, will bring these things to the home.

All *vratas* are vows taken by women on special festival days. Let us now examine what are the key holidays and festivals observed by all Hindus.

Festivals and Holidays

Hindus make use of both solar and lunar calendars, as well as a calendar based on twenty-seven different constellations. All three calendars are consulted to determine when festivals and holidays will be observed. Many Hindu festivals link mythic events to the agricultural cycle. There are also innumerable holidays and observances that commemorate saints and sages, historical events, and sacred sites of regional interest.

Three popular Hindu festivals that are celebrated with many regional variations serve to illustrate the diversity of observances in Hinduism.

Navaratri or Dashera *Navaratri* ("nine nights") or *Dashera* ("ten days") is a holiday cycle celebrating the end of the monsoon season in India. In some regions, *Dashera* also commemorates the conclusion of a great war between Rama and the demon-king, Ravana. In other regions, such as southern India and in Bengal, the festival celebrates Devi's battle against the buffalo-demon, Mahisha (p. 135). To commemorate this conquest, altars are set up with images of the Goddess. For the first three days of the festival, devotees worship Devi in her manifestation as Durga. They then turn their attention to worshipping her as Lakshmi. On the concluding three days, she is worshipped as Sarasvati, the embodiment of knowledge. In Bengal, the eighth day is especially important, as it celebrates Durga slaying Mahisha and is marked with the sacrifice either of black goats or a substitute sacrifice of pumpkins. The festival culminates with street processions of large painted clay icons of Durga that are later dissolved in the nearby river or the sea. The "victorious tenth day," *Vijaya Dashami*, is celebrated all over India as Rama's final victory over the demon Ravana.

Diwali *Diwali*, the five-day "Festival of Lights," is celebrated in October. For many Hindus, it commemorates Rama's rescue of Sita and their heroic return to Ayodhya. Other myths are invoked as an explanation for the festival in different regions of India. At Diwali, oil lamps are set out on doorsteps and window ledges, and floating lamps are placed as offerings in rivers and reservoirs to signify the triumph of good over evil. Fireworks are lit on the night of the new moon, when Lakshmi is worshipped. The third day of *Diwali* marks the end of the harvest season, and *Lakshmi Puja* is performed to thank the goddess for the abundance that she has given. New clothes are worn and gifts are exchanged. *Diwali* is also celebrated by Sikhs and Jains.

Holi The spring festival of *Holi*, always celebrated at the vernal equinox, is Hinduism's most colorful holiday. Celebrated in either February or March, its festivities take place over two days. On the first night, bonfires are lit, and coconuts are offered as a sacrifice. The following day is a carnival celebration during which social and gender hierarchies are temporarily inverted, as crowds of young and old alike frolic in the streets, spraying colored water and staining one another with brightly colored powders.

Fun and frolic characterize the spring festival of *Holi*, as participants mischievously smear colored powders or spray colored water on each other.

Performance Traditions

There is a multitude of performance traditions in Hinduism, many of which cross over into the realm of ritual. Even the act of publicly reciting the *Ramayana* in Hinduism is believed to transform the performance site into sacred space. Hindu sacred performance traditions include many different genres: theater, puppetry, dance, music, storytelling, processions, and street festivals.

Ram Lila The *Ram Lila* (*The Play of Rama*) is one of Hinduism's most popular performance traditions. During the month of September, northern Indian villages and cities host *Ram Lila* festivals to coincide with the festival of *Dashera*.

A performance in Mumbai, India, of *Ram Lila*, the very popular enactment of the *Ramayana*.

These festivals, lasting anywhere from ten days to a month, are costume dramas based on the *Ramayana*. The most famous and elaborate *Ram Lila* is sponsored by the Maharaja (the hereditary ruler) of Ramnagar, a city located across the Ganges from Varanasi. The Ramnagar *Ram Lila* attracts pilgrims from all over northern India who come not only to participate in this annual festival but also to have *darshan* of Rama. The roles of Rama, Lakshmana, and Sita (the three principal characters of the *Ramayana*) are played by young upper-caste boys. For the duration of the *Ram Lila*, these boys are worshipped as the embodiments of divinity. Every evening, a priest waves a lamp, illuminating the principal characters who give *darshan* to the assembled pilgrims and devotees. Just as in a temple, where God is actively present in the icon, here too the very act of performing the *Ramayana* enables the young boys to embody divinity.

Sacred Songs: *Bhajan* and *Kirtan* The term *bhajan* refers specifically to devotional songs in Hinduism and Sikhism. The *bhajan* helps the gathered community to contemplate the divine. This is usually achieved through repetition of key phrases and lines and also through a call-and-response format of singing. Often, profound mystical concepts are presented in simple language that everyone may understand.

Bhajan may be contrasted to *kirtan*, which is neither formal in form nor structure, nor is it constrained by setting. *Kirtan* may be performed in lively sing-along processionals that roam the streets. Instruments are not necessary for *kirtan* performance, although they are often used. There are two different types of *kirtan* performances: in one type, the *kirtan* leader and the chorus alternate singing the divine name; and in the other, a hymn is communally recited, usually with an opening invocation, and then the body of the composition that describes the pastimes of the deity. For Hindu devotees, *kirtan* is a key spiritual practice, and it continues to be popular today, particularly for *Vaishnava* sects.

Storytelling An important way in which Hindus learn about the content of their religion is through storytelling. Even today, as in centuries past, professional storytellers continue to travel particular routes throughout India to visit local festivals, where they sing the epics and other myths in all-night performances.

Modern Hindus enjoy sacred narratives through new and equally vibrant media, such as movies, television, and even comic books. Throughout the history of Hinduism there have been numerous versions of sacred narratives, the *Ramayana* being perhaps the most obvious example. In recent decades, sacred narratives have been invigorated through print, radio, and television, as well as the Internet, with ever-new and imaginative retellings of these ancient stories.

CONCLUSION

Throughout this chapter, we have explored the rich diversity of the Hindu tradition. The extent of this diversity has prompted some observers to remark, "There are as many Hinduisms as there are Hindus." But we also have noted aspects of Hinduism that tend to unite Hindus. For example, all seek *moksha,* the ultimate liberation from *samsara,* and the realization of the true nature of the self and its relationship to the whole of reality. Hindus traverse three main paths to liberation, *karma marga, jnana marga,* and *bhakti marga.* In these various paths, we see diversity and unity together, with three different sets of teachings and practices all leading to the same goal. We see a similar blending of diversity and unity when we consider the detailed system of *varnashrama dharma,* which assigns to each individual Hindu a specific place and stage in life, while asserting the overall duty to conform to that which upholds the cosmic and social order. The history of Hinduism, therefore, exhibits a succession of inventions and reinventions in thought and practice with respect to these teachings.

For the most part, Hinduism developed in a rural setting, in small villages, and even (as we have noted) in the forest. In recent decades, however, there has been a pronounced shift in population from rural to urban settings. Furthermore, India, the world's second largest country and its largest democracy, is fast becoming a leader in high-tech industries, with cities like Bangalore and Mumbai rapidly developing as epicenters of international corporations. Hinduism is facing significant challenges brought on by modernization and the accompanying phenomenon of globalization. The religion is being constantly reshaped. But as this chapter has shown, the diversity of the Hindu tradition is integral to its identity, in the present just as in the ancient past. Whatever shape Hinduism takes in the future, it is likely to thrive, drawing on its age-old ability to adapt and to reform with even greater diversity and vitality.

SEEKING ANSWERS

What Is Ultimate Reality?

Monistic Hindus believe that *Brahman* is the supreme, unitary reality, the ground of all Being. Understood as undifferentiated and without attributes, *Brahman* manifests itself as the world, in all its particular forms. Thus, all things are inherently divine. Humans are unable to apprehend this ultimate reality because of attachment, delusion, and identification with the limited ego-self. For dualistic or devotional Hindus, ultimate reality is typically understood to be fully embodied in a deity, such as Vishnu or Shiva.

(continued)

SEEKING ANSWERS (continued)

How Should We Live in This World?

Powerfully attracted to the *samsaric* realm of particulars—our egoistic selves, our relationships, our possessions, and the seemingly countless objects of our desires—we are caught up in the continual cycle of death and rebirth. Hinduism prescribes living in a manner that moves the self toward liberation from *samsara*. Three paths (*margas* or *yogas*) lead to *moksha*: *karma* (action), *jnana* (knowledge), and *bhakti* (devotion). All the while, Hindus are required to live in conformity with *dharma*, upholding the cosmic and social order.

What Is Our Ultimate Purpose?

Moksha is liberation from *samsara*—the continuous cycle of death and rebirth, and the this-worldly realm in which this cycle recurs. Impossible fully to describe from the perspective of this world, the experience of *moksha* is said to be one of infinite awareness and eternal bliss. For monistic Hindus, *moksha* involves the full realization of the identity of the self with *Brahman* rather than with the world. For dualistic or devotional Hindus, *moksha* is the complete realization of the soul's perpetual and deep loving relationship with God.

REVIEW QUESTIONS

For Review

1. What were the essential features of Vedic religion? How was it different from Hinduism as it is practiced by most Hindus today?
2. In what ways do Hindus seek an experience of the divine?
3. What is the relationship between the ideas of karma, *samsara*, and *dharma*?
4. Describe the three *margas*, or paths, to liberation.
5. Describe the *Vedas*, *Upanishads*, epics, and *Puranas*. What are the most important features of each?

For Further Reflection

1. What are the various ways in which Hindus understand divine reality? How do these compare with those of other religions?
2. What is an avatar? How does the concept of avatar compare with the ways in which other religions speak of God on earth?
3. How does the traditional system of *varnashrama dharma* compare to systems of social organization with which you are familiar?
4. How were Hindus and Hinduism affected by British colonialism?
5. What are the most important turning points or milestones in the history of Hinduism?

GLOSSARY

arati (aah-ra-tee; Sanskrit) Worship with light, involving the waving of a lamp in front of the deity.

atman (aat-mun; Sanskrit) The eternal self or soul that is successively reincarnated until released from *samsara* through *moksha*.

avatar (ah-vah-taahr; from Sanskrit *avatara*) A "descent" of God (usually Vishnu) to earth in a physical form with the specific goal of aiding the world.

bhakti marga (bhah-k-tee; Sanskrit) The path of devotion.

Brahman (braah-mun; Sanskrit, "expansive") For monistic Hinduism, the supreme, unitary reality, the ground of all Being; for dualistic Hinduism, *Brahman* can refer to the supreme God (e.g. Vishnu).

brahmin (braah-mun; Sanskrit) A member of the priestly class of the *varna* or caste system.

dalit (daah-lit; Sanskrit, "oppressed"; Marathi, "broken") Self-designation of people who had traditionally been classified as untouchables or outcastes.

darshan (dur-shaan; Sanskrit, "to see") Worship through simultaneously seeing and being seen by a deity in the presence of its image.

dharma (dhur-mah; Sanskrit) Duty, righteousness, "religion"; basis for living in a way that upholds cosmic and social order.

hindutva (hin-doot-vah; Sanskrit, "Hindu-ness") A modern term that encompasses the ideology of Hindu nationalism.

jati (jaah-tee; Sanskrit, "birth group") One of thousands of endogamous groups or subcastes, each equal in social and ritual status.

jnana marga (nyah-nah mar-guh) The path of knowledge.

karma (kur-mah; Sanskrit, "action") Action; also the consequences of action.

karma marga (kur-mah mar-guh) The path of ethical and ritual works, or "action."

kshatriya (kshut-ree-yuh; Sanskrit) A member of the warrior and administrator class of the *varna* or caste system.

mantra (mun-trah; Sanskrit) A ritual formula recited to produce a spiritual effect.

maya (my-yah: Sanskrit, "magic" or "illusion") In the *Vedas*, the magical power the gods used to create this world; in *Vedanta* philosophy, illusion that veils the mind.

moksha (mohk-shah; Sanskrit, "release") Liberation, the final release from *samsara*.

OM (oh-m) (from three Sanskrit letters: *A-U-M*) The primordial sound through which the universe is manifested.

puja (poo-jah; Sanskrit, "worship") Generally, worship; usually the offering before an image of the deity of fruit, incense, or flowers.

Purana (pooh-raa-nah; Sanskrit, "ancient") A compendium of myth, usually with a sectarian emphasis.

samsara (sum-saah-rah; Sanskrit) The continuing cycle of birth, death, and rebirth; also the this-worldly realm in which the cycle recurs.

sannyasi (sun-nyaah-see; Sanskrit) Renouncer in the fourth stage (*ashrama*) of life.

Shaiva (shay-vah; Sanskrit) A devotee of Shiva.

Shakta (shah-k-tah; Sanskrit) A devotee of the Great Goddess, Devi.

shruti (shroo-tee; Sanskrit, "that which is heard") Term denoting the category of Vedic literature accepted by orthodox Hindus as revealed truth.

shudra (shoo-druh; Sanskrit) A member of the servant class of the *varna* or caste system.

smriti (smree-tee; Sanskrit, "tradition") Term denoting the vast category of Hindu sacred texts that is not *shruti*.

Upanishad (ooh-pah-nee-shud; Sanskrit, "sitting down near [a teacher]") A philosophical text from the later period of Vedic literature, also called *Vedanta* ("end of the *Vedas*").

Vaishnava (vie-sh-na-vah; Sanskrit) A devotee of Vishnu and his avatars.

(continued)

GLOSSARY *(continued)*

vaishya (vie-sh-yuh; Sanskrit) A member of the producer (farmer and merchant) class of the *varna* or caste system.

varna (vaar-nah; Sanskrit, "color") Caste or class; the four main classes form the basis of the traditional hierarchical organization of Hindu society.

Vedas (veh-duh; from Sanskrit *veda*, "knowledge") Broadly, all Vedic literature; narrowly, four ancient collections (*samhitas*) of hymns and other religious material.

Vedanta (veh-daan-tah; Sanskrit, "end of the *Vedas*") Synonym for *Upanishads*; prominent Hindu philosophical school.

yoga (yoh-gah; Sanskrit, "yoking" or "uniting") Generally, uniting of the self with God; sometimes used as an alternative to *marga* when referring to the three main paths to liberation; also (normally capitalized: Yoga) one of the six philosophical schools, focusing on moral, physical, and spiritual practices leading to liberation.

SUGGESTIONS FOR FURTHER READING

Eck, Diana. *Darsan: Seeing the Divine Image in India.* New York: Columbia University Press, 1998. An excellent discussion on the significance of *darshan* and traditions of Hindu temple worship.

Flood, Gavin. *An Introduction to Hinduism.* Cambridge, UK: Cambridge University Press, 1996. A concise and in-depth study of Hinduism.

Flood, Gavin, ed. *The Blackwell Companion to Hinduism.* Oxford, UK: Blackwell, 2003. A presentation on select special topics that are key to understanding Hindu belief and practice.

Hawley, John Stratton, and Mark Juergensmeyer. *Songs of the Saints of India.* Oxford, UK: Oxford University Press, 2006. A survey of the lives of medieval *bhakti* saints, with excellent translation of some of their poetry.

Hawley, John Stratton, and Vasudha Narayanan, eds. *The Life of Hinduism.* Berkeley: University of California Press, 2006. Special topical articles that explore personal voices and perspectives on Hindu life experience.

Klostermaier, Klaus K. *Hindu Writings: A Short Introduction to the Major Sources.* Oxford, UK: One World Publications, 2000. A keen survey of excerpts from many of the important textual sources that inform Hindu belief.

Knipe, David M. *Hinduism: Experiments in the Sacred.* New York: HarperCollins, 1991. A dependable and clear study organized based on the history of the tradition; includes a helpful timeline and glossaries.

ONLINE RESOURCES

The Internet Sacred Text Archive of Hinduism
www.sacred-texts.com/hin/
The Internet Sacred Text Archive of Hinduism provides an excellent array of the many genres of Hindu sacred texts with multiple public domain translations of key works.

The University of Wyoming Hinduism Website
http://www.uwyo.edu/religionet/er/hinduism/index.htm
The University of Wyoming Hinduism website offers concise but in-depth discussions on numerous aspects of Hindu tradition, literature, and belief.

(continued)

ONLINE RESOURCES *(continued)*

Understanding Hinduism

www.hinduism.co.za/index.html

An informal collection of articles and information on key topics offering some range of viewpoints.

The Sri Vaishnava Homepage

www.ramanuja.org

The Sri Vaishnava homepage is a unique resource for adherents to this important sect of Hinduism, yet is accessible and informative for outsiders.

The Shaivam.org Site

www.shaivam.org/index.html

The Shaivam.org site is a unique resource in that it explores multiple sectarian views of Shaivism yet is vast in scope and rich in detail.

The Internet Sacred Text Archive on Yoga

www.sacred-texts.com/hin/yoga/index.htm

The Internet Sacred Text Archive offers an extensive array of works on yoga, including both original sacred texts in translation and modern explorations of the subject.

BUDDHISM

IN A ZEN BUDDHIST MONASTERY IN NEW MEXICO, a young Buddhist nun named Jisen has spent years preparing for her ordination as a Zen priest. For the past week, she has spent each night sleeping outdoors under a tree that her fellow monks and nuns honor as the living embodiment of an ancient monk named Jizo, a bodhisattva famed for his compassion and devotion to others. Now the day has arrived for Jisen to take her vows. It is her hope that, as a priest, she will be better able to follow in Jizo's footsteps, working to alleviate suffering in the world by helping others to understand the workings of the mind and the nature of reality.

Before dawn, Jisen walks from the tree down to the river. There, in a rite called the tonsure ceremony, a small group of monks and nuns from her monastery shaves her head, leaving only a single strand at the crown. The tonsure ceremony symbolizes the letting go of worldly attachments, a step Buddhists believe is necessary on the road to enlightenment.

Jisen next joins a procession of monks and nuns who make their way to the temple, where the ordination ceremony will be completed. As she kneels before the altar, the monastery's Preceptor, or principal teacher, invokes all the buddhas, bodhisattvas, and earlier teachers of this lineage of Zen Buddhism. Then the Preceptor turns and addresses Jisen:

"Jisen, clinging and delusion do not cease, yet your original true nature has been revealed. After entering the priesthood, heaven neither covers nor does the earth sustain. Having nothing with which to cover your round

Tonsure ceremony of a Buddhist nun in Vietnam.

Significant sites of early Buddhism.

head and your robes embodying enlightenment, you stand out. . . . You will now be able to dedicate this life freely to the welfare and service of all beings."

An ordination robe is placed in Jisen's outstretched arms, and the elder nuns and monks help her to put it on. The Preceptor then continues, "Now, the last of your hair will be cut. Will you allow me to cut it?"

The Preceptor repeats this question three times, and each time Jisen answers "I will." Finally, as the Preceptor cuts the final strand of hair, Jisen recites her vows, pledging to let go of all attachments while helping to end the suffering of others. The Preceptor then ceremoniously invests Jisen with the begging bowl of a Zen priest and calls her to atone for any harmful actions done in both this and all of her previous lives. Having formally committed herself to observing the Buddhist precepts of her order, Jisen is now an ordained priest. ☀

Jisen is one of nearly 500 million Buddhists in the world today, about 7% of the population.[1] They belong to a vast number of Buddhist groups. Each has its distinctive characteristics, and their differences are sometimes remarkable, but all trace their origins back to the life and teachings of the Buddha, our point of departure for this chapter. We will then briefly survey the history of Buddhism and, finally, take note of the more important features of the Buddhist way of life.

THE TEACHINGS OF BUDDHISM

The **Buddha**, the "Awakened One," lived in northern India more than 2,500 years ago. It was the Buddha who set in motion the "wheel of the **Dharma**," the body of teachings about the cause and end of suffering that lies at the heart of Buddhism.

The Life of the Buddha

There is little we know with certainty about the life of the Buddha. The many accounts we have are legendary rather than historical, although their agreement on many points suggests they are based on a genuine historical figure. As much as reliable historical sources might do to satisfy our curiosity about the course of the Buddha's life, the legends about him are more helpful to us here. This is because they are didactic in character, telling the story of the Buddha in a way that educates us about the essential features of his teaching.

Because both Sanskrit and Pali (another language of ancient India) were so instrumental in the early transmission of accounts of the Buddha's life and teaching, we will make occasional use of both, aiming in each instance to provide only what is most helpful.

The Early Life of the Buddha
Siddhartha Gautama, who was to become the Buddha, was probably born in the sixth century B.C.E. Western scholars have traditionally set the dates for his life at 583–463 B.C.E., though good arguments can

be made for moving them as much as a century earlier or later. According to tradition, Siddhartha's father was the ruler of a small kingdom that straddled part of what is now the border of India and Nepal. It is said that astrologers and seers observed auspicious marks on the infant Siddhartha's body, indicating that he was destined to

---

TIMELINE
Buddhism

c. 563–483 B.C.E. Traditional dates for the life of the Buddha

c. 483 B.C.E. First Buddhist Council.

c. 383 B.C.E. Second Buddhist Council.

c. 360 B.C.E. Council of King Mahapadma.

c. 272–231 B.C.E. Reign of Ashoka in India.

c. 247 B.C.E. Third Buddhist Council.

250–200 B.C.E. Buddhism arrives in Southeast Asia.

65 C.E. Buddhism arrives in China.

100–200 Composition of the *Lotus Sutra*.

300–400 Buddhism arrives in Korea.

400–450 According to tradition, Bodhidharma brings Chan (Zen) Buddhism from India to China.

552 Buddhism arrives in Japan.

775 The first Buddhist monastery in Tibet is built at Samye.

c. 800 Borobudur Stupa built in Java.

c. 1200 Destruction of Buddhist universities at Nalanda and Vikramasila.

1185–1333 Pure Land, Zen, and Nichiren flourish in Japan during the Kamakura period.

c. 1500 Virtual disappearance of Buddhism in India.

1890–1921 T. W. Rhys-Davids, professor of Pali at the Universities of London and Manchester, translates Buddhist texts into English.

1899 The Buddhist Churches of America founded in San Francisco by Japanese immigrants of the Jodo Shinshu sect.

1900 Over 40,000 Buddhist and Daoist texts are rediscovered in a cave at Dunhuang, in western China.

1956 Indian social activist B. R. Ambedkar (1891–1956) converts to Buddhism along with 400,000 others to protest Hindu oppression of "untouchables."

1959 The 14th Dalai Lama flees to India from Tibet.

conquer the world. But there was a question: Would he conquer the outer world as a victorious monarch, or the inner world as a holy sage?

Siddhartha's father was determined that his son would follow in his footsteps. Fearing that Siddhartha would be drawn to the spiritual life if he became aware of the existence of suffering in the world, the king went to great lengths to shield him from the harsh realities of life. And so Siddhartha grew up surrounded by palace walls, living an idyllic life in which every pleasure was made available to him and there was no hint of pain. In time, he married a beautiful princess, Yasodhara, whom he loved deeply and with whom he had a son. It was what many would consider a perfect life—and yet Siddhartha grew restless.

Finally, at the age of twenty-nine, Siddhartha ventured outside the sheltered world of the palace. Accompanied by his charioteer, he saw things that were to change the course of his life. Buddhists call these the "Four Sights." The first was a frail old man, bent and leaning on his staff. Siddhartha, who had never seen old age, asked if he, too, would become old and decrepit. He was dismayed when his charioteer assured him that he would. The second sight was a man afflicted by disease. Sickness, said the charioteer, is also a part of human life. The third sight, a corpse being carried off to a cremation, was terrifying. Death, too, said the charioteer, is something no one can escape. Siddhartha now saw through the illusion that his father had perpetrated. Filled with horror and disgust by the inescapable truths of old age, sickness, and death, he fell into despair. It was not until he witnessed the fourth sight that he found some reason to hope. Sitting by the side of a road, he saw a wandering ascetic, homeless and without possessions, who seemed to be content.

Siddhartha cuts his hair. Mural depicting the Life of Buddha, Jogyesa Temple, Seoul, South Korea.

The "Great Going Forth" For Siddhartha, the ascetic pointed the way. To return to life within the palace would be to hide from the truth. He resolved instead to face it. He would renounce the life he had lived, take up the life of an ascetic, and search for the truth about suffering. One night, he arose from his bed, kissed his sleeping wife and son good-bye, and silently slipped away. As soon as he was alone in the forest, he took off his expensive clothing and used his sword to cut off his hair, symbolically severing the bonds that tied him to his old life.

At first, Siddhartha turned to ascetic sages who were acknowledged for their wisdom, becoming a disciple first of one, then another. They taught him meditation techniques and yogic disciplines, but although he mastered these, they left him unsatisfied. He then committed himself to extreme asceticism. After a time of wandering, he found a grove of trees watered by a river. Joined there by five other ascetics who wished to follow his example, he began to practice severe austerities in the hope that they would somehow clarify his thought. For five years, Siddhartha wore rags. Never cleaning himself, he allowed filth to cover his body. He slept on thorny brambles and in cemeteries strewn with half-burned corpses. Weakened by eating as little as a single grain of rice a day, he became a skeletal figure whose eyes had withdrawn into their sockets and whose distorted mind was tormented by searing pain and thunderous sound.

One day, after a long period of intense fasting, Siddhartha set out for the river. On the way, he overheard a music teacher explaining to his student that an instrument string wound too tight will break, whereas one that is too loose makes no sound at all. These words brought Siddhartha to the realization that neither sensual indulgence nor self-denial is helpful in the quest for understanding and liberation from suffering. Because both weaken the body and the mind, the best path lies between them, between attachment and aversion. This principle of the **Middle Way** was to become foundational in Buddhism. According to tradition, it was at just this moment that a young woman from a nearby village came to Siddhartha with a bowl of porridge. He accepted her offer of nourishment, ate it, and bathed himself. He then returned to his ascetic companions, but they left him when they learned he had abandoned their way of life.

Enlightenment Siddhartha's determination was now absolute. At a village in northern India now known as Bodh Gaya, he sat down beneath a fig tree and vowed to remain there in meditation until he gained the understanding he sought. Restored to health by his practice of moderation, he sat for forty-nine days, moving into ever-deeper states of awareness. Then, during his meditation in the course of a single night, his enlightenment came. In a series of psychological breakthroughs made possible by the power and clarity of his mind, Siddhartha first recalled all of his past lives. He then saw how **karma**—the law of actions and their consequences—had been at work throughout time, conditioning the existence of all beings as they took form and then passed away. Finally, Siddhartha realized that desire is the cause of suffering and that for suffering to end there must be an end to desire.

According to Buddhist tradition, Siddhartha was not the first to attain enlightenment. Buddhists believe that others before and after him became, and will become, buddhas. But it is from *this* buddha that they have received the Dharma, and so for them he is *the* Buddha, the "Awakened One." His enlightenment brought an end to the desire that causes suffering. It also brought freedom from rebirth, which results from attachment to the world. Freed from the disturbances caused by attachment, his mind came to rest in its natural state, and he was filled with joy. He had attained **nirvana**, the "extinguishing" of desire and suffering. For many days the Buddha remained close to the site of his enlightenment. Then, moved by compassion for others, he set out to teach what he had learned.

"Calling the Earth to Witness." According to tradition, the demon Mara afflicted the Buddha with powerful temptations to give up his quest for enlightenment. Ignoring them, the Buddha touched his right hand to the ground, thereby calling upon the earth to witness his unshakeable resolve. Immediately thereafter, he experienced nirvana.

Rock-cut reclining statue of the Buddha preparing to enter *parinirvana*, in a cave shrine at Ajanta, Maharashtra State, India. Fifth century C.E.

Beginnings of the Buddhist Community He went first to a deer park at Sarnath (near modern Varanasi in India), where the five ascetics who had earlier abandoned him were still practicing harsh austerities. Seeing that he had broken through to some new understanding, they gathered around the Buddha, who gave them his first teaching. This was the "Sermon in the Deer Park," in which he told them of the Middle Way and set forth the Four Noble Truths and the Noble Eightfold Path, which describe the cause and cure of suffering (pp. 151–152). Having heard him, the ascetics became followers of the Buddha, the first Buddhist monks and the first members of the Buddhist **Sangha** (Pali, "community").

From Sarnath, the Buddha began to retrace his steps back home, attracting more followers to the Sangha along the way. Many were relatives, including his father and his son, Rahula. A cousin, Ananda, became one of the Buddha's most devoted disciples and later played such an important role in remembering and transmitting his teachings that he has been called the "Guardian of the Dharma." The Buddha wandered across northern India for more than four decades, teaching, ordaining monks and nuns, accepting lay followers, and inviting doubters to test his teachings in order to see for themselves if they had merit.

The Death of the Buddha The life of the Buddha came to an end forty-five years after his enlightenment. He was eighty. He and Ananda had been on their way to Kusinara, not far from Varanasi, when they stopped to eat at the home of a blacksmith. Something in the meal was tainted—some accounts say pork, some say a nut or a mushroom—causing the Buddha to become fatally ill. In a grove on the outskirts of the village, Ananda made a bed for him between two trees. According to some accounts, as the Buddha lay down, the trees suddenly burst into bloom and showered him with their petals. At the same time, fragrant sandalwood powder fell from the sky, and the air was filled with celestial music. His monks soon began to gather at the scene, frantically seeking a final fragment of the Buddha's wisdom. When they asked what they would do without him to teach them, he responded that the Dharma would always be their guide. Then, closing his eyes, the Buddha went deep into meditation and died. Without attachments to the world, and unbound by karmic forces that would have brought another incarnation, he passed into ***parinirvana***, the complete and final entry into nirvana.

The Essentials of the Buddha's Teaching

The Buddha's motive for embarking upon the spiritual life had been to find the truth about human suffering. What was its cause? How could it be ended? His enlightenment had brought answers to these questions, and these answers constitute the core of the Dharma. We saw in Chapter 4 that in Hindu usage, the Sanskrit word *dharma* has a wide range of meanings, including "law," "duty," and "righteousness." In Buddhist contexts, *dharma* (Pali, *dhamma*) in its broader sense refers to nature and its laws, but it is more often and more narrowly used to describe the body of the Buddha's teaching, passed down through the centuries. The difference between the broader and narrower meanings of *dharma* is not as great as one might imagine. As we will see, the teachings of the Buddha are based on his observations of nature and its laws.

Interdependent Origination We will begin our investigation of the Buddha's teaching with the doctrine of **Interdependent Origination** (Pali, *Panicca-samuppada*), also known as Dependent Origination, because so much of the Dharma is based upon it.

To most of us, the world seems to be a composite system consisting of different and separate things. The chair you are sitting in certainly appears to exist on its own, apart from all other things in the room. And it is likely that you see yourself as existing independently from everyone and everything else you encounter.

Looking deeply into reality, the Buddha saw things very differently. He taught that reality is a complex of interrelated and interdependent phenomena in which nothing exists apart from anything else. Instead, all things depend on other things for their coming-into-existence—that is, for their origination. Of course, everyone recognizes at some level that this is the case. Someone built your chair, for example, and your parents had something to do with you. But the Buddha's teaching, augmented by later Buddhist thinkers, goes far beyond this in identifying a cycle of twelve causal factors (such as ignorance, desire, and rebirth) that bring about a coming-into-existence once any one of them is set in motion.

Of course, things also *remain* in existence—or at least they *seem* to. How can this be explained? And what *are* things, really? Here, again, the Buddha taught that all things are interdependent; so much so, in fact, that they have no existence whatsoever *in and of themselves*. Once again, take your chair as an example. Looking deeply, you will find that it is constituted of different elements: height, width, leather, legs, texture, firmness, color, and so on. But you will not find "chair." Instead, your chair exists only as a complex of "not chair" elements, and only for as long as these constituent parts remain together. And so it is with all things. Each thing exists as a collection of other elements, having no independent existence of its own.

The Three Marks of Existence Building on his teaching about the interrelatedness and interdependence of things, the Buddha taught that there are **Three Marks of Existence**—Impermanence, Suffering, and No-Self.

The Buddha's doctrine of **Impermanence** (Pali, *anicca*) holds that all things are always changing. Nothing remains the same, even for a moment. All things are always in a state of *becoming*. For example, imagine a blade of grass. Although it may seem static, the truth is that it is growing and therefore becoming a *different* blade of grass in every moment.

The Buddha's teaching about suffering (Pali, **dukkha**) is central to the Dharma. He once said, "I have taught one thing and one thing only, suffering and the cessation of suffering." Although *dukkha* is usually translated as "suffering," it can also mean "unease" and "dissatisfaction," as well as specific forms of unease and dissatisfaction (such as anxiety, fear, doubt, and so on).

Suffering is caused by the desire to hold on to things when, in fact, nothing can be held. Uncomfortable with constant change and the impermanence of things, we want them to remain as we want them to be. Buddhists describe this wanting in a variety of ways—as desiring, craving, clinging, and thirsting (the literal meaning of the Pali *tanha*, commonly translated as "desire"). However it is described, desire is made possible by ignorance (and, in particular, ignorance of impermanence) and can take the form of an attachment to something we want in our lives or an aversion to something we don't want. These three qualities of attachment, aversion, and ignorance (also referred to as greed, hatred, and delusion) are known as the "Three Poisons." The suffering that arises from them can take innumerable forms. Wanting is suffering. Lacking is suffering. Fearing that something you have might one day be lost is suffering. Believing that you cannot be happy unless you have something is suffering. Being averse to something is suffering. Wanting things to stay the same is suffering. Wanting things to be different is suffering. Stress and worry are suffering. Envy and jealousy are suffering. Anger, hatred, grief, loneliness, and frustration are suffering. Finally, the unhealthy effects many of these mental or psychological states have on the body constitute suffering.

The third of the Three Marks of Existence is the doctrine of **No-Self** (Sanskrit, **anatman**; Pali, *anatta*). Of all the things we desire, it is likely that our greatest attachment is to our notion of self. As we saw in Chapter 4, Hinduism includes the belief that at the core of one's self is the unchanging and eternal *atman*, which survives the death of the body through successive incarnations. The Buddha rejected this idea, teaching that just as there are no other things that remain unchanged, there is no static self that remains the same, even from moment to moment. The doctrine of No-Self does not mean that there is no "you." Clearly, you exist. You have a body, a mind, movement, interests, and other qualities. The Buddha taught that these are rooted in the **skandhas** (Sanskrit, "bundles" or "heaps"), the five basic components of every self: the body, perception, feelings, innate tendencies shaped by karma, and thought—all of which are always in flux. Thus the Buddha taught that each of us is a shifting self that is always changing in response to changes happening elsewhere in the great web of interrelated, interdependent, and impermanent phenomena that make up reality.

It can be difficult to accept this idea. After all, most of us are quite attached to our individual identities and to the notion that for as long as we live (and, perhaps, even after we die) there are some ways in which we remain the same. No-Self might seem to imply a destruction or annihilation of something we like very much—ourselves. But this is not the case. Instead, the Buddha urged only that his followers recognize that the self is not concrete, permanent, or independent of all other things. The great

THE FOUR NOBLE TRUTHS

1. Suffering is inherent in life.
2. The cause of suffering is desire.
3. There is a way to put an end to desire and suffering.
4. The way is the Noble Eightfold Path.

benefit he saw in this teaching is that it opens the way to living without the suffering that arises from a false notion of self and from clinging to things that cannot be held. The Buddha found the full realization of this ideal in his enlightenment and in the bliss of nirvana.

The Four Noble Truths and the Noble Eightfold Path We saw earlier that the first teaching the Buddha offered to the Sangha was the Sermon in the Deer Park, in which he told the five ascetics who had been his companions about the **Four Noble Truths** and the **Noble Eightfold Path**. Like a physician dealing with some illness—in fact, his followers often spoke of him as the *Bhisakko*, or "the Peerless Physician"—he structured his most fundamental teaching about suffering as if it were a medical diagnosis and prescription for a cure. The Four Noble Truths follow the four steps ancient Indian doctors used to diagnose and treat illness: (1) identifying a symptom, (2) discovering its cause, (3) determining if there is a way to remove the cause, and (4) prescribing a therapy to effect a cure. As a process of identifying and treating the disease of suffering, the Four Noble Truths empower those who follow them to understand the root cause of suffering and to cure themselves.

Now that we have investigated some of the Buddha's other teachings, we are in a good position to understand the Four Noble Truths. In teaching that suffering is inherent in life, the Buddha was pointing to the inevitability of suffering and its everyday presence in its many forms in people's lives. In identifying the cause of suffering as desire, the Buddha was not teaching that all forms of desire are unhealthy. Satisfying our desire for nourishment, employment, and a decent place to live certainly makes sense. But when we desire to grasp and hold on to things that cannot be held, we will always be disappointed. The good news is that there is a way to deal with desire and to minimize, even to end, the suffering it causes.

The Buddha's prescription for a cure for suffering is the Noble Eightfold Path. In treading the Eightfold Path, one follows in the footsteps of the Buddha in eradicating attachment, aversion, and ignorance, putting an end to desire, and ultimately achieving enlightenment and nirvana, just as the Buddha did.

The eight aspects of the Noble Eightfold Path are sometimes divided into three divisions, each with its own goal. The first is the *prajna* (Sanskrit, "wisdom") division,

Compare the Buddha's teachings about the self or soul with the teachings of other religions.

THE NOBLE EIGHTFOLD PATH

1. **Right View**: seeing things as they are, in accordance with the Buddha's teachings.
2. **Right Intention**: cultivating an unshakeable commitment to tread the path to enlightenment in accordance with the Buddha's teachings.
3. **Right Speech**: cultivating the virtue of addressing others with kindness, while abstaining from lying, divisive or abusive speech, and idle chatter.
4. **Right Action**: abstaining from killing, stealing, and sexual misconduct.
5. **Right Livelihood**: making a living in a way that harms no one and benefits all.
6. **Right Effort**: striving to abandon all thought and action that is harmful to oneself or others and to cultivate virtues that benefit oneself and others.
7. **Right Mindfulness**: focused awareness of the body and mind and the phenomena arising within and affecting each.
8. **Right Concentration**: cultivating the four stages of concentration leading to equanimity beyond pleasure and pain.

which includes Right View and Right Intention. Here, the aim is to ensure that one understands and accepts the Buddha's teachings about Interdependent Origination, Impermanence, and Suffering and is committed to striving for goals consistent with them. The second division has the purpose of cultivating ethical conduct (Sanskrit and Pali, *sila*) through Right Speech, Right Action, and Right Livelihood. The Buddha taught that unethical conduct is an obstacle to mental clarity. For this reason, destructive speech, immoral behavior, and making a living in a way that does not benefit oneself and others are to be avoided. The third division promotes concentration (Sanskrit and Pali, *samadhi*). Through Right Effort, one seeks to eliminate all qualities of the mind that give rise to unwholesome thought and action and to encourage those that produce more positive effects. Right Mindfulness is the observation of thoughts, feelings, and all other phenomena that occur in the body and mind. Finally, Right Concentration involves progress through four stages of concentration until one achieves a state of nonattachment and equanimity.

Karma and Rebirth The Buddha taught a doctrine of rebirth that differed from the Hindu view in denying that there is an eternal and unchanging soul (*atman*) that passes through many incarnations. According to his doctrine of No-Self (*anatman*), one's sense of self arises from the interrelationship of the five *skandhas* and exists only for as long as they function together in such a way as to give rise to that sense of self. When they separate at death that sense of self ceases to exist, and so there is nothing substantial that passes from one incarnation to another. And yet there is a definite connection between one life and the next; there is a type of rebirth. The Buddha's teaching on this point is obscure and much debated. What *is* clear is that one's actions and the karma they generate bring about the conditions for the coming-into-existence of a new set of *skandhas*. This, in turn, gives rise to another sense of self. Nothing concrete passes from one life to the next; only the karmic and character-related elements of the previous life, which shape a new life in some ways consistent with the old. There are a variety of analogies Buddhists have used to illustrate this idea. According to one, rebirth is much like what happens when one candle is used to light another. A light appears where none had existed before, and yet nothing has passed over other than the energy (which we might compare to karmic energy) generated by the first candle.

Of course, these teachings about karma and rebirth do not apply to those who have found enlightenment. The Buddha taught that these individuals no longer set in motion the karma that leads to rebirth and are also freed entirely from the karma produced in earlier lives. There is no rebirth for them. Only those who continue to thirst for things and to seek to satisfy their desire through attachment to them are reborn in **samsara** (Pali, "perpetual wandering"), which, just as it is in Hinduism, has for Buddhism two closely related meanings: the continuous cycle of birth, death, and rebirth and the this-worldly realm in which this recurs.

Nirvana The ultimate goal of Buddhist practice, nirvana is liberation from suffering in the cyclic existence of samsara. A Sanskrit word, nirvana means a "blowing out" or "extinguishing" and can refer to the extinguishing of desire and of suffering. The Buddha taught that all people have the potential to attain nirvana. Buddhists employ a variety of techniques for attaining nirvana but agree that its attainment brings perfect bliss and an end to suffering. Beyond this, any description of nirvana is uncertain. Being utterly unlike anything one might experience with ordinary awareness, no comparison is possible. For this reason, the Buddha said very little about nirvana, as it is something that must be experienced in order to be understood.

Gods in Buddhism? It is often said that Buddhism is an atheistic religion. And indeed, some Buddhists are atheists. Many others, however, believe in a wide variety of divine beings.

The Buddha had little to say about the gods and discouraged devotion to them. He urged his followers instead to focus their attention on the Dharma and devote themselves to putting its precepts into practice. The Buddha's perspective on the gods is perhaps best described as *transtheistic*[2] (see the Introduction, p. 12), in the sense that he acknowledged the existence of gods; but when it comes to the truly crucial issues of the quest for enlightenment and nirvana, the gods are not helpful.

Later forms of Buddhism tend to acknowledge the existence of supernatural beings—celestial Buddhas and bodhisattvas—who are the objects of devotion and who are believed to bestow benefits on their followers. Whether or not these supernatural beings are "gods" depends on how one defines the term. We will explore the ideas of celestial Buddhas and bodhisattvas in more detail below.

Katherine Sei is an American Buddhist who lives in California. She is a practitioner of Vajrayana Buddhism and has been a student of Lama Lodru Rinpoche for nearly three decades. She is the facilitator of a Buddhist study center in Sacramento.

Katherine Sei

As a Buddhist, what is the most important aspect of human existence? What should Buddhists do or focus on in life?

The most important aspect of human existence, to me, is that we have an opportunity to evolve as beings. This evolution encompasses uncovering our true nature. This true nature is comprised of a spontaneous, natural compassion and a clear wisdom as to "what is really going on here." I've found through all the years of meditation that we all tend to really limit our minds, and the expression of our true wise and benevolent nature. As I uncover and begin to understand my mind's true nature, and learn to let go of my limiting definitions of self, others, and events in my life, suffering diminishes. Life becomes more joyful, more peaceful, and I feel more interconnected with everyone. Life also becomes very, very interesting as I begin to become aware of all the interconnections of karmic causes and effects, and I can relax into the "play" of events.

Does Buddhism give you a unique outlook on life? How so or why?

I'm not sure if Buddhism gives a unique outlook as much as a useful outlook on life in this culture. The teachings of Lord Buddha are not necessarily unique to Buddhism—I think many aspects of Hinduism, Christianity, Judaism, and Islam provide a framework for becoming a more loving and wise person. What may be unique in terms of Buddha's teachings is that one can examine one's mind and one's life through meditation practices. It's more like a science than a religion, analogous to a physicist learning mathematics to explore the universe. I've found through meditation that life isn't quite as rigid as we often make it out to be. Knowing that, one can learn to let go of many of the emotional habits and knee-jerk reactions. One can find many creative solutions to life's problems, big and small, from "What is death?" or "What does it all mean?" to "How do I deal with my angry boss?" "How do I deal with the stress in my life?" and so on.

What single event in your life would you characterize as your most meaningful religious experience?

It's hard to pick one single event in my life that I consider most meaningful. Three come to mind. First would be when I took refuge with Trungpa Rinpoche in the 1980s. At that time, I discovered that I could treat others and myself with more gentleness. The second event would be when I met Ven. Lama Lodru Rinpoche, my direct teacher for the past twenty-seven years. Lama Lodru has taught me the same meditation practices that Tibetan lamas go through in a formal three-year retreat, but spread out over fifteen years. In doing this, he demonstrated that anyone can learn to meditate and apply it in their day-to-day life.

One doesn't have to become a monk or nun to become liberated. The third event was having the nature of my mind pointed out by Mingyur Rinpoche. Mingyur Rinpoche is a Tibetan lama who had to overcome panic attacks when he was a teenager. He showed me how applicable Buddha's teachings on meditation are to all aspects of life.

THE HISTORY OF BUDDHISM

In this section we explore the early history of Buddhism in India, its expansion into other parts of Asia and beyond, and the developments of new forms of Buddhism, each interpreting in its own way the teachings of the Buddha. Along the way, we pause to consider in some detail each of the three main forms: **Theravada**, **Mahayana**, and **Vajrayana**.

The Period of the Buddhist Councils

According to traditional Buddhist accounts, immediately after the death of the Buddha a council was convened at the town of Rajagriha in northeast India. It was the first of a series of such councils, which would define Buddhism by addressing key doctrinal and practical issues as they arose at particular times and places in its history.

Diffusion of Buddhism across Asia.

The First and Second Buddhist Councils

The First Council, convened c. 483 B.C.E., shortly after the Buddha's death, was made up of his direct disciples, who wished to ensure that they all accurately remembered his teaching. The First Council formalized an oral canon, thereby establishing an authority for a community that had lost its teacher.

During the Buddha's lifetime, he and his *bhikkus*, or monks, had been wanderers, remaining in one place only during the annual rainy season. This changed in the centuries after his death as formerly itinerant monks and nuns began to settle in permanent monastic communities. Over time, these communities became increasingly insular and geographically dispersed. Without a unifying authority above them, there was a proliferation of variations in practice and doctrine that led in turn to sectarian splits. This tendency is apparent as early as the Second Buddhist Council (c. 383 B.C.E.), which was convened to address issues relating to discipline; some monks, for example, had begun to accept money for services they performed for their lay followers.

A few early Buddhist sources allude to another council held c. 360 B.C.E., shortly after the Second Council. On this occasion, the monks assembled to address the issue of the authority of the Buddhist canon. A majority, known as the *Mahasanghika* (Sanskrit, "Great Community"), held that the canon was not absolutely authoritative and that there were other legitimate means for the transmission of the Dharma. The minority held that the canon did indeed faithfully preserve the Buddha's teachings. This group, who called themselves the *Sthaviras (*Sanskrit, "Elders"), was a precursor of Theravada Buddhism. In the years following, subdivisions within both groups arose that foreshadow the events of Ashoka's Third Buddhist Council.

Ashoka and the Third Buddhist Council

The renowned emperor of the Mauryan Dynasty, Ashoka (r. c. 272–231 B.C.E.), embodies the ideal of Buddhist kingship. He united the subcontinent of South Asia on a scale unseen either before or after his time. It was not until the British colonized India in the eighteenth and nineteenth centuries that such a large portion of the subcontinent would again be unified under a single ruler.

Despite his success as a conqueror, Ashoka later profoundly regretted the violence involved in his conquests. According to legend, he underwent a conversion experience immediately following a military triumph over his rivals in 260 B.C.E. He abandoned his expansionist policies and began to channel his efforts into social reform grounded in Buddhist ethics.

Although Ashoka had been influenced by Buddhist ideals even before his victory, his conversion was clearly the pivotal moment of his reign. His sincerity was evident in his edicts, which promoted moral purification, self-awareness, nonviolence, and respect of all religious viewpoints. The edicts were promulgated across his empire. Often carved on stone pillars (some of which are still preserved today), these edicts are our earliest evidence for the widespread promotion of Buddhist ideals.

Ashoka convened the Third Buddhist Council in his capital at Pataliputra c. 247 B.C.E. Those present attempted to settle disputes regarding doctrinal departures of some monks

ACTIONS TAKEN DURING EACH OF THE BUDDHIST COUNCILS

First Council (c. 483 B.C.E.): preserved the teaching and created a Buddhist canon
Second Council (c. 383 B.C.E.): preserved vows and banned handling money and the selling of selling religious services
King Mahapadma's Council (c. 360 B.C.E.): according to some sources, asserted that the

Dharma teaching is not bound by canon and can be modified
Third Council (c. 247 B.C.E.): defined what the "authentic" view of the Buddha is and acknowledged the later Theravada sect as representing that view (under Ashoka's reign)

from the teachings of the Buddha. The council ultimately concluded that one sect (*Vibhajyava*), which eventually gave rise to Theravada Buddhism, represented the authentic and orthodox viewpoint of the Buddha.

Theravada is the only modern form of Buddhism that can trace its origin back to the years immediately following these disputes. The study of philosophical texts, combined with cosmological speculations and new ways of thinking about the Buddha, brought about the emergence by the first century C.E. of Mahayana Buddhism. By the seventh or eighth century C.E., new symbolism and ritual techniques contributed to the development of Vajrayana Buddhism, which gained a particularly powerful foothold in Tibet. Let us now examine the distinctive features of these three primary Buddhist paths and the sacred texts that inform them.

The Brahmi script is an ancestor of all modern Indian scripts. This example is from the sixth edict of Emperor Ashoka, 238 B.C.E.

Theravada Buddhism

Theravada (Sanskrit, "way of the elders") views itself as representing the original and authentic teaching of the Buddha. Theravada is also known as *Hinayana* (Sanskrit, "Lesser Vehicle"), although this name is sometimes considered to be derisive. There are over 100 million Theravada Buddhists around the world today. Theravada is the predominant Buddhist tradition in Sri Lanka, Thailand, Cambodia, Laos, and Burma.

Theravada emphasizes pursuit of nirvana through the individual's own efforts. The Buddha is revered as one who achieved nirvana and provided his teachings, the Dharma, so that others could do the same. But the Buddha himself is beyond the reach of the individual and no longer available to provide direct assistance. Theravada stays true to the Buddha's last words: "Work out your salvation with diligence."[3] The individual pursues nirvana primarily through meditation, for which the monastic lifestyle is best suited. Theravada therefore also emphasizes the central role of the monastic community, or Sangha.

With its emphasis on the monastic community, Theravada naturally incorporates a hierarchy that separates the ordained—monks and nuns—from the laity. There are at least ten times as many monks in Theravada as nuns, and monks have always tended to exert the most influence over the Sangha. Both nuns and monks, however, devote themselves through study and meditation to attaining nirvana. Those who do attain it are known as **arhats**, who represent the religious ideal for Theravada. In many countries where Theravada is dominant, the monastic body acts as an advisor to governments or rulers and provides teaching to the lay community, while its monks also serve as ritual specialists during festivals, at funerals, or in rites that confer blessings and supernatural protection. The central role of the monastic community can also be seen in the support it receives from laypeople, who seek to accumulate karmic merit by making offerings to the monastic community.

Theravada Texts   Theravada lays claim to following the original teachings of the Buddha, contained within the early canonical group of Buddhist texts known as the **Pali Canon**, or **Tripitaka**. According to tradition, four centuries after the Buddha's death a group of 500 monks met in Sri Lanka to commit his teachings to writing for the first time. As there were already significant differences in reports of what the Buddha had said, these monks labored to finally fix his teaching in written form. The Sanskrit term *Tripitaka*, which means "three baskets," refers to the fact that in ancient times, manuscripts were written on palm leaves, which were then stored in baskets. Theravada's collection is the only complete version of the *Tripitaka* that has survived to the present day.

The first of the three baskets, the *Vinaya Pitaka* (Sanskrit, "Discipline Basket"), contains hundreds of monastic rules reportedly prescribed by the Buddha and stories that illustrate how these rules originated. The second basket, the *Sutra Pitaka* (Sanskrit, "Basket of Discourses"), consists of many teachings of the Buddha. The term **sutra** generally means a Buddhist text but often is used to refer specifically to the contents of the *Sutra Pitaka*. Although one cannot assume that everything recorded in the *sutras* is the literal word of the Buddha, their overall content is remarkably consistent in portraying the Buddha's teaching, suggesting to a significant extent the ideas, practices, and personality of the Buddha himself. The third basket is the *Abhidharma Pitaka*; the basket of "that which is above or about the Dharma."[4] These texts seek to reorganize and systemize the teaching in the *Sutra Pitaka* while also elaborating upon them, exploring the nature of consciousness, epistemology (the nature of knowledge), cosmology, and meditation.

The opening verses of the *Dhammapada*, a collection of aphorisms on Buddhist morals and one of the texts in the *Sutra Pitaka*, afford a glimpse into the way *sutras* are structured and how they poetically present ideas. They also illustrate a key feature of Theravada thought: we are responsible for our own happiness.

> What we are today comes from our thoughts of yesterday, and our present thoughts build our life of tomorrow: our life is the creation of our mind.

If a man speaks or acts with an impure mind, suffering follows him as the wheel of the cart follows the beast that draws the cart.

What we are today comes from our thoughts of yesterday, and our present thoughts build our life of tomorrow: our life is the creation of our mind.

If a man speaks or acts with a pure mind, joy follows him as his own shadow.[5]

Mahayana Buddhism

With origins in the early years of the Common Era, the period to which we can trace its earliest sutras, Mahayana Buddhism soon grew to become the largest of the Buddhist traditions. This is suggested by its very name—the Sanskrit word *mahayana* means "Great Vehicle"—as is its great variety of schools and sects, which make Mahayana a large and accommodating "vehicle" with room for Buddhists of all kinds. Mahayana Buddhism sees itself as a tradition that penetrates the teachings of the Buddha more deeply than does Theravada. Its careful analysis and elaboration of the many aspects of the Dharma help to explain its expansive doctrines, which are sufficiently elastic to allow for an easy coexistence among the many sects within the Mahayana tradition. Sometimes called "Buddhism for the masses," Mahayana, unlike Theravada, understands everyone as being capable of attaining nirvana, not only monks and nuns. Today, the great majority of Buddhists belong to the Mahayana tradition, which is the dominant form of Buddhism in East Asia and in parts of Southeast Asia.

As we have seen, Theravada Buddhism regards Gautama the Buddha as only a man, albeit an extraordinary man. Mahayana Buddhism understands the Buddha as something far greater: the earthly expression of ultimate reality. In the Mahayana view, reality exists at three levels called "Buddha Bodies." At the lowest level is the *Nirmanakaya,* the "earthly body," which is ultimate reality expressed rather crudely in material forms. These can be personal and are always limited by factors such as time and space. Gautama Buddha, the man who was known to other human beings as he traveled and taught across northern India, was ultimate reality expressed at this level. The second Buddha Body is the *Samboghakaya,* or "bliss body." This is ultimate reality expressed at what we might think of as a "heavenly" level, at which particulars exist but are beyond space and time. This is the level at which many bodhisattvas and "celestial buddhas" exist. At its highest level, the *Dharmakaya,* or "truth body," ultimate reality exists as it is: undifferentiated, impersonal, absolute—and completely beyond all forms and labels. Mahayana Buddhists describe ultimate reality at this level in a variety of ways: Void, Consciousness, Nirvana, Buddha Nature, and Buddha Mind.

Understood in this way, the universe is the great setting in which the Mahayana ideal of compassion makes enlightenment and freedom from suffering possible for everyone. Instead of having to "go it alone" in seeking nirvana, the Mahayana Buddhist can benefit from the compassion of others.

Indeed, one of the characteristics that distinguishes Mahayana from Theravada is its teaching that compassion for others and working to bring about their liberation is a higher goal than attaining one's own enlightenment. Many Mahayana Buddhists take a "bodhisattva vow" to subject themselves to rebirth until all other beings have been liberated from suffering. Whereas Theravada Buddhism makes the *arhat* its spiritual hero in recognition of his detachment from the world and attainment of nirvana, Mahayana recognizes as its ideal figure the compassionate and selfless bodhisattva, who remains devoted to others in the samsaric realm of suffering.

Bodhisattvas In the early years of Buddhism, **bodhisattva** (Sanskrit, "enlightenment being") was a term used to denote Gautama the Buddha in the lives he lived prior to that in which he achieved enlightenment. It was also used to refer to future buddhas (in fact, many Buddhists today look to the bodhisattva Maitreya as the next buddha to arise in the world). Later, Mahayana Buddhists began to describe a multitude of bodhisattvas. Some were simply people who had taken a bodhisattva vow to help

Gilded bronze Sitting Maitreya icon. Maitreya ("Loving-kindness") is the future Buddha. Like Rodin's Thinker, he is seated on his throne in deep contemplation with his hand touching his chin. Three Kingdoms period, seventh century. National Museum, Seoul, Korea.

"Manjushri, Bodhisattva of Wisdom" appearing with the flaming sword of discrimination and a copy of the *Prajnaparamita Sutra* in the blooming lotus of enlightenment. Kopan monastery, Kathmandu, Nepal.

others. This was done by practicing the "Six Perfections" (generosity, morality, patience, energy, meditation, and wisdom), thereby generating merit that could be transferred to those not as advanced on the path to enlightenment. Other bodhisattvas were figures who had already attained insight and power nearly equivalent to that of a buddha. Many legends describe them intervening in the lives of both ordinary people and aspiring saints with their pithy wisdom, psychic powers, and skillful magic. Some of these legendary bodhisattvas no longer required human bodies, dwelling instead in heavenly realms and appearing to those who prayed to them.

One of the earliest and most popular bodhisattvas is Manjushri, Patron of Buddhist Scholars and Lord of Wisdom. He is often represented with his flaming sword of discriminating insight in one hand and the *Perfection of Wisdom Sutra* in the other. Without a doubt, the most widely venerated of all the bodhisattvas is the Bodhisattva of Compassion, Avalokiteshvara. A male deity in South Asia, in East Asia this bodhisattva is known as Guanyin, the Goddess of Mercy. The bodhisattva Jizo (Ksitigarbha), mentioned at the beginning of this chapter, is also popular. As guardian of the dead in the underworld, he provides a safe journey to their next incarnation.

Mahayana Texts Mahayana schools revere a wide array of texts that build upon the Pali Canon, or *Tripitaka*. These vary widely in the subjects they address. Some investigate the profound states of consciousness reached during meditation. Others elaborate on the implications of doctrines such as Interdependent Origination. Still others analyze the qualities of bodhisattvas or explain the benefits of calling upon various buddhas. All are thought to be thoroughly grounded in the teachings of the Buddha, whose implications they identify and explain.

One of the earliest Mahayana texts is the *Perfection of Wisdom Sutra*, which probably dates from the first century B.C.E. (with longer versions appearing in the centuries that followed). Between 300 and 700 C.E., important condensed versions arose, such

"The Laughing Buddha." This form of Maitreya is popular in China, where his fatness symbolizes prosperity and joy. It is customary for Buddhists to rub his belly for good luck. Here, people try to improve their luck by touching an image of Maitreya during the New Year fair at the Huayan Temple on the Laoshan Mountain in Qingdao, China.

Frontispiece of the Diamond Sutra of Dunhuang, 868 C.E. This manuscript is the oldest known printed book in the world; it appeared 587 years before the Gutenberg Bible.

Buddhist bodhisattvas can be understood as intermediary figures who serve others. What kinds of intermediary figures exist in other religions and what are their functions?

as the *Diamond Sutra* and the *Heart Sutra*. Both emphasize the cultivation of **bodhichitta** (Sanskrit, "awakened thought"), the aspiration to achieve enlightenment in order to benefit others. They also emphasize the Six Perfections, which were to become very important in relation to the ideal of compassion in the bodhisattva path.

Among the most widely venerated Buddhist works in East Asia is the *Lotus Sutra*, composed in Sanskrit in the second century C.E. While exploring the path of the bodhisattva, it places particular emphasis on skillful means, the thoughtful application of knowledge and insight in making decisions related to ethics and spiritual progress. Another interesting feature of the *Lotus Sutra* is its teaching that the death of the Buddha did not bring about his absolute dissolution. Instead, he is an eternal entity who remains in the cycle of samsara in order to benefit those who have not yet achieved liberation. Another important Mahayana text, the *Lankavatara Sutra* (fourth century C.E.), provides a detailed study of the nature of consciousness and explores how the mind has both the propensity to generate illusory, dualistic misperceptions and the potential to clearly apprehend the unity of existence. Another theological innovation appears in the *Pure Land Sutras* (second century C.E.), which describe Amitabha Buddha, "The Buddha of Boundless Light," who brings those who call upon him to rebirth in his Buddha Realm, "the Pure Land." The Pure Land is a kind of heaven where the faithful enjoy happiness and affluence. The *Pure Land Sutras* became foundational to Pure Land Buddhism (also known as Jodo Buddhism).

Two Mahayana Schools: Pure Land and Zen In fact, Pure Land Buddhism, popular throughout East Asia, is arguably the most important of all the schools within the Mahayana tradition. Based on belief in the infinite compassion of the Amitabha Buddha—known in China as Amito and in Japan as Amida—this tradition is best known for its practice of "reciting the Buddha's name" (Chinese, *nianfo*; Japanese, *nembutsu*) as a way of guaranteeing entry into his Pure Land at death. For those who join Amitabha in his Pure Land, there will be no more rebirth in the samsaric world. Instead, their reward for their devotion to him is happiness in his heavenly paradise. There is also the possibility of attaining full and complete enlightenment in Amitabha's Pure Land. Pure Land Buddhism's total reliance on the grace of Amitabha Buddha is in stark contrast to Theravada Buddhism's insistence on self-reliance and individual effort.

One of the best-known Mahayana Buddhist schools in the West is **Zen** Buddhism (known in China as **Chan**). Although Zen traces its teachings back to the Buddha himself, it traditionally holds that it became a distinct school when the South Indian sage Bodhidharma (early fifth century C.E.) brought it to China. From China, it spread throughout the rest of East Asia.

Zen emphasizes practice over doctrine, considering doctrine to be a distraction from the sudden, spontaneous experience of enlightenment called *satori*. Even devotion to the Buddha can be an obstacle to *satori*. This helps to explain the well-known Zen saying: "If you meet the Buddha on the road, kill him." Any form of attachment, even to the Buddha, is an obstacle. The Zen sayings called *koans* present the mind with paradoxes. Two well-known examples of *koans* are: "What is the sound of one hand clapping?" and "Show me your Original Face before your mother and father were born." Seeking to resolve these paradoxes through deliberate, logical thought, the impotence of rational cognition is exposed—and ultimately abandoned. What remains is direct intuition of reality, which is enlightenment.

Zen practitioners often use artistic mediums such as poetry, calligraphy, and garden design to enable the insights gained in meditation to find articulation outside the constraints of language. This creative aspect of Zen, its deeply ingrained sense of humor, and its emphasis on direct apprehension over doctrine helped to popularize this form of Buddhism in American pop culture and subculture. This is particularly evident in its influence on the 1950s "Beat" poets Gary Snyder and Allen Ginsberg.

Zen asserts the total efficacy of the mind rather than unswerving devotion to a savior figure as the only path to enlightenment and liberation. In other words, it rejects the Pure Land reliance on the Buddha's compassion for salvation in favor of gaining personal insight into the true nature of all things. Zen is the most radically self-reliant tradition among all Buddhist traditions.

Vajrayana Buddhism

Although **Vajrayana** Buddhism began in India in the sixth or seventh century C.E., it has little presence there now. Today, it is the dominant form of Buddhism in Tibet, Nepal, Bhutan, and Mongolia. Although it is generally understood as deriving from Mahayana Buddhism, Vajrayana Buddhists say their tradition can be traced back directly to the Buddha, who began expounding its teachings sixteen years after his enlightenment. Whatever position one might take on this issue, one thing is clear: Vajrayana is a unique form of Buddhism that combines elements of Mahayana—and, in particular, the bodhisattva ideal—with secret teachings found in the Tantras, ancient Indian texts that teach esoteric knowledge about special methods for attaining enlightenment and liberation.

The Tantric texts reveal Tantra as a system of thought and practice based on the idea that the material world is a manifestation of divine energy. Practitioners of Tantra seek to gain control of this energy and to channel it in ways that will allow them to break through the confines of the ego, thereby finding enlightenment and liberation. Some of the most prominent features of Tantra are its emphasis on secret knowledge, ritual use of mantras and mandalas, worship of deities, visualization of deities and identification with them, and the deliberate breaking of taboos. Taken together, these and other features of Tantra are said to give practitioners powerful and even shocking means for shattering the illusion of self. One scholar has defined Tantra as "a technique for magically storming the gates of Buddhahood."[6]

As a Buddhist tradition that combines Tantra with Mahayana Buddhism and shamanism, Vajrayana was originally conceived as a spiritual method of such intense power that it could catapult an ordinary person to the level of an advanced bodhisattva—a level of awareness that would normally take many eons to attain—in a single lifetime. Adherents of this tradition refer to it as the "Diamond Vehicle" because of the clarity of its wisdom and its ability to cut through all misperceptions of reality. It is also known as the "Thunderbolt Vehicle" because of its power and as Tantric Buddhism. Among Vajrayana's most visible features are its *lamas*, the spiritual teachers (such as the Dalai Lama) in Tibetan Buddhism; its devotion to vast arrays of buddhas and bodhisattvas and to fierce gods and goddesses; its complex rituals; and its special meditation techniques, whose purpose is to propel one to the status of bodhisattva and, ultimately, to full enlightenment and buddhahood.

The most fundamental practice in Vajrayana Buddhism is "deity yoga." This exercise, which involves visualizing oneself as a deity, ultimately leads to the experience of becoming one with the deity and attaining its heightened perspective of reality. In "guru yoga," the practitioner seeks to unite his mind with that of his guru, or teacher, thereby gaining and experiencing his wisdom. Other forms of Vajrayana practice take advantage of states in which the mind is more attuned to the true nature of things and well positioned to gain enlightenment. These can occur in meditation, while dreaming, during sex, and at death. "Death yoga," for example, is based on the belief that there are moments during the death process in which the mind's vision is especially clear. If the dying person makes skillful use of such a moment to meditate on the "emptiness" (*shunyata*) of all things—that is, the absence of any enduring identity or quality in them, as the Buddha taught—then enlightenment can be achieved.

Vajrayana Texts Tibetan Buddhism preserves two large canonical collections of sacred texts, including traditional *sutras* (such as those found in the Pali Canon and Mahayana *sutras*), as well as Buddhist Tantras. In addition, Tibetan Buddhism has also maintained a tradition (dating back to the eleventh century C.E.) of "hidden texts." Often called "hidden treasures," these texts are attributed to Padmasambhava, the tantric master who is credited with bringing Vajrayana Buddhism to Tibet in the eighth century. According to Tibetan tradition, these texts were hidden away by Padmasambhava with the intention that each would be found at the proper time. The "treasure finders" who discover them do so only when Padmasambhava's "time-lock" spells unravel—always at a time when the world is ready for a new revelation.

What general tendencies do you see in the Theravada, Mahayana, and Vajrayana forms of Buddhism? Do you see similar tendencies in divisions within other religions?

Buddhism in India

During the centuries after Ashoka, Buddhism thrived in India and expanded into Central, East, and Southeast Asia. We will soon turn to the story of Buddhism's expansion, but it is important first to say something about its early history in its Indian homeland.

The Theravada, Mahayana, and Vajrayana traditions all began their historical development in India. Of these three, Theravada, which traces its origins back to the Sthavira sect in the time of the Buddhist Councils, had the least impact in India. As we will see, its future lay instead in Sri Lanka and Southeast Asia. Mahayana and Vajrayana maintained a longer cultural presence in India.

The Mahayana tradition, which originated in the first centuries of the common era, was fortunate in receiving financial and political support from the Gupta Dynasty (320–550 C.E.) of northern India. As we saw in Chapter 4 (pp. 117–118), the Guptas succeeded in bringing about a partial restoration of the great empire of Ashoka. Many Indian monasteries adopted Mahayana ideas and practices during the Gupta period. This is made clear by records of donations made to monasteries, some of which describe the support of monastic leaders for "Great Vehicle" teachings and the praise they offered their monks for becoming Mahayana adepts. The vibrancy of Mahayana in India is also attested to by the fact that from the fifth century onward East Asian monks regularly traveled to India to study and bring home copies of Mahayana texts such as the *Lotus Sutra*. The accounts of these East Asian pilgrim monks confirm that Mahayana ideas and practices were widespread among Indian Buddhists. By the seventh century, many of India's monasteries had formally allied themselves with the growing Mahayana tradition, with the greatest concentration of these being in northern India.

By that time, some influential teachers in northeast India were promoting Vajrayana Buddhism. A number of Buddhist universities were founded in this period. From these, Vajrayana was transmitted to nearby Tibet and Nepal, and subsequently to Mongolia and Bhutan, as well as to parts of East and Southeast Asia.

The Decline of Buddhism in India

Even as Mahayana and Vajrayana were flourishing in India, the forces that were to bring about their decline had already been set in motion. The fall of the Gupta Empire in the mid-sixth century brought political fragmentation and an end to much of the royal support and protection given to Buddhists and Buddhist institutions in earlier years. At the same time, Indian Buddhism had to contend with a resurgence of Hinduism. The Hindu Brahminical establishment began making concerted efforts to regain and enforce its supremacy in Indian society and culture. In southern India, Buddhism was challenged by the flourishing *bhakti* movement (Chapter 4). By the tenth century, Hinduism had won back both royal and popular support across India, and Buddhist monasteries had fallen into a decline from which they would never recover.

The final stage in the decline of Indian Buddhism was initiated by Muslim Turks, whose raids into northern India in the eleventh and twelfth centuries disrupted all of society but were particularly damaging to Buddhist monasteries and universities. The Turkish destruction of the Buddhist universities at Nalanda and Vikramasila around 1200 delivered the final blow. When the Tibetan Buddhist monk Dharmasvamin wrote of his travels in India the mid-thirteenth century, he despaired that almost no one would openly profess to being a Buddhist. Nevertheless, small pockets of Buddhism did endure in India, particularly in its southern regions, until the seventeenth century.

Buddhism Beyond India

Even as the light of Buddhism dimmed in India, it was thriving and spreading along three major routes that took it far from its homeland: a southern transmission into Sri Lanka and Southeast Asia, a northern transmission into Central Asia and East Asia, and a western transmission in the colonial period that brought Buddhism into contact with Europe and North America.

The Southern Transmission   Sri Lankan legend recounts that King Devanampiyatissa (250–210 B.C.E.) was converted to Buddhism by Ashoka's own son, Mahinda. The newly converted king had a huge monastery complex built in his capital at Anuradhapura. Ashoka's daughter, Sanghamitta, also came to the island to plant a sapling from the Buddha's *bodhi* tree and to establish the first order of Sri Lankan nuns.

From the beginning, monastic institutions were strong in Sri Lanka. Monasteries competed with each other for royal patronage, sometimes causing disputes and schisms within the Sangha. Despite such periodic disruptions, Sri Lanka has been renowned for more than a millennium as a bastion of Theravada Buddhism.

Lokeshwara peers out in all directions from the temple towers at the Angkor Wat temple complex in Cambodia. These colossal faces were identified both as Shiva and as Avalokiteshvara by their worshippers.

In Burma, the pivotal moment for Buddhism occurred in 1057 when Anwar, the Bamar king of Pagan, invaded the Mon kingdom of the south to establish the first Burmese empire (1057–1287). Along with other spoils of his conquest, he carried off Buddhist relics (believed to be fragments of the Buddha's remains), Pali texts, and a retinue of monks to whom he granted control of the Sangha. As a result, Theravada became the state religion of this new empire. These events spurred the spread of Theravada Buddhism throughout Southeast Asia. In Thailand, Laos, and Cambodia between the twelfth and fifteenth centuries, an earlier mingling of various Buddhist sects, Hinduism, and indigenous traditions gave way to state-sponsored Theravada.

It is important to note that Mahayana also had a significant place in the history of these regions. In Cambodia, kings frequently identified themselves as bodhisattvas, and the worship of Lokeshvara (another name for Avalokiteshvara) was of prime importance during the latter part of the Angkor period (twelfth–fifteenth centuries C.E.). Mahayana also reigned supreme in

Indonesia and on the Malay Peninsula. By the seventh century, sites such as Srivijaya in Sumatra were important centers of Buddhist training and attracted monks from as far away as China. The renowned Indian monk Atisha (982–1054) came to study in Srivijaya under the great master Dharmakirti before journeying in 1042 to Tibet, where he founded the Kadampa sect of Vajrayana, from which the Gelugpa school of the Dalai Lamas eventually arose.

In Java, Mahayana Buddhism was promoted by the native Sailendra Dynasty, which ruled much of Indonesia, including Sumatra and Bali, in the eighth and ninth centuries. One of the great monuments built by the Sailendras is the Borobudur Temple (c. 800). This gigantic complex includes 540 statues of the Buddha, some of them hidden within perforated screens of stone. There are also 2,672 relief sculpture panels depicting the Buddha. Buddhism thrived alongside Hinduism in Indonesia until both were eclipsed by Islam, originally introduced by Muslim traders, in the thirteenth through fifteenth centuries.

The earliest known image of the Buddha appears on the reverse of a coin minted by the second-century Kushan king, Kanishka I. Previously, the Buddha was not ever portrayed in physical form but was depicted more as an absence than a presence, symbolized with images such as footprints or an empty chair.

The Northern Transmission

Buddhist communities were also founded in Central Asia during the time of Ashoka's reign (c. 272–231 B.C.E.). Ashoka sent Buddhist missionaries to Afghanistan. Legend says that he sent his son, Kustana, to the region northwest of Tibet, where he founded the Buddhist kingdom of Khotan in 240 B.C.E. Later, the Central Asian ruler Kanishka I (r. c. 110–139 C.E.), after inheriting the portions of Bactria and northwest India conquered by his Kushan predecessors, is said to have embraced and vigorously supported Buddhist tradition in the second century C.E. Some of the earliest Buddhist images date from the period of his reign. Indeed, the oldest extant image of the Buddha appears on a coin of Kanishka.

Buddhism Comes to East Asia

Buddhism may have first appeared in China as early as the first century C.E., brought by monks and missionaries from Central Asia who accompanied merchants along the Silk Road to China. When Buddhism arrived in the refined world of China's Han Dynasty (206 B.C.E.–220 C.E.), it was received as an exotic import.

China The first dated proof of Buddhism's entry into China is found in the Han chronicles, which assign this event to 65 C.E. In that year, they say, the Han emperor Ming dreamed of an encounter with a golden-robed flying figure his diviners later identified as the Buddha. The chronicles also describe imperial relatives and aristocrats making offerings to the Buddha. Three years later, the emperor built the famous White Horse Temple in his capital city of Luoyang. According to a well-known tale, he did so to honor two missionary monks from Central Asia who brought the first Buddhist texts to make their way into China on the back of a white horse. Translation of Buddhist texts into Chinese

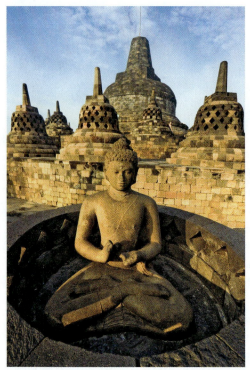

Borobudur Temple, Java, Indonesia, c. 800 C.E. Here, one of the hidden statues of the Buddha is revealed. In order to see others, pilgrims would have to peer through holes in bell-shaped stupas, such as those visible in the background.

began as soon as they appeared in China. This was especially true of texts relating to meditation and breath control techniques. These were of great interest to Daoists (Chapter 8), who at first regarded Buddhists as like-minded seekers of physical health and immortality. Daoist interest in the new religion diminished only when Buddhism's teachings were better understood and after its differences with Daoism had become apparent.

To a great degree, Buddhism established itself in China through adaptation and accommodation to the Chinese cultural landscape. The Central Asian missionary translator An Shigao is a good example of this adjustment. He was one of the first to translate Mahayana works into Chinese in the latter half of the second century C.E. Not unexpectedly, the process of translation often produced a fair amount of deviation from the original sources. Early on, for example, Daoist equivalents stood in for Buddhist philosophical terms; only later were new Chinese words coined to better convey abstract Buddhist concepts.

After the fall of the Han Dynasty (c. 220 C.E.), the Chinese empire split into a north-south division that lasted another three and a half centuries. The north was ruled by successive groups of non-Chinese tribes, while the south was colonized by the fleeing native Chinese elites who also founded their successive dynasties there. The Chinese Buddhist community experienced a similar split. Many Buddhist clerics and their followers stayed in the north, while others followed the Chinese authorities and fled to the south, taking the Dharma into new territory, where it quickly found acceptance among locals. Confucianism (Chapter 8), which had always supported the aims of the state, had lost some of its influence in the wake of China's political upheavals, and Buddhism was primed to take its place. Moreover, Buddhism appealed to the Chinese in both the north and the south because it reflected the contemplative and mystic introversion of native Daoism. In northern China, Buddhist intellectualism had given way to an emphasis on practice. "Barbarian" kings who ruled in the vacuum created by the fleeing native Chinese rulers patronized Buddhist ascetics and magicians who had roots in Central Asian traditions. In the south, there was an intense expression of faith and piety in the plea for Buddha's compassion, as well as an incipient movement toward meditation and enlightenment.

The golden age of Buddhism in China lasted from the fifth to the eighth centuries C.E. As we have seen, many Mahayana texts were translated during this period into Chinese by eminent scholars, both native and foreign. Pilgrim monks from China also took long and often dangerous journeys to India in search of Buddhist wisdom from its point of origin. New *sutras* were authored by Chinese patriarchs to proclaim equal authority with the Indian and Central Asian texts. Of the Mahayana schools of today, many took on their definitive forms in China. In particular, the Mahayana convention of devotion to a particular text can be clearly seen as informing the primary character of these schools.

The two major schools that would eventually arise to signal the final stage in the Chinese transformation of Buddhism into a native faith were Pure Land and Chan (Japanese, Zen, Korean, Seon). Pure Land appeared at the start of the fifth century C.E. According to its own tradition, Chan was introduced to China by the legendary Bodhidharma in the fifth century C.E. It was in the eighth century, however, that it began to make its mark on the Chinese religious scene thanks to a succession of Chinese patriarchs (masters of a particular sect of Buddhism), most notably the Sixth Patriarch, named Huineng (c. 638–713 C.E.). An illiterate firewood vendor who allegedly attained enlightenment after merely hearing a neighbor's chanting of the *Diamond Sutra*, Huineng gained full patriarchal status after correctly discerning the ultimate message of the Buddha's original teaching.

Korea and Japan Buddhism arrived in Korea in the fourth century C.E. and closely emulated the text-based Chinese systems by developing the Five Doctrinal Schools. The new religion from China soon blended with native Korean shamanism, with the result that it took on a very distinctive flavor. Many Buddhist temples, for example, also became centers for the veneration of Korean mountain spirits and local deities. Moreover, Korean Buddhists eventually adopted a holistic approach to their belief by ignoring many of the sectarian differences that plagued the Indian and Chinese Buddhist establishments. Seon (Chan, Zen) has long been the dominant form of Buddhism in Korea.

In Japan, Buddhism was first introduced in 552 C.E., when the Korean king of Paekche presented Emperor Kinmei of Japan (r. 531–571) with a gift of *sutras* and an icon of the Buddha. The leader of a clan with the least vested interest in native Shinto (Chapter 9), Kinmei embraced Buddhism and promoted its adoption by the imperial family. Its success was evidenced by the accomplishment of Prince Shotoku (574–622), a prominent member of this clan. According to tradition, Prince Shotoku produced for the newly institutionalized Japanese state a constitution that stressed the ideals of the Buddhist Three Jewels as well as the Confucian virtue of harmony. By the Nara period (710–784), six schools of Buddhism had been imported directly to Japan from China. In the Heian period (794–1185), Tantric Buddhism and the Tendai sect were added, and by the Kamakura period (1185–1333), Pure Land, Zen, and the Nichiren sect came to essentially define the sectarian complexity of Buddhism in Japan. Among these, Pure Land would later have the most enduring and greatest impact on Japanese culture and values. Today, its presence is ubiquitous in almost every Japanese home. Zen Buddhism is embraced by the Japanese cultural and military elite and has influenced many Japanese art forms.

Vietnam Mahayana Buddhism also made major inroads in Vietnam. Because of Vietnam's cultural and geographical proximity to China (it was twice annexed by China and sent tribute to China for much of its premodern history), Vietnamese Buddhism shares a great deal with its Chinese counterpart. Because Vietnam served as the point of convergence between the northern and southern routes of Buddhist expansion out of India (north from China and south from Sri Lanka and Indochina), Vietnamese Buddhism displays Theravada influence as well.

Tibet Although Buddhism took root in Tibet later than in China, its transmission came directly from India. Since its arrival in Tibet (around 650 C.E.), the region has remained a stronghold of Vajrayana Buddhism. Initially, the new religion met with resistance, for the shamans and court wizards of the indigenous Tibetan *Bön* religion had strong influence over the nobility. But legend has it that when King Songtsen Gampo (c. 617–649) arranged alliances with the king of Nepal and the emperor of China through marriages to their daughters, he found that his new wives were Buddhists. Their presence began to soften Tibetan attitudes to Buddhism, and so it was not long before the king built Tibet's first Buddhist temple and made arrangements for the translation of *sutras* into Tibetan. As monks and teachers poured into Tibet, Buddhism flourished. Trisong Detsen (c. 742–798), Tibet's first Buddhist king, consecrated the Samye monastery in 775 C.E. and also ordained members of the Tibetan aristocracy.

In the early ninth century, Buddhism was again under siege in Tibet and forced underground during the reign of King Lang Darma (r. 838–842 C.E.). When the king was assassinated and his dynasty collapsed, Buddhism was blamed for instilling weakness in the military. The scholarly monk Atisa, who arrived in Tibet in 1042 C.E., provided Tibet with an effective synthesis of the Theravada, Mahayana, and Tantric forms of Buddhism and united the Tibetan *Sangha*. Atisa instituted the practice of formal initiation into lineages of tantric teachers, which still characterizes Tibetan Vajrayana today.

During the thirteenth century, Tibetan Buddhist masters entered into a "patron-priest" relationship with the Khans (descendants of Genghis Khan) who ruled an empire that extended from China to eastern Europe. In 1578 C.E. the head of the Gelugpa monastery, Sonam Gyatsho (1543–1588), converted Altan Khan, the ruler of the Mongols. The Great Khan bestowed upon Sonam Gyatsho the title *Dalai Lama* (Mongolian, "Ocean [of Wisdom] Teacher"). Because this title was later assigned to two of his predecessors, tradition calls him the third Dalai Lama. It was the fifth Dalai Lama (1617–1682) who took full advantage of Mongol patronage. Backed by Mongol troops, he took over all of Tibet and sent other sects with conflicting political aspirations fleeing to other parts of the Himalayas. By the seventeenth century, with the Dalai Lama as the primary ruler of Tibet, great efforts were made to identify and reinstate him in this role each time he died and took rebirth.

Across all of these regions and countries, Buddhism adapted to local cultures and integrated indigenous beliefs. These patterns of transformation have also extended to Buddhism's encounter with Europe and America in the modern and postmodern contexts.

The Western Transmission

It has been during only the last two centuries that Buddhist traditions have come to the attention of the West. Many of those who were among the first to understand Buddhist teachings and practices and share them with Western audiences were also among the first Western converts to Buddhism. These early Western Buddhists both anticipated and inspired the growing popularity of the religion in Europe and America today.

Some say that the story of the Western transmission begins in the early nineteenth century, when T. W. Rhys-Davids (1843–1922), a British colonial administrator, first "discovered" Buddhist teaching while stationed in Sri Lanka. His translations of Buddhist texts sparked the interest of an English-speaking audience, many of whom saw the Buddha as embodying the modern values of the era as a radically independent, rugged individual who relied only on his own introspection and insight. These early Western readers of Buddhist texts preferred to characterize Buddhism primarily as a philosophy that radically contrasted with the perceived antirational dogmas of Western religion.

In recent years, Western adherents have increasingly come to value a deeper commitment to particular lineages of Buddhist teachers and a more well-rounded understanding of the subtle complexities of specific systems of Buddhist practice.

Although Chinese and Japanese immigrants had established Buddhist institutions on American soil many years earlier, the first notable conversion of an American to Buddhism did not occur until 1893. In that year, Charles T. Strauss formally converted, following a series of lectures on Buddhism delivered at the World Parliament of Religions in Chicago. But it was the American subcultures of the 1950s and 1960s, and particularly those of the Beats and hippies, that helped catalyze a deep and abiding

In 1963, the Vietnamese Buddhist monk Thich Quang Duc, while seated in meditation, burned himself to death in Saigon's Market Square to protest his government's religious policies.

As the young Thich Nhat Hanh, a Vietnamese monk, looks on, Dr. Martin Luther King, Jr., calls for a halt to the bombing of Vietnam (May 31, 1966).

interest in Buddhism among Americans. The perception of Buddhist leaders as political dissidents and peace activists helped to inspire new generations of American Buddhists. Martin Luther King Jr.'s nonviolent approach to civil rights activism was informed in part by Buddhist thought and practice. King's admiration for the Vietnamese Buddhist monk and peace activist Thich Nhat Hanh (b. 1926), whose commitment to community service helped to heal the emotional wounds of many American veterans of the Vietnam War, led King to nominate Hanh for a Nobel Peace Prize in 1967. The ever-growing popularity of the fourteenth Dalai Lama, Tenzin Gyatso (b. 1935), who was awarded the Nobel Peace Prize in 1989, also exemplifies the identification of Buddhism with peaceful political dissidence in America.

Buddhists in the World Today

Today, teachings about the Dharma are delivered as podcasts. Apps that help Buddhists time their meditations or look up specific *sutras* are available for mobile devices. In Japan, vending machines sell pocket-sized plastic replicas of some of the most revered Buddhist icons. Chinese animated hagiographies of saints and bodhisattvas can be easily downloaded. In America, Trey Parker and Matt Stone, creators of the television show South Park, offer online versions of old Zen lectures by Alan Watts (a twentieth-century philosopher and proponent of Buddhism), accompanied by their own "cartoon commentaries."[7] In the world of American comic books, an increasing number of superheroes are turning Buddhist (such as "Xorn" of the X-Men; even Batman has been revealed to have received Buddhist training in Tibet). Even as far back as the 1930s and

World Buddhist population.

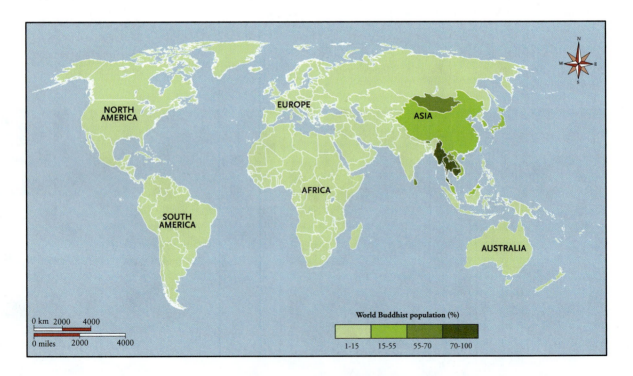

World Buddhist population (%)

| 1-15 | 15-55 | 55-70 | 70-100 |

1940s there were mystic American heroes trained in Buddhist practice, such as the Shadow and the Green Lama, who appeared in pulp magazines, radio serials, and comic books.

Today, no scribes are needed to copy *sutras,* as the vast majority of the Buddhist canon is available online. It is possible to visit virtual temples and meditation halls without stepping outside your front door. New technologies and media challenge Buddhists to adapt, expand, and explore new environments. But Buddhism has encountered a multitude of cultures in its spread throughout Asia (and beyond) over the past 2,500 years and has always found skillful ways of applying new technologies. Buddhists continue to develop innovative ways to integrate modern realities into an ancient Buddhist worldview, as they convey traditional teachings through contemporary media that preserve the sacred *sutras*, stories, and songs that comprise Buddhist traditions.

A modern Cambodian monk at work on his computer.

BUDDHISM AS A WAY OF LIFE

Buddhists put the teachings of the Buddha into practice in many ways. Seeking to observe the ethical principles he taught, they aspire to proper conduct in daily life. Seeking to observe the workings of the mind and to see reality more clearly, many make use of meditative disciplines. Some become members of monastic orders. All Buddhists participate in festivals that commemorate important events and engage in rituals that mark important transitions in life, from birth to death. In this part of our investigation, we will look at several Buddhist practices in order to gain an understanding of the meaning they have for followers of the Buddha.

Who Is a Buddhist?

You will recall that the first followers of the Buddha were the five ascetics who had once practiced severe austerities with him. Convinced by his example and by his Sermon in the Deer Park that he had found what they, too, had been looking for, they became the first members of the Sangha. Their formal conversion was solemnized by their recitation of the "Three Refuges," also known as the "Three Jewels":

> I take refuge in the Buddha.
> I take refuge in the Dharma.
> I take refuge in the Sangha.

Since then, all followers of the Buddha have affirmed their Buddhist identity by reciting this formula, Buddhism's most fundamental ritual practice and the closest thing the Buddhist tradition has to a creed. The Three Refuges are recited throughout one's

Pema Chodron is an American-born Buddhist nun whose books, such as *When Things Fall Apart: Heart Advice for Difficult Times*, address skillful ways to cope with everyday suffering and how to keep one's heart open in the face of adversity.

life, and often daily. To take refuge in the Buddha is to acknowledge the Buddha as the supreme example of the potential of human life. To take refuge in the Dharma is to recognize it as the path to enlightenment and an end to suffering. To take refuge in the Sangha is to recognize one's reliance on the Buddhist community—and, in particular, the order of monks—as the custodian of the Dharma, responsible for its preservation and transmission.

The Buddha's Teachings on Ethics and "Skillful Means"

As we have seen, the path to nirvana requires ethical conduct. This may be as simple as serving the Buddhist community and supporting its institutions. Some Buddhists formally commit themselves to observing the Five Precepts. These are (1) not killing or causing harm, (2) not stealing, (3) not committing inappropriate sexual acts, (4) not lying, and (5) not using intoxicants.

Beyond these formal precepts, the Buddha also taught a practical approach to ethical conduct in which the first and most important consideration is one's intention. Conduct intended to benefit oneself or others, or at least not to do harm, is ethical conduct. To put this another way, ethical conduct is conduct that does not arise from the Three Poisons of greed, hatred, and delusion. For the Buddha, the distinction between "ethical" and "unethical" was not something that could be discerned with reference to traditional standards of "right" and "wrong." Such standards, which often hold that an action is *always* right or wrong, do not necessarily result in ethical behavior when applied in particular circumstances. Thus, one must bring creativity and insight to every situation in order to skillfully consider one's intention in determining how to behave. In later forms of Buddhism, **upaya** (Sanskrit, "skillful means") was developed into a formal practice that encourages the individual to thoughtfully apply knowledge and insight in making decisions related to ethics and spiritual progress.

Meditation and the Cultivation of Mind

The Buddha encouraged his followers to practice meditation, which enables practitioners to identify, understand, and eliminate patterns of thought that perpetuate desire and suffering. In fact, it is sometimes said that the full implications of the Buddha's teaching cannot be understood without devoting oneself to meditative practice. Of course, most of the Buddha's followers were monks and nuns who had given up ordinary life in order to devote themselves entirely to monastic practices. For them, there was no obstacle to meditation. Others, who continued to meet their obligations in ordinary society, had to be content with offering support to monastic communities in the hope of gaining merit and a more favorable rebirth. This remains the case today. Most Buddhists do not meditate regularly. Instead, they seek to make spiritual progress by supporting Buddhist causes, including monastic orders, and by doing their best to put Buddhist principles into practice in their daily lives. They are inspired by the great achievements of monastics who have developed a remarkable range of meditative techniques, as well as an impressive body of literature on meditation, over the past 2,500 years.

Meditation: *Shamatha* and *Vipassana* From the beginning, Buddhists have made extensive use of two basic types of meditation: *shamatha* (Sanskrit, "calm abiding" or "stabilizing meditation") and *vipassana* (Sanskrit, *vipashyana*, "insight"). These are still widely practiced today and are often employed by the same practitioner. Both are practiced in a variety of forms by the many Buddhist sects.

Shamatha cultivates the ability to focus awareness upon a single object of concentration. This focal point is very often the breath, but any object or sensation is appropriate as it is concentration upon *something* that matters, not the nature of the thing itself. Focused awareness stabilizes the mind, making it less easily disturbed by the disruptive influences of thoughts and feelings.

By comparison, the object of *vipassana* meditation, often called "mindfulness meditation" or "insight meditation," is awareness itself. Typically, the practitioner begins with a focus on the breath, which brings focused concentration and a stable mind. These make it possible to move beyond the thoughts, feelings, daydreams, and other concerns that normally occupy the attention of the mind and to calmly observe, as if from a distance, the unfolding of all mental and physical phenomena—neither obsessing, reacting, nor judging, but simply allowing them to be. In doing so, the practitioner gains insight into the workings of compulsive and restless thought and the ability to move past the suffering they cause.

Walking Meditation The Buddha taught that there are four postures in which one should practice meditation: sitting, standing, walking, and lying down. Any activity, he asserted, is an opportunity for meditation. Many Buddhist traditions encourage walking meditation as a means for making the serenity and insight found in the meditation hall possible out in the everyday world as well. The foundation of this practice is simply being mindful of and content with what one is doing:

> When walking, just walk.
> When sitting, just sit.
> Above all, don't wobble.
>   —Yunmen (d. 949 c.e.; Tang Dynasty founder of the Yunmen school of Chan
>   Buddhism)[8]

According to the Vietnamese monk Thich Nhat Hanh, who has written extensively on meditation, walking meditation involves relinquishing the impulse to "get somewhere"

A large contemporary image of the Walking Buddha in Thailand. Thai images often stylistically craft his right arm to represent the graceful swaying trunk of an elephant.

and to practice instead the mindful enjoyment of each breath and each step. To emphasize the spontaneity and naturalness of walking meditation, he often alludes to the Chinese Zen master Linji (d. 866), who taught that whereas most people think it is a miracle to walk across burning hot coals, to walk on water, or to walk through the air, the real miracle is simply to be walking upon the earth.

Some forms of Buddhism, such as Zen, are quite formal in their approach to walking meditation. In most *Zendo*s, or "meditation halls," meditators execute prescribed movements very slowly and deliberately in order to be completely aware of each subtle shift in posture, breathing, and sensation.

Visualization, Deity Yoga, and Inner *Mandalas*   Another important form of meditation entails the practice of visualization. Practices involving the mental contemplation of the body of the Buddha developed early in the history of Buddhism. The visualization of buddhas and bodhisattvas came to occupy a central place in the meditation practices of such Mahayana sects as Pure Land Buddhism. But undoubtedly it is in Vajrayana Buddhism that a true virtuosity in employing visualization techniques developed. By means of a combination of visualization and mantra recitation, "deity yoga" (as it in known in the West) or "actualization" (as it is called in Tibet) creates conditions in which the very substance of the practitioner's mind comes to embody the deity that is invoked.

Other visualization techniques employ the contemplation of **mandalas**. *Mandalas* are circular cosmological diagrams that often map out how a Buddhist deity or group of deities manifests both *in* and *as* the universe. These deities embody the function and interaction of archetypal forces within the sphere of being. As with deities, mandalas are also venerated externally as *tankas* ("tapestries"), sand paintings, and three-dimensional models, such as the Borobudur Stupa in Java.

Mantra, Liturgical Ritual, and Chanting

Perhaps the most widespread of Buddhist rituals is chanting, which is practiced by almost every Buddhist group. The Three Refuges, in which Buddhists declare their reliance on the Buddha, the Dharma, and the Sangha, are often chanted. Most Buddhist services include liturgical chanting that reflects the philosophical orientation of that particular tradition. The content of the chant and its function can vary greatly. Some forms of chanting consist of entire *sutras*, whereas others focus on key passages in particular philosophical texts. Still other varieties of chant make use of ritual formulas or simple **mantras** (sacred sounds or syllables).

Conversion and Ordination

As noted earlier, most Buddhists consider a simple heartfelt recitation of the Three Refuges to be sufficient in declaring oneself a "Buddhist." A striking example of this occurred in 1956 at Pune, India, when thousands of protesting *dalits*, the oppressed "untouchables" of Hinduism's lowest caste, recited the Three Refuges and converted to Buddhism en masse under the leadership of the *dalit* activist Dr. B. R. Ambedkar (1891–1956).

In most cases, Buddhists seeking to make their conversion public or to be ordained as priests, monks, or nuns participate in formal rites conducted in the presence of the Sangha and a revered senior monk, lama, or spiritual teacher.

Typically, there are two different levels of ordination as a monk or nun. The first is that of the novice, which can be conferred on children as young as seven or eight in Theravada. The novice agrees to abide by ten precepts and essentially functions as a student under the direct guidance of a Preceptor. The second, higher ordination of an adult monk requires candidates to be at least twenty years of age. In both cases (but to varying degrees) the recipient of the ordination makes a commitment to embody, maintain, and transmit the Buddhist Dharma.

At the beginning of this chapter we had a glimpse into the form and structure of an ordination ceremony in which the nun Jisen became a priest. The authority conferred in this kind of ceremony is primarily transmitted through the formal acknowledgment that the initiate is part of a lineage of teachers that can be traced directly back to the Buddha. Sometimes a scroll or document tracing this spiritual genealogy is presented to the newly ordained. We can imagine how moving it must be to see one's name at the bottom of a list headed by the Buddha, indicating that one has been formally admitted into the Buddha's own "Dharma family."

Women in Buddhism

For much of its history, Buddhism's institutions were formed and controlled primarily by men. In mainstream monasteries nuns did not have much of a place in the preservation and transmission of the Dharma. But Buddhist women did take on more central roles outside of monasteries, both as lay Buddhists and as wandering ascetics, and their significance is acknowledged in many sources. Powerful political figures such as the Empress Wu Zetian of Tang Dynasty China (late seventh century C.E.) and Camadevi (seventh century C.E.), the legendary queen of Haripunjana in northern Thailand, have left an indelible mark in the history of Buddhism as patrons whose support and example helped to spread Buddhist traditions.

But beyond the historical influence of Buddhist women as powerful secular leaders, several important female spiritual leaders emerged even at the very beginnings of Buddhism. In the early formation of the Pali Canon, one collection called the *Khuddaka Nikaya* canonized a group of early saints in two collections of poems: the *Theragatha* ("Poems of Male Elders") and the *Therigatha* ("Poems of Female Elders"). Thus, even in Buddhism's very early years, the tradition acknowledged and preserved the compositions of its women saints. Later, other women saints, particularly in Vajrayana Buddhism, stood out as great virtuosos and innovators of the highest esoteric practices.

In 2003 there were approximately 125,000 Buddhist nuns worldwide. However, centuries ago lineages of Buddhists nuns in many regions either disappeared (such as in the eleventh century in Sri Lanka) or never existed in the first place (as in Thailand). Only in China, Korea, Taiwan, and Vietnam have nuns traditionally been given full ordination and regarded with the same respect as their male counterparts. In other countries, only novitiate ordination (that is a beginning or trial ordination) has been conferred on women. Elsewhere, women have not been eligible for ordination at all. In Tibet, for example, nuns were originally allowed to take only the vows prescribed for laypeople.

Resistance to women taking an active role in Buddhist monastic institutions goes all the way back to the time when Mahaprajapati, the Buddha's stepmother, petitioned for women to be allowed ordination. Though the Buddha eventually relented, he noted that allowing nuns into the order would only hasten the demise of the Buddhist teaching. Even those regions that allowed nuns placed additional constraints on female monastics.

Where there have been some nunneries attached to Theravada monasteries, the nuns have often been relegated to serving the domestic needs of monks, primarily by cooking and cleaning for them. Some women, like the *maechi* (female renunciants) of Thailand, have preferred a solitary ascetic life to the limitations of ordination in the male-dominated monastic institutions.

Recently, in most of the Theravada world, full ordination of women has begun to be revived. Women renouncers have been proactive in these regions, adopting ascetic disciplines and formal vows on their own or forming small groups of female practitioners. And there has been an explosion in the number of notable women Buddhist leaders in the West, who have profoundly influenced and empowered Buddhist women around the world. Because of their efforts, new opportunities for women to receive ordination have begun to open up in many countries as women are transforming the Buddhist institutional landscape.

One such example is that of Ayya Khema (1923–1997), who organized the First Council of Buddhist Nuns. Born to a Jewish family in Berlin, Ayya Khema was evacuated from Germany along with hundreds of other children in 1938. Her parents eventually escaped to China, where she was reunited with them in Shanghai. When the Japanese invaded Shanghai, the family was placed in a prisoner-of-war camp. Ayya Khema's father died in the camp before the Americans liberated it. After these life-altering experiences, Ayya Khema traveled extensively and spent time studying meditation in the Himalayas. The experiences that grew out of her meditation practice led to her taking ordination as a Buddhist nun in Sri Lanka in 1983. She founded an international training center for Buddhist nuns in 1983 in Sri Lanka, and in Germany she helped organize thirty-seven different meditation groups. But Ayya Khema is most widely remembered for organizing the first international council for nuns in Buddhist history. This conference led to the founding of a worldwide Buddhist women's organization called Sakyadhita ("Daughters of the Buddha"). In May 1987 Ayya Khema became the first Buddhist nun to ever address the United Nations.

Sacred Places and Objects of Veneration

Like adherents of other religions, Buddhists recognize special places and objects as having a sacred character that makes them worthy of reverence and veneration. The most important of these are places where particularly important events in the life of the Buddha occurred and that contain the relics of the Buddha.

The principal sacred sites in Buddhism are Lumbini (in modern Nepal), the site of the Buddha's birth; Bodh Gaya, the place where he attained enlightenment; Sarnath, where he preached his first sermon, the "Sermon in the Deer Park"; and Kusinara, the place of the Buddha's death and passing into *parinirvana*. These sacred places are visited by thousands of pilgrims each year.

According to the *Mahaparinibbana Sutra*, the Buddha's followers collected the relics that remained after his cremation. Apparently, they intended to keep all of the relics in a single place, but conflict arose when local kings made claims to them. In the end, they were divided into eight portions so that they could be distributed equally among the claimants. According to another account, in the time of Ashoka the relics were divided again, this time into 84,000 portions that were taken to all parts of the Indian subcontinent. Although we cannot be certain of the accuracy of every detail in these stories, there is good evidence that soon after his death the relics of the Buddha were divided and placed in reliquary mounds called **stupas**. In time, the custom arose of placing the relics of Buddhist saints in *stupas* as well. Today, most *stupas* are large and impressive hemispherical structures that resemble the original mounds built on the sites where they stand. As symbols of the achievements of others in grasping truth and bringing an end to suffering, the relics they preserve have a powerful and inspiring effect on those who venerate them.

Because the Buddha said that his teaching would serve as his Dharma-body after his passing, many Buddhists venerate the sacred texts in which the Dharma is preserved. For example, some Mahayana groups place manuscripts of sutras in images of the Buddha or in the structures of shrines, making them a part of ritual worship. The thirteenth-century Japanese teacher Nichiren advocated worship of the title of the *Lotus Sutra* in the form of a calligraphic mandala.

Early Buddhist arts and artifacts tended to represent the Buddha more as an absence than a presence. For example, the Buddha was often indicated by an empty chair, a pair of footprints, or the *bodhi* tree he sat under when he obtained enlightenment. In time, though, Buddhists began to make extensive use of images to recall more vividly the physical form of the Buddha and to visualize appearances of other buddhas and bodhisattvas. Many of these images make use of subtle iconographic cues—such as hand gestures and postures—to symbolize events and functions associated with the Buddha and other enlightened beings.

From the beginning, Buddhists also venerated images that represent important events in the life of the Buddha and aspects of his teaching. To this day, in fact, fig trees continue to be objects of reverence, as it was beneath the shade of a fig tree that the Buddha achieved enlightenment. Another commonly venerated symbol is the wheel.

The Great Stupa of Sanchi, India. Early Andhra Dynasty, first century B.C.E.

Cherry trees in front of Goju-No-To Pagoda. Built in 1407 on the island of Miyajima, this Japanese adaptation of the Indian *stupa* has a central shaft with stylized umbrellas that extends down through all five stories to a reliquary casket below.

With its eight spokes, the "Dharma Wheel" is an ancient Buddhist symbol that represents the Noble Eightfold Path. The prayer wheel, commonly used in Vajrayana ritual, is a device filled with printed scrolls believed to emit thousands of prayers and mantra recitations when they are rotated.

Holidays and Festivals

The Buddhist year is filled with holidays, festivals, and other special observances. In most countries, their dates are determined by the lunar calendar and therefore fall on different days each year. The most important occasions are commemorations of key events in the life of the Buddha, but there are also celebrations of the birthdays of bodhisattvas, remembrances of historical events, and seasonal observances that have taken on a religious significance.

Vesak By far, the most important Buddhist celebration is *Vesak*. Although it originally commemorated the day on which the Buddha was born, *Vesak* has also become a celebration of the Buddha's death and *parinirvana*. It occurs on the day of the first full moon in the month of *Vesakha*, usually in May. On *Vesak*, Theravada Buddhists decorate local shrines and light lamps to symbolize the Buddha's enlightenment and the spreading of his insight throughout the world. People send out greeting cards that depict key events in the life of the Buddha. Some lay Buddhists stay up all night in meditation as the Buddha had done on the night of his enlightenment.

In Tibet this festival is called *Saga Dawa*. Tibetan Buddhists light lamps and, like Buddhists in other countries, express their devotion by circumambulating shrines and *stupas*. They also show reverence and seek to acquire merit through repeated prostrations—lying face down in supplication before a sacred site or object. Many Tibetan Buddhists observe *Saga Dawa* by taking turns bathing an image of the infant Buddha. In Japan, *Vesak* is known as *Hana Matsuri* ("The Flower Festival"). Celebrated on April 8, when it coincides with the blooming of the cherry blossoms, *Hana Mutsuri* also involves the practice of bathing images of the infant Buddha. In some regions, this bathing ritual occurs at other times of the year, usually as a rite of purification.

Father and child bathe an image of the Buddha as a baby in a Taipei temple during the April 2001 celebration of the Buddha's birth in Taiwan.

Asala   In Theravada Buddhism, *Asala* is a holiday that originally marked the beginning of the three-month rainy season. During this time, monks would cease their wandering and remain in a monastery for an extended period of meditation and introspection. Today, many lay Buddhists in Burma and Thailand take temporary ordinations and live as monks for this three-month period. *Asala* also commemorates the "First Turning of the Wheel of the *Dharma*," when the Buddha gave his first teaching. Many sermons are given to laypeople at this time.

Other Festivals   The conclusion of the three-month retreat season coincides with other festival observances. During the *Kathina* ceremony, observed by Theravada Buddhists, the laity offer new robes to monks and make special requests for spiritual guidance and intervention. The Tibetan form of this holiday is called *Lhabap* and is characterized by feasting and visits to temples.

There are many important culturally specific festivals that lack corollaries in other regions. To mention just one interesting example, during the "Festival of the Hungry Ghosts" in China and Japan's "Feast of the Dead," the spirits of ancestors are placated with food offerings, and monks are called upon to recite *sutras* in order to aid the departed in securing a favorable rebirth.

Funerary Rites

When the death of a Buddhist approaches, family and friends will often come and sit in the dying person's room to offer comfort and assurances that death is a natural part of the life cycle. They may speak of the good deeds that he or she has done and note that these are likely to bring a favorable rebirth. In some cases monks may be

Prime Minister Abhisit offers Kathina robes to monks at a 2010 Kathina ceremony in Bangkok, Thailand.

invited to chant comforting *sutras*. A small statue of the Buddha is often placed near the head of the dying person.

Buddhists practice both cremation and burial. Funeral services may be held either before these events or, in the form of a memorial service, after them. Whatever form a funeral takes, it is always a solemn and dignified affair. Funerals are not appropriate occasions, as other important events might be, for displays of emotion or wealth. A photograph or other image of the deceased is usually set upon an altar at the front of the room in which the service is held, as are flowers provided by family and friends. When entering the room, mourners approach the altar, bow with their hands pressed together in a prayerful manner, spend a moment in quiet reflection, and then take their seats. It is customary for monks, family, and friends to speak, offering eulogies to honor the deceased. In most cases there is also chanting, led either by monks or family members.

VISUAL GUIDE
Buddhism

The Buddha achieved enlightenment while seated beneath a fig tree that came to be known as the Bodhi Tree ("Enlightenment Tree"). The fig tree was already considered a sacred tree long before the Buddha lived, but during his lifetime it came to symbolize his enlightenment. Here, monks gather at Bodh Gaya in India, the site of the Buddha's enlightenment, to venerate a descendant of the original Bodhi Tree under which he sat.

Before the Buddha himself was first depicted in works of art, Buddhists venerated his footprints, which symbolized his path into nirvana. Although Buddha statues that actually depict his form later become common, the convention of

(continued)

CONCLUSION

We began this chapter by reflecting on the life of the Buddha, which offers his followers an example worthy of emulation. The life of the Buddha was a journey from the sorrow inherent in clinging to impermanent things to the ineffable joy and freedom that spring from understanding and accepting reality as it is. The Buddha's teaching is intended to dislodge the mind from clinging to the illusion of permanence and to empower each individual to find the joy and freedom this realization brings.

Through its history, Buddhism has adapted itself to diverse cultural contexts. Much of its versatility was fostered by the teaching of the Buddha, who insisted that wherever the Dharma is transplanted, local custom, convention, and religious observance should always be maintained. This allowed Buddhism to syncretize easily with regional beliefs and customs, as its predisposition was not to displace but to augment. New ways of understanding and practicing the Buddha's teachings proliferated as the Dharma took root in new settings. These sometimes created divisions within the Sangha, but Buddhists have always tended to see diversification as a natural and wholesome development in which the versatility of the Dharma was demonstrated even as its essential features were maintained. Many Buddhists believe that there are ultimately as many "Buddhisms" as there are beings in the universe. Each Buddhist must rely on his own understanding of the Dharma and make his own way. As the Buddha once said to his disciple, Ananda: "Be a lamp unto yourself."

In the modern context, Buddhism has inspired productive and progressive forms of social dissidence and political liberation, as in the mass conversion of *dalits* to Buddhism in 1956. But, as with other religions, Buddhist institutions have also at times functioned as mechanisms of social control and state-sponsored violence, as may be seen in the fact that there have often been "fighting monks" in Tibetan and East Asian monastic traditions that developed various martial arts traditions, often to enforce both sectarian and political agendas.[9] Nevertheless, many modern Buddhist leaders have come to exemplify the power of nonviolent modes of resistance and reform, such as the Burmese Buddhist dissident Aung San Suu Kyi (b. 1945), whose commitment to peaceful resistance resulted in her receiving the Nobel Peace Prize in 1991, among other awards and accolades.

A new development in the modern context—and one that has emphasized the teaching of Interdependent Origination—views ecology as a primary model for understanding and embracing the interconnectedness of all things. This trend, which sees the individual and the environment in perpetual relationship, embraces a timely and essential evolution of the Dharma.

venerating his footprints continues today. The Buddha's footprints, which remind Buddhists of the immediacy of Buddha and the law of Impermanence, are inscribed with the sacred marks said to have been present on the body of the infant Siddhartha.

Buddhists of all sects demonstrate their reverence for the Buddha by bowing and prostrating themselves. In the Tibetan Nongdro (*sngon'gro*) or preliminary practices of Vajrayana, some Buddhists will perform 100,000 prostrations as an act of purification. Others show reverence while walking to a sacred site by bowing or prostrating themselves every step of the way.

As in Hinduism and Jainism, the lotus in Buddhism is a symbol of both purity and enlightenment. The lotus has its roots in the mud of the world but rises up as its pure blossom expands in the light of the sun.

While *mandalas* are used in Hinduism, where they also function as cosmological diagrams used for meditation, some Buddhists utilize them in other ways. In Vajrayana Buddhism, monks spend weeks constructing sand *mandalas* such as the Avalokiteshvara Mandala shown here. The sacred image will then be swept toward the center and destroyed as a reminder that art, like all other things, is impermanent.

SEEKING ANSWERS

What Is Ultimate Reality?

Buddhists often use the word *dharma* in its broader sense (that is, as nature and its laws) to refer to ultimate reality, or reality as it is (rather than as it usually perceived, or misperceived). According to the doctrine of Interdependent Origination, reality is a web of interrelated and interdependent phenomena in which nothing comes into existence independently of other things. Instead, the origination, or coming-into-existence, of things depends on all other things, as does their continued existence. All things are constituted of elements of other things. Nothing exists in and of itself. Further, according to the Buddha's doctrine of Impermanence, all things are in a constant state of flux and without any underlying or enduring essence or identity.

How Should We Live in This World?

Believing that there is stability and permanence in the world, we seek to possess what we want and to avoid what we do not want. Our inability to do so results in suffering that arises from our ignorance of the true nature of reality. Accordingly, the Buddha's guide to life, the Noble Eightfold Path, begins with the acceptance of a correct view of reality. The importance of striving for goals consistent with this understanding and living according to corresponding ethical principles follows. Finally, the Eightfold Path enjoins Buddhists to cultivate awareness and concentration that lead to enlightenment and an end to suffering.

What Is Our Ultimate Purpose?

For Buddhists, one's ultimate purpose is to break free of *samsara* and to achieve the end of suffering that is found in nirvana. But Buddhists also recognize that suffering is a condition that afflicts all sentient beings. Moved by compassion for others, they seek to live in a way that allows and encourages them to follow the path that will lead to their own enlightenment and liberation from suffering.

REVIEW QUESTIONS

For Review

1. Describe some of the distinctive ways in which Buddhism differs from other religions.
2. What are the implications of the Buddha's doctrine of Interdependent Origination?
3. What are the Three Marks of Existence? How do they relate to the doctrine of Interdependent Origination?
4. Describe some of the different ways in which adherents of various Buddhist groups put the teachings of the Buddha into practice.

5. What did the Buddha mean by "suffering" (*dukkha*)? How does following the Noble Eightfold Path bring an end to suffering?

For Further Reflection

1. It is sometimes said that Buddhism is a philosophy rather than a religion. Do you agree? Why or why not?
2. What are the most significant ways in which the teachings of the Buddha deviated from those of Hinduism?

3. In what specific ways do the teachings of Mahayana and Vajrayana Buddhism elaborate on those of Theravada?
4. Why is the principle of the Middle Way essential to Buddhism?
5. To what extent are the Buddha's teachings about the nature of reality in agreement with those of modern science?
6. Would you find it difficult to accept the Buddha's doctrine of No-Self? Why or why not?

GLOSSARY

anatman (un-aat-mun; Sanskrit) The doctrine that there is no independent, eternal self or soul underlying personal existence.

arhat (ar'hut) In Theravada Buddhism, one who has attained enlightenment.

bodhichitta (bow-dhi-chit-ta; Sanskrit, "the awakening mind or heart") In Mahayana Buddhism, the wise and compassionate intention to attain Buddhahood for the sake of all other sentient beings.

bodhisattva (bow-dhi-sut-tva; Sanskrit, "enlightenment being") One who is on the verge of enlightenment. In Mahayana Buddhism, a bodhisattva is one who has taken a "bodhisattva vow" to remain in samsara in order to work for the enlightenment of all sentient beings.

Buddha (bood-dha; Sanskrit, "the Awakened One") A fully enlightened being.

Chan or Zen (chah-aahn/Zehn) Respectively, the Chinese and Japanese names for the "meditation" school of Buddhism that values meditative experience far and above doctrine.

Dharma (dhur-mah; Sanskrit, "that which upholds") In the Buddhist context, Dharma refers both to Buddhist teaching and Buddhism as a religion.

dukkha (doo-kah; Pali, "suffering") Usually translated as "suffering," it can also be understood as the anxiety, unease, and dissatisfaction caused by desire.

Four Noble Truths The four truths that form the basis of the Dharma: Suffering is inherent in human life, suffering is caused by desire, there can be an end to desire, the way to end desire is the Noble Eightfold Path.

Impermanence According to the Buddha's doctrine of Impermanence, all phenomena are in a constant state of change.

Interdependent Origination (Sanskrit: *pratitya-samutpada*, "arising on the ground of a preceding cause") The doctrine that reality is a complex of interrelated and interdependent phenomena in which nothing exists independently; instead, the origination of all things depends on other things.

karma (kur-mah; Sanskrit, "action") Action; also, the consequences of actions.

lama (laah-mah; Tibetan) In Tibet, a teacher of the Dharma.

Mahayana (muh-haah-yaah-na; Sanskrit, "great vehicle") Also known as the "Great Vehicle," Mahayana is the form of Buddhism most prominent in China, Japan, Mongolia, Tibet, and Korea.

mandala (muhn-daah-la; Sanskrit "circle") Typically, a circular diagram representing the entire universe. Often used as an aid in meditation.

(*continued*)

GLOSSARY (continued)

mantra (mun-trah; Sanskrit) A sacred sound or syllable used as a focus for meditation, as an invocation of a deity, or as a protective spell.

Middle Way The Buddha's principle of the path between extremes of asceticism and self-indulgence that leads to enlightenment.

nirvana (nihr-vaah-nah; Sanskrit, an "extinguishing" or "blowing out") The ultimate goal of Buddhist practice, nirvana is the extinguishing of desire and the suffering it causes.

Noble Eightfold Path The Buddha's prescription for a way of life that leads to enlightenment. Based on the principle of the Middle Way, it is also defined by eight virtues.

No-Self The doctrine that there is no independent, eternal self or soul underlying personal existence. See also **anatman**.

Pali Canon Also known as the **Tripitaka** (Sanskrit, "Three Baskets"), the Pali Canon is the first canon of Buddhist texts. It consists of three "baskets" or collections of sutras.

parinirvana (pah-ree nihr-vaah-nah; Sanskrit, "supreme release") The full entry into nirvana that occurs at the death of one who has achieved nirvana in his or her lifetime.

samsara (sum-saah-ra; Sanskrit, "continuous flow") The continuing cycle of birth, death, and rebirth; also, the this-worldly realm in which the cycle recurs.

Sangha (suhn-ghaah; Sanskrit, "community") The worldwide community of Buddhists. Alternatively, the order of Buddhist monks or the membership of a particular Buddhist congregation.

skandhas (skuhn-dhaah; Sanskrit, "heaps" or "bundles") The five components (body, perceptions, feelings, innate tendencies, and thought) that give rise to a sense of self.

stupa (stooh-puh; Sanskrit, "heap") A reliquary mound in which the relics of the Buddha or a Buddhist saint are buried and venerated.

sutra (sooh-trah; Sanskrit, "a thread") Verses of text or scripture.

Theravada (thair-ah-vaah-duh; Pali, "the Way of the Elders") The form of Buddhism that is most prominent in Sri Lanka, Cambodia, Laos, and Vietnam.

Three Marks of Existence The Buddha's teachings on impermanence, suffering, and the nonexistence of an eternal unchanging self or soul.

Tripitaka (see *Pali Canon*)

upaya (ooh-paah-ya; Sanskrit, "expedient means") "Skillful Means" was developed into a form of Buddhist practice that encourages imaginatively applying wisdom to whatever circumstances one is in to assist in easing suffering or cultivating insight.

Vajrayana (vaah-jiraah-yaah-nah; Sanskrit, "Diamond Vehicle" or "Thunderbolt Vehicle") Often described as a form of Mahayana, Vajrayana is the most prominent form of Buddhism in Tibet and Nepal. It incorporates both Mahayana and tantric ideas and practices.

SUGGESTIONS FOR FURTHER READING

Byrom, Thomas. *The Dhammapada: The Sayings of the Buddha*. New York: Vintage Books, 1976. A very accessible and readable version of a key early Buddhist text.

Faure, Bernard. *Buddhism*. New York: Konecky and Konecky, 1977. A richly illustrated and descriptive introduction to Buddhism.

Lopez, Donald. *Buddhist Scriptures*. London: Penguin Books, 2004. A survey of Buddhist scriptures.

Skilton, Andrew. *A Concise History of Buddhism*. Birmingham, UK: Windhorse Publications, 1994. An excellent and accessible history of Buddhism.

(continued)

Snelling, John. *The Buddhist Handbook: The Complete Guide to Buddhist Schools, Teaching, Practice and History*. Rochester, VT: Inner Traditions, 1998. A guide to Buddhism that includes a detailed directory of contemporary institutions.

Suzuki, Shunryu. *Zen Mind, Beginner's Mind*. New York: Weatherhill, 1997. An excellent introduction to meditation practice.

Williams, Paul. *Mahayana Buddhism: The Doctrinal Foundations*. 2nd ed. New York: Routledge, 2008. A history of Mahayana that places emphasis on the veneration of certain Buddhist texts.

ONLINE RESOURCES

The Wikipedia Buddhism Portal

en.wikipedia.org/wiki/Portal:Buddhism
The collection of articles in the Wikipedia Buddhism series are generally quite reliable and extensive in scope.

Access to Insight: Readings in *Theravada* Buddhism

accesstoinsight.org/canon
Includes very helpful summaries and substantial translated portions of the Pali *Tripitaka*.

The Berzin Archives

berzinarchives.com/web/en/index.html
An excellent collection of translations, teaching, and scholarship on the Vajrayana tradition.

JAINISM

IN A SMALL VILLAGE in the southern Indian state of Karnataka, a middle-aged man stands silently in the main room of the home of Mr. and Mrs. Chandra, lifelong residents of the village and followers of the Jain religious tradition. Mr. Chandra carefully places small amounts of food in the cupped hands of his visitor. Other family members look on reverently, respectful and admiring both of the man who is receiving the food and of all that he represents—even though they have not met him before this day. These morsels of food—thirty-two altogether—and the small amount of water to follow are the only things he will ingest on this or any other day. His sole possessions consist of a gourd for drinking water and a broom for sweeping the path before him as he walks, lest he accidentally destroy a living being even as small as an ant. As a monk of the **Digambara** (literally, "sky-clad") sect of Jainism, this visitor does not even possess clothing. He stands naked before the Chandra family and, during his annual eight-month period of wandering about the land, goes naked before the elements.

Along with illustrating the austerities of the Jain monastic life, this ritual of giving, known as *dana*, indicates certain distinctions between ascetics (which includes both monks and nuns) and laypeople. The Chandras and the other laypeople who have gathered to participate in this *dana* represent the great majority of Jains in the world today.

Jains worship in a temple at Ranakpur, India. Splendid marble temples such as this are a common feature of the Jain tradition.

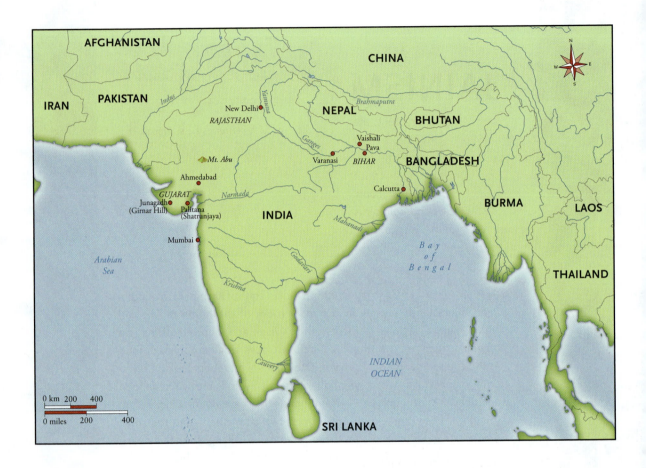

Significant sites in the development of Jainism.

As members of the laity, their religious duties differ from those of the ascetics, who exemplify Jainism's highest ideals of nonviolence and self-denial. The layperson depends on the ascetic for spiritual nourishment. But this in no way diminishes the sanctity or relevance of the lay religious life. The reverence shown by the roomful of admirers is as true to Jainism as is the monk's extraordinary self-discipline as he follows the ascetic path. Through such acts as *dana*, the lay participants can positively affect their **karma** ("action") and its consequences that determine prospects for a good rebirth. At the same time, the ascetic depends on laypeople like the Chandras for physical nourishment and support.

Viewing the scene from a more distant perspective, we can note other features of Jainism. For one thing, Mr. and Mrs. Chandra painstakingly prepared the food and carefully strained the water in preparation of the ritual, in order to avoid harming any living organism such as a tiny plant or insect in the water. They had invited the monk to partake of the food, for it would not befit one so venerated as a Digambara monk actually to have to beg for his food. The monk's accepting of the offerings was not a foregone conclusion. Had he for any reason found the circumstances objectionable and refused, the Chandras' reputation would have been damaged. In other words, the ritual of *dana* is played out within an interwoven network of religious and social ideas and forces. The fact that the monk stands naked with cupped hands is proof that he is a member of the Digambara sect, the more prevalent sect in southern India. In any number of households across India on this very morning, we could find similar scenes, but with some variations. Members of Jainism's **Shvetambara** sect, for example, don white robes and hold alms bowls for receiving their food. Or the ascetic could be a nun, in which case she would be clothed, even if of the Digambara sect.

Stepping back even further as we view this ritual of *dana*, we can observe a number of correlations with other South Asian religions. A nonviolent ethical stance, the ascetic path, karma, rebirth, and *dana* are also prominent aspects of Hinduism and Buddhism. Compared with those two religions, Jainism is a very small one, with just over 5 million adherents, the great majority of whom live in India. Because it rejects the authority of the *Vedas* (Chapter 4), Jainism (along with Buddhism) is considered to be distinctive relative to the Hindu traditions. Through the centuries, Jainism has earned a special reputation for having exemplified the ideal of nonviolence. ※

This chapter sheds light on the main elements of Jainism, with regard to both the ascetics and the laity—and the interplay between the two groups. We have already identified some central Jain teachings: nonviolence, the need for an ascetic lifestyle, and the ultimate need to attain perfect knowledge. In the following section we explore in more detail these central elements and how they relate to the Jain understanding of the nature of the universe, the human condition, and the quest for spiritual deliverance. But first we will look to the distant past, to the foundational figures whom all Jains revere as the *jinas* (Sanskrit, "conquerors"), those the Jains believe have shown the way to spiritual deliverance.

TIMELINE
Jainism

c. Eighth century B.C.E. Probable period of Parshva, the twenty-third *tirthankara*.

Sixth or fifth centuries B.C.E. Probable period of Mahavira (Shvetambara traditional dates 599–527 B.C.E.; Digambaras date Mahavira's death at 510 B.C.E.; current scholarly opinion holds that he died in app. 425 B.C.E.).

(From antiquity through the medieval period, there is scant evidence for historical events, though there is much evidence for general involvement by Jains in the cultural life of India, through the building of temples and monuments, founding of schools and sects, and interaction with other religions.)

1313 C.E. Pillaging of Mount Shatrunjaya by Turkish invaders.

Fifteenth century Period of Lonka, precursor of Sthanakvasi and Terapanthi sects.

1526 Founding of the Mughal Empire.

1556–1605 Akbar the Great (Mughal emperor who maintained good relations with Jain leaders).

Seventeenth century Period of the founding of the Sthanakvasi sect.

1726–1803 Acarya Bhikshu, founder of the Terapanthi sect.

1867–1901 Shrimad Rajacandra (also spelled Rajchandra) teacher and mystic, friend of Mohandas (Mahatma) Gandhi.

1893 Lecture on Jainism delivered by Virchand Gandhi at the World Parliament of Religions at Chicago.

1900–2000 Period of geographical expansion of sizable Jain communities outside of India.

THE TEACHINGS OF JAINISM

Most of the world's religions look to a glorious founding figure, who is typically regarded both as an exemplar of the religious life and as the revealer of the religion's most significant teachings; the Buddha, Confucius, Jesus, and Muhammad are examples of such founding figures. Jainism looks not to just one but to a series of founding figures, the **tirthankaras**, "makers of the ford (or river crossing)." Each is considered to be a *jina*, "conqueror"—whence comes the name Jainism. Through having conquered the realm of *samsara*, the continuing cycle of death and rebirth (also a concept prominent in Hinduism and Buddhism), the *tirthankara* has, metaphorically, successfully crossed the river from the worldly realm to the beyond—the realm of the liberated.

The most recent of the *tirthankaras*, Mahavira, is especially significant. We begin this section by considering his captivating and highly influential life story.

Mahavira, the Twenty-Fourth and Last *Tirthankara* of This World Cycle

Nataputta Vardhamana, popularly known as Mahavira ("great hero"), was probably born near Vaishali (located in the northern Indian state of Bihar). He lived, according to the Shvetambara sect, from 599 to 527 B.C.E., although the Digambaras date his death at 510 (and scholars tend to date it later still, to sometime in the second half of the fifth century B.C.E.). The earliest biography of Mahavira is from the ninth century C.E. (the Sanskrit work *Vardhamanacarita*, by the poet Asaga), and so it is not possible to determine with historical certainty the details of his life. One thing, though, is agreed on by all: Mahavira was a contemporary or near-contemporary of Gautama the Buddha, who lived in the same area of northern India and preached his last sermon at Vaishali. There is no record of the two having met, but their legendary biographies are strikingly similar.

Vardhamana is said to have been born into the ruling class (the *kshatriyas*), the second son of a *rajah* or local ruler who was also a pious Jain. Vardhamana grew up amidst the luxuries of the palace, eventually marrying a princess named Yashoda (although the Digambara sect denies that he married), with whom he had a daughter. Eventually, however, he yearned for more than his princely life could offer, and so at age thirty he asked for permission to leave and become a monk. He joined a group of Jain ascetics who were followers of Parshva, the last *tirthankara* to have lived prior to Mahavira.

Vardhamana soon set off from the other ascetics and wandered about for over twelve years, naked and exposed. Fasting, going for long periods without sleep, withstanding the verbal and physical abuse of human opponents, and enduring the bites of insects rather than doing them harm, Vardhamana exemplified the ideals of nonviolence and asceticism, thereby earning his epithet "great hero," Mahavira.

In the thirteenth year of his ascetic wanderings, Mahavira is believed by Jains to have attained the state of **kevala**, or omniscience, the complete and perfect knowledge that leads at the time of death to liberation from the realm of *samsara*. The tradition recounts that Mahavira attained this enlightenment after spending two and a half days fasting in the heat of the sun, squatting near a tree but out of its shade. With these acts of extreme asceticism, his steadfastly nonviolent approach to life, and his supreme spiritual achievement of attaining *kevala*, Mahavira exemplifies Jainism's central ideals.

Now perfectly enlightened, Mahavira set about preaching the tenets of Jainism. His followers included eleven *ganadharas*, or disciples, who had been Hindu *brahmins* before hearing Mahavira's message. All of them eventually attained *kevala*, ending with Jambu, who is regarded as the last human being ever to attain *kevala* in this world cycle.

Mahavira preached for some thirty years until, at the age of seventy-two, he died in the town of Pava (like Vaishali, located in the northern Indian state of Bihar). Now liberated from his body, Mahavira's perfected soul is said to have ascended to the top of the universe in a state of eternal bliss.

Sculpture of Mahavira in the cave temples of Ellora, India.

It is helpful at this point to recall the similarities between the Buddhist accounts of Gautama's path to enlightenment (Chapter 5) and Mahavira's path to *kevala*. Both men practiced severe austerities. But whereas Mahavira continued on the path of strict asceticism to the very end of his life, Gautama, at the time of his enlightenment, rejected strict asceticism and instead embraced the Middle Way, which calls for moderation in the treatment of one's body. The distinction is highlighted during the climactic moments of each story, for while Gautama is said to have sat underneath the *bo* (or *bodhi*) tree when he experienced enlightenment, Mahavira is said to have squatted in the scorching heat of the sun, near a tree but apparently intentionally avoiding its shade.

Whatever the historical accuracy of these accounts, clearly the two traditions diverged over the question of the degree of ascetic rigor. Indeed, Buddhists typically held Jains in contempt for their extraordinary rigor, which for Jains has always been the hallmark of their religion and a mark of honor. And so, even though Buddhism and Jainism have a considerable amount in common doctrinally and even in terms of practice, the two traditions seem not to have engaged much with each other. Apparently it was this way from the beginning, for while Mahavira and Gautama the Buddha seem to have been at least near-contemporaries, none of the texts claim that they ever met.

An Eternal Succession of *Tirthankaras*

Jainism, like Hinduism and Buddhism, is categorized by scholars as being an "eternal" religion in the sense that it subscribes to an ongoing succession of world cycles, without beginning or end. Jains believe that twenty-four *tirthankaras*, or *jinas,* have appeared in this current world cycle. Mahavira is the latest in an infinite line of previous *tirthankaras*, but he is not expected to be the last.

All twenty-four *tirthankaras* of this world cycle are known by name and by their specific symbols: Mahavira by the lion, for example, and Parshva—of whom there are

Sandstone sculpture of Parshva, the *tirthankara* most commonly depicted in Jain art.

more sculptures in India than of any other *tirthankara*—by the serpent. Along with Parshva and Mahavira, however, the only additional *jinas* who play a prominent role in the scriptures and in the tradition generally are the first, Rishabha (symbolized by the bull), and the twenty-second, Nemi (symbolized by the conch shell). Rishabha, who is clearly legendary and not historical, is believed to have been the father of Bharata, whom Jains regard as the first world emperor of this world cycle. Nemi, in addition to being the predecessor to Parshva, is traditionally thought to be a relative of Krishna, whom many Hindus revere as an avatar (human incarnation) of the god Vishnu (Chapter 4). The nineteenth *tirthankara*, Malli (symbolized by the jar), is also especially notable, for according to the Shvetambara sect, Malli was a woman. The Digambaras, who in general are more conservative, deny this, regarding this *tirthankara* as a man by the name of Mallinatha.

Jainism and Hinduism

Throughout the centuries, Jainism has coexisted with Hinduism. The list of interesting and relevant points of contact between the two religious traditions is almost endless. Here we shall make note of just a few, in order to shed some light on the cultural interplay.

Jains commonly worship deities of the Hindu pantheon, and they tend to think of them in similar ways. There are, however, certain rather glaring exceptions. For example, Hindus would probably be surprised to learn from one popular Jain text that Rama and Krishna were both pious Jains. Also, the various Jain renditions of the *Mahabharata*, the great epic poem that, in its more standard form, is regarded with devotion by almost every Hindu, transform Krishna into a devious trickster. On the other hand, the *Bhagavad Gita*, which forms a very small portion of the *Mahabharata* and is typically regarded as Hinduism's most popular text, has been very favorably received by Jains. As for Hinduism's part in this cultural interplay, devotees of the god Vishnu have at times adopted the *tirthankara* Rishabha as being an avatar of their god. These few examples suffice at least to indicate the extensive interaction between Jain and Hindu religious and other cultural aspects.

Cultural interaction and similarities notwithstanding, Jainism is very much its own tradition. Among its more distinctive features is the very special status assigned to the *tirthankaras*. Jains believe them to be human—not gods or avatars of gods—but nevertheless to deserve the highest degree of veneration.

Jain reverence for twenty-four *tirthankaras*, as opposed to focusing on just one founding figure, is instructive with regard to some basic elements of the religion. Why, one might wonder, would more than one *jina* be needed? Human nature, Jainism would answer, is depraved to the point of needing repeated assistance from these spiritual masters. In a related manner, Mahavira is the last *jina* of the present world cycle because human nature has become continually *more* depraved. In the present state of affairs, *kevala* is no longer a possibility in this world, having been attained for the last time by Jambu, the disciple of Mahavira.

So, the next logical question is, what hope do human beings have if they are confined to this realm of *samsara*? What needs to happen before a *tirthankara* once again appears to show humanity how to cross the river from this shore to the beyond, the eternal realm of complete freedom and perfect bliss? Answers to such questions call for an analysis of Jain teachings.

We will now turn to a brief survey of Jain scriptures, the main source of Jain teachings. All Jains agree that, originally, there were fifty-eight books of scripture based on the preaching of Mahavira, who in turn based his views on the earlier *tirthankaras*. These books are divided into three categories: *Purva*, *Anga*, and *Angabahya*. But much is believed to have been lost. The Digambaras believe that only excerpts from one of the books of *Purva* survive; these excerpts, together with later commentaries written about them, constitute Digambara scripture. The Shvetambara sect, on the other hand, officially rejects the Digambara texts and follows instead eleven books of *Anga* and thirty-four books of *Angabahya*.

Ahimsa and Asceticism: Jainism's Ideals

We have observed how, in the ritual of *dana* ("giving") and in the ascetic practices of Mahavira, the principle of nonviolence functions as a basic ethical norm in Jainism. This principle, commonly known by its Sanskrit name **ahimsa**, is prevalent throughout the traditional religions of India. Hindus and Buddhists, for instance, all tend to favor vegetarianism because of its relative nonviolence. Jainism emphasizes the place of *ahimsa*, the "pure, unchangeable, eternal law" in this well-known passage from the *Acarangasutra*, the first book of the *Angas*:

> All breathing, existing, living, sentient creatures should not be slain,
> nor treated with violence, nor abused, nor tormented, nor driven away.
> This is the pure, unchangeable, eternal law which the clever ones, who
> understand the world, have proclaimed.[1]

All aspects of life are set in the context of avoiding injury toward "sentient creatures," an extensive category that includes not only human beings and animals but also plant life. Jain ascetics expand the category nearly to its logical extreme, striving even to avoid harming the atomic particles believed to pervade the natural elements.

The most distinctive characteristic of Jain doctrine, then, is *ahimsa*, the avoidance of doing injury to any life form. Or, put differently, Jains strive toward constant friendship with all fellow living creatures. As this striving becomes more intense, an ascetic lifestyle emerges naturally. Denying the body anything beyond what is necessary to sustain life lessens the risk of injuring other forms of life. Restricting one's diet to vegetables, for example, avoids doing violence to animals. On a more subtle level, straining one's water before drinking it (as we saw in this chapter's opening account of the Chandra household) and, indeed, drinking only as much water as is absolutely necessary further decreases violence, in this case to the small organisms that live undetected in drinking water.

Interrelated aspects of *ahimsa* are helpfully set forth by two other Jain concepts: *anekantavada* ("nonabsolutism") and *aparigraha* ("nonpossessiveness"). As stated in this introductory section of *Jain Way of Life*, a publication of the Federation of Jain Associations of North America, these three concepts—AAA—set forth the foundations of Jain teachings:

> Jainism is a religion and a way of life. For thousands of years, Jains have been practicing vegetarianism, yoga, meditation, and environmentalism. Jains have three core practices: Non-Violence, Non-Absolutism, and Non-Possessiveness (Ahimsa, Anekantvad, and Aparigraha—AAA).
>
> **Non-Violence** is compassion and forgiveness in thoughts, words, and deeds toward all living beings. For this reason, Jains are vegetarians.
> **Non-Absolutism** is respecting views of others. Jains encourage dialog and harmony with other faiths.
> **Non-Possessiveness** is the balancing of needs and desires, while staying detached from our possessions.[2]

In what ways is the teaching of nonviolence relevant for other world religions?

Another basic doctrine of Jainism is the need to diminish karma through limiting one's actions. In order to understand karma and Jain beliefs regarding spiritual fulfillment, it is best first to consider Jain cosmology, or its theory of the universe.

Theory of the Universe

According to tradition, Mahavira taught extensively and in detail about the nature of the universe, its makeup, and its functioning. He did so not merely as an intellectual exercise, but because, as he saw it, understanding the universe had sweeping implications for the spiritual quest. Thus, to understand Jain doctrine, one must understand Jain cosmology. We begin with considering the Jain concept of time, which incorporates the notion of eternally recurring cosmic or world cycles. Then we examine the makeup of the universe and all that exists within it.

Cosmic Cycles of Generation and Degeneration

In keeping with the general Indian notion of *samsara*, Jainism conceives of time as cyclical and envisions the cycles as upward and downward turnings of a wheel. During the upward turning of the wheel (which proceeds through six spokes, or ages), the world is in a state of ascendancy, with all aspects of existence, notably including the moral propensity of human beings, in the process of improvement. The three upper spokes are considered to be a golden age of goodness and prosperity. Once passing the top of the wheel and entering into its downward turning, however, things begin gradually to decline, until the end of the age of the sixth spoke, at which point the universe reaches utter moral deprivation. Then the wheel once again begins its turn upward. And so it continues, eternally.

The traditional length of each of the six ages is 21,000 years. The world currently is in the age of the fifth spoke of the downward turning, called *Kali Yuga*, to be followed by the sixth, final period of degeneration. In this sixth age, the theory goes, people are more prone to immorality, and they become physically smaller. The consequences for the spiritual quest are pronounced, for human beings can no longer hope to attain *kevala* in this world until the wheel has once again begun its upward turning. Mahavira is the last of the *tirthankaras* of the turning of the wheel in which we now live, and his eleven *ganadharas*, ending with Jambu, are the last people to achieve liberation during this cycle. The wheel will need to advance considerably into its upward motion before anyone else can hope again to attain *kevala* in this world.

Notably, Rishabha, the first *tirthankara* of this downward turning of the world cycle, is believed to have appeared during the third spoke. Before that, the world was so healthy morally and spiritually that human beings did not need a *jina* to show them the way to liberation. Rishabha and the other early *tirthankaras* are understood to have been of greater physical stature than their successors.

The concept of *Kali Yuga* and the continuing downward turning of the wheel gives rise to a fundamental and serious question. If indeed *kevala* is no longer a possibility, what purpose is there in continuing to pursue the religious life? Thinking again of the *dana* ritual, why should laypeople like the Chandras go to the effort of giving so conscientiously to monks? And why would anyone opt to undergo the physical hardships of the ascetic life? Part of the answer depends on the nature of karma, which we will address next. Another part of the answer is provided through consideration of the composition of the universe, which Jains call the **loka** and regard as containing within it three distinct lands inhabited by human beings.

The *Loka*   The *loka* is understood to be vast almost beyond description. Over the centuries, Jains have speculated as to just how vast the *loka* is, deriving a unit of measure known as the "rope," which is strikingly similar to the "light year" of modern astrophysics. According to one account, the *loka* is fourteen ropes from top to bottom. This means, according to traditional Jain calculations, that it would take a god, flying at the speed of 10 million miles per second, seven years to traverse its full span. These attempts at specifying the size of the universe are probably to be taken figuratively rather than literally. Still, a tendency toward something like scientific understanding is in keeping with the Jain belief that perfect and complete knowledge is attainable and indeed has been attained—namely, by Mahavira, his disciples, and the countless numbers of those who have achieved enlightenment before them.

The *loka*, then, is a vast and yet a finite space, within which all beings dwell. Beyond the *loka* there is nothing but strong winds. The *loka*, together with everything in it, has always existed and will continue to exist eternally. Jainism thus does not believe in a creator god.

Jains sometimes depict the *loka* as a diagram in the shape of a giant man, the *purusha*. Across the midsection runs a relatively small band known as the Middle Realm, which contains a series of oceans and continents, three of which together form the region inhabited by human beings. This region is further divided into various lands, one of which is India and another of which, Mahavideha, is not affected by the corruption of this world cycle and therefore continues to be the home of *tirthankaras* and of human beings who still can attain *kevala*. This notion is crucial when considering the quest for spiritual liberation that takes place in this corrupt world. As we shall discuss in more detail shortly, living a good life that is true to Jain ideals leads to a good rebirth, perhaps even in a land like Mahavideha, where *tirthankaras* currently reside and where *kevala* is a possibility.

Below the Middle Realm is a series of progressively darker hells, whose denizens suffer agonizing torments. At the very bottom of the *loka*, below the lowest hell, there are only clouds. Above the Middle Realm is a series of progressively brighter heavens, inhabited by deities who enjoy pleasures not unlike those of earthly rulers. For both the denizens of hell and the deities, their stays in those realms are only temporary, as they will eventually be reborn in another realm. In other words, just as in Hinduism and Buddhism, the realm of *samsara* extends well beyond the human domain. Because only humans can ever attain *kevala*, however, the Jains believe that even being reborn as a deity in one of the brightest heavens is ultimately not as fortunate as it might seem. The best rebirth is as a human being, so that the quest for spiritual fulfillment can be continued.

At the top of the *loka*, in the crown of the head of *purusha*, is a roof that is described as having the shape of an umbrella. Called the "slightly curved place," this is the eternal home of the souls that have been liberated from the realm of *samsara*.

Categories of Existence: *Jiva* and *Ajiva*

Jain scriptures spell out the categories of existing things in meticulous detail (in keeping with the belief in the omniscience of Mahavira and others who have attained *kevala*). The categories of existence can be said to begin with a simple distinction: that between the living, which is termed **jiva**, and the nonliving, **ajiva**. The nonliving is further divided into four: motion, rest, atoms, and space. These four basic entities plus the *jiva* are the five building blocks of all that exists in the universe. The entities interact, but forever maintain their individual existence. This view contrasts with the main form of Hindu cosmology, which envisions an ultimate union of all being. Furthermore, Jainism holds that the universe has an infinite number of atoms, forever distinct from one another, along with an infinite number of *jivas*, or souls.

Each *jiva* ("soul") is eternal, completely without form, and yet capable of interacting with the atoms of the body it inhabits in such a way that it can control the body's mechanisms. While avoiding the notion that the *jiva* is in any way dependent upon the body, Jainism does posit a complex integration of soul with body. Thus, while bodies do act, it is the soul that wills actions and therefore is held responsible for their moral quality.

All *jivas* are essentially equal, regardless of the bodies they inhabit. For example, the *jiva* of an insect is considered to be of identical quality to that of a large animal or a human being. This belief has significant implications with regard to the doctrine of *ahimsa*, as it encourages equal treatment of all living beings.

The great variety of bodies inhabited by the *jivas* produces many different life forms. Jainism's detailed classification of these life forms is among its most fascinating features, and one that shows remarkable similarities to the modern field of zoology. A simple twofold approach distinguishes life forms that are stationary, such as plants, from those that are moving. Another approach categorizes life forms based on the number of senses they have. In the words of one text:

> Up to the vegetable-bodied ones, selves have one sense [i.e., touch].
> Worms, ants, bumblebees, and men each have one more than the one preceding.[3]

Human beings are thus categorized with life forms having five senses: deities, denizens of hell, and most animals aside from insects. Flying insects (bumblebees and the like) are thought to lack the sense of hearing, while most that crawl on legs also lack sight. Along with such insects as worms, shellfish are thought to have only the senses of touch and taste. Plants and "microbes" (a large category of the most basic life forms) are devoid of all sensations but touch.

More elaborate systems of classification abound in Jain scriptures. This fascination with the intricacies of life forms supports the religion's general concern for their welfare and for maintaining the attitude and practices that secure this welfare as best possible. To some extent, the attitude and practices of the religious life are expected of nonhuman life forms as well. Lions, for example, are said to be able to learn to fast. Even plants and the simplest microbes are believed to have some basic religious capacity that they can apply toward spiritual advancement. Ultimately, however, all *jivas* must be reborn as human beings before they have any chance of attaining *kevala* and release from the realm of *samsara*.

Liberation and Salvation

Many religions typically emphasize teachings concerning salvation or liberation, and Jainism is no exception. As our account will make clear, salvation depends on understanding the challenges of *samsara* and how to overcome them.

To begin, salvation in no way depends on the power of a deity. Just as Jainism has no creator god, neither does it have one to assist with the all-important quest for liberation. Some would thus label Jainism an atheistic religion, but this is not quite accurate. We have seen that in the Jain cosmology, deities inhabit the various heavens. Many of their names would be recognizable to the student of Hinduism, for the pantheons are similar. Thus Jainism might best be labeled *transtheistic*[4] in the sense that there are gods (in fact, a great variety of gods), but ultimately the religion moves beyond them when it comes to the truly crucial issues of salvation. To understand why this is, let us first examine Jainism's concept of karma.

Karma and the Human Condition Notwithstanding the intricate categories of existence, so far as the human condition is concerned, Jainism is best understood in terms of two categories: soul (*jiva*) and matter (*ajiva*). As noted earlier, the *jiva* is essentially pure and formless. And yet, for reasons that defy explanation, souls have become entwined with impure matter, causing them to be weighed down and bound to *samsara*. Human beings are born into this state. The religious life strives to clean away the dirt that tarnishes the *jiva*, returning it to its original state of pristine purity and releasing it from *samsara*, so it can ascend upward to the "umbrella" ceiling of the *loka*, the realm of liberated souls.

For Jains, the term karma refers to the process in which matter dirties the soul. In both Hinduism and Buddhism, karma is commonly understood as being the consequence of action per the law of cause and effect. This general definition applies to Jainism as well, but here the term's more literal meaning of "action" is stressed. Because all actions encumber the *jiva* with matter, whenever the soul wills an action, it risks tarnishing itself. Immoral actions, those that violate the principle of *ahimsa* or other Jain ethical teachings, are especially damaging because they dirty the *jiva* with heavier impurities. Highly virtuous actions, on the other hand, bring about only small quantities of light matter that neither cling to the soul nor weigh it down.

Along with this emphasis on the material aspects of karma, Jainism also emphasizes the intentions behind one's actions. That is, the immorality that tarnishes the soul with heavy matter lies mainly in the evil intention, not in the consequence of the action. Similarly, an action that might appear to have evil consequence could be considered moral if good was intended. For example, the accidental killing of microbes, provided proper means were taken to avoid it, would generally not be immoral and thus would not lead to the dirtying of the *jiva*.

Kevala: Omniscience That Leads to Liberation *Kevala* is best translated as "omniscience"; one who has attained this state is a *kevalin*. Whereas Buddhist enlightenment (*bodhi*) incorporates the sort of knowledge that is vital for spiritual perfection (Chapter 5), Jain *kevala* is knowledge of everything: the nature of one's inner self, of one's past lives, and of the external world and all things, including fellow living beings (and their past lives and future lives) that inhabit it. Little wonder that Jainism so boldly sets forth cosmological explanations, based as they are on the omniscience of Mahavira and the other *tirthankaras*.

The most significant feature of *kevala* is that it frees the *jiva* completely from the tarnishing effects of karma so that it may be liberated. The final experience of liberation or release is known as *moksha* (as it is in Hinduism). *Moksha* and *kevala* are distinguishable in that one who has attained *kevala* normally goes on living in the physical body, confined to the realm of *samsara*, while one who achieves *moksha* is liberated from the body. Mahavira, like the *jinas* before him, passed many years as an enlightened one (sometimes referred to in Jainism, as in Buddhism, as *arhat*) before experiencing *moksha* at the time of his death, which finally freed him completely from any impurities that would bind him to the material world.

One might ask at this point whether omniscience leads to the purity of the soul or whether purification of soul brings about omniscience. A Jain might respond by asserting that the two work together harmoniously. This notion of religious impulses working in harmony is embodied in the Jain concept of the Three Jewels of the religion: right faith (*darshana*), right knowledge (*jnana*), and right practice (*caritra*). All three are integral to the religious quest. Right faith, which for Jainism involves a proper outlook or mindset, the correct way of "seeing" (which is the root meaning of *darshana*), nurtures right knowledge and practice. Likewise for the other Jewels; they function together like three legs of a stool.

The Quest for a Heavenly Rebirth   We have noted that Jambu, the last of Mahavira's eleven disciples to attain *kevala*, is believed to be the last person of this world in the current cycle ever to achieve liberation. But this does not imply that for Jains living since Jambu's time it is meaningless to seek liberation. Every living being remains destined for rebirth, and the nature of rebirth depends on karmic status. A good rebirth, into the delights of one of the heavens or back into the human realm, therefore requires living a good life.

In contrast to Hindu and Buddhist beliefs, Jainism understands rebirth as occurring immediately after death. This has various implications that set Jainism apart from Buddhism and Hinduism, especially in regard to the need to perform rituals on behalf of the dead. For Jains, such rituals are deemed superfluous—which is not to say that Jains forgo mourning rituals or that they fail to honor their deceased loved ones. But the most crucial thing, the destiny of the deceased's soul, is determined as soon as the person dies. In fact, the soul is believed immediately to begin animating another life form.

Having examined the primary teachings of Jainism, we now turn our attention to the various ways these teachings have been manifested in Jain society and rituals.

THE HISTORY OF JAINISM

In the previous section, we have focused attention on Jain teachings. Turning now to a study of Jain history, we begin by considering the general place of Jainism in the context of Indian religions.

The Indian Historical Context

Earlier in this chapter we learned about the traditional understanding of Jainism's founding figures: the *tirthankaras* of this world cycle, most notably Mahavira. Here, our attention shifts to the scholarly understanding of Jainism's historical foundations, so we can observe some features of Indian religious culture that help situate the stories of the *tirthankaras* within a broader context.

Jains themselves do not regard Mahavira as having founded their religion. Historians, too, tend to agree with the traditional view that Mahavira himself followed an already established form of Jainism—possibly that of Parshva, the twenty-third *tirthankara* of this world cycle. Scholars situate Parshva's lifetime in the eighth century B.C.E. As noted previously, there are more sculptures in India of this *tirthankara* than of any other, Mahavira included, indicating his great popularity as an object of Jain devotion.

In the eighth century B.C.E., the probable period of Parshva, Indian civilization was beginning an important transition. The Vedic period, named for the Sanskrit texts that form the scriptural foundation of Hinduism, was ending, as was the domination of the priestly leadership of the *brahmin* caste (Chapter 4). Now began a period of religious diversity that included philosophical speculation on the *Upanishads* (themselves, technically, the last section of the Vedic corpus) and religious movements that eventually gave rise to Buddhism and the devotional forms of Hinduism that continue today. Parshva, and Mahavira after him, fit into a general category of religious movements that emphasized asceticism as a means of spiritual development.

Perhaps because of Jainism's belief in a never-ending succession of world cycles, Jains have not kept a detailed historical record of their own tradition. As we have seen, the dates for the lifespan of Mahavira are a matter of dispute, and so, too, is the place of his birth. The texts that contain the accounts were written hundreds of years after the fact. Much of the story of Jainism through its early centuries similarly does not lend itself to precise historical reckoning. With the religious changes of the period around 1000 C.E., the historical record begins to become clearer.

> Jains' lack of emphasis on maintaining a detailed historical record seems to be based on religious belief—specifically, belief in a never-ending succession of world cycles. What is the relationship in other religions between religious beliefs and the relevance of history?

The Legacy of the *Tirthankaras*: Jainism through the Centuries

In the ninth century C.E., about the time that the influence of Buddhists was severely diminishing in India, the country's religious landscape was undergoing a rather sudden shift with the influx of Islam. Muslim rule was established in 1192 in the form of the Delhi Sultanate, which was succeeded in 1526 by the Mughal Empire. During the early centuries of Muslim rule, relations between Muslims and Jains were not always friendly. There are accounts of large-scale destruction of sacred Jain sites, for example, the pillaging by Muslims in 1313 of Mount Shatrunjaya, a major Jain pilgrimage site in the western state of Gujarat. But during the period of Mughal rule, and especially at its apex during the reign of Akbar the Great (1556–1605), remarkably close relations developed. Akbar himself was the close friend of a Jain leader, and he issued several decrees promoting the protection of animals, motivated apparently by learning about the Jain emphasis on *ahimsa*.

During the eighteenth and nineteenth centuries, Jainism became somewhat more diverse through the establishment of the Sthanakvasi and Terapanthi sects. In the twentieth century, immigration led to the establishment of Jain communities in various places around the globe.

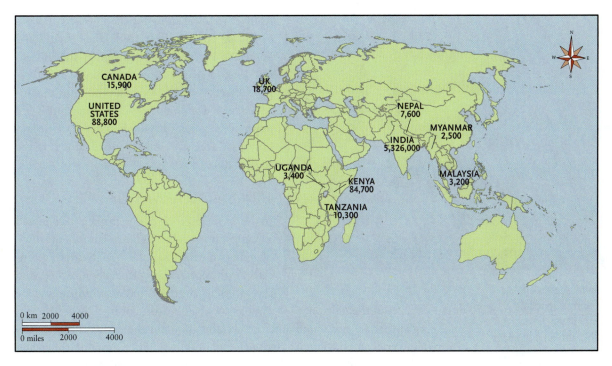

CANADA
15,900

UK
18,700

UNITED
STATES
88,800

NEPAL
7,600

MYANMAR
2,500

INDIA
5,326,000

UGANDA
3,400

KENYA
84,700

MALAYSIA
3,200

TANZANIA
10,300

0 km 2000   4000

0 miles   2000   4000

World Jain population.

Jainism in Today's World

The total number of Jains today is about 5.6 million, with all but about 275,000 living in India. Still, in India Jainism is dwarfed numerically by the Hindu population, which now numbers near 1 billion. In light of these numbers, the influence that Jainism has on Indian culture is quite remarkable. To some extent, this influence can be measured in financial terms. For centuries, Jains have been very successful in business, perhaps because of their religiously motivated focus on trade as opposed to agriculture. Also, the Jain community is highly respected for its charitable giving. In keeping with their profound emphasis on *ahimsa*, Jains commonly take in and care for animals that are maltreated or are targeted for slaughter. Although they generally do not actively seek converts to their religion, Jains tend to be outspoken advocates of universal vegetarianism, and so have exercised wide influence in this regard.

Among Jains of recent times, Shrimad Rajacandra (1867–1901; also spelled Rajchandra) is especially known outside India because of his connection to Mohandas (Mahatma) Gandhi. Both from the state of Gujarat, they met in 1891, and according to Gandhi's autobiography, Rajacandra made a strong impression and had a very positive impact on his spiritual development. Gandhi, of course, is perhaps the most famous advocate of *ahimsa* the world has ever known, even though he never overtly adopted Jainism as his religion.

Jain influence has also reached well beyond India through the Indian diaspora population. Their centuries-old focus on business has made life in the modern world a

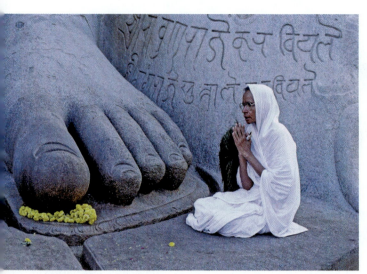

Jain ascetics and impressive religious monuments, such as this nun on pilgrimage at Shravanabelagola, are common sights in India. Through its diaspora population of some 275,000 people, Jainism also has a significant presence outside of India.

relatively natural thing for the Jain laity. For ascetics, of course, life outside their traditional homeland is especially challenging; and indeed, it is quite rare, as only the Sthanakvasi and Terapanthi sects even allow monks and nuns to journey in the world at large. The Terapanthis are responsible, too, for having founded the first Jain university, recently established at Ladnum in the state of Rajasthan.

JAINISM AS A WAY OF LIFE

In the opening section of this chapter, we glimpsed a moment in the religious life of Jainism, the ritual of giving known as *dana*. While illustrating concern for the central Jain principles of *ahimsa* and the ascetic path, the ritual also indicates some of the diversity of the religion. For example, we noted features of the Digambara version of *dana* that are not found among Shvetambaras, and the basic distinction between the ascetics and the Jain laity was evident. In this section, we examine in greater detail these varieties of Jainism and consider other significant practices and characteristics of the Jain religious life.

Digambaras and Shvetambaras

Before highlighting those things that distinguish the Digambaras from the Shvetambaras, it is important to acknowledge the many things they share in common, including a general heritage of teachings and similar forms of practice. Still, the differences are interesting and instructive, helping to illustrate Jainism's rich diversity.

We have noted some differences at earlier points in the chapter. The two sects posit differing dates for the death of Mahavira (527 B.C.E. for Shvetambaras, 510 B.C.E. for Digambaras). The Digambaras deny that Mahavira ever married. In keeping with their generally more conservative views, Digambaras do not agree that the nineteenth *tirthankara,* whom the Shvetambaras know as Malli and the Digambaras as Mallinatha, was a woman.

The most obvious issue differentiating the two sects involves clothing. Digambara (or "sky-clad") monks, as their name infers (and as we have witnessed in the *dana* ceremony), go about naked; Digambara nuns do not, donning simple white garments like their counterparts in other Jain sects. From the Digambara perspective, wearing clothes puts monks back into the ordinary category of the laity. Nuns are not esteemed quite as highly as monks, and in general, Digambara doctrine is more severe than the other sects when it comes to spiritual deliverance of men versus women. In short, women (including nuns, even though they perform the same ascetic practices as monks) are deemed incapable of attaining *kevala;* they must await rebirth in a male body in order to reach the potential of final deliverance.

VOICES: An Interview with Girish Shah

Girish Shah was born in the Indian state of Gujarat, which is home to many Jains and to important pilgrimage destinations. He attended college in Mumbai and then left India to attend graduate school in the United States, where he now lives. A founding member and director of the Jain Center of Northern California and the Federation of Jain Associations in North America, Mr. Shah is dedicated to educating people about his religion.

What do you consider to be the most important reason for living a proper Jain religious life?

The goal is to become free of karma. To make your soul and its properties of infinite knowledge, infinite vision, infinite strength, and infinite capacity to character "clean," you have to get rid of all the karmas that are polluting it. For one to live a religious life it is important to achieve that. . . . But for me, the more important part of living the proper religious life is that it is the way you will support each other, it is the way you will serve each other. You are helping each other grow, and you are reciprocating, giving back. We need to have empathy toward everyone. Forgiveness is not for those who have done nothing to you; forgiveness is for someone who has hurt you.

Girish Shah

Do you consider Jainism to be an atheistic religion?

I think the question is what you mean by "atheistic religion." If you mean by atheistic religion god the creator and god the controller and god the sustainer; that there is an entity that created the world, that controls the world, that sustains the world, and that judges everybody, then no. We do not believe in god in that sense, but we do believe in the quality of the soul, which is godliness. Infinite compassion—that is the characteristic of soul. The knowledge, the vision, and working with and relating to everybody, comes from infinite compassion. And that has the power, that has the godlike characteristics. It doesn't control anything. Even our enlightened or *tirthankaras* cannot make me achieve *moksha*. They can show me the path, but cannot say, such as the gods will say, "I bless you." There is no blessing. There is no divine grace that anyone can give. Forgiveness has to be done by you, by your own action. The burden is on you completely, but you can achieve it. Jainism is the religion that says: "I am god" (if we call the *tirthankara* "god," which is the common word that we use). No other religion tells you that you can become god. But Jainism says everyone can become god.

How important to you are vegetarianism and other forms of *ahimsa*?

Very important. The idea is to minimize the amount of *himsa* that you are doing, and so you give up some of these things—at least for the important religious days, if not all the time. Some people will take vows to give up this or that for their entire lifetime. Increasingly I am becoming vegan, knowing that there is so much *himsa* in dairy. I have not become fully vegan, but hopefully some day I'll get there. Traditionally, milk was okay, because of the way cows were treated before. Now things have changed, and so we have to evolve and look at it. It's just sensitivity to it. Here is another example. I ask myself: "Why am I wasting natural resources?" I have a nice home. I have never felt the need to go beyond. This is my first house and my last house. I have no attachment to the house. People say, "Girish, you should be living in a beautiful big home," and I say, "What beautiful big home? Why do I need one?" It's all internalizing. I don't have the need. I have a four-bedroom house; it's big enough. That's plenty of space, 1,800 square feet. Why do I need a 7,000-square-foot house, why do I need a 10,000-square-foot house? Just because I can afford it doesn't mean that I should have it. . . . This is all part of *ahimsa*. It's all part of *ahimsa* because then you are not wasting your resources. Charity is a form of *ahimsa* because you are now using money that you made for the benefit of others, for their growth, their progress, their betterment of life. People need to have betterment of life beyond their basic needs in order for them to spiritually think. If you don't have enough even to eat and to think, you're not going to have spirituality.

You immigrated to the United States from India. What do you consider to be the most notable differences between being a Jain in India and being a Jain in the United States?

For Jains in India, things are taken for granted, whereas being a Jain here, you have to put up with a lot of issues. Every time I go shopping, it takes a half hour reading the ingredients to see how many animal products are in it. There is no green mark on food packaging here like we have in India, where you can look at it and say, green—it is vegetarian. Also, I can't walk to places here. In India, you walk to places. You don't have to use the car. To go shopping, to go to the temple, you walk. Here in California you have to drive, particularly when you drive here in summer, your car windshield is filled with all those butterflies that you're killing on the way. And so my wife refuses to travel at night. You're going to get up in the morning and go. You're not going to kill all those butterflies, just to get there at night.

Another identifying feature of the Digambara sect involves the ascetics' avoidance of alms bowls as means of collecting food, using instead only their cupped hands. The reasoning is based in the principle of *ahimsa:* washing of bowls presumably would bring about greater harm to living beings. The same reasoning supports the "sky-clad" practice of monks, for the washing of dirty clothes causes harm. Finally, as previously noted, the Digambaras have their own official collection of scriptures.

A sizable majority of Jains are Shvetambaras. Since about the thirteenth century c.e., they have followed their set of forty-five sacred texts as authoritative. Unlike the Digambaras, they use alms bowls when begging for food; they accept the possibility of a woman attaining *kevala;* and, of course, they wear clothing (monks and nuns alike), consisting of upper and lower white garments.

Interestingly, even Shvetambara texts make clear that Mahavira and his early male followers went about naked. Gradually the opinion arose among Shvetambaras that the wearing of clothes was an option. One text from the second or third century C.E. designates three specific factors making this permissible: embarrassment; causing others to feel disgust; and inability to endure hardships caused by nakedness.[5]

Sthanakvasis and Terapanthis

Within Shvetambara Jainism, two distinctive sects, the Sthanakvasi and the Terapanthi, have features that distinguish them somewhat from their parent. Most significantly, they both reject the worship of images, which is a common religious practice among the majority of Shvetambaras. Ascetics of both sects constantly wear the *muhpatti* ("mouth-shield"), a cloth that protects insects from accidentally being inhaled as the monks and nuns traverse the land. And both sects allow monks and nuns to travel abroad.

The Sthanakvasis trace their origins to the seventeenth century. Today there are over 3,000 Sthanakvasi ascetics, about five-sixths of whom are nuns. A relatively liberal sect, the Sthanakvasis allow nuns to travel unaccompanied by monks.

The Terapanthis revere as their founder the Shvetambara reformer Ācārya Bhikshu (1726–1803; *ācārya* is a general term in Jainism for "leader" of a group of ascetics). He implemented what is perhaps the most characteristic Terapanthi teaching: drawing a strict distinction between the worldly sphere and the religious sphere, Bhikshu declared that it is not possible to earn merit through deeds involving the worldly sphere. For example, whereas most Jains consider it highly meritorious to purchase animals from butchers in order to set them free, the Terapanthis reject this.

The Ascetic Life

Through their biographies and teachings, the *tirthankaras*, "makers of the river crossing," show the way to liberation to all Jains. However, as neither the *tirthankaras* nor any Jain deities can bestow salvation, all individuals must make their own spiritual progress and eventually attain their own deliverance. Moreover, as noted, Jains believe that the ascetic life offers the spiritual path that best replicates the lives and follows the

VISUAL GUIDE
Jainism

Jain emblem. Incorporating a variety of symbols, the Jain emblem's outline represents the *loka*, or universe. The swastika, an ancient and common symbol in Hinduism, Buddhism, and other religious traditions, is very prominent in Jainism; its four arms represent the four realms of life (heavens, human realm, animal realm, hells). The hand represents *ahimsa*.

Tirthankara. Sculptures of *tirthankaras*, like this one of Rishabha, whom Jains revere as the first of the current world cycle, are objects of Jain worship.

Whisk. Shown here with a book of Jain scripture, the whisk is used by ascetics to clear away, and thus to protect, insect life. It symbolizes *ahimsa*.

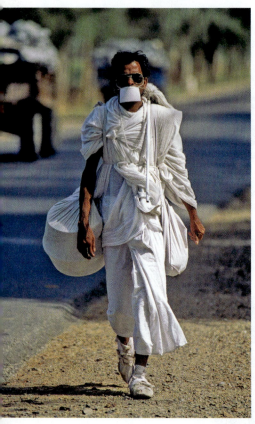

A Jain monk wearing the *muhpatti* in order to prevent unnecessary harm to airborne insects.

teachings of the *jinas*. Still, no one expects the average Jain to enter upon this arduous path. Simply having entered into the human realm does not imply that one is ready for the ascetic life. A Jain takes this life on gradually, after having become an accomplished layperson who fulfills all religious duties successfully and with a pure disposition. When the circumstances are right, whether in this lifetime or in a future lifetime, the decision to renounce the lay life and become an ascetic is made.

It almost goes without saying that the decision of renunciation is not to be made lightly. The initiation ritual, *diksha*, marks the point at which the individual becomes completely committed to the ascetic life. Through the centuries, minimum age requirements have been imposed—young adulthood for the Digambara sect, younger for the Shvetambaras (historically, as young as age 6, although today only the Terapanthi sect permits the initiation of young children). The ceremony includes a symbolic removal of hair (via the traditional method of being pulled out tuft by tuft) and presentation to the initiate of the whisk and other implements of the ascetic life, such as the alms bowl for Shvetambaras. *Diksha* is overseen by a teacher, who typically continues to provide guidance to the new ascetic. The ritual marks the symbolic rupturing of the participant's past and future lifestyles, usually involving total separation from one's family, although Shvetambara nuns are on occasion allowed to interact with family members.

Ascetics depend on the almsgiving of the Jain laity, and sometimes of Hindus, in order to eat. Usually wandering in groups, they spend eight months of the year traversing the land, and then four months, during the rainy season, with lay communities. By remaining settled during this wet period, the ascetics do not jeopardize the well-being of life forms, which tend to be on the roads in greater numbers because of the rains. So, once again, the principle of *ahimsa* underlies Jain practice.

The Five Great Vows All ascetics commit to five "Great Vows" that serve as the doctrinal groundwork of both their inner purity of intention and their outer purity of action:

1. Avoid inflicting violence (*ahimsa*) on other life forms.
2. Abstain from lying.
3. Do not take what has not been given.
4. Renounce sexual activity.
5. Renounce possessions.

Jain texts expand on these vows in great detail, elaborating on the subtleties of their content and means of satisfactorily fulfilling them. As you might expect, most attention is devoted to the first vow, as *ahimsa* is understood to be the foundation of the entire ethical outlook of Jainism. Each of the other four vows is interrelated to *ahimsa*. For example, the third vow (not to take what is not given) is interpreted to mean, in its most profound sense, not to take a life. The fifth vow is understood also to imply avoidance of violence, for to renounce possessions is to deflect the passion that arises through attachments to them. Passion is thought to be a primary cause of violence.

Ascetic Practices   The basic impulse toward asceticism, so pervasive throughout the history of Jainism, is grounded in two objectives: the avoidance of further dirtying of the *jiva* with karmic matter and the eventual burning off of the matter that has already tainted it. Specific practices are prescribed in Jain texts, notably the Six Obligatory Duties, which for the Shvetambara sect are enumerated as follows (the Digambara list differs only slightly):

1. Equanimity, achieved through meditation
2. Praise of the *tirthankaras*
3. Veneration of teachers
4. Repentance
5. Laying down the body (standing or sitting motionless for varying periods of time)
6. Abandonment (renunciation of specific foods or activities for a certain period of time)

The Six Obligatory Duties are to be performed by all ascetics and, ideally, by laypeople as well. Specifics of each duty are developed in the texts. The duty of repentance, for example, involves acknowledging wrongdoings before one's teacher twice daily and ends with the recitation of a passage well known to Jains: "I ask pardon from all living creatures. May all creatures pardon me. May I have friendship for all creatures and enmity towards none."[6]

Perhaps the most startling Jain ascetic practice in the view of outsiders is *sallekhana*, the intentional fasting of oneself to death. Although this practice was quite common in earlier times and is believed to have been the form of dying adopted by Mahavira and other great ascetics of the past, today it is rare. Insistent that *sallekhana* is in no way suicidal, Jains argue that, because the act of eating generally involves the risk of harming other life forms, fasting even to the point of ending one's own life is a highly effective means of warding off karma. In general, an individual's mindset at the moment of death is considered to be a significant factor for the prospects of rebirth, and so *sallekhana*, lacking the passion and violence that regularly accompanies suicide and instead fostering a tranquil and meditative state, is thought to provide an ideal means of dying.

Jain laypeople look to monks and nuns as exemplars of Jain ideals. What similar sorts of exemplars are present in other religions?

Jainism and Women

We have observed that among Jain ascetics the places and roles of women and men vary considerably. The relatively conservative Digambaras allow only monks, not nuns, to go about naked, and they deny that women can attain *kevala*. They, unlike the Shvetambaras, also insist that the nineteenth *tirthankara* was a man. In general, there tend to be fewer distinctions between monks and nuns among Shvetambara Jains. The Sthanakvasi subsect, in which nuns outnumber monks by about five to one, can be said to be relatively liberal, even among Shvetambaras. One Sthanakvasi group has recently taken the unprecedented step of promoting a nun, Candanājī, to the rank of *ācārya*.

The long history of Jainism reveals some diversity with regard to the places and roles of women and men. One ancient text states that the original group of Mahavira's followers, both the laity and the ascetics, was composed mostly of women. It also states that during Mahavira's lifetime 1,400 women, as opposed to 700 men, attained *kevala*.[7]

For most of Jain history, however, women have tended to be regarded as less spiritually capable than men, even among the Shvetambaras. Recently, attitudes have begun to shift. For example, the long-standing assumption that women are prone to lead men away from virtuous lives by tempting them and arousing passions has gradually subsided. Today, the moral fortitude of the chaste Jain woman provides a role model for the proper behavior of women and men alike.

It almost goes without saying that Jain laywomen occupy vital roles within the family and community, roles that, especially until recently, have tended to differ from those of men, but that have been vital nonetheless. In the chapter's opening vignette we entered the home of the Chandras and observed the ritual of giving known as *dana*. It is difficult to imagine such a scene without the presence of the wife, who takes a leading role in managing the household affairs and raising the children. The fact that women tend to be less involved than men in business and other professional concerns means that they tend to have more time and energy to devote to the important lay religious practice of fasting.

The Dilwara Temple on Mount Abu in the state of Rajasthan is famous for its exquisite, delicate carvings and architectural design.

The Religious Life of the Jain Laity

Although Jainism is best known for its asceticism, a balanced understanding of the religion demands a careful look at the role of the laity. For one thing, lay adherents constitute the great majority of Jains. Also, even as the laity looks to the monks and nuns as exemplars of Jain ideals, the ascetics themselves depend on the lay community for their livelihood and support. These two components, in other words, function hand in hand. The worship activities of the Jain laity are rich and diverse and have for centuries been a vital part of the religious life of India.

Jain worship occurs on two separate levels. At the more mundane level, the objects of worship are various gods who, as we have noted, tend to be the same as those worshipped by Hindus. While having nothing to do with the ultimate religious pursuit of liberation, the gods are believed to respond to material needs, such as providing weather favorable for agriculture and cures for health maladies.

On a more sublime level, Jains worship the *tirthankaras*—even though they, like the gods, are unable actively to assist a worshipper in achieving salvation. Nevertheless, worship of the *tirthankaras* nurtures a properly devout religious attitude; its net effect is to burn off the dirtying karma that weighs down the soul. It is this second level of worship that warrants our consideration here.

Religious Places In its most visible form, Jain worship concentrates on images of the *tirthankaras*, although, as we have observed, the Sthanakvasis and Terapanthis shun this. Most of this worship takes place in temples, some of which rank among India's most impressive architectural achievements. For example, the Dharna Vihara at Ranakpur in the state of Rajasthan, which is dedicated to the *tirthankara* Rishabha, is remarkable for its unique four-directional design, four-faced image of the *tirthankara*, and 1,400 carved columns. Along with such spectacular temples as the Dharna Vihara, many temples coexist with shops and offices on city streets, indistinguishable from the neighboring buildings.

Jain sacred places also include various sites in the countryside, such as Mount Shatrunjaya in Gujarat in western India, one of five sacred mountains for Shvetambara Jains. Hundreds of shrines are located at Mount Shatrunjaya, and one textual tradition predicts that nineteen future *tirthankaras* will spend time preaching there.

Pilgrimages to places like Mount Shatrunjaya constitute an important aspect of lay worship. In fact, every Jain strives to make at least one pilgrimage in his or her lifetime. Typically undertaken at considerable expense, the pilgrimage offers each lay individual an opportunity to experience, through the interruption of normal life and the rigors of journeying to the site, an ascetic lifestyle for a temporary period. This experience allows for the concentration of effort in gaining karmic merit. Traditionally, pilgrimages were made on foot, and this is still the mode of transportation for ascetics. Today, laypeople often travel by train or other modern means. Sometimes the expenses for entire groups of pilgrims are paid for by one person, who is thought to gain much karmic merit through the act of benevolence.

Shatrunjaya, a hill near the town of Palitana, India, and for centuries an important Jain pilgrimage site, features 863 temples of various sizes and styles.

Rituals and Observances In addition to the relatively rigorous periods of pilgrimage, the religious life of the Jain laity overlaps with that of the ascetics in some everyday aspects. All Jains are careful with regard to their eating habits. They are diligently vegetarian, and go well beyond abstaining from meat by avoiding such things as eggs, vegetables, and fruits with a large number of seeds in order not to destroy life forms unnecessarily. Fasting, a very common practice among ascetics, also is quite common among the laity, especially, as we have seen, among women.

These similarities notwithstanding, it is easy to observe that in almost every way, the ascetics' religious life demands significantly more by way of exertion and endurance of physical hardships than does the religious life of most laypeople, who strive mainly to behave morally in order to ebb the flow of harmful karma and thus to foster a good rebirth. As we observed at the outset of this chapter, the ritual of *dana* (the giving of food to monks and nuns) provides one opportunity to be a good Jain layperson and to enhance one's karmic status. A somewhat similar practice involves bidding for the right to sponsor rituals, with any extra money being donated to charitable causes and the winning bidder gaining in social esteem. Whenever a new image of a *tirthankara* is erected or installed in a temple, for example, rituals are performed to celebrate each of the "five auspicious events" of a *tirthankara's* life: conception, birth, renunciation, attainment of *kevala*, and *moksha*. The person who sponsors the building of such an image and funds the rituals is said to acquire very positive karmic merit, so that the person likely will be born into a world blessed with a living *tirthankara*.[8]

A formalized system of religious observance features the Twelve Vows for the layperson. The first of the Vows, for instance, makes clear that it is the intentionality, rather than specific action, that most matters with regard to *ahimsa*. Proper intentionality is involved, for example, in choosing the right profession, one that would not likely result in violence toward sentient life forms. As a result, Jains through the centuries have tended to engage in trade and other forms of business. Obviously harmful occupations such as hunting and fishing are strictly prohibited; farming is acceptable because it can be done without *intentionally* harming life forms. Trade and business, however, are generally considered optimal because they can be done without causing any harm at all.

CONCLUSION

In this chapter, we have learned about Jainism's teachings, historical development, and way of life. One of the world's oldest traditions, Jainism today remains relatively small, with only about 5.6 million adherents, and also relatively confined to its place of origin, with the great majority of Jains living in India. This tendency for the tradition to maintain itself demographically and geographically is natural for Jains, who do not actively seek converts to Jainism and, even when living outside of India, tend to maintain strong ties to the motherland.

Like every religion in the world today, however, Jainism has become diverse, as indicated by the differences between the sects. Some aspects of the religion are more adaptable to modernization, pluralism, and other contemporary forces, and some are less adaptable. In this regard, Jainism as a whole can perhaps best be summed up as a tradition that is both eternally constant and constantly evolving. At one extreme, a group of monks and nuns wandering the countryside, sweeping ahead of their bare feet with their whisks, hardly fit into the picture of the modern world. Paradoxically, these same ascetics carry on a tradition of cosmology that appears remarkably modern relative to most traditionally religious points of view. Moreover, the social consciousness of Jains—expressed in their advocacy of vegetarianism and other forms of nonviolence—is in step with many who are concerned over the state of the world, the environment, and humanity's plight.

SEEKING ANSWERS

What Is Ultimate Reality?

Like Hinduism and Buddhism, Jainism maintains belief in *samsara*, the wheel of life. Time is conceived of as being cyclical, such that this world is but one in an eternal sequence of worlds that have come to be. The Jain perspective on space features the *loka*, a vast expanse that includes three realms inhabited by human beings. Jainism does not emphasize the importance of deities, even to the point of appearing atheistic; it can be considered a *transtheistic* religion. Souls (*jivas*) and matter (*ajiva*) are believed to exist eternally. Ultimate reality for Jainism might best be identified as *kevala*, the supreme state in which the eternal soul is perfectly pure.

How Should We Live in This World?

Jainism bases its ethical teachings on the principle of *ahimsa* (nonviolence) and on the accompanying value of asceticism. Both are exemplified by Mahavira and the other *tirthankaras*, and Jain monks and nuns continue to act as exemplars. Jainism understands human beings—like every other sentient being—to be made up of a soul (*jiva*) combined with bodily matter (*ajiva*). This matter is believed to contaminate the soul and thus to weigh it down and to prevent it from attaining spiritual perfection. Jains explain this through their doctrine of karma, understanding the term in its literal sense as "action."

What Is Our Ultimate Purpose?

Jains believe that eventually every soul will become perfectly pure, allowing it to rise to the top of the *loka* in the transcendent state of *kevala*, the Jain equivalent of Buddhist nirvana or Hindu *moksha*. Jains also believe that the soul that does not experience *kevala* is destined for rebirth, which is understood to occur immediately after death and is determined by the adequacy of one's spiritual and moral life in this world. Death, then, does not "end it," and mortality for Jains involves the prospect of a good rebirth.

REVIEW QUESTIONS

For Review

1. What is the role of Mahavira as one of Jainism's *tirthankaras*?
2. How do Jain practices of asceticism promote the cause of *ahimsa*?
3. What is the *loka*?
4. Identify and briefly describe the various Jain sects.
5. Differentiate the main religious duties of the Jain laity from those of the ascetics, and explain what religious advantages a monk or nun might have over members of the laity.

For Further Reflection

1. Compare the biographies of Nataputta Vardhamana (Mahavira) and Siddhartha Gautama (the Buddha), focusing especially on the episodes of attaining enlightenment.
2. What is the relationship between Jain cosmology and the Jain perspective on spiritual liberation? Consider especially the classification of reality into *ajiva* and *jiva* and how this relates to the quest for spiritual liberation.
3. What is *kevala*? How does it compare to Buddhist *nirvana*? To Hindu *moksha*?

GLOSSARY

ahimsa (ah-him'suh; Sanskrit, "nonviolence," "not desiring to harm") Both the avoidance of violence toward other life forms and an active sense of compassion toward them; a basic principle of Jainism, Hinduism, and Buddhism.

ajiva (uh-jee'vuh; Sanskrit, "nonsoul") Nonliving components of the Jain universe: space, time, motion, rest, and all forms of matter.

dana (dah'nuh; Sanskrit, Pali, "giving") Ritual of giving.

Digambara (dig-ahm'buh-ruh; Sanskrit, "those whose garment is the sky") The second largest Jain sect, whose monks go about naked so as to help abolish any ties to society; generally more conservative than the Shvetambara sect.

jina (ji'nuh; Sanskrit, "conqueror") Jain title for one who has "conquered" *samsara;* synonymous with *tirthankara*.

jiva (jee'vuh; Sanskrit, "soul") The finite and eternal soul; also the category of living, as opposed to nonliving, entities of the universe.

karma (Sanskrit, "action") "Action" and the consequences of action; determines the nature of one's reincarnation; in Jainism, all activity is believed to involve various forms of matter that weigh down the soul (*jiva*) and thus hinder the quest for liberation.

kevala (kay'vuh-luh; shortened form of Sanskrit *kevalajnana*, "isolated knowledge" or "absolute knowledge") The perfect and complete knowledge or omniscience that is Jain enlightenment; marks the point at which one is free from the damaging effects of karma and is liberated from *samsara*.

loka (loh'kah; Sanskrit, "world") The Jain universe, often depicted as having the shape of a giant man.

Shvetambara (shvayt-ahm'buh-ruh; Sanskrit, "those whose garment is white") The largest Jain sect, whose monks and nuns wear white robes; generally more liberal than the Digambara sect.

tirthankaras (teert-hahn'kuhr-uhs; Sanskrit, "makers of the river crossing") The Jain spiritual heroes, such as Parshva and Mahavira, who have shown the way to salvation; synonymous with *jinas*.

SUGGESTIONS FOR FURTHER READING

Dundas, Paul. *The Jains*. 2nd ed. London: Routledge, 2002. A thorough and scholarly study that has become a standard reference work for students and academics alike.

Jain, Satish Kumar, and Kamal Chand Sogani, eds. *Perspectives in Jaina Philosophy and Culture*. New Delhi: Ahimsa International, 1985. Helpful insights from within the Jain tradition.

Jaini, Padmanabh S. *The Jaini Path of Purification*. 2nd ed. Columbia, MO: South Asia Books, 2001. The first comprehensive work in English that offers a sympathetic study of the religion, this modern-day classic has been revised and updated.

Lopez, Donald S. Jr., ed. *Religions of India in Practice*. Princeton, NJ: Princeton University Press, 1995. Offering some translations for the first time, this anthology presents a wide range of texts well beyond the usual collections of sacred writings.

Radhakrishnan, Sarvepalli, and Charles A. Moore, eds. *A Sourcebook in Indian Philosophy*. Princeton, NJ: Princeton University Press, 1957. A standard anthology of sacred texts in English translations.

ONLINE RESOURCES

The Wabash Center

wabashcenter.wabash.edu/resources

The Wabash Center, a trusted resource for all aspects of the academic study of religion, offers links to a wide variety of dependable Internet resources on Jainism.

The Jaina

jaina.org

The Jaina (Federation of Jain Associations in North America) website is especially useful for studies of Jainism in North America.

SIKHISM

MANJIT KAUR, a sixteen-year-old girl, and Sandeep Singh, a fourteen-year-old boy, stand in the **gurdwara**, the place of Sikh worship, in their small village in northwestern India. Here in the region known as the Punjab, Sikhism's ancestral homeland, Manjit and Sandeep are members of the majority religion, and *gurdwaras* are common sights in the farming villages that dot the land. Most of the village has gathered together to witness the proceedings, and Sandeep and Manjit have spent the morning preparing for this momentous event—their initiation into the Sikh **Khalsa**, or community of "Pure Ones." They have both bathed and washed their long hair carefully and have dressed especially for the occasion. Most notably, they both don the five articles of faith, known as the Five Ks: uncut hair, a comb, a steel wristlet, a short sword, and a pair of shorts.

Manjit and Sandeep join a group of five older villagers who also don the Five Ks and who for this ceremony play the part of the *Panj Piare*, or "Beloved Five." They are established members of the Khalsa and will oversee the initiation. The grouping of five recalls the founding of the Khalsa centuries ago, when Guru Gobind Singh (1675–1708 C.E.), the tenth in a line of Gurus going back to Guru Nanak (1469–1539 C.E.), chose five original initiates who had distinguished themselves for their loyalty to the Guru and for their commitment to Sikh ideals. On this day of *Amrit Sanchar*, the Khalsa initiation ceremony, the stirring memory of

The five Sikh men who participate in the *Amrit Sanchar* represent the original "Beloved Five" in commemoration of the founding of the Khalsa.

these founding figures and the ideals they embody is palpably felt. But the most vital presence of all is a large book, lying open on a special platform. It is Sri Guru Granth Sahib, or the **Adi Granth**, the sacred scripture of Sikhism, and the Sikhs' **Guru**, or spiritual teacher, from the time of Guru Gobind Singh forward.

Sandeep and Manjit stand before the *Panj Piare*, one of whom explains the basic principles of Sikhism. They agree to accept these principles by nodding, the ritual action that makes the initiation official. The new members of the Khalsa are then served **amrit** ("immortalizing fluid"), a special drink made from water and sugar crystals, which has been mixed by the *Panj Piare* in an iron bowl and stirred with a two-edged sword. Meanwhile, hymns from the Adi Granth are sung by the congregation. The *amrit* is drunk and sprinkled on the eyes and heads of the initiates, who recite the **Mul Mantra**, the summary of Sikh doctrine that comprises the opening lines of the Adi Granth. The *Panj Piare* then instruct Manjit and Sandeep about the ethical requirements of the Khalsa. These include prohibitions against the cutting of one's hair, the eating of meat that has been improperly slaughtered, extramarital sexual relations, and the use of tobacco. The initiates are also told that all Sikhs are brothers and sisters and that there should not be any distinctions made on the basis of caste.

Significant sites in the history of Sikhism.

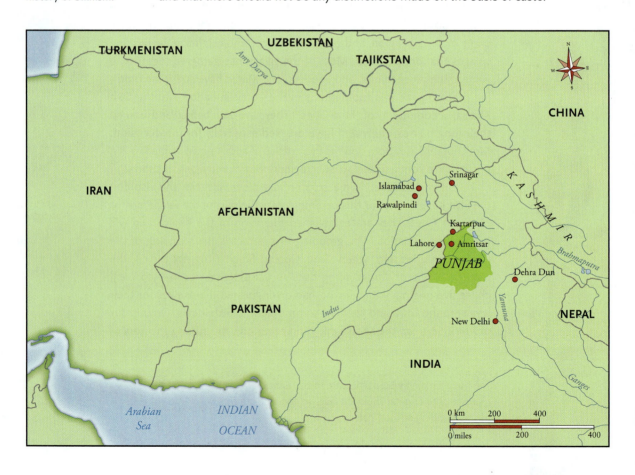

Manjit and Sandeep are among a minority of Sikhs, approximately 15 percent, who undergo the traditional ceremony of initiation into the Khalsa. Some 70 percent of the approximately 25 million Sikhs in the world,[1] however, are popularly considered to be members of the Khalsa, insofar as they observe the Five Ks, or at least the one that is generally deemed most important: not cutting one's hair.[2] And regardless of percentages or degrees of membership, the traditional ways of the Khalsa greatly influence the practices and customs of the entire **Panth**, or Sikh community. We can thus glimpse in this ceremony, with its powerful ties to tradition and its rich symbolism, key aspects that are at the heart of Sikhism. ☀

TIMELINE
Sikhism

1469 C.E. Birth of Guru Nanak, founder of Sikhism.

1520s Establishment by Guru Nanak of the township of Kartarpur, the first Sikh community.

1539 Death of Guru Nanak.

1606 Death (execution?) of Guru Arjan, under Mughal emperor Jahangir.

1675 Execution of Guru Tegh Bahadur, under Mughal emperor Aurangzeb.

1699 Founding of the Khalsa by Guru Gobind Singh.

1708 Death of Guru Gobind Singh and establishment of the Adi Granth as Guru.

1799 Establishment of independent Sikh kingdom by Ranjit Singh.

1849 Annexation of Sikh kingdom by the British.

1947 Partition of Punjab with the establishment of India's independence.

1984 Indian army attacks and occupies Sikh holy sites, including the Darbar Sahib (or Golden Temple).

1999 The Panth celebrates the third centennial of the establishment of the Khalsa.

2004 Manmohan Singh elected prime minister of India, the first Sikh to attain this office.

I n this chapter we shall study these and other key aspects, attending in turn to the founding of Sikhism and its primary doctrines, its historical development, and its most prevalent rituals and worship practices. By virtue of its size alone, Sikhism is among the major religions of the world. Theologically, Sikhism's intermixing of concepts that are common to some Hindu traditions on one hand and to Islam on the other make it a very interesting subject for the comparative study of religion. And with nearly 2 million Sikhs living outside of India, and Sikh communities being found today in most of the large cities of the West, Sikhism clearly is a global tradition that has a significant impact on the world.

THE TEACHINGS OF SIKHISM

The term *Sikh* is derived from an ancient Sanskrit term that means "disciple." Sikhs are thus disciples, specifically of the ten Gurus, beginning with Guru Nanak and ending with Guru Gobind Singh, founder of the Khalsa. Since then, Sikhs have been disciples of Sri Guru Granth Sahib, the traditional name for their most important sacred text, the Adi Granth. A sound understanding of Sikhism therefore must begin with a consideration of the origins of this line of Gurus.

By the time Guru Nanak had come on the scene, the important role of the guru had long been established within Hindu traditions of northern India. A guru is a spiritual teacher. *Guru* is actually used in three slightly different ways in Sikhism. Along with being the title of Guru Nanak and his successors and of the sacred text (Sri Guru Granth Sahib), it is used as a name for God. (In fact, *Vahiguru*, "Praise to the Guru," is the most common name for God used by Sikhs today.) In each case the guru functions as the teacher of God's will. As Sikhs believe that God lovingly reveals the divine will to humans, God, too, thus functions as Guru.

We now consider the career of the guru of northern India whose extraordinary life experiences and bold spiritual leadership were to have such a profound impact that a new religion would arise.

The Life of Guru Nanak

Nanak was born in 1469 C.E. in the small village of Talvandi (modern-day Nankan Sahib, located near Lahore, Pakistan). He was born to Hindu parents of a mercantile caste who probably were worshippers of Vishnu (for more information about the caste system and the worship of Vishnu, see Chapter 4). His parents arranged for him to marry early, when he was still in his teens, as was customary at the time. Nanak and his wife, Sulakhani, moved to Sultanpur, where Nanak's older sister Nanaki lived. Soon Nanak and Sulakhani had two sons.

Sultanpur, located on the main rode between Lahore and Delhi, was a religiously diverse community, with residents and visitors who practiced varieties of Hinduism and Islam. Nanak, who is said to have been dissatisfied with traditional forms of religion, gravitated toward a religious outlook similar to Hindu *bhakti*, the path of devotion (see Chapter 4). Nanak believed in the oneness of God and in the need to move closer to God. This could best be accomplished, he believed, through meditation and singing hymns in praise of God. Eventually Nanak began composing his own hymns. With his friend Mardana, a Muslim musician, accompanying him on the *rebab* (a stringed instrument), Nanak sang his hymns at communal worship gatherings. These hymns are included in the Adi Granth and are sung in Sikh services today.

Sikhs pay homage to Guru Nanak, the founder of Sikhism, in a crowded room in Lahore, Pakistan.

According to tradition, Nanak became recognized as a spiritual leader early in his life. He would rise before dawn and bathe in the river, meditate, and then lead others in singing hymns of praise. When Nanak was about thirty years old, he underwent a crucial experience that led to the origin of the Sikh tradition.

Receiving God's Revelation One morning while Nanak was bathing in the river, he did not resurface from the water. He was presumed drowned, and yet his body was not found. Three days and three nights later, however, Nanak emerged from the river, and, returning to the village, he proclaimed: "There is neither Hindu nor Muslim so whose path shall I follow? I shall follow God's path. God is neither Hindu nor Muslim and the path which I follow is God's."[3]

When he explained what had happened, Nanak said that he had been escorted to the court of God, who gave him a cup of *amrit* (the same drink that is used in the Khalsa initiation ceremony) and said to him:

> This is the cup of the adoration of God's name. Drink it. I am with you. I bless you and raise you up. Whoever remembers you will enjoy my favor. Go, rejoice in my name and teach others to do so. I have bestowed the gift of my name upon you. Let this be your calling.[4]

The Journeys of Guru Nanak Deeply moved by this revelation, Guru Nanak spent the next stage of his life, from age thirty to about age fifty, traveling far and wide and learning about a variety of religious customs, including Hindu, Muslim, and Jain. He is said to have undertaken four long journeys: eastward to Assan; southward to Sri Lanka; northward to the Himalayas; and westward, reaching as far as Mecca and Baghdad. He visited holy sites and encountered a wide variety of religious people. He also proclaimed and practiced his own teachings, sometimes to hostile audiences.

Several incidents during Guru Nanak's travels illuminate the new message he proclaimed. On one occasion, while visiting a Hindu shrine in Haridwar, India, he found himself among *brahmins* throwing water toward the rising sun as an offering to their dead ancestors. Nanak turned and threw water the other way, explaining, "If you can send water to your dead ancestors in heaven, surely I can send it to my fields in the Punjab."[5] On another occasion, Nanak was awakened from sleep by an angry Muslim who chastised him for sleeping with his feet pointing toward the Ka'ba in Mecca, the most sacred site in Islam. (Showing the soles of one's feet is considered by many Muslims to be a grave insult.) Nanak responded: "Then turn my feet in some other direction where God does not exist."[6]

Such stories as these illustrate a general theme of Nanak's religious outlook. He consistently rejected traditional rituals and "proper" religious protocol, whether Hindu or Muslim.

Founding the Sikh Community Drawing from his revelation experience and years of journeying, Nanak continued proclaiming his own religious ideals, among them monotheism; lack of distinctions based on gender, caste, or creed (for example, whether Hindu or Muslim); and doing good deeds. Nanak attracted a large following. At about the age of fifty, he established a new settlement called Kartarpur ("abode of the creator") in what is now Pakistan. Here he and his followers formed the first Sikh community and instituted the lifestyle that has characterized Sikh society to this day.

Guru Nanak erected a special building, a *dharamsala* ("abode of faith"), for worship. In so doing, he provided the prototype of the *gurdwara*, which today is the central structure of any particular Sikh community. (The term *dharamsala* gradually was replaced in the eighteenth century with *gurdwara* to designate the Sikh place of worship.) Nanak welcomed people from all segments of society to reside in Kartarpur and to work together to maintain it. Nanak himself joined in the work, which was primarily agrarian. And though in most respects a regular member of the community, Nanak sat on a special seat when addressing the congregation. Followers recognized the nature of the Guru as merely human and yet also as very spiritually advanced.

On September 22, 1539, after leading the Kartarpur community for about twenty years, Guru Nanak died. According to the traditional account the Guru, aware of his approaching death, settled a dispute regarding the proper disposal of his body.

> Hindus and Muslims who had put their faith in the divine Name began to debate what should be done with the Guru's corpse. "We shall bury him," said the Muslims. "No, let us cremate his body," said the Hindus. "Place flowers on both sides of my body," said Baba Nanak, "flowers from the Hindus on the right side and flowers from the Muslims on the left. If tomorrow the Hindus' flowers are still fresh let my body be burned, and if the Muslims' flowers are still fresh let it be buried."
>
> Baba Nanak then commanded the congregation to sing. They sang *Kirtan Sohila* and *Arati*. . . . Baba Nanak then covered himself with a sheet and passed away. Those who had gathered around him prostrated themselves, and when the sheet was removed they found that there was nothing under it. The flowers on both sides remained fresh, and both Hindus and Muslims took their respective shares. All who were gathered there prostrated themselves again.[7]

Even with his death, Guru Nanak encouraged Hindus and Muslims to transcend their differences and to let peace prevail.

Guru Nanak's example powerfully informs the beliefs and practices of Sikhs up to the present day. We will next turn our attention briefly to Sikh scripture, the collection of texts that contains the doctrinal position as set forth by Guru Nanak and his successor Gurus.

Sikh Scripture

We have previously identified the Adi Granth, commonly known as Sri Guru Granth Sahib, as Sikhism's most important sacred text. This is without question true for all Sikhs today. There are, however, other texts that most Sikhs would classify as scripture, of which the most important are the Dasam Granth and the Rahit, both of which we consider here. In addition, works by two disciples of the Gurus are granted sufficient status to be recited in the *gurdwara:* Bhai Gurda (disciple of Guru Arjan and Guru Hargobind) and Nand Lal (disciple of Guru Gobind Singh). A collection of stories about the life of Guru Nanak, called the *Janam-sakhi*, also deserves mention. The account of Guru Nanak's death cited in the previous section is from the *Janam-sakhi*.

The Adi Granth   Compiled by Guru Arjan in 1603–1604, the Adi Granth contains the works of his four predecessors, along with his own hymns and various works by poets,

Compare Guru Nanak to founding figures of other religious traditions, with regard to establishing teachings and way of life and to the founding figure as a role model for others to follow.

such as Kabir (c. 1440–1518). Through the centuries, the Adi Granth has occupied a central place in Sikhism. Whereas the Gurus once sat on a special seat amid Sikh disciples, since the time of the tenth and last historical Guru, Gobind Singh, the Adi Granth has occupied the same type of seat in the middle of any place of worship. And whereas the Gurus were once the authorities on religious matters, now Sikhs consult the Adi Granth.

The name "Adi Granth" ("the Original Volume" or "the First Book") is standard among scholars. Sikhs commonly express their reverence for the scripture by referring to it as Sri Guru Granth Sahib (*sahib* is a title of respect). Every copy is identical in both script and page number; there are 1,430 pages in every copy. It was composed using the Gurmukhi script and a variety of languages that were used in northern India at the time, most prevalently Punjabi. It also contains some words in Arabic, Persian, Prakrit, and Sanskrit. All of these factors render the Adi Granth somewhat difficult to read, as well as difficult to translate. Today, however, English and French translations are available. Many Sikh families have at least a condensed version of the Adi Granth, containing all of the works used in daily prayers, including Guru Nanak's *Japji*, which is the only portion of the entire Adi Granth that is chanted, rather than sung. For Sikhs, the Adi Granth rings with brilliance when it is set to music and proclaimed in its original language. In the words of one commentator: "The poetic excellence, the spiritual content, and the haunting, lilting melodies of the hymns of the Adi Granth are Sikhism's greatest attraction to this day."[8]

A Sikh reads from Sri Guru Granth Sahib, here occupying its customary place on a cushion within a *gurdwara*.

The Dasam Granth The composition of the Dasam Granth ("Volume of the Tenth Master") has been traditionally attributed to Guru Gobind Singh, although many Sikhs today regard only some parts to have been authored by the Guru. The first compilation of works into the Dasam Granth is thought to have taken place in 1734 (twenty-six years after the death of Guru Gobind Singh), although in the ensuing decades variant versions appeared. In 1902, the version that is used today was officially authorized.

During the eighteenth century, the Dasam Granth was considered to be Guru alongside the Adi Granth. Today, however, only one group of Sikhs, the Nihangs, bestow equal honor on the Dasam Granth. Nevertheless, the sections of the text that all Sikhs attribute to Guru Gobind Singh can safely be categorized as Sikh scripture. These sections include the well-known *Jap Sahib* and the *Ten Savayyas;* both are recited daily in morning prayers.

The Rahit In the chapter's opening, we observed that the *Amrit Sanchar*, the Khalsa initiation ceremony, is undertaken only by a minority of Sikhs, even though the Khalsa continues to exemplify the ideals of Sikhism. These ideals are spelled out in written form in *rahit-namas*, texts composed over the centuries and collectively referred to as the **Rahit**. Traditionally, the contents of the Rahit are believed to stem from the teachings of Guru Gobind Singh himself. In both this section on Sikh doctrinal teachings and the following section on Sikh religious life, we shall draw frequently from the contents of the Rahit.

On God, the Human Condition, and Spiritual Liberation

More than anything else, Sikhism is a religious path to spiritual liberation through devotional praise of God, most especially by way of meditation on the divine Name. This meditation is often done through prayerful recitation of sacred words. In this section, we take up in more detail three main aspects of Sikh teachings that will shed light on this religious path: the nature of God and the "divine Name"; the nature of the human condition and its need, through the aid of the Guru, to move from darkness to enlightenment; and the nature of liberation, which is release from *samsara*, the cycle of death and rebirth.

Sikhism teaches that the ultimate purpose of life is to attain ***mukti*** (spiritual liberation). This liberation is similar to Hindu *moksha*, "release" from *samsara*, the cycle of death and rebirth (a concept Sikhism also adopted from Hinduism). This release is believed to bring about an experience of being in the presence of God, a state of eternal bliss.

God: Formless One, Creator, True Guru   Guru Nanak's understanding of the nature of God is the center from which all Sikh teachings emerge. It is fitting that the Adi Granth begins with a concise summary of Sikh theology. This summary is known as the *Mul Mantra*, the passage recited by initiates to the Khalsa (as we noted in the beginning of the chapter) and by most Sikhs daily as part of their morning prayers.

> There is one Supreme Being, the Eternal Reality, the Creator, without fear and
>   devoid of enmity, immortal, never incarnated, self-existent, known by grace
>   through the Guru.
> The Eternal One, from the beginning, through all time, present now, the
>   Everlasting Reality.[9]

As this description suggests, Sikhism is similar theologically to the monotheistic religions Zoroastrianism, Judaism, Christianity, and Islam. God is one, eternal, self-existent, and "Creator." The Punjabi term that the Gurus used for God is *Akal Purakh*, "The One Beyond Time." Guru Nanak sometimes used the name *Nirankar*, "Without Form." For Sikhs, then, God is without form and beyond all attributes that humans use to describe reality. God is without gender and is referred to as "he" in Sikhism only begrudgingly and when grammatically necessary because of the limitations of language; there is no neuter pronoun in Punjabi. Sikhs actively strive to avoid assigning such human attributes to God.

For reasons beyond the grasp of human comprehension, God decided to create the world and all that is in it, including human beings. Akal Purakh (we'll use this traditional name, although modern Sikhs commonly refer to God as *Vahiguru*, "Praise to the Guru"), in addition to being the Creator, is also the Preserver and the Destroyer. Sikhism here draws from the important Hindu triad of gods and their respective functions: Brahma (Creator), Vishnu (Preserver), and Shiva (Destroyer). All Sikhs, though, insist that their God is one. These three functions are thus different aspects of the one God. For Hindu *Vaishnavas*, Vishnu similarly incorporates all three functions within his own being (Chapter 4, p. 112).

In God's primary state, to which Guru Nanak referred when he used the name *Nirankar* ("Without Form"), God is distinct from his creation in much the same way that an artist remains distinct from her or his artwork. And yet God dwells within creation—within nature and within human beings. God is thus said to be immanent, or indwelling (as opposed to transcendent, or beyond creation). In this state of immanence, Akal Purakh is personal and approachable through loving devotion. Because of God's immanence in creation, it is possible for humans to make contact with God and to come to know God. To extend our analogy, one can know something of an artist by seeing the artist's works. So too can one come to know Akal Purakh through experiencing God's creation. Indeed, part of the ongoing purpose of creation is that God, through loving grace, might reveal the divine self to human beings. It is in this capacity that God is referred to as Guru, for in this manner God delivers humans from darkness to enlightenment.

The Human Condition: Self-Centered and Bound to *Samsara*

Human beings are especially near to Akal Purakh. Though Sikhism advocates kindness to living things, it also holds that other creatures are here to provide for us. (Unlike most Hindus and all Jains, therefore, Sikhs are not opposed to eating meat—although vegetarianism is the preference of many.) More importantly, Akal Purakh is believed to dwell within all human beings and is actively concerned about their spiritual welfare. Humans, however, tend to neglect the need to center their lives on God.

Rather than being God-centered, humans are inclined to be self-centered and to depend on the powers of the mind. The Sikh term for this self-centeredness is **haumai**, which causes one to resist submitting to Akal Purakh. When life is dominated by *haumai*, its five accompanying vices—lust, anger, greed, attachment, and pride—tend to run rampant. *Haumai* and its vices increase the distance between the person and God and at the same time cause attachment to the charms of the world.

As long as *haumai* and its accompanying vices persist, humans are destined to remain in *samsara*, the ongoing cycle of death and rebirth.

Spiritual Liberation through Union with God

The quest for spiritual liberation is a constant struggle between *haumai*, the self-centeredness to which humans are naturally inclined, and the call to live in accordance with the will of God. Akal Purakh plays an essential role in determining the outcome of this struggle. God is immanent in creation through *hukam*, the divine order. It is through *hukam* that Akal Purakh asserts the divine will and communicates truth. Through Akal Purakh's grace, humans acquire the potential for perceiving this truth, and therefore for perceiving God. In the words of the *Mul Mantra* cited earlier, Akal Purakh is "known by grace through the Guru"—the Guru being either one of the historical Gurus or Sri Guru Granth Sahib. (Because the *Mul Mantra* was composed by Guru Nanak, we can assume that the original meaning was the historical Guru.) Through humbling oneself, thus denying the normally dominating powers of *haumai*, a person is opened to the power of God's grace. Having received God's grace, the task is to respond in loving devotion through meditation on the nature of God. The term most often used in the Adi Granth to denote the nature of God is *nam*, the "divine Name." Meditation on the *nam* or recitation of the *nam* is prescribed repeatedly as the path to spiritual liberation. A chapter of the *Japji* sets forth these points:

> The Eternal One whose Name is Truth speaks to us in infinite love. Insistently we beg for the gifts which are by grace bestowed. What can we offer in return for all this goodness? What gift will gain entrance to the hallowed Court? What words can we utter to attract this love? At the ambrosial hour of fragrant dawn meditate on the grandeur of the one true Name. Past actions determine the nature of our birth, but grace alone reveals the door to liberation. See the Divine Spirit, Nanak, dwelling immanent in all. Know the Divine Spirit as the One, the eternal, the changeless Truth.[10]

The significance of the *nam* for Guru Nanak, and thus for the entire Sikh tradition, can hardly be overstated. In the words of one modern commentator, "Anything that may be affirmed concerning Akal Purakh constitutes an aspect of the divine Name, and a sufficient understanding of the divine Name provides the essential means to deliverance."[11]

Mukti, spiritual liberation, brings about the eternal, infinitely blissful state of being in the presence of God. It should be noted that Sikhism's doctrine of spiritual liberation is not dependent in any way on one's caste status or gender. Also, the focus is on inward meditation and piety, rather than on outward forms of worship, such as festivals or pilgrimages—although Sikhism is not entirely without such forms of worship, as we shall consider shortly. But before we move on from this section on Sikh teachings, we next consider elements introduced with the foundation in 1699 of the Khalsa, the community of "Pure Ones," and take up the crucial question of the relationship of the Khalsa to the Panth or Sikh community at large.

Teachings of Guru Gobind Singh and the Khalsa

The teachings that Guru Gobind Singh proclaimed to the *Panj Piare*, the "Beloved Five" who became the first initiates into the Khalsa, are believed by Sikhs to make up the Rahit, the regulatory code that spells out correct belief and behavior for members of the Khalsa.

The Rahit contains vital teachings pertaining to the religious life. As we observed in the opening of the chapter, Manjit and Sandeep, as part of their initiation into the Khalsa, were taught certain norms of behavior, all of which are contained in the Rahit. Among the teachings are four cardinal prohibitions (*kurahit*): cutting one's hair, eating meat that has been improperly slaughtered (specifically, slaughtered according to Muslim regulations), engaging in extramarital sex, and using tobacco. Along with these and other prohibitions, the Rahit also sets forth requirements, including the requirement to don the Five Ks, so named because all five of the items begin in Punjabi with the letter "k." The Five Ks are:

- *Kes*, uncut hair, symbolizing Sikh belief that one should not interfere with natural, God-given form
- *Kangha*, a small comb worn in the hair, a reminder of cleanliness
- *Karā*, a steel wristlet, affirming constant connectedness with God
- *Kirpan*, a sword, a sign of devotion to truth and to the defense of just causes
- *Kachh*, a pair of shorts tied with a drawstring, symbolizing chastity.

To some extent, both the meaning and the practical implications of the Five Ks have varied somewhat through the centuries. At the time of the founding of the Khalsa, for example, the wearing of a sword would have suggested true preparedness to fight. Today, the *kirpan* is usually only five to eight inches long and often is concealed underneath clothing in order not to appear threatening.

Study of Sikh teachings has led us naturally to a consideration of some historical aspects of the Sikh tradition. In the next section, we take up in more detail significant events from the time of Guru Nanak to the present.

Gurbaj Singh Multani (right) wears a ceremonial dagger, known as a *kirpan*, after a news conference on Parliament Hill in Ottawa on March 2, 2006. Multiculturalism and religious freedom trumped safety concerns in a Canadian Supreme Court decision that allows orthodox Sikh students to carry traditional daggers to school.

THE HISTORY OF SIKHISM

Guru Nanak has remained the most prominent and revered of the ten Gurus of the Sikhs. Yet his nine successors contributed significantly to the development of the religion. Young Sikhs like Manjit and Sandeep learn about all of them as a natural part of their upbringing, celebrating their heroic life stories.

Guru Nanak's Successors

All ten Gurus are considered to have been revealers of truth and to have been linked to one another through sharing the same divine essence. This made them spiritually more adept than ordinary people. They were not, however, thought to be divine incarnations

THE TEN GURUS

The guruship of each begins with the death of his predecessor.

1. Guru Nanak (1469–1539)
2. Guru Angad (1504–1552)
3. Guru Amar Das (1479–1574)
4. Guru Ram Das (1534–1581)
5. Guru Arjan (1563–1606)
6. Guru Hargobind (1595–1644)
7. Guru Hari Rai (1630–1661)
8. Guru Hari Krishan (1656–1664)
9. Guru Tegh Bahadur (1621–1675)
10. Guru Gobind Singh (1666–1708)

of God. The Gurus thus are not to be worshipped by Sikhs, though they are greatly revered. Guru Nanak constantly stressed his human limitations, humbly referring to himself as God's slave. All the Gurus were highly prestigious persons. They were revered for their spiritual gifts and acquired much worldly prestige as well. The Mughal (therefore, Muslim) emperors who ruled northern India knew the Gurus personally and tended to respect them, in some cases developing strong friendships with them.

Nanak's successors are responsible for a wide variety of impressive accomplishments that gradually transformed the Sikh community. Arjan, the Fifth Guru (from 1581 to 1606), deserves special mention. For one thing, he compiled the scripture that would come to be known as the Adi Granth ("the Original Volume," distinguishing it from the later Dasam Granth), thus giving the Sikhs their most important sacred scripture. He included, by traditional count, 2,312 of his own compositions, beautifully melodic hymns that are considered to be among Sikhism's most impressive musical accomplishments. Arjan also constructed at the city of Amritsar the Hari Mandar ("Temple of God"), now called Darbar Sahib ("Court of the Lord") or the Golden Temple. This provided the Sikhs with a geographical center.

The Darbar Sahib remains one of the world's most impressive and important religious buildings. Along with being architecturally magnificent, it is rich in symbolic meaning, beginning with the building process itself. At Arjan's invitation, Mian Mir, a Muslim Sufi saint, laid the foundation stone. Even as the Sikh community was gaining independence from its Muslim and Hindu neighbors, Sikhism served as a bridge between religions. In contrast to Hindu temples, which typically have only one door, Arjan designed the Darbar Sahib with four doors. Traditionally this is interpreted as representing Sikhism's openness to all people—to adherents of all four of northwestern

India's major religious traditions of the time (Hinduism, Islam, Buddhism, and Sikhism); to people of all four classes of the prevalent Hindu caste system; and to people of the north, south, east, and west. In light of this, it is ironic that, in recent times, the Darbar Sahib has become associated with controversy and discord, having been the site of the bloody military action in 1984 known as Operation Blue Star, which we shall consider in more detail below.

Guru Gobind Singh and the Khalsa

The tenth Guru, Gobind Singh (1666–1708), is revered as the greatest Guru after Nanak. His strength of character and spiritual adeptness made him a successful and memorable leader. By the time he became Guru at the age of nine, he had already begun training in the art of warfare and hunting, along with the ways of religion. A modern history of the Sikhs makes note of the enduring impression made by the Guru's appearance:

> Every description of Guru Gobind Singh's person delineates him as a very handsome, sharp-featured, tall and wiry man, immaculately and richly dressed as a prince. Decked with a crest upon his lofty, cone-shaped turban with a plume suspended behind from the top, he was ever armed with various weapons, including a bow and a quiver of arrows, a sword, a discus, a shield and a spear. His choice steed was of bluish-grey color and on his left hand always perched a white hawk when he sat on the throne or went out hunting.[12]

Whereas Guru Nanak is traditionally depicted as being contemplative and the master of things spiritual, Guru Gobind Singh is depicted as a worldly prince, ever ready for battle.

Guru Gobind Singh contributed significantly to the growth of Sikh militarism and engaged in many armed conflicts during a period when revolts against the Mughals, which had been occurring periodically for about a century, were common. Due to his success in consolidating and strengthening the Panth, the Sikhs had a realistic possibility of establishing independent rule. Most notably, Guru Gobind Singh brought about two innovations that forever changed the structure of Sikhism. As we have already noted, he instituted the Khalsa, which would redefine the Panth, and he installed the Adi Granth, the sacred scripture, as Guru, which radically altered the nature of leadership.

A woman prays at the Golden Temple in Amritsar, India.

Founding the Khalsa The traditional story of this momentous event is set forth in this account by twentieth-century Sikh historians Teja Singh and Ganda Singh. Note the story's emphasis on the virtues of loyalty and unity of the Sikh community, with its details concerning various castes and livelihoods.

On the Baisakhi day, March 30 of 1699, [Guru Gobind Singh] called a big meeting at Anandpur. When all were seated, he drew out his sword and cried, "Is there anyone here who would lay down his life for dharma?" At this the whole assembly was thrown into consternation; but the Guru went on repeating his demand. At the third call, Daya Ram, a Khatri of Lahore, rose from his seat and offered himself. The Guru took him into an adjoining enclosure, where a few goats were kept tied, and seating him there cut off a goat's head. He came out with the dripping weapon and flourishing it before the multitude asked again, "Is there any other Sikh here who will offer himself as a sacrifice?" At this Dharam Das, a Jat of Delhi, came forward and was taken into the enclosure, where another goat was killed. In the same way three other men stood up one after another and offered themselves for the sacrifice. One was Muhkam Chand, a washerman of Dwarka; another was Himmat, a cook of Jagannath; and the third was Sahib Chand, a barber of Bedar. The Guru after dressing the five in handsome clothes brought them before the assembly. He baptized them with sweetened water [i.e., *amrit*] stirred with a dagger and called them his Beloved Ones.[13]

Sikh devotees celebrate the 345th birth anniversary of Guru Gobind Singh on January 1, 2011, in the northern Indian city of Jammu.

Guru Gobind Singh, after preaching to the crowd about the unity of the Sikh community, asked the *Panj Piare*, the "Beloved Ones" (or "Beloved Five"), to baptize him—a surprising request given the traditional elevated standing of the Guru. The five baptized the Guru, thus forming the original Khalsa, the community of "Pure Ones" (as we noted in the chapter's opening description of the initiation ceremony). Over the course of the next few days, some 80,000 were baptized. All the men were given the additional name Singh, which means "lion," and all the women were named Kaur, which means "princess." To this day, these names indicate a family's affiliation with the Khalsa (although they no longer imply that one has undergone initiation).

By the time of his death in 1708, Guru Gobind Singh had managed to befriend the Mughal rulership and to ease tensions between the peoples, although his own death came at the hands of a Mughal assassin. Before dying, he is said to have declared that he was to be succeeded, not by another individual, but by the Adi Granth and by the Panth, to both of which he assigned the title "Guru."

Sikhs and Nationalism

Over the centuries, the Punjab has tended to be a volatile region, marked by political and military strife. In the century following the death of Guru Gobind Singh in 1708, the Sikhs struggled through a period of especially violent confrontations with the Mughal Empire, eventually managing to establish independent rule. Under the leadership of Ranjit Singh (1780–1839), who ascended to the throne in 1792, the Sikh community thrived as a sovereign kingdom in the Punjab. In 1849, the kingdom was annexed by the British, who had established control over India and had commenced the period known as the British Raj.

When India gained independence from the British in 1947, the Punjab was divided, with India gaining control of the east and Pakistan gaining control of the west. Most Sikhs living in the western region migrated eastward, favoring the Hindu-dominated India over the Muslim-dominated Pakistan. These Sikhs left behind their traditional homeland and many significant sites, including Nanak's birthplace.

In recent times, a new nationalist movement for independence, commonly called "Khalistan," has involved the Sikhs in conflict, both within and outside the Sikh community. The most violent tragedy of all took place in 1984 when, in an attempt to control the more radical aspects of the independence movement, the Indian government launched "Operation Blue Star," which culminated in the occupation of Sikh holy sites, most notably the Darbar Sahib (or Golden Temple), by Indian forces and the death of as many as 10,000 Sikhs. (Estimates of the death count vary widely, with various sources citing from 500 to 10,000.) This led to the assassination of Indian Prime Minister Indira Gandhi by two of her Sikh bodyguards on October 31, 1984. Today, the Khalistan movement is not nearly so prevalent as it was in the 1980s. That in 2004 a Sikh, Manmohan Singh, for the first time became India's prime minister perhaps signals a new degree of assimilation of Sikhism within Indian society.

Sikhs in the Diaspora

Sikhism clearly has become a global religion. For most Sikhs, traditional aspects of the religion as it has been practiced for centuries in its homeland, especially as defined by the Khalsa, tend to endure. At the beginning of this chapter, we noted that there are approximately 25 million Sikhs in the world,[14] of which approximately 70 percent follow at least the basic requirement of the Khalsa and do not cut their hair. Only about 15 percent of Sikhs have undergone the traditional ceremony of initiation into the Khalsa.

With nearly 2 million Sikhs now living in the diaspora[15] (that is, outside of the Punjab and of India), issues of these Sikhs have gained prominence. Many of the traditional practices taken for granted in the Punjab simply are not feasible—or, in some cases, even legal—in other lands. Consider, for example, Sikh funeral rituals.

All religious traditions feature important persons, in addition to founding figures, who have made significant contributions as innovators, institutional leaders, and so forth. Thinking of Sikhism's nine successors to Guru Nanak, compare other religions on this issue of the contributions of important persons.

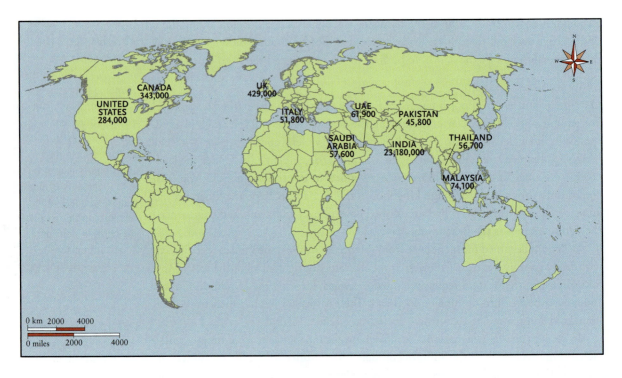

World Sikh population.

According to the Rahit, and in keeping with long-standing tradition, the body of the deceased is to be borne to the pyre on a bier, not in a coffin, and the fire is to be lit by a close relative or friend. In countries such as the United States, such a practice is not permitted; as a result, adjustments are made. The ceremonial departure for the cremation site is replaced by placing the coffin into a hearse, which then proceeds to a crematorium. (Or the ceremony is held at a funeral home that is equipped with a crematorium.) The lighting of the pyre is replaced by the chosen person pushing the button that conveys the coffin into the cremation furnace.

Other challenging situations for Sikhs in the diaspora involve the Five Ks. Wearing the turban, for example, which is based on the requirement of uncut hair and is almost universal among male Sikhs in their traditional homeland, is an important symbol of Sikh identity. But in many places in the diaspora, wearing a turban is not so easily done. In the United States, for example, there are laws requiring that helmets be worn when driving a motorcycle. A Khalsa Sikh who wishes to don the *kirpan* (the sword or knife, one of the Five Ks) when traveling by plane must be prepared for varying rules governing security practices at airport screenings.

In some cases, governments attempt to accommodate Sikhs. In the United Kingdom, for example, motorcycle helmet laws have been modified. But in many situations, such traditional practices as wearing the turban have led at least to inconvenience and sometimes even to tragedy. In the aftermath of the attacks on the World Trade Center and the Pentagon of September 11, 2001, Sikhs have been mistaken (presumably because of the wearing of the turban) for Muslims and have become targets of hate crimes, including murder.

For Sikhs living in the diaspora, this issue of identity needs to be weighed against practical concerns, sometimes even involving one's safety. Whereas most Sikhs in the Punjab continue to follow the injunction not to cut their hair, most living in Western countries do not. The Panth, as a global religious community, must contend with this complex mix of issues and concerns.

SIKHISM AS A WAY OF LIFE

One aspect of Guru Nanak's teachings was the rejection of the outward forms of religion that he found troubling in the Islam and Hinduism of his day. Focused as he was on seeking the indwelling God through meditation on the divine Name, Guru Nanak regarded the external forms of religion as useless.

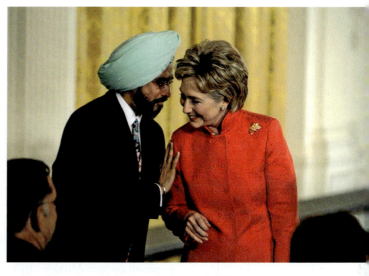

A Sikh man greets Hillary Clinton, at the time a senator from New York, at the United States National Day of Prayer ceremony in 2007.

Guru Nanak's rejection of outward forms of religion, however, has not resulted in complete avoidance by Sikhs of religious observances. For one thing, Sikhs through the centuries have continued to celebrate annual festivals that are generally features of northern Indian culture. We noted previously that Guru Gobind Singh founded the Khalsa on the day of an important annual festival, Baisakhi Day, which is the first day of the Indian year (according to the Western calendar, this day occurs in March or April). For Sikhs, Baisakhi Day has the special significance of commemorating the founding of the Khalsa. Another important festival celebrated by Sikhs, as well as by Hindus and Jains, is Divali, the Festival of Lights (which takes place in October or early November). Other religious observations were instituted by the Sikh Gurus, most notably by Guru Gobind Singh, and are unique to Sikhism.

VOICES: An Interview with Onkar Singh

Onkar Singh is a Sikh who was born and raised in the Punjab; earned a Ph.D. (Entomology) from the University of California, Berkeley; and served in India, Nigeria, Sudan, Liberia, and Indonesia before immigrating to the United States and becoming a U.S. citizen. He has devoted his retirement years to educating his fellow citizens about Sikhism.

What is the significance of the Name of God, and does the fact that your name, "Onkar," is one of the Sikh names of God have special significance?

God's name is used to remember Him, to meditate on Him, to pray to Him, and to seek His blessings. People are named after different names of God (*Bhagwan, Govind, Hari, Indra, Kartar, Eshwar, Ram,* etc.) or gods and prophets (*Krishan, Shiva, Jesus, Moses, Mohamed,* etc.). I was named Onkar, after the most

Onkar Singh

common name of God in the Sikh Holy Scriptures, following the tradition of choosing a name starting with the first letter of the hymn when Sri Guru Granth Sahib is opened at random.

What is the primary purpose of prayer?

The primary purpose of Sikh prayer is to thank God (*Vahiguru*) for all His blessings thus far and to seek His blessings for the success of the task about to be started. Sikhs also ask for His continued blessings so that they submit to His Will and continue to remember Him at all times. The prayer ends with a request for their optimism and for the welfare and prosperity of the entire humanity.

How does wearing the turban relate to your religious beliefs?

In South Asia and Southwest Asia, the turban is a symbol of dignity, honor, respect, and responsibility. Guru Hargobind, the sixth Sikh Guru, asked his followers to wear turbans, carry arms, and ride horses, in opposition to a ban imposed on non-Muslims by the rulers. Further, in 1699, Guru Gobind Singh, the tenth Sikh Guru, prescribed the five articles of faith including uncut hair (and the turban) mandatory for the Khalsa. I wear a turban as per the dictates and practice of my Sikh faith.

To what extent are the Golden Temple and the Sikh homeland of Punjab in general of special meaning for you, living in the United States?

The Golden Temple, Amritsar, is the most visited Sikh shrine. More people, of different faiths, castes, etc., visit the Golden Temple than the Taj Mahal. Guru Arjan Dev, the fifth Sikh Guru, built this temple. He invited a famous Sufi saint, Mian Mir, to lay its foundation stone. Further, he compiled, edited, and installed the first edition of the Sikh Holy Book in this temple in 1604. The Golden Temple Complex houses the SGPC (Shromani Gurdwara Parbandhak Committee) and includes the Akal Takht and some historic *Gurdwaras*. Besides the Golden Temple, the Sikh homeland of Punjab has three *Takhats* and numerous historic *Gurdwaras*. Sikh Americans, irrespective of the country of their birth, look upon Punjab as the Land of their Gurus, who preached Unity of God, practiced equality of humanity, and worked lovingly to unite the populace.

What is the most important thing that non-Sikhs in the United States need to understand about your religion?

Non-Sikhs in the United States should understand that almost all who wear turbans in America are followers of Sikhism, which is not a branch of another religion (e.g., Hinduism or Islam) and has its own founder (Guru Nanak) and Holy Book (Sri Guru Granth Sahib) and worship places (*Gurdwaras*), where all are welcome.

In this section we focus on the ideals of the religious life, paying attention to the actual degree of participation among Sikhs today.

Daily Devotional Practices

Guru Nanak emphasized the importance of *nam simaran*, "remembrance of the Name." This can be done simply by repeating one of the names used to refer to God. Recall that Guru Nanak composed many hymns; *kirtan*, the singing of hymns, is another form of *nam simaran*. A third form involves meditation practices designed to contemplate the divine Name and ultimately to bring one into perfect harmony with God. On one hand, these methods are straightforward and easy to practice on one's own. On the other hand, to make significant progress normally takes years of diligence.

Daily prayers are another form of devotional practice that can (and should) be done by every Sikh. The Khalsa Rahit, which spells out the ideal regimen for much of the religious life, gives the following instructions:

> A Sikh should rise early (3 A.M. to 6 A.M.) and having bathed he should observe *nam japan* by meditating on God. Each day a Sikh should read or recite the order known as the "Daily Rule" (*nit-nem*). The Daily Rule comprises the following portions of scripture: Early morning (3 A.M.– 6 A.M.): *Japji*, *Jap*, and the *Ten Savayyas*. . . . In the evening at sunset: *Sodar Rahiras*. . . . At night before retiring: *Sohila*. At the conclusion of the selections set down for early morning and evening (*Sodar Rahiras*) the prayer known as *Ardas* must be recited.[16]

To follow such a regimen requires much diligence and much time: altogether, these prayers cover about twenty pages in English translation. Whereas some Sikhs, especially those more advanced in age, commonly do this on a regular basis, the majority do not.

Sikh Worship in the *Gurdwara*

Gurdwara literally means "doorway of the Guru" (a variant translation is "by means of the Guru's [grace]"). Any building that contains a copy of the Adi Granth is,

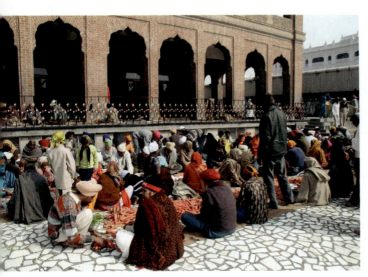

Volunteers prepare food for the *langar* meal at the Golden Temple in Amritsar. Many thousands of people share meals together here daily, at no cost to the visitor.

Compare the daily ritual practices of Sikhism with those of other religions.

technically speaking, a *gurdwara*, a Sikh house of worship. There is at least one *gurdwara* in virtually every village in the Punjab. Most *gurdwaras* have a characteristic Sikh style, with minarets and chalk-white paint. Aside from the presence of the Adi Granth, which usually sits atop cushions and under a canopy, there are no specific requirements regarding the interior.

The *gurdwara* serves mainly as a place for Sikh men, women, and children to congregate for worship. This they do frequently, on no particular day of the week. Worship usually takes place in the evening, though the early morning is also a popular time. Worship in the *gurdwara* is preceded by bathing and consists of singing the Gurus' hymns, reading from the Adi Granth, or telling a story about one of the Gurus. No formal requirements govern the exact nature of worship. It generally ends, though, with a sharing of a special pudding made of wheat flour, sugar, and ghee (clarified butter), known as *karah prasad*. This act is symbolic of the unity of the Panth.

The sharing of food is an important feature of Sikhism. Each *gurdwara* typically has within it a community kitchen, called the *langar*, where Sikhs gather at various times to share in the preparation and consumption of a meal. The food served in the *langar* is strictly vegetarian; even eggs are not allowed. Again, this sharing of food symbolizes the equality of all. It also provides food for the needy.

Life Cycle Rituals

In the chapter's opening description of the *Amrit Sanchar*, the Khalsa initiation ceremony, we witnessed an example of a Sikh ritual that marks a certain point in the individual's life and does so through detailed actions and rich symbolism that are steeped in tradition. Having already considered the Khalsa initiation ceremony in some detail (and bearing in mind that only about 15 percent of Sikhs undergo initiation), we now turn to considering other important rituals of the life cycle.

Birth and Naming
On the birth of a child, Khalsa Sikhs can choose to undertake a ritual that resembles an aspect of the initiation ceremony. A sweet drink is made by stirring water and sweets with a *kirpan* (the short sword, one of the Five Ks), while reciting from the *Japji*. A few drops are given to the baby, and the rest is drunk by the mother.

A short time after giving birth, the parents and child proceed to the *gurdwara*, where hymns are sung and the Adi Granth is opened randomly. The child's first name is chosen based on the first letter that appears on the left-hand page of the Adi Granth, the letter with which the name is to begin. If the child is a girl, she is also given the name Kaur; if male, he is given the name Singh. The names Singh or Kaur normally correspond to an English last name. No distinction is made between girls' and boys' first names. The "last name" of Kaur or Singh serves to make this distinction.

Tying a Turban When a boy reaches the age of ten or eleven, Sikh families often undertake a ceremonial tying of his first turban. This symbolizes the great respect that Sikhs hold for the turban. Even though wearing the turban is not technically required, it is regarded as a natural corollary of *kes*, not cutting one's hair (one of the Five Ks). Indeed, because one's hair is typically kept inside the turban, it is really the turban, not the hair, that is the most visible sign that one is a Sikh.

Traditionally, the turban is tied in a specific way that is both easy to do (once one has learned how) and effective, keeping the turban securely on the head. The style and color of the turban may sometimes indicate regional, political, or religious affiliation. The turban is generally considered to be highly practical, providing protection both from the summer sun and from the cold of winter. Women rarely wear turbans; instead, they traditionally wear a scarf or veil that can be used to cover the head.

Marriage Proper Sikh marriage, according to the traditions established by the Khalsa, is arranged by the parents of a child of marriageable age through the assistance of a relative, who seeks out a suitable spouse and sets up meetings with the families. The parents thus can become acquainted with their child's potential bride or groom. The same type of meeting takes place with the other set of parents. Once both families have agreed on a match, the marriage ceremony is planned. According to the Rahit, a Sikh woman is only to be married to a Sikh, but no account whatsoever of caste status is to be taken into consideration. In actual practice, however, there are many exceptions. Caste status commonly dictates the choice of marriage partners, and Sikhs (men more commonly than women) sometimes marry outside the tradition. As we have remarked previously, common practice by no means always complies with Khalsa ideals.

The ceremony takes place at the *gurdwara*, with Sri Guru Granth Sahib the central focal point, just as it is in everyday worship. First seated before the Adi Granth during the singing of hymns, the couple then stands and receives instruction in the teachings of the Gurus on marriage, nodding their assent to the Adi Granth, and afterward walking around it. This focus on the scripture exemplifies the central role that the Adi Granth is to play in the life of the married couple.

The ceremony concludes, like other worship services in the *gurdwara*, with the distribution of *karah prasad*, the special pudding made of wheat flour, sugar, and ghee.

Death Traditional Sikh mourning rituals center around the process of cremation. The body is washed and dressed in clean clothing and adorned with the Five Ks.

A hymn is recited, and the body is carried to the cremation grounds, which women do not enter. The funeral pyre is lit by a son or other male relative or friend, while the other mourners sing funeral hymns. The *Kirtan Sohila*, the prayer that is recited daily when retiring for the evening, is then sung.

Once the fire has burned out, the ashes are recovered and are either buried there at the cremation site or immersed in running water. Then the entire Adi Granth is read, within a period of ten days if possible. (The Rahit specifies that a full reading takes forty-eight hours, if done without interruption.)

As noted previously in the section on Sikhs in the diaspora, such traditional practices are modified today in places where laws prohibit outdoor cremations.

Worship, Work, and Charity

Like every global religion, Sikhism is continually in contact with people of other traditions. In this chapter, we have seen how Guru Nanak inspired followers who were both Muslims and Hindus. Although the common notion that Sikhism somehow resulted from the mixing of Islam and Hinduism is not an accurate one, clearly Guru Nanak and Sikhs after him helped to bridge differences among these two major religions of India. Sikhism has generally maintained peaceful relations with other religions and with other peoples, both in their homeland and abroad. Indeed, Sikhs have a well-deserved reputation for reaching out and helping to improve their communities. From its beginnings, Sikhism has been on the side of religious freedom and justice for oppressed people. Justice is carried out partly through the regular donation of one-tenth of one's income to charitable causes.

Three guiding principles of Sikh life are worship, work, and charity, as embodied in the popular Punjabi proverb, *nam japo, kirat karo, vand chhako*: "Repeat the divine Name, work, and give a share [of your earnings to the less fortunate]."[17] An outsider need only pay a visit to a Sikh *gurdwara* and witness the worship and afterward partake of the carefully prepared food in the *langar* to experience these guiding principles in action.

Women and Sikhism

Sikhism, like every religion, has both its ideals and its practical realities. Such is the case with the place of women over the centuries. The ideals are set forth straightforwardly, for instance in these words by Guru Nanak:

> From women born, shaped in the womb, to women betrothed and wed,
> We are bound to women by ties of affection; on women man's future depends.
> If a woman dies he seeks another, source of society's order and strength.
> Why then should one speak evil of women, they who give birth to kings?
> Women also are born from women, as are all who have life and breath.[18]

Sikhism has always maintained this ideal of gender equality with regard to the crucial issue of spiritual liberation (*mukti*). Sikh teachings from the beginning rejected practices such as female infanticide, which were common in the Punjab in Guru Nanak's time. The Rahit emphasizes that women are to participate fully in the religious life. But teachings alone do not always ensure equality in society, even in religious society.

Sikh society, through the centuries and up to the present day, has tended to be quite patriarchal, with positions of institutional power occupied by men. (Notably, the ten Gurus were all men.) The wedding ceremony that we have considered suggests a certain patriarchal tendency with its prescribed vows. The groom promises to be "protector" of the bride and her honor; the bride promises to accept her husband as "master of all love and respect."

On the other hand, the social history of Sikhism includes many examples of equal participation by women in religious matters and of women who serve as role models. Sulakhani, the wife of Guru Nanak, certainly is portrayed as a role model—not only in the domestic domain of the household but also as a confidant and advisor to her husband. Evidence exists showing that wives of other Gurus participated to some degree in administration of the Panth.

As is the case with all of the world's major religions, the degree of gender equality in Sikhism varies from circumstance to circumstance. Generally speaking, modern times have brought changes. In 1977, a wedding ceremony took place in a small town in the Punjab in which the bride led the groom in the final walk around the Adi Granth—a surprising incident, but no one was able to find anything in Sikh scripture to provide an objection based on doctrinal grounds. In another example of changing times, in the late 1990s women began to take on the traditionally male practice of ritual washing of the Golden Temple at midnight.[19]

The rapid growth of the Sikh diaspora in places where gender equality is held up as an ideal suggests that such changes will bring new opportunities for women to occupy roles of power in Sikh religion and society. With regard to the issue of gender equality, too, the Panth will need to continue to make adjustments as it orients its way as a global religion.

Sikh Identity

This chapter has assumed all along a rather flexible definition of who is a Sikh. On one end of the spectrum, we have considered the rigorous regimen of observance as spelled out in the Rahit, which calls for the recitation of some twenty pages of prayer every morning before six o'clock. At the other end of the spectrum, there are those who cut their hair, and yet one cannot go so far as to deny that they are Sikhs.

This flexible definition is in keeping with the Sikh perspective. Every religious tradition sets forth ideals that are not necessarily put into practice by all of its followers. Sikhism openly acknowledges this. It is also important to recognize that "Sikh" can refer broadly to an ethnic group, without necessarily implying adherence to the religion of Sikhism. For centuries, Sikhs maintained a society in the Punjab that was quite distinctive, and the vast majority of today's Sikhs are themselves descendants of Punjabi Sikhs. There is thus both a societal and a hereditary aspect of being Sikh, neither of which necessarily involves the explicitly religious aspects of belief or conduct.

CONCLUSION

In this chapter, we have learned about the teachings, the way of life, and the historical development of Sikhs and their religion. Founded by Guru Nanak (1469–1539), Sikhism is relatively young compared to other major world religions. It nevertheless is firmly rooted in tradition that is historically rich, theologically and ritually sophisticated, and adorned with impressive musical and architectural achievements. Especially because of the central role of the Khalsa, with its Five Ks and other standards for Sikh behavior and identity, the Panth tends to be a community with well-defined ideals. All of these factors contribute to the considerable holding power of Sikh tradition, even as the modern world invites—and sometimes forces—adaptations.

Sikhism today is a global religion, as vital in such places as Toronto, Canada, and the central valley of California as it is in its ancestral homeland of the Punjab. As it continues to draw upon the richness of its eventful historical tradition, Sikhism shows every sign of continuing also to adapt to modernity in the various places across the globe that it has come to call home.

SEEKING ANSWERS

What Is Ultimate Reality?

Sikhism is strictly monotheistic, emphasizing the oneness of God, while also teaching that God dwells within creation. For reasons that cannot be understood by human beings, God created the world. Knowing the divine nature can be considered as analogous to knowing the nature of an artist through contemplation of her artwork. Sikhism holds that the world is good, that God is immanent in the world, and that the world is permeated with divine order, called *hukam*. If this divine order can be recognized, it stands to reason that human beings can come to know God.

How Should We Live in This World?

Sikhs believe that God dwells within everyone. Humans tend, however, to be self-centered, rather than God-centered, a concept known as *haumai*, the self-reliance or pride that poses

(continued)

SEEKING ANSWERS (continued)

the primary obstacle to spiritual fulfillment. Sikhs further believe that the world is permeated with *hukam*, or divine order. To live in accord with *hukam* naturally requires proper ethical conduct. The Khalsa, though technically made up of only a minority of Sikhs, continues to be the authoritative source for ideals on the right way to live.

What Is Our Ultimate Purpose?

Immanent in creation, God is knowable to human beings. The flaws of *haumai* can be overcome through attention to the presence of the divine, most effectively through meditation on *nam*, the Name of God. As the term suggests, liberation (*mukti*), which for Sikhism is being in the presence of God, is the complete overcoming of the human condition. Sikhism teaches that the ultimate purpose of life is to attain spiritual liberation, and thereby release from *samsara*, the cycle of death and rebirth.

REVIEW QUESTIONS

For Review

1. What is the meaning of the term "guru"?
2. Identify at least three of the names for God in Sikhism. Why do you think there is more than one name? What is the relationship of the names to each other?
3. Compare the contributions of Guru Nanak and Guru Gobind Singh for the development of Sikhism.
4. What is the Khalsa? What is its ongoing relevance for Sikhism?
5. How do the "Five Ks" of Sikhism serve to strengthen Sikh identity?

For Further Reflection

1. What aspects of the Sikh God would Jews, Christians, or Muslims find familiar?
2. Describe *mukti*, spiritual liberation. How does this compare to forms of spiritual liberation in other religions—for example, to Hindu *moksha* or Buddhist *nirvana*?
3. Compare Sikh worship in the *gurdwara* with the forms of worship in religions with which you are familiar, either through studies or through personal experience. What are the notable similarities and differences? What do these comparative points regarding worship suggest about the nature of the religions, in general?

GLOSSARY

Adi Granth (ah'dee gruhnth; Punjabi, "first book") Sikhism's most important sacred text and, since the death of Guru Gobind Singh in 1708, Sikhism's primary earthly authority; traditionally known as Sri Guru Granth Sahib.

amrit (ahm-reet; Punjabi, "immortalizing fluid") A special drink made from water and sugar crystals, used in the Khalsa initiation ceremony.

gurdwara (goor'dwah-ruh; Punjabi, "doorway of the Guru" or "by means of the Guru's [grace]") A building for Sikh worship that houses a copy of the Adi Granth; the central structure of any Sikh community.

Guru (goo'roo; Sanskrit, "venerable person") A spiritual teacher and revealer of truth, common to Hinduism, Sikhism, and some forms of Buddhism. When the word *Guru* is capitalized, it refers to the ten historical leaders of Sikhism, to the sacred text (Sri Guru Granth Sahib, or Adi Granth), and to God (often as True Guru).

haumai (how'may; Punjabi, "self-reliance," "pride," or "egoism") The human inclination toward being self-centered rather than God-centered, which increases the distance between the individual and God.

hukam (huh'kahm; Punjabi, "order") The divine order of the universe.

Khalsa (khal'sah; Punjabi, "pure ones") An order within Sikhism to which the majority of Sikhs belong, founded by Guru Gobind Singh in 1699.

Mul Mantra The summary of Sikh doctrine that comprises the opening lines of the *Japji*, Guru Nanak's composition that in turn comprises the opening section of the Adi Granth. (See p. 224 for an English translation of the full text.)

mukti (mook'tee; Punjabi, "liberation") Spiritual liberation bringing on the eternal and infinitely blissful state of being in the presence of God; sometimes the Sanskrit term *moksha* is used instead.

Panth (puhnth; Punjabi, Hindi, "path") The Sikh community. In lower case, *panth* ("path") is a term applied to any number of Indian (primarily Hindu) religious traditions.

Rahit (rah-hit'; Punjabi) The *rahit-nāmā*, a collection of scripture that specifies ideals of belief and conduct for members of the Khalsa and, by extension, for Sikhism generally; the current authoritative version, the *Sikh Rahit Maryādā*, was approved in 1950.

SUGGESTIONS FOR FURTHER READING

Cole, W. Owen, and Piara Singh Sambhi. *The Sikhs: Their Religious Beliefs and Practices.* 2nd rev. ed. Brighton, UK: Sussex Academic Press, 1995. A highly readable and informative account, organized in such a way as to make easily accessible the main figures and ideas.

Mann, Gurinder Singh. *Sikhism.* Upper Saddle River, NJ: Prentice Hall, 2004. A clear and up-to-date overview, with focus on modern times.

McLeod, Hew. *Sikhism.* London: Penguin Books, 1997. A detailed yet accessible overview of the religion, with a helpful appendix of primary source material.

McLeod, W. H., ed. and trans. *Textual Sources for the Study of Sikhism.* Totowa, NJ: Barnes & Noble Books, 1984. A helpful collection of source material that goes well beyond the Adi Granth and presents texts in such a way as to clarify the identity of authors.

Singh, Khushwant. *A History of the Sikhs.* 2 vols. Princeton, NJ: Princeton University Press, 1963–1966. A detailed and authoritative resource.

ONLINE RESOURCES

Wabash Center

wabashcenter.wabash.edu/resources

The Wabash Center, a trusted resource for all aspects of the academic study of religion, offers links to a wide variety of dependable Internet resources on Sikhism.

SikhNet

sikhnet.com

SikhNet offers an extensive "insiders' view" on Sikhism, with information on many aspects of the religion.

CHINESE RELIGIONS: CONFUCIANISM and DAOISM

TODAY IS *QINGMING*, a "pure and bright" day (the literal meaning of this Chinese compound word) that arrives once a year, 105 days after the winter solstice. It is a day for all Chinese families to remember their dead relatives and ancestors in a very public way. Spring is definitely in the air. The days have been getting longer and warmer. The rice seedlings, standing in neat rows in ankle-deep water in the paddy fields, wave gracefully in the gentle breeze. Their luxuriant greenness is most pleasing to the eyes of Chen Liang,[1] a peasant from Southern China in his early fifties. He and his two sons have been working hard in the past couple of months to plow and flood the paddy fields, seed the nursery plots, and then transplant the young seedlings one at a time into their current location. It is a tedious and backbreaking job that the Chen family has been doing for generations.

But today there will be no work in the fields. *Qingming* marks the renewal of spring. It also celebrates the rekindling of the kitchen fire. Two days earlier the old fire was put out, so only cold food had been served. Chen Liang and his wife get up today at the crack of dawn to light a new fire in the kitchen. Leftovers from the previous days' cold meals are wrapped in rice pancakes and fried, making "spring rolls" that many Chinese restaurants the world over serve regularly on their appetizer menu. They prepare for an important family gathering at the ancestral graves of the Chen clan. During this annual event, family members gather at and sweep

Woman making offerings in front of her ancestor's tomb.

Important Confucian and Daoist sites in China.

the graves of their relatives and ancestors to renew their kinship ties with both the dead and the living. Platefuls of fruits, freshly steamed chickens, a whole roasted pig, bottles of wine, bundles of incense sticks and bright-red candles, and strings of fire-crackers, as well as piles of make-believe paper money and paper clothing for the dead, are all ready to be carried to the lineage burial ground just outside the village.

At the gravesite, where several generations of the Chen clan are buried, Chen Liang meets up with his three brothers, his five cousins, and their families. The children, numbering more than twenty, are all dressed in brightly colored clothing, giggling and playing. They help remove overgrown weeds, clean the tombstones, and arrange food in front of the graves. Then, by generation and birth order, all members of the Chen clan take part in the annual ritual. They bow before their ancestors, address them in silent prayers, offer them wine and food, send them clothing and stacks of under-world money by burning paper imitations of those goods, and set off firecrackers to scare off wandering ghosts unrelated to the family.

Afterward a picture is taken of the entire gathering in front of the graves. The fami-lies divide up the fruits and the meats to be consumed later back at their respective homes. The men linger to talk about the weather and the crops, the women catch up on family news, and the children play. ☼

TIMELINE
Daoism and Confucianism

Era in Chinese History	Daoism	Confucianism
Shang–Zhou dynasties (c. 1600–256 B.C.E.*)	Ancient Chinese religion Shamans	Ancient Chinese religion Beginning of Ru tradition
Spring and Autumn (c. 722–481 B.C.E.)	World-escaping recluses and hermits	Confucius (551–479 B.C.E.)
Warring States (c. 480–221 B.C.E.)	Zhuangzi (365–290 B.C.E.*), *Daodejing* (earliest extant ed. c. 300 B.C.E.)	Mencius (371–289 B.C.E.*.), Xunzi (c. 310–238 B.C.E.*.)
Early Han Dynasty (206 B.C.E.–9 C.E.)	Worship of Xiwangmu (Queen Mother of the West)	Confucianism declared orthodox (136 C.E.); Five Classics designated
Later Han Dynasty (25–220 C.E.)	Laozi deified as Taishang Laojun. Tianshi [Celestial Master] movement founded by Zhang Daoling (142 C.E.) *Laozi bianhua jing* (Classic of Laozi's Transformations) (170s*)	Confucian classical commentaries and Scholasticism
Period of Disunion (221–589)	Shangqing [Highest Clarity] movement (fourth century) Lingbao [Numinous Treasure] Movement (fourth century)	Confucian texts introduced to Korea, and subsequently to Japan
Tang Dynasty (618–907)	First attempt at compiling canon State patronage of Daoism Daoism merged with Chinese folk religion	First stirring of Neo-Confucianism
Song Dynasty (907–1279)	Quanzhen [Complete Perfection] movement founded by Wang Zhe (1113–1170)	Neo-Confucianism: Zhu Xi (1130–1200)
Yuan Dynasty (1279–1368)		*Four Books* designated as civil service examination curriculum (1313)
Ming Dynasty (1368–1644)	*Daozang* compiled (1445) Daoist sacrificial rituals and notions of health influenced both elites and commoners in Korea, Japan, and Southeast Asia	Wang Yangming (1472–1529), an alternative Neo-Confucian view to Zhu Xi's Confucianism became state orthodoxy in Joseon dynasty (1392–1897) Korea Confucianism also became state ideology in Tokugawa Japan (1600–1868)
Qing Dynasty (1644–1911)		Civil service examination abolished (1905) Confucianism became dominant ideology in Nguyen dynasty Vietnam (1802–1945)
Early twentieth century	Chinese intellectuals criticized Daoism as superstition	Chinese intellectuals rejected Confucianism as feudal and reactionary
Communist China (1949–present)	Cultural Revolution (1966–1976) devastated Daoism Daoism gradually recovering since 1980s	Cultural Revolution (1966–1976) devastated Confucianism Confucianism gradually recovering since 1980s

Note: Asterisks indicate contested or approximate dates.

G atherings similar to that of the Chen extended family are replicated millions of times throughout China in observance of *qingming*. It is through this activity of paying homage to the ancestors and reaffirming kinship relations that the Chinese act out one of their most basic religious assumptions. At the core of this ritual is the Confucian notion of filial piety (honoring parents and ancestors) and of the centrality of the family in Confucian teaching. Equally on display is the Daoist (Taoist) attentiveness to changes in season and in nature, as well as the practice of warding off unwelcome ghosts through thunderous explosives. From this single family ritual we see that Confucianism and Daoism can coexist quite harmoniously among the Chinese, with no sense of incompatibility or mutual exclusivity. Indeed, except for extreme partisans in each tradition, most Chinese often embrace both religions with no sense of tension or conflict. How is that possible?

In this chapter you are invited to step into the religious world of the Chinese and to see how these two native Chinese religions both rival and complement each other. (Even though Buddhism is the third main religious tradition in China, we only give passing notice to it in light of its alien origin and its totally different worldviews; see Chapter 5 for a complete treatment of Buddhism.) By focusing on the teachings, history, and practices of Confucianism and Daoism, we can appreciate the true religious nature of the two traditions as well, even though in content and expression they may differ from most other world religions.

THE TEACHINGS OF CONFUCIANISM AND DAOISM

It should be observed from the outset that before Confucianism and Daoism arose, an ancient religion already existed in China. This ancient Chinese religion took shape no later than 1600 B.C.E., fully a thousand years prior to the rise of the two traditions. In fact, both Confucianism and Daoism may be regarded as two divergent extensions or outgrowths of this ancient Chinese religion, with the former focusing on human social relationship, whereas the latter emphasizes individual physical and spiritual well-being. In order to understand the religious nature and practice of Confucianism and Daoism, therefore, this ancient Chinese religion needs to be examined first.

Ancient Chinese Religious Views

The *Book of Changes,* the *Yijing* (*I Ching,* traditionally believed to have been compiled by the end of the second millennium B.C.E.) represents the earliest expression of the Chinese religious mindset. It conveys a worldview that has been described as "organismic,"[2] meaning that every single component of the cosmos belongs to an organic whole and that all the component parts interact with one another in a continuous self-generating process. Unlike the foundational texts of most religions, the *Book of Changes* does not include a creation myth. This absence of a creation myth may be attributed to the dominance of the spirit of honoring ancestors in China since antiquity. When most of the spirits who populate the supernatural world are former human beings who share the same qualities as the living, the sense of mystery and "otherness" of a creator being may be difficult to envision. Instead, from an original state of "undifferentiated chaos" (*hundun*),[3] two polar yet complementary energies known as **qi** ("breath," "energy," or "force") emerged. One is called **yang** (literally the south-facing, sunny side of a mountain) and the other **yin** (the north-facing, shady side of a mountain). Representing all binary entities and concepts (such as day and night, male and female, hot and cold), *yang* and *yin* interact and alternate ceaselessly to form a continuum or spectrum, generating the myriad elements of the creation.

The *yin-yang* symbol best represents the Chinese religious mentality. This worldview recognizes differences but also harmony among the differences.

In this kind of a worldview, nothing exists outside the cosmos; therefore, everything is subject to its operating principles. This absence of a "wholly other" creator in the early Chinese cosmological myth has very significant implications. That is, the classical Chinese view uses the metaphor of procreation or giving birth, not creation or fashioning something out of nothing, for the beginning of the universe. In the Chinese view, the lack of any notion of a wholly transcendent ultimate cause makes it difficult to produce the idea of an almighty god preceding and existing outside of creation. Correspondingly, the notion of an active evil dedicated to undermining the plans of a supposedly benevolent creator is absent in the Chinese cosmological view. In other words, no frighteningly personified devil competes with a benign god to win the hearts and minds of humans. In this world without sin (at least sin as understood by the Abrahamic faiths of Judaism, Christianity, and Islam), humanity is released from an acute sense of guilt. Instead, harmony and balance are good and preferable. Disharmony and imbalance are not.

The cosmic tango of *yang* and *yin*, spontaneous and unceasing, is manifested in the **wuxing** ("five elemental phases"), the five paradigmatic states of metal, wood, fire, water, and soil. These five states or elements correlate with many categories in nature. In the human body, they correspond to the Five Viscera (heart, liver, spleen, lungs, and kidneys). In the sky they are represented by the Five Planets (Venus, Jupiter, Mercury, Mars, and Saturn), and then there are the Five Colors (red, blue, yellow, white, and black) and the Five Flavors (sour, sweet, bitter, spicy, and salty). These five states are at the same time mutually nurturing and mutually destructive. Water sustains wood, wood feeds fire, fire reduces everything back to ashes (soil), soil produces ores (metal), and ores melt into liquid (water). Conversely, water douses fire, fire melts metal, metal chops down wood, wood draws nutrients from soil, and soil blocks water. Ultimately, like the swinging of the pendulum, what drives this dynamic process is the principle of alternation: when one extreme is reached, it reverts to the other. Such is the way the cosmos operates.

Notice in the photo that the two halves of the circle are not perfectly divided right down the middle. Instead, they are interlocked and mutually penetrating. Each half also contains the seed of the other. Thus the entire cosmos is involved in a ceaseless flow of alternation and change.

Human Body and Soul As fundamental energies of the cosmos that constantly interact with each other, *yin* and *yang* make solid matter when they coalesce and remain immaterial when diffused. Thus their interplay can manifest in coarse and materialistic things, as well as in subtle and spiritual entities. It is in this context that the constitution of human beings can be understood.

All humans have a physical body, seen as the corporal manifestation of the interplay between *yin* and *yang*. But all humans also have an immaterial aspect, subdivided into *hun* and *po*. *Hun* reflects the *yang* component, being light, pure, and upward-rising. *Po*, on the other hand, indicates *yin*, being heavy, turgid, and downward-sinking. *Hun* and *po*, introduced into the physical body when the fetus is gestating, together make up the spiritual aspect of the individual. For lack of a better term, they constitute the soul matter of the individual. As long as they stay with the human body, with only short and temporary absences during the dream state or when in a coma, the individual remains alive. At death, however, *hun* departs from the body permanently, rising skyward, and *po* settles down on earth alongside the interred and decomposing body. Both *hun* and *po* eventually dissipate and become reconfigured in different proportions to form future beings.

The Spiritual World of Gods and Ghosts

After death, as long as the energy remains to keep the current identity of *hun* and *po* intact, the spirit of the deceased lingers. Though only a pale shadow of its former self, the spirit of one who dies at a ripe old age and is properly cared for by the descendants may become **shen**, a benevolent power that protects and brings benefit to the living. On the other hand, the spirit of one who dies tragically or prematurely, and one who is not given a suitable burial or sacrifice, will become **gui**, a vengeful and malevolent ghost who visits disasters on people. *Shen* is a generic term for all kindly deities and gods whose power and efficacy are sought to fulfill people's wishes for health, wealth, progeny, and status. Conversely, *gui* refers to all spiteful ghouls, demons, and ogres who wreak havoc in people's lives. Motivated both by longing and fear, the Chinese from the ancient times to the present strive to cultivate good relations with both *shen* and *gui*. This, of course, is in addition to their primary obligation in the commemorating and honoring of their ancestors. The line of demarcation between the spirits and humans thus cannot be sharply drawn. Humans can indeed possess or exhibit qualities that in other cultures or beliefs may be considered spiritual, or even divine.

The Ancient Chinese Concept of Honoring Ancestors and the Divine

To the ancient Chinese, the ancestors were not just dead, buried, and forgotten. Instead, they continued to play an active role in the lives of their living descendants. They were consulted often on matters both major and minor. From the very beginning, then, Chinese religious practice focused on kinship ties and practical living. It was not exclusively located in a separate "sacred" realm.[4] The ancestors' presence in the lives of their descendants has remained a central and characteristic aspect of Chinese civilization. It is in this sense that the depiction of *qingming* at the opening of this chapter is so demonstrative of Chinese religious behavior.

During the Shang Dynasty, the earliest verifiable historic period in China to date, whose traditional dates are 1600–1046 B.C.E., the spirits of the ancestors were sometimes asked to carry messages to a higher deity for decision and response. This higher, more authoritative deity was **Shangdi**, the Lord on High, who was the most powerful god in the Shang spiritual world and who also happened to be the ancient ancestor of the Shang imperial house. This Lord on High was the controlling power in the cosmos. Along with the spirits of the ancestors, *Shangdi* monitored the behavior of the royal descendants, dispensing rewards and meting out punishments as appropriate. It was precisely for this reason that the Shang rulers needed to maintain close contact and good relationship with *Shangdi* and the other ancestral spirits, for the spirits were their source of kingly power. This power was termed **de**, commonly translated as "virtue," but more accurately as "potency." It was through the timely and correct performance of sacrificial rites to the ancestors and to *Shangdi* that each Shang ruler could claim this power, which may be more appropriately understood as the charismatic influence he possessed. With *de* the Shang king ruled with authority and legitimacy.

But sometime near the end of the second millennium B.C.E., a former minister of the court staged a rebellion that overthrew the Shang Dynasty and founded the next regime, the Zhou Dynasty (1122–256 B.C.E.). This power shift was rationalized primarily in religious terms. The defeat of the Shang, as the victorious Zhou founders explained it, was in fact sanctioned by *Shangdi*, who turned out to have a different name and was, in fact, a different kind of deity. *Shangdi* was now known as **Tian**, literally, "the sky," but more properly "the force above." (Regrettably, most books and articles written in English on Chinese religion and philosophy translate *Tian* as "Heaven," which is both inaccurate and misleading. In this chapter we continue to use the term *Tian* rather than any English equivalent in order to avoid any mistaken notion of *Tian* being a paradise-like location.)

Tian was believed to be the source of all things in the universe (not as a creator, but rather as a procreator), the ultimate divine entity that provided order throughout the cosmos. More significantly, *Tian* was also a "will" that would support only the morally deserving as king. This made *Tian* radically different from *Shangdi*, who was understood to be partial to the Shang kings and subject to their sacrificial "bribery." *Tian* was not swayed by claimed blood ties or sacrificial offerings; instead, it insisted on the demonstration of moral uprightness as the only condition for its award of political authority and legitimacy, which was labeled **ming**, or **Tianming**. This was the "mandate" or "charge" given by *Tian* to the person and the imperial line that was to rule on *Tian*'s behalf. Moreover, this *ming* could be revoked and withdrawn and could be transferred to another person or family any time its provisional holder was found wanting in morality. This event was known as "*geming*," the revocation of the "*ming*." To this day, *geming* in Chinese means "revolution—the withdrawal of the current regime's mandate to rule."

According to the religious mindset of the Zhou, *Tian*'s workings in nature and in the human world are its **dao**, its "way" or "path." It is the *dao* of *Tian* that provides order and regularity in nature and in human society. By following and obeying this *dao*, both the natural and the human worlds would reach their optimal fulfillment. This implementation of the *dao* of *Tian* is the duty and obligation of the human ruler. Thus what had happened to the Shang regime actually validated this belief in *Tian's* mandate. Shang's last ruler, who was, according to the Zhou founders, a corrupt and immoral individual, was no longer fit to exercise *Tianming*, hence his violent removal from power.

As the chosen deputy of *Tian* in the human world, the Zhou king (and all subsequent imperial rulers in China) called himself *Tianzi* ("Son of *Tian*"), the person who had been entrusted with the power to rule *Tianxia* ("domain under *Tian*," i.e., the entire known world). The king was therefore not just a political leader exercising power over both territory and people; he was also a religious figure who served as intermediary between *Tian* and humanity, as well as the natural world. To fulfill his roles as both king and priest, the Zhou ruler had to observe a set of behavioral practices collectively referred to as **li** ("rituals" or "rites"). It was the correct and sincere performance of *li* that would convince *Tian* of the ruler's moral worth, ensure *Tian's* continuous favor, and guarantee the ruler's power through his *de*, his "potency." *Li* covered every aspect of kingly behavior—from matters of state to relation with ancestors to conduct on important familial occasions such as marriage and funerals and even involving military campaigns. It would in time govern all the ritual conduct of the king's ministers as well, as their proper behavior also contributed to the stability and legitimacy of the regime.

Ancient Chinese Texts Such prescribed rites for the king and his ministers would later be codified into a text known as the *Record of Rites* (*Liji*). However, the beliefs in the source of kingly power and the underlying assumptions of imperial moral obligations are fully addressed in two other texts, the *Book of Odes* (*Shijing*)[5] and the *Book of History* (*Shujing*).[6] The former is an anthology of poems and ballads expressing the sentiments of both nobles and commoners, whereas the latter consists primarily of recorded activities and pronouncements of kings and aristocrats. Another work, the previously mentioned *Book of Changes* (*Yijing*), contains early Chinese views of cosmology and the supernatural. Collectively, these texts, which existed in some form after the founding of the Zhou regime, provide most of the information on the ancient Chinese religion from which Confucianism and Daoism would evolve. The Confucians, in particular, would revere these texts as classics and as sacred texts. The four just mentioned, along with the *Spring and Autumn Annals* (*Chunqiu*), purportedly compiled by Confucius himself, would constitute the Confucian **Five Classics**. The Daoists, while fully aware of the authority of these texts, especially the *Book of Changes*, would create their own corpus of scriptural works focusing more on the constitution of the human body, the basic elements of nature and the cosmos, and the ideal human relationship with the spirits, as we shall see in later sections.

The Teachings of Confucius

In this chapter, the term Confucianism is used with reluctance. The Chinese refer to this tradition as the "Teaching of the **Ru**" (scholars and ritualists). Even though Confucius has been rightfully credited with giving this tradition prominence and profound religious meaning, he is by no means its founder, nor is he worshipped as a supernatural savior figure like Jesus Christ in Christianity or the Buddha in Mahayana Buddhism. Therefore, "Confucianism" is quite a misleading term. In fact, the name "Confucius" is equally problematic, as it is actually a Latinized way of representing the Chinese reference to "Kong Fu Zi," the honorific way of addressing "Master Kong." Master Kong's full name is Kong Qiu, whose dates are conventionally given as 551–479 B.C.E. We will take a closer look at his life and times later in this chapter; here, we turn to an examination of his teachings.

Confucius inherited the entire package of ancient Chinese religious views discussed in the preceding pages. This is made clear in the single most important work that contains his main teaching, the *Lunyu*. Literally meaning "comments and sayings" but customarily translated as the *Analects*, this text is believed to have been compiled by Confucius's leading disciples after his death. It serves as a record of statements he had made, exchanges with students he had conducted, and even remarks some of the students had offered. As such it is an authoritative source for the examination of Confucius's teaching. Despite the possibility of later interpolations and the apparent lack of organization, the extant twenty "Books" of the *Analects*, taken as a whole, reflect a coherent picture of Confucius's major concerns and aspirations. A careful analysis of the content of the *Analects* shows that, while accepting many of the preexisting cosmological notions and religious beliefs of ancient China, Confucius and his immediate followers offered many new insights and creative interpretations regarding them. In the end, these "comments and sayings" contributed to the formation of a distinct tradition with unique views on humanity and its relationship with the divine. The following are some of the most notable topics addressed in the *Analects*.

The Primacy of *Tian* Confucius lived during the last centuries of the Zhou regime, which was a period of unmistakable dynastic decline. The notion of the possible revocation and transfer of *tianming* could not be too far from the minds of the weak Zhou ruler, the ambitious feudal lords serving under him, and the "men of service" who were seeking new opportunities for social and political advancement. Confucius was no exception. What he has conveyed in the *Analects* is a reinvigorated and fresh understanding of *Tian*, *Tianming*, and their relationship to humans, especially the moral elite.

The *Tian* of early Zhou, as we have seen, was an august and aloof divine power whose interaction with human beings was largely confined to the ruler, who alone could worship it. By contrast, the *Tian* of Confucius was a far more intimate religious and ethical entity. It had a conscious will that no longer reached out to the Zhou rulers and the various feudal lords (as it had done in the past), but to moral and noble men of diverse backgrounds so that they might revive a moral order that once existed.[7] Confucius saw himself, and encouraged his followers to become, a member of this moral vanguard.

Tian's message to the moral elite is not verbal or revelatory. Unlike the biblical God or the Qur'anic Allah, *Tian* silently manifests itself in the course of the seasons and in the records of human events to allow perceptive individuals to detect the full content of its command. Once the individual moral person firmly understands that imperative, a special relationship with *Tian* becomes possible. That person feels that *Tian* "knows" him and that he in turn has direct access to *Tian*. He becomes an obedient mouthpiece through which *Tian*'s message will be spread, resulting, hopefully, in a general uplifting of society. Various passages in the *Analects* attest to this faith in the primacy of *Tian* in Confucius's life and teachings. The following are particularly illustrative.

TIAN IN THE ANALECTS

A border official from the town of Yi requested an audience with the Master. . . . After emerging from the audience, he remarked [to the Master's disciples], "The world has long been without the ideal Way. *Tian* intends to use your Master like a wooden clapper for a bell [to awaken the world]."

—*Analects 3:24*

When Huan Tui, the Minister of War of the principality of Song, tried to kill Confucius (who was visiting), Confucius exclaimed, "It is *Tian* who has endowed me with virtue. What harm can Huan Tui do to me?"

—*Analects 7:23*

When under siege in the principality of Kuang, the Master declared, "With King Wen (founder of Zhou Dynasty) dead, does not civilization rest now on me? If *Tian* intends to have civilization destroyed, those who come after me will have nothing. But if *Tian* does not intend to have civilization destroyed, then what can the men of Kuang do to me?"

—*Analects 9:5*

The Master lamented, "Alas, there is no one who understands me." Zigong said, "How is it that no one understands you?" The Master continued, "I do not complain against *Tian*, nor do I blame my fellow men. I study what is mundane to reach what is transcendent. If there is anyone who understands me, it is *Tian*!"

—*Analects 14:35*

What these passages show collectively is the centrality of *Tian* in Confucius's thinking. *Tian* is clearly the highest religious authority, as well as ultimate reality, in the *Analects*. The *Analects* suggests a conscious *Tian* who "intends" human beings to have civilization in the form of a perfect order. To that end it reaches out to a few noble individuals. It does so not by direct revelation but through the quiet natural course of nature, as well as through human events, and it charges those individuals with the mission to sustain and protect human civilization. This is *Tian*'s mandate or imperative (*ming*). *Tianming*, to Confucius, is no longer an endowment of dynastic power and legitimacy for the political power holders but a call to moral perfection and close relation with the divine ultimate for the spiritual elite.

Some scholars of Confucian studies have noted the "prophetic voice" in Confucius and his followers. William Theodore de Bary of Columbia University is a forceful advocate of this aspect of the Confucian tradition.[8]

To be sure, unlike Moses or Muhammad, Confucius did not see himself as the messenger of a personal God; nevertheless, he criticized the authorities of his time and condemned their departure from the normative ideal by appealing to *Tian*. He invoked his own power as someone who, because of his endowment with *Tian*'s command, had that right to do so. In effect Confucius changed the very nature of *Tianming*. It became the self-ascribed duty of the moral individual to serve as mouthpiece to a *Tian* that did not speak itself, to be inspired and motivated by the sense of mission, indeed of commission, by *Tian*. The men of virtue, the *Analects* insists, must be "strong and resolute, for their burden of responsibility is heavy and the journey is long. Taking upon themselves the burden of humaneness, is that not heavy? Stopping only at death, is that not long?" (*Analects* 8:7). *Tian* in the *Analects* spurned the power holders of a decadent age and instead entrusted the awesome responsibility of protecting the ideals of the human order to a nonruler like Confucius.

How is the Confucian *Tian* different from the Judaic Yahweh, the Christian God, and the Islamic Allah?

The Content of *Tian*'s Imperative—the *Dao*

Just what is this message that *Tian* seeks to convey through the spiritual elite? It is the *Dao*, the Way. Confucius often complains in the *Analects* that the "*Dao* is not in practice" (*Analects* 5:7), or the "*Dao* does not prevail in the world" (*Analects* 16:2). What he means by the *Dao* is the total normative social-political-ethical order with the prescriptions for proper ritual behavior publicly, as well as moral rectitude privately. However, when men in power were incapable or unwilling to uphold this order, as was the case during Confucius's time, men of virtue and uprightness must take it upon themselves to protect and preserve this ideal or civilization would be doomed. It is for this reason that Confucius regards the search for and embodiment of the *Dao* to be the ultimate, paramount task in life. He proclaims: "If I can hear the *Dao* in the morning, I will die contented that evening!" (*Analects* 4:8).

As *Dao* represents the entire normative human order, Confucius focuses on certain key aspects for detailed discussion: *ren* and *li*.

Ren

Perhaps the single most important article of faith held by Confucius is **ren** (benevolence, humaneness, virtue)—the kernel of humanity that exists in all human beings. It is the germ of moral consciousness that enables human beings to form a perfect human order. Etymologically, it points to the interrelatedness among humans, for in writing it is a combination of the character for person (人) and the character for the number two (二), signaling that it is in a "state of person-to-person" that *ren* (仁) can be enacted. Throughout the *Analects* the importance of *ren* in Confucius's teaching is evident. Many of his leading disciples ask him about it, and he gives various answers to drive home the idea that *ren* is all-rounded and multifaceted. Indeed, *ren* is so fundamental a concept that Confucius allows the giving of one's life in order to preserve it (*Analects* 15:9), implying that a life without *ren* is meaningless.

People who can preserve and develop their *ren* can be entrusted to carry out the imperative of *Tian*. "When the root is firmly established, the *Dao* will grow. Filial piety and brotherly deference, are they not the basis of *ren*?" (*Analects* 1:2). It is the cultivation and nurturing of this root of moral propensity that constitutes the actualization of the *Dao*. Note that Confucius here is not asserting the perfection of all human beings. Rather, he is advocating their perfectibility through self-effort. This inner moral disposition needs to be expanded and developed before it can sustain the *Dao*. What is remarkable about this view is the belief that this moral potentiality is not a monopoly of those in power, or those of noble birth, but is in fact possessed by all humans. This universal accessibility makes it possible for someone like Confucius to teach others how to achieve *ren* and how to become men of virtue themselves.

Furthermore, this goodness is exemplified by filial piety (**xiao**) and brotherly deference, as well as by a sense of dutifulness (*zhong*) and reciprocity (*shu*). Filial piety honors one's indebtedness to the family elders and to the parents, and brotherly deference acknowledges the natural hierarchy in birth order among siblings. Thus it is within the family that humans first acquire their moral education. Outside the family, one should interact with other people according to the principle of exerting one's utmost effort in fulfilling one's diverse roles in society. This effort arises from one's sense of dutifulness and "not doing unto others what one does not want done unto oneself" (*Analects* 15:24), which is the height of reciprocity. *Ren* is thus the entire human moral repertoire, which, when developed and enacted, will produce harmony in the human world and in the relationship that humans maintain with *Tian*.

Li *Ren* alone, however, is not enough to enable one to preserve the *Dao*. This inner potentiality for goodness and benevolence has to be manifested by an external performance of prescribed behavior within the family, the community, the entire human society, and the spiritual world beyond. This is referred to as *li* (rites, rituals, normative behavior) in the *Analects*, a word that in ancient China meant only the sacrificial and behavioral rituals of the kings and the nobles. The ideograph for *li* shows a sacred ritual vessel, indicating that the etymological origin of the word has something to do with sacrifice to the gods or the ancestors (禮). In Confucius's understanding of the term, *li* encompasses the entirety of proper human conduct vis-à-vis other human beings, dead ancestors, and the spirits. *Li* cultivates a learned pattern of behavior that, when combined with the moral propensity present in each individual, will produce a "magical power" in human relationships, as well as in relations with the spirits. Once a ritual gesture is initiated in the proper ceremonial context and performed with grace and sincerity, the magical result of goodwill, trust, and harmony will follow. This is the irresistible and invisible power of ritual itself.

The *Analects* is most optimistic about the efficacy of *li*: In a famous response to his favorite student's question about *ren*, Confucius states: "Restraining oneself and returning to *li*, this is *ren*" (*Analects* 12:1). Only through ritualized interaction with others and with the spirits can one realize one's full potential as a human being. The mastery and performance of *li*, then, is in fact a "process of humanization."[9] *Li* is the externalization of *ren*. Conversely, *ren* is the inner source of *li*. This is why Confucius asks rhetorically: "A man who is not *ren*, what has he to do with *li*?" (*Analects* 3:3).

Junzi Confucius uses the term **junzi** (the noble man, the man of virtue, and the superior man) for the noble *ru* on whose shoulders rests the burden of reviving and preserving the *Dao*. This is Confucius at his most creative and revolutionary in the usage of terminology. Originally used to refer to the scions of feudal rulers, *junzi* in Confucius's refashioning comes to mean men of moral rectitude. From someone highborn, *junzi* becomes someone high-minded. From those of noble birth, *junzi* now means those of noble worth. They are the prophet-like individuals who, though holding no political office or having no privileged positions, nevertheless heed *Tian*'s call. They undertake the most arduous task of implementing *Tian*'s *Dao* in the human world. The *Analects* puts the issue most plainly: "Without knowing the imperative of *Tian*, one cannot be a *junzi*" (20:3).

The self-cultivation of the *junzi* will earn them a power (*de*) similar to that possessed by the ancient sage rulers. It is a charismatic, noncoercive, potent influence that both inspires and persuades, and coaxes and shames, people into doing what is right. In the *Analects* Confucius confidently declares: "The *de* of the *junzi* is like wind, while that of the common people is like grass. When the wind blows over the grass, the grass cannot help but bend in the direction of the wind" (*Analects* 12:19). The epitome of the *junzi* is the sage (**shengren** or simply **sheng** 聖), the rarest of human beings who are perfect in their moral standing and kingly in their worldly accomplishments. The traditional Chinese character for sage contains three components: ear, mouth, and ruler (耳, 口, 王).

The sage is someone who hears or listens to the Way of *Tian*, reconveys it through the mouth, and acts in the capacity of the ancient ruler whose job it is to link up the three realms of Heaven, Earth, and Humankind. Thus the sage is decidedly a religious figure, a saintly person who is at once a messenger of *Tian* to the human world and an exemplar of human perfection in the eyes of *Tian*.

The Religious Vision of the *Analects* Taken as a whole, the vision of the *Analects* offers an amazingly clear picture of Confucius's ultimate concern. The religious aspect of this Confucian vision is unmistakable. It has been justly pointed out that, unlike many other religious figures, Confucius envisaged no escape from the world and human society, nor did he insist on ascetic self-denial as a precondition for spiritual progress. In a similar vein, Confucius did not consider concern with the afterlife or with the spirits to be of primary importance. The following exchange between him and his student Zilu on that subject is famous: "Zilu asked about serving ghosts and spirits. The Master said, 'When we are not yet able to serve fellow humans, why worry about serving the ghosts and spirits?' 'What about death?' [Zilu persisted]. 'When we do not yet know enough about life, why worry about death?' [the Master replied]" (*Analects* 11:12).

Then in what sense is the Confucian teaching religious? Confucius has an abiding faith in the transcendent ultimate *Tian*. He feels an intimate relationship with it. He has a keen awareness of its command (*ming*) given to the moral and spiritual elites (*junzi*) to create the ideal human order (*Dao*). He firmly believes in the *Tian*-endowed human capacity for perfection and genuine humanity (*ren*) through self-cultivation, and enthusiastically participates in sacrificial rituals and familial and social rites (*li*). These are all components of his religious outlook. To be sure, this religiosity does not express itself in faith in a personal God and the need for salvation through divine grace. Rather, it distinguishes itself as a form of "this-worldly transcendentalism." It treats the "secular as sacred,"[10] and it imparts deeply religious meaning to participation in the mundane. Thus it expresses a different mode of religiousness. For this reason, it has been paradoxically labeled a "humanistic religion" and a "religious humanism."[11] The distinction between the human and the divine, clearly drawn in the Abrahamic traditions, is not found here. For Confucius, the ultimate goal for humans is to heed the instruction of *Tian* by transforming themselves from potential to actual goodness. This process of transformation toward the absolute is the religious nature of the Confucian teaching, and it is right there in the *Analects*.

Admittedly, this religiousness of the Confucian *Analects* has been largely overshadowed by its familial, social, and political emphasis throughout the course of Chinese imperial history, so much so that Confucianism as a religion is not readily recognized. However, the discussion that follows should further confirm the intrinsic religiosity of the Confucian tradition as it unfolded.

The *Mencius* Mencius (a Latinized rendition of "Master Men") (371–289 B.C.E.?) was born a full century after Confucius's death. Claiming to be the rightful successor to Confucius, Mencius reaffirmed moral cultivation as a religious calling. He provided the moral elite with a strong sense of mission. Mencius also made one lasting contribution to the Confucian belief system with his insistence on the basic goodness of human beings, thus upholding Confucianism's optimistic view of human perfectibility.

Next to the *Analects*, the *Mencius* (likewise compiled by some of Mencius's leading disciples) is significant as a Confucian scriptural text. Unlike Confucius, who does not regard himself as a sage—a title he reserves only for the few legendary rulers in ancient China—Mencius not only boldly declares his predecessor's sageliness but also insists on his own. Indeed, he considers every human being a potential sage, as he deems that each possesses all the innate qualities to become one. It is based on that assumption that he asserts the intrinsic goodness of human nature, which he compares to the natural tendency of water to flow downward (*Mencius* 6A, 2:2). This is Mencius's fundamental article of faith.

Identifying four "sprouts of morality" in all humans—the inborn sentiments of commiseration (inability to bear to witness the suffering of others), shame, deference and yielding, and sense of right and wrong—Mencius proclaims them to be the roots of benevolence (*ren*), righteousness (*yi*), propriety (*li*), and wisdom (*zhi*), respectively. With this belief as his religious premise, he constructs a logical progression from moral cultivation to the ultimate attainment of divine spirituality. He states, "That which is sought after is called 'good.' To have it in oneself is called 'true.' To possess it fully is called 'beautiful,' while making it shine forth with brilliance is called 'great.' To be great and be able to transform others is called 'sage.' To be sage and be beyond understanding by others is called 'spiritually divine'" (*Mencius* 7B, 25). Through our moral progress, Mencius suggests, we can become not only good, true, beautiful, and great, but also sagely and ultimately divine. With utter conviction, then, he maintains, "Probing one's heart/mind to the utmost, one will know one's nature. Knowing one's nature, one will know *Tian*. To preserve one's heart/mind and nurture one's nature is to put one in the service of *Tian*" (*Mencius* 7A, 1:1). Once one has embodied the moral imperatives of *Tian*, Mencius reasons, one will find all other concerns secondary. In one of his most celebrated statements, Mencius declares: "I like fish, and I also like bear's paw. If I cannot have both, I will give up fish and keep the bear's paw. Life is what I desire, but so is righteousness. If I cannot have both, I will give up life but cling to righteousness" (*Mencius* 6A, 10:1). With morality as his ultimate concern, Mencius is willing to sacrifice his own life in order to preserve it. This is certainly reminiscent of Confucius's commitment to benevolence (*ren*), for the preservation of which he, too, is willing to suffer death. This is demonstrative of the spirit of the martyr and a deeply held religious sentiment.

The *Great Learning* and the *Doctrine of the Mean*

The remaining two texts of the **Four Books**, completing the Confucian religious corpus designated by a later Confucian scholar (see the section on the history of Confucianism later in this chapter), are the *Great Learning* and the *Doctrine of the Mean*, supposedly compiled by two of Confucius's prominent students. Both are chapters from the *Book of Rituals* that have been excerpted as independent texts because of their religious significance. The former refers to learning about what is of primary importance. It prescribes a practical step-by-step road map for self-cultivation, starting with individual inquiries and ending with the transformation of humanity as a whole. Listing eight steps in personal cultivation, the *Great Learning* outlines a sequence of individual and social effort made to manifest "illustrious virtue," "love the people," and reach the "ultimate good," which is nothing short of the *Tian*-ordained perfect world order. Thus learning involves far more than the acquisition of knowledge, but is actually an ethical-religious program of personal and societal perfection.

The *Doctrine of the Mean* begins with a bold declaration: "What *Tian* has ordained is called human nature. Following this nature is called the *Dao*. Cultivating the *Dao* is called teaching" (*Doctrine of the Mean* 1:1). These three statements articulate the fundamental Confucian articles of faith, representing what Confucianism regards as self-evidently true. The text asserts that humans are born with a benign nature imparted by *Tian*, the ultimate religious authority. This nature provides them with the inner strength to reach their fullest potential as perfect beings. Furthermore, when extended beyond the individual, this human nature can bring about an ideal social-political-ethical order, the actualization of which is the purpose of education. The text further maintains that the real possibility for achieving perfect goodness exists because of the special relationship between human beings and *Tian*. There is a logical progression from self-generating moral effort to the perfection of the faithful and the world around them: "The *junzi* [noble person] cannot avoid not cultivating his person. Thinking of cultivating his person, he cannot neglect serving his parents. Thinking of serving his parents, he may not avoid knowing other humans. Thinking of knowing other humans, he cannot ignore knowledge of *Tian*" (*Doctrine of the Mean* 20:7). It is clear that human beings must fully engage themselves with others in order to actualize their genuine humanity and divine potential.

There are five cardinal human relations for such interaction—three within the family and two outside of the family: that between father and son, husband and wife, elder and younger brothers, ruler and subject, and friends. All these relations obligate individuals to perform their respective roles in society—the father has to be kind while the son is respectful; the husband has to be caring while the wife is submissive; brothers need to be mutually deferential; the ruler needs to have the people's welfare in mind while the subjects need to be obedient; and friends must maintain fidelity toward one another. It is therefore the entire human community that provides the setting for the Confucian religious quest. The *Doctrine of the Mean* offers a climactic conclusion to the process of self-cultivation:

> Only the most authentic and genuine person can fully develop his nature. Able to fully develop his nature, he can then thoroughly understand the nature of other people. Able to fully understand the nature of other people, he can develop the nature of things. Able to fully develop the nature of things, he can assist in the transforming and nourishing process of *Tian* and *Di* (earth, counterpart to *Tian*). When he assists in the transforming and nourishing process of *Tian* and *Di*, he forms a trinity with them!
>
> —*Doctrine of the Mean* 22:1

This euphoric assurance of the final outcome of human moral cultivation is breathtaking in its grandeur. Not only does the person who realizes his own nature to the full become a paradigm of genuine humanity, but also he actually becomes a "coequal" with *Tian* and *Di* through his participation in their nurture and sustenance of the myriad things. Forming a trinity with the ultimate numinous entity in the cosmos is without a doubt the highest accomplishment for any religious seeker in the Confucian mode.

In the preceding paragraphs, we have analyzed the content and the religiosity of the Four Books. These four texts neatly annotate the later Neo-Confucian goal of *neisheng waiwang*—inner moral cultivation and external skillful management of society and state (see the section on the history of Confucianism later in this chapter). This is believed to reflect the original vision of Confucius, namely, to pursue a personal relationship with the ultimate reality through moral improvement, culminating in an ordering of society and state in accordance with the Way ordained by *Tian*. This religious mission is best expressed by a famous Neo-Confucian scholar by the name of Zhang Zai (1020–1077):

> To establish the mind of *Tian* and *Di*
> To inculcate an understanding of [*Tian*'s] command (*ming*) for the multitudes
> To revive and perpetuate the teachings of the sages of the past
> To provide peace and stability for all future generations.

This is indeed the social-political, as well as religious, aspiration of Confucianism in a nutshell!

Confucianism and Women

The issue of Confucianism and sexism needs to be addressed. Despite its lofty religious teaching, Confucianism has often been criticized for its dismissive and negative attitude toward women. The single most notorious statement made by Confucius regarding women is truly incriminating: "Women and the petty men are alike, in that they are both hard to deal with" (*Analects* 17:23). In addition, one of the most prominent features of Confucianism during the Han Dynasty (206 B.C.E.–220 B.C.E.) and beyond is the submissiveness of the female to the male. Cleverly manipulating the traditional *yin-yang* belief into an argument for the priority of *yang* over *yin*, hence the male over the female, Han Confucians and their successors in later dynasties insisted that women submit to their fathers when young, their husbands when married, and their sons when old and widowed. This aspect of Confucianism in imperial China became a major cause of criticism of the tradition in the modern period. Since the beginning of the twentieth century, Confucianism has been portrayed as a sexist, patriarchal ideology responsible for the oppression of women in China. The insidious Chinese practices of foot binding (the crushing of the feet of young girls with long binding cloth to make their walking willowy and feminine), concubinage (the keeping of multiple wives by one man), disallowance of women-initiated divorce, prohibition against remarriage, and encouragement of widow suicide have all been blamed on Confucianism.

However, this view of Confucianism may be too simplistic in characterizing the two thousand years of Chinese gender history. It makes no distinction between theory and practice, as well as ideal, normative values versus actual, living experiences. Furthermore, it also overlooks the very intellectual and religious dynamism of Confucianism as a teaching of human improvement and self-cultivation with no gender specificity. Some contemporary scholars have taken note of the parallels between Confucian and feminist ethics. Confucianism as a state orthodoxy whose central purpose is social control and political manipulation is indeed incompatible with modern values. However, Confucianism as an ethical and religious teaching with an emphasis on mutual care, empathy, responsible government, and communal welfare shares many similarities with feminist care ethics.[12]

Laozi riding on the back of a water buffalo as he retires into the realm of the immortals.

The Teachings of Daoism

We have pointed out earlier that Daoism evolved out of the same ancient Chinese religious mindset as Confucianism did. But instead of regarding *Tian* as the Absolute Ultimate, as the Confucians do, Daoists from the beginning hold *Dao* to be supreme. It should be recalled that the term *Dao* is also central to the Confucian tradition. However, the Daoists articulate a very different understanding of the *Dao*. It is this alternative apprehension of the *Dao* that serves as the point of departure for their entirely different mode of religious experience from that of the Confucians.

Laozi (Lao-tzu) and *Zhuangzi* (Chuang-tzu)   Traditionally, the best known and earliest identifiable Daoists were Laozi (Master Lao) and Zhuangzi (Master Zhuang). The former, more of a composite figure than an actual person, was the reputed author of the **Daodejing** (*Tao-te Ching*; The Scripture of the Way and Its Potent Manifestation),[13] alternatively known as the *Laozi*. The latter was an obscure individual active in the late fourth century B.C.E. who was credited with authorship of the second most influential Daoist text, the *Zhuangzi*. Both texts are more representative of certain modes of thinking than of individual thinkers, as they are actually anthologies containing different strands of thought rather than coherent and logical teachings of single authors. One thing, however, is clear: they are self-consciously non-Confucian in that they express a decidedly alternative understanding of the *dao* and of ideal human action. In addition, both the *Daodejing* and the *Zhuangzi* also contain descriptions of perfected human beings who possess amazing powers of magic and immortality. Both texts suggest

that, through intense inner psychic journeying and mystical conditioning of the human body, individuals can acquire impressive powers of transformation and invulnerability to the decaying agents in nature.

The *Daodejing*   The eighty-one-chapter *Daodejing* is undoubtedly the most translated and most popular Chinese text in the West. Virtually all the different movements and sectarian lineages within Daoism regard this work as the founding scripture of the tradition.

In contrast to the Confucian *Dao* being the ideal ethical-social-political order ordained by *Tian* for human beings, the *Dao* of the *Laozi* antedates *Tian* and acts as the basis of the natural order. Here *Dao* is the primordial entity that exists in an undifferentiated state prior to the coming into being of the myriad things, including *Tian* and *Di*, which now stand for nothing more than nature itself. The lofty primacy of the Confucian *Tian* is supplanted by the nebulous *Dao* of the *Daodejing*, as indicated by the following celebrated passage:

> There was something undifferentiated and yet complete, which existed
> before *Tian* and *Di*
> Soundless and formless, it depends on nothing and does not change
> It operates everywhere and does not stop
> It may be regarded as the "Mother of the world"
> I do not know its name; I call it *Dao*.
> —*Daodejing, Chap. 25*

In one broad stroke, the entire Confucian cosmological scheme is turned upside down. It is *Dao*, not *Tian*, that gives birth, like a mother, to the myriad things. It is *Dao*, not *Tian*, that serves as the primal source of the cosmos. Echoing the cosmogonic (concerning the origin of the cosmos) view of the *Book of Changes*, the *Daodejing* gives an even terser summary of the generating process of the cosmos:

> The *Dao* gives birth to the One [Being, Existence]
> The One brings forth the Two [*Yin* and *Yang*]
> The Two give rise to the Three [*Tian, Di*, and Humans]
> The Three engender the Ten Thousand Things [world of multiplicity
> and diversity]
> —*Daodejing, Chap. 42*

Again, the primacy of the *Dao* as the procreator of the entire universe and everything in it is unequivocally asserted here. As the ground of all beings, this *Dao* is compared to a "mysterious female," "water," "infant," and "uncarved block," all alluding to the beginning of life and form. However, unlike the Confucian *Dao*, which requires superior human beings (the *junzi* [men of virtue] and the *shengren* [sages]) to exert their utmost effort to actualize its ideal design, the *Dao* of the *Daodejing* can only maintain its pristine form when humans leave it alone. Thus the ideal course of action for insightful and wise human beings is to observe **wuwei** (actions without intention) and **ziran** (natural spontaneity) in their attempt to return to the *Dao*. These two ideal approaches to life are indicative of the *Daodejing*'s belief in the innate perfection and completeness of the *Dao*. *Wuwei* calls for a minimalist and noninterventionist attitude in human action, whereas *ziran* rejects any artificiality and contrived undertaking as detrimental to human well-being. Ultimately, the *Dao* in the *Daodejing* is indescribable, for it defies verbalization and precise definition. "The *Dao* that can be [verbally] expressed is not the constant *Dao*," insists the *Daodejing* in its first verse.

Yet the transcendent *Dao* is, at the same time, manifested in the myriad things through its presence in them as *de*—the very "potent manifestation" of each thing. In contrast to the *de* of the Confucians, which is the charismatic power of the moral elite, the *de* of the *Daodejing* points to the concrete expression of the *Dao* in all things. *De* is the "thingness" of a thing—that which makes a thing what it is. The combination of *Dao* and *de*, then, helps to bridge the gap between the transcendent and the immanent for the author(s) of the *Daodejing*. The *Dao* is the transcendent ground of being, yet through its expression in the *de* of the myriad concrete things, it is also fully immanent.

The *Zhuangzi*

The extant version of the *Zhuangzi* consists of thirty-three chapters divided into three sections—"Inner," "Outer," and "Miscellaneous." The first seven Inner chapters are generally believed to be the authentic writings of Zhuang Zhou, the putative author. Yet as in the case of the *Daodejing*, we have only a vague biographical account of Zhuang Zhou, and little of substance is known about him.

The *Zhuangzi* is overall a different kind of text from the *Daodejing*. Whereas the latter is terse and aphoristic in language, the former is effusive and vividly narrative. The *Daodejing* idealizes the feminine and regards the *Dao* as mother, but the *Zhuangzi* does not. The *Daodejing* gives much emphasis to politics and the techniques of rulership; the *Zhuangzi* is overtly adverse to politics. The *Zhuangzi* tells stories with a witty, playful, irreverent tone that is totally absent in the *Daodejing*. In terms of basic worldview and cosmological assumptions, however, the *Zhuangzi* shares much in common with the *Daodejing*, hence their grouping together by later historians and bibliographers as representatives of the "School of the *Dao*."

In the *Zhuangzi*, the *Dao* is not only the ineffable transcendent entity that gives rise to all things but also the immanent core that exists in all things, from the loftiest perfected beings to the lowliest broken tiles and excrement. It is therefore omnipresent, making all things ultimately equal. As such, the *Dao* transcends all polarities, dichotomies, and dualities that the human mind is inclined to create. Hence the use of the human cognitive and rational approach to apprehend the *Dao* is futile and unproductive, as it can only be realized intuitively through the abandonment of the intellect. The mind must be able to be free from all conventional distinctions and established views, hence the advocacy of "carefree wandering" (*xiaoyao yu*) in the *Zhuangzi*. In this connection the discussion of "fasting the mind/heart" (**xinzhai**) and "sitting and forgetting" (**zuowang**) becomes pertinent, as both practices dispense with rationality and deliberative cognition in order to arrive at the perfect intuitive understanding of the *Dao*.

Elements of Physical Invulnerability in the *Daodejing* and the *Zhuangzi*

Although both the *Daodejing* and the *Zhuangzi* are best known (in China and in the West) for their sophisticated philosophical discussions of the *Dao*, much less known is their commentary on the physical prowess of the Daoist practitioners. They hint at invulnerability to harm, longevity, and even immortality—the very goals of a Daoist religious movement that began no later than the second century C.E.

We next explore the impact the two have had on the content of Daoism as a religion. The following passages from both texts are highly suggestive:

EXCERPTS FROM THE *DAODEJING*

He who does not lose his proper place lasts long
He who dies but does not perish has longevity.

—Daodejing, Chap. 33

I have heard that people who are good at preserving their lives will not encounter wild bulls or tigers when traveling on land, and will not need to protect themselves with armor when in the army. Wild bulls will find nowhere to thrust their horns, tigers will have no place to sink their claws, and weapons will find no point to insert their cutting blades. And why is that? Because in them there is no room for death.

—Daodejing, Chap. 50

He who is richly endowed with *de* is comparable to a newborn baby: poisonous insects will not sting him, ferocious beasts will not seize him in their claws, and birds of prey will not snatch him with their talons.

—Daodejing, Chap. 55

EXCERPTS FROM THE *ZHUANGZI*

Far away on Mt. Guye there dwells a divine person (*shenren*) whose skin is like ice and snow, and who is gentle and shy like a young girl. He does not eat the five grains; but [only] inhales the wind and drinks the dew. He ascends the clouds, mounts flying dragons, and wanders beyond the four seas. His spirit is focused, thus he saves creatures from sickness and plagues, and guarantees bountiful harvests.

—Zhuangzi, Chap. 1

The ultimate person (*zhiren*) is spirit-like. Though the great marshes are set ablaze, they will not make him hot. Though the rivers and streams freeze up, they cannot chill him. Though violent thunder splits the mountains and howling gales churn the ocean, they will not frighten him. A man like this rides the clouds and mist, mounts the sun and moon, and goes beyond the four seas. Death and life have no effect on him, how much less will profit and loss?

—*Zhuangzi, Chap. 2*

The perfected individuals (*zhenren*) of old . . . could go up to high places without getting frightened, enter water without getting wet, and go into fire without feeling hot. Only those whose knowledge ascends the height of the Dao can be like this. . . . The perfected breathe with their heels, while the ordinary men breathe with their throat.

—*Zhuangzi, Chap. 6*

Blowing and breathing, exhaling the old and inhaling the new, [imitating the postures of] bear strides and bird stretches—these are all undertaken for the purpose of longevity. They are pursued with fondness by people who practice gymnastic calisthenics (*daoyin*) and body nourishments (*yangxing*) in hope of [attaining the longevity] of Patriarch Peng.

—*Zhuangzi, Chap. 15*

A Daoist immortal flying through the clouds, 1750. Portrayed is the sage mother of Dongling, who studied the Way and could cure illnesses. One day, amidst a throng wishing to thank her, she ascended to the clouds.

These passages on *Daoist* adepts describe their amazing magical power and physical invulnerability.

What these two texts suggest, at the very least, is that the numinous *Dao* (the holy) is accessible by potent (that is, healthy) individuals and that holiness and robust health are closely related. As described by the *Daodejing* and *Zhuangzi*, the early practitioners of the *Dao* were people who, through their use of various bodily techniques, acquired powers that enabled them to experience the divine. These techniques and powers would very much become the concern of later Daoists. In short, the *Daodejing* and the *Zhuangzi* can be perceived as "proto-Daoist" texts by virtue of their distinctive view of the *Dao* and their reference to various practices and powers that anticipate those of the later organized Daoist groups.

Immortality and Alchemy One later Daoist preoccupation is with the notion of **xian** (immortal or transcendent), long a folk religious fascination but articulated most eloquently in the *Baopuzi* (Master Who Embraces Simplicity), a text authored by

Ge Hong (283–343 C.E.). Central to this belief in *xian* is the conviction that physical transformation, invulnerability to disease, longevity, and ultimately immortality, can be acquired through proper diet, physical exercise, and drugs. People with the right recipe, formula, or prescription (**fangshi**) would teach these esoteric techniques and provide ready-made elixirs to those who had the financial resources and the necessary devotion to secure their services.

Inherent in the belief in immortality are the ancient Chinese assumptions about the human body and the measures that can be taken to keep it healthy and even immortal. The ancient Chinese believed that the human body is the microcosm that reflects the macrocosm of the cosmos. In other words, there is a direct correspondence and parallel between the human body and nature. All the myriad things in the universe are produced by the interaction of the vital energies (*qi*) of *yin* and *yang*. They also manifest the qualities of the five elemental phases (*wuxing*), follow the principle of alternation and constant return, while maintaining balance and harmony with one another. This belief was retained by Daoism and Chinese folk religion. According to this view, there are three central nodal points in the human body called **dantian** (locations for the production of pills of immortality)—in the head, the chest, and the abdomen—connected by meridian circuits through which the *qi* (energy) flows. And, because the body is the cosmos writ small, just as there are gods and deities inhabiting the physical world outside, there are also numerous spiritual beings residing in various organs of the human body.

Based on this whole series of assumptions, the techniques of **yangsheng** (nourishing life) are developed. First mentioned in the *Zhuangzi*, *yangsheng* has the goal of refining the body so that it can overcome its earthly limitations and be in perfect harmony with the *Dao*, making it last as long as the universe. It involves an entire spectrum of exercises, including deep meditation, controlled breathing, therapeutic gymnastics, dietary regimens, even sexual techniques. All these measures of nourishing life have been practiced by religious Daoists since the second century C.E. and are grouped under the general heading of **neidan** (internal alchemy).

While these *yangsheng* techniques aim at the regeneration and reinforcement of the human body by making use of what the body originally possesses, the *fangshi* also focus on the compounding and refining of elixirs with substances (herbal and mineral) from nature. References to "refining gold" (*lianjin*) and transmuting cinnabar (mercury sulphate) in some Han Dynasty texts indicate a growing practice of alchemy for the purpose of attaining longevity and immortality. This pursuit of alchemical manufacturing of *dan* with minerals and plants would eventually lead to the **waidan** (external alchemy) tradition in Daoism.

A Daoist view of the major nodal points in the human body through which the *qi* (energy) flows.

Figurine of Lord Guan as seen in many Chinese restaurants.

All the internal and external alchemical techniques discussed here are intended to produce a new body that grows within the old so that, in time, the old self will be replaced by the new in the same way cicadas and snakes regenerate themselves.

Daoist Deities As the Daoist tradition matured, the most exalted god in the Daoist pantheon became the *Yuanshi tianzun* (Celestial Venerable of Primordial Beginning), who is head of a trinity of Three Purities (*sanqing*). Below the *sanqing* are innumerable deities of both genders who fill up various ranks in a mind-boggling celestial bureaucracy that loosely corresponds to its human counterpart.

The lowliest among the spiritual bureaucrats is the local earth god (*tudi gong*), and the head of the celestial government is the Jade Emperor (*Yuhuang*). Many of them have divine origins, of course, but many also are former humans whose merits warrant their promotion to godly status. Some of the deities have national appeal, such as Lord Zhenwu [Perfect Martiality] of Mt. Wudang, whereas others are more local in influence, including the Stove god (*zaojun*) in each household. One ubiquitous Daoist deity, Lord Guan, is honored by business owners as their protector and benefactor. A human turned god, Lord Guan can be seen in the form of a heroic figure with a red face and a cascading black beard, sporting a long robe and holding a long blade. An altar or alcove containing a figurine of him can be found in most Chinese restaurants in North America, where he is worshipped as a patron deity.

Daoist deities not only reside in the heavens, on earth, in the underworld, and in the homes but also inside the human body. They are supposed to protect all the major internal organs from the decaying effect of unwholesome food and old age. The entire pantheon of Daoist deities can be accessed and appealed to through ritual performance for assistance in warding off evil, improving health, guaranteeing harmony in family and community, and attaining immortality.

Daoism and Women

Because of the feminine emphasis of the *Daodejing*, it is generally assumed that Daoism, unlike Confucianism, treats women fairly and kindly. Yet the situation is more complicated than it might appear at first thought. The positions and roles of women in organized Daoism have to be examined in the larger context of Chinese society, which until recent times has indeed been patriarchal and sexist. It is therefore not surprising that women only play limited roles even in Daoism.

And yet it is also undeniable that because of women's believed greater sensitivity to the spirits and their keener communication ability with the divine and invisible world, they do have access to roles and positions denied to most women in Chinese society at large. Women's special power to intercede with the deities often makes some of them more outstanding and influential practitioners of Daoism than men.

A Daoist movement known as the Celestial Masters (**Tianshi**; see more details in the section on the history of Daoism in this chapter) identified five classes of women suited to be Daoist practitioners: young unmarried women, women unable to marry because of their inauspicious horoscopes, women forced into marriage, rejected (divorced) wives, and widows. All these were vulnerable individuals to whom the Celestial Masters offered an escape and a way to assert their worth. In the Tang Dynasty (618–907 C.E.), women from aristocratic families became Daoist nuns in substantial numbers, either between marriages or as widows. There were also imperial princesses ordained as Daoist priestesses.

Xiwangmu (Queen Mother of the West) is one of the most prominent female Daoist deities. She rewards her devout followers with immortality by feasting them with magical peaches.

Equally noteworthy are a number of major Daoist goddesses who play key roles in the religion. Chief among them are Xiwangmu (Queen Mother of the West), best known for her granting of the power of immortality to the faithful, and Mazu, the virginal protectress of fishermen and merchants who is still very popular in southeast China and Taiwan today. Some women were actually founders of Daoist sects, most notably Wei Huacun (252–334 C.E.) of the Shangqing [Highest Clarity] tradition and Zu Shu (most active during 889–904 C.E.), who initiated the Qingwei [Pure Subtlety] tradition. Sun Bu'er (1119–1182 C.E.) was a famous female disciple of the founder of the Quanzhen [Complete Perfection] sect who became a senior leader in the movement with the power to teach and ordain other female practitioners. (We examine these other Daoist groups more closely later in this chapter.)

No comparable number of women can be identified as prominent Confucians. It is thus accurate to conclude that women generally fare better in Daoism than in Confucianism.

THE HISTORY OF CONFUCIANISM AND DAOISM

The earliest time in Chinese history for which we have both written records and archaeological evidences is the Shang Dynasty, whose traditional dates are 1600–1046 B.C.E. Representative of these records and evidences are the "oracle bone inscriptions," carved messages on smoothed-out oxen shoulder blade bones or tortoise shells that include questions put to (and supposed answers from) deceased members of the Shang royalty. The questions covered a wide spectrum of issues, from actions to be undertaken by the ruler (such as the decision to go to war) to intimate, personal matters of the imperial family (such as the gender of royal offspring about to be born). After the questions were put forth, heat was applied to a predrilled hole in the bone or shell, causing cracks to appear. Patterns formed by these cracks were read by the shaman-diviner, and

A Chinese oracle bone made of tortoise shell.

occasionally the Shang ruler himself, and were interpreted as answers to the original questions posed.

As indicated in the section on teachings in this chapter, the head of the Shang spiritual world was *Shangdi*, the ultimate benefactor of the royal house. Eventually, around the end of the second millennium B.C.E., the Shang dynasty was toppled by the Zhou. While retaining the ancestral focus of the Shang, as well as its belief in the religious underpinning of political authority, the Zhou founders nevertheless replaced *Shangdi* with *Tian* as the overarching spiritual authority. They exercised political power with the claim that it was a mandate they received from *Tian*, ostensibly because of their moral worthiness. Early Zhou society was reportedly well-ordered and harmonious, presided over by men of virtue. This impression was projected by the Zhou texts, collectively labeled as the Confucian Five Classics mentioned earlier in this chapter, which would serve as the prototypical source of the Confucian teachings.

The History of Confucianism

At the time of Confucius's birth, the entire political system and moral framework put in place by the early Zhou kings, as described in the previous section, was in disarray. Powerful feudal lords jockeyed for position to become the next *Tianzi*, the son of *Tian*, and to replace the current Zhou king. The more capable and ambitious among them actively sought the service of talented men outside the hereditary aristocratic circles, thereby creating upward social mobility for some among the commoners. Conversely, powerful lords could become commoners overnight as a result of their defeat by their rivals, creating a downward social spiral as well.

These critical social developments gave rise to the increasing prominence of a class of experts and specialists known as **shi** (men of service). Drawn from lower aristocratic or commoner backgrounds, they entered the employ of feudal lords and imperial rulers. The *shi* performed two major categories of duties: military and civil. The military men of service, the knights, were referred to as *wushi*, whereas their civilian counterparts, the scholars, were known as *rushi*, or simply **ru**. *Ru* were scribes and record keepers, masters of rituals and ceremonies, as well as diviners and religious professionals. To perform their duties well, *ru* had to acquire expertise in history, poetry, religious rites, divination, dance, and music.

Confucius was just such a *ru* who was born into a family of former aristocrats in the feudal domain of Lu (located in present-day Shandong province in North China). His father died when he was still an infant, so he had to do menial work as a young man to support himself, his sickly older brother, and his widowed mother. What enabled Confucius to lift himself up from poverty and anonymity was his desire for and success in scholarship. He apparently had an extraordinarily inquisitive mind and a voracious appetite for study, especially of the ancient texts of history, rituals, and poetry. By the age of thirty he was well known for his expertise as a *ru*. His service in government was limited to a number of minor posts, but his greatest accomplishment was in his vocation as a teacher. Confucius offered fresh insight into the human condition, creatively reinterpreting the belief system he inherited from the early Zhou. In addition, he communicated a forceful message of the need for improvement of individuals and society through moral cultivation and benevolent government. Aided by an intense and charismatic personality, Confucius became a popular private teacher with a huge following.

After age fifty, as he realized that the feudal lord of his native Lu did not value his service, Confucius left with a number of trusted disciples in tow and headed for other feudal domains. His hope was that other lords would embrace his ideas and would implement his political blueprint for restoring order to the world. For the next thirteen years he traveled all across Northern China, going from one feudal domain to another in search of opportunities to carry out his reform proposals. He was met with disappointment everywhere, at times suffering much indignity, deprivation, and even physical danger. In the twilight years of his life, he returned to his home state of Lu with his political ambition unfulfilled and devoted the remainder of his life to teaching, writing, and editing the ancient texts. Confucius died in his early seventies.

Confucius is believed to have put the major classical works into their final form. He supposedly edited the *Book of Odes* and the *Book of History*, wrote important commentaries on the *Book of Changes*, and contributed to the *Record of Rites,* as well as the no-longer-extant *Book of Music*. He also supposedly authored a book on the history of the late Zhou period from the vantage point of his native state of Lu, which is titled *Chunqiu (Spring and Autumn Annals)*. The work covers the years 722–481 B.C.E., a period that since has been known as the Spring and Autumn period in Chinese history.

Statue of Confucius at the entrance to the Confucian Academy in Beijing, China.

Toward the end of his long life, Confucius gave a telling summary and assessment of his intellectual development as recorded in the *Analects*, a work compiled by his followers that contains his celebrated sayings:

> At fifteen I set my mind on learning
> At thirty I had become established [as a *ru*]
> At forty I was free from doubts
> At fifty I knew the decree of *Tian* (*Tianming*)
> At sixty my ears became attuned [to what I heard from *Tian*]
> At seventy I could follow my heart's desires without transgressing what
> was right
>
> —*Analects 2:4*

This intellectual and spiritual autobiography of Confucius illustrates the pattern of his development from a scholar to a religious figure. His biography shows that he was a fully human figure with no claim to supernatural origin or power and was the consummate representative of the *ru* tradition and an exemplary teacher. Eventually, however, Confucius would be honored as a sage and the founder of China's most important philosophical and religious tradition.

Later Defenders of the Faith   The Chinese world after Confucius took a turn for the worse. Warfare among the feudal states became even more frequent and brutal. The centuries between Confucius's death in 479 and 221 B.C.E. are known as the Warring States period in Chinese history. Confucius's original vision of moral cultivation and benevolent government seemed impractical and quixotic. Internally, the Confucian tradition was rocked by self-doubt and resignation, as his *ru* followers became mere functionaries for the feudal lords, enjoying little influence or self-esteem. Externally, rival traditions such as Daoism and other more pragmatic schools competed for attention and attacked many of the Confucian ideas.

Into this picture came Mencius (371–289 B.C.E.?), the second most important figure in the Confucian tradition. As the most ardent defender of the faith, he articulated views that would be revered as definitive interpretations of what Confucius had outlined. We have already examined his contribution to the tradition in the section on the teachings of Confucianism in this chapter. His ideas would become orthodox for most future Confucians.

A younger contemporary of Mencius was Xun Qing (310–238 B.C.E.?), or Master Xun (Xunzi), who actually exerted far greater influence on the Confucian movement through the second century C.E. than Mencius did. Xun Qing's rationalism and pragmatic approach to rituals and learning had given a decisively secular and worldly bent to the Confucian tradition, resulting in a noticeable neglect of its religious nature. His view of human nature as evil also contradicted the Mencian version. Nevertheless, Xun Qing shared with Mencius an abiding faith in the transformative influence of moral cultivation and the perfectibility of humanity through self-effort. Eventually, however, Xun Qing was rejected by later Confucians as heterodox, and the text bearing his name was never recognized as a Confucian scripture.

Confucianism as Orthodoxy   When China was unified by the Qin (Ch'in) state in 221 B.C.E., the Confucian tradition was initially a target of state persecution. Its call for benevolent government and individual moral autonomy was rejected by the First Emperor of Qin as impractical and subversive. But the Qin Dynasty soon fell, replaced by the Han (206 B.C.E.–220 C.E.), a much more hospitable regime for Confucian teaching. By the middle of the second century B.C.E., the Confucian tradition finally surpassed all its competitors by becoming the state-designated orthodoxy, in recognition of its usefulness in fostering effective governance and enhancing social cohesiveness. Yet its orthodox status also necessitated fundamental changes in its orientation. From a teaching that called for high-minded personal moral cultivation and benevolent government, Confucianism in the Han Dynasty became a scholastic tradition and a tool for state control and patriarchal authoritarianism. In fulfilling that role, Confucius was showered with grandiose titles by subsequent generations of Chinese rulers who scrambled to outdo one another in their adoration of him, culminating in the breathtakingly exuberant title of "Ultimate Sage of Greatest Accomplishment, King of Manifest Culture" given to him by an emperor in 1308. "Temples" dedicated to Confucius were built in all the administrative and political centers throughout the empire. Nevertheless, these temples served more as memorials, such as those dedicated to Thomas Jefferson or Abraham Lincoln, than as places of worship, and Confucius himself remained by and large an exemplary human figure worthy of veneration, rather than a god promising salvation and demanding pious submission.

The Neo-Confucian Tradition   Though Confucianism served nominally as China's orthodoxy from the second century B.C.E. to the beginning of the twentieth century C.E., a span of over 2,000 years, it coexisted with Daoism and Buddhism during that entire period, and at times was even overshadowed by them. Since the twelfth century C.E., however, through a revitalization movement known in the West as Neo-Confucianism, it regained the initiative over its Daoist and Buddhist rivals and became the predominant religious tradition in China until the modern era. Indeed, as advocated by its most eloquent representative, the scholar Zhu Xi (1130–1200), its new scriptural corpus, the Four Books, composed of the *Analects*, the *Mencius*, the *Great Learning*, and the *Doctrine of the Mean*, would constitute the main curriculum upon which the civil service examination of late imperial China would be based. Between 1313 and 1905, all aspiring scholars and government officials in China had to study and were examined on their mastery of this set of canonical works, which provided the basis of their worldview and their outlook on life. To be sure, there would be other voices within the Neo-Confucian movement that challenged Zhu Xi's interpretations, notably that of Wang Yangming (1472–1529). They differed primarily in how best to attain the same goal of "inner sagely moral perfection and outer political ability and administrative skills" (**neisheng waiwang**). Personal moral perfection and universal transformation of the human community formed one continuum in their ultimate religious quest.

Beginning in the fourteenth century, as China entered the late imperial period, the Confucian tradition became fossilized and rigid. The examinations were formulaic wordplays instead of genuine expressions of moral insight or sound administrative proposals. The entire Confucian tradition was turned into a mere tool of state control and social climbing. Political autocracy, patriarchal authoritarianism, and social exploitation were all carried out in its name.

Confucianism as Pan-Asiatic Tradition   Confucian texts had found their way beyond China no later than the turn of the Common Era, along with China's

The Apricot Platform (Xingtan) is traditionally identified to be the location where Confucius lectured to his students.

Confucian influence in
East Asia.

outward expansion both culturally and territorially. But it was in the form of
Neo-Confucianism that this religious and philosophical tradition had exerted its most
significant impact on China's neighbors such as Korea, Japan, and Vietnam. Thanks
to the dynamic influence of Zhu Xi and his intellectual successors, Confucianism
became the dominant philosophy and state orthodoxy, beginning with the Yi Dynasty
in Korea (fourteenth century), the Tokugawa Shogunate in Japan (seventeenth century),
and the Nguyen Dynasty in Vietnam (nineteenth century). The social organizations,

bureaucratic cultures, and religious assumptions of these Asian neighbors of China echoed much that existed in China during her late imperial period (fourteenth to twentieth centuries).

Confucianism in the Modern World Confucianism entered a period of sharp decline in the modern age. This process began after the Opium War of 1839–1842, in which China was handily defeated by Great Britain. Other foreign powers quickly followed suit to demand enormous concessions from a weakened and disgraced China. For China's patriotic young generation of intellectual elite, this humiliating development exposed the shortcomings of their Confucian heritage. Confucianism was blamed for China's political, social, and economic backwardness. As a result, the New Culture Movement that began in the second decade of the twentieth century made Confucianism their main target of assault. "Down with Confucius and sons!" was now the popular call for rebellion against the tradition. The logic was that unless the roots of the Confucian tradition were eradicated completely, China would not survive the challenge of modernity. Indeed, the birth of the Chinese Communist movement was in part attributable to this rebellious mode of thinking. From the perspective of the radical revolutionaries, Confucianism was a reactionary ideology of the ruling elite in China's feudal past that should be cast into the dustbin of history.

But the obituary for Confucianism appears to have been written prematurely. Despite repeated and sometimes violent attempts to rid China of the harmful influence of Confucianism, the "anti-Confucius" campaign of the Cultural Revolution period (1966–1976) on mainland China being the most glaring example, the tradition has survived. As the opening vignette demonstrates, Confucianism as a religious tradition is still very much alive in contemporary China. The central importance of the family, the persistence of ancestral remembrance, and the value placed on education and self-improvement are evidence of the resilience of the Confucian ethos among many Chinese, and even East Asians in general. Some argue that the economic and industrial progress of the "Four Dragons" of Taiwan, South Korea, Hong Kong, and Singapore since the 1980s, and a similar development under way in China as well, might have been brought about by the Confucian heritage in these East Asian countries.

At the same time, an emergent group of "New Confucians," both inside and outside China, has been active as advocates for the revival of the Confucian teaching on philosophical and religious grounds. This group finds a new relevance for the Confucian tradition in the postmodern world on the ground that it expresses values of universal significance. These new defenders of the Confucian faith seek to rearticulate Confucianism for our time in the same way Confucians of the past had rearticulated it for theirs.

Equally notable is the new popularity enjoyed by Confucianism in China within the last decade, in part endorsed by the Chinese government. Academies devoted to the study of the Confucian tradition have been established, instruction on and the memorization of the *Analects* for school-age children are widely promoted, and even

TV programs dedicated to the explanation of the relevance of Confucian teaching to contemporary Chinese society are eagerly viewed by a growing audience. The Chinese government also provides partial funding for the establishment of "Confucius Institutes" in European and North American universities to encourage interest in Chinese and Confucian studies.

The History of Daoism

As we learned in the section on teachings in this chapter, Laozi and Zhuangzi, traditionally recognized as early founders of the Daoist tradition, were shadowy figures whose books bearing their names were actually anthologies containing divergent strands of thought. At best they could only be considered proto-Daoists. Laozi, historically believed to have been an older contemporary of Confucius, was a mysterious figure who was already an old man at the time of Confucius's birth (hence his name "Laozi," which literally can mean "old baby"). Late in his life he reportedly left China beyond her western borders, but not before he dictated to a follower what came to be known as the *Daodejing*. Zhuangzi, whose historicity was more accepted, was believed to have been a fourth-century B.C.E. figure whose wit and irreverence made his comments on the Dao some of the most well-known and celebrated ones. His dreaming of being a butterfly, and upon waking, his questioning of the validity of his human identity was of course the most famous example of his relativistic thinking. There were, as well, numerous other early commentators of the Dao who contributed to the formation of a "Daoist school" or "Daoist tradition" no later than the second century B.C.E.

The Deification of Laozi

A crucial development that led to the rise of Daoism as an organized religion was the divinization of Laozi. Sometime between the second century B.C.E. and the second century C.E., Laozi was revered as a human incarnation of the *Dao*. Remarkably, a belief arose that the *Dao* could now intervene in human affairs and directly and personally impart teaching to the faithful through its human form. As the *Dao* incarnate, Laozi was the object of worship, thereby making the *Dao*, for the first time, a human-like being that demanded and received religious devotion. In a text entitled *Laozi bianhua jing* (*Scripture of the Transformations of Laozi*), compiled around the middle of the second century C.E., the various incarnations of Laozi over time were recounted. One such incarnation was in the form of a messianic figure dedicated to the salvation of the world, and the title Laozi assumed in this case was *Taishang Laojun*, the Venerable Lord of the Most High.

Even more significantly, Laozi as *Taishang Laojun* could give instructions to selected individuals on the esoteric secrets of the *Dao* as part of his scheme to save the world. This deified and messianic Laozi thus turned the Daoist teaching into a divine revelation on salvation, which has since become a major tenet of organized Daoism. Once Laozi was venerated as the *Dao* incarnate, as well as a dispenser of redemptive instructions, Daoism became a salvational faith. A whole pantheon of deities, both in nature and within the human body, came to be worshiped as physical manifestations of the *Dao* and as agents of deliverance.

Beginning in the middle of the second century C.E., Daoism became an organized and large-scale movement among the common people. In the year 142 C.E., a man by the name of Zhang Ling (or Zhang Daoling) allegedly had a fateful encounter with the deified Laozi, who indicated to him that the world was in great trouble and that he was the one who would be taught the right knowledge and proper practice to save it. He was to adopt the title of **Tianshi** (Celestial Master; see the section on the teachings of Daoism in this chapter), and the teaching he was to transmit would be called *Zhengyi* (Orthodox Unity).

Zhang Ling later transferred the *Tianshi* title to his descendants down through the ages until the present day (in Taiwan). The movement would be known variously as "Celestial Master," "Orthodox Unity," or "Five Bushels of Rice," the last derived from the amount of contributions members were expected to make to the organization at their initiation. During the second half of the second century C.E., the movement acted as a theocratic shadow government, providing material aid and physical healing services to its membership, in addition to offering a vague hope of messianic salvation. A contemporary and parallel movement, alternatively known as "Great Peace" (*Taiping*) and "Yellow Turbans" (more accurately, Yellow Kerchiefs) (*Huangjin*), took the messianic message more seriously and rebelled against the Han court in an attempt to usher in a new age. This movement was ruthlessly suppressed, even though the dream of *taiping* would live on.

Later Daoist Historical Development The Celestial Masters made an arrangement with the government in 215 C.E. whereby it abandoned its theocratic base in southwestern China and migrated closer to the political center in the north. But soon the Han Dynasty fell, and the subsequent short-lived regimes failed to maintain their power in the face of devastating invasions by nomadic non-Chinese groups such as the Huns, forcing the political and cultural elite to flee south toward the Yangzi River basin. The Celestial Masters followed, and became popular there as well, setting up its headquarters on the Dragon and Tiger Mountain in Jiangxi province in southeast China. During the ensuing Period of Disunion, three centuries when China was politically divided between north and south, Daoism entered a most creative period.

First, both the *Daodejing* and the *Zhuangzi* were given new philosophical interpretations that downplayed, if not totally eliminated, the religious elements on meditative transformations and magical physical transmutations in the two texts. Then someone who was much more closely related to the Celestial Masters, a certain Ge Hong (283–343 C.E.), who styled himself the "Master Who Embraces Simplicity" (*Baopuzi*), vigorously asserted the possibility of attaining physical perfection in the form of immortality through various techniques involving alchemy.

But the most significant development in Daoism was in the area of textual revelations and ritual reforms. Responding both to the competition offered by a rapidly expanding Buddhism and to the need to distinguish itself from the "uncouth" and "coarse" practices of popular religion, Daoist leaders from aristocratic families created new texts and devised new rituals that they claimed were revealed to them through ecstatic encounters with an ever-growing number of Daoist deities.

In the south, the Shangqing (Highest Clarity) and the Lingbao (Numinous Treasure) set of texts and rituals began to emerge almost simultaneously in the fourth century c.e. While the former emphasized individual experiences of spiritual fulfillment through meditation and mental visualization, the latter focused on ritual precision and use of talismans for the purpose of universal salvation, though there was considerable overlapping between the two as well. In the north, similarly intense and creative activities also took place under the claim of new revelations from *Taishang Laojun*, the deified Laozi. A Tuoba (a people outside of the Great Wall) ruler, Emperor Taiwu of the Northern Wei Dynasty, was touted as the "Perfect Lord of Great Peace" (*Taiping zhenjun*) and declared that the ideal world had arrived.

Common among the various Daoist groups of this period was the belief in and anticipation of an impending cataclysmic disaster that would radically transform the existing world. There was an anxious yet exciting expectation of the imminent arrival of a savior-like figure who would protect the devout followers from harm and ensure them a safe journey to the world to come—a perfect world populated by the faithful alone. This eschatological (vision of the end of time) and apocalyptic (revelation of a secret divine design) feature of the Daoist movement resembles many millennial traditions in other cultures.

Because of the proliferation of revelatory texts and the diverse array of rituals, the Period of Disunion also witnessed the first attempts made to classify and standardize them. The Lingbao master Lu Xiujing (406–477 c.e.) was the first to propose the notion of the "three caverns" (*sandong*) to categorize the growing corpus of texts. This tripartite principle of organization was a conscious imitation of the *Tripitaka* (Three Baskets), the canonical corpus of Buddhist texts. Subsequent centuries and regimes would see the organization of the texts become more elaborate with the addition of "four supplements" (*sifu*). This form of classification would constitute the framework of the entire Daoist canon, known as the **Daozang**, the most complete and monumental version of which was printed in 1445 c.e. in 480 sections, 1,120 titles, and over 5,300 volumes.

During China's medieval period, lasting from the seventh to the fourteenth centuries, organized Daoism enjoyed imperial patronage and became very much a part of the cultural life of the elite. Along with a very popular Buddhism and the nominal state ideology of Confucianism, it was one of the "three teachings" (*sanjiao*) of the realm. Its emphasis on nature and a free spirit informed much of the art and literature of the time. The breathtaking monochrome landscape paintings and cursive calligraphic art of the elite scholars reflected central Daoist values.

Several new orders also gained prominence during this time, the most influential among them being the *Quanzhen* Sect (Complete Perfection). Founded by a man named Wang Zhe (1113–1170 c.e.), this school of Daoism embraced elements from both Confucianism and Buddhism. From Confucianism it took moral values, and from Buddhism it adopted monasticism and clerical celibacy. In addition to the *Daodejing*, the Confucian *Classic of Filial Piety* and the Buddhist *Heart Sutra* were given the highest prominence by this tradition. The *Quanzhen* Sect was the most popular religious organization in Mongol Yuan China (1279–1368 C.E.), even overshadowing Buddhism. It is one of the only two Daoist groups that still exist today, the other being the Celestial Masters.

During the late imperial period in Chinese history (fourteenth to nineteenth centuries), Daoism was put on the defensive by the triumphant Neo-Confucians. Its clergy was tightly controlled by the state through the highly regulated issuance of ordination certificates. Though individual emperors might have supported Daoism, as evidenced by the printing of the complete *Daozang* in 1445, as a religious tradition it was overshadowed by Confucianism. Although the Confucian elite grudgingly acknowledged the "philosophic" brilliance of the *Daodejing* and the *Zhuangzi*, they regarded organized Daoist groups as nothing more than a degenerated form of pristine, original Daoism. Organized Daoism was marginalized as superstition, unworthy of elite attention. This contempt for Daoism continued beyond the imperial period, was intensified in the early twentieth century, and was adopted as official policy under the Communist regime since 1949.

This painting, *Wind among the Trees on the Riverbank* by Ni Zan (1306–1374), is best known for the quietude and balance in nature it expresses. China, Yuan Dynasty (1271–1368), dated 1363.

Daoism as a Pan-Asiatic Tradition Like its Confucian counterpart, Daoism is not confined to the Chinese mainland. The proto-Daoist texts of *Laozi* and *Zhuangzi* had certainly reached Korea no later than the Goryeo Period (918–1392), even though Buddhism was the dominant faith of the time. By the ensuing Joseon Dynasty (1392–1897), when Confucianism was the state orthodoxy, Daoism in the form of shamanism, mountain worship, and immortality practices had become an integral part of Korean folk religion. Even today, the national flag of South Korea contains the Taegeuk symbol of yin-yang complementarity and four of the eight divinatory trigrams. In Japan, similarly, Daoism was never a dominant, independent tradition when compared with Confucianism and Buddhism. Rather, in its diffused form, it has combined with certain Buddhist groups and indigenous Shinto cults to form specific folk religious traditions since the Tokugawa period (1600–1868). Specifically, the Shūgendō (shamanistic mountain ascetics) and the Kōshin religious practice of controlling the decaying agents of the human body to prevent them from shortening human life span display unmistakable Daoist influences. In Southeast Asia as well, Daoism has found its way into the beliefs of the Xiantian Dao (Way of Prior Heaven) of Malaysia and the Caodai (High Power) tradition in Vietnam.

Daoist influence
in East Asia.

Both are movements promising deliverance from the current age of decadence and corruption.

Daoism Today Because of elite hostility and government neglect, if not active persecution, Daoism as a religious tradition has fared generally very poorly in the modern period. Although the intellectuals still recognized the philosophical ideas in the *Laozi* and the *Zhuangzi* as properly Daoist, they totally ignored the meditative exercises and amazing magical powers of the Daoist seekers of perfection discussed in the two texts, along with the entire corpus of the *Daozang*, the Daoist canon. Daoism was lumped with shamanic popular religion and viewed with disdain. The New Culture Movement of the 1910s and 1920s regarded both Daoism and Confucianism as unwelcome remnants of China's feudal past. The Cultural Revolution (1966–1976) that did so much damage to Confucianism also proved devastating to Daoism. Many historic Daoist shrines and sites were destroyed or sacrilegiously defaced, and all performances of Daoist rituals and liturgies were banned. For all intents and purposes, Daoism as an organized religion ceased to exist in mainland China. Yet the tradition survived amidst China's nebulous folk religion. It also continued to exist, if only barely, outside China among Chinese communities in Taiwan, Hong Kong, and Southeast Asia. Since the late 1970s, however, a Daoist revival of sorts has begun. Daoist ceremonies are once again openly observed in China, and a new generation of Daoist priests has been trained to carry on the tradition and to rebuild the shrines. Academic study of Daoism, primarily by Japanese and French scholars at the beginning, and now joined by Americans and Chinese themselves, has created new understanding of the tradition both from the point of view of doctrines and practices. Some of the scholars have actually become ordained Daoist priests of either the Celestial Master or the Complete Perfection tradition to access more accurate and authoritative interpretations of Daoism. In recent decades, *qigong* exercises (meditation and respiration techniques designed to enhance the body's vital energy), martial arts, and food therapy are popular both in China and abroad. Though not strictly associated with organized Daoism, such phenomena are nevertheless in part based on and inspired by Daoist views on nature and the human body. Respective Daoist practices in breath circulation, gymnastics, and dietetics, discussed in more detail in the next section, attest to the continued relevance of Daoism in the modern world.

This painting of the poet Li Bo (Li Bai, 701–762) shows him as a Daoist immortal.

Both Confucianism and Daoism have been embraced by political authorities to legitimize their rule and to impose order on society. How did they fare when compared with other major world religions?

CONFUCIANISM AND DAOISM AS WAYS OF LIFE

The two Chinese religions discussed in this chapter are not just a collection of precepts and beliefs. More important, they are lived and practiced traditions. It is in the living and practicing of the two traditions that their true meaning and value can be gauged.

Confucian Rituals

From the very beginning, the Confucian tradition has put great emphasis on ritual as a crucial expression of humanity. As "moral behavior," ritual teaches people to conduct themselves with dignity and decorum, making them authentically human. As "holy rites," ritual enables them to communicate effectively with the spiritual powers and interact harmoniously with one another. It is in the latter, more overtly religious sense that Confucian ritual is addressed in this section.

In addition to the mundane rituals of familial and social interaction with other human beings in accordance with the prescribed rules outlined in the classic texts, the most important aspect of religious ritual in Confucianism in the premodern period was the sacrifice (*jisi*), or the making of offerings to the spirits, including ancestors, in the form of animals, other food and drink, even jade and silk. These sacrificial rituals were performed at different levels—the state, the community, and the family. The grandest of the rituals were, of course, conducted at the state level. And chief among the state rituals were those connected with sacrifices to *Tian* and *Di*—and to Confucius once his teaching was exalted to orthodoxy.

Sacrifice to *Tian* and *Di*   *Tian*, it should be recalled, had been the source of legitimate political power since the Zhou Dynasty. As son of *Tian* (*Tianzi*), the Chinese

The Temple of Tian (*Tiantan*), where the Chinese emperor prayed to *Tian* on behalf of his subjects and in his capacity as "Son of Tian," is now a popular park in Beijing.

The Hall of Praying for an Abundant Harvest (*Qi'nian dian*), Temple of Tian (*Tiantan*), Beijing. The whole complex was built in 1420 under the emperor Yongle and restored in 1530 and 1751. Here the emperor celebrated the sacrifice to *Tian* for a good harvest. The decorated ramp between the two stairways was reserved for the emperor's palanquin.

VOICES: An Interview with Jason Ch'ui-hsiao Tseng

Jason Ch'ui-hsiao Tseng is a Taiwanese man in his fifties with a master's degree from an American university. He engages in educational exchange for Chinese students wishing to study in the United States.

Do you consider yourself a Confucian or a Daoist?

I do not consider myself exclusively one or the other. Both have influenced me deeply and I regard their teachings as equally valid and complementary.

How is that possible, as their teachings often conflict with each other?

They are not in conflict. They merely represent the polar opposite of the other. They complete each other. For most Chinese, there is no necessity to choose one or the other. We think of them as the two sides of a coin—without both there is no coin. The two together constitute our native Chinese religious outlook. As a matter of fact, we also consider Buddhist teaching a third way of guiding our religious life. These teachings are generally not jealous of one another. They do not demand total exclusive devotion. They provide meaning to different aspects of our lives. There is religious pluralism for most Chinese.

Jason Ch'ui-hsiao Tseng

How is that so?

We do not believe that one teaching alone corners the market. As a respectful son and an upright citizen, I embrace Confucian values. They teach me to put family and society ahead of myself and to value education as the most important undertaking to improve myself. In my views on how my body works, how my health can be maintained, how different ingredients should be used to achieve balance in my food, and how I can relate to the spirits in the invisible world, I follow the Daoist teaching. And Buddhism gives me hope for a good afterlife. Together they make me a complete person.

ruler carried out *Tian*'s mandate (*Tianming*) to exercise his imperial prerogatives over the entire realm under *Tian* (*Tianxia*). The worship of *Tian* thus became the ruler's exclusive privilege and obligation. Later, with Confucianism imbued with *yin-yang* cosmological ideas in the Han Dynasty, *Tian*, the *yang* element, was paired up with *Di* (earth), the *yin* element, and worship of *Di* was added, though with much less pomp and ostentation.

In late imperial China, the worship of *Tian* and *Di* took place annually. On the day of the summer solstice, the emperor made sacrifice to *Tian* at the Temple of Tian (*tiantan*) located in the southern suburb of Beijing. Correspondingly, on the day of the winter solstice, worship of *Di* was conducted at the Temple of Di (*ditan*) located at the northern suburb of the capital. The rituals involved nine steps, including the purification of the participants, the performance of dance and music, the reading of prayer documents, and the offering of sacrifices.

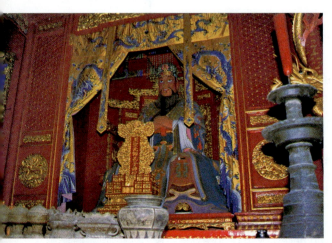

Confucius serves as an object of veneration and commemoration. He is the "Utmost Sage and Late Teacher," as the tablet in front of his statue declares.

A far more elaborate rite known as "*feng* and *shan*" has only been performed a total of six times in all of Chinese history.[14] *Feng*, literally meaning "to seal," was the rite of worshipping *Tian* atop Mt. Tai, the "Sacred Eastern Peak" located near Confucius's native town of Qufu in modern Shandong province. *Shan*, literally meaning "to yield" or "to clear away," was the ritual of sacrificing to *Di* at the lesser peak of Liangfu at the foot of Mt. Tai. The ultimate purpose of the *feng* rite was to seal a new covenant between the ruler and the numinous Absolute that gave him his legitimacy to rule. Similarly, the *shan* performance was meant to establish a bond with the earth. Because of the huge expenses and elaborate arrangements involved, *feng* and *shan* were conducted consecutively on the same trip.

Sacrifice to Confucius   The state cult of Confucius began in the Han Dynasty with the designation of Confucianism as orthodoxy. The descendants of Confucius were first given a hereditary fief, and later the Master himself was given increasingly laudatory titles and ducal honors. Finally temples commemorating Confucius were ordered to be built in every county and major city throughout the empire. In time, wooden tablets commemorating some of his prominent students, as well as those of successive generations of Confucian worthies such as Mencius and Zhu Xi, were installed in these temples. Though the frequency and elaborateness of the sacrificial rites conducted at these temples varied with time and locale, the traditional birthday of Confucius (the twenty-seventh day of the ninth month) was generally observed. These rites involved dance and music accompanied by drums and bells, proclamations and didactic lectures given by local dignitaries and government officials, and offerings of incense and animals. It should be noted that Confucius's divinity was never claimed at these ceremonies, nor was his intervention sought in solving human problems. Rather, they were expressions of veneration and respect for a human cultural hero who had helped to define Chinese civilization.

The most magnificent Temple of Confucius, as can be expected, is located in his native county of Qufu, not far from Mt. Tai. Built and maintained at state expense, the Qufu Confucian Temple has a main building with a palatial design supported by dragon-decorated pillars, all meant to accord the Master the highest honor comparable to that of a ruler. Stone steles are engraved with the calligraphy or essays of various emperors in Chinese history, all lauding the moral and cultural accomplishments of the sage. This Confucian Temple in Qufu was a pilgrimage site for generations of scholars and aspiring literati and is still popular among tourists today.

Family Rituals   Commemorating and honoring of ancestors in China goes back to the very dawn of recorded Chinese history. But Confucianism lent further theoretical support to the practice with its discussion of *xiao* (filial piety). The Confucian teaching maintains that one's filial obligation to parents and ancestors is the core of one's humanity. Thus while the state monopolized the worship of *Tian/Di* and the educated elites controlled the sacrifice to Confucius, all people could participate in the family ritual of honoring parents and ancestors. Sacrifice to ancestors, in particular, is important because it gives the descendants a sense of belonging and continuity and thereby a religious appreciation of the chain of life that links them to their forebears.

In the *Family Rituals* (*Jiali*), compiled by the Neo-Confucian scholar Zhu Xi, detailed step-by-step liturgies are provided for ceremonies associated with ancestor worship. Chapters describe daily "looking in" on the ancestors; more elaborate semimonthly "visits," "reports" on major family events such as births, weddings, and deaths; and formal "offerings" on festival days and seasonal sacrifices. What follows is a summarized version of Zhu Xi's instructions for the rites of making seasonal offerings to the ancestors.[15]

Confucius's tombstone boldly declares that he is the "Ultimate Sage of Greatest Accomplishment, King of Manifest Culture."

In the preparatory phase, the date for the sacrifice is selected by divination performed in front of the ancestral shrine in the preceding month. Then, three days before the event, the designated leading man and woman will each lead family members of their respective gender to perform purification rituals in their designated quarters, men in the outer and women in the inner. The men also make the main hall sparkling clean and arrange the place settings for each generation properly. The women will set the incense burner and incense box, as well as prepare wine racks and containers, along with meat plates for the ancestors.

On the day of the event, when the sun is fully up, the wooden tablets containing the names of the different generations of ancestors, separated by gender, are moved to their proper places in the main hall. Then the spirits of the ancestors are greeted, and food is offered to them three times. The ancestors are entreated to eat the food and are given privacy to do so, with everyone from the presiding man on down exiting the main hall, and the door is closed. After a suitable interval, the master of ceremony coughs three times to announce his intention to reenter; then he opens the door, and everyone else comes back in. Tea is offered to the ancestors to supposedly cleanse their mouths. Then the presiding man receives the sacrificed food from the master of ceremony. With reverence the presiding man bows and prostrates himself to taste the food and drink the wine. Then the entire group takes leave of the ancestral spirits, returns their tablets back to their original locations, and clears away the offering tables. The presiding man supervises the division of the sacrificial food to be consumed by all the family members later that day. This brings an end to the ritual of the ancestral sacrifice. The intended effect of this ritual is apparent—to create familial cohesiveness and

This is an iconic image of Confucius as a learned scholar and an exemplar of human moral accomplishment. Traditionally the Chinese did not see religion as a separate realm of activity, hence the pursuit of scholarship and the enactment of moral behavior within the family and community were very much part of their religious experience.

Though not strictly Confucian, this yin-yang symbol surrounded by the eight trigrams does reflect the Chinese belief in the complementarity of opposites and the harmonious unity of the cosmos. More than any other visual symbol, it represents Chinese religiousness.

Family cohesion and respect for elders are central Confucian values. A daughter and her husband pay a visit to her parents on Chinese New Year's Day to renew her kinship tie with her natal family.

Statue of Laozi carved out of a huge rock in Fujian province, China. This legendary founder of Daoism symbolizes wisdom and irreverence for conventional thinking. He is understood as the yin to Confucius's yang, and the image of passive acceptance of what nature has ordained to Confucius's active attempt at improving society.

(continued)

to recognize the unseverable bond between the living and the deceased family members. You may notice that the opening scene of *qingming* observance at the beginning of this chapter has similar rituals.

Daoist Practices

As can be deduced from our discussion of Daoist beliefs, Daoism is essentially lived, not merely believed. Whether it is the amazing feats of the immortals and perfected beings in the *Daodejing* and the *Zhaungzi*, or whether it is the physical-spiritual regimens and alchemical techniques of the later Daoists, there is always an understanding and expectation that the beliefs need to be put into practice to be truly meaningful. Returning to the *Dao*, warding off physical deterioration, and attaining actual immortality involve a whole spectrum of undertakings and practices.

Daoist Communal Festivals and Liturgies

To ordinary believers—those who have no hope of going through the rigor and the expenses of pursuing immortality—the Daoist religion as practiced by the Celestial Master sect offers the promise of health, long life, even collective salvation. Membership in these organized movements during the tumultuous centuries after the collapse of the Han Dynasty meant a special sense of belonging to a select group destined to survive those trying times. Noteworthy in their beliefs was the idea of chosenness—that they constituted a special group of people who, because of their embrace of an apocalyptic ideology, were favored by the gods. Referred to as *zhongmin* (seed people), they confirmed their "elect" status through their participation in collective rituals called *zhai* (fasts). Lasting several days each, these fasts involved abstinence from food, public performance of penance for past moral transgressions, submission of written memorials to request pardon from the deities, and communal prayers for the salvation of the faithful.

The Fast of Mud and Soot (*tutan zhai*) in China's medieval period reflected the general tenor of *zhai* rituals. With hair disheveled and face smeared with soot, believers prostrated themselves like condemned criminals before a raised altar to ask for forgiveness from the gods. Moved by their emotions, many fell to the ground and rolled about amidst loud wailings. Such public acts of penance were performed to earn pardon and spiritual merit. Another liturgical ritual was the Fast of the Yellow Register (*Huanglu zhai*), during which the participants performed penitence for their ancestors going back seven or nine generations. The names of deceased ancestors, entered in registers, were read by the officiating priests and were then considered to have gained postmortem immortality. In this way the filial obligation of the faithful was ritually expressed.

Another communal ceremony, the ***jiao*** (offering), is popular even down to the present day. It is a public liturgy performed usually by the Daoist priests on behalf of the entire community to petition the gods to bestow good fortune, health, and prosperity on all. Sometimes labeled as a rite of cosmic renewal, the *jiao* brings together the community to participate collectively in a religious ritual that is loud, colorful, and dramatic. Depending on the needs of the community, a *jiao* is conducted at periodic intervals (ranging from once a year for the affluent communities to once every sixty years for the poor communities) or to give special thanks to the deities for having successfully protected the entire community by, for example, warding off an epidemic.

A *jiao* ceremony usually lasts several days. The dates are chosen for their astrological auspiciousness. Daoist priests are contracted to perform the ritual with efficacy and precision. Prior to the official dates of the ceremony, "memorials" are submitted by the priests to the celestial bureaucracy of the gods to give notice of the scheduled *jiao*. Then the location at which the liturgy takes place, usually both the inside and the outside of the largest local temple or shrine, is marked off by hoisted lanterns to signal the enclosure of the sacred space. Afterward the local deities are invited to take their honored seats within the enclosure; their statues or wooden tablets are carried there by community elders. The procession of the deities through the community is accompanied by lion or dragon dances, made even more boisterous with lots of firecrackers. Then the ritual proper begins in earnest.

A group of Daoist priests perform a ritual service for a member of the community.

Reenacting the beginning of the cosmos in a ritual called *fendeng* (spreading the light), the chief Daoist priest, in full vestment, blows on a buffalo horn and rings his "thunder" bell, to the accompaniment of an entire music ensemble, and repeats the forty-second chapter of the *Laozi* by announcing that "the *Dao* gives birth to the One [Being, Existence]; the One brings forth the Two [*Yin* and *Yang*]; the Two give rise to the Three [*Tian, Di,* and Humans]; and the Three engender the Ten Thousand Things [world of multiplicity and diversity]." Entering a meditation-induced trance, he transforms his body into the body of the *Dao*. He takes prescribed steps that are dancelike, spins on himself, and sanctifies the ritual enclosure by requesting the dispatch of heavenly troops to guard the place. At the same time, to placate the wandering ghosts in the neighborhood and to warn them against intrusion into the sacred ground, he provides a feast for them while lecturing them on the reasons for their suffering.

At some point during the ceremony, the names of every member of the community will be posted on a roster and read aloud by the priests to signal their financial and spiritual support of this elaborate and expensive event, as well as to ensure that they will receive their share of the benediction of the gods. There is great interest among the community members in checking the posted name list to make sure that the names are written accurately and that they have not been inadvertently left out.

The climax of the ceremony occurs when the highest of the Daoist deities, the Three Purities and the Jade Emperor, are invited to take part in the ceremony. Piercing prepared talismans with his sword, the chief Daoist priest burns them with great dramatic effect to appeal to the august deities. Once the gods are properly seated, a blanket pardon of every immoral act committed by every member of the community between the last *jiao* and the present one is announced. In grateful response, the community performs a public charitable act of "releasing life"—setting cages of captured birds free and returning to a stream a bucket full of live fish. On the last night of the ceremony, a grand feast for all ghosts trapped in hell is hosted by the community. Once again, the Daoist priests exhort the ghosts to behave themselves and to refrain from wreaking havoc in the lives of the living. Balance is restored among the worlds of humans, gods, and ghosts. The rite concludes with the sending off of the celestial gods and the local deities and the distribution of food and buns to the spectators and the performance of operas for the entertainment of all.[16]

> Confucianism and Daoism have together shaped personal conduct and social behavior in China. How do the Chinese allow themselves to be guided by two very distinct religious traditions in their daily lives without much sense of tension and conflict?

CONCLUSION

In this chapter we have invited you to explore the religious world of the Chinese through a study of their two native religious traditions—Confucianism and Daoism. We have highlighted the religious nature of both traditions. In the case of Confucianism, we have established that it is not just a teaching of ethics and good government but is in fact informed by a deep religious faith in a numinous Absolute—*Tian*. This faith, moreover, mandates dedicated human effort to transform the individual and the world. We have also documented the historical unfolding of this tradition over the course of more than two thousand years. At the same time, we have also identified the ritual dimensions of this tradition, from the ornate and solemn state observations of the past to the simple familial ceremonies that are still practiced today.

As for Daoism, we have clarified that it is not confined to the metaphysical discussions of the *Daodejing* and the *Zhuangzi*, but that it is richly informed by an elaborate belief in the cosmological importance of the human body, a salvational message of communal redemption, and an abiding yearning for physical transformation and perfection. Moreover, we have examined the historical progression of this tradition as it meandered through the different periods in China. We have also documented the colorful ritual performance of Daoism in the community.

Both Confucianism and Daoism (along with a Chinese version of Buddhism and a syncretized amalgamation of the three teachings in the form of folk religion) have contributed to the shaping of the Chinese religious mindset. Both have experienced ups and downs in their respective history, at times being the dominant ideology of the realm and at times being eclipsed by other traditions in influence. Nevertheless, both have maintained their central importance to the Chinese people, at no time risking irrelevance or extinction. Despite suffering a brutal critique and rejection in the twentieth century by the modern Chinese intellectual elite in the name of rationalism and egalitarianism, both have remained resilient among the common people. In fact, there are signs of their revival and rejuvenation at the dawn of the twenty-first century. Confucian values continue to inform Chinese familial ethics and social and political behavior, and Daoist concerns for the well-being of the human body and harmonious relationship with the spiritual world shape contemporary Chinese attitudes toward health, medicine, cuisine, and the environment.

Most important, we have attempted to justify the inclusion of both Confucianism and Daoism in the study of world religions. Confucianism treats the fulfillment of the human potential as an ultimate concern. The tenacity with which Confucianism exhorts people to strive for human perfection in our mundane lives as a form of divine calling—thereby making the secular sacred—demonstrates an interesting type of religiosity. Its assertion of human coequality with the divine offers an intriguing contrast with other religious traditions as well. Daoism is similarly a significant world religion. Its perception of the divine Absolute as a life-generating, feminine entity; its call for a harmonious coexistence between humans and nature; its emphasis on healthy improvement of the human body as a religious mission; and its promotion of communal cohesiveness through ritual participation make it all the more relevant in a postindustrial world.

SEEKING ANSWERS

What Is Ultimate Reality?

Confucianism and Daoism share the same cosmological myth, inherited from ancient China. The natural world is not in a fallen state. There is no almighty creator, nor is there a demonic counterpart. There is no definite beginning of the world, and there is no predicted end. Instead, the world unfolds cyclically and operates like a pendulum, arcing between two extremes and alternating between two polar but complementing opposites. Human beings are not caught in a tug of war between good and evil, and the side they choose does not result in a permanent fate in paradise or hell. Emphasis is placed on balance, coexistence, and harmony. For the Confucians, ultimate reality is *Tian* (Neo-Confucians sometimes use the term *Taiji*, Supreme Ultimate). *Tian* is the procreator of the cosmos and all the myriad things in it. Moreover, *Tian* has a special relationship with humans and communicates with chosen individuals its grand design for humanity. This communication does not occur through dramatic and ecstatic encounters such as that between god and the prophets in Abrahamic traditions. Instead, *Tian*'s message is discerned by perceptive and insightful human representatives through their keen observation of nature and diligent study of human affairs as recorded in history and enacted in the present. It is in this sense that Confucianism is not a revelatory religion in the conventional sense. In contrast, Daoism, in its organized form, is a revelatory religion. Its ultimate reality is the *Dao*, the "mother of the universe." Originally formless and undifferentiated, it later takes on human and divine forms, giving instructions and revealing texts to the faithful. Daoism can also be salvational in its message, complete with prescriptions for repentance and thanksgiving.

(continued)

How Should We Live in This World?

Both Confucianism and Daoism inherit the ancient Chinese religious view regarding the human condition: human beings are, like everything else in the cosmos, the product of the interaction between *yin* and *yang*. They have a corporeal aspect (the body) and an incorporeal aspect (the "soul"), consisting of *hun* and *po*. There is no notion of any alienation from or disobedience of an almighty god, thus a total absence of sin. However, this does not mean that human beings are already perfect and need no improvement from their current state. There is still a yawning gap between human beings as they are and human beings as they should or can become. For the Confucians, the right way to live is to live ethically, in accordance with the moral dictates of *Tian*. Humans alone have the responsibility to model and exemplify *Tian*'s moral imperative, thereby making themselves partners in creating harmony and prosperity throughout the cosmos. In concentric circles extending outward from the individual, moral behavior will transform the family, the community, and the world at large. "Do not do unto others what you do not want done to you" is the minimal moral guide for correct living in Confucianism. For the Daoists, the right way to live is to live healthily. To be sure, ethical behavior is part of desirable living, but Daoists also emphasize the human body as a microcosm reflecting perfectly the macrocosm of the cosmos. Thus taking care of one's body through both internal and external "alchemical" means is a way of living life properly in accord with the Dao. Similarly focusing on the intimate connection between the individual, the community, and the cosmos, Daoists prescribe diet, exercise, and preservation of health and energy as a way of approaching the holy.

What Is Our Ultimate Purpose?

Confucians and Daoists differ in their answers to this question. For the Confucians, humans are potentially perfect and inclined toward the good. Yet this potentiality and inclination need to be rigorously nurtured and developed through scholastic learning, moral introspection, and ethical behavior. Learning to be authentically human, to enact the "way" of *Tian*, is the way to improve the human condition and to perfect it. The highest achievement of human endeavor is to become the coequal of the divine ultimate—*Tian*.

Daoists regard humans on the same level as all the myriad things—they are all concrete expressions of the *Dao*, the numinous Absolute. Through their ignorance or negligence, however, humans dissipate their primordial endowment of the vital energy, the *qi*, resulting in their vulnerability to disease and death. Consequently, the Daoist prescription for improving the human condition is to engage in exercises and rituals designed to replenish the body and the spirit, making it once again as immortal as the *Dao*. Confucians and Daoists also diverge in their beliefs about what happens after we leave this life. Confucius himself

(continued)

SEEKING ANSWERS *(continued)*

famously brushed aside a student's inquiry on death. He just did not consider it an issue worthy of exploration. His priority was to pay exclusive attention to life and how to improve it. This "prejudice" has affected all subsequent Confucians, none of whom showed any strong interest in addressing death or its religious meaning. Even the Confucian practice of ancestor worship and respecting the dead can be explained as a way of bypassing the issue, as dead ancestors are treated very much as living members of the lineage and the family. Daoists, on the other hand, confront the topic of mortality by emphasizing the possibility and the desirability of immortality. Even with the appearance of death as inevitable, Daoists explain it as a stage of transformation to a higher plane of existence, a way of attaining true immortality. Thus the deeper meaning of death is equally ignored by Daoists.

REVIEW QUESTIONS

For Review

1. Why should the term "Confucianism" be used with caution? In what way may it be a misnomer?
2. How do Confucianism and Daoism define such terms as *Tian*, *Dao*, and *de* differently?
3. Why is Daoism more than the teachings of the *Laozi* and the *Zhuangzi*?
4. Why is Confucianism a religious tradition despite its lack of concern for the afterlife?

For Further Reflection

1. In what ways do Confucianism and Daoism complement each other, and in what ways do they oppose each other?
2. Compare and contrast the Confucian notion of *Tian* with the Christian concept of God.
3. Compare and contrast the Daoist notion of *Dao* with the Hindu concept of Brahman.
4. Having examined Confucianism and Daoism, have you arrived at any conclusion regarding Chinese religiosity? How does it differ from that of other religious traditions?

GLOSSARY

dantian (dahn'-tee'ən) "Fields for the refinement of the immortal pill"; major nodal points in the human body where the "pill" of immortality can be refined through alchemical means.

dao (dow) A fundamental concept in Chinese religion, literally meaning the "path" or the "way." In Confucianism, it specifically refers to the entire ideal human order ordained by the numinous Absolute, *Tian*. In Daoism, it is the primary source of the cosmos, the very ground of all beings.

Daodejing (dow'-duh-jing) Basic Daoist scripture, lit. "The Scripture of the Way and Its Potent Manifestation"; also known as the Book of *Laozi*, the name of its purported author.

(continued)

GLOSSARY (continued)

Daozang (dow' zahng) Literally "Treasury of the Dao," this is the Daoist Canon that contains the entire corpus of Daoist texts. The most complete version, still in use today, was first published in 1445.

de (duh) Another fundamental concept in Chinese religions, meaning "virtue" or "potency." In Confucianism, it is the charismatic power of the ruler or the man of virtue, while in Daoism it means the concrete manifestation of the *dao*.

fangshi (fahng-shər) "Magicians" who allegedly possessed the recipe for immortality.

Five Classics The five canonical works of Confucianism designated in the Han Dynasty. They are *Book of Odes*, *Book of History*, *Book of Changes*, *Record of Rites*, and *Spring and Autumn Annals*.

Four Books The four texts identified by the Neo-Confucian Zhu Xi as fundamental in understanding the Confucian teaching. Between 1313 and 1905, they made up the curriculum for the civil service examination. They are *Analects*, *Mencius*, *Great Learning*, and *Doctrine of the Mean*.

gui (gwei) Ghosts and demons, malevolent spirits.

jiao (jee'au) Daoist communal sacrificial offerings to signal cosmic renewal and collective cohesion.

junzi (ju'un zee) The personality ideal in Confucianism; the noble person.

li (lee) Etiquette and proper manners; rituals and holy rites.

ming (see ***Tianming***)

neidan (nay'-dahn) Daoist "internal" alchemy designed to attain immortality through meditation, breath control, gymnastics, diet, and massage.

neisheng waiwang (nay'-sheng' wī'-wahng) Neo-Confucian ideal of "inner sagely moral perfection and outer political skills."

qi (chee) Breath, force, power, material energy.

ren (rən) Human-heartedness, benevolence; the unique moral inclination of humans.

ru (rōō) Scribes and ritual performers of the Zhou period; later used exclusively to refer to Confucians.

Shangdi (shahng'-dee) The August Lord on High of the Shang period.

shen (shən) Gods and deities; benevolent spirits.

shengren (shəng rən) (or ***sheng***) The Confucian sage, the epitome of humanity.

shi (shər) Men of service; lower-ranking civil and military officials in the Zhou period.

Tian (tee'ən) The transcendent, numinous entity in ancient Chinese religion; the conscious Will that regulates the cosmos and intervenes in human affairs; conventionally translated as "Heaven."

Tianming The mandate or command of *Tian* that confers political legitimacy to the ruler; also understood by Confucians as the calling to morally improve oneself and to transform the world.

Tianshi (tee'ən shər) "Celestial Master"; reference to a Daoist salvational figure, as well as an organized movement.

waidan (wī dahn) Daoist "external" alchemy involving refining of "pills" with herbs and minerals for ingestion so that immortality can be attained.

wuwei (wōō way) Daoist notion of action without intention; actionless action.

wuxing (wōō shing) The five elemental phases of metal, wood, water, fire, and soil that mutually support and overcome one another.

xian (shee'ən) Daoist immortals and perfected individuals.

xiao (shee'au) Filial piety; respect and care for parents and ancestors.

xinzhai (shin jī) "Fasting of the Mind" in the *Zhuangzi*.

yang (young) Lit. the south-facing side of a mountain, representing the energy that is bright, warm, dry, and masculine.

(continued)

GLOSSARY (continued)

yangsheng (young shəng) Daoist techniques of nourishing life and attaining immortality.

yin Lit. the north-facing side of a mountain, representing the energy that is dark, cold, wet, and feminine.

zhai (jī) Daoist "fasts" designed to seek redemption of transgressions by the gods.

ziran (zee'-rahn) Daoist notion of natural spontaneity.

zuowang (zoh'-wahng) "Sitting and Forgetting" in the *Zhuangzi*.

SUGGESTIONS FOR FURTHER READING

de Bary, William Theodore. *The Trouble with Confucianism*. Cambridge, MA: Harvard University Press, 1991. A thought-provoking discussion of the "prophetic voice" in Confucianism.

Fingarette, Herbert. *Confucius: The Secular as Sacred*. New York: Harper Torchbooks, 1972. A creative interpretation of the Confucian notion of *li* as holy rites.

Gardner, Daniel K., trans. *The Four Books: The Basic Teachings of the Later Confucian Tradition*. Indianapolis, IN: Hackett Publishing, 2007. A handy translation of important excerpts from the scriptural corpus of Confucianism.

Gardner, Daniel K. *Confucianism: A Very Short Introduction*. New York: Oxford University Press, 2014. A pocket-size introduction to the Confucian tradition for beginners.

Kirkland, Russell. *Taoism: The Enduring Tradition*. London: Routledge, 2004. An impassioned monograph by a specialist to correct many of the misconceptions regarding Daoism and its history.

Kohn, Livia, ed. *Daoism Handbook*. Leiden, Netherlands: Brill, 2000. A magisterial and encyclopedic collection of essays on various aspects of Daoism, ranging from history to schools to texts.

Sun, Anna. *Confucianism as a World Religion*. Princeton, NJ: Princeton University Press, 2013. An authoritative monograph on the issue of Confucianism's religious content and labeling.

Schipper, Kristofer. *The Taoist Body*. Berkeley: University of California Press, 1993. An authoritative discourse by an ordained Daoist priest on the rituals and practices of Daoism as they relate to the texts and teachings.

Taylor, Rodney L. *The Religious Dimensions of Confucianism*. Albany: State University of New York Press, 1986. A convenient collection of mostly previously published essays by the author to argue for the religiousness of Confucianism.

Yao, Xinzhong. *An Introduction to Confucianism*. Cambridge, UK: Cambridge University Press, 2000. An authoritative basic text on the entire Confucian tradition.

ONLINE RESOURCES

Research Centre for Confucian Studies

cuhk.edu.hk/rih/confucian

This useful website for Confucian studies is maintained by the Research Center for Confucian Studies, Chinese University of Hong Kong. It contains a rich resource guide for Confucian studies.

The Daoist Foundation

daoistfoundation.org

The Daoist Foundation was created by two American academics who, having studied and practiced Daoism for many years, "are committed to fostering the flourishing of authentic and tradition-based Daoist practice, community, and culture with attentiveness to the needs and concerns of Western students."

Center for Daoist Studies

daoistcenter.org

This useful website is the education and research branch of the Daoist Foundation.

SHINTO

IT IS THE LAST DAY of the three-day Sanja Festival in Asakusa, a historic precinct in Tokyo. The climax of the festival is the wild parading of **mikoshi**, portable shrines carrying the "essence" of the patron deities of the various neighborhoods and merchant groups.[1] As one of the most popular annual festivals in Tokyo, the Sanja Festival attracts upward of half a million spectators and participants during the three-day festivities.

At 5 A.M. on the third Sunday in May, Satoshi Tanaka, a young grocery clerk in his twenties, is waiting expectantly outside the Asakusa Shrine. Along with hundreds of other young men (and some brave women), he has signed up months in advance to form teams of shrine carriers sponsored by local merchants and civic groups. Though ordinarily preferring to sleep late, Satoshi finds himself in a state of excited anticipation and alertness this morning. Dressed in colorful shirts and shorts with matching headbands, he waits with others to receive their purification by the Shinto priests so that he will be considered spiritually clean and ready for the sacred task ahead. Even though he does not see himself as a seriously religious person, Satoshi feels perfectly comfortable in being a shrine carrier at this Shinto festival. It is his way of interacting with his community and with the deities he believes are present.

The job of these carriers is to carry the *mikoshi* through the streets of Asakusa so that all in attendance can share a moment of intimacy with the deities temporarily housed in these portable shrines. These ornately

Throngs of portable shrine carriers with their respective
mikoshi outside the Asakusa Shrine in Tokyo.

Significant sites in the history of Shinto.

decorated *mikoshi* rest on poles that are carried on the shoulders of the carriers. Shouting and grunting in unison, to the accompaniment of much drumming, cymbal clanging, and loud cheers from the crowd, the carriers attempt to move the portable shrines along. But because no one among them is in total control of the direction of the *mikoshi*, all the carriers move back and forth or sideways more or less blindly. The movement of the portable shrines can thus be wild and unpredictable, subject to the unconscious collective will of the entire group of carriers (or, supposedly, that of the deity inside). This cumbersome and potentially dangerous parade lumbers down narrow streets and broad boulevards amidst large crowds.

Quite frequently one shrine will cross paths with another, resulting in great commotion and competition for attention from the throngs of spectators. Sweating profusely and hoarse from too much shouting and chanting, individual shrine carriers drop out and are quickly replaced without disrupting the progress of the shrines. Thirsty and hungry, the temporarily retired carriers sit or lie on the ground in total exhaustion. Meanwhile, the spectators watch, take pictures, applaud, cheer, visit the main shrine, purchase the sundry food, drink, and souvenirs offered by enterprising street vendors, and make a day of it. ✳

The preceding scene is typical of a ***matsuri***, a Shinto festival in contemporary Japan that helps to create religious awareness and social solidarity within the entire community. The *matsuri* is both a religious and a social occasion. Though the oldest surviving religion in Japan, Shinto has, by and large, coexisted with Buddhism and Confucianism since the sixth century C.E. The two latter traditions were introduced into the country from China by way of Korea. Although there has been rivalry and competition among the three religions over the centuries, there has also been accommodation and mutual acceptance. There is an observation about Japanese religious behavior that describes perfectly the eclectic attitude of the Japanese. It says that the Japanese are born and wed in Shinto, die Buddhist, and live in accordance with Confucian ethical principles. In other words, most Japanese do not see the three religions as mutually exclusive or incompatible. Rather, they regard them as mutually reinforcing and relevant in separate aspects and stages of their lives. In this chapter, we invite you into the life of the Shinto believers as they practice their religion in the context of recognizing, and sometimes actually embracing, the other faiths. We do so by discussing its beliefs, history, and ritual practices. As Shinto is practiced almost exclusively in Japan, this chapter does not include a map showing global distribution of Shinto adherents.

TIMELINE
Shinto

10,000–300 B.C.E.* Jōmon period.

300 B.C.E.–300 C.E.* Yayoi period.

300–500 C.E.* Kofun period.

538 Introduction of Buddhism and Confucianism, possibly also Daoism, to Japan.

593 Prince Shōtoku becomes regent.

712 *Kojiki* (Record of Ancient Matters) completed.

720 *Nihon-shoki* or *Nihongi* (Chronicles of Japan) completed.

794 Heian (present-day Kyoto) becomes the permanent capital.

1185 Beginning of samurai rule in Japan.

1339 Kitabatake Chikafusa publishes the *Jinnō shōtōki*.

From 1750s* Rise of *Kokugaku* (National Learning, Neo-Shinto).

From 1780s* Birth of founders of New Religions.

1868 Meiji Restoration begins creation of State Shinto.

1937 Beginning of Pacific War, fought in the name of Emperor Hirohito.

1945 Japan surrenders to Allies, Shinto separated from state.

Note: Asterisks indicate contested or approximate dates.

THE TEACHINGS OF SHINTO

The term **Shinto** is an elegant reference to the longest existing religion in Japan. "*Shin*" is the Japanized pronunciation of the Chinese word "*shen*," which refers to gods and deities (see Chapter 8). "*To*," alternatively "*dō*," is the Japanese way of pronouncing the Chinese word "*dao*," which suggests the "way." Hence Shinto literally means "the way of the gods." As a matter of fact, the term Shinto did not come into existence until the Japanese used it to distinguish their preexisting religion from Buddhism, which, when first introduced into the country in the middle of the sixth century C.E., was known as "*Butsudō*," "the way of the Buddha." In more colloquial form, Shinto is known as *kami-no-michi*, "the way of the **kami**," as the core of Shinto is the belief in the existence and power of *kami*, a broad term that suggests a whole range of meanings.

The Meaning of *Kami*

The complexity of the word *kami* is best illustrated by the great eighteenth-century Japanese scholar Motoori Norinaga (1730–1801). As an articulate advocate for the revival of Shinto in a Japan dominated by Confucian orthodoxy and Buddhist piety, Motoori points out the diverse meaning of the term *kami*:

> I do not yet understand the meaning of the term *kami*. Speaking in general, however, it may be said that *kami* signifies, in the first place, the deities of heaven and earth that appear in the ancient records and also the spirits of the shrines where they are worshiped. It is hardly necessary to say that it includes human beings. It also includes such objects as birds, beasts, trees, plants, seas, mountains, and so forth. In ancient usage, whatsoever was outside the ordinary, possessed superior power, or was awe-inspiring, was called *kami*.[2]

Put simply, then, *kami* refers to anything that is out of the ordinary, awe-inspiring, mysterious, powerful, marvelous, and beyond human control or comprehension. The awe and marvel accorded the *kami* seem to date back to the earliest times in Japanese history. A closer examination of the Shinto beliefs and practices will bear this out.

Belief is the least precise aspect of Shinto, as this religion has no identifiable founder, nor does it have a sacred book similar to the Bible. Our discussion of Shinto beliefs cannot then rely on a professed creed or doctrine. Rather, it is based on a set of highly revered texts, dating back to the eighth and ninth centuries C.E. The **Kojiki** (*Record of Ancient Matters*, completed in 712 C.E.) and the **Nihon shoki** (alternatively known as *Nihongi, Chronicles of [the Land Where] the Sun Originates*, compiled in 720 C.E.) are the two authoritative texts for the study of ancient Shinto mythologies and beliefs. The following narrative is primarily based on the former.

Creation Myth in the *Kojiki*

The *Kojiki* begins with several generations of invisible divinities at the beginning of time, all of whom have titles that end with the word *kami*, until the primordial pair, **Izanagi** and his wife **Izanami**, appear. The couple is credited with bringing the world out of its original chaos. Standing on the Heavenly Floating Bridge, they lower a jeweled spear to stir the ocean below. When they lift up the spear, the brine dripping down from its tip forms an island. In like manner, "the grand eight islands" of the Japanese archipelago are created. The divine couple then descends to take up residence there, and through their sexual union they produce the various nature deities.

Izanami is burned to death while giving birth to her last child, the fire god. Izanagi follows his wife to Yomi, the underworld of the dead, where, upon seeing her putrefied and decomposing body, he is horrified and beats a hasty retreat. After his return to the world of the living, Izanagi washes himself in a stream. From his eyes are born the solar goddess **Amaterasu**-no-Ōmikami (The Great August Kami who Shines in the Sky)[3] and the lunar god Tsukiyomi. From Izanagi's nose comes the violent and ill-tempered storm god Susa-no-o.[4]

When the *Kojiki* continues, the focus shifts to the relationship between Amaterasu and her brother Susa-no-o. Petulant and mischievous, Susa-no-o gives much grief to his sister. He ravages her heavenly domain, destroys her rice fields, and desecrates her house. Annoyed and frightened, Amaterasu retreats into a cave, thereby plunging the world into darkness. The other deities try to lure her back out with all sorts of tricks, but to no avail, until a goddess by the name of Uzume performs a lewd dance that causes so much raucous laughter among the gods that the curious Amaterasu is finally enticed to emerge from her hiding. (This is an ingenious Shinto attempt at explaining solar eclipse.) Susa-no-o is forced to apologize to his sister and is banished to Izumo, a region facing the Japan Sea (alternatively referred to as the East Sea) on the other side of the main island from Ise, the future home of Amaterasu's grand shrine. In Izumo Susa-no-o settles down and locates a sword, which he presents to Amaterasu as a token of his apology and goodwill. The sword will later become one of the "three imperial regalia" Amaterasu bestows on her descendants who occupy the Japanese throne.

The final cycle of the narrative in the *Kojiki* deals with the successors of Susa-no-o and the descendants of Amaterasu. Ninigi, grandson of Amaterasu, is instructed by her to rule all of Japan. But his mission is thwarted by Susa-no-o's successors in Izumo, who refuse to yield to the Amaterasu line until she promises to honor her young brother by building him a grand shrine. After Izumo's accommodation with the Sun Goddess group, the descendants of all the other deities then fall in line, and Ninigi's own grandson, the Emperor Jimmu, is the first human ruler to claim imperial authority over all of Japan. He is provided with the three imperial regalia of the sword, the mirror, and the curved jewel as symbols of his power, which he is believed to have exercised in the Yamato region near present-day Nara. According to tradition, this momentous event took place in 660 B.C.E., and the imperial line has supposedly continued uninterrupted to the present time.

From the *Kojiki* story just outlined, major themes of Shinto belief can be identified: the divine creation of Japan, a concern with fertility and purification, the importance of the feminine, an absence of ethical teachings, a corresponding lack of absolute good or radical evil, and a profound intertwining of divinity with imperial power.

Japan as a Divine Creation
The core belief of Shinto centers on the *kami* and Japan's unique relationship with them. Representative of the Shinto notion of the sacred or the holy, *kami* are mysterious and tremendous powers in nature and in the human world, powers that have been the object

The Meoto-iwa (Husband and Wife rocks) in Mie Prefecture is an iconic landmark in Japan that symbolizes the union between Izanagi and Izanami.

of worship in Japan since prehistoric times. Most *kami* are believed to be the source of blessing and protection, hence worship of them is understood either as thanksgiving or as pleading for more divine gifts. But some *kami* are ill-tempered and even ill-intentioned, so worship of them is a necessary and prudent act for preventing disaster.

Kami are most evident in nature. Illustrious objects in the sky such as the sun and the moon, majestic mountains such as Fuji, serene waterfalls such as the Nachi, and strange-shaped rocks are all regarded as *kami*.

Furthermore, the *Kojiki* story of creation reflects a fundamental Japanese sentiment that their island nation was created by the *kami* as a paradise on earth. Nature, then, with its awesome power and captivating beauty, is the very expression of divine presence. Human beings, who themselves are also descendants of divinity, have the duty to respond in celebration and adoration to the gifts and blessings of the *kami*. The *kami* among humans—the ancestors of clans and communities, the heroes and powerful individuals, the emperors and some of their high officials, all exemplify godly qualities. They therefore equally deserve veneration and worship.

In the prehistoric or quasi-historic periods prior to the fifth or sixth century C.E., when Japan had no centralized imperial rule or institutionalized governmental structure, only clans and communities existed. With the ascendancy of the Yamato clan that claimed descent from the Sun Goddess Amaterasu, the chiefs and heads of the various clans and communities surrendered their power to the Yamato ruler in return for recognition and position in the divine/political power structure. The result was the entire country of Japan forming a network of *kami* with strong local identities that were loosely linked to the worship of the emperor as a deity.

Fertility and Purification   Early Shinto is centrally concerned with fertility. In the *Kojiki* cosmogonic (explanation of how the cosmos came about) myth, the main function of the primeval pair of *kami* is to "fertilize" the land and to procreate the other gods. Much emphasis is placed on the sexual union between Izanagi and Izanami in the population of the world, especially Japan, with plants, animals, and people. This procreative power of the original divine couple continues even after the death of the wife, when Izanagi, on his own, manages to bring forth more deities through ritual washing. At the same time, this mythic story highlights the Shinto fear of contamination and defilement, as well as its emphasis on purification. Despite the love that he has for his wife, Izanagi is so horrified and repulsed by Izanami's decomposing form after her death that he abandons her in the netherworld and hurries back to the world of the living. Death, disease, and blood are thus seen as polluting; persons connected to those things are considered spiritually impure and must be ritually purified before they can approach the *kami*. The arrangement of the typical Shinto shrine and the main ritual responsibility of the Shinto priests illustrate well this vital aspect of Shinto belief, as we shall see later in this chapter.

The Feminine in Shinto   It is highly noteworthy that in the Shinto myth, the sun, the most illustrious object in the sky, is portrayed as female, this despite the later patriarchal (male-dominated) nature of Japanese society. It is equally significant that the Sun Goddess Amaterasu is also the ancestress of the Japanese royal family and that, at least up through the tenth century C.E., it was not uncommon for the imperial ruler to be a woman. Also prominent in early Shinto is the role of the shamanic figure, often a female. The ecstatic dance of the goddess Uzume to lure Amaterasu out of hiding, thereby saving the world from perpetual darkness caused by solar eclipse, is indicative of the power of the female shamanic dancer. In addition, both the *Kojiki* and the *Nihongi* mention the mother of Emperor Jimmu, the first human ruler of Japan, whose name is Tama-yori-hime. This name suggests her role as a female shaman, as it literally means "a princess (*hime*) in whom dwells (*yori*) the spirit (*tama*) of the *kami*." Equally noteworthy is the account of Emperor Sujin in the *Nihongi*, whose rule is assisted by two female diviners, one being his own aunt, and the other a charismatic commoner named Ōtataneko, the favorite woman shaman of the deity of the Yamato region. It is the latter who is credited with the peace and prosperity of Sujin's reign, as she is known for her capacity to commune with the *kami* and be possessed by them.

The high prestige of female shamans in ancient Japan is further attested by the story of Empress Jingō, also recorded in the *Nihongi*. Jingō is a capable shamanic diviner for her husband, Emperor Chūai, who, after his death, personally leads an armada to invade Korea because of the oracle of assured victory she receives from the gods. It is the extension of Japanese political control over Korea that paves the way for the powerful reign of her son, Emperor Ōjin. Scholars today speculate that Empress Jingō's legendary account is modeled after the story of Himiko in Chinese historical records dating back to the fourth century C.E. They describe a female shamanic ruler of a region called Yamatai (suspected to be a variation of Yamato) in the country of Wa (Japan) whose bewitching control over the people is the source of her power. One possible interpretation of the term Himiko is "*miko* of the Sun (*hi*)." At the same time, **miko** to this day refers to unmarried women attendants at Shinto shrines who possess shamanic power to communicate with the *kami* through dance and other ritual performances. Himiko's central role as medium for the Sun Goddess can thus be imagined. Jingō's possible association with Himiko only highlights the critical importance of female diviners in ancient Shinto.

Ethics, Good, and Evil   Conspicuously absent in early Shinto belief is any reference to ethics. Although much emphasis is placed on fertility and purity, *Kojiki*'s cosmogonic story does not address the issue of morality at all. The fire god, though causing the death of his mother Izanami, is not depicted as a villain. Izanagi, though abandoning his wife in the eternally dark and terrifying underworld, is not blamed for being a heartless spouse. Susa-no-o, though causing much distress to his sister Amaterasu with his destructive and willful behavior, is not portrayed as an evil culprit. Likewise, the explicitly lewd behavior of the *kami* in drawing Amaterasu out of her hiding is not seen as immoral. In other words, the early Shinto account of creation and the relationship between the gods gives no emphasis on proper ethical conduct. There is no supreme god giving moral instructions and laws. Nor is there any hint of a cosmic struggle between good and evil. Whether in the primeval divine realm of the gods, in the natural world, or within the human community that comes into being afterward, there is no existence in Shinto beliefs of a radical evil entity that is bent on subverting the will and the handiwork of a benevolent creator god. Divine and human actions are judged only as fertile or unproductive, pure or impure, desirable or undesirable. Wayward behavior can be remedied and impurities can be removed. What are most offensive to the gods are not sin and guilt, but pollution and defilement.

The notable absence of ethical concerns in early Shinto myth by no means signals that the Japanese are not governed by moral principles in their behavior. What it does mean is that Japanese ethics came from other sources, primarily Buddhism and Confucianism. The introduction of these two alien traditions in the history of Shinto is discussed later.

State Shinto   One controversial issue in Shinto that must be addressed is the religion's tie to the imperial state and to the worship of the emperor. As early Shinto texts make clear, the divine origin of the imperial family and of the reigning emperor had been asserted right from the beginning. As descendant of the Sun Goddess Amaterasu, the Japanese ruler (both male and, not infrequently, female—at least up to the tenth century C.E.) traditionally wielded both political and religious power. As a matter of fact, government affairs and government in general were originally referred to as *matsurigoto*, "matters relating to festivals." Meanwhile, the principle of **saisei-itchi**, "the unity of the religious and the political," theoretically guided government operations. Sentiments showing strong advocacy of Japan's special position and the emperors' sacred nature based on Shinto beliefs were expressed by nationalists and royalists from the fourteenth century on. In a work entitled *Jinnō shōtōki* (*Direct Succession of Gods and Sovereigns*), published in 1339 by Kitabatake Chikafusa (1293–1354), the superiority of Japan and the divine status of the emperors were forcefully asserted: "Great Japan is the divine land (*shinkoku*). The heavenly progenitor founded it, and the Sun Goddess bequeathed it to her descendants to rule eternally. Only in our country is this true; there are no similar examples in other countries."[5] But it was during the eighteenth and nineteenth centuries C.E., when an intense Shinto revivalist movement took hold in Japan, that such sentiments came to be even more extravagantly expressed. Known as National Learning (*Kokugaku*), this movement aimed at preserving the very essence of Japanese culture by ridding the country of all foreign elements, including Confucian and Buddhist influences. These concepts were advanced in the National Learning writings of Motoori Norinaga (1730–1801) and Hirata Atsutane (1776–1843).

> Our country's Imperial Line, which casts its light over this world, represents the descendants of the Sky-Shining Goddess [Amaterasu]. And in accordance with that Goddess' mandate of reigning "forever and ever, coeval with Heaven and Earth," the Imperial Line is destined to

rule the nation for eons until the end of time and as long as the universe exists. That is the very basis of our Way. That our history has not deviated from the instructions of the divine mandate bears testimony to the infallibility of our ancient tradition. It can also be seen why foreign countries cannot match ours and what is meant by the special dispensation of our country.

—Motoori Norinaga

[A]s a special mark of favor from the heavenly gods, they gave birth to our country, and thus there is so immense a difference between Japan and all the other countries of the world as to defy comparison. Ours is a splendid and blessed country, the Land of the Gods beyond any doubt, and we, down to the most humble man and woman, are the descendants of the gods. . . . Japanese differ completely from and are superior to the peoples of China, India . . . and all other countries of the world, and for us to have called our country the Land of the Gods was not mere vanity. . . . This is a matter of universal belief and is quite beyond dispute.[6]

—Hirata Atsutane

These chauvinistic sentiments, buttressed by a revived nationalistic Shinto, became a prime motivating force that eventually brought down the last feudal military government and ushered in an imperial Restoration in 1868. With the help of Shinto nationalism and deep respect for the imperial line, the fifteen-year-old Meiji emperor emerged from the shadow of centuries of domination of the royal family by military commanders to reclaim his divine right to rule. A "State Shinto" was implemented to promote the worship of the emperor as a living *kami*, at once sacred and inviolable, and to propagate a form of ethnocentric nationalism. It was this State Shinto that was responsible for the cult of emperor worship and the rise of ultra-nationalism in Japan in the twentieth century, a subject to which we return in the section on the history of Shinto later in the chapter.

How has Shinto managed to maintain its independent identity in light of the overwhelming influence of Buddhism and Confucianism in Japan since the beginning of its recorded history?

VOICES: An Interview with Watanabe Minoru

Mr. Watanabe Minoru is a Shinto priest in his fifties at a shrine in the Nerima district of Tokyo.

Why did you want to become a Shinto priest?
My family has been in charge of a shrine at my native city of Shizuoka for generations. Both my grandfather and father were chief priests there. So, ever since my childhood, I have been expected to carry on this family profession also.

Did you have to go to a special school in order to be a Shinto priest?

After high school, I attended the Kokugakuin University in Tokyo to learn all about being a Shinto priest. The university is pretty much like all other universities, except that it is one of the two main training centers for Shinto priests, the other being Kōgakkan in Mie prefecture, near Ise. In addition to Shinto culture and practices, the university offers numerous other disciplines, including economics and law. I led a typical college student's life. I was even president of the judo club during my senior year.

What does it mean to be a Shinto priest?

To me, being a Shinto priest is more than knowing all the Shinto teachings and ritual performances. Most important, it is to serve as "cement" for the community by bringing all the neighbors together through year-round shrine activities. The shrine should be a place where people can come and interact with the *kami* and one another on all sorts of occasions and for all kinds of needs whenever they want to. It is a fundamental aspect of Shinto to have a sense that *kami* is so close to us that we can communicate with it whenever we need guidance and protection. Respect of the *kami* and closeness to it either as an individual or as a community form the very basis of our Japanese cultural identity. As a Shinto priest I consider it my solemn duty to preserve this identity and to invite people to appreciate and respect this identity.

THE HISTORY OF SHINTO

The long history of the Shinto tradition can be divided roughly into three periods: ancient, medieval, and modern. The ancient period lasted from prehistoric times to the unification of the country by the Yamato leaders sometime prior to the sixth century C.E. We have already discussed the major tenets of this ancient Shinto as revealed in the classical works of the *Kojiki* and the *Nihongi*, compiled in the eighth century C.E.

Medieval Shinto

By the time the *Kojiki* and *Nihongi* had been compiled, Shinto had actually begun its second (medieval) stage of development. This stage was marked by the new religious and political challenge from the continental culture of China by way of Korea. In the year 538 C.E., Confucianism and Buddhism were formally introduced into Japan by the Yamato leaders, who had consolidated their power over all other rival clans. This was an accomplishment confirmed by the mythological accounts that describe the submission of the various *kami* (who were believed to be the founding ancestors of these clans) to Amaterasu, the ancestress of the Yamato rulers.

Confucianism and Buddhism gave a great jolt to the established Shinto faith, addressing issues it had ignored or had no interest in. Confucianism (see Chapter 8) provided an ethical framework for state, society, and family, and Buddhism (see Chapter 5) gave special attention to the issues of suffering and death. The clearest evidence of the influence of the two alien traditions can be seen in the "Seventeen Articles Constitution" promulgated in 604 C.E. by Prince Shōtoku, regent to his aunt the Empress Suiko.

More a vision statement than a constitution in the modern sense, the document clearly acknowledges the strengths of Confucianism and Buddhism in giving guidance to harmonious living and purpose in life. Article One declares the primacy of Confucian harmony as the operating principle of both state and society, while Article Two professes hearty adherence to the Buddhist Three Treasures: the Buddha, his teachings (the *dharma*), and the community of monks he created, the *Sangha*.

In the face of strong challenge from such potent rivals, the reaction of Shinto practitioners was accommodation and adaptation. With no clear inherent ethical orientation (as noted earlier), Shinto adopted Confucian moral principles with little resistance. With respect to Buddhism, the Shinto reaction was more complicated. The Buddha was initially vehemently rejected as a foreign *kami* with no relevance to Japan. In time, however, when Buddhism began to be fully embraced by the Japanese court during the Nara period (710–784 C.E.), Shinto *kami* became guardians and protectors of the newly arrived Buddha and his various manifestations. Sometime later, Buddhas and *bodhisattvas* in turn became saviors of the *kami!* It was common for Buddhist scriptures to be recited before the altar of *kami*, and conversely Buddhist monks were in charge of Shinto shrines. At the end, though, the accommodation between Shinto and Buddhism became nearly a total merger, when Shinto *kami* were worshiped as Buddha or *bodhisattva* and the alien Buddhist deities were likewise regarded as Japanese *kami*. Using the Tōdaiji temple in Nara as an example, the Vairocana Buddha housed there is known as Dainichi, the "Great Sun," a conscious effort to equate and identify with Amaterasu the Sun Goddess. By the Heian period (794–1191), a perfect amalgamation of Shinto and Buddhism was complete.

One interesting form of this Shinto-Buddhist merger at the folk level was the emergence of a lay Buddhist and occult Shinto group known as Shūgendō ("The Way of Cultivating Magical Power"). Practitioners of this faith usually underwent austere training in the mountains to acquire mysterious powers of healing, divination, and exorcism. Commonly referred to as *yamabushi* ("those who sleep in the mountains"), Shūgendō members were ascetics with no formal affiliation with either established Shinto or Buddhism but were revered as shamanic healers and exorcists, as well as guides for pilgrims making their way to remote sacred sites.

The convergence of Shinto and Buddhism (and Confucianism, for that matter) in Japan has been credited with the formulation of the *samurai* ("sword-wielding warriors") code of conduct in premodern Japan. Known alternatively as *Bushidō* ("Way of the warrior"), this *samurai* ethic emphasizes purity of the heart and soul, contempt for pain and death, and undying loyalty to the feudal lord. It aims to combine the best elements of Shinto, Buddhism, and Confucianism within Japan's cultural heritage.

The Modern Period

The modern period of Shinto history began with its attempt at recovering its pristine past and its claim of superiority over the non-native traditions. Stirrings of this sentiment can be detected after the unsuccessful Mongol invasions of Japan in 1274 and 1281. The near disasters aroused in the Japanese a strong sense of national consciousness, resulting in their reevaluation of their native beliefs and those coming from abroad. The aforementioned nationalistic sentiment of Kitabatake Chikafusa, whose writing insisted that Japan was superior to all other countries because of its single line of emperors descended from the gods, reflected this trend in the political realm.

With the rise of the *Kokugaku* (National Learning) movement in the eighteenth century, a call was made for the return of Japan to the pristine beliefs and practices of ancient times before the introduction of "inferior" alien traditions such as Buddhism and Confucianism had contaminated Japanese culture. Meanwhile, with reinvigorated effort, the priests of the Grand Shrine at Ise actively promoted pilgrimage to the shrine by groups from all over Japan. This helped create a sense of national unity, binding all Japanese together under one common Shinto faith.

State Shinto   All these developments paved the way for the establishment of State Shinto after the Restoration of the Meiji Emperor in 1868. In 1870, the Meiji government proclaimed that "the Way of the *Kami*" would be the guiding principle of the nation. Reversing the previous Tokugawa military regime's practice of requiring all households to register in Buddhist temples, the new government mandated every household to enroll in the shrine of the local *kami*. The government also actively encouraged Shinto funeral rites in a deliberate effort to deprive Buddhism of its monopoly in conducting funeral services. Indeed, Buddhism was forcefully separated from Shinto, and Buddhist monks who had been affiliated with Shinto shrines were ordered to return to secular life.

But it was the Meiji government's promotion of the emperor cult that constituted the core of State Shinto. The emperor was venerated as a "living *kami*"—a god in flesh and blood. During the Meiji reign, a special shrine was built in Tokyo (formerly known as Edo), the seat of power of the just-toppled Tokugawa shogunate, which had become the new capital. The shrine, named Yasukuni Jinja ("Shrine for the Pacification of the Nation"), was dedicated to those who had sacrificed their lives for the royalist cause in toppling the last feudal regime and the restoration of imperial authority in 1868. All of them had been elevated to *kami* status, as would others who were subsequently enshrined there after each of Japan's foreign wars in the twentieth century, including the Russo-Japanese War of 1904–1905 and World War II. Because of its close association with State Shinto and the emperor cult, both of which have been blamed for Japan's imperialistic expansion in Asia (the colonization of Taiwan and Korea in 1895 and 1910, respectively; the occupation of Manchuria in the 1930s; and the outright invasion of China and Southeast Asia during the Pacific Wars of 1937–1945), the Yasukuni Shrine has become a controversial symbol. That it also houses the remains of some of the most notorious government leaders and commanders at the end of World War II makes matters even more sensitive. Japan's neighbors (China and Korea, in particular), who were victims of Japan's ultra-nationalistic aggression in the first half of the twentieth century, invariably file official complaints whenever prominent Japanese political figures (such as the prime minister) pay formal visits to the Yasukuni Shrine.

State Shinto has also been blamed for the fanatical nationalism among many Japanese, particularly among the rank and file of the military, during World War II. Japanese soldiers ravaged much of Asia in the name of their imperial ruler, Emperor Hirohito (r. 1926–1989). They considered their foreign aggression a divine mission, to be carried out without remorse or hesitation. Even when Japanese defeat appeared inevitable by the early 1940s, the military commanders sent suicide pilots to plunge their planes into Allied battle ships in a desperate attempt to reverse the fortune of the war. Calling the pilots *kamikaze* ("divine wind"), they tried to evoke the memory of the Japanese defeat of the invading Mongol troops in 1274 and 1281 thanks to the alleged assistance of the divine storm (*kaze*) sent by the *kami* to protect the nation. State Shinto's hold on Japan during those war years was unmistakable.

But the best illustration of the emperor cult in State Shinto was the building of the Meiji Shrine that began in 1915 and was completed in 1920. Constructed to enshrine the *kami* spirits of the Meiji emperor and his wife, the shrine was a tremendous undertaking, funded by the government. Located in the heart of Tokyo, the Meiji Shrine covers close to 200 acres of prime real estate, surrounded by elaborate gardens and wooded areas. It remains to this day a popular site for New Year's celebrations and other festivals.

Sect Shinto   The Modern period of Shinto also saw the rise of Sect Shinto and other new religions. A combination of Shinto, Confucianism, Buddhism, Shūgendō, and folk beliefs, Sect Shinto arose at the end of the Tokugawa period and became popular throughout the Meiji period. Thirteen such sects have gained official recognition. Grouped with other eclectic religious organizations that arose in the 1920s and 1930s under the general category of "New Religions," they include such influential sects as Tenrikyō ("Teaching of Heavenly Principles"), Konkōkyō ("Teaching of Golden Light"), and Kurozumikyō ("Teaching of the founder, Kurozumi Munetada" [1780–1850]).

Although different in doctrine and practice, these religious groups share a number of common features. Their founders were charismatic individuals steeped in the shamanic tradition of Shinto, the esoteric teachings of Buddhism, and a whole host of other folk beliefs. A noticeable number of them were women. Mostly of farming origin, they appealed to the anxiety and unease experienced by the lower classes during a time of rapid social change and political upheaval, as was the case in much of modern Japanese history. Explaining that calamity and disaster emanate from disturbances in people's spiritual state, they offered their shamanic powers to bring peace, harmony, health, and prosperity to their followers. The emphasis on worldly benefits was often accompanied by the promise of the impending arrival of a new age and a new world. To impress the faithful and the larger society around them, they have built imposing headquarters and even whole cities of great beauty. Their teachings generally stress clean living, hard work, moral conduct, familial cohesion, and social solidarity. The sectarian nature of these groups has made their believers more fervent than members of the established traditions of Shinto and Buddhism.

Shinto in Japan Today

Japan's defeat at the end of World War II in 1945 fundamentally changed the religious landscape of the country. The State Shinto that sponsored the cult of the emperor and government support of the shrines was, in theory at least, abolished. The divinity of the Japanese emperor was officially disavowed. Yet the imperial family continues to enjoy great affection from the majority of the Japanese people. Public reference to members of the emperor's family, even children, has to be couched in honorific language, and great throngs of people visit the grounds of the Imperial Palace on New Year's Day to greet the imperial family. The emperor opens each session of the parliament as the constitutional monarch and officially receives each new prime minister upon his assumption of office (a female prime minister is yet to be elected in Japan). Members of the imperial household, particularly the Crown Prince, visit the Grand Shrine at Ise periodically to signal their claimed lineage tie to the Sun Goddess Amaterasu.

Meanwhile, Sect Shinto in the form of the many new religions discussed previously has flourished. With their charismatic leaders and their emphasis on this-worldly benefits, the various Shinto-inspired groups attract large followings by serving the practical needs of the faithful. Local, regional, and even national shrines are maintained largely with nonofficial sources of funding, providing quiet locations of escape from the hustle and bustle of urban living and scenic sanctuaries where people can commune with the numinous forces in nature. Shinto values continue to give the Japanese people their sense of identity and aesthetics, as well as solace and comfort after disasters. In the aftermath of the 9.0 earthquake and its subsequent nuclear leak and devastating tsunami that wreaked so much havoc in northeastern Japan in March 2011, Shinto beliefs about life renewal and rejuvenation, as well as its emphasis on purification and decontamination, have provided the Japanese people with the purpose and resolve to carry out a massive program of reconstruction and revival of the stricken areas. Shinto remains at the core of Japanese culture. As the opening vignette illustrates, it is the ritual and social functions of Shinto that continue to provide solidarity for the Japanese people and justify the relevance of this religion for the Japanese nation.

> Given that religious justification of political rule is a common phenomenon in world history, in what ways is Shinto's justification of the Japanese imperial system unique?

SHINTO AS A WAY OF LIFE

Far more important to Shinto than beliefs are ceremonies and ritual practices. Some scholars even argue that Shinto beliefs are "more acted out than thought out."[7] It is often the case that many Japanese perform some of the Shinto rituals and daily habits without full knowledge or consciousness of their doctrinal and theoretical underpinnings. It is certainly the rituals, both public and private, that enable Shinto practitioners to directly experience the presence of the divine *kami* and to recognize their bond with the *kami,* as well as with one another. The young shrine carrier Satoshi Tanaka, whom we met at the beginning of this chapter, is representative of this Shinto mindset. Though he does not consider himself a deeply religious man, he finds fun and meaning in his participation in the Sanja Festival. Let us examine how the Shinto beliefs discussed in the previous section of this chapter are lived and acted out in the daily lives, as well as the ceremonial occasions, of the believers.

Fertility Rites

A major emphasis of Shinto is fertility. In villages throughout Japan, one can still find phallic symbols and representations of the female sex organ on display and worshipped. The Shinto ritual calendar to this day gives prominence to ceremonies revolving around fertility and productivity. In early spring, the *kinensai* (festival for praying for good harvest) is celebrated when the fertility-dispensing *kami* are believed to be physically present in their shrines. Processions of worshippers greet these deities, carry them into the fields on portable palanquins, and dance to celebrate their divine powers while rice seedlings are being planted or transplanted. In the fall, the *niiname matsuri* (harvest festival), the largest event of the ritual year, is observed, when the *kami* are honored and thanked for the bounteous crops with joyous and boisterous celebrations.

The harvest festival is also closely linked with the Shinto belief in divine kingship. The Japanese emperor, the *tennō* ("august heavenly ruler"), had until 1945 both religious and political responsibilities, as he was regarded as a direct descendant of the Sun Goddess Amaterasu and thereby entrusted to rule over the land. One such religious responsibility was the guarantee of fertility of the soil and bountiful harvest. This is consummated ritually each fall at the *niiname* festival, presided over by the emperor as high priest. The most spectacular expression of this magical power of the Japanese ruler is the *daijosai* ("the great food festival"), which is performed by a new emperor the year after his ascension to the throne. In an elaborate and ancient ritual, rice and wine from specially cultivated fields are presented by the new ruler to the deities in the middle of the night, a gesture that consecrates the emperor's religious power and political legitimacy. This rite, still performed as the climax of a royal accession in modern Japan, marks the very distinctive religious foundation of the Japanese imperial institution.

Women in Shinto

As we have seen in an earlier discussion of the feminine in Shinto, its mythology includes many powerful female figures and forces. It should also be noted that, though small in number and usually more junior in rank, Shinto priestesses constitute an integral part of the Shinto clergy and can be found in many of the larger shrines all over Japan. They participate fully in all the Shinto rites performed by their male counterparts, though serving as chief ritualist remains rare. Yet it is also true that the most supreme religious figure at the Grand Shrine of Ise, the home of the Sun Goddess Amaterasu, is the *saishu*, the female priestess who is usually a relative of the imperial family and is ranked above even the chief priest there!

The role of the *miko* (unmarried female shrine attendants) cannot be overlooked. Practically all Shinto shrines have *miko* performing a variety of important, though subordinate, functions. Because of the persistent belief in the shamanic power of these young women to communicate with the *kami*, they are entrusted to perform the sacred dance of *kagura* (music of the *kami*) at festivals and other ritual occasions as an indispensable complement to the prayers and purifying acts of the priests. In addition, they serve as secretaries in shrine offices, sell amulets and other trinkets at shrine gift shops, and generally interact with the public by providing a feminine touch on behalf of the shrine.

Last but not least, a noticeable number of the founders of Japan's New Religions are women. These new religious groups are heavily indebted to Shinto beliefs and motifs, even though they also borrow substantially from other traditions, such as Buddhism and Daoism. As a religious tradition, Shinto recognizes the considerable power and potency of women.

Rites of Purification, Presentation, Petition, and Participation

The Shinto ritual event generally involves a four-step sequence of purification, presentation, petition, and participation. The first three steps are performed by priests, and the last one involves the "congregation" in attendance. The rationale for the sequence is first to make the participants (both clergy and laity) physically and spiritually clean for their encounter with the *kami*. The second step is to present food offerings to the *kami* in an attempt to show respect and good will and to pave the way for the next act. This is to formally plead with the *kami*, through beautiful and correct words intoned with reverence and awe by the chief priest, for the concrete benefits being sought. Finally, the last sequence of the ritual is to have the entire worshipping audience fully participate in the ceremony through the watching of performances, sharing of ritual drinks, and the gift of shrine souvenirs.

Entry of the bridal procession at a Shinto wedding, walking through the shrine gate, led by *mikos*. Yasaka Shrine, Maruyama Park, Kyoto, Japan.

The Japanese word for the purification ritual performed by the Shinto priest is **harae**, the purpose of which is to please and soothe the *kami*. The ceremony is deemed necessary to prepare the faithful for their encounter with the deity or to remove the defilement that results from any contact with pollutants. All sorts of occasions call for the performance of *harae*, which may take place at the shrine; otherwise, the priest may go to the place where it is needed. It is common to call in the Shinto priest to perform the *harae* before moving into a new home, occupying a new office building, opening a new highway, or even driving a new car. The priest, dressed in sacramental vestments, waves an *onusa* (the wand of stripped paper or an evergreen branch) over the person(s) or the object(s) to be purified, first on the left, then the right, and finally back to the left. Ritual bathing is another form of purification. In a practice known as **misogi**, Shinto believers purify themselves by standing under a waterfall or immersing themselves in ocean water. As is well known, the Japanese are a meticulously clean people who enjoy long and frequent baths during which they scrupulously clean and scrub themselves. This national trait certainly has Shinto roots.

Salt also plays an important role in the *harae*. Its snow-like appearance symbolizes purity, and its potency as a purifying agent is widely accepted in Japan. The Shinto priest often sprinkles salt over the place, the people, or the object to be purified. Sumo wrestlers, whose characteristic Japanese spectator sport has strong Shinto connections, are purified with salt before each match. This belief in salt as spiritual purifier also makes its way into many aspects of Japanese life. After attending a funeral service, people sprinkle salt in the doorway before reentering their homes so as not to carry the defilement of death inside. Shop owners also put small mounds of salt on either side of their storefronts to ward off evil spirits. The Shinto concern with purification is evident in these examples.

The presentation component involves the offering of rice, fish, fruit, rice wine, water, and salt to the *kami*. It should be pointed out that there is absolutely no blood sacrifice in the offerings, as blood is considered repulsive and polluting in Shinto. (For the same reason, menstruating priestesses cannot participate in the *harae* ritual, thus making them less available and qualified to officiate at Shinto rites.) The petition takes the form of the priest reverently reciting the **norito** (prayers or "words spoken to the *kami*"), which is usually written in advance in very elegant and flowery language and read aloud with a rhythmical cadence, ending with a vowel that slides down an octave in pitch with the volume tapering off slowly. The worshippers' participation in the ritual event includes receiving purification by the priest, watching the dance of the *miko*, listening to the performance of the musicians, and, when over, taking small sips of rice wine called *omiki*, as well as bringing home leafy sprigs of the native Japanese *sakaki* tree to complete their encounter with the divine. All of these activities are designed to create bonding between the worshippers and their *kami*, as well as among themselves.

The Shrine   The Shinto shrine is generally the location where Shinto rituals are carried out. It is referred to as the **jinja**, the "dwelling place of the *kami*." It is here that the *kami* can be approached and worshipped. In early Shinto and in some remote, isolated sacred locations today, the *jinja* can be a tree, a waterfall, or an extraordinarily shaped rock, which local people believe to be a source of spiritual power. These *kami* dwellings are filled with awe-inspiring mystery and great natural beauty. They are often marked with nothing more than a pile of rocks, or sometimes an ornamental rope to suggest the approach to sacred space. Most *jinja*, however, are enclosed areas with a few simple structures. Entry into them requires a purified body and, ideally, a purified mind, as godliness in Shinto is synonymous with cleanliness. Thus the shrine is a holy space, of which the visitor is immediately reminded by two guardian stone lions, one on each side of the entry approach. (In the case of the shrines of the grain goddess Inari, the stone lions are replaced by foxes, which are believed to be her preferred messengers.) The entry path then passes under the distinctive Shinto crossbar gateway, known as the **torii**, whose literal meaning is "bird dwelling," probably reflecting the earliest function of it as a roost for sacred birds.

In its most characteristic form, the *torii* of today is painted red and consists of two upright posts joined by one or two crossbeams, with the upper crossbeam gently curved in the middle toward the ground. This use of red paint and the curved line in the upper crossbeam indicates both Chinese and Buddhist influence and would not have been found in the early days of Shinto. The *torii* is not meant merely to be a decorative gateway. It is a magical protective device that guards the shrine against all impurities and contaminants. Sometimes visitors have to pass under multiple *torii*, and on occasion an extended series of them are set so close together that they form a veritable tunnel.

There is an ancient belief that every part of the island of Itsukushima is so sacred that even the hills and surrounding waters are gods. When the tide is high, the main sanctuary and other structures appear to be floating. The shaded sanctuary's stage is used for events such as Noh performances.

Once inside the shrine grounds, all visitors perform a simple purification ritual by approaching a basin or trough of purified water called **temizuya** (usually a natural stone basin filled with clear water from the mouth of a sculpted dragon) and, using a bamboo dipper, taking a ladleful of water to rinse their mouth and hands. They are now ready for communion with the *kami*. The *jinja* generally has two buildings—the *haiden* and the *honden*. The former, the "worship sanctuary," is the more public of the two. As its name implies, the *haiden* is where the faithful can approach and worship the *kami*. One very noticeable feature of the *haiden* is the **shimenawa**, a huge rope made of rice straw that marks the boundaries of the building that has been purified or an area in which the kami might be present. Strips of paper called *shide* are hung from the rope.

Worshippers stand in front of the building, clap their hands twice, and ring a suspended bell to attract the attention of the deity. Then they bow their heads and, with hands clasped and sometimes eyes closed, silently utter their prayer of requests or thanksgiving. Occasionally they also deposit offerings into a money chest. The *haiden* is also the place where the priests conduct their ordinary ceremonies on specific occasions on behalf of the community or the state but sometimes also purely private matters for individuals or small groups.

In the courtyard facing the *haiden*, visitors display their interaction with the *kami* through two specific objects: the **ema**, wooden tablets on

The Fushimi Inari-taisha Shrine in Kyoto, Japan, is dedicated to the god of rice and sake. Here, a tunnel of *torii* arches is guarded by a pair of foxes.

which are written their pleadings with the *kami* for success in marriage, childbirth, investment, and entrance examinations; and the **omikuji**, paper fortunes wrapped around tree branches as a form of divination to gauge the future outcome of an undertaking.

Beyond the *haiden* and more hidden from public view is the *honden* ("main sanctuary"), the place where the *kami* resides. It is generally raised higher than any other structure on the premises and has steep access stairs in front and at the sides. Only priests can enter this building, for it is regarded as the shelter of the **shintai**, the "body of the deity" that is the very physical embodiment of the *kami*. This *shintai* is the kernel of sacredness, the symbolic representation of the *kami* honored at the shrine. In and of itself the *shintai* has little intrinsic value. It may be a stone, a scroll, a mirror, a sword, or a small statue. Yet it is regarded with such awe and reverence that even the priests are prohibited from gazing upon it or handling it except on special occasions. As the soul of Shinto holiness and cleanliness, the *shintai* is both invio-lably sacred and pure.

The Grand Shrine at Ise, the main sanctuary of the Sun Goddess Amaterasu and official shrine of the imperial family, deserves special mention in connection with this Shinto concern for purity and cleanliness. Though originally built more than thirteen centuries ago, it is completely torn down and rebuilt every twenty years for the purpose of regular purification and renewal. According to tra-dition, this practice was inaugurated in 690 C.E. by Emperor Jitō. The design, however, is meticu-

lously copied each time. The shrine we see today is supposedly an exact replica of the original one, and it was freshly built in 2013.

The carpenters for the Ise Shrine come from families that have been hereditarily entrusted to undertake the task. Only natural cypress wood is used for the main struc-tures, and only hand tools are allowed to work on the wood. There are no metal braces or nails used in construction, and the different parts of the shrine are held together by complex and intricate wooden joints. The cypress wood is carefully selected years in advance of the rebuilding and is paraded through different communities throughout

Top: The *shimenawa* marks off a sacred space at a Shinto shrine. Bottom: These prayer plaques express the hopes, aspirations, and requests for blessing of the shrine visitors.

The inner shrine of Amaterasu at Ise.

Shrine visit is a regular practice of most Japanese, even though many of them do not regard it as an overt or deliberate religious act. How does it reflect Shinto's intertwining relationship with the Japanese way of life?

Japan to drum up support for and interest in the shrine rebuilding project. Thus the Ise Shrine is simultaneously the oldest and the newest, as well as the purest, shrine in Japan.

Religious Observances throughout the Year

Because of the diversity in Japanese religion, the yearly round of customary ritual observances (*nenjū gyōji*) is correspondingly diverse in religious orientation. Excluding the various local festivals that pay tribute to particular Shinto *kami* and Buddhist feasts that honor the Buddha and specific *bodhisattvas*, the following are the most popularly observed annual ritual occasions.

New Year (*Oshōgatsu*) People prepare for the New Year each January 1 by cleaning their houses thoroughly in an attempt to get rid of both physical and spiritual dirt. On New Year's Eve near midnight, they visit one of the major Shinto shrines such as the Meiji Shrine in Tokyo or a prominent Buddhist temple such as the Honganji in Kyoto to welcome in the New Year. Beginning on New Year's Day, they visit friends and relatives to offer their greetings and renew their relationship.

The Turn of the Seasons (*Setsubun*) This festival is observed on February 3, the last day of the winter season. A special purification ritual is performed by the entire family, which involves the throwing of roasted beans from the house into the yard, yelling *Oni wa soto!* (Demons get out!) and, from the yard into the house, calling out *Fuku wa uchi!* (Fortunes come in!). Shinto shrines in the community do the same, though on a much larger scale.

Doll Festival (*Hina Matsuri*) March 3 is devoted to the celebration of girls and daughters in the household. A notable feature of the observance of this special day is the prominent display of tiers of dolls with elaborate costumes that represent the styles of the court ladies of the ancient imperial period. These dolls are expensively made and are seen as a reflection of the family's financial standing.

Boys' Day (*Tango no Sekku*) This counterpart of the Doll Festival is celebrated on May 5. Dedicated to celebrating the healthy growth of boys, this day refers to the annual festival (*sekku*) held on the day of the horse (*go*) at the beginning (*tan*) of May. It also involves the display of figurines of armored fighters and the flying of carp-shaped paper or fabric streamers on a tall pole.

Star Festival (*Tanabata*) This festival was introduced from China to commemorate the romantic story of two stars, Vega and Altair, personified respectively as a young weaver maiden and her lover the cowherd, who are allowed this one-time-a-year rendezvous in the heavens. Observed on July 7, it is a festival for young lovers and for unmarried girls who want to improve their chances of marriage by honing their skills in weaving, sewing, and embroidery or any arts and crafts requiring manual dexterity.

Ghost Festival (*Obon*) Unlike the other festivals listed here, the Ghost Festival's date each year is not determined by the solar calendar. Instead, it falls on the fourteenth day of the seventh month in the lunar calendar. This is the Japanese

VISUAL GUIDE
Shinto

This image contains three major aspects of Japanese religiosity—the sun, the Shinto torii, and cherry blossoms. The sun is the chief deity responsible for the rise of the Japanese state, the torii (lit. "bird perch," hence the bird atop the arch) marks off the sacred space of the Shinto shrine ground, and cherry blossoms convey the Japanese sense of fragile beauty and transience.

Mt. Fuji is probably the most recognized mountain in the world, with its perfect cone shape and white top for a good part of the year. It is also believed by the Japanese to be a kami—a deity with awesome power. Framed by blooming cherry blossoms in early spring, it offers a breathtaking sight.

The *shimenawa* in front of a Shinto shrine. A giant rope made of rice stalk, the *shimenawa* marks off the sacred space within the shrine complex. Worshippers believe that beyond the line resides the spirit of the *kami*.

The Nachi Waterfall in Kumano, Japan. Like Mt. Fuji, the Nachi Fall is an iconic Shinto symbol long revered in Japan. Also considered a *kami*, it is a popular site for Shinto pilgrims who appreciate not only its magic power but also its scenic beauty.

A Shinto priest at the Itsukushima Shrine in Miyajima, Japan. The priest acts as bridge between the worshippers and the *kami* housed at the shrine. He makes presentation to the deity on behalf of the community, purifies the shrine visitors with prescribed rituals, and presides over community events.

version of the *Yülanpen*, a Chinese Buddhist festival. *Bon* is the Japanese pronunciation of the Chinese word *pen* (bowl of offerings), and *o* is the honorific. This is the festival to welcome the ancestral spirits to return home with food and offerings. Families clean the graves of their ancestors and wash the headstones. On the previous evening, people build a small fire outside the gate of their homes to greet the returning spirits. Sometimes Buddhist monks are invited to the house to recite *sutras* to soothe the souls of the deceased and comfort the living. Over the next two days, people participate in communal folk dances called *bon odori* to please the spirits and to enhance communal solidarity.

Harvest Festival (*Niiname-sai*)   This giving of thanks by the community for rice harvest occurs on November 23. In modern Japan, it is renamed "Labor Thanksgiving Day" (*Kinro kansha no hi*) and designated a national holiday. Celebrating the harvest with the people, the Japanese emperor traditionally would taste the newly ripened rice and would offer it to the *kami* on behalf of his subjects. The festival also links all local shrines to the imperial court, as the emperor is believed to be the representative of the people to thank the *kami* for providing fertility and bountifulness.

CONCLUSION

We have established in this chapter that Shinto is the longest surviving and most distinctive religious tradition in Japan. It pervades much of Japanese life and informs much of Japanese behavior. It also provides a sense of identity and unity to the Japanese people. Shinto belief in the ubiquitous presence of the *kami*, both in nature and in human society, makes the Japanese view nature and human community with awe and respect. Though lacking an ethical code and detailed understanding of the afterlife, Shinto is complemented by Confucianism and Buddhism to allow the Japanese the full experience of a religious life.

SEEKING ANSWERS

What Is Ultimate Reality?

According to Shinto, the world is a sanctified place divinely created and ordained by the *kami*. The *kami* reveal themselves in living and nonliving things, in nature and in the human world. They are responsible for the fertility of the world, and they prefer purity and cleanliness. Humans, some of whom are *kami* themselves, must pay constant attention to their relationship with the *kami*, for that is the only way that life can be fulfilled. Because the world is the creation of the *kami*, humanity is obligated to maintain the world's sanctity by acting as its guardian and caretaker. Shinto believers are

(continued)

extremely sentimental about nature and are easily moved by its beauty. Many Japanese literary compositions express this Shinto affirmation of the divine and sanctified nature of the world.

How Should We Live in This World?

Original Shinto gives little emphasis on morality or ethical living. There is no revealed moral code. Instead, it teaches right living primarily as fertile and pure living. The human condition is defined more in terms of purity and defilement. Death, blood, improper food, or improper behaviors are sources of contamination that make humans unfit to interact with the *kami*. However, these are temporary conditions. Constant attention to maintaining cleanliness and purity will ensure favor from the deities. As a result, rituals of purification and sanctification are meticulously performed by Shinto believers to seek good interaction with the *kami*.

What Is Our Ultimate Purpose?

Unlike many other religions, Shinto does not perceive the human condition as a fallen state or intrinsically flawed by sin. Humans are therefore not evil by nature; thus there is no need for improvement or transcendence. Conversely, Shinto has no belief in an almighty benevolent God who has made humans in an initial state of perfection. Humans are therefore not good by nature, either. Instead, humans are very much a part of nature, striving to live in harmony with it through interaction with its various spiritual manifestations, the *kami*.

REVIEW QUESTIONS

For Review

1. What is the Shinto version of creation?
2. Why is the concept of *kami* so central to Shinto beliefs?
3. How does Shinto view death?

For Further Reflection

1. If Shinto does not address ethics in its original outlook, what is the source of morality for the Japanese?

2. Discuss the role played by women in Shinto.
3. What role does Shinto play in bolstering the nationalistic sentiments of the Japanese people?
4. Although there are rivalry and competition among the three major religions in Japan, there has been a conspicuous absence of religious wars based on doctrinal or theological differences. Please explain.

GLOSSARY

Amaterasu (ah-mah'-te-rah'-soo) "Deity that shines in the sky," the Sun Goddess in Shinto. Enshrined at Ise, Amaterasu is the *kami* of the imperial family. As the Sun Goddess, she is the most august of all deities. Her descendants are considered the only rightful rulers of Japan.

ema (∂-mah') Wooden tablets expressing pleadings to *kami* for success in life.

harae (hah-rah'-∂) Shinto purification.

Izanagi (ee-zanah'-gee) The male *kami* who is the procreator of the Japanese islands.

Izanami (ee-za-nah'-mee) The female *kami* who is the procreator of the Japanese islands.

jinja (jin'-ja) Shinto shrine.

kami (kah-mee) Shinto deity and spirit with awe-inspiring power.

Kojiki (koh'-jee-kee) *Record of Ancient Matters*, compiled in the eighth century c.e.

matsuri (mah-tsu'ree) Shinto religious festival.

miko (mee'-koh) Unmarried female Shinto shrine attendants.

mikoshi (mee-koh'-shee) Portable shrine temporarily housing a Shinto deity.

misogi (mee-soh'-gee) Shinto ritual of purification with water.

Nihon shoki (nee-hohn shoh-kee) *Chronicles of [the Land Where] the Sun Originates.*

norito (noh-ree'-toh) Invocational prayer offered by Shinto priests to the *kami.*

omikuji (oh'-mee-koo-jee) Paper fortunes wrapped around tree branches at shrines.

saisei-itchi (sai-sei ik'-kee) Unity of the religious and the political realms.

shimenawa (shee-m∂' nah-wa) Huge rope hung in front of the worship sanctuary of a shrine.

shintai (shin-tai) The "body" of a *kami* housed in a shrine or temporarily in a *mikoshi.*

Shinto (shin-toh) The Way of the Gods. Traditional Japanese religion that acknowledges the power of the *kami.*

temizuya (te mee' zoo-ya) Purification fountain at a shrine.

torii (toh- ree' ee) Cross-bar gateway leading up to the Shinto shrine.

SUGGESTIONS FOR FURTHER READING

Ashkenazi, Michael. *Matsuri: Festivals of a Japanese Town.* Honolulu: University of Hawaii Press, 1993. An anthropological and sociological description of Shinto in practice at Yuzawa, a town in Japan's northern region.

Bellah, Robert N. *Tokugawa Religion: The Cultural Roots of Modern Japan.* New York: Free Press, 1985. A classic sociological study of the religious roots of modern Japan, with an in-depth look at possible parallels to the Protestant ethic.

De Bary, William Theodore, et al., eds. *Sources of Japanese Tradition.* 2nd ed. 2 vols. New York: Columbia University Press, 2001, 2005. Though not exclusively focused on religious writings, this two-volume anthology is a gold mine of information for the study of Japanese religion.

Earhart, H. Byron. *Religion in the Japanese Experience: Sources and Interpretations.* 2nd ed. Belmont, CA: Wadsworth, 1997. An informative collection of source materials on Japanese religion, arranged topically and with insightful comments.

Ellwood, Robert, and Richard Pilgrim. *Japanese Religion: A Cultural Perspective.* Englewood Cliffs, NJ: Prentice Hall, 1985. A concise volume for the cultural study of Japanese religion.

Kasahara, Kazuo, ed. *A History of Japanese Religion.* Tokyo: Kosei, 2002. An English translation of a two-volume work in Japanese that contains chapters written by scholars on different stages in the historical development of Japanese religion.

Kitagawa, Joseph M. *Religion in Japanese History.* New York: Columbia University Press, 1990. A detailed historical narrative of the development of Japanese religions.

Nelson, John K. *A Year in the Life of a Shinto Shrine.* Seattle: University of Washington Press, 1996. An ethnographical description of the ritual cycle at the Suwa Shrine in Nagasaki.

Ono, Sokyo. *Shinto: The Kami Way.* Tokyo: Charles E. Tuttle, 1962. This remains a very convenient single volume on Shinto.

ONLINE RESOURCES

Encyclopedia of Shinto

eos.kokugakuin.ac.jp

This useful, English-language resource is maintained by the Kokugakuin University in Japan. In addition to the *Encyclopedia of Shinto*, it includes various images and video clips of Shinto objects and rituals.

Tsubaki Grand Shrine of America

tsubakishrine.com

The Tsubaki Grand Shrine, located near Seattle, is the North American branch of one of the most ancient Shinto shrines in Japan. This English-language website provides information about Shinto, as well as a schedule of observances at the Tsubaki shrine.

ZOROASTRIANISM

WITH THE WHITE-ROBED PRIEST standing behind her and with family members and friends seated in the living room of her parent's home, Yasmin recites the last stanzas of the prayer she had learned just for this very important occasion: the investiture ceremony, or Sudreh-Pooshi. Yasmin is about to receive the **kusti**, the sacred cord that will serve from this day forward as the visible symbol of her full membership in the Zoroastrian community. Still only nine years old, Yasmin now looks forward to fully participating in the rituals and religious life that her ancestors have embraced since the time of the ancient Iranian prophet and poet **Zarathustra**—whom the Greeks called Zoroaster—some three millennia ago.

Prior to this point in the ceremony, the priest has recited a confession of sins on behalf of Yasmin. She then commenced to recite the prayers that she had spent the past several months memorizing. In preparation for tying the *kusti* cord around Yasmin, the priest provided her with a white cotton vest, or *sudreh*. The *kusti* cord is woven from seventy-two threads of lamb's yarn—seventy-two also being the number of chapters in the **Yasna**, one of Zoroastrianism's most ancient sacred texts. The *kusti* cord had been carefully produced by women in Yasmin's community and then consecrated by a priest. For the rest of her life, wearing the *sudreh* and *kusti* on a daily basis will constitute one of Yasmin's most important religious duties.

Once the priest has assisted Yasmin with tying the *kusti* cord around her waist, he will draw a red mark on her forehead and then bless her. Afterward, Yasmin's family and friends will congregate for a celebration,

Parsi children participate in Navjote, the Zoroastrian investiture ceremony, in Mumbai, India (known as Sudreh-Pooshi in Iran). The priests assist with tying the *kusti*, the sacred cord.

Significant sites in the development of Zoroastrianism.

at which she will receive gifts. Investiture into the Zoroastrian community is a happy occasion for all involved.

Yasmin lives in Iran, the original homeland of Zoroastrianism. Today there are more Zoroastrians living in India, where they are called Parsis, and where the investiture ceremony is called Navjote and is less common for girls (but standard for all boys). Such differences in investiture ceremonies are among the many distinctive characteristics that distinguish Zoroastrianism as experienced in various places.

Even in Iran, and especially in India, the Zoroastrian population is dwindling—and so young people like Yasmin bear a special responsibility to help maintain the vitality of their religion. In order to be true to traditional norms that have been upheld through the centuries, Yasmin will need to marry a Zoroastrian man—and in our contemporary world this sort of tradition faces stiff challenges. Furthermore, a proper Zoroastrian life calls for practices—such as wearing the *kusti* cord—that do not necessarily conform to modern modes of living. To cite a more extreme example, traditionally Zoroastrians have disposed of the bodies of the dead by exposing them to the open air so that the flesh can be cleaned away by scavengers. Such a practice is no longer even legal in some places where Zoroastrians live. Tensions like this, between tradition and modernity, inevitably present people like Yasmin with hard choices. ☀

This chapter explores the teachings, history, and way of life of Zoroastrianism—or Mazdaism, as it is sometimes known. Arguably the world's oldest living religion, Zoroastrianism's long history, together with the geographical distribution just noted, has resulted in much diversity. There are various ways of being Zoroastrian. This introductory study, while acknowledging diversity, presents the religion mainly as it is practiced today by the majority of its followers. We begin by focusing on its principal teachings.

THE TEACHINGS OF ZOROASTRIANISM

Through the centuries, Zoroastrians have lived in evolving cultural circumstances—most notably the rise of Islam in the seventh century C.E. and the subsequent migrations of Zoroastrians to India and other lands. In this chapter's later section on the history of Zoroastrianism, we explore some of these circumstances in more detail, paying careful attention to Zoroastrian texts from different eras and how they reflect changing perspectives. Here, we describe in more general terms the central teachings of Zoroastrianism that have endured until today. Some of these teachings date from the religion's origins, whereas others have developed in much later periods.

> ### TIMELINE
> Zoroastrianism
>
> **2000 B.C.E.** Indo-Iranian tribes migrate to the Iranian Plateau.
>
> **1300–550 B.C.E.** Most scholars place the life of Zarathustra within this period.
>
> **1300–550 B.C.E.** Composition of the *Avesta*.
>
> **550–330 B.C.E.** Persian (Achaemenid) Empire. Most of the Achaemenid kings were Zoroastrians.
>
> **247 B.C.E.– 224 C.E.** Parthian Empire. Zoroastrianism loses its royal endorsement, existing as one of many religions.
>
> **224–651** Sassanid Empire. Sassanid kings declare Zoroastrianism to be the official state religion.
>
> **651** Arab invaders topple Sassanid dynasty. Islam begins to eclipse Zoroastrianism in Iran.
>
> **700–900** Composition of most chapters of the *Bundahishn*.
>
> **c. ninth century** Iranian Zoroastrians flee to western India, where they are known as Parsis (Persian for "Persians").
>
> **900–1000** Composition of the *Denkard*.
>
> **1860** Martin Haug publishes the first translation of the *Gathas* into a European language (German).
>
> **1878** The first fire temple in America is built in Florence, Arizona.

The most significant of all Zoroastrian teachings is cosmic **dualism**—the ongoing opposition between the forces of order and chaos, of good and evil, understood to be played out on a cosmic level.

Cosmic Dualism

Before examining dualism, it must be pointed out that many contemporary Zoroastrians likely would not cite this as being their religion's most characteristic feature. Instead, they would emphasize that they are monotheists, believing in the one God **Ahura Mazda**. And on the surface, it might seem that a dualism that features opposing forces of good and evil cannot be compatible with a monotheism that features one God who is perfectly good and is ultimately in control of all things.

But in fact, monotheism and dualism are not necessarily incompatible—and, depending on how strictly one defines "monotheism," Zoroastrianism is an especially intriguing example of these two doctrines fitting together harmoniously. Its teachings provide a remarkable solution to the so-called "problem of evil": How can a perfectly good, all-powerful God *and* evil exist at one and the same time? Zoroastrian's explanation is simple but at the same time profound: Ahura Mazda is the only God, and ultimately order and goodness will win out over chaos and evil. But in the meantime the existence of evil cannot be denied, and so it must be addressed. A great cosmic struggle is being played out, with forces of evil aligned against forces of good. Ahura Mazda, while not responsible for the origin of these forces of evil, orchestrates the gradual process by which the cosmos will be purged of evil and good will prevail for all eternity.

We will investigate this cosmic struggle in detail shortly. First we note that Zoroastrianism embraces not just one but two forms of dualism. Interrelated with the dualism of good and evil is the dualism of spirit and matter.

Spirit and Matter Zoroastrianism teaches that reality is divisible into two realms: that of spirit and thought and that of matter and physicality. Everything in existence embodies both realms. Readers familiar with Platonic philosophy will recognize similarities with Zoroastrian spirit/matter dualism—and, indeed, Greek philosophy, Platonic and also Aristotelian, might have influenced Zoroastrian beliefs.

Human beings must orient themselves toward the spiritual realm in order to live righteously and in accordance with order and ultimately to achieve salvation. And yet, Zoroastrianism teaches a healthy regard for the body and its enjoyments, within appropriate limits. The realm of spirit and thought is the true origin of human life, but embodiment is not a negative thing. In fact, as we will consider in more detail later in the chapter, it is a general religious duty for Zoroastrians to have children, thereby furthering the embodiment of the realm of spirit or thought within the realm of matter or body. And ultimately, the final triumph of good over evil depends on this. But in order to understand Zoroastrian teachings on this final triumph, we must first examine the dualism of good and evil and the opposing forces at work in the cosmos.

Order and Chaos The Zoroastrian dualism of order and chaos involves two key concepts. *Asha* is "order," the true, cosmic order that pervades both the natural and social spheres of reality, encompassing the moral and religious life of individuals. *Asha* is symbolized by light, and therefore by the sun and by fire.

Asha is opposed by the "Lie," or *druj*. Whereas *asha* gives rise to good thoughts, words, and deeds, *druj* gives rise to evil thoughts, words, and deeds. The two are fundamentally incompatible and locked in a cosmic struggle. Soon we will focus on the relevance of this struggle for human beings. First, we investigate how this dualism divides the Zoroastrian pantheon of divine beings.

The Divine Realm

Earlier we noted that most Zoroastrians today consider their religion to be monotheistic. This section on the divine realm might therefore come as a surprise, given the extensive array of deities and other supernatural beings that it describes. But in fact, the case of Zoroastrianism is not so different from that of other notable monotheistic religions. The Bible makes many references to supernatural beings—seraphim, cherubim, angels—other than the one God of Judaism and of Christianity. Likewise the Qur'an, while strongly emphasizing belief in only one God, Allah, assumes the existence of other supernatural beings, namely angels, devils, and *jinn* (who can be good or evil; see Chapter 13). All three of these monotheistic religions acknowledge the existence of an Evil One, named Satan.

Ahura Mazda   Zoroastrianism emerged from an earlier Iranian religious perspective that undoubtedly was polytheistic. Zarathustra seems to have been responsible for declaring that one god is primary and qualitatively above all others: Ahura Mazda, the "Wise Lord" (*ahura* in ancient Iranian means "lord"; there is no other known ancient usage of the term *Mazda*). In later centuries, Zoroastrians came also to use the name Ohrmazd to refer to their God.

Zarathustra worshiped Ahura Mazda as the only eternal deity, responsible for the creation of the world. This is not to say that Ahura Mazda is responsible for the evil that also has existed since the beginning of time. Zarathustra taught that Ahura Mazda ultimately will overcome evil, and that to do so he created this world. It is in the realm of the physical world that the embodied forces of order and good do battle against the embodied forces of chaos and evil. The final triumph will be accomplished through the forces of good aligned with Ahura Mazda.

Divine Forces of Good   Especially prominent among the forces of good are the seven **Amesha Spentas**, the "Beneficial Immortals," angels who help Ahura Mazda govern creation. Chief among these seven is **Spenta Mainyu**, Ahura Mazda's Holy Spirit. The *Amesha Spentas* function together as semi-independent powers, all of them in service of Ahura Mazda. Among them is *Asha*, the cosmic principle of order that we have already encountered. Each of the *Amesha Spentas* constitutes an element of the cosmos; *Asha*, for example (whose full name is *Asha Vahishta*, "Best Order"), constitutes fire.

The seven *Amesha Spentas* are assisted by a large number of deities called **yazatas**, "ones worthy of worship." Eventually the number was fixed at thirty, so that each day of the Zoroastrian month is represented by a different *yazata* (this includes the seven *Amesha Spentas*, who sometimes are classified along with the *yazatas*). One of the most important among them is Mithra, a god of light who works to keep human beings in harmony with *asha*. As we will see in the later section on the history of Zoroastrianism, Mithra was to become a very popular

Integration of the dualism of spirit/matter and the dualism of order (good)-chaos (evil). The spirit of *asha*, personified in the *yazatas* ("ones worthy of worship"), is embodied in the physical world; so too is the spirit of *druj*, personified as the *daevas*, embodied in the physical world—the stage on which the cosmic struggle between good and evil is played out.

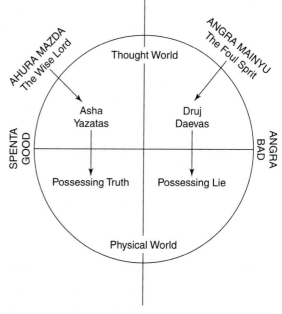

god in Roman culture, in the mystery religion of Mithras (his Greek and Latin name). Another *yazata* of particular note is Sraosha ("Obedience"), the caretaker of the souls of the dead who also plays an important role in overseeing ritual practices.

The "Lie" and Forces of Evil   From the beginning of time, Spenta Mainyu, Ahura Mazda's Holy Spirit, has battled against his adversary **Angra Mainyu**, the "Foul Spirit," who in later texts also is named Ahriman. This battle is at the basis of the cosmic dualism between order and chaos, also manifested in the struggle between *asha* and the "Lie," or *druj*. One of Zoroastrianism's earliest texts provides us with insight regarding the battle and its participants:

> Truly there were two primal Spirits, twins renowned to be in conflict.
> In thought and word, in act they are two: the better and the bad. And
> those who act well have chosen rightly between these two, not so the
> evildoers. And when these two Spirits first came together they created
> life and not-life, and how at the end Worst Existence shall be for the
> wicked, but (the House of) Best Purpose for the just man. Of these two
> Spirits the Wicked One chose achieving the worst things. The Most Holy
> Spirit, who is clad in hardest stone, chose right, and (so do those) who
> shall satisfy Lord Mazda continually with rightful acts. The Daevas indeed
> did not choose rightly between these two, for the Deceiver approached
> them as they conferred. Because they chose worst purpose, they then
> rushed to Fury, with whom they have afflicted the world and mankind.
> —*Yasna 30.2–6, from the Gathas*[2]

The ***daevas*** mentioned here are the various demonic powers (*daevas* in ancient Iranian originally meant "gods," but eventually came to mean "demons"). Notably, as this text reports, the *daevas* came to be demonic because they *chose* "worst purpose." As we will see, this same opportunity for choice presents itself throughout the lifetime of each human being.

Compare other religions with Zoroastrianism on how they deal with the problem of evil.

Creation and the Nature of the World

Zoroastrianism cosmology, or teachings on the nature of the world, posits three progressive phases: the creation of the physical world; the mixing in the physical world of the embodied spirits of evil forces with those of good forces; and the final transformation, in which the world will be cleansed of all evil.

According to Zoroastrianism's most prominent creation myth, in the beginning Ahura Mazda conceived a plan for creation and also secured the support of the ***fravishis***, preexisting higher souls and guardian spirits of individual human beings. Distinct from the lower souls that exist together with human bodies, the *fravishis* were to descend into the material world once it was created, where they combat the forces of evil and gently guide human beings toward ethical lives and the realization of their true nature.

After Ahura Mazda had taken these initial steps he over-
came Angra Mainyu, who fell into a kind of stupor for
3,000 years, and then created the *Amesha Spentas* ("Beneficial Immortals"). He also created *asha*, the cosmic order
that underlies the universe, intended to serve as a bulwark
against the destructive actions of Angra Mainyu.

During this period of 3,000 years, Ahura Mazda
and the *Amesha Spentas* created the physical world. As
the primary textual account makes clear, the process of
creation took place in seven stages:

> When the Evil Spirit was helpless in prostration, he lay prostrate for
> 3,000 years. During the helplessness of the Evil Spirit, Ohrmazd cre-
> ated the creation materially. First, He created the Sky as a defence;
> second, He created Water, to defeat the demon of thirst; third, He cre-
> ated the all-solid Earth; fourth, He created the Plant, to help the ben-
> eficient Animal; fifth, He created the beneficent Animal, to help the
> Just Man; sixth, He created the Just Man, to smite the Evil Spirit to-
> gether with the devs and to make them powerless. And then He cre-
> ated Fire and linked its brilliance to the Endless Light.
> —*Bundahishn 1a.1–4*[3]

The best-known symbol
of Zoroastrianism, the
Faravahar is believed to
represent the *fravishis*.
This example is from
Yazd, Iran.

The "Just Man" is the first human being. (The "devs" are the *daevas* we have already
discussed.) The "Fire" of the seventh stage is represented by the sun.

According to the same account, the entire span of time between creation and the
final triumph of good over evil will be 12,000 years. After the 3,000-year period
during which the physical world was created comes the period of the Mixture, during
which Angra Mainyu is again active and the evil spirit forces are mixed together with
the spirit forces of good—hence the cosmic struggle that currently is ongoing. Angra
Mainyu and the evil forces destroyed the primordial Plant, Animal (a bull), and Just
Man. But these victories would prove to be only temporary.

Eventually there will ensue the period leading up to the final triumph of good over
evil. This will be achieved through the separation of the evil from the good, culminating in complete purification. The ultimate purpose of human life is to help bring about
this purification through leading virtuous lives according to Zoroastrian teachings.

Human Nature and Human Destiny

Dualism, the most significant feature of Zoroastrian teachings, lies at the heart of the
religion's perspective on human nature and human destiny. As is detailed in this section, the meaning of life rests in ethical choice: whether to comply with Zarathustra's
revelations and live in accordance with *asha,* cosmic order, or to deviate from this and
succumb to the evil ways of *druj,* the Lie.

Dualism in Human Life: Ethical Choice Zoroastrianism teaches that human beings are free to choose to live in harmony with *asha*. This way of living involves making Ahura Mazda, the transcendent God, immanent in one's own being, a blessing made possible through Spenta Mainyu, the Holy Spirit of Ahura Mazda, whose worldly creation is humankind.

Zoroastrian teachings regarding human nature and destiny can be simplified by considering a few parallels involving the basic dualism of good and evil. *Asha* is opposed to *druj*. Spenta Mainyu and Angra Mainyu are, respectively, spirits of good and evil because of the choice they made. This choice is the prototype of the ethical choice confronting every individual.

Judgment of the Soul The ethical choices made in life determine the fate of the soul in the afterlife. The outcome of these ethical choices is knowable by the individual's thoughts, words, and deeds. The goodness of these three must outweigh the evil if the individual is to be saved and to live for eternity in heaven. The alternative is eternal torment in hell.

Zoroastrian teachings on the judgment of the soul involve two aspects that are especially notable: the **Daena** and the **Chinvat Bridge**.

The Daena is a feminine being who embodies the individual's ethical quality and who appears to the soul after death. If the individual has lived in harmony with *asha*, then the Daena appears as a beautiful young woman. To the soul of an evil individual, however, the Daena appears as an ugly old hag.

The Chinvat Bridge needs to be crossed by the soul in order to reach the afterlife. For the good individual, the Chinvat Bridge is wide and easy to cross. But for the evil, it is razor-thin, causing the soul to plummet down into hell.

The Final Triumph The ultimate purpose of individual striving for righteousness transcends the salvation of the individual soul. The combined efforts of each individual's striving will eventually overcome evil, bringing about the purification of the world and the final triumph.

At some point (the date is uncertain), new teachings arose that involved elaboration on this doctrine of the final triumph. These teachings asserted that a messianic savior figure, named Saoshyant, a son of Zarathustra (whose semen is said to have been miraculously preserved in a lake), will appear to usher in the events that will transform the wicked world into the glorious and eternal kingdom of Ahura Mazda. The cosmic struggle will culminate in a battle between the *yazatas*, allied with righteous human beings, and the *daevas*, allied with evildoers, in which the good will emerge victorious. Then the dead will be resurrected, and all souls will be judged, the evil being burned in molten metal. The righteous will be saved, to live forever in the presence of Ahura Mazda.

THE HISTORY OF ZOROASTRIANISM

Its roots reaching back 3,000 years to the ancient Iranian tribes, Zoroastrianism by the sixth century B.C.E. had become the dominant religion in Iran. But the rise of Islam in the seventh century C.E. changed the religious culture of the Middle East, pushing Zoroastrians into corners of the world where their numbers have dwindled. Still, Zoroastrianism persists as a living religion, and its teachings and practices continue to fascinate scholars and other observers.

The Background of Zoroastrianism

The Indo-Iranians At some time about 2000 B.C.E., two nomadic peoples related by language and religion began moving southward from their ancestral home in Central Asia. One was the Indo-Aryans, who migrated to what are now Pakistan and western India. There, joining with the indigenous population, they produced Vedic culture and laid the foundations of Hinduism. The other was the Indo-Iranians, who found a new homeland on the Iranian Plateau just east of Mesopotamia. Living apart from their cousins, these ancient Iranians formed a religious tradition very different from Hinduism. And yet both retained vestiges of their common past. Consider, for instance, a linguistic example with clear religious implications: Iranian *daevas* and Indian *devas* both mean "gods" or "spirits."

Iranian Peoples and Languages There were several early Iranian peoples whose languages became the languages of Zoroastrianism. Avestan, spoken by tribes of northeastern Iran, is the language in which the earliest Zoroastrian text, the **Avesta**, is written. In fact, the development of the *Avesta* over time resulted in some parts being written in Old Avestan and others in Younger Avestan.

Developing alongside Avestan was Old Persian, a language from the southwestern region of Pars (also Parsa), from which "Persia" derives. Old Persian texts relating to Zoroastrianism are mostly cuneiform inscriptions written on clay tablets and seals between 600 and 300 B.C.E. A later form of Old Persian is Middle Persian, usually called Pahlavi in connection with Zoroastrian texts. Inscriptions in Pahlavi can be dated as early as the third century C.E. Most of the Zoroastrian scriptures were written in Pahlavi in the eighth and ninth centuries C.E. after circulating orally for centuries.

Pre-Zoroastrian Religion Ancient texts tell us that early Iranian religion had marked similarities with early Hinduism as described in the *Vedas* (Chapter 4). They describe worship of the *daevas* as widespread in Iran, just as devotion to the *devas* was common in India. The *daevas* were personifications of the aspects of nature on which all people depend: sky, sun, earth, fire, water, wind, and so forth. There was also a higher order of deities, known as *ahuras* ("lords"), responsible for maintaining order in the universe as a whole. These included Intar, a war god known as Indra in the

Hindu *Vedas*; Mithra (Vedic Mitra), a god of light who gave cattle and children to the Iranians; and Yima (Vedic Yama), ruler of the dead. Finally, our sources describe belief in *asha*, an underlying natural and moral order that promoted goodness in all its forms—most notably light, truth, and justice. At times, order would be overcome by chaos in its many aspects—such as darkness, falsehood, and injustice—only to reestablish itself later. The universe was the setting for an unending struggle between order and chaos.

Human beings could support the forces of order through religious practices designed to strengthen them: sacrifices of cereal grains and, more commonly, animals; fire worship; and the preparation and consumption of **haoma**, a sacred drink made from the sour, milky juice of the soma plant (and similar to the *soma* drink described in the *Vedas*). In time, however, the violence involved in animal sacrifices, the cost of sacred rituals, and the power of the priests who conducted them became oppressive to many of the early Iranians. One of them was Zarathustra.

Zarathustra

Scholars cannot agree on where and when we should locate the life of Zarathustra. Some scholars go so far as to argue that he was not a historical figure at all. Most plausibly, Zarathustra is indeed a historical figure, who lived in eastern Iran or in Central Asia at some point between 1300 and 550 B.C.E.

Legends preserved in Zoroastrianism's sacred texts say that Zarathustra displayed religious inclinations even as a child and that at the age of twenty he left his family and the wife they had found for him in order to search for truth. Ten years later he had a vision of Ahura Mazda. Lifted out of his material body, Zarathustra was taken up into a heavenly court, where he beheld Ahura Mazda, the "Wise Lord," attended by his angels. Calling upon Zarathustra to be his prophet, Ahura Mazda, leader of the forces of *asha* (order), revealed the grave threat posed by Angra Mainyu, the "foul spirit" and leader of the forces of chaos. In additional visions occurring over the next eight years, each of the six principal angels of Ahura Mazda appeared to Zarathustra and elaborated on the content of the first vision. By the time the visions ended, Zarathustra understood the message Ahura Mazda wanted him to proclaim to human beings: Ahura Mazda was the Supreme Being and the power upon which order depended. Human beings could join in the struggle against Angra Mainyu by resolving to live lives of exemplary morality. Any other decision would establish them as allies of Angra Mainyu. At the end of time every human being would be judged on the moral quality of his or her life and assigned to an eternity either in the paradise of Ahura Mazda or the hellish pits of Angra Mainyu.

There was much that was new in the revelations Zarathustra had received. Ahura Mazda, formerly on equal terms with other *ahuras*, was now raised to a level far above them. Ethical conduct on the part of the individual now displaced sacrificial rituals performed by priests as the most significant form of human activity. Human beings were now understood as full participants and no longer as semiengaged bystanders in the cosmic struggle between order and chaos, good and evil.

The unfamiliarity of ideas like these no doubt helps to explain the difficulty Zarathustra encountered in finding converts to the new religion—the one true religion—he had learned from Ahura Mazda and his angels. It is also likely that many people resented certain reforms made by Zarathustra, who forbade sacrifices to the *daevas*, whom he saw as agents of Angra Mainyu, and sought to put an end to the drinking of the intoxicating *haoma* at animal sacrifices because of the erratic behavior and sexual license that resulted from this combination. It is said that he suffered through many years of discouragement and that Angra Mainyu himself urged him to give up. But then Zarathustra came to the court of King Vishtaspa, whom legend describes as a good man surrounded by a class of wicked priests. Profiting from their bloody animal sacrifices and from popular belief that their magic could ensure good harvests and protection from the raids of nomadic tribes, the priests were able to arouse so great an opposition to Zarathustra that he was thrown into prison. But when Zarathustra managed to perform a miraculous cure for Vishtaspa's favorite horse, the king took a stand against the priests and converted his kingdom to Zarathustra's new religion. From this point on, Zarathustra and his followers had great success in bringing it to other parts of Iran. According to Zoroastrian scripture, Zarathustra died at the age of seventy-seven, killed by a nomadic raider in the city of Balkh (in modern Afghanistan) while performing a ritual at his fire altar.

Compare the role of Zarathustra as founder of Zoroastrianism with the roles of other founders of world religions: for example, the Buddha, Mahavira, Guru Nanak, Confucius, or Muhammad.

Zoroastrian Scriptures

The *Avesta* The oldest and most important of the Zoroastrian scriptures is the *Avesta*, a collection of sacred texts that preserve the teachings given to Zarathustra by Ahura Mazda and a great deal besides. The history of the *Avesta* is described in later texts written in Pahlavi. According to the tradition, the *Avesta* we have today is a remnant of a much larger collection of texts said to have been destroyed when Alexander the Great conquered the Persian Empire in the fourth century B.C.E.

The *Avesta* is organized into five parts. The *Yasna* consists of material recited by priests when performing their liturgical functions. At the core of the *Yasna* are the *Gathas*, hymns attributed to Zarathustra. Written in a very ancient dialect, the *Gathas* are the part of the *Avesta* thought to most accurately reflect the life and thought of Zarathustra. The *Visperad* is a collection of texts recited along with the *Yasna* in order to solemnize seasonal celebrations, such as the Zoroastrian New Year's Day. Unlike the *Yasna* and *Visperad*, which are liturgical collections, the primary purpose of the *Vendidad* is to describe the many ways in which the *daevas* work evil in the world and various means for confounding them. The *Vendidad* also contains stories about the creation of the world, the first human being, and the temptation of Zarathustra by Angra Mainyu. The *Yashts* constitute a collection of hymns that venerate Zoroastrian virtues such as wisdom, truth, justice, and obedience and the angels associated with them. Originally, there were thirty *Yashts*, one dedicated to each day of the month.

Only twenty-one survive today. The final part of the *Avesta* is the *Khordeh Avesta*. Sometimes called the "concise *Avesta*," it consists of selections from the rest of the *Avesta* that are used by laypeople in the course of their daily lives. These include *Yashts* and special prayers recited during the five parts of the day, before undertaking certain tasks, and before eating and drinking.

Pahlavi Texts In addition to the *Avesta*, there are numerous later texts written in Pahlavi. Two of the most important are the *Denkard* and the *Bundahishn*. The *Denkard* is a compendium of materials relating to Zoroastrian beliefs and customs, some of them much older than the *Denkard* itself. It includes doctrines; instructions for ethical behavior; the writings of Zoroastrian sages; observations on the arts and sciences, as well as on philosophical and theological topics; a history of the world up to the time of Zarathustra; and substantial material on Zarathustra himself. The *Bundahishn* ("Primal Creation") is technically not scripture, though it elaborates on ideas found in the *Avesta*. Earlier in this chapter we studied the myth of creation as presented in the *Bundahishn*.

Zoroastrianism through the Centuries

We will return soon to Zoroastrianism as a living religion, but it is important first to survey the course of its history from ancient times to the present. As we do, we will pause briefly to take note of the great deal it had in common with other ancient religions and to comment on the fascination Zarathustra and Zoroastrianism have held for Western artists and thinkers.

Zoroastrianism in the Persian Empire (550–330 B.C.E.) The history of Zoroastrianism in the period immediately following the time of Zarathustra is uncertain. The historical record begins in the sixth century B.C.E. with the *Histories* of Herodotus, a Greek who lived a century later. Herodotus's interest in the Persian Empire—so-called because the ancestral home of its Achaemenid Dynasty was Pars ("Persia") in southwestern Iran—can be explained by the fact that it invaded Greece twice in the early years of Herodotus's own century. Wanting to provide his countrymen with an account of the culture of the enemy, Herodotus included his observations on the religion of the Persians and, in particular, the Magi. These appear to have been members of a powerful Zoroastrian priestly caste in the empire of the neighboring Medes, which was annexed to the newer Persian Empire by its founder, Cyrus the Great, in 550 B.C.E. Owing to the unwelcome political intrigues of the Magi, Cyrus and his son Cambyses II curtailed their influence and sometimes persecuted them. But Zoroastrianism began to gain momentum with the accession of Darius I (r. 549–485 B.C.E.), who credited Ahura Mazda with bringing him to power. Thereafter, the religious culture of the Persian Empire became thoroughly Zoroastrian, and the role of the Magi as priests was secured. Surviving monuments and inscriptions testify to the influence of Zoroastrianism, as do a number of Avestan texts from this period.

Zoroastrianism in the Parthian Empire (247 B.C.E.–224 C.E.)

Achaemenid Persia fell to the Greeks and Macedonians under Alexander the Great in 330 B.C.E. A century later, Iran made a resurgence under a new dynasty of rulers from the region of Parthia. At its height, the Parthian Empire encompassed Iran, Mesopotamia, and parts of the Arabian Peninsula and what is now Turkey. Its culture was heterogeneous, combining the Iranian and Greek cultures with features of many others found within its borders. This can be seen, for example, in the Parthian tendency to equate Iranian and Greek deities. Thus Ahura Mazda was identified with Zeus and Angra Mainyu with Hades.

This wall carving features a Faravahar, thought to represent the *fravishis*. The wall is located in Persepolis, the ancient ceremonial center of the Achaemenid Empire.

Because the Parthian kings did not give Zoroastrianism the endorsement it had enjoyed under the Achaemenids, its status during this period was somewhat diminished. Still, there is evidence that some Parthian rulers built fire altars to honor Ahura Mazda and had Magi serve as priests in their courts. The Magi (sometimes translated "wise men") described in the Gospel of Matthew as coming to visit the infant Jesus would have begun their journey in Parthian Iran.

Zoroastrianism in the Sassanid Empire (224–651)

Much larger than that of the Parthians, the Sassanid Empire included all of today's Iran, Iraq, Armenia, and Afghanistan, as well as parts of Turkey, Syria, the Arabian Peninsula, and Central Asia. It was the last of the Iranian empires before the conquest of the Middle East by Muslim Arabs and the only one to formally adopt Zoroastrianism as the state religion. This was, however, a Zurvanite Zoroastrianism that differed from the traditional Mazdean form in teaching that Ahura Mazda (now known as Ohrmazd) and Angra Mainyu were twin brothers produced by Zurvan, a higher creator god. Thus Zurvanism departed from orthodox Zoroastrianism in demoting Ahura Mazda from his status as the Supreme Being and in creating a link between good and evil that was denied by other Zoroastrians, who saw these two principles as being completely separate and absolutely opposed to each other. The Sassanids also encouraged the worship of some of the old Iranian gods, such as Mithra, the god of light, and Anahita, goddess of water and the moon.

The Sassanid rulers aggressively promoted their form of Zoroastrianism. With their support, the basic features of its rituals were established, and a priestly hierarchy was created, with the chief priests assigned to every region being supervised by a high priest. The most important duty assigned to priests was the tending of the sacred flame of Ahura Mazda in fire temples. Because fire, like water, was considered an agent of purity, great care was taken to avoid pollution; thus Zoroastrian priests adopted the habit of wearing cloth masks that covered the mouth and nostrils to prevent any unclean element from coming into contact with the fire. Because the bodies of the dead had the potential to pollute fire, earth, and water, they were exposed on high places, such as mountaintops, where vultures and other scavenging animals would pick the bones clean before putrefaction could begin.

Zoroastrianism and Other Ancient Religions

One of the most striking features of Zoroastrianism is the number of features it shares with other ancient religions.

The number of points of similarity in the Zoroastrian, Jewish, and Christian scriptures is especially impressive. There are far too many to mention here, but a few good examples will make the point. Just as the Zoroastrian Ahura Mazda is an all-powerful, all-knowing, and eternal being who exercises his creative power in the world through his Spenta Mainyu (Holy Spirit), the God of Jews and Christians makes his presence known in the world through the Spirit of God (Judaism) or Holy Spirit (Christianity). All three religions imagine God, supported by angels, locked in a struggle with Evil, backed by demons. All three anticipate an end of the world that will involve the coming of a savior, the resurrection of the dead, judgment, the restoration of the world to a state of perfection, and life everlasting. All three describe God as intervening in human affairs in order to communicate his nature and will to human beings. The scriptures of all three religions describe human beings as descended from a single, primordial couple. Finally, not long after their creation, a great catastrophe destroys all of humanity except for a single righteous individual and his family—in Zoroastrianism (according to one Avestan text), it is a cataclysmic winter; in Judaism and Christianity, a great flood.

Although noting such similarities is easy, explaining them is difficult. As it is well known that Jews and Iranians were in close contact beginning in the sixth century B.C.E., most scholars believe that the religion of the Jews (and, through them, that of the Christians) was influenced by Zoroastrianism. Claims that Jews influenced Zoroastrians have not won significant support. A more successful argument has been that the shared beliefs of the two religions reached the forms they take in their respective scriptures at roughly the same time, and so their similarity can be explained as the result either of a collaborative creativity or of a parallel development nourished by a shared cultural milieu.

The matter of influence is much clearer with respect to Manichaeism, a religion that appeared shortly after the founding of the Sassanid Empire in the mid-third century. At that time Mani, an itinerant prophet, began preaching an extreme form of dualism that combined elements of Zoroastrianism with aspects of other Iranian religions and Christianity. Manichaeism enjoyed great success in the third through fifth centuries, when it was one of the most visible religions in the Roman Empire and was practiced as far east as China. Manichaeism's central teaching, that the world is divided by the struggle between the forces of light and darkness, clearly derives from Zoroastrianism. It is also true that Zoroastrian deities were included in its pantheon. But Mani's teaching that all matter is evil and only spirit is good cannot have come from Zoroastrianism, which teaches that spirit is indeed sometimes evil—most notably of course in the case of Angra Mainyu. Similarly, Mani's claim that all material reality is formed from the substance of Satan differs radically from the Zoroastrian teaching that matter was created by Ahura Mazda, the source of all good things.

A final ancient religion with Zoroastrian associations is Mithraism. Based on devotion to the ancient Iranian god Mithra, known as Mithras in the West, Mithraism thrived in the Roman Empire in the second and third centuries C.E. It was one of the mystery religions of the Greco-Roman world, so-called because membership was limited to initiates (in this case, only men) into the secrets of their underlying myths. From Roman times until the late twentieth century, Mithraism was understood as an Iranian religion that had managed to make its way westward. But recent scholarship has shown that although Mithras and his iconography (such as his slaying of a divine bull) had their origins in ancient Iran, where Mithra was included in the Zoroastrian pantheon, the actual content of the religion was more closely related to the speculations of intellectuals in what is now southeastern Turkey about the stars and their relationship to human events. Still, the mere presence of Mithra in the West speaks to the influence and prestige of Zoroastrianism far from its Iranian homeland.

The *tauroctony* ("bull-slaying") was the universal symbol of Mithraism. The symbol includes several features drawn from ancient Iranian religion, including the slaying of a primordial bull and the figure of Mithras himself, known in Zoroastrianism as Mithra, one of the *yazatas* ("ones worthy of worship").

Zoroastrianism and the Coming of Islam

In the seventh century the Sassanid Empire was overthrown by the Arabs, converts to Islam who were then conquering much of the Middle East. Although the Zoroastrians of Iran now found themselves living under an Islamic government, they managed at first to cope with their new circumstances because the Qur'an called upon Muslims to be lenient in their treatment of non-Muslims to whom God had given a book of scripture. The Arab conquerors were satisfied that the *Avesta*, like the Jewish and Christian scriptures, qualified as just such a book. Zoroastrians were required to pay a special tax imposed on all non-Muslims, and there were occasional acts of violence against them, but there was security in the fact that they remained the majority in Iran.

But the position of Zoroastrians had deteriorated markedly within a century after the arrival of the Arabs. Zoroastrians were subjected to harassment and violence, priests were executed, fire temples were destroyed or turned into mosques, and books of scripture were burned. Worse, Zoroastrians lost their status as a "People of the Book" and the protections it offered. The dangers of their situation were enough to persuade many Zoroastrians to capitulate and convert to Islam. Conversion was made easier by a legend invented to link Shi'a Islam, the dominant form in Iran, with the Zoroastrian royalty of the Sassanid Empire. According to the story, the fourth Shi'a imam was the son of Husayn, Muhammad's grandson, and a Sassanid princess. The effect of these and other factors on Iran's Zoroastrians was dramatic. By the end of the eighth century they had become a religious minority.

By the tenth century Arab rule of Iran had come to an end. It was replaced by a series of Iranian dynasties, some with Turkish or Kurdish associations, that lasted until the overthrow of the Pahlavi dynasty in 1979. Throughout this period the number of Zoroastrians in Iran continued to decline steadily. Those who remained faithful to their religious traditions continued to suffer discrimination, periodic persecutions, and economic hardship.

Zoroastrianism in the Modern World

There is some irony in the fact that there has been a fascination with Zarathustra among artists and thinkers in the modern West—a time and place in which few people have any contact with Zoroastrianism. In fact, the number of sizable communities of Zoroastrians anywhere in the world is very small.

Zarathustra in the West   Since the beginning of the early modern era in the sixteenth century, Zarathustra has made appearances in well-known works of art, music, and literature, some of which make use of his image in ways he would certainly have found surprising.

In *The School of Athens* (1510), the Italian painter Raphael placed Zarathustra in a gathering of ancient Greek philosophers. Voltaire, an eighteenth-century leader of the French Enlightenment, misunderstood the teachings of Zarathustra as a form of rational religion resembling the deism of his day. A leading character in Mozart's opera *The Magic Flute* (1791), "Sarastro," is a wise and benevolent ruler who triumphs over darkness and the Queen of Night. In his philosophical work *Also Sprach Zarathustra* ("Thus Spake Zarathustra," 1885), the German philosopher Friedrich Nietzsche

World Zoroastrian population.

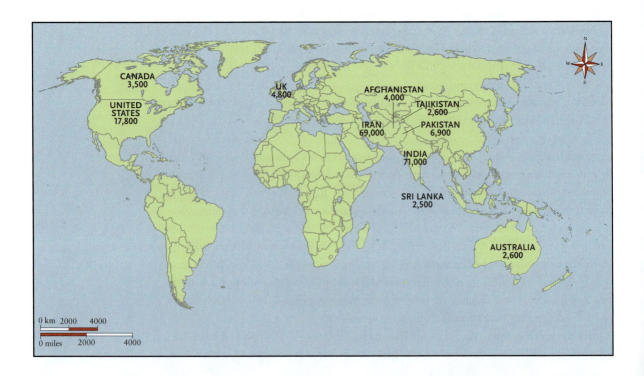

described a new Zarathustra, rather unlike his namesake, who condemns conventional morality and its conceptions of good and evil. Inspired by Nietzsche's work, the German composer Richard Strauss composed a tone poem also titled *Also Sprach Zarathustra* (1896). Its initial and memorable fanfare ("Sunrise") became a best-selling recording and earned a place in American popular culture after being featured in Stanley Kubrick's 1968 science-fiction film *2001: A Space Odyssey*.

Zoroastrians Today The largest community of Zoroastrians today is in western India, and particularly in the area of Mumbai. Known as Parsis ("Persians"), they are the descendants of Zoroastrians who fled Iran in the ninth century to escape Muslim persecution. The Parsis thrived in the more tolerant Hindu environment. The British, who established rule over the Indian subcontinent in the mid-nineteenth century, tended to favor Zoroastrians, in part because they rejected distinctions based on caste and because they placed a high value on education. Today, they are among the most affluent of Indian ethnic groups and are highly regarded for their success as industrialists and their generosity as philanthropists.

Zoroastrian Centre in London. With 4,800 Zoroastrians, the United Kingdom is one of several countries across the world with sizable communities.

The second largest group of contemporary Zoroastrians is in Iran. Known to themselves as Iranis and Zarathushtis, their history throughout most of the modern era has been one of continued marginalization and, in some cases, persecution. Like the Parsis, the Iranis have been tenacious in hanging on to traditional beliefs and rituals. Many still speak Dari, an Iranian language that is distinct from the Farsi (Persian) spoken by other Iranians. As non-Muslims, the government prohibits Zoroastrians from being elected to any representative body in government except for the few seats set aside for religious minorities in the Islamic Consultative Assembly (the Iranian parliament). On the other hand, it appears that Zoroastrians have been gaining greater acceptance among the general population because they represent a part of Iranian history in which Muslims, as well as Zoroastrians, can take pride.

Zoroastrian populations in other parts of the world are much smaller. As immigrants, or the descendants of immigrants, most continue to identify themselves as either Parsis or Iranis/Zarathushtis. Major Zoroastrian populations are indicated on the map on page 338; Zoroastrian communities can also be found in Australia, Singapore, Hong Kong, and other places in East Asia. The total worldwide Zoroastrian population is about 194,000.

The number of Zoroastrians in the world is dwindling. For example, in the mid-twentieth century there were about 115,000 Parsis in India, compared with 71,000 today. One reason for the decline might be that Zoroastrians have no interest in proselytizing. Another reason, mentioned in this chapter's opening, involves rules against marrying non-Zoroastrians. Furthermore, some Zoroastrians choose to leave the religion because they find its strictures burdensome or its ancient teachings difficult to accept.

Because of the long-term decline in their numbers, Zoroastrians are concerned about the future of their religion. Various opinions are voiced. Conservatives say that adherence to tradition is the key to the survival of Zoroastrianism. Liberal Zoroastrians remind conservatives that Zarathustra himself was a reformer who broke with tradition. They find the essence of their religion in the *Gathas*, the Avestan hymns said to have been composed by Zarathustra, and take less interest in the beliefs, doctrines, laws, and rituals that became a part of tradition after him.

ZOROASTRIANISM AS A WAY OF LIFE

Like most any religious tradition, Zoroastrianism includes many rituals, festivals, and rites of passage, the most important of which we will consider in this section. But more so than most other religious traditions, perhaps because of its status as a minority religion, the Zoroastrian way of life is based in a tightly knit sense of community and the routine practice of well-established customs. These customs in turn can be seen to integrate fundamental religious teachings. For example, Zoroastrian reverence of fire means that candle flames are not extinguished but rather allowed to burn out (although today birthday candles commonly are blown out). More generally, the deep-seated preference for light over darkness leads Zoroastrians to speak a blessing when a light is lit and to avoid killing roosters once they have begun to crow, for a rooster crowing signals the break of dawn and the return to daylight. Other customs are based straightforwardly on Zoroastrian respect for life, which implies a general attitude of kindness toward animals. Custom dictates, for instance, that at meal time dogs be fed prior to people.

As we turn to considering religious rituals, festivals, and rites of practice, we will observe how consistently these same fundamental teachings—reverence for fire, light, and life itself—tend to underlie many aspects of the Zoroastrian way of life.

Ritual Practices

We have seen that Zarathustra opposed traditional forms of Iranian ritual practice, notably animal sacrifice and the ingestion of *haoma*. Within the first few centuries of the Zoroastrian tradition, however, such ritual activities were revived. To this day, Zoroastrianism is a tradition rich in ceremony and ritual, with regular activities carried out both within temples or other religious buildings and without. The most commonly practiced ritual activity is prayer.

VOICES: An Interview with Rustom Ghadiali

Rustom Ghadiali is a resident of Singapore, home to a community of about 200 Zoroastrians. This community was founded in the early twentieth century by Parsis who immigrated from India. Mr. Ghadiali is a Zoroastrian priest with a strong interest in the history and transformations through time of the tradition.

Zoroastrianism is an ancient religion. Has it taken steps to adapt to new conditions in the modern world?

The Zoroastrian religion has taken steps to adapt to new conditions in the modern world in some countries. In Iran, as it is difficult to get young boys to join religious orders and become priests, eighteen girls for the first time have become initiated as priests and carry out all rituals. Zoroastrians in India are still very orthodox and do not accept the same.

What are the greatest challenges faced by Zoroastrians and Zoroastrianism today?

The greatest challenges faced by Zoroastrians and Zoroastrianism is that their numbers are dwindling. This is because of late marriages, not having children, and not being allowed to marry outside the community.

What features of Zoroastrianism are most important to you in your daily life? Why?

Prayers are the most important in our daily life, and thanking God for good health and happiness.

How common is the traditional Zoroastrian practice of exposing the bodies of the dead, and how it is carried out?

The practice of exposing the bodies of the dead to the birds is followed in India today, but it is slowly disappearing, as it is difficult to have vultures in urban settings. Also, vultures are dying as the bodies of sick Zoroastrians contain medicine which kills the vultures. The orthodox Zoroastrians in India are struggling to accept changes in traditional practices and to accept burial or cremation. It is only a matter of time when the practice of exposing the dead will disappear and burial or cremation will be accepted.

You are a Zoroastrian priest. What are your most important responsibilities in worship and in serving the Zoroastrian community?

The most important responsibilities of the priest are the carrying out of rituals and praying for any and all Zoroastrians. The religion as practiced in India and as practiced abroad has a lot of variance. If all were to follow the *Gathas*, the original verses of the Prophet, then there would be harmony. Scholars and the High Priest, however, enforce their own views. Also, the priests are not being looked after by the temples where they work and must depend on the community to pay them as they pray. They prefer to study and get educated in commercial subjects, so that they can earn and be independent.

Rustom Ghadiali

Prayer and Purification Zoroastrians pray five times daily, during five periods determined by the position of the sun: dawn until noon, noon until mid-afternoon, mid-afternoon until sunset, sunset until midnight, and midnight until dawn. For many Zoroastrians, this amounts to more than one hour of prayer per day. Zarathustra himself, despite his antiritual tendencies, is believed to have prescribed formal prayer. Its importance has endured throughout the centuries.

Daily prayers often coincide with the *kusti* ritual, which also should be performed several times per day. This involves untying and tying the *kusti* cord while standing in a lighted space and reciting ritual texts. Recalling Yasmin's investiture ceremony described in this chapter's opening, we can see that the *kusti* ritual is a repetition in shorter form of this very important rite of passage.

The *kusti* ritual and the recitation of prayers require that the worshipper undergo ritual purification using water, washing the face, forearms, hands, and feet. Zoroastrians thus are expected to undergo rituals of purification on a daily basis. These ritual ablutions take only a few minutes. Longer, more elaborate rituals of purification also should be undertaken occasionally. The Barashnum, for example, takes ten days and must be performed by a priest during the daylight hours and in rooms especially designated for this purpose. Special substances are consumed, including pomegranate leaves, ashes from a sacred fire, and consecrated bull's urine. The Barashnum is needed in cases of severe pollution or as preparation for major ceremonial events, such as marriage or initiation into the priesthood.

Where Zoroastrians Worship   The strong emphasis on purity is evident in the designation of certain spaces as appropriate for worship. By definition, temples and other sacred precincts are set apart from the impurities of the world outside. Spaces such as private homes can be used for religious activities so long as they are pure in a religious sense— that is, there are no non-Zoroastrians present. And, indeed, rituals often are performed in private homes, especially in Iran. Older homes, especially, are believed to be inhabited by the spiritual presence of deceased ancestors—making these spaces desirable for rituals performed on the souls' behalf. In India, most religious activities occur in temples.

Temples include rooms and water wells specifically designed for purification rituals. All temples provide a source of clean water. Special kitchens are equipped for preparation of food, some to be used in rituals and some to be consumed in communal meals. Temples have various other rooms, including at least one meeting hall. The most important rooms are the ceremonial room and the fire chamber.

In the ceremonial room, site of several important rituals, the floor is inscribed with grooves that demarcate a rectangular space 3.5 meters by 2 meters. The rituals performed within this space are of a special category, and are named "inner liturgies."

Open to the outside, the fire chamber consists of a stone floor with a domed covering, vented in order to permit the fire to burn. This in turn is protected from rain and from the sun's rays by a partial roof.

> Compare the Zoroastrian temple with places of worship in other religions.

Sacred Fire   The supreme significance of fire for Zoroastrianism is clearly evident in the meticulous categorization and care of fire and in its central role in ritual activities.

A fire is consecrated through ritual practices. Once consecrated (and thereby sacred), the dying out of the fire is held to be a catastrophe. Sacred fires therefore are tended very carefully. As we have already observed, the fire chamber in a temple is covered over in such a way as to prevent rain from falling on and extinguishing the fire. We have also seen that fires generally are not extinguished but rather allowed to burn out. Fires are protected from coming into contact with various polluting objects, including corpses and the bodily fluids of the living, such as saliva. Fires are tended and fed with dried wood several times per day.

There are three main categories of sacred fires, the highest of which is the Atash Bahram ("victorious fire"). In India, where by the twentieth century there were over 100 Zoroastrian temples, only eight of these fires exist, all having been consecrated in the late eighteenth or early nineteenth centuries. Consecration of the Atash Bahram takes a group of priests nearly a full year to accomplish, involving intricate steps of purification.

Fire is employed in various ways in ritual practices. The most important of the inner liturgies, those that are performed within the specially marked rectangular space in a temple's ceremonial room, is Yasna, the sacrifice of the sacred drink *haoma* before a fire. The extensive preparations for Yasna include the preparation of the *haoma*, a mixture of water, pomegranate, ephedra, and goat's milk. During the three-hour ritual the entire *Yasna*, the seventy-two-chapter portion of the *Avesta*, is recited while the sacred fire is fueled.

Parsi priests tend the sacred fire within a temple in India.

Priests   The Yasna liturgy and other ritual activities in the temples are orchestrated by priests. As we have observed in Yasmin's investiture ceremony, priests also lead rituals outside of the temple—in that case, in the family's home.

Priests have throughout the history of Zoroastrianism occupied an important place in the religious society. As we have observed, the ancient Greek historian Herodotus included in his account reference to Zoroastrian priests, whom he called Magi. The training and precise roles of priests and the organizational features of priesthoods have varied widely depending on cultural circumstances. Throughout the centuries, priesthoods have been made up of men.

Today, the nature of the priesthood varies somewhat between India and Iran. In India, training for initiation into the priesthood mainly involves memorization of sacred texts used in rituals. The training normally begins when the candidate for initiation is still a youth, and it takes several years. In Iran, where in general Zoroastrians are less insistent on maintaining traditional rituals, priests are not expected to be expert in the performance of rituals, and many work as priests in addition to having careers. It is normal for all Zoroastrian priests to marry and raise a family, although until the twentieth century priests were expected to marry within priestly families.

Women and Zoroastrianism

As with most religions, the status of women in Zoroastrianism is much different today than it was even a century ago. Traditionally, the religion has been highly patriarchal. Texts such as the *Arda Viraz Namag* make clear that women are to be subordinate to men. Even a woman who is virtuous in every other way but who has not been obedient to her husband is said to have no chance of crossing the Chinvat Bridge and proceeding to heaven. Next to an obedient wife, the most important role for a woman is to be a caring mother. Women have not been allowed to enter the priesthood until very recently in Iran, where this measure has been thought necessary to preserve the religion. In India, women still are not allowed to become priests.

Special ethical norms and ritual practices apply to women, many of them stemming from Zoroastrianism's stance on menstruation as being highly polluting, basically in the same category as contact with a corpse. The *Avesta*, for example, sets forth rules governing the conduct of a menstruating woman, including the need to stay at least fifteen steps away from water, fire, religious implements, and men. At the end of her period the woman is to be cleansed with bull's urine, which was used as a disinfectant in ancient times.

In the modern period, such rules as these have become largely obsolete. Most Zoroastrians today support a general attitude of egalitarianism, even if some limits are still imposed because of ritual regulations and other traditional aspects. The rationale for this attitude is not necessarily a modern invention. The *Gathas* sometimes address women and men together, suggesting a type of equality in the time of Zarathustra. As we have observed, girls undergo the investiture ceremony (not as commonly in India as in Iran) and become full members of the Zoroastrian community, thereafter wearing the *kusti* cord and partaking in the *kusti* ritual and daily prayers. Women have equal right of access to temples—unless they are menstruating, in which case still today they are not permitted to enter. In recent times, a category of rituals that can *only* be performed by women has become popular. Called Sofre-rituals, after the cloth (*sofre*) on which Iranian meals traditionally have been served, they involve the consumption of special foods and drinks. Overseen only by a select group of qualified women, the foods and drinks are consecrated through recitation of Zoroastrian miracle stories.

One notable sign of women lagging behind men in terms of participation involves positions of leadership. Women hold far fewer seats than men on committees in Zoroastrian organizations, regardless of the location. Among the Parsis of India, women are not allowed to become priests. The degree to which Zoroastrianism becomes fully egalitarian obviously remains to be seen.

Holy Days and Rites of Passage

To this point we have considered Zoroastrianism's strong emphasis on ritual activities as they are practiced daily and occasionally on a random basis. Here we consider the array of rituals and ceremonies that occur at specific times—on the various days of the year that are designated as especially holy, and at the crucial points in a person's lifetime that are marked out as rites of passage from one stage to another, as, for example, the investiture ceremony we observed in the chapter's opening.

The Zoroastrian Calendar Most religions feature their own special calendar of holy days and periods. The Zoroastrian calendar is more elaborate than most, connecting days of the month and months of the year to various deities.

Since ancient times, the Zoroastrian calendar has been based on twelve months of thirty days each, although during the Achaemenid period five days were added to the twelfth month. (Today, because of attempts at various times to align the calendar with the solar year, there are three Zoroastrian calendars, one or the other favored by each community.)

The first day of the month is named for (and dedicated to) Ahura Mazda. The next six days are named for the other six *Amesha Spentas*. The other days are named for various *yazatas*; for example, the sixteenth day is named for Mithra. The twelve months also bear names of divinities. Whenever one of the days aligns with the month, such that the same deity is honored for both, Zoroastrians celebrate a feast for that deity. And so, for example, the sixteenth day of the seventh month (September/October) is celebrated in honor of Mithra. To cite another example, the fifth day of the twelfth month (February/March) is celebrated in honor of Spenta Mainyu, the Holy Spirit of Ahura Mazda.

Annual Holy Days Zoroastrians observe seven obligatory holy days, traditionally believed to have been established by Zarathustra. Each of these holy days honors one of the *Amesha Spentas*, and each celebrates aspects related to its divine benefactor. For example, the holy day associated with Spenta Mainyu is named All Souls and celebrates, along with the Holy Spirit of Ahura Mazda, humankind, Ahura Mazda's primary creation.

Of the seven obligatory holy days, the one that is most popularly observed is **Nowruz** (or No Ruz), the Zoroastrian New Year's Day. Nowruz honors the *Amesha Spenta* Asha Vahishta ("Righteousness"), who is associated with the creation of the very special element, fire. Nowruz originally was celebrated at the time of the vernal (spring) equinox and still is by most Zoroastrians, regardless of which of the three calendars they use. Throughout western Asia, people of all religious and ethnic backgrounds celebrate New Year's Day at the time of the vernal equinox. Even for non-Zoroastrians, these New Year's celebrations tend to show vestiges of Zoroastrian influence, for example, the symbolic significance of fire.

For Zoroastrians, the spring equinox is a symbol writ large of the triumph of light over darkness. The holy day of Nowruz features a sense of renewal of personal commitment to righteousness and of communal ties. It is richly celebrated, with a special meal made up of seven items, each with names beginning with the same Persian letter: wine, sugar, milk, syrup, honey, candy, and rice pudding.

Death and Funeral Rites In this chapter's opening we witnessed the investiture ceremony of Yasmin, a nine-year-old Iranian girl. This is Zoroastrianism's primary rite of initiation, marking the passage from youth to adulthood. The most elaborate religious activities marking a rite of passage occur at death.

According to Zoroastrian teachings, death involves the separation of the soul, the spiritual element of the person, from the physical body. As we have seen, the soul is believed to undergo judgment by crossing the Chinvat Bridge, where it encounters the Daena, a feminine being who embodies the individual's ethical quality. Zoroastrian funeral rites are intended to free the soul for this journey, while also attending to the body in a manner that ensures as much purity as possible.

The *dakhma*, or "Tower of Silence," provides a space for exposure of the dead body to vultures and to the sun. This *dakhma* is located in Yazd, Iran.

In Zoroastrian perspective, a corpse is inevitably a polluting object. It needs to be kept at a distance from water, fire, plants, and even fertile ground. This insistence on the attempt to maintain purity helps to explain the famous Zoroastrian practice of exposing corpses on *dakhmas*, or "Towers of Silence" (a British neologism from the colonial period), elevated circular structures with a platform at the top on which bodies would be left. Rather than cremating

VISUAL GUIDE
Zoroastrianism

Zarathustra. Copies of this painting of Zarathustra are found in fire temples and Zoroastrian homes throughout the world. The original is found in the fire temple in Yazd, Iran.

Zoroastrian symbols: the sun, a fire, the moon, and the Faravahar, thought to represent the *fravishis*. These symbols adorn a Parsi temple in Ahmadabad in the state of Gujarat, India.

Ateshkadeh Fire Temple. The Atesh-kadeh Fire Temple in Yazd, in central Iran, is perhaps the most famous of the Fire Temples found worldwide in Zoroastrian communities. Although the structure itself was built in the twentieth century, the sacred flame inside is said to have burned continuously since 470 C.E. Zoroastrians believe that fire is symbolic of purity and of Ahura Mazda.

or burying their dead—as fire is holy and unfit for contact with a corpse, and the ground is sacred because it bears life—corpses are exposed to the elements, to be devoured by vultures and other scavengers. This is deemed to be the manner of disposal that best maintains purity. Today, in part because of laws prohibiting this traditionally preferred manner of disposal, sometimes bodies are buried, provided that burial vaults are used that prevent any chance of contact between the corpse and the earth. A form of electric cremation, devoid of flames, is also sometimes used.

The Zoroastrian Community: Social and Ethical Responsibilities

At the outset of this section on the Zoroastrian way of life, we noted the relatively tightly knit sense of community and practice of traditional customs that continue to characterize the tradition. Many other features typify Zoroastrian social life. As we have seen, religious festivals such as Nowruz involve community and family celebrations. The same is true of the other holy days throughout the year and of rites of passage such as the investiture ceremony. Zoroastrian communities take pride in the care of their temples and other religious buildings and also in their social and cultural achievements. All Zoroastrians are expected to marry and to raise families, and responsibilities for caring for family members extend even beyond this life: individuals' moral behavior affects the fate of their deceased ancestors' souls.

Ethical responsibilities have always been a central feature of Zoroastrian life. Traditionally, even such daily activities as eating food have been regulated by prescribed rituals, for example, by the religious requirements to maintain purity. Zoroastrian texts from ancient times have spelled out specific ethical requirements. The early medieval text *Arda Viraz Namag* (*The Book of the Righteous Viraz*) is one notable example. Similar to Dante's *Divine Comedy* (and, in fact, this book was one of Dante's influences), the *Arda Viraz Namag* recounts a seven-day journey of the righteous Viraz through the afterlife, where he encounters the spirits of Ahura Mazda and Angra Mainyu and many instances of souls of the righteous enjoying heavenly rewards and souls of the evil suffering horrible torments in hell. In each instance, the specific virtue or vice is identified. The book strongly condemns such vices as lying, greediness, and cruelty to animals.

Today, although general ethical norms such as admonition against these three vices still guide behavior, many of the traditional rules and regulations tend to be overlooked. With regard to the once prevalent purification rituals—some of which are still very much in effect—a newfound emphasis on personal hygiene has become the equivalent of the older insistence on "purity." And rather than focusing on traditional lists of virtues and vices, a more basic ethical outlook has taken hold, based on the "motto" of the Zoroastrian religion: "good thoughts, good words, good deeds." Along with aspiring to base their lives on these ideals, Zoroastrians are to practice daily confession of sins, mostly as a means of improving upon their moral behavior.

CONCLUSION

For Zoroastrians today, their motto, "good thoughts, good words, good deeds," is much more than just a catchy slogan. Etched into the walls of some temples, this "triad of good" provides a platform for Zoroastrian life in the modern age. And underlying this platform is something more basic, and something that Zoroastrians have embraced since ancient times: thoroughgoing emphasis on individual choice. As we have seen, following in the pattern of the primordial spirits Spenta Mainyu and Angra Mainyu, all human beings have freedom of choice between good and evil. This choice not only determines the individual's fate in the afterlife, but also contributes to the ultimate fate of the cosmos itself.

Much of the world now embraces individual freedom of choice, but for most cultures this has happened only recently. That it has been a central tenet of Zoroastrianism from the time of its origins attests both to the profound insight of its founder, Zarathustra, and to the special nature of the Zoroastrian religion down to the present day.

SEEKING ANSWERS

What Is Ultimate Reality?

Zoroastrians believe that Ahura Mazda, eternal and all-powerful, created the world and human beings. Ahura Mazda, allied with forces of order (asha) and good, continues to oversee the world. Also preexistent, however, is Angra Mainyu, the "Foul Spirit" who leads the forces of chaos and evil—those on the side of druj, the Lie. The cosmos is currently in a state of struggle between these opposing forces. This is cosmic dualism, the basis of Zoroastrian teachings. Zoroastrians believe, however, that in time good will triumph over evil.

How Should We Live in This World?

Human beings are constantly presented with a choice: to live righteously according to cosmic order (asha) or to live according to the Lie (druj). Zoroastrian texts contain many

(continued)

SEEKING ANSWERS (continued)

specific ethical commands. Today, however, many Zoroastrians focus on the more general ethical ideals set forth in the motto: "good thoughts, good words, good deeds."

What Is Our Ultimate Purpose?

Human beings are believed to participate in the cosmic struggle currently ongoing, and therefore to play a part in the future triumph of good over evil. In the meantime, each individual strives for a heavenly afterlife, anticipating after death the judgment of the soul on the Chinvat Bridge through the soul's encounter with the Daena, a feminine being who embodies the person's ethical quality.

REVIEW QUESTIONS

For Review

1. Describe and distinguish between Zoroastrianism's two types of dualism.
2. Explain Zoroastrian teachings on creation and cosmology.
3. Summarize the historical relevance of Iran (or Persia) for Zoroastrianism.
4. Why is fire such an important symbol in Zoroastrianism? In what specific ways does fire play a part in the practice of the religion?
5. Describe Zoroastrian funeral rites, noting how Zoroastrian teachings relate to practices.

For Further Reflection

1. Many Zoroastrians today consider their religion to be monotheistic. Do you agree?
2. Why do you think Westerners find Zarathustra such a fascinating figure?
3. Imagine a Zoroastrian student talking about religion with Jewish, Christian, and Muslim students who know nothing about Zoroastrianism. Assuming the student wants to point out teachings Zoroastrianism has in common with their religions, what do you think he or she would say?

GLOSSARY

Ahura Mazda (uh-hoo'rah moz'dah; "Wise Lord") The God of Zoroastrianism; also known as Ohrmazd.

Amesha Spentas (ah-mesh'-ah spent'ahs; "Beneficial Immortals") Seven angels—including Spenta Mainyu, the Holy Spirit of Ahura Mazda—who help Ahura Mazda govern creation.

Angra Mainyu (ang'grah mine'yoo; "Foul Spirit") Evil adversary of Ahura Mazda; also called Ahriman.

asha (ah'shah) The true, cosmic order that pervades both the natural and social spheres of reality, encompassing the moral and religious life of individuals; opposed to *druj*.

Avesta The oldest and most important of Zoroastrian scriptures, consisting of a collection of texts including the *Yasna* and *Gathas*.

Chinvat Bridge The bridge that needs to be crossed by the soul in order to reach the afterlife, wide and easy to cross for the good, razor-thin and impossible to cross for the evil.

(continued)

GLOSSARY *(continued)*

Daena (die'nuh) The feminine being who embodies the individual's ethical quality and who appears to the soul after death.

daevas (die'vuhs) The various demonic powers aligned with Angra Mainyu.

druj (drooj; "lie") Cosmic principle of chaos and evil, opposed to *asha*.

dualism In Zoroastrianism, of two types: cosmic dualism of order and chaos (or good and evil); dualism of spirit and matter (or thought and body).

fravishis (frah-veesh'ees) Preexisting higher souls and guardian spirits of individual human beings.

haoma Sacred drink made in ancient times from the sour, milky juice of the soma plant; in modern times from water, pomegranate, ephedra, and goat's milk.

kusti (koo'stee) Sacred cord that is to be worn daily by Zoroastrians who have undergone the initiatory rite of the investiture ceremony.

Nowruz (now-rooz') Zoroastrian New Year's Day coinciding with the vernal equinox, the most popularly observed annual holy day; celebrated in varying ways throughout western Asia by people of all religious and ethnic backgrounds.

Spenta Mainyu (spen'tah mine'yoo) Ahura Mazda's Holy Spirit; one of the seven *Amesha Spentas*.

Yasna Seventy-two-chapter section of the *Avesta* containing material recited by priests in rituals; includes the *Gathas*. The Yasna liturgy, an important ritual, is the sacrifice of the sacred drink *haoma* before a fire.

yazatas (yah-zah'tahs; "ones worthy of worship") A large number, eventually fixed at thirty, of deities on the side of Ahura Mazda and order/good.

Zarathustra (zare'ah-thoos'trah) Called Zoroaster by the ancient Greeks; ancient Iranian prophet and poet, founder of the Zoroastrian religion; dates uncertain (between 1300 and 550 B.C.E.).

SUGGESTIONS FOR FURTHER READING

Boyce, Mary. *Textual Sources for the Study of Zoroastrianism*. Manchester, UK: Manchester University Press, 1984. An anthology of Zoroastrian sacred texts, suitably thorough for an in-depth study of the religion, and with reliable translations and commentary.

Rose, Jenny. *Zoroastrianism: An Introduction*. London and New York: I. B. Tauris, 2011. A very engaging, dependable, and quite in-depth introductory study, organized by historical period and geographical locations.

Stausberg, Michael. *Zarathustra and Zoroastrianism: A Short Introduction,* trans. Margret Preisler-Weller. Postscript by Anders Hultgård. London: Equinox, 2008. First published in German in 2005 (by Verlag C. H. Beck oHG), this slim volume provides a concise yet remarkably informative, clearly written overview.

ONLINE RESOURCES

Religion Facts: Zoroastrianism

http://www.religionfacts.com/zoroastrianism/index.htm

A good resource for, as the site states, "just the facts."

The World Zoroastrian Organisation

http://www.w-z-o.org/

Created and maintained by Zoroastrians, a dependable resource that provides an "insider's" perspective on the religion.

JUDAISM

IT IS A SATURDAY morning, and Seth is waiting to read from the Torah—the most ancient of Jewish Scriptures. Seth has spent the past ten months preparing for this moment, and he is about to become a **Bar Mitzvah** (Hebrew, "son of the commandment"). In late antiquity, a young Jewish male became a Bar Mitzvah simply by turning thirteen years old, but by the later Middle Ages a formal rite of passage had developed that signaled a young man's entry into religious manhood. By demonstrating that he can read directly from and comment on the Torah, Seth is proclaiming, before an entire congregation of worshippers, his intention to enter the Jewish community as a literate adult.

Moving a silver pointer shaped like an outstretched hand and index finger across the Torah scroll, Seth reads the passage assigned for that particular Sabbath morning. The sacred text before him is especially difficult to decipher because, as in ancient times, it is written in the consonantal script (that is, without vowels of Hebrew); however, Seth has reviewed this passage many times and has practically memorized it. After the service, Seth will be joined by friends and family who will celebrate his accomplishments with a party, gifts, and lavish praise. This coming-of-age ritual has been enacted countless times over the centuries in Jewish communities throughout the world, but it is only recently—since the 1920s—that the privilege of participating in this ritual

The *Bar Mitzvah* stands behind a lectern, facing an open Torah scroll, preparing to read his scriptural passage in Hebrew.

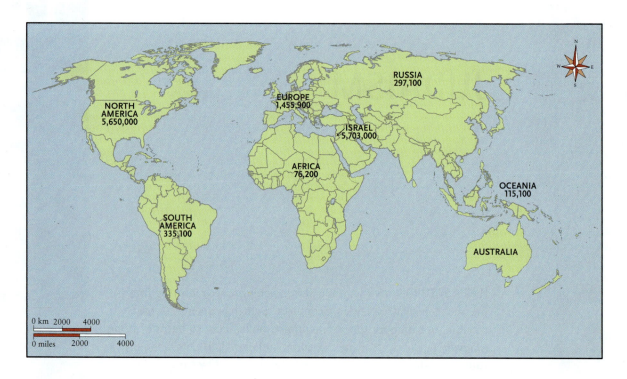

RUSSIA
297,100

EUROPE
1,455,900

NORTH
AMERICA
5,650,000

ISRAEL
5,703,000

AFRICA
76,200

OCEANIA
115,100

SOUTH
AMERICA
335,100

AUSTRALIA

0 km 2000   4000

0 miles   2000   4000

Total number of Jews presently living throughout the world.

has been extended to young women (in which case the young woman in question becomes a **Bat Mitzvah**—a "daughter of the commandment"). Nevertheless, it has become quite common today for twelve- and thirteen-year-old Jewish girls to perform the same ritual acts that their male counterparts do and to receive the same recognition.

Of all of the life-cycle events in Judaism, the Bar and Bat Mitzvah rite is the one ritual occasion at which we see the most fundamental of Jewish beliefs on display. For at the core of the Judaic belief system is the assumption that a very special historical and spiritual relationship—referred to, traditionally, as a *covenant*—exists between the one God of heaven and earth and the people of Israel. By demonstrating both a degree of religious literacy and a willingness to freely embrace a life of sacred duties and obligations, adolescent Jewish boys and girls renew that covenant in a public and deliberate way.

The Bar or Bat Mitzvah ritual is not, however, a prerequisite for membership in the Jewish community. Historically, the one and only precondition of Jewish identity has been biological: that is, whether or not one has been born to a Jewish mother. Although Judaism has always accepted converts, the majority of the world's Jews have been persons whose ancestors are also Jewish. Nevertheless, this rite of passage has achieved its present popularity precisely because it symbolizes a commitment to a communal religious life and to Judaism as the collective faith experience of the Jewish people. ☀

Judaism is one of the world's oldest extant religions. In addition to examining the teachings and practices of the Jewish religion, we will also survey the historical context out of which they emerged and to which they responded. But first, an overview of Judaism's teachings.

THE TEACHINGS OF JUDAISM

Judaism has undergone many changes in its long history. For the purposes of our study, however, we will start by looking at those concepts and values that the majority of Jews living today would regard as "normative" or "enduring." Having done that, we will consider the diversity of belief that increasingly characterizes Judaism in the present age, beginning with Judaism's concept of God.

God

The Jewish religion is most commonly referred to as a type of **ethical monotheism**, as it assumes the existence of a Creator-God whose benevolence and goodness are reflected in His love of humanity and who has imparted to the Jews ethical principles by which they (and the rest of the human race) are expected to live.

As Jewish philosophy developed over the centuries, an understanding of God's nature deepened, and additional qualities—such as **omniscience** and **omnipotence**—were added to the composite portrait of the deity. Most important for Judaism, however, is the concept of divine "oneness," which can be understood to mean that there is only one divine Being in the universe; this one Being is truly incomparable, and no human being (or anything we can possibly imagine) can be compared to this Being. Judaism's idea of divine **transcendence** presupposes that a fundamental difference in reality exists between God and the world He has brought into existence, and that this difference precludes the possibility of God's embodiment or "incarnation" in a particular human personality.

Yet for all its emphasis on God's "otherness," Judaism is not lacking a sense of God's nearness, or **immanence**. The very fact that Jews pray to God—and do so with the expectation that their prayers will be heard and that those prayers may move the deity to respond—suggests that there are limits to the distance between the divine reality and human consciousness. Moreover, the ancient liturgical tradition of addressing God through the use of masculine nouns and pronouns (still preserved in many prayer books today) suggests that, at the level of common speech, Jews have long thought of God in human terms. As we shall learn, contemporary feminist critics of traditional Judaism have repeatedly challenged this practice, arguing that the attribution of gender—that is, employing masculine metaphors (or capitalizing the masculine pronoun) to speak of God—subverts God's transcendent character. Humanist critics have also challenged this practice, arguing that any anthropomorphic imaging of the divine is a false representation of an unknowable reality. Such contending views constitute part of an ongoing conversation within modern Judaism over the nature of the one God Jews have long proclaimed.

One of the great constants in Jewish theology, however, has been its assumption that the Creator-God was also the shaping force or will behind our universe and our human world. Judaism has never conceived of God as a deity who abandoned the universe once it was brought into being. On the contrary, Jews have always assumed that God is determined to see His creative purposes fulfilled in time. Judaism assumes, therefore, that God is moved to respond by every human act of goodness and contrition.

The Problem of Evil How such a God can tolerate the continued existence of evil in a world that He has created is a question that has troubled Jewish philosophers for many centuries. Like their counterparts in other monotheistic faiths, they have sought various solutions to this possibly insoluble enigma. The oldest Judaic response to this question—a question that philosophers today often refer to as the "problem of evil"—takes the familiar form of an accusation: the people of Israel have sinned against God by violating His Covenant, and therefore God has no alternative but to punish those who have rejected Him and His laws.

However, the Nazi genocide against the Jews during World War II has prompted many Jewish theologians to reexamine this traditionalist argument and to reject this cause-and-effect pattern of thinking. For some, the spectacle of mass murder or, even worse, the possibility of global annihilation makes the biblical idea of a just, compassionate, and omnipotent Creator-God insupportable; indeed, according to this argument, such a God-concept is no longer acceptable to a post-Holocaust Judaism.[1] Still others, unwilling to embrace the agnosticism (or atheism) this argument inevitably leads to, insist on reviving the biblical idea of a divine "eclipse": the belief that God periodically conceals Himself from human understanding, thereby creating a seeming void in which evil, for a time, may prevail.[2]

Nevertheless, according to this counterargument, even during this period of divine "absence," God remains present in many human hearts, and in time God will "return" to our world in the form of humanity's moral striving and severe self-judgment. This alternative view of God's role in the world holds that reconciliation with God, and a renewal of those divine values that reside within all enlightened human cultures, is still possible, and that one should never doubt God's continuing love for, and anguish over, the human race.

Torah

In addition to a commitment to monotheism, Judaism also claims to be a "revealed" religion, in that its most basic teachings are believed to be the result of divine revelation. Most of the books that make up the Hebrew Bible— twenty-four in total— advance this claim. Furthermore, when Jews employ the Hebrew word *torah* (Hebrew, "teaching") in its most inclusive sense, they are referring to the totality of God's revelation to the people of Israel. The very fact that Judaism possesses a sacred scripture presupposes a belief in divine-human communication, as well as a belief in the trustworthiness of those individuals—whether prophets or sages—who served as instruments of divine speech and understanding.

The word **Torah**, however, has secondary and even tertiary meanings, and all of them are crucial to an understanding of Jewish faith. Thus, when reference is made to the scrolls of the Torah (which Seth read from at the beginning of this chapter), what is meant are the parchment copies of the first five books of the Hebrew Bible (known in English as Genesis, Exodus, Leviticus, Numbers, and Deuteronomy). Such scrolls can be found in any synagogue in the world. Jews view this portion of Judaism's ancient scriptures with particular reverence because these scrolls contain virtually all of the sacred legislation contained within the Hebrew Bible, and given the centrality of the idea of sacred law in traditional Judaism, it is hardly surprising, then, that the word Torah has often been translated as "the Law."

An even more expansive use of the word Torah can be found in the practice of referring to a comprehensive collection of commentaries on biblical law as the "Oral Torah." This multivolume anthology of interpretive and folkloristic writings, more commonly called the **Talmud**, represents the final extension in Jewish history of the idea of revelation. The teachers—known as rabbis—whose comments are preserved in these volumes claimed to be passing on the oral instructions of the biblical Moses, to whom God originally imparted His laws at Mt. Sinai. Though not every community of Jews has accepted this claim as historically or theologically valid, the vast majority of the world's Jews have accorded to the Talmud a degree of sanctity and intellectual authority almost equal to that of the biblical Torah, thereby making the Talmud a virtual second scripture in Judaism. Much of the education of rabbis today consists of studying the Talmud, as well as a vast body of interpretive literature (commentaries upon a commentary) that has grown up around the Talmud.

Compare the idea of *mitzvot* in Judaism to the concept of divine commandments in Christianity and Islam.

Mitzvot   At the core of the Torah tradition (whether understood as written or oral) lies the concept of the **mitzvot** (Hebrew, "commandments"), and it would not be unreasonable to describe Judaism as religion of "divine commandments." By the Rabbinic (or "Formative") Age, the number of such commandments that can be found in the first five books of the Hebrew Bible was fixed at 613, and each of these *mitzvot* was viewed as an essential link in a chain of religious laws that could not be broken. Over many centuries, rabbinic commentators have attempted to categorize these commandments into positive and negative precepts, but the simple fact today is that at least half of these laws are no longer applicable, either to contemporary society or to a Judaism without a Temple in Jerusalem, and therefore without a priesthood and a system of animal sacrifice.

However, at the heart of this vast network of sacred laws lie the Ten Commandments, which can be found in two slightly different forms in the books of Exodus and Deuteronomy. For all Jews, in every age and in every land, these ten pronouncements have served not only as the bedrock of their faith but also as the basis of their social and philosophical ideals.

However, just like the term "Torah," the word *mitzvot* (singular, *mitzvah*) has taken on another, more informal meaning—that of "good deeds." In ordinary conversation, Jews routinely refer to any act of generosity or good will as a *mitzvah*. In fact, a glance at a traditional prayer book will reveal exactly which good deeds the rabbis expected every adult to feel especially bound by in everyday life. The list includes honoring one's parents, visiting the sick, outfitting a bride, and peacefully resolving quarrels between neighbors. But the greatest *mitzvah*, the rabbis go on to explain, is the study of Torah, because it contains all the moral wisdom God has imparted to the Jewish people.

Nevertheless, there are practical limits to how far anyone can go in the performance of a good deed or the fulfillment of a divine commandment. Those limits are formally acknowledged in rabbinic law under the principle of *pikuach nefesh*, or "the preservation of life." Thus the rabbis taught that whenever carrying out a *mitzvah* entails imminent risk to one's life or health, one is released from that obligation until the threat to life has passed. The only exceptions to this rule—and these exceptions became the basis for the concept of martyrdom in Judaism—are those situations in which a Jew is commanded to worship another god, to commit adultery, or to murder an innocent human being. In all other cases, the traditionalist view is that laws may be bent, but not permanently broken, to accommodate exigent circumstances.

Covenant and Election

Throughout its long history, Judaism has thought of God's relationship with the Jewish people as an intimate contractual relationship (rather like a marriage), freely granted by God and freely entered into by the biblical Israelites and all their remote descendants. In Hebrew this type of relationship is referred to as a *b'rit*, commonly translated into English as a "Covenant."

THE TEN COMMANDMENTS

1. I the Lord am your God who brought you out of the land of Egypt.
2. You shall have no other gods besides Me. You shall not make for yourself a sculptured image, or any likeness of what is in the heavens above, or on the earth below.
3. You shall not swear falsely by the name of the Lord your God.
4. Remember the Sabbath day and keep it holy.
5. Honor your father and your mother.
6. You shall not commit murder.
7. You shall not commit adultery.
8. You shall not steal.
9. You shall not bear false witness against your neighbor.
10. You shall not covet anything that is your neighbor's.

In the Hebrew Bible, Israel's covenant with God is often portrayed as a kind of treaty, with reciprocal obligations and expectations. On God's side, an unconditional promise is given to the patriarch Abraham that his "seed," or descendants, would be numerous and that they would inhabit the land God had given Abraham as a legacy. The people of Israel, however, are expected to live up to all of God's demands and to obey His *mitzvot*. The penalty for disobeying God is a temporary dissolution of the covenant connection, coupled with such punishments as famine, defeat in war, and ultimately exile from the very land first promised to Abraham and his heirs. Clearly, this later understanding of the covenant idea is conditional and even punitive in nature, and for many centuries it provided a theological rationale for the worldwide dispersion of Jews and their subsequent statelessness. Since the establishment of the State of Israel in 1948, contemporary Jewish theology tends to deemphasize that theme and to stress, instead, the bond of enduring love, trust, and forgiveness that exists between Israel and God.

Much more problematic than the covenant idea, however, is the accompanying belief in Israel's **election**, or, as this idea is more commonly expressed, a belief that the Jewish people have been "chosen" by God to receive His laws and to live in His presence. No concept in Judaism has evoked more hostility and misunderstanding; yet despite the controversy, it would be difficult to imagine a historically credible form of Judaism that completely lacked this concept. On one level, all that the idea of election in Judaism affirms—and all that the Hebrew Bible attests to—is God's decision to reveal Himself to the people of Israel in a way that is qualitatively different from the way He has related to any other people on earth.

On yet another level of understanding, however, the covenant demands that Israel actively serve God's purposes in history: first, by becoming a "holy nation," completely obedient to His will, and, second, by representing God to the peoples of the world who have no knowledge of His existence. This latter understanding of the doctrine of election is precisely what the biblical prophet Isaiah had in mind when he spoke of Israel becoming a "light to the nations," and after long centuries of living in a stateless Diaspora, Jews have come to see their "chosenness" simply as an obligation to serve both God and humanity, rather than as an assertion of moral or religious superiority.

Historically, Jews have thought of the Covenant in ancestral terms, as most Jews are persons born to Jewish parents. Nevertheless, conversion to Judaism has long been open to any non-Jew who wishes to assume the responsibilities (and the hazards) that are a part of membership in the covenant community. Those who enter Judaism by choice are required by tradition to prove their sincerity and to undertake a term of study to prepare for full participation in Jewish religious life. The final stage of conversion customarily entails circumcision for men who are not already circumcised and, for both men and women, immersion in a ritual pool (known as a **mikveh** in Hebrew). From that moment on the convert is known as a "son" or "daughter" of Abraham, and no Jew by birth is permitted to treat such a convert as anything but a spiritual equal. Paradoxical as it may sound, therefore, it is possible for anyone to choose to become part of the "chosen people." Nevertheless, because Jewish religious identity is traditionally traced through the mother's line (matrilineal descent), the conversion of a prospective bride is absolutely critical to determining the Jewishness of her offspring. Though the Reform Movement in the United States has attempted to trace Jewish identity through the male line as well (patrilineal descent), the standard practice in most Jewish communities worldwide remains, at present, matrilineal.

Israel

Since 1948, the word "Israel" has been used to identify the Middle Eastern nation-state that bears that name. But for many centuries, beginning with the Hebrew Bible, "Israel" connoted both a political and a spiritual community, a double frame of reference that is still preserved within the synagogue liturgy. In the latter sense, therefore, Israel is that covenant community to whom God imparted Torah and to whom He is bound by promise and affection. Like the idea of election, however, the notion of peoplehood implicit in the concept of Israel has seemed to some either confusing or simply archaic, and its use today can still generate controversy.

Biblical writers, however, had no difficulty reconciling ethnic identity and religious affiliation: God's covenant, they believed, was established with the *b'nei yisrael*—literally, "the children of Israel" (that is, the lineal descendants of the patriarch Jacob)—and that contractual bond was thought to be unique and therefore without precedent in history. As a consequence, Jews continued to think of themselves over the centuries as members of a single extended family *and* as a faith community held together by a common set of beliefs.

However, during the modern era Jews found themselves faced with a political dilemma that soon took on religious implications: they could receive citizenship within the now largely secular nation-states of Europe, but only at the expense of their collective historical identity, and by denying all other "political" loyalties. For many Jews, eager to assimilate into modern society and determined to secure civil rights that had been denied them for centuries, the demand that Judaism redefine itself as a religious creed and nothing more seemed a small price to pay for political emancipation.

On the other hand, Orthodox Jews, generally suspicious of secular values and distrustful of the process of acculturation, viewed this new understanding of Jewish identity with alarm. In addition, by the end of the nineteenth century, a very different group of secular dissident Jewish intellectuals—early advocates of Zionism, for example, such as Theodor Herzl—also rebelled, though for completely different reasons, against the notion that Jews had no claim to nationhood and were just another religious denomination among thousands in the world.

Today, many of those who practice Judaism are comfortable with their double identity as members of both a religious and an ethnic community, while at the same time recognizing the inevitable tension between these two perspectives. For those Jews who have chosen to make *aliyah* (Hebrew, "to ascend")—that is, to immigrate to Israel and become citizens of a Jewish state—this tension almost disappears, though secular/nationalist and religious values continue to clash with one another in contemporary Israeli society. For those Jews who remain in the Diaspora—a majority of the world's Jewish population—the need to establish a balance between national and religious self-identification remains a challenge.

The Messiah and the Messianic Age

One idea that emerged from the matrix of ancient Judaism that has had a profound impact upon the Western world is the idea of a messiah. From its very beginnings in the Hebrew Bible, however, this concept has meant different things to different audiences. At its root, the term *mashiach* (Hebrew, "anointed one"; translated into English as "messiah") means any person who was ceremonially anointed with oil in preparation for becoming a priest or a king, and when most biblical writers used this term literally, that was all they had in mind.

Nevertheless, later prophets such as the Second Isaiah (c. late sixth century B.C.E.) began to extend the use of this term metaphorically by applying it to either non-Israelite kings or to an unnamed future "prince" who would redeem his people from subjugation to foreign nations. As the beginning of the Common Era approached, the idea of a messiah continued to evolve. In works that lie outside of the Hebrew Bible, such as the First Book of Enoch and the Fourth Book of Ezra, the term *mashiach* took on explicitly supernatural meanings, signifying a heavenly redeemer figure sent by God to rescue Israel and the world from evil. This more imaginative use of the messiah concept was linked in such books with end-of-the-world visions, complete with predictions of a new world order emerging from a final era of chaos and destruction. Such writers saw the Messiah as an instrument of divine power through whom God would accomplish both the final judgment and the ultimate renewal of life on earth.

When Christianity identified Jesus of Nazareth with this redemptive-supernatural messiah tradition, it prompted the rabbis of the Talmud to reevaluate the very notion of a "messiah." What followed in their writings on this subject was a remarkably diverse collection of views, with some religious authorities identifying the biblical king Hezekiah (late eighth century B.C.E.) as a "messiah," whereas others deferred the appearance of an equally human messiah (albeit one from the line of David) to the indefinite future. Yet despite this uncertainty over the Messiah's precise identity, a lively debate ensued, within and beyond rabbinic literature, on which tasks such a messiah might be expected to accomplish and whether his mission would be accomplished within the span of human history or only at the "end" of time. Not surprisingly, centuries of longing for the fulfillment of these messianic visions have produced a succession of "false" messiahs in Judaism; what is more remarkable is the persistence of that belief into the modern era and its active advocacy among traditionalist communities within contemporary Judaism.

The Afterlife

Of all the basic beliefs of Judaism, belief in an afterlife (Hebrew, *Olam Ha-Bah*—in rabbinic literature, the "world to come"), along with accompanying beliefs in the resurrection of the dead and the immortality of the soul, are among the most elusive. Historically viewed, these beliefs are largely postbiblical in their origin, or at least are not fully articulated until the period of the Talmud. For most biblical writers, the death of the body entailed the passage of the soul into an underworld (Hebrew, *Sheol*; "pit" or "abyss"), where it would remain forever. Still, various biblical texts contain hints of a countertradition; for example, the Second Book of Kings depicts the prophet Elijah as ascending directly into heaven on a fiery chariot (2 Kings 2:1–12). But such miraculous transitions from life to a mysterious afterlife are exceptional, and it is only in a very late biblical work, the Book of Daniel, that we come upon an explicit reference to the dead rising again to life.

By the rabbinic era, however, mainstream Judaism had already embraced the idea of a postmortem existence in the "world-to-come," though the rabbis who espoused this belief were notoriously vague as to just what this belief entailed. Thus questions such as whether the departed enter the world-to-come automatically upon death or only after some ultimate judgment has been passed upon that soul by God, or whether a general resurrection of mankind would precede or follow the Messianic age, were left unanswered.

By the modern era, many reform-minded Jews, bent on reevaluating traditional Judaic beliefs, concluded that any belief in an existence beyond this world was either an archaic folk belief or an insupportable, unscientific hypothesis. Yet despite such opposition, the classic phraseology of the afterlife, along with references to the resurrection of the dead, persists within most contemporary prayer books. In Orthodox communities, Jews continue to insist that these beliefs are an integral part of the Judaism they uphold.

Jewish Mysticism

The origins of mystical thinking in Judaism can be found in the Hebrew Bible, in which at least one prophet, the sixth-century figure of Ezekiel, recorded visionary trances in which God appeared to him as a figure of infinite mystery, seated upon a throne:

> Above the expanse . . . was the semblance of a throne, in appearance like sapphire; and on top, upon this semblance of a throne, there was the semblance of a human form. From what appeared as his loins up, I saw a gleam as of amber—what looked like fire encased in a frame; and from what appeared as his loins down, I saw what looked like fire. There was a radiance all about him. Like the appearance of the bow which shines in the clouds on a day of rain, such was the appearance of the surrounding radiance.
>
> —*Ezekiel 1:26–28*

Visionary passages like these testify to a tradition of ecstatic meditation in biblical Judaism in which a prophetic writer experiences the presence of God in a manner that is at once direct and mysterious. For centuries, Ezekiel's vision of the heavenly throne (which is also a chariot) served as an inspiration to mystics who sought a comparable glimpse of God and of the heavenly beings who, according to biblical tradition, surround His throne.

Another popular biblical text that served as inspiration for Jewish mystics was the opening chapter of the Book of Genesis, in which the creation of the world and of mankind is described. What distinguished the Kabbalistic school of mystical writers from other visionaries was a fascination with the mysterious process of world creation and a deep curiosity over the role of the Creator in this process. This type of mystical inquiry is often accompanied by some form of esoteric biblical interpretation, and it often incorporates some of the boldest kinds of cosmological speculation Jewish writers have ever indulged in.

Key to the writings of the Kabbalah (Hebrew, "received tradition") is one underlying cosmic metaphor, the image of the *Sephirot*. The *Sephirot* are ten in number, and they can be visualized as connected "spheres" of divine power, or as stages in a process of divine self-revelation. As such, they come to represent at least one of two things: the primary attributes of God and the dynamic emanations of His creative force.

However, the goal of mystical meditation in Kabbalah goes well beyond a desire to describe God or His relation to our world in quasi-mythological terms. The kabbalists were united in their desire to reconnect heaven and earth through a process of contemplative prayer and restorative moral actions. Thus every blessing that a Jew utters in praise of God, or every *mitzvah* that is performed in strict accordance with tradition, they taught, can now be invested with an almost magical power to "heal" the world (Hebrew, *tikkun olam*) and is directly related to the soul's longing to reunite

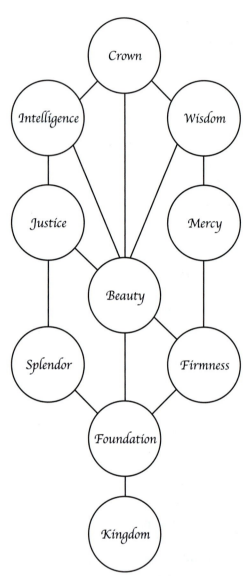

The traditional arrangement of the *Sephirot* is designed to evoke either the tree of life or the human body.

with its Creator. The end goal of this longing, kabbalists believe, is *devekut*, or a "clinging" to God that represents the highest state in mystical Judaism of the covenant relationship.

The Lurianic system of Kabbalah, in particular, has had tremendous appeal. In the "beginning" before creation, Rabbi Isaac Luria taught, God (whom kabbalists refer to as the *Ein Sof*, or "Infinite One") withdrew into Himself, thereby creating an empty space within which a material universe could take shape. Having performed this voluntary act of self-contraction (Hebrew, *tzimtzum*), the Creator then allowed rays of light to penetrate the void, resulting in a concentration of this creative force into ten spheres (the *Sephirot*). However, the ten "vessels" God had prepared to hold this *Sephirotic* light mysteriously shattered, leaving the material universe in disarray. According to Luria, this cosmic event was the true origin of evil and disorder in the world, and this partly inexplicable catastrophe resulted in the scattering of divine "sparks" throughout the cosmos and within the human soul. Within each of us, therefore, is an intermingling of good and evil; even the worst human beings, he believed, retain some small portion of divine goodness. With the coming of the Messiah, all of these sparks would be reunited with God. Until that eschatological event transforms the world forever, each person has the potential to liberate that divine "spark" for himself or herself through a process of repentance and return to God (Hebrew, *teshuvah*).

Ideas and images derived from Kabbalah continue to exert some influence on contemporary Jewish thought, and particularly for those associated with the Jewish "Renewal" movement.[3] Admirers of Rabbi Abraham Joshua Heschel (1907–1972) and, more recently, followers of Rabbi Zalman Schachter-Shalomi (1924–2014)—who are determined to bring about a reinvigoration of Jewish spirituality—insist that such concepts as *teshuvah* and *tikkun olam* cannot be confined to the synagogue or to a life of conventional religious observance. For some, *teshuvah* entails a sincere and disciplined internalizing of our longing for God in the form of true piety, affecting every aspect of our behavior. For others, however, *tikkun olam* means, quite literally, actions that benefit humankind and promote peace in the world.

THE HISTORY OF JUDAISM

The earliest reference we have to the Jews—known variously as "Hebrews," "Israelites," and "Judeans" (depending on the era and the context)—dates from the late thirteenth century B.C.E. On a commemorative stone, inscribed at the request of the reigning

Ancient Israel.

Egyptian ruler, Pharaoh Merneptah (c. 1210 B.C.E.), the following inscription appears: "Israel is laid Waste, its seed is no more." No other reference to "Israel" or the "Israelites" appears in Egypt or anywhere else for centuries. Most of what we know about ancient Israel, as well as the beliefs and religious practices of the ancient Israelites, is derived from Jewish Scriptures, referred to in Hebrew as **Tanakh**. In English we refer to these books as the Hebrew Bible, though Christians commonly refer to these books as the "Old Testament."

Dispersion, Assimilation, and Collective Identity

The composite portrait of ancient Israelite society and its faith that one finds in the books of the Hebrew Bible is one of seemingly endless conflicts and successive divine revelations. For the authors of the Hebrew Bible the central conflict was over one issue: Would Israelites remain loyal to their one God (referred to, in Hebrew, by the consonants **YHWH**), or would they worship the deities of the nations that surrounded them? This was a politically relevant question, as well as a spiritual one, as the people of ancient Israel struggled to maintain their political and cultural independence for several centuries. Eventually, however, the tides of imperial Near Eastern politics swept over them, and after a series of devastating military defeats—first at the hands of the Assyrians in 722 B.C.E. and later at the hands of the Babylonians in 587 B.C.E.—the once-independent Israelite kingdoms of Israel and Judah were destroyed. Thousands of the Israelites were driven into exile or simply absorbed into the Assyrian and Babylonian empires.

Yet despite this history of conquest and dispersion, the Israelites retained their national identity and their collective memory, and while living in exile they began to assemble a continuous history of their people and of their relationship with their God. Once completed, that history became part of their sacred scriptures. With the earliest copies of these books in hand, exiles from the kingdom of Judah began returning to their homeland after 538 B.C.E., believing that YHWH had at last forgiven them. Over the next few centuries, Jewish communities could be found not only in the historical land of Israel (which Greek and Roman geographers later named "Palestine") but also in Mesopotamia and throughout the Mediterranean. These communities were referred to as the Jewish **Diaspora**, and in the many centuries that followed, the number of Jews living outside of their historic homeland ultimately far exceeded those living within its borders.

For more than two millennia, therefore, dispersion, acculturation, and resistance to total assimilation have formed the larger pattern of Jewish life and must serve as the backdrop to any discussion of Judaism as a historical religion.

The Biblical Period

It has become customary to segment the history of Judaism into several discrete "epochs," each marked by certain key events that help to shape the direction of Jewish religious behavior and thought. The earliest of these epochs is the Biblical period, which can be dated (speculatively) from the eighteenth century B.C.E. to the sixth century B.C.E. The key events of this era are the rise of the Patriarchs (Abraham, Isaac, and Jacob); the **Exodus** from Egypt; the formation of the monarchy; and the rise and fall of the two kingdoms—Israel and Judah—that followed. Viewed historically, the Patriarchal period remains shrouded in myth and legend, with the towering figures of Abraham as the principal bearer of the **Covenant** that YHWH first establishes with the people of "Israel."

The Exodus from Egypt remains a problematic event for which little credible historical evidence exists today. Nevertheless, in the minds of biblical writers—and in the consciousness of Jews for centuries thereafter—it remained one of the crucial turning points in the history of Judaism. For whether or not it occurred exactly as described in the Hebrew Bible, the escape of Israelite slaves from Egypt marked a significant reversal of fortune for the tribes that called themselves "Israel," and it served as proof of God's power and willingness to intervene in history on their behalf.

More than that, however, the Exodus also marked a decisive moment in Israel's history of divine revelation and lawgiving, for it was on a mountain peak in the Sinai peninsula (variously identified as Mt. Horeb or Mt. Sinai) that divine instruction was provided to their leader **Moses**, who then imparted these teachings to the assembled

Israelite masses. From this era on, "Israel" could no longer regard itself as a simple tribal society, cherishing memories of remote patriarchal leaders. The moment Israel encountered YHWH at Sinai it became a "confessional" community, bound together by a common faith in a Creator-God and committed to His service. As for the land the Israelites were poised to invade, that was understood to be a gift from YHWH, as well as the fulfillment of promises made to their ancestor Abraham. But it was theirs only as long as they remained faithful to the God who had brought them into their "Promised Land" and true to the Covenant He had established with them.

Kingdoms of Israel and Judah As a nation in the making, Israel began to emerge as a distinctive political entity only in the tenth century B.C.E., with the establishment of the dynasty of King David (c. 1000–961 B.C.E.). For a time, David managed to unite a warring tribal society under his leadership, finally passing on the throne to his son Solomon (c. 961–922 B.C.E.), whose even more exalted reign—at least in the eyes of biblical writers—brought a united monarchy to its height of power and fame.

The most important achievement of Solomon's reign, however, was not the extent of his legendary wealth and power, but rather the construction of the First Temple—a permanent sanctuary, designed to replace the portable tent (or "Tabernacle") of Moses's time, wherein prayers and animal sacrifices were offered to YHWH. By building this Temple in the capital city of Jerusalem, Solomon ensured not only that the political and religious life of Israel would be geographically concentrated within one "holy" city but also that the Davidic monarchy would forever be associated with the most sacred site in Judaism.

Following Solomon's death, the northern tribes seceded to form a kingdom of their own, subsequently identified as the kingdom of Israel. The southern tribe of Judah remained loyal to the house of David and his descendants, and it bore the name of the kingdom of Judah. Both of these kingdoms, as we have noted, were relatively short-lived, and each in turn was overrun by the armies of more powerful empires. Of the two invasions, it was the second, by the Babylonians (587 B.C.E.), that resonated most powerfully with Jews for centuries thereafter, if only because it was the occasion of the destruction of Solomon's Temple. In time, the loss of the First Temple and of the kingdom of Judah became the archetype of all later tragedies of displacement that the Jews were to endure and would be commemorated in both prayer and practice.

The Second Temple Period

The second great epoch in the history of Judaism, known as the Second Temple period, began with the gradual return of a relatively small band of Judean exiles from Babylonia, following the Persian conquest of the Babylonian Empire in 539 B.C.E. The rebuilding of the First Temple (c. 516 B.C.E.), which the Babylonians had earlier destroyed during their siege of Jerusalem in 587 B.C.E., signaled the renewal of a centralized ritual life for Jews in what was formerly the kingdom of Judah, now merely a province within the Persian empire. However, the movement of Jews between

Babylonia and "Yehud" (as the Persians called Judah) not only provided for the re-population of Jerusalem and its restoration as a center of religious life but also provided for the passage of ideas and literature from Mesopotamia to the land of Israel.

Even at the beginning of the Second Temple era, a "canon," or collection of sacred Jewish writings, was slowly taking shape. Thus the formation of Tanakh can be dated most reliably from this period, and the persons most likely responsible for the gathering and editing of these books were scribes and priests. Using the historical and theological perspectives of earlier prophets as their guides, these priestly editors selected works that embodied a recurrent pattern of teachings about divine promise, judgment, and hoped-for restoration, binding together this diverse collection of sacred works with an archetypal vision of Israel's past and anticipated future.

Though politically turbulent, the Second Temple period saw both the growth of the Jewish Diaspora and an increase in the Jewish population of Palestine. In the absence of a Jewish nation-state, religious leadership within the Jewish community fell to the priesthood and to an intellectual class connected to the priesthood. These two groups are said to have formed a leadership "council," known as the "Men of the Great Assembly." Tradition assigns to this body the decision to "close" the canon of divinely revealed (or inspired) Scripture. Scholars differ today on the probable period in which religious authorities—whether in Jerusalem or Babylonia—considered the period of prophecy (and therefore the process of revelation) to have ended. However, it is commonly assumed that by the third century B.C.E. the writing and editing of the Torah had already reached a sufficient state of finality to allow Greek-speaking Jews to translate it from Hebrew into Greek. In time, additional portions of Tanakh were translated from available texts; this translation is referred to as the Septuagint, and it played a significant role in introducing Judaism to the larger Greek-speaking world. It was this version of Jewish Scriptures, rather than the Hebrew original, with which most early Christians were familiar.

Division and Revolt One important development within the Second Temple period was the increasing tension within the Jewish community between those who favored social and intellectual assimilation into Greek (and, later, Roman) culture and those who resisted such assimilation in favor of preserving "traditional" values and religious practices. This struggle became openly violent during the Maccabean revolt of 167–164 B.C.E., as the leaders of the revolt found themselves fighting against not only Syrian-Greek armies but also their more assimilated countrymen who sided with the Syrian king, Antiochus IV (c. 215–164 B.C.E.). Although this conflict finally resulted in the reestablishment of an autonomous Jewish state (c. 140–63 B.C.E.), one of the results of this internal struggle was the gradual appearance of religious "parties" whose influence on Jewish belief and practice grew during the period of Roman domination and occupation of Palestine.

The first-century Jewish historian Josephus (37–c. 100 C.E.) identified the most important of these parties as the Pharisees, who appear to have commanded the attention and the loyalty of the Jewish masses. Central to the Pharisees' form of Judaism was their belief in the "Oral Torah"—that is, a body of teachings imparted by God to Moses on Sinai (but never written down) and subsequently transmitted orally to later generations. For the Pharisees, these interpretive readings of Scripture were an integral part of "Scripture" itself, and therefore just as binding. Thus the Pharisees taught that *torah*—that is, the totality of divine revelation to the Jews— incorporated a belief in both the immortality of the soul and the resurrection of the dead. In the eyes of the common people, the Pharisees' knowledge of the biblical text and their familiarity with biblical law made them more reliable guides than the often corrupt and politically compromised priesthood, and it is from the followers of the Pharisees that we derive our sense of what the dominant form of Judaism may have been like by the end of the first century C.E.

A second group that Josephus identified were the Sadducees, whose influence upon the Judaism of the time was much weaker. Drawing their constituents largely from priestly families, the Sadducees regarded the written Torah as exclusively sacred and authoritative and therefore rejected the very notion that an "Oral Torah" existed. Unlike the Pharisees, the Sadducees tended toward literalism in their understanding of Scripture and therefore could find no warrant for believing in either immortality or resurrection. In politics, they tended to be sympathetic to—or at least accommodating of—Roman authority and therefore less likely than the Pharisees to favor revolutionary leaders.

The third, and most reclusive, community Josephus refers to is that of the Essenes, a general term designating groups of devout Jews who had withdrawn from society in protest against the moral and spiritual corruption of their contemporaries. These traditionalists viewed the Temple priesthood with disgust and held the radical view of history that the "End-Time" of divine judgment and global catastrophe was at hand. Such beliefs, which religious scholars refer to as **eschatological**, had become increasingly widespread during the late Second Temple era, particularly when coupled with a belief in a **messiah**. Although such beliefs were well known throughout the Jewish world, Essenes held to their faith in the imminence of the world's end with particular fervor, and they looked forward to a Messianic Age, when the Temple would at last be purified and the Romans defeated by armies of angels.

Many historians today associate the Essenes with a community of sectarian Jews who withdrew from Judean society and built a settlement near the northwestern shore of the Dead Sea, at a place called Khirbet Qumran, sometime during the second century B.C.E.[4] The religious literature written and preserved by this group was hidden away in caves near their settlement, and it was not until 1947–1956 that these ancient scrolls were discovered. Collectively, they are referred to as the **Dead Sea Scrolls**, and almost half of these are fragments of books from the Hebrew Bible. These copies of biblical texts are the oldest copies of the Jewish Scriptures known to exist today.

Last, and most transitory in their influence on Judaism, were those revolutionaries Josephus termed the Zealots. Like the Pharisees and the Essenes, the Zealots were eager to see the Romans driven from the land of Israel and looked forward to a restoration of Israel's sovereignty and of its monarchy. However, believing that God would fight on their side, the Zealots sought to expel the Roman army through direct action, and Zealot agitation and rebellion were underlying causes of the First Jewish War against Rome (66–70 C.E.). Even after this war ended in the defeat of Jewish forces and in the destruction of the Second Temple, a group of Zealots contin-

Masada was the last stronghold Zealots held before taking their lives rather than yielding to the Roman army (73 C.E.).

ued to hold out against the Romans until 73 C.E., when their mountain fortress of Masada was besieged and overrun by the Roman army. Rather than surrender, the remnant of the Zealot fighters, along with their women and children, committed suicide (according to Josephus) rather than be taken alive by their enemy.

The Formative Age

The fall of Jerusalem and of Masada, and the destruction of the Second Temple, signaled the end of the Second Temple era and the beginning of the third epoch of Judaism's history, known variously as the Rabbinic Age and the Formative Age (c. late first century C.E.–sixth century C.E.). As long as the Temple stood, it served as both a treasured symbol of Israel's biblical past and the operational center of Jewish ritual life throughout the world. Once it lay in ruins, however, the Jewish people needed a new institutional center—a replacement sanctuary, until such time as the Temple could be rebuilt. The **synagogue**, whose remote origins can be traced back to the beginning of the Babylonian exile, provided just such a substitute, but unlike the Temple it was never a place of animal sacrifice, nor was it under the control of a priesthood. In all likelihood, the synagogue began simply as a place of assembly at which Judean exiles could meet and study together. With the Temple gone, however, Jews turned increas-

The Touro Synagogue, built in Newport, Rhode Island, in 1759, is the oldest synagogue in the United States.

ingly toward the synagogue as the place for religious leadership or for communal prayer.

Unlike the Temple, which could stand in only one place (namely, Jerusalem), a synagogue could be built anywhere. Moreover, almost anyone could build a synagogue or serve as a communal leader. Priests had no role to play in the ritual or social life of a synagogue, which made it a more democratic institution from the start.

The Rabbis   In time, the synagogue acquired a clerical leadership all its own, which brings us to the second major historical change that defines the Formative Age: the emergence of a class of religious intellectuals known as Rabbis (Hebrew, "my master"). The word was a term of honor conferred on someone whose piety and learning caused him to stand out among his contemporaries and whose teachings (or legal rulings) were sufficiently memorable that subsequent generations viewed him with respect and even reverence.

One such figure, who had come from Babylonia to study in Jerusalem, was Hillel (fl. 30 B.C.E.–4 B.C.E.), whose compassionate nature was as remarkable as his scholarship. According to legend, it was Hillel who, when asked (mockingly) by a pagan to teach him *torah* while he stood on one foot, replied: "What is hateful to you, do not do to your neighbor; the rest is commentary"—a version of the so-called Golden Rule. Like Hillel, many of the early Rabbis saw themselves as more than just legal scholars whose expertise in biblical law allowed them to advise common folk on matters of correct observance. They also saw themselves as sages or wisdom teachers whose insights into human nature complemented their knowledge of divinely revealed law.

The Compilation of the Talmud   The signature accomplishment of the rabbinic scholar class during the Formative Age was the writing and compilation of the Talmud, a composite work that, in time, was seen as a second Torah, or at the very least, as an indispensable addendum to the Tanakh. On one level, the Talmud is a collection of expansive (and occasionally imaginative) interpretations of biblical law. The format of the Talmud is often dialogical (that is, a series of question-and-answer exchanges). Nearly every page consists of some portion of a rabbinic debate over the alternative ways in which a particular biblical statute can be understood or implemented. The practical objective of all these debates was the creation of an authoritative form of ritual behavior—referred to in Hebrew as ***halacha***—that would enable the observant Jew to sanctify daily life and fulfill the commandments imparted to Moses on Sinai. God gave *torah* to Israel, the Rabbis believed, and now it was their responsibility to clarify its terms and relate them to daily life. In the section of this chapter on sacred practices, we will see how *halacha* informs the ways many Jews today live their faith.

The Babylonian version of the Talmud, compiled at the beginning of the sixth century C.E., consists of sixty-three separate volumes covering a wide range of legal issues. The historical process by which these volumes came into being, however, can be studied in two stages: the earlier stage, known as the *Mishnah* (Hebrew, "repetition"), is written in Hebrew and consists of economical formulations of *halacha*, often accompanied by an attribution to a particular rabbinic scholar; the later stage, referred to as the *Gemara* (Hebrew, "completion"), is written in Aramaic (a Semitic language, very close to Hebrew), and the rabbinic debates recorded there often take up where the Mishnah leaves off.

This process of recording and summarizing rabbinic debates continued, in both Palestine and Babylonia, during a period of roughly four centuries. As the body of rabbinic commentary evolved toward the next stage of completion—first in Jerusalem in the fifth century C.E. and later in Babylonia at the beginning of the sixth century C.E.— the Mishnah was combined with the far more elaborate text of the Gemara. Together these two scholarly works make up the Talmud. Judaism's greatest challenge during this period, however, was not simply that of preserving the teachings of its religious elite but was, more important, that of protecting itself from a rival "sister" religion—namely, Christianity—whose political might increased throughout the Roman empire in the course of the fourth and fifth centuries, at the same time that Judaism's declined.

The Conflict between Judaism and Christianity

Christianity, as you will learn in Chapter 12, began life as a splinter movement within Judaism, following the death by crucifixion of its central figure, Jesus of Nazareth, in 30 C.E. Over the next two generations the early Christian community gradually pulled away from mainstream Judaism and redefined both the nature and role of Jesus in Christian thought, largely under the influence of an ex-Pharisee known as Paul of Tarsus. Those early followers of Jesus, who may have thought of him as a prophet, or even as a Messiah-figure, were soon displaced by those who saw Jesus as the "Son of God," and who eventually came to believe in him as the incarnate human form of YHWH. As the letters of Paul (mostly written between 50 and 64 C.E.) clearly testify, most contemporary Jews viewed these teachings as heresy and quickly banished Jewish followers of Jesus from the synagogue. By the turn of the second century the split between Judaism and Christianity was irreversible, and out of the matrix of Judaism a new (and largely antagonistic) faith had been born.

The philosophical conflict between Judaism and Christianity sprang from a number of incompatible views on the nature of God, the covenant, salvation from sin, and the proper interpretation of biblical texts. For rabbinic Judaism, any material representation of God—either in the form of an image or a living human being—was barely acceptable, and even then only as metaphor. For Christianity, on the other hand, the embodiment of the divine in Jesus as the "Christ" soon became a central doctrine of the early Church. As for God's covenant with Israel, Paul argued that the Christian community had—at least at that moment in time—displaced the Jews as true heirs of the biblical promises made to the Patriarchs and the prophets; the Jews, he insisted, had alienated God by their rejection of Jesus and had (if only temporarily) forfeited their intimate relation to the deity. That the Christian and Jewish communities would, before long, rejoin each other in an expanded covenanted relationship with God was Paul's fervent wish and expectation. However, the first four centuries of the Common Era saw only a widening theological and social gap between the two communities.[5]

With the Roman Emperor Constantine's conversion to Christianity early in the fourth century, Judaism found itself facing not only a determined religious antagonist in the Christian Church but also an even more powerful political antagonist, as a succession of Christian emperors sought to stifle Judaism throughout the Roman Empire by imposing punitive legislation on the Jews and by condoning acts of violence against synagogues. In the eyes of the late fourth-century Christian theologian St. John Chrysostom (c. 347–407 C.E.), the Jews were the devil's spawn, their synagogues the dwelling places of all evils, and any civil relations between Christians and Jews, he argued, represented a betrayal of God.[6] Against such a background of institutionalized hatred, the Jews of Christian Europe struggled for the next millennium to maintain not just their faith, but their very lives.

The Age of Philosophy and Mysticism

The fourth great epoch in the history of Judaism, extending from the Early Middle Ages (sixth–seventh centuries C.E.) to the Early Modern period (sixteenth–seventeenth centuries C.E.), can be thought of as the Age of Philosophy and Mysticism. During this period the Jewish Diaspora stretched from China and India in the East to England in the West. Historians frequently employ the following terms to identify these historical/cultural groupings: Ashkenazim, representing those Jews living in Europe; Sephardim, or Jews living in Spain, Portugal, and parts of North Africa; and Mizrachim, or Jews living in various parts of the Middle East. Each of these communities underwent periods of prosperity and decline, but throughout most of this period some of the most creative developments in Judaism took place: first in Babylonia (present-day Iraq) and later in Spain.

As the Palestinian Jewish community dwindled in numbers and prestige in the course of the sixth and seventh centuries, the center of Jewish intellectual life shifted to Babylonia and to the principal rabbinic academies of Sura and Pumpeditha. And it was Sura, in the early tenth century, that gave rise to one of the major figures in Jewish philosophy: Rabbi Saadiah ben Joseph (882–942). Two challenges faced Saadiah during his career—the first, from within the Jewish community; the second, from an entirely new religion.

The Karaites The challenge from within the Jewish community came from a group of anti-rabbinic Jews, known as Karaites, who (like the Sadducees of the first century) rejected the very notion of an "Oral Torah," and therefore rejected both the Talmud and whatever claims to religious authority the Rabbis had asserted since the beginning of the Common Era. For Karaite scholars the only sacred texts in Judaism were those books that made up the Hebrew Bible, and no work of commentary could possibly claim equal, or near equal, status.

Such views clearly threatened the existence of the rabbinical class, and as a representative of the rabbinical tradition, Saadiah rose to its defense. The interpretation of Scripture, he argued, rested not only on a profound knowledge of the language of Scripture but also on "reliable tradition," as no generation of scholars could claim a monopoly upon insight or knowledge. In addition, unlike the Karaites, Saadiah did not encourage his contemporaries to believe that the Messiah would arrive momentarily or to assume that the End of Days was at hand. His comparatively realistic view that the Messiah would arrive when the time was right—whenever that might be—made the rest of his views on the Torah seem that much more reliable to his readers.

The Encounter with Islam Saadiah's second great challenge came from outside Judaism altogether, in the form of a competing faith—namely, that of Islam (Chapter 13). The founder of Islam, Muhammad (570?–632 C.E.), claimed to have received a new work of Scripture—the Qur'an—in the form of oral communications from the Angel Gabriel, and which he saw as a more reliable revelation than that given to either the Christians or the Jews. Viewing himself as one in a long line of prophets that included both Moses and Jesus, Muhammad clearly expected the Jews of Arabia to accept his claim to be the last (or "seal") of the prophets and to embrace his revelation as the definitive message of God (or "Allah" as the one Creator-God is referred to in Arabic) to humanity.

When it became apparent that the Jews of Mecca would accept neither him nor his new *torah*, Muhammad turned his full attention to his pagan audience, whom he found more receptive to a new monotheistic faith. Muhammad's success in propagating his religious message was matched by his military success in defeating many of his more powerful enemies (which included some of the prominent Jewish tribes of Arabia), and after his death the faith of Islam spread rapidly throughout many of the lands in which Jews had settled centuries before. Although Muhammad's attitude toward the Jews, as expressed in the Qur'an, remained understandably ambivalent, from the eighth century on Jews were accorded a degree of tolerance within Muslim societies that they rarely encountered in Christian lands.

Like many Jewish scholars of his generation, Saadiah had learned a great deal from reading Muslim philosophical literature of the ninth and tenth centuries. Foremost among Saadiah's concerns, therefore, was the need to present Judaism to an educated Jewish audience already familiar with the teachings of both Islam and Greek philosophy, and to do so in a way that did not contradict Jewish Scriptures.

The result of this investigation, which Saadiah published as *The Book of Beliefs and Opinions* (933), is the earliest example of scholasticism in Jewish thought—that is, a systematic attempt to reconcile faith and reason by relating mainstream religious beliefs to contemporary philosophical arguments. Thus Saadiah sought to prove the unique character of God's revelation to Israel, as well as the rational character of many (though not all) biblical commandments, and thereby strengthen Jewish belief in the uniquely trustworthy nature of Judaism's Scriptures.

Maimonides The tradition of philosophical inquiry produced at least one more intellectual giant during this period: Moses ben Maimon, better known as **Maimonides** (1135–1204). In Maimonides, Judaism found one of its supreme philosophers; much of Orthodox Jewish theology derives directly from his writings. Maimonides, the son of a respected rabbinic scholar, was well prepared by his background and early education for this role. When his family was forced to flee their native city of Cordoba, Spain, to escape the tyrannical rule of a militant Muslim regime, they found refuge in Egypt under the more tolerant rule of the celebrated Muslim ruler Salah ad-Din

(c. 1138–1193). Maimonides was better known to his Muslim hosts as a physician than as a philosopher, though it is the latter role that concerns us here.

Maimonides's passion for logic and intellectual clarity is evident in all of his writings. In his *Mishneh Torah*, for example, he listed every single one of the 613 biblical commandments, revealing (even to the casual reader) that many of these *mitzvot* could no longer be fulfilled in the absence of the Temple in Jerusalem. Similarly, in his *Commentary to the Mishnah*, Maimonides clearly describes what he believed to be the thirteen essential "articles" of Jewish belief, thereby creating a dogmatic framework for any subsequent discussion of Judaism as a faith system.

Though not universally acceptable, even during and after Maimonides's lifetime, this compact statement of belief still serves as a useful reference point in any discussion of what today is called "Torah-true" (or "Orthodox") Judaism.

Ironically, Maimonides's most celebrated work, *The Guide for the Perplexed*, evoked considerable controversy when it finally became public, though Maimonides had not intended it originally for widespread publication. In this philosophical treatise, Maimonides attempted to grapple with some of the more problematic philosophical issues of his day: the existence and attributes of God, the nature of creation and prophecy, the problem of evil, divine providence, and the purpose of human existence. Throughout the *Guide*, Maimonides makes it clear that he distrusts any comparison between humanity and the eternal creator. At best, he argued, we can speak of God mostly in negative terms. For example, instead of saying that God is a being who lives forever, Maimonides advises that it is preferable to say that He has no temporal limits. This particular approach to theology (and, inevitably, to biblical interpretation) emphasizes God's "otherness" and tends to remove God from the material world and beyond the limitations of the human mind.

Like many of his Jewish contemporaries, Maimonides looked forward with some eagerness to the advent of the Messianic Age, though he was shrewd enough not to assign a date to that hoped-for event. Interestingly, however, Maimonides's view of both the Messiah and the era of his arrival is largely naturalistic, and it contrasts sharply with the more supernaturalist traditions that both preceded and followed him:

> The "days of the Messiah" refers to a time in which sovereignty will revert to Israel and the Jewish people will revert to the land of Israel. Their king will be a very great one, with his royal palace in Zion. . . . All nations will make peace with him, and all countries will serve him out of respect for his great righteousness and the wonders which will occur through him. . . . However, except for the fact that sovereignty will revert to Israel, nothing will be essentially different from what it is now.

> —*Helek Sanhedrin, Ch. 10*

This demythologized version of messianic Judaism was Maimonides's principal legacy to future generations of acculturated Jews. But one important segment of the Jewish community, those drawn to mystical thinking, rejected Maimonidean scholasticism and its celebration of reason and sought to restore to Judaism some of its rich mythological past.

The Kabbalah Collectively, the many diverse traditions that make up the world of Jewish mysticism are sometimes referred to as **Kabbalah**, but when historians use that term they are thinking primarily of a school of mystics whose beginnings can be traced to twelfth-century France and thirteenth-century Spain. Common to all these writers was an acknowledgment that the hidden "essence" of YHWH—as Maimonides taught—cannot be fully grasped, and certainly never directly perceived or represented.

In a late thirteenth-century work many regard as the "bible" of Kabbalah—the **Zohar**—this entire structure of divine qualities and emanations is laid out in the form of a biblical *midrash*, that is, an extended interpretation of select passages from the Book of Genesis. Central to this form of mystical thought is the idea that however imperfect the human race may be, we are still capable of interacting with, understanding, and even influencing God. This theology of immanence—or, more precisely, of divine-human interaction—is quite obviously at odds with Maimonides's view of a profoundly transcendent Creator. Consequently, the kabbalists felt free to evoke the Creator in explicitly anthropomorphic language (i.e., portraying God in very human terms).

MAIMONIDES'S 13 ARTICLES OF JEWISH BELIEF

1. God the Creator exists.
2. God is uniquely "one."
3. God is incorporeal (and therefore all scriptural images of a divine "body" are mere figures of speech).
4. God is eternal.
5. God alone is worthy of worship and obedience.
6. The teachings of the biblical prophets are true.
7. Moses is the chief of all prophets.
8. The Torah comes directly from God (through Moses).
9. Both the Written and the Oral Torah represent the authentic word of God, and nothing can be added or taken away from either.
10. God is omniscient.
11. God rewards the good and punishes the wicked.
12. The Messiah will undoubtedly come (though no exact date can be known for his coming).
13. The resurrection of the dead will occur in the World-to-Come.

By the sixteenth century, the kabbalistic system had matured to the point that a powerful and highly imaginative cosmology emerged, mainly through the teachings of one man: Rabbi **Isaac Luria** (1534–1572). The *Ari* (or "holy lion"), as he was known to his disciples, left no writings at the end of his short life, but his followers disseminated his thought throughout much of the Jewish world, and of all the many variants of Kabbalah, the "Lurianic" system is at once the most influential and the most complex. Luria taught that the individual believer could liberate the divine "spark" within by careful observance of the divine commandments and acts of self-discipline and meditation. In addition, in sharp contrast to mainstream Jewish belief, Luria envisioned each soul undergoing a series of reincarnations, as the soul constantly strives to return to its Source.

The potential danger—as well as the enormous appeal—of Lurianic Kabbalah became quite apparent a century after the Ari's death in the sensationalistic career of a messianic pretender, Shabbetai Tzevi (1626–1676). A Turkish Jew of obviously unstable temperament, Shabbetai became convinced early in life of his extraordinary spiritual powers after studying Lurianic texts. At the encouragement of one of his most fervent disciples (a self-styled prophet named Nathan of Gaza, whom he had met on a visit to Palestine), Shabbetai declared himself the "King Messiah." In 1666, he presented himself before the Sultan of Turkey, asserting his messianic credentials and his "royal" right to the historic land of Israel. The Turkish response to this would-be savior was, first, to imprison Shabbetai for a year, and then to offer him a minor position at court following his conversion to Islam. Shabbetai's acceptance of this offer not only exposed him as an apostate, but it also sent shockwaves throughout the Jewish world, particularly among those who had firmly believed that Shabbetai was indeed the messianic deliverer he claimed to be.

The Rise of Hasidism   Shabbetai Tzevi was neither the last nor even the most important religious figure to base his teachings on Lurianic thought, however. Within two generations of Shabbetai's death yet another mystical teacher arose, this time in Poland. The **Baal Shem Tov** (c. 1700–1760) also taught the necessity of releasing the sparks of holiness within, thereby hastening the approach of the Messiah. His given name was Israel ben Eliezer, but his disciples commonly referred to him as the "Master of the Good Name" (Hebrew, *Baal Shem Tov*), a title that conveyed to contemporaries the belief that he possessed secret "names" of God that he could use in incantations. Orphaned as an infant, the Baal Shem Tov was given a rudimentary education, and at no time during his career as a spiritual guide was he regarded as a great scholar. Instead, his fame derived from his faith healings and exorcisms. In time, the Baal Shem Tov gave up the life of an itinerant healer and began to attract a growing number of disciples who were drawn by his reputation for wisdom and spirituality.

At the heart of the Baal Shem Tov's teachings was a profoundly immanental vision of God's omnipresence. For the Baal Shem Tov and his followers—who were soon called **Hasidim** (Hebrew, "pious ones")—God could be found everywhere, and everyone was at least potentially capable of spiritual communion with the Creator. To worship God properly, the Baal Shem Tov taught, one need not be a master scholar; the most ordinary of everyday acts, he insisted, if performed with an awareness of God's nearness and in a spirit of joy and love, become acts of spiritual devotion and serve to make everyday life sacred. No one was too humble or too depraved to turn (or return) to God, who required only a burning desire to perform His will.

At the communal level, the key to success within this system of mystical devotion lay with its leadership, and the Baal Shem Tov urged his disciples to choose a spiritual guide, or *tsaddik* (meaning "righteous one"), to provide a living example for themselves and the rest of the community of what it is like to live a life of intense religious commitment and intimacy with God. After the Baal Shem Tov's death, the Hasidic movement he helped to create spread rapidly throughout Russia and much of Eastern Europe. In each major geographical center of Hasidic activity, *tsaddikim* appeared to carry on the teachings of the Baal Shem Tov. Each of these leaders formed a "court," or spiritual circle of followers. In time Hasidic dynasties appeared, as one generation followed another and as the loyalty to the father was transferred to the son. Many of these dynasties, formed in the nineteenth century, still exist today, with the result that virtually all Hasidic communities are centered around the personality and religious leadership of one man—often referred to in Yiddish as the *Rebbe*—whose authority in all things is largely unchallenged.

Opposition to the Hasidic movement arose soon after the Baal Shem Tov's death, and for the next two generations established rabbinic authorities in Russia and Poland sought to stifle popular interest in Hasidic teachings. Their principal fear was that Hasidism would lead to a revival of a messianic cult like that which formed around Shabbetai Tzevi. Yet despite the determined opposition of the rabbinic establishment, Hasidism flourished, and by the mid-nineteenth century official opposition to Hasidism waned as Europe's rabbinic leadership realized that it faced a far more formidable opponent in the Jewish reform movements that suddenly emerged in response to Enlightenment values during the late eighteenth and early nineteenth centuries.

The Modern Era

The modern era in Judaism can be studied on at least two levels—the political and the philosophical—for until the Jews of western Europe had achieved a certain degree of political emancipation, they were unable to fully acculturate within European society or benefit from the intellectual revolutions of the seventeenth and eighteenth centuries. For centuries, Jewish life in the West was characterized by both physical and cultural containment, the most visible symbol of which was the Jewish Quarter of many cities (or Ghetto, as it was known after the sixteenth century), where Jews were forced to reside. By law, Jews were also restricted to certain

Compare the Baal Shem Tov with the Buddha. How are their teachings alike, and how are they different?

A young Israeli Hasid with curled sideburns, commonly worn by men in his community.

trades and professions, especially money lending, but by the late eighteenth century many of these restrictions began to be removed. As more prosperous and highly educated Jews were permitted to intermingle (and, increasingly, intermarry) with their Christian contemporaries, Judaism itself began to change.

Moses Mendelssohn   No better example of this pivotal transformation in Jewish life can be found than Moses Mendelssohn (1729–1786), the son of a Torah scribe and the principal representative for his time of the Age of Enlightenment (referred to in Hebrew as the *Haskalah*). Because Jews were not yet permitted to attend universities, Mendelssohn was largely self-taught in modern philosophy and several European languages. Before long, his philosophical writings began to attract the attention of non-Jews within his native Germany and beyond. His impact on the Jewish community was just as profound, and through his translation of the Hebrew Bible into modern German and his various other publications, Mendelssohn became one of the most effective advocates for educational reform and the modernization of Jewish intellectual life.

What Mendelssohn is best remembered for today, however, is his eloquent defense of religious freedom, coupled with a defense of the Jewish faith, in a volume entitled *Jerusalem* (1783). In this polemical masterwork, Mendelssohn entered a plea on behalf of religious tolerance and in defense of the integrity of Judaism. He argued that all higher religions share certain common beliefs (such as the existence of a benevolent Creator-God, or the immortality of the soul) and that because Judaism also held such beliefs, it was as much an expression of the "common religion of humanity" as Christianity or Islam.

What was distinctive to Judaism, Mendelssohn proposed, was not so much its belief system as its sacred legislation—its *Torah*, understood here strictly as divinely revealed law—and its emphasis on doing God's will rather than professing correct ideas about God or the afterlife. The essence of Judaism, Mendelssohn insisted, was orthopraxy (correct conduct), and not orthodoxy (correct beliefs). This interpretation of Judaism, it should be noted, was not acceptable to more conservative religious authorities, but it did appeal to more secularized Jewish readers who were prepared, in the next generation, to carry the logic of Mendelssohn's argument even further and to attempt to transform the belief structure of Judaism in more radical ways.

Reform Movements in Europe and the United States

The European Enlightenment, and the revolutionary political changes it inspired, affected Judaism in various ways, but its most direct influence can be seen in the early stages of the Reform Movement in the first decades of the nineteenth century. Beginning in Germany, where admirers of Moses Mendelssohn called for the political "emancipation" of European Jews and their gradual assimilation to Western society, the idea of "reforming" Judaism drew support both from lay community leaders and from a younger generation of rabbis who had been permitted to receive a university education. From the outset, the Reform Movement sought to accomplish two goals: first, the modernization of Jewish thought and ritual practice, and second, the acculturation of Jews to the secular culture of nineteenth-century Europe and America. As in any "reformation," however, a split soon developed between those who were determined to achieve these objectives by radical means and those who were not.

At first, reformers seemed content with largely ceremonial innovations, insisting, for example, that rabbinic sermons be delivered in the vernacular language of the nation in which they were living (rather than in Yiddish, the Germanic language of European Jews) or that men and women be permitted to sit together in synagogue during religious services (as opposed to separate seating, which had been the norm for hundreds of years). By the 1840s, however, the demands of the more aggressive reformers became increasingly anti-traditionalist and theologically innovative, as reformist rabbis increasingly embraced the idea of Judaism as an evolving religious culture. All of these changes were opposed vigorously by more traditionalist rabbis, who, from this time forward, came to be described as "Orthodox" religious authorities.

Reform Judaism This more radical type of reformist thinking flourished in the United States after the Civil War. By the late 1880s Rabbi Kaufmann Kohler (1843–1926) had drafted a set of principles and objectives—known today as "The Pittsburgh Platform of 1885"—that defined the "essence" of Judaism for Kohler and many of his reformist contemporaries. The most important features of this "platform" can be found in its most negative statements, namely, that the Reform Movement rejected the biblical idea of a direct, finite, and exclusive revelation from God—the traditional understanding of the concept of *torah*. The reformists opted instead for the concept of an evolving (and therefore universal) revelation, an idea that was easily gleaned from the writings of Moses Mendelssohn. This way, Kohler and his colleagues were able to renounce the dietary code and all other forms of "Mosaic legislation" deemed unacceptable to the Reform rabbinate (such as circumcision and rigorous Sabbath observance) on the grounds that they were "not adapted to the views and habits of modern civilization." And in language designed specifically to suppress any sympathy for Jewish aspirations to return to the historic land of Israel, the Pittsburgh Platform declared boldly that the Jews were no longer a nation and therefore no longer desired to return to, or to restore, a nation-state in Palestine.

Conservative Judaism However acceptable these innovations may have seemed to those American Jews who identified with the Reform Movement, they were clearly unacceptable to the overwhelming majority of European Jews who began to immigrate to the United States in rapidly increasing numbers during the last two decades of the nineteenth century and the first decade of the twentieth century. As the Jewish population of America increased exponentially, the religious diversity of that community increased as well. By the middle of the twentieth century, the American Jewish community found itself largely divided into three movements: Reform, Orthodox, and Conservative. Of these three, the Conservative Movement had emerged, by the

1950s, as the Reform Movement's principal rival, and its appeal can be explained, historically, as a "counterreformation" both within and outside of the Reform Movement itself.

Thus, for those Jews who were initially drawn to reformist ideals but who found the more extreme changes advocated by the early Reform Movement distasteful, Conservative Judaism offered a more moderate departure from traditional (or what is now called "Orthodox") beliefs and practices. Like their Reform counterparts, Conservative rabbis acknowledged the evolutionary character of Judaism and embraced the need for substantive change; unlike the leading reformists, however, they were not willing to abandon either principles of faith or religious behaviors that had defined Judaism for many centuries. The result was the formation of a "third way" of responding to the challenges facing Judaism in the modern era, in which a high level of adaptation to secular culture was combined with a selective relaxation of *halacha*.

However, in its formative stages, the most obvious difference between Conservative Judaism and its Reform and Orthodox counterparts was the public support of both its rabbis and laity for **Zionism**. Throughout its more than 100-year existence, the Conservative Movement has been a fervent advocate for both the formation of a Jewish nation-state in what is now Israel and for the emigration of American Jews to this state.

Reconstructionist Judaism   One of the most important offshoots of Conservative Judaism first emerged in America in the 1930s. Known today as Reconstructionism, this new school of thought centered on the teachings of Rabbi Mordecai Kaplan (1881–1983). By the 1960s, however, the Reconstructionists had formally separated themselves from Conservative Judaism, first by writing their own prayer book and later by establishing their own rabbinical seminary. Though few in number, Reconstructionists have had a far-reaching effect on the thought and religious practices of non-Orthodox Judaism in the United States.

Philosophically, Reconstructionism occupies a position somewhere between Conservatism and Reform. Unlike their Reform counterparts, Reconstructionists held firm to the concept of Jewish nationhood; in fact, for Mordecai Kaplan, the idea that Jews constituted a separate and distinctive *civilization* was central to his belief system. What followed from that assumption was a desire to retain as many traditional "folkways"—which was Kaplan's way of referring to such ritual practices as the dietary code and circumcision—as modern Jews found meaningful. As a consequence, the Reconstructionist Movement tended to place greater emphasis upon the historical continuity of religious customs than did Reform Judaism.

At the same time, Reconstructionism developed a much more naturalistic conception of God than either Conservativism or Reform were willing to support. For Kaplan and his followers, God could no longer be thought of as a noun—that is, as a metaphysical "entity," separate from humanity—but rather as the expression of whatever moral and spiritual potential human beings possess in their search for holiness and righteousness. Kaplan's virtual abandonment of the traditional concept of divine transcendence signaled a dramatic break with the Orthodox faith in which he was raised.

For many Jews, Reconstructionist theology seemed to be a contradiction in terms: lacking a true Judaic concept of God, it could be nothing more than a disguised form of secular humanism, and as such, a heretical rejection of *torah*. Kaplan's defenders, however, insisted that, as an "evolving religious civilization," Judaism's understanding of God and of the covenant would have to change as well, and in the process absorb contemporary scientific views of the cosmos and of the human mind.

THE VARIETIES OF MODERN JUDAISM

ORTHODOXY
- "Torah True": belief in divine revelation at Sinai and in rabbinic interpretation of Torah.
- Strict observance of *halachah,* allowing for limited adaptation to changing conditions of life (Sabbath, family purity, and dietary laws).
- Literal belief in the afterlife, immortality of the soul, resurrection of the dead, messianic redemption of Israel and the world.
- Some ambivalence toward Israel; fervent opposition toward secular Zionism.
- Gender separation and differentiation: separate seating for women in synagogue; opposition to rabbinic ordination of women.
- Retention of Hebrew as language of prayer and strict adherence to traditional prayer routines.

CONSERVATISM
- "Positive-Historical" Judaism: belief in divine inspiration of Scriptures and acceptance of historical process in the formation of *halachah.*
- Serious commitment to observance of *halachah,* combined with a significant degree of adaptation to changing circumstances of modern life.
- A historical-critical approach to Tanakh and Talmud, coupled with a generally nonliteral belief in the afterlife, immortality of the soul, and resurrection of the dead.
- Retention of Hebrew as the language of prayer and preservation of most traditional prayer routines coupled with innovative practices (e.g., Bat Mitzvah).
- Rejection of gender separation and differentiation; mixed seating in synagogue and ordination of women.
- Enthusiastic support of Zionism and Israel.

REFORM
- "Progressive Judaism" committed to an evolutionary view of Jewish belief and religious practice.
- Skeptical view of any literal belief in divine revelation, afterlife, resurrection of the dead; figurative view of immortality of the soul and messianic redemption.

(continued)

THE VARIETIES OF MODERN JUDAISM (*continued*)

- Liberal view of *halachah*, generally regarding Sabbath and dietary laws as optional observances.
- Initial opposition to Zionism and use of Hebrew prayers changes in the course of the twentieth century to greater enthusiasm for both.
- Rejection of all forms of gender separation and differentiation; first to ordain women as rabbis, and eager adoption of the Bat Mitzvah.

RECONSTRUCTIONISM

- "Humanistic Judaism" rooted in the belief that Torah is the expression of the religious creativity of the Jewish people.
- A respectful but liberal view of *halachah*, coupled with a view of religious practices as "folkways" and facets of Judaism as a civilization.
- Generally agnostic view of any belief in a personal God, combined with a fervent belief in the creative potential of human beings.
- Intense interest in Jewish "peoplehood" and enthusiastic support for cultural and political Zionism.
- Rejection of all gender separation and differentiation: ordains women as rabbis and first movement to support the Bat Mitzvah.

The *Shoah* and the State of Israel

During the twentieth century two of the most extraordinary events in Jewish history occurred: one traumatic, the other transformative. Both events have had a profound effect on the beliefs and practices of contemporary Judaism. The first event, referred to in Hebrew as the *Shoah*—or, more commonly, as the **Holocaust**—can be seen as the single greatest tragedy of modern Jewish life: the most successful attempt in history by anti-Semites to rid the world of both the religion Judaism and the Jewish people.

The *Shoah* The word *Shoah* itself requires some explanation, if only because it has a different connotation than the more familiar word "Holocaust." In Hebrew the word *shoah* literally means "whirlwind," and as a metaphor it captures—as well as any image can—the insane rage of anti-Semitic hatred that was loosed on Europe's Jews during World War II. Many Jews prefer this term, unfamiliar as it may be to English-speaking audiences, precisely because it avoids the connotation of a divinely commanded sacrifice, which is exactly what the biblical term "holocaust" (or "burnt offering") brings to mind.

For centuries Jews had been the targets of Christian and occasionally Muslim hostility and persecution, but until Adolf Hitler and Nazi Germany embarked on the

The entrance gate at
Auschwitz.

"Final Solution," no ruler or regime ever entertained the idea of total extermination. In Hitler's autobiography, *Mein Kampf* (1925), he described the Jews as a disease organism within the body of European society that he and his followers proposed to destroy forever. The genocidal policies that his government pursued represented a logical outcome of this essentially racist conception of the Jews and their faith. To carry out this genocidal campaign, Hitler mobilized not only the resources of Germany but also the support of willing collaborators throughout Europe. There is little doubt that had German armies defeated the United States, Britain, and the Soviet Union during World War II, the annihilation of the world's Jewish population would have been one of Hitler's proudest accomplishments. Even in defeat, however, the Nazis destroyed roughly one-third of the world's Jewish population, and the legacy of torture and mass murder they left behind has deeply scarred the Jewish consciousness.

Contemporary Jewish philosophers have responded in remarkably diverse ways to the tragedy of the *Shoah*. For one theologian in particular, Ignaz Maybaum (1897–1976), the slaughter of innocents can be seen as a kind of *churban* (Hebrew, "divinely willed sacrifice"), through which the Jews perform an act of vicarious atonement for the sins of the world.[7] For theologian Richard Rubenstein (b. 1924), on the other hand, such logic is morally insane. Rubenstein insists that the random killing of six million Jews (not to mention the untold suffering and murder of many more millions of non-Jews) challenges, at the most fundamental level, Judaism's belief in a just and benevolent Creator who values every single human life. In his book *After Auschwitz*, Rubenstein insisted that Judaism's historic God-concept is "dead" and that no religious philosophy that is still committed to biblical ideas of divine justice and retribution can withstand scrutiny in an age of genocide and mass destruction.[8] For philosopher and rabbi Eliezer Berkovits (1908–1992),[9] however, the mystery of God's presence in history is deepened by the *Shoah*, not refuted by it, and ours is not the first generation to reflect on God's "hiddenness" or on the terrible consequences of human freedom. For human beings to be capable of choice, he argues, God must "restrain" Himself and allow His human agents to exercise their moral will, even if the consequences of divine restraint are catastrophic.

None of these theologians, however is willing to see the *Shoah* as an instance of merited (and therefore inevitable) divine punishment. Their refusal to accept that now-archaic model of God's judgment and response to human sin marks a definitive break with traditional Jewish thought. If much of the world's Jewish population can no longer declare—in the words of the traditional liturgy—"because of our sins were we exiled from the land," then what model of covenant relations can now be invoked to make both human suffering and world redemption meaningful?

For theologian Abraham Joshua Heschel, the only defensible Jewish theology after the *Shoah* is one that posits God's need for, and yearning after, humankind. The covenant relationship, as Heschel understands it, is a reciprocal one in which human moral intelligence and divine "pathos" join in the act of worship and of love. God's longing for us does not, Heschel insists, annul the reality of evil or the terrible freedom with which human beings have been invested. It does, however, establish what Heschel calls an "analogy of being," that is, a hint of divine likeness in every soul, and thereby the capacity to mend a broken world. If all we knew of God, Heschel argues, was a theory of omnipotence or omniscience, then the *Shoah* might very well sweep away that merely conceptual reality. But the truth is, he continues, that we know God at a much deeper level of moral consciousness, and that form of the divine presence abides even in the midst of the most appalling evils.[10]

Statehood for Israel The second pivotal event of modern Jewish history is the establishment of the State of Israel in 1948, what one philosopher has called the "the Jewish return into history."[11] The Zionist philosophy on which the State of Israel rests is really several philosophical/religious arguments in one. In its earliest form, "Zionism" is simply a feeling of attachment to an ancestral homeland in which a vast majority of Jews, past and present, have never lived. Even though a comparatively small population of Jews continued to live in Palestine for centuries after the Exodus, most Jews were content to sing "next year in Jerusalem" at the Passover *Seder* without ever really contemplating a return to the land of biblical Israel.

A decisive shift in such thinking occurred, however, in the course of the nineteenth century. Two Orthodox Rabbis—Yehudah Hai Alkalai (1798–1878) and Zvi Hirsch Kalischer (1795–1874)—argued passionately for a messianic view of Jewish history, urging their contemporaries to emigrate to Palestine in the expectation that the redemption of Israel was about to be accomplished, but only if the Jews took the first practical step of occupying and restoring the land.[12] Their writings were largely ignored within their lifetimes, but the arguments of an assimilated Austrian Jew, writing near the end of the century, attracted much greater attention.

For Theodor Herzl (1860–1904), the rapid growth of anti-Semitism had made the condition of Eastern European Jews so precarious that something had to be done—apart from continuing mass emigration to the United States—to deal with the poverty and desperation of the Jewish masses. Herzl's solution was the establishment of an internationally recognized Jewish state, either in Palestine or Argentina. He laid out his ideas in an extended tract entitled *The Jewish State* (1896)[13] and later in a utopian novel, *The Old New Land* (1902).[14] Herzl, who died in 1904, never lived to see any of his ideas come to fruition. The Zionist movement he helped to found continued to

This painting of Herzl is one of many that appear on Israeli currency.

solic it support for his ideas, and in 1917 British Zionists found a sympathetic advocate in the foreign minister of Great Britain, Lord Arthur Balfour (1848–1930).

Balfour's private letter—now known as the Balfour Declaration—to the most prominent Jew in England, Lord Walter Rothschild (1868–1937), is the earliest sign that any major power was willing, for whatever reasons, to validate Zionist claims to a political stakehold in Palestine. In carefully guarded diplomatic language, Balfour declared his government's willingness to establish a "national home for the Jewish people," provided that "nothing shall be done which may prejudice the civil and religious rights of existing non-Jewish communities in Palestine."[15] Within a decade of this proclamation, however, both Great Britain and the rapidly growing Jewish community in Palestine discovered just how intense Palestinian Arab opposition to increased Jewish immigration really was. By the late 1930s, as Great Britain sought to limit sharply the number of Jews who could legally enter Palestine, the stage was set for a succession of wars between Arabs and Jews—wars that have continued to the present day.

As a secular ideology, Zionism (in all its variations) rests on a few basic assumptions. The first assumption holds that anti-Semitism may abate from time to time, but it will never disappear, and as long as Jews are hated anywhere in the world, their lives are in peril. The second assumption is that the only guarantee of physical survival in a hostile world is national sovereignty—because only a nation-state can effectively defend its citizens. Third, the guest-host relationship Jews have lived under, whether in Christian or in Muslim lands, has always been inherently unstable, and on occasion threatening to Jewish survival. If Jews are to have any hope of a secure future, they will have to regain their collective autonomy, which can be accomplished only through political means. And if one adds to all of this the specifically religious belief that the rebirth of the State of Israel represents the beginning stage of messianic redemption of the world, one has a totality of ideas that have been employed to rationalize the transformation of the world Jewish community back into a politico-religious entity. Viewed from this perspective, Jewish history has come full circle in our time, as Jews search for ways to reconnect their religious lives with their enduring sense of peoplehood.

The Future of Judaism in the Contemporary World

During the last three decades of the twentieth century, and at the dawn of the new millennium, Judaism faced a number of formidable challenges. The sheer loss of human life following the *Shoah* meant more than just a sharp reduction in the Jewish world population. For some Jews, the possibility of collective annihilation carried with it the secondary possibility of the "end" of Judaism itself, or at the very least the dwindling away of what was once a global community. For others, however, the threat of cultural extinction inspired a reexamination of their most basic philosophical assumptions and institutional behaviors. Two of the most far-reaching challenges came from two largely unrelated movements: feminism and radical humanism.

The Challenge of Humanist Judaism Probably the most far-reaching critique of traditional Jewish concepts and religious practices at the end of the twentieth century came from a very different quarter: the rejection of Judaism's central God concept by secular Jews who found any form of theism philosophically untenable. For some, the renunciation of Judaism's God was a logical response to the insane violence of the *Shoah* and the absurd wastefulness and cruelty of a world that seemed perpetually at war. No truly just or beneficent God, they argued, could possibly tolerate such slaughter. Therefore, the only reasonable and morally compelling response was to assume that no such deity ever existed—except perhaps in the human imagination.[16]

Of course, anyone who has studied the development of atheism in the modern era has encountered arguments like these. What was new can be found in the insistence of humanist advocates such as the American rabbi Sherwin Wine (1928–2007) that one can remain a Jew, culturally and sociologically, while at the same time rejecting any belief in a supernatural Creator.[17] Taking their cue from Mordecai Kaplan and Reconstructionism, humanistic Jews insist that since Jews are a people first, and only secondarily a religious community, their disbelief in a God should not exclude them from the company of their fellow Jews or prevent them from embracing Jewish ethics and folkways.

At present, the appeal of this approach to Jewish life and values appears to be small. Institutionally, very few communities throughout the world have identified themselves with this form of radical humanism or have made the effort to revise their religious calendars and liturgies accordingly. Still, no survey of contemporary Judaism would be complete without some recognition of this radical alternative to mainstream Jewish faith.

Women and Judaism

Traditionally, the status of women in Judaism has been that of a respected but subordinate member of the religious community, and for many centuries Jewish women lived in a male-dominant culture. Though two of the books of the Hebrew Bible are named for women (the Book of Ruth and the Book of Esther), and though Jewish identity is traced through the mother's line, nevertheless religious leadership in Judaism has historically been a male preserve. The Orthodox *Siddur* instructs Jewish males to thank God that they were not born women, and rabbinic tradition released women from all time-bound religious obligations (such as fixed prayer times), based on the assumption that a woman's chief responsibility was the raising of children and maintenance of the home. In fact, the only ritual obligations that women were expected to fulfill were those of baking challah, lighting the Sabbath lights, and attending the mikveh. And though women were never prevented from attending synagogue, their very presence necessitated a physical barrier to separate them from male worshippers, who, it was feared, would otherwise be distracted by their presence. Moreover, the privilege of advanced religious study was reserved exclusively for men, who were thought to be better equipped by nature for the mental rigors of scholarly debate.

The Western feminist movements of the 1970s totally rejected such views on the grounds that they embodied a "patriarchal" view of woman's place in society, and as the influence of feminist thought made its presence felt throughout the Jewish community—particularly in the United States—the exclusion of women from positions of religious authority soon came to an end. The American Reform Movement took the lead by conferring the title of Rabbi on Sally Priesand (b. 1946) in 1972, and shortly thereafter both the Conservative and Reconstructionist Movements in the United States admitted women to their rabbinic seminaries. However, even more transformative changes were under way, affecting the very language and root concepts of traditional Judaism.

At the same time that women were being admitted to the rabbinate in greater numbers, a new approach to both religious language and the interpretation of biblical literature was beginning to manifest itself within the non-Orthodox spectrum of the Jewish community. Feminist scholars in particular focused on the gendered vocabulary that surrounded the biblical idea of God, as well as echoes of a distinctly masculine image of the Deity in traditional prayers, where God is consistently referred to as "Father," "Lord," and "King." Reform liturgists began to experiment with gender-neutral words such as "Eternal One" and "Source of Life" as alternatives to the obviously patriarchal terminology of the traditional *Siddur*. In addition, the elimination or revision of prayers that implied the spiritual superiority of the male or that excluded women from the prayer community by omission became part of the same revisionist project. Not all of these innovations have proven universally acceptable, but collectively they represent a serious effort to bring the religious discourse of Judaism into the contemporary world.[18]

JUDAISM AS A WAY OF LIFE

As Judaism has historically placed great emphasis on the sanctification of time, any consideration of Judaism as a "way of life" should begin with the ways in which Jews mark the passage of time. Like many ancient peoples, Jews in antiquity employed a modified lunar calendar, which allowed them to celebrate each month's appearance of a new moon while at the same time periodically adjusting the lunar year to the solar year. They dated this calendar from what they presumed to be the moment of the world's creation, with the result that the year 2014 in our secular calendar overlaps with the Jewish year 5774. And within this sacred calendar, certain seasons were designated as "Sabbaths," or occasions for religious celebration, during which the Jewish community reaffirms its covenant relationship with God.

The Major Festivals

At the core of this system of seasonal religious observances are five major festivals, all linked to each other and to the cycle of nature—**Rosh Hashanah**, **Yom Kippur**, **Sukkot**, **Pesach**, and **Shavuot**—plus a host of relatively minor festivals interspersed throughout the year. Each major festival is biblical in origin, and on each of these occasions Jews are commanded to cease working and devote themselves to prayer. That said, each major *chag* (Hebrew, "sacred occasion") is as individual as the season it celebrates and the ritual function it performs.

Rosh Hashanah Commonly referred to as the Jewish New Year, Rosh Hashanah is traditionally celebrated for two days at the beginning of the month of Tishri (September–October), and it is regarded as both a solemn and a joyous occasion. Though there is some evidence that, in biblical times, the agricultural year began in the early spring, by the rabbinic era, the start of the religious year had already shifted to the early fall. This shift placed a greater emphasis on the internal rhythms of the human heart and a need for self-reflection, as opposed to a celebration of the seasonal harvests.

As a consequence, the year begins with a period of self-reflection, signaled by the blowing of a ram's horn (Hebrew, *shofar*) during the synagogue service. The sound of this instrument, which can be heard 100 times during the service, is designed to awaken the conscience of the worshipper to the need for repentance and reconciliation with God. For that reason Rosh Hashanah is referred to in the liturgy as *Yom Hazikaron*, or the Day of Remembrance. At the same time, the mood created during the two days of Rosh Hashanah is a generally happy and expectant one, and it is customary to eat a dish of apples and honey as an expression of hope that the coming year will be one of sweet fruitfulness and fulfillment. It is also customary on this occasion for Jews to greet each other, at the conclusion of religious services, with the words *l'shanah tovah tikatevu*—"may you be inscribed for a good year"—alluding to the ancient belief that, during the ten-day period between Rosh Hashanah and Yom Kippur, God writes the names of those who will live for another year in a "Book of Life." The hope is that all those who sincerely repent their sins will be inscribed in the Book of Life.

Covered in a large *tallit*, this Yemenite Jew blows the *shofar* on Rosh Hashanah.

Yom Kippur Also known as the Day of Atonement, Yom Kippur is unquestionably the most solemn day in Judaism's sacred calendar and its most important fast day. The purpose of both the dusk-to-dusk fast and the penitential prayers that are recited on Yom Kippur was made clear by the rabbis centuries ago: "For transgressions against God, the Day of Atonement atones; but for transgressions of one human being against another, the Day of Atonement does not atone until they have made peace with one another" (Tractate Yoma 8:9). For repentance (Hebrew, *teshuvah*) to be effective, therefore, some restorative action must accompany the process of prayer and self-examination. As a result, the liturgy for Yom Kippur asks forgiveness for a rather lengthy list of all the sins that people are likely to commit against one

VISUAL GUIDE
Judaism

The Torah scroll is placed on a table where the reader will use a *Yad* (a pointer) to read each word aloud.

The Palm Branch, the Willow, and the Myrtle make up the Lulav; the Lemon (or Etrog) and the Lulav are held together during Sukkot prayers.

The Passover plate is prepared for the *Seder*, with an egg, a shank bone, parsley, chives, and bitter herbs.

The Star of David is a medieval symbol of Jewish identity placed in the center of the flag of Israel.

another, as well as all the acts of defiance that people are likely to display toward God. These confessional prayers, which are recited throughout the day, are collective expressions of guilt and remorse ("Our father, our King, *we* have sinned before You"). But although it is the norm in Judaism to pray as a part of a community, each worshipper is nevertheless expected to internalize the act of repentance and strive for reconciliation with neighbors and with God.

On Yom Kippur a number of restrictions, in addition to fasting, are commonly imposed on those who observe this holy day. Thus, in Orthodox communities it is customary for married couples to abstain from intimacy, for men to wear white garments (symbolic of purification) to synagogue, and to neither shave nor bathe (as if one were in mourning). In addition, no work of any kind may be performed on Yom Kippur, from the evening in which the holy day begins until the following evening when it ends. However, all fasting on Yom Kippur ceases the moment one's health is imperiled, and the norm is that any seriously ill person will first consult with a physician before undertaking a twenty-four-hour fast. Children under 13 and women who are actively nursing infants are generally exempt from the rigors of this day.

Sukkot Five days after the conclusion of Yom Kippur, Jews undertake a week-long fall harvest celebration known as Sukkot ("booths"). As with any harvest festival, Sukkot displays symbols of the season, the most important being the palm frond (Hebrew, *lulav*), the citron (Hebrew, *etrog*), and leaves of the willow tree (Hebrew, *aravah*) and the myrtle (Hebrew, *hadassah*). It is customary to adorn the *sukkah*—or temporary hut, from which Sukkot derives its name—with each of these plants while leaving the roof of this structure partly open to the sky. During the seven days of this holiday Jews are encouraged (weather permitting) to eat and sleep in the *sukkah*, so as to reenact, symbolically, the biblical Exodus (i.e., the passage of ancient Israelites through the desert after escaping

VOICES: An Interview with Rabbi Brad Bloom

Rabbi Bloom, of Temple Beth Yam, Hilton Head, South Carolina, is a graduate of the Hebrew Union College (a Reform Rabbinic seminary). He holds a Master's degree in social work, and for almost thirty years he has served congregations in Illinois and California.

How do the High Holy Days evoke feelings of wonder and awe, for you and your congregation?

Rosh Hashanah and Yom Kippur lie at the very core of Jewish religious con-sciousness. These "Days of Awe," as they are called, challenge us to assess our relationship to God and to each other. We are obliged to ask hard questions and recognize our human frailties, and hopefully discover whatever inner strength we possess to change for the better. The awe and wonder we experience during this period of repentance come from two sources: from our encounters with God and from our communal experience and collective memory, woven together to create a moment of special sanctity.

Of course, our prayers and special rituals are an essential part of that experi-ence. Listening to the *Kol Nidre* chant, for example, we are moved as much by the beauty of the traditional melody as by the thought of unfulfilled vows to God. And similar feelings arise on Rosh Hashanah when the *shofar* is sounded, echo-ing throughout the sanctuary. These are all sensory responses, but they evoke powerful emotions and even more powerful moments of introspection.

Rabbi Brad Bloom

And how does a sense of God's presence enter into these rituals?

For some, God occupies the center stage in this drama; for others, he is thought of as working behind the scenes, eliciting deep feelings of empathy and belong-ing through our interaction as a congregation. And for still others, God is not present at all; instead, they experience the assembled presence of *K'lal Yisrael*— the worldwide community of Jews joined in solidarity. Taken together, all of these experiences represent the continuum of awe and wonder that are central to the High Holy Days.

from slavery in Egypt). Sukkot thus becomes one of three festivals (the other two being Pesach and Shavuot) that recall the Exodus narrative.

It is traditional religious practice to attend synagogue during the first two days and the last two days of the festival, offering thanksgiving prayers attuned to the fall season. To that end, each worshipper is required to carry a *lulav* and an *etrog* to morning ser-vices, and in the course of this ceremony both the *lulav* and the *etrog* are waved in six directions, signifying God's presence throughout the universe. In addition, the biblical book of Ecclesiastes is read on the Sabbath of Sukkot, highlighting some of the major themes of this festival, namely, the passing of the seasons and the providence of God. At the conclusion of Sukkot an eighth day of prayer and celebration, known as Shemini

A decorated *sukkah*, ready for a midday meal.

Atzeret (or "the Eighth Day of Assembly"), is added to the seven days of Sukkot as a culminating moment in the process of expressing one's gratitude to God for the bounty of the world.

Traditionally, Jews living outside Israel divide up Shemini Atzeret into two days, with the second day referred to as *Simchat Torah* (Hebrew, "Joy of the Torah"); on that day, the annual reading of the first five books of the Hebrew Bible comes to an end, and the cycle of weekly readings begins again. In Israel, and in many Reform congregations, Shemini Atzeret and Simchat Torah are telescoped into a single day of observance, characterized by a festive atmosphere in which both children and adults join in celebrating the "gift" of Torah while singing and dancing with their congregation's Torah scroll in their arms.

Pesach   More commonly known as "Passover" in English-speaking countries, Pesach is the second of three pilgrimage festivals, the first being Sukkot and the third being Shavuot. In ancient times, as long as a Temple stood in Jerusalem, Jews made a pilgrimage to it to offer prayers and animal sacrifices to God. With the Roman destruction of the Second Temple in 70 C.E., Jews were left with nothing but a memory of this rite, and the practice of celebrating the Exodus from Egypt then shifted exclusively to the synagogue and to the home. And it is in the home, then, that Jews gather on the first two nights of this week-long festival to recount the Exodus story and to celebrate this event through a ceremonial meal known as a **Seder**—a practice that may well have begun in biblical times.

Like Sukkot, Pesach is celebrated for either seven or eight days during the month of Nisan (March–April), depending, once again, on whether one lives in Israel or in the Diaspora, or whether one follows the Orthodox custom of celebrating Pesach for eight days or the Reform custom of limiting observance to a week. In either case, the first two and the last two days are subject to the same restrictions that govern any *chag*—no work and limited travel. In addition, however, Pesach imposes one more strictly dietary requirement: no foods containing yeast may be consumed during this period (reflecting the fact that Jewish slaves, escaping from Egypt, had no time to allow their bread to rise). In most observant Jewish households it is the custom, therefore, to rid the home of all breads and foods that contain leavening agents and to prepare for this occasion by either boiling one's dishes and silverware or using a separate set of dinnerware and utensils that are reserved for use on Pesach alone. As is discussed later in this chapter, the dietary rules and regulations collectively known as kashrut are fundamentally important to Jewish practice. The number of foods sold in supermarkets bearing a "Kosher for Passover" label testifies to the seriousness with which this practice is observed by many Jews today.

Observance of Pesach begins in the evening in the home, where the *Seder* is celebrated by a gathering of family and friends, followed the next morning by a festival service in the synagogue. The *Seder* consists of two rituals in one: a festive meal, featuring biblical and seasonal foods that reflect the Exodus story, and a liturgy, found in an ancient text called the *Haggadah* (Hebrew, the "telling"). The *Haggadah* contains both the story of Israel's escape from Egypt and a collection of hymns and songs and rabbinic commentaries in praise of God, who made that deliverance possible. One of the principal goals of this highly ritualized meal is to leave each participant in the *Seder* with a sense of engagement in the biblical story. Ideally, each person should identify with the enslaved generation that witnessed not only the liberation from bondage but also the giving of the Torah at Mt. Sinai.

Because the Pesach *Seder* is essentially a family event, children play a very prominent role in this rite by being given questions to ask, songs to sing, and stories to listen to. Most temptingly of all, during the initial ceremony that precedes the meal, the prayer leader takes a piece of *matzah* (a type of unleavened flatbread that, according to biblical writers, the escaping Israelites baked in haste while fleeing Egypt) and breaks it in half, hiding one half of this piece—known as the *Afikoman*—so that children can find it by the end of the meal and exchange it for a gift.

In addition to *matzah*, several other foods are either displayed or consumed during the *Seder* meal, including bitter herbs (a reminder of the bitterness of slavery); a mixture of wine, chopped nuts, and apples (symbolically representing the mortar used by Israelite slaves to build cities and pyramids); a roasted lamb shank bone (recalling the sacrifice of lambs by the Israelites before their departure from Egypt); and a roasted egg, a green vegetable (usually parsley), and an additional herb or vegetable. These items all reflect the ancient agricultural context of this celebration—namely, the early spring harvest and the lamb-shearing season that often accompanied that harvest. Finally, participants consume four small symbolic cups of wine during the *Seder* meal, each serving as a reminder of the many blessings God bestowed upon ancient Israel and continues to bestow upon the Jewish people. A fifth cup is set aside for the prophet Elijah, whose symbolic presence at the *Seder* represents the hope that a messiah will some day appear and bring peace and justice into the world.

Shavuot Seven weeks separate Pesach from the last of the three pilgrimage festivals, Shavuot (Hebrew, "weeks"). (This holiday is often referred to by Christians as "Pentecost.") Between the second day of Passover and the first day of Shavuot, it was the practice in biblical Israel to bring a sheaf of new grain to the Temple, and an obvious connection exists between this festival and the later spring harvest. However, during the rabbinic era Shavuot became associated with the giving of the Torah on Mt. Sinai, and from that moment on Shavuot became a part of the ongoing liturgical reenactment of the Exodus that we have traced through Sukkot and Pesach. Given this new historical association, we can understand why the rabbis decided that the high point of the synagogue liturgy for Shavuot would be the public reading of the Ten Commandments.

Traditionally, Shavuot is celebrated for two days (the sixth and seventh of the month of Sivan [May–June]), though the festivities associated with Shavuot are considerably less elaborate than those connected to Pesach or Sukkot. It is common practice on Shavuot to decorate the synagogue with flowers and to serve meatless meals with honey as a key ingredient—the idea being that the reading of the Torah should be sweet upon the lips, though neither of these practices is obligatory. More common is the public reading of the Book of Ruth, which tells the story of a young Moabite widow who is welcomed into Israelite society and who, centuries later, became the prototype of the ideal convert to Judaism. Finally, there is a custom of staying up the entire first night of the *chag* for the purpose of studying some portion of the Torah. This practice was established for the first time by a community of mystics living in sixteenth-century Safed (northern Israel) who believed that the celebration of the Torah on Shavuot should be preceded by a process of mental and spiritual preparation.

The Minor Festivals

In contrast to the major festivals we have just reviewed, a number of relatively "minor" festivals serve to fill out the Jewish religious year. Yet despite their historically subordinate status, they are no less beloved by Jews and are sometimes observed with equal attention. The distinction between them is mainly ceremonial: the observance of many of these festivals does not entail restrictions on labor, diet, or any other activities. In addition, these festivals were never really integrated into the agricultural cycle that is so clearly embedded within the calendar of major holidays, though some indirectly reflect the season in which they appear.

Hanukkah Of all of Judaism's minor holidays, Hanukkah is probably the best known throughout the Western world, if only because of its proximity to Christmas. It is also one of the most historically oriented, as it is linked directly to a historical event. Hanukkah commemorates the Maccabean rebellion that began in 167 B.C.E. against the tyrannical rule of the Syrian monarch, Antiochus IV, who sought to suppress the practice of Judaism within Palestine and who "defiled" the Temple in Jerusalem by rededicating it to the Greek gods. For the next two years an armed insurrection, led first by a rural priest named Mattathias and after his death by his eldest son, Judah the Maccabee, wrested control of the Temple from Antiochus's army.

The key event that Hanukkah celebrates, however, is the recovery and cleansing of the Jerusalem Temple and the miracle of the lights that Jewish tradition records. According to this legendary account, once the Temple was in Jewish hands it became necessary to rededicate the sanctuary—yet only one flask of the oil necessary to keep lamps lit could be found. Miraculously, however, this one flask continued to burn for eight days, thus attesting to the renewal of God's presence within the Temple. In commemoration of that miracle, Jews light a candle each night for eight nights until a ceremonial lamp (known in Hebrew as either a *menorah* or a *hanukkiah*) is completely lit. This candle-lighting ceremony is accompanied by the chanting of prayers, the singing of songs, and, in more recent times, the giving of gifts. In addition, a traditional game of chance is played with a four-sided top known as a *dreidel*, on whose sides are inscribed four Hebrew letters, which stand for the words meaning "a great miracle occurred there." In contemporary Israel, however, *dreidels* bear a slightly altered message: "a great miracle occurred here," referring to the establishment of the Jewish state in 1948.

Purim   Another history-oriented festival, and one that exhibits an even more secular character than Hanukkah, is Purim, which occurs on the fourteenth day of the month Adar (February–March). Purim is a carnival-like holiday whose origins can be found within the biblical Book of Esther. Like Hanukkah, Purim celebrates a victory, this time over an antagonist named Haman, who appears in the Book of Esther as a would-be destroyer of the Jewish people. However, unlike Hanukkah, the underlying festival narrative appears to have little or no historical basis. Still, Purim tells an interesting story of adaptation and survival against all odds, and it is a story that has gripped the Jewish imagination for centuries.

On the final night of Hanukkah, all the candles are lit while children play with the dreidel, a game with toy coins.

For Orthodox Jews, Purim begins with a fast on the thirteenth of the month of Adar. Once the fast is over, however, the festive aspects of Purim begin. These include a reading of the *megillah* (the book or scroll) of Esther. While this scroll is being read, congregants interrupt the narration with shouting and foot stamping every time Haman's name is read aloud. In addition, the rabbis, many centuries ago, sanctioned the practice of drinking to excess on Purim, thereby contributing to an atmosphere of barely controlled anarchy. This near-riotous behavior is coupled with the practice of dressing children in costumes that suggest the principal characters in the Esther story, so it is easy to see why this holiday is sometimes referred to as the Jewish Mardi Gras.

However, Purim also has its more sedate customs: the sending of gifts to friends, or to the poor, and the eating of triangular-shaped fruit-filled cookies known as *hamantaschen*, variously thought to represent Haman's ears, or hat, or pockets. Finally, although there is no prohibition against working on Purim, many Orthodox communities will devote the entire fourteenth of Adar to celebrating this festival.

Tu B'Shevat   The fifteenth day of the month of Shevat (January–February) is identified in rabbinic literature as the "New Year's Day of Trees," and it is often referred to today as the Jewish version of Arbor Day. Typically, trees are planted on this day (especially in modern Israel), and monies are set aside for the poor. In some communities Jews hold a special *Seder* on Tu B'Shevat consisting of recitations from the Bible and the Talmud, combined with the eating of certain fruits and nuts (chiefly figs, dates, carobs, almonds, and pomegranates) that are native to the land of Israel.

Tisha B'Av   The ninth day of the month of Av (Hebrew, *Tisha B'Av*) is, after Yom Kippur, the most solemn day in the Jewish calendar because it commemorates the destruction of both the First Temple by the Babylonians in 587 B.C.E. and the Second Temple by the Romans in 70 C.E. Each of these events was a tragic turning point in Jewish history, leading to the loss of national sovereignty and the subsequent exile of the Jewish masses from their homeland. On Tisha B'Av (commonly celebrated in July or August), Jews fast from sunset to sunset as they remember not only these tragedies but other terrible losses that they have suffered during their long history. Like Yom Kippur, Tisha B'Av is a day of collective contrition and virtual mourning, as Jews gather in synagogues to read from the Book of Lamentations and sing hymns that reflect on the double loss of Jerusalem and Jewish nationhood.

Yom HaShoah Holocaust Memorial Day, or *Yom HaShoah* in Hebrew, is the most recent addition to the sacred calendar in Judaism. In 1951 the Israeli Parliament selected this date (the twenty-seventh day of Nisan [March–April]) as a remembrance day for the millions of Jews who were victims of Nazi genocide during World War II. This date was chosen because it coincides with the beginning of the Warsaw Ghetto Uprising of 1943, and today the overwhelming majority of Jewish communities throughout the world observe this day of collective mourning and reflection. Yom HaShoah, however, is not a fast day, and unlike Tisha B'Av there are no prohibitions on work or other activities. Nevertheless, it has become customary in recent years for Jews to gather on the evening of the twenty-seventh of Nisan and to recite memorial prayers for the roughly one-third of the Jewish world population who lost their lives during the war.

The Sabbath

Though it is neither a major nor a minor festival, strictly speaking, the weekly Sabbath (Hebrew, *Shabbat*) forms the core of the sacred calendar in Judaism. Like the major festivals, it is a day of prayer and rest, with its own liturgical tradition and pattern of observance; but, unlike any other sacred occasion in Judaism, its observance is explicitly mandated in the Ten Commandments. The Torah, in fact, provides two different rationales for Shabbat: in the Book of Exodus (20:8–11) it is identified as the day on which God rested from His creative labors; in the Book of Deuteronomy (5:12–15), however, it is associated with the Exodus from Egypt and liberation from slavery. Each of these explanations, of course, provides a distinctive interpretation of the meaning of Shabbat; the former is supernatural, whereas the latter is historical. For both interpretations, however, the commanding lesson of the Sabbath remains the same: God's actions, whether at the beginning of human time or at a turning point in the history of Israel, serve as a model for human behavior. The Creator/Liberator has separated sacred time from ordinary time, and so must we.

Shabbat begins at dusk on Friday and concludes at sundown on Saturday (according to tradition, when three stars appear in the sky). This 24-hour period is ushered in by the lighting of two candles in the home, reminiscent of the first act of creation. Customarily it is the woman of the house who lights these candles. Once the Sabbath formally begins, observance shifts to the synagogue, where the *Erev Shabbat* (Sabbath evening) service is conducted. The liturgy for Sabbath evening identifies the Sabbath itself as a "bride," and the feelings aroused by the "joy of the Sabbath" are similar to the emotions evoked by a wedding. With the return of the family from prayer, the Sabbath meal begins with a prayer of sanctification recited over wine and a blessing said over two loaves of bread. Sabbath bread is called *challah*, and it is usually baked in a shape that suggests a woman's braided hair (yet another allusion to the Sabbath "bride").

Sabbath morning observance shifts, once again, to the synagogue, where, in addition to the Shabbat liturgy, a weekly portion of the Torah is read, accompanied by a portion from the prophetic books. That service concluded, the remainder of the day is spent in quiet study or in rest until the evening, when the last two worship services of the day are celebrated, and a separation ceremony, known as *Havdalah*, is celebrated with a cup of wine, a braided candle, and a spice box—all reminiscent of the sweetness and calm of the Sabbath that has just departed. The rabbis of the Talmud once observed that it was not just Israel that had kept the Sabbath but the Sabbath that had kept Israel; as the most direct link to the ancient past, Shabbat serves as one of Judaism's primary symbols of historical and spiritual continuity.

A Jewish mother and daughter light the Sabbath candles.

Life-Cycle Events

Virtually all religious cultures attempt to locate the sacred within the context of everyday life, and Judaism is no exception. At each stage in the cycle of living and dying, Judaism offers a distinctive ceremony that marks the passage from birth to death. The ultimate object of these rites of passage is the sanctification of human life and the desire to deepen the covenant relationship between Israel and God.

A table set for Shabbat: Challah, candlesticks, and wine.

Birth The ritual process of entering the Jewish community begins, for male babies, on the eighth day of life with the rite of circumcision. Jews are not the only people today who circumcise male infants (nor were they in antiquity), but in Judaism circumcision is much more than a medical procedure. It is, in fact, a very basic *mitzvah*, a divine commandment imparted to the biblical patriarch Abraham and incumbent upon all of his male descendants from that time forward.

Historically, circumcision has been one of the distinctive physical marks of Jewish identity, and its importance for the overwhelming majority of Jews can be gauged by the fact that the circumcision ritual takes precedence over the Sabbath or any other holy day in the sacred calendar; indeed, the only thing that would delay the performance of this *mitzvah* would be concern for the health of the child. During this ceremony, after the *mohel* (a ritual circumciser, who is usually a medically trained professional) has removed a portion of the infant's foreskin, the newborn receives his Hebrew name, which traditionally consists of the child's own name and that of the father (for example, Isaac son of Abraham). From this moment on, this is the name by which the child will be known in the Jewish community, particularly on ritual occasions. In many Conservative and Reform communities, it has become the custom to add the mother's name to the father's, thereby assigning equal weight to the matrilineal source of the child's identity.

Baby girls enter the Jewish community under slightly different circumstances. There has never been any form of female circumcision in Judaism, nor any fixed naming ritual for the infant female. However, one very popular custom today among Jews worldwide is the practice of bringing the newborn to the synagogue on the first (or, in some communities, the fourth) Sabbath after birth. On that occasion, either the child's father or both parents are called up to the Torah and recite the customary blessings. Then the baby girl is given a Hebrew name, and, like her male counterpart's, it is the name that she will use on all ritual occasions for the rest of her life. This ceremony is sometimes referred to, in Hebrew, as a *brit hayim*, or "covenant of life."

Bar/Bat Mitzvah and Confirmation

As you learned from Seth's story at the beginning of this chapter, Jewish males traditionally enter the stage of religious maturity at the age of thirteen, whether or not they have engaged in the *Bar Mitzvah* ceremony. There is no reference to such a ritual in the Hebrew Bible, nor do the rabbis of the Talmud make mention of any specific rite of passage that marks a young man's assumption of responsibility for fulfilling the *mitzvot* incumbent on an observant Jew. Nevertheless, by the later Middle Ages, something like the *Bar Mitzvah* ceremony practiced today had already begun to evolve, consisting of some demonstration of Hebrew literacy and an ability to read a weekly portion of the Torah. And of all the commonly practiced rituals of contemporary Judaism, the *Bar Mitzvah* is the one ritual that is likely to be familiar to non-Jews.

Regarded as the culminating point of years of study, the young man who becomes a *Bar Mitzvah* is taught to see himself as a scholar-in-training whose entry into adult Jewish life is just the beginning of a lifelong program of study. Though the celebration that follows is often joyous, there is a serious underlying purpose: the preparation of a young person to assume what the rabbis have called the "yoke of Torah." Thus, in addition to reading a portion from both the Torah and the prophetic literature, a *Bar Mitzvah* is expected to deliver a *d'rash*, or brief scholarly explanation of the portion he has just read, thereby demonstrating a mature comprehension of Jewish Scriptures.

The practice of requiring young women (between the ages of twelve and thirteen) to furnish similar proof of both literacy and religious commitment is of much more

Compare the *Bar* or *Bat Mitzvah* in Judaism with the confirmation ceremony in various forms of Christianity. How are they alike, and how do they differ?

recent origin. The first *Bat Mitzvah* to be performed in the United States was conducted in 1922 for Judith Kaplan, daughter of Rabbi Mordecai Kaplan, the founder of the Reconstructionist Movement. Beginning as a somewhat radical gesture designed to affirm gender equality in modern Judaism, the *Bat Mitzvah* soon evolved into an alternative form of the *Bar Mitzvah* ritual, and today the *Bat Mitzvah* ceremony is as common as the *Bar Mitzvah* in non-Orthodox communities.

Another innovative practice, known as a Confirmation, is almost as commonplace today in non-Orthodox communities as the *Bar* and *Bat Mitzvah*, and it too involves a process of study and ritual performance by both young men and young women. The Confirmation ceremony can be traced back to the early decades of the Reform Movement in nineteenth-century Germany, where some Reform-minded rabbis attempted to find an alternative rite of passage for adolescents rather than the traditional *Bar Mitzvah*, believing that the latter had become little more than a ceremonial occasion. Their solution was to borrow a practice from the Christian church and to require sixteen-year-old males (and later females) to make a profession of faith during the Shavuot service, thus connecting their religious coming of age with the traditional celebration of the giving of the Torah at Mt. Sinai. Curiously, however, this intended departure from normative Jewish practice was finally reintegrated into the traditional life cycle after World War II, as many Reform and several Conservative congregations added the Confirmation ceremony to the now-lengthened process of Jewish education. Thus, instead of supplanting the *Bar Mitzvah*, the Confirmation ceremony simply became a secondary stage of the passage to adulthood.

Marriage and Divorce In Judaism, marriage is a contractual relationship between a man and a woman, rooted in mutual love and respect, and presumed to be both monogamous and enduring—a relationship on which divine blessings can be invoked. However, like all contracts, the marriage contract can be dissolved.

Over time Jews have devised formal procedures for regulating and solemnizing the processes of marriage and divorce. Many centuries ago, the marriage ceremony consisted of two separate rites: the betrothal and the actual nuptials. According to this ancient custom, the future bride and groom became engaged to one another through the exchange of a ring. The couple then returned to the homes of their respective parents for a year, at which time the bride and groom gathered, along with their families, under a marriage canopy (known as the *chuppah*). A rabbi would recite seven blessings, praising God and sanctifying the union, and only at the conclusion of this ceremony would the marriage be consummated. Today, these two ceremonies have been combined and are accompanied by other, largely symbolic rituals: first, having the bride and groom drink from the same wine cup, and second, having the groom present the bride with her marriage contract (Hebrew, *ketuvah*). Finally, at the conclusion of the ceremony, the groom crushes a wine glass with his shoe—traditionally understood to symbolize the destruction of the two Temples—whereupon the attending guests shout *Mazel Tov* (Hebrew, "good luck").

The bride and groom will stand under this canopy during the wedding ceremony.

From a traditional point of view, the presentation of the *ketuvah* by the groom is the core of the marriage rite in Judaism because it states publicly and clearly the groom's intention to provide for his bride's comfort and well-being while he lives and her financial security after he dies, or after they divorce. The *ketuvah*, in short, is a "prenuptial agreement," and its principal purpose is to provide for the future bride so that, in the event of divorce or the groom's death, she will not be left destitute. Traditionally, the groom alone vows to set aside monies in escrow as "marriage insurance," but many modern Jewish couples have opted for a very different kind of *ketuvah*, vowing mutual commitment and support, symbolized by an exchange of rings.

Jewish divorce proceedings are no less formal (albeit much sadder) than the marriage ceremony. After marital counseling has been tried and failed, the couple comes before a rabbinic court (Hebrew, *bet din*) that consists of three rabbis who hear the case. The divorce document (Hebrew, *get*) is then drawn up, releasing both parties from any future obligation to one another. At that moment, the husband (or his representative) must hand the *get* to his soon-to-be ex-wife. He is then declared free of their union and eligible to marry again—that very day, if he chooses. The wife, however, must wait three months to marry again, on the presumption that she may be pregnant and therefore carrying the child of her former spouse. Moreover, if her husband refuses to grant her a divorce—or cannot do so because he is missing—traditional Jewish law leaves her few options for dissolving the marriage. She may find herself bound by religious law to a husband who has abandoned her or who may have died in some distant land without witnesses to his death. In rabbinic parlance, such a woman is an *agunah* (Hebrew, "chained woman"), and Orthodox communities continue to struggle with this legal dilemma today.

Death and Mourning It is the custom in Judaism to treat the deceased with as much dignity as the living, and every effort is made to ensure that the ceremonies associated with the burial of the dead and mourning are invested with sanctity and respect. Whenever possible, a Jewish burial will take place within twenty-four hours of death (unless the Sabbath or a festival intervenes, delaying burial for a day or two). The body is prepared for burial by being bathed and wrapped in a shroud, then traditionally placed in a simple pine box, thus discouraging ostentation. It is customary during the burial service for mourners to express their sorrow by a symbolic tearing of their clothes—often wearing a strip of torn black cloth, pinned to a garment—while reciting prayers of praise for God and comfort for the soul of the deceased in the afterlife. During this ceremony mourners are consoled by family and friends and gently discouraged from showing excessive grief.

Once burial occurs, those mourners who were closest to the deceased—parents, siblings, children, or spouse—enter into a week-long period of intensive mourning known as *shivah* (Hebrew, "seven"), interrupted only by the Sabbath. During this period, mourners do not work, remain at home, and receive well-wishers who join with the mourning family in "sitting *shivah*." Because mourners are not expected, during this week, to attend synagogue, it is customary for friends to form a prayer quorum (Hebrew, *minyan*) in the home so that morning and evening prayers may be recited.

Once *shivah* is over, however, mourners are expected to return to the world and everyday obligations, with the understanding that for the remainder of that month mourners will abstain from entertainments of all kinds and remain in a somber state of mind. Once this thirty-day period of diminished mourning is completed, restrictions on the mourner's participation in celebratory events are lifted, though most Orthodox Jews continue a modified mourning protocol until the first anniversary of a parent's death has passed. The erecting of a tombstone does not normally occur until eleven months have passed; thereafter, close relatives are expected to visit the grave at least once a year—usually on the anniversary of the death of that family member—as well as to recite prayers in memory of the dead during memorial services held during all the major festivals. Finally, it is customary to light candles in the home at the time of the yearly anniversary of a loved one's death, and, whenever possible, to place small stones on the gravestone as a sign of one's remembrance of the deceased.

Other Sacred Practices

As a way of life—and not just a creed—Judaism seeks to shape every facet of one's behavior: from the food one eats (or doesn't eat) to the way husbands and wives relate to one another. To someone outside these traditions, these religious practices might seem intrusive, but to those living within those traditions they provide a sense of meaning and order, endowing all of life's activities with an aura of holiness.

The Dietary Code   Since antiquity, Jews have observed a restricted diet. Although the details of that diet have changed somewhat over the centuries, the underlying assumptions behind these practices have not. In the Torah, the people of Israel are told, repeatedly, that God wishes them to be in a state of "holiness," and when that principle is applied to diet, it becomes a multiform discipline of selective food consumption and careful food preparation.

The essentials of the Jewish dietary code—known in Hebrew as *kashrut*—are as follows:

1. The only animals that may be eaten are those that have been properly slaughtered; no animal that has been killed by another or that has died a natural death may be consumed.
2. The only quadrupeds that may be eaten are those with split hooves who also chew the cud (like cows or goats), and, once properly slaughtered, their blood must be drained away.
3. No fish may be eaten that does not have both fins and scales.
4. No insects may be consumed at all.
5. No meat dish may be eaten at the same time as a milk dish.

The practical consequences for anyone who observes this diet are obvious: no one who is serious about *kashrut* will walk into a restaurant and order a cheeseburger, nor will that person dine at a stranger's home without first inquiring whether the food about to be served is really "kosher" (meaning in conformity to rabbinic standards of food selection and preparation) and whether the plates and cooking utensils are also completely free of contamination from forbidden foods. In fact, within all Orthodox and many Conservative Jewish homes it is customary to find not only kosher foodstuffs on the table but also, on occasion, duplicate sets of ovens, refrigerators, and dinnerware to make it easier to separate meat dishes from milk dishes. Kosher restaurants carry this process one step further by ordering only meat prepared by kosher butchers and by obtaining rabbinical certification that all food preparation procedures have been followed scrupulously. The phrase "kosher-style" food is therefore a deceptive misnomer; foods and cooking processes are either kosher or nonkosher, but never both.

It is interesting to note, however, that all fruits and vegetables are kosher, and that certain foodstuffs—such as Jell-O or margarine—are "neutral" with respect to meat-milk distinctions. Such "neutral" foods are known by the Yiddish term *pareve*, and they may be eaten at either a meat-based or a milk-based meal. Over the centuries, attempts have been made to rationalize this system of food taboos and culinary practices by suggesting an underlying concern with food safety and dietary well-being, but whatever side benefits may be derived from not consuming infected meats, such benefits are largely peripheral to the primary intent of the dietary code, namely, that of separating the observant Jew from a nonobservant food-consuming culture, thereby making the commonplace act of eating a religiously self-conscious event.

Family Purity All Orthodox, and some Conservative and Reform, women, in addition to maintaining kosher homes, are also equally attentive to the practice of ritual "purity," and as a consequence attend a *mikveh* (Hebrew, "pool") at the conclusion of their menstrual periods. In fact, in a truly orthodox Jewish home, husband and wife abstain from sexual intimacy not only during the entire period of menstruation but for seven days thereafter, and only then will the wife attend the *mikveh*. The purpose of this rite of purification, however, is not to remove biological impurities from a woman's body; that can be accomplished simply by bathing. Immersion in a *mikveh* is, rather, a symbolic act of spiritual preparation—somewhat similar to the practice of baptism in Christianity, which clearly derives from antecedent Jewish practices—and although the *mikveh* is used primarily by women preparing to resume sexual relations with their husbands, it is also used for conversion ceremonies and by orthodox males on the afternoon before Yom Kippur.

The rabbinical laws governing this entire process are referred to as *taharat hamish-pachah* (Hebrew, "purity of the family"), and the remote origin of these practices can be found in the Hebrew Bible, where men are warned against having intimate relations with a menstruating woman. Nowhere, however, in either the Hebrew Bible or in rabbinic literature does Judaism suggest that women's bodies are "unclean" in a hygienic or biological sense. As with the dietary code, so with the laws of family purity: the ceremonial discipline of traditional Judaism requires a heightened degree of self-awareness about the routines of everyday life. Among Reform and Reconstructionist Jews, however, such practices are rarely observed, and today rigorous application of the purity laws is only a distinguishing mark of family life within the Orthodox Jewish home.

Prayer

From its earliest beginnings, Judaism developed a distinctive culture of prayer. In the Hebrew Bible one can find numerous examples of the principal types of prayer that make up the traditional Judaic liturgy: prayers of praise, confession, petition, and thanksgiving. In the Book of Psalms, for example, the legendary King David (to whom much of that book is attributed) petitions God in the following prayer-like poem:

> Hear my cry, O God,
> Heed my prayer.
> From the end of the earth I call to You;
> When my heart is faint,
> You lead me to a rock that is high above me.
> For you have been my refuge,
> A tower of strength against the enemy.
> O that I might dwell in Your tent forever,
> Take refuge under Your protecting wings.
> —*Psalms 61:2–5*

In poems like this, biblical writers repeatedly addressed God in a language that is at once intimate and awestruck, praising His providential care of those who trust in Him, while requesting His continued protection against evil and misfortune. But no matter what the character of any particular prayer, all prayers in Judaism are addressed directly to God, and all assume His compassion and just concern.

With the destruction of the Second Temple in 70 C.E., the principal site of Jewish prayer shifted to the synagogue, where prayer alone, disconnected from animal sacrifices, became the norm. From that point on, the practice of offering prayer—now no longer primarily the privilege of Temple priests—became more democratic. Each community constructed its own house of worship, and before long a recognized liturgy emerged that consisted, in part, of selections from the Hebrew Bible and prayers for various occasions composed by rabbinic authors. By the Middle Ages these prayers were collected in a single volume, known in Hebrew as the *Siddur*, that became the primary source of the synagogue liturgy for weekdays, the Sabbath, and festivals.

The daily routine of prayer appears to have been established during the late biblical period, where we find the exiled Daniel, living in Persia, praying three times a day while turning toward Jerusalem (Daniel 6:11). The architectural arrangement of early synagogues echoed this practice by orienting the entire building in the direction of Jerusalem, though in later centuries Jews were content with placing the Ark—a large, upright cupboard designed to hold several scrolls of the Torah—on the eastern wall. As the rabbinic protocol of prayer developed during the early Middle Ages, the rules governing thrice-daily prayer became increasingly elaborate and formalized, with an additional early afternoon service added on the Sabbath.

Holding a prayer book and wearing a *tallit*, *tefillin*, and a *kipah*, a young man prepares to recite morning prayers.

The most common setting for prayer in Judaism is communal, and although individual (and even spontaneous) prayer is always valid, the full complement of prayers in any prayer service can only be said once a quorum of worshippers has assembled, either in the home or, more commonly, in a synagogue. That quorum is referred to in Hebrew as a *minyan*, and in Orthodox communities it consists of at least ten males thirteen years of age or older; in Conservative and Reform synagogues, a minyan consists simply of ten adults of either gender.

During the morning service (Hebrew, *shacharit*), men traditionally wear a prayer shawl (Hebrew, **tallit**) and phylacteries or prayer-amulets (Hebrew, **tefillin**) throughout, and then remove them at the conclusion of prayers. On the Sabbath it is customary, even in many Reform synagogues, to wear the *tallit* during prayer services, with *tefillin* worn only during weekday prayers. In most synagogues today, a head covering (known variously as a *kipah* or a *yarmulke*) is worn during prayer, chiefly by males, and as a sign of respect. Prayer services are conducted in the late afternoon

(Hebrew, *minchah*) and early evening (Hebrew, *maariv*) as well, and, like the morning service, they consist of certain fixed prayers that represent a succinct summation of the Jewish faith.

One of the most powerful, and the most revered, of all the prayers that are recited during the morning and evening services is the *Shema*, which consists of biblical verses that first declare the unity of God and then declare Israel's commitment to His service:

> Hear O Israel, the Lord is our God, the Lord is one!
> Blessed is God's glorious kingdom forever and ever!
> And you shall love the Lord, your God with all your heart, with all your
> soul, and with all your might. Set these words, which I command you
> this day, upon your heart. Teach them faithfully to your children; speak
> of them in your home and on the way, when you lie down and when
> you rise up. Bind them as a sign upon your hand, and let them be
> symbols before your eyes; inscribe them on the doorposts of your
> house and upon your gates.
>
> *—Deuteronomy 6:4–9*

This passage is one of the first prayers taught to children at the earliest age of religious instruction, and it is, traditionally, the last prayer one utters before death. It is one of a repertoire of "statutory" prayers that are recited every day in the week, on major festivals, and on the Sabbath.

In Orthodox and many Conservative congregations, it is customary to read aloud a portion from the Torah every week, on Monday and Thursday mornings, and especially on the Sabbath (morning and late afternoon). In addition, an extra passage from the prophetic books is read on both the Sabbath and the major festivals. On each occasion the portion selected from the prophetic books either echoes the themes of the Torah portion or reflects the themes of the festival itself. All these readings are normally recited or chanted in Hebrew, with translations in the local language freely available to the congregation. Today, all Jewish communities employ quite a bit of Hebrew in both the recitation of prayers and in readings from the Torah, though the ratio of Hebrew to the vernacular will vary considerably, with Orthodox synagogues conducting services almost entirely in Hebrew and Conservative, Reform, and Reconstructionist communities employing a variable mixture of Hebrew and the congregation's native language.

CONCLUSION

Judaism has not merely survived over a period of three millennia (in itself a remarkable achievement); it has also evolved, responding and adapting to changing circumstances as it developed from a geographically and philosophically circumscribed religious culture into a global faith. As the oldest of the Abrahamic religions, it carries within itself the longest memory of formative events and personalities, and with it an abiding sense of the divine purposefulness of human history. Judaism exists, therefore, at a point of intersection between history and theology, as the life experiences of a people intertwine with their experience of the sacred.

At the summit of Jewish faith lies a singular Creator-God—at once familiar and mysterious, judgmental and forgiving—whose very existence guarantees the order and meaning of the universe; at the heart of Jewish faith lies a covenanted relationship between that God and those who are committed to serving and obeying His will. And even those who doubt the very existence of that God, but who persist in identifying themselves with Jewish history and values, continue to believe in a moral covenant that makes all human communities possible.

SEEKING ANSWERS

What Is Ultimate Reality?

The one God of Jewish faith is understood to be not only the source of all created things but also the highest and most complete form of reality the human mind can imagine. Jewish mystics often refer to this transcendent reality as the *Ein Sof*, or Infinite One. Traditionalists believe that God revealed Himself to the people of Israel at Mt. Sinai and that Jewish Scriptures provide a reliable account of that revelation. The biblical view of Creation is, initially, positive: when God views the world He has brought into being He declares it "very good" (Genesis 1:31). However, later mystics, like Rabbi Luria, traced the evil in the world back to a mysterious cosmic error that subverted the design for the created world that God had originally intended. Nevertheless, the presence of divine "sparks" in each of us inspires us to believe that goodness and not evil will prevail.

How Should We Live in This World?

The divine commandments that make up the core of the Torah are designed to enable human beings to achieve true righteousness, that is, to bring the human moral will into conformity with God's will, and thereby ensure that justice and peace will prevail in the world. All ideas of right and wrong—such as the Ten Commandments—must, therefore, be referred back to God's revelation of His will at Sinai and the Torah's laws that govern human conduct. Both biblical writers and their rabbinic commentators believed that human beings are created in the "image of God" and, at the same time, are torn between good and bad impulses. In the mystical tradition this conflict can be resolved through study, prayer, and meditation, all of which draw us closer to God.

(continued)

SEEKING ANSWERS *(continued)*

What Is Our Ultimate Purpose?

Judaism has never believed that human beings are hopelessly evil, nor does it support the view that humanity can never make moral progress. The High Holy Days are dedicated to the belief that both individuals and whole societies are capable of changing their behavior and that, through active repentance, they are even capable of drawing closer to each other and to God.

Jews have long believed that the soul is immortal and survives death. The fate of the soul in the "world to come" and God's judgment of that soul remain a subject of speculation and wonder, even today; some, however, regard these beliefs as obsolete and no longer a part of contemporary Jewish faith.

REVIEW QUESTIONS

For Review

1. What are *mitzvot*, and where can they be found?
2. What does the word *Torah* literally mean, and how many other meanings can be derived from it?
3. What are Maimonides's thirteen Principles of Faith?
4. Who was Mordecai Kaplan, and to which movement in modern Judaism is he connected?
5. What does the term *Shoah* mean, and how is it different from the word "Holocaust"?

For Further Reflection

1. What are the implications for Judaism of the concepts of election and covenant? Do Jews see themselves as the only people with whom the Creator-God has communicated? Is it ever possible for a non-Jew to enter into a covenant relationship with Israel's God?
2. How did Judaism recover from the loss of the Jerusalem Temple in 70 C.E.? Why do you think that some Jews living today are hoping to rebuild the Temple and resume the practice of animal sacrifice? Why are the majority of the world's Jews content with the synagogue and its prayer routines?
3. How does Maimonides's approach to both God and Torah differ from that of the mystics? Do the kabbalists really believe that it is possible for human beings to seek union with God or to find the presence of God within oneself?
4. Among the varied responses to the *Shoah* that modern Jewish philosophers have proposed, which response seems the most compelling to you? If you were a Holocaust survivor, what would your view of life and of

faith be now? Would you still find it possible to believe in a just and loving God?

5. What does the word Zionism refer to, and what role did Theodor Herzl play in promoting Zionist ideas?

6. What are the Ten Commandments, and where can they be found?

7. What is the Talmud, and how many volumes (or tractates) does the Babylonian Talmud contain?

GLOSSARY

Baal Shem Tov (1698–1760) A charismatic faith healer, mystic, and teacher (whose given name was Israel ben Eliezer) who is generally regarded as the founder of the Hasidic movement.

Bar/Bat Mitzvah A rite of passage for adolescents in Judaism, the *Bar Mitzvah* (for males age thirteen) and the *Bat Mitzvah* (for females ages twelve to thirteen) signal their coming of age and the beginning of adult religious responsibility.

Covenant A biblical concept that describes the relationship between God and the Jews in contractual terms, often thought of as an eternal bond between the Creator and the descendants of the ancient Israelites.

Dead Sea Scrolls Religious literature hidden in caves near the shores of the Dead Sea (c. second–first centuries B.C.E.).

Diaspora A Greek word in origin, it refers to those Jewish communities that live outside of the historical land of Israel.

election The belief that the biblical God "chose" the people of Israel to be His "kingdom of priests" and a "holy nation." This biblical concept is logically connected to the idea of the Covenant, and it entails the belief that the Jews' relationship with God obliges them to conform to His laws and fulfill His purposes in the world.

eschatological Any belief in an "End-Time" of divine judgment and world destruction.

ethical monotheism A core concept of Judaism: it is the belief that the world was created and is governed by only one transcendent Being, whose ethical attributes provide an ideal model for human behavior.

Exodus The escape (or departure) of Israelite slaves from Egypt as described in the Hebrew Bible (c. 1250 B.C.E.).

halacha An authoritative formulation of traditional Jewish law.

Hasidism A popular movement within eighteenth-century Eastern European Judaism, Hasidism stressed the need for spiritual restoration and deepened individual piety. In the course of the nineteenth and twentieth centuries the Hasidic movement spawned a number of distinctive communities that have physically separated themselves from the rest of the Jewish and non-Jewish worlds and who are often recognized by their attire and their devotion to a dynasty of hereditary spiritual leaders.

Holocaust The genocidal destruction of approximately six million European Jews by the government of Nazi Germany during World War II. This mass slaughter is referred to in Hebrew as the *Shoah*.

Immanence The divine attribute of in-dwelling, or God being present to human consciousness.

Kabbalah One of the dominant forms of Jewish mysticism, kabbalistic texts begin to appear in Europe during the twelfth and thirteenth centuries. Mystics belonging to this tradition focus on the emanative powers of God—referred to in Hebrew as *Sephirot*—and on their role within the Godhead, as well as within the human personality.

Luria, Isaac A sixteenth-century mystic who settled in Safed (Israel) and gathered around him a community of disciples. Lurianic mysticism seeks to explain the mystery surrounding both

(continued)

GLOSSARY *(continued)*

the creation of the world and its redemption from sin.

Maimonides A twelfth-century philosopher and rabbinic scholar whose codification of Jewish beliefs and religious practices set the standard for both in subsequent centuries.

Messiah A possibly supernatural figure who will judge and transform the world.

mikveh A ritual bath in which married Jewish women immerse themselves each month, after the end of their menstrual cycle and before resuming sexual relation with their husbands.

mitzvot Literally translated, the Hebrew word *mitzvot* means "commandments," and it refers to the 613 commandments that the biblical God imparted to the Israelites in the Torah (i.e., the first five books of the Hebrew Bible).

Moses The legendary leader and prophet who leads the Israelite slaves out of Egypt, Moses serves as a mediator between the people of Israel and God in the Torah and is later viewed as Israel's greatest prophet. It is to Moses that God imparts the Ten Commandments and the teachings that later became the Torah.

omnipotence The divine attribute of total and eternal power.

omniscience The divine attribute of total and eternal knowledge.

Pesach An early spring harvest festival that celebrates the liberation of the Israelites from Egypt, Pesach (better known as "Passover" in English) is celebrated for seven days in Israel and eight days in the Diaspora. The first two nights are celebrated within a family setting.

Rosh Hashanah The Jewish New Year, it is celebrated for two days in the fall (on the first day of the month of Tishrai) and accompanied by the blowing of a ram's horn (a *shofar*, in Hebrew). It signals the beginning of the "ten days of repentance" that culminate with Yom Kippur.

Seder A ritualized meal, observed on the first two nights of Pesach, that recalls the Exodus from Egypt.

Shavuot A later spring harvest festival that is celebrated for two days and is associated with the giving of the Torah at Mt. Sinai. Along with Pesach and Sukkot, it was one of the "pilgrimage" festivals in ancient times.

Siddur The prayer book that is used on weekdays and on the Sabbath.

Sukkot A fall harvest festival that is associated with the huts (in Hebrew, *sukkot*) in which the ancient Israelites sought shelter during the Exodus. It is celebrated for seven days in Israel (eight days in the Diaspora). During that time Jews take their meals and, if possible, sleep in huts that are partly open to the sky.

synagogue Jewish houses of worship. The focal point of every synagogue is the Ark, a large cabinet where scrolls of the Torah are stored.

tallit A prayer shawl that is worn during morning prayers (traditionally by men). The fringes of this shawl represent, symbolically, the 613 *mitzvot* found in the Torah.

Talmud A multivolume work of commentary on the laws of the Torah and on the teachings of the entire Hebrew Bible, composed in two stages: the Mishnah (edited in approximately 200 C.E.) and the Gemara (edited, in its Babylonian version, around 500 C.E.). Traditionally, Jews refer to the Talmud as the "Oral Torah" and regard it as an extension of sacred scripture.

Tanakh An acronym standing for the entire Hebrew Bible: **T**orah (the first five books of the Hebrew Bible); **N**eviim (or "Prophets," which includes works of both prophecy and history); and **Kh**etuvim (or "Writings," a miscellaneous gathering of works in poetry and prose). Taken together, the twenty-four books that make up this collection constitute the core "scriptures" of Judaism.

tefillin Taken from the word for "prayer," the term *tefillin* refers to two small boxes to which leather straps are attached. Traditionally, Jewish males from the age of thirteen wear *tefillin* during

(continued)

GLOSSARY (continued)

weekday morning prayers. Inside each of these boxes is a miniature parchment containing biblical verses; one box is placed on the forehead and the other is placed on the left arm, signifying that the individual's mind and will are devoted to God.

Torah Literally, the word *torah* means "teaching," and in its most restrictive sense it refers to the first five books of the Hebrew Bible. Less restrictively, it signifies the totality of God's revelations to the Jewish people, which includes not only the remaining books of the Hebrew Bible but also the writings contained in the Talmud.

transcendence The divine attribute of being above and beyond anything human beings can know or imagine.

YHWH These four consonants constitute the most sacred of names associated with the biblical God.

The exact pronunciation of this name, according to ancient Jewish tradition, was known only to the High Priest, but after the destruction of the Second Temple the precise vocalization of these letters was lost—only to be recovered in the days of the Messiah.

Yom Kippur Referred to as the "Day of Atonement," it is the most solemn of all of the fast days in the Jewish religious calendar.

Zionism A modern political philosophy that asserts a belief in Jewish national identity and in the necessity of resuming national life within the historic land of Israel.

Zohar A kabbalistic *midrash* based on the biblical Book of Genesis (c. 1280 C.E.).

SUGGESTIONS FOR FURTHER READING

Akenson, Donald Herman. *Surpassing Wonder: The Invention of the Bible and the Talmuds.* Chicago: University of Chicago Press, 2001. An ambitious, and sometimes argumentative, history of the evolution of biblical and rabbinic literature.

Ariel, David. *What Do Jews Believe?* New York: Schocken Books, 1995. An accessible and nuanced account of traditional and nontraditional Jewish beliefs.

Bauer, Yehuda. *A History of the Holocaust.* New York: Franklin Watts, 2001. A well-researched and readable account of the Holocaust, written by the "dean" of contemporary *Shoah* historians.

Eisenberg, Ronald. *The JPS Guide to Jewish Traditions.* Philadelphia: The Jewish Publication Society, 2004. A well-researched and comprehensive guide to traditional and nontraditional Jewish religious practices.

Fredricksen, Paula. *From Jesus to Christ.* New Haven, CT: Yale University Press, 1988. A close scholarly reading of the gospels that traces the separation of emergent Christianity from normative Judaism of the first four centuries.

Neusner, Jacob, and Alan J. Avery-Peck, eds. *The Blackwell Companion to Judaism.* Oxford, UK: Blackwell, 2003. A collection of diverse articles on the history of Judaism, written by some of the leading scholars in Jewish studies.

Robinson, George. *Essential Judaism: A Complete Guide to the Beliefs, Customs and Rituals.* New York: Pocket Books, 2000. A well-written and comprehensive description of Jewish beliefs and practices.

Sarna, Jonathan D. *American Judaism: A History.* New Haven, CT: Yale University Press, 2004. The best account to date of the historical development of the Jewish community in the United States.

Strassfeld, Michael. *The Jewish Holidays.* New York: HarperCollins, 1985. A nicely illustrated presentation of major and minor Jewish festivals with detailed accounts of religious observances from around the world.

ONLINE RESOURCES

My Jewish Learning
myjewishlearning.com
A well-researched site for historical subjects and religious practices.

The Jewish Virtual Library
jewishvirtuallibrary.org
A good site for contemporary subjects such as Israel and the Holocaust.

CHRISTIANITY

STEVE AND RENEE WALKER have had a lot to look forward to during the past two years. First there was the long-awaited arrival of little Simone, who brings gladness to her parents and her brother, Brent. Today there will be another exciting event as the Walkers present Simone for **baptism** into a spiritual family that Christians call the Church.

Whereas some Christians prefer to baptize adult believers who understand and accept the essential teachings of Christianity, others such as the Walkers believe that baptism is a special means by which God's love begins to grow even within small children. Wanting Simone to be touched by God in this way, they have arranged for her baptism to take place at St. James's Episcopal Church, where they have found friendship and fellowship with others.

Now the church is filled with worshippers whispering quietly in rows of pews while waiting for the service to begin. When it does, the organist fills the building with resplendent strains of music that seem to shake its foundations, the congregation launches into a favorite hymn, and a procession of clergy and their attendants makes its way to the front of the church. After welcoming everyone, the priest, Father Robert, pronounces a blessing upon them. Then all eyes turn toward the baptismal font, an elevated basin of water. Steve, Renee, and Brent are waiting there, with Renee holding Simone in her arms.

A priest baptizes a baby girl as her family looks on.

Father Robert now enters into a formal dialogue with Steve and Renee, asking if they will bring up Simone in the Christian faith, if they renounce evil in all its forms, and if they put their trust in the grace and love of Jesus Christ. Answering for themselves and on behalf of Simone, they respond affirmatively. Then, dipping a small silver cup into the water of the baptismal font, Father Robert pours a bit of it three times on Simone's forehead. As he does so, he says, "Simone, I baptize you in the name of the Father, and of the Son, and of the Holy Spirit. Amen." Then, placing his hand on Simone's forehead, he marks the sign of the cross and adds, "Simone, you are sealed by the Holy Spirit in baptism and marked as Christ's own forever. Amen."

Now that the baptismal ritual is complete, Simone's family return to their seats to await the end of the service. Soon they will be on their way home to join friends and relatives for a festive dinner and celebration of the new life that Simone will live, not just with the Walker family but in communion with more than 2 billion Christians worldwide. ☀

There are three great traditions within Christianity. Historically, the **Roman Catholic Church** has been the dominant **church** in the West. In the East, most Christians have belonged to the **Orthodox Church** (also known as the Eastern Orthodox Church). **Protestant Christianity**, which consists of thousands of "denominations," grew out of the Roman Catholic tradition in the sixteenth century. Although these churches have been shaped in different ways by complex historical and

World Christian population.

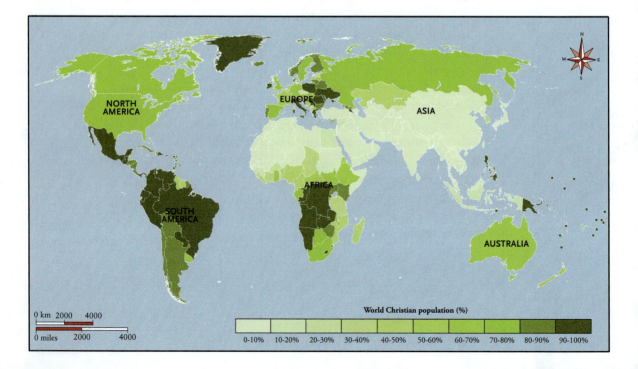

World Christian population (%)

| 0-10% | 10-20% | 20-30% | 30-40% | 40-50% | 50-60% | 60-70% | 70-80% | 80-90% | 90-100% |

cultural forces, they are united by shared beliefs that lie at the heart of Christianity. Christians acknowledge a personal and transcendent God, the creator and sustainer of the universe. The Christian doctrine of the **Trinity** describes God as one in essence, but consisting in three "persons": Father, Son, and Holy Spirit. Christians believe that communion with God, in this life and in eternity, is the ultimate purpose of human existence. But there is an obstacle to be overcome: sin. The violation of God's will in thought or action, **sin** is common to all humanity. Worse, sin separates the individual from God. What is needed is the forgiveness that God gives to all who believe that the sacrificial death of Jesus Christ, the Son of God, atoned for all sin. For Christians, the sacrifice of Christ is the supreme expression of divine love. Similarly, they see in his resurrection and ascension into heaven a sign that not even death can separate from God those who respond to God's love. Although they remain imperfect, Christians believe that the destructive power of sin is no longer the primary force in their lives, for they have been baptized into a new "life in Christ."

We begin our investigation of Christianity with a survey of its teachings. We then trace the history of Christianity from the earliest days after the death of Jesus to the present time. Finally, we explore the practices by which Christians give outward expression to their beliefs in their daily lives.

THE TEACHINGS OF CHRISTIANITY

By the first century (as was discussed in Chapter 11), Palestinian Jews had endured centuries of oppression under foreign conquerors, always struggling to preserve their unique religion and culture. Their situation became especially dangerous with the arrival of the Romans (63 B.C.E.), whose brutality fueled a bitter resentment that ultimately led to a Jewish rebellion. Tragically, the revolt ended with the destruction of the Jerusalem Temple, the center of Jewish religious life, in 70 C.E.

TIMELINE
Christianity

c. 30 C.E. Crucifixion of Jesus.

c. 46–60 Paul's missionary journeys.

70–100 Gospels of Matthew, Mark, Luke, and John written.

313 Constantine decrees religious freedom for Christians.

325 Council of Nicea declares God the Son to be "of the same substance as God the Father."

354–430 Augustine of Hippo, first great theologian of the West and author of the *Confessions* and *City of God.*

367 Contents of New Testament established.

529 Benedict of Nursia writes the *Benedictine Rule.*

949–1022 Simeon the New Theologian and the beginning of Hesychasm.

c. 1000 Conversion of Russia to Orthodox Christianity begins.

1054 The Great Schism divides the churches of East and West.

1095–1272 Western Crusaders repeatedly attempt to free the Holy Land from Muslim rule.

1184 Pope Lucius III inaugurates the Inquisition.

1198–1216 Height of papal power under Innocent III.

1265–1274 Thomas Aquinas writes the *Summa Theologica.*

1453 Constantinople, capital of the Byzantine Empire, falls to the Ottoman Turks.

1517 Reformation begins when Martin Luther posts his Ninety-Five Theses.

1534 King Henry VIII establishes Church of England.

1545–1563 Council of Trent, at which the Roman Catholic Church responds to the Protestant movement.

1647 George Fox founds the Society of Friends (Quakers).

1703–1791 John Wesley, founder of the Methodist movement.

1804–1814 Napoleon, Emperor of the French, acts to strip the Roman Catholic Church of its influence.

1834 The Spanish Inquisition, the last stage of the Inquisition, is formally abolished.

1869–1870 First Vatican Council declares doctrine of papal infallibility.

1962–1965 Second Vatican Council.

1948 Founding of the World Council of Churches.

The Jewish people responded to these pressures in different ways. Pharisees defended Jewish tradition through strict observance of the Torah. Sadducees cooperated with the Romans in the hope of preserving social stability. Zealots advocated anti-Roman violence. Essenes withdrew to the desert lands outside Jerusalem to wait for divine deliverance.

Believing that God would soon bring an end to unrighteousness, many Jews looked for the coming of a **Messiah** who would inaugurate a new era of justice and peace. Originally, *messiah* ("anointed one") was a title given to Israel's kings, who were anointed with oil as a sign of God's favor. Later, it came to mean the deliverer God would send to save the Jewish people from oppression. Some looked for a supernatural Messiah. Others watched for a descendant of David, ancient Israel's greatest king. Most believed the Messiah would rule as king and judge the wicked and the righteous.

The first Christians were Palestinian Jews who believed that Jesus of Nazareth was the Messiah—in Greek, the *Christos*, or "Christ." They proclaimed him as a deliverer not from earthly oppression but from the power of sin. In Jesus, these long-oppressed people saw the beginning of a new era of righteousness and peace evident in his teachings, miracles, death, and resurrection.

The Life of Jesus

Our most important sources for the life and teachings of Jesus are the **gospels** of Matthew, Mark, Luke, and John. Written between approximately 70 and 100 c.e., the gospels are early Christian proclamations of the "good news" ("gospel," from Middle English *godspel*, translates the Greek *evangelion*, "good news") about Jesus's teachings, suffering, death, and resurrection. Because their interests are more theological than biographical, the gospels leave much unsaid about the life of Jesus. Still, their essential agreement on many points does allow us to establish the general outlines of his career and teachings.

The gospels report that Jesus was born in the Judean city of Bethlehem (most scholars place his birth between 4 and 1 b.c.e.) and spent his youth in the Galilean village of Nazareth. At about the age of thirty, he made his way south to the Judean wilderness, where he was baptized by John the Baptist in the River Jordan. A prophetic figure who warned of God's imminent judgment, John called on sinners to repent and be baptized in water as a sign of spiritual cleansing.

Mass baptism of Christians at Yardenit, the site on the Jordan River in Northern Israel where Christian tradition says Jesus was baptized by John the Baptist.

After his baptism, Jesus began a ministry that lasted no more than three years. The gospels say that as he traveled throughout Galilee he performed healings and miracles that testified to God's presence within him. The gospel accounts also describe Jesus as a charismatic teacher who spoke with authority on the scriptures and urged repentance and baptism in anticipation of the coming **kingdom of God**, a new era of peace and holiness. He was accompanied by an inner group of disciples, sometimes called "the twelve," led by three Galilean fishermen (Peter, James, and John), as well as by people from towns, villages, and the countryside. There were also Galilean women among Jesus's disciples who supported his ministry with their own resources. Indeed, women figure prominently in the gospel accounts of Jesus's ministry. Rejecting the social norms of his time, he befriended women and spoke and ate with them both in public and in private. When even the twelve abandoned Jesus in his final days, it was only the faithful women among his followers who remained with him.

As enthusiasm for his teachings and miracles grew, Jesus's popularity aroused resentment and opposition among members of the religious establishment. Jesus himself appears to have understood that dark days lay ahead. As he prepared to leave Galilee for Jerusalem, he warned his disciples that rejection, suffering, and death awaited him there.

Jesus arrived in the holy city just before Passover. The gospels describe a triumphal entry in which crowds greeted him as the Messiah. Entering the Temple, he caused a great stir by driving out those who did business there, accusing them of making the sacred place a "den of robbers." For several days Jesus taught in the Temple, but then events took an ominous turn. After celebrating a "Last Supper" (perhaps a Passover Seder meal) with his disciples, Jesus was brought before a council of Jewish leaders and

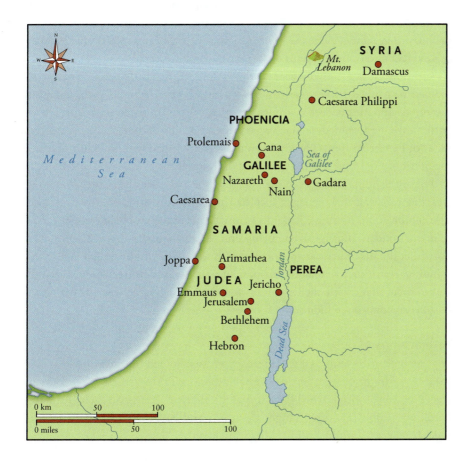

Palestine during the time of Jesus.

then handed over to Pontius Pilate, the Roman governor. Fearing that Jesus was a threat to public order, Pilate ordered his execution. Jesus was crucified less than a week after he had entered Jerusalem.

The gospels add theological reflections to this historical outline. Matthew and Luke assert that Jesus's mother, Mary, was a virgin who conceived miraculously in fulfillment of prophecy (Isaiah 7:14). All four of the gospels say that the Spirit of God, or the Holy Spirit, descended upon Jesus at the time of his baptism. According to Matthew, Mark, and Luke, a voice from heaven then declared: "This is my Son, the Beloved, with whom I am well pleased" (Matthew 3:17). In this way, the gospels link Jesus to King David, who is described in Psalms 2:1–7 as God's "anointed" and "son." The gospels also identify Jesus as the "servant" of God who would suffer for the sake of humanity, as foretold by one of Israel's prophets (Isaiah 42:1–4; 53:10–12). In making these connections, the gospels reveal their understanding of the kind of Messiah Jesus was to be: a Son of God who, filled with the Spirit of God, would suffer for the sins of others. Finally, the gospels report that women who had followed Jesus found his tomb empty at dawn on the Sunday following his crucifixion. They and the other disciples were overjoyed when Jesus appeared to them and they remembered what he had once told them: "The Son of Man must undergo great suffering, and be rejected by the elders, chief priests, and scribes, and be killed, and on the third day rise again" (Luke 9:22). Convinced that he was indeed God's Messiah, they began to proclaim the good news that God had acted through Jesus for the salvation of the world.

According to the Acts of the Apostles (found in the Christian scriptures), Jesus remained with his disciples for forty days after his resurrection. Then, having sent them out as **apostles** (Greek *apostolos*, "one who is sent out") to preach to Jews and Gentiles alike, he ascended into heaven. Several days later, as they celebrated the Jewish holiday of **Pentecost**, Jesus's followers were suddenly "filled with the Holy Spirit," the same Spirit of God that had descended upon Jesus at his baptism (Acts 2:2–4). Empowered by the Spirit to carry out the mission Jesus had given them, they found themselves able to speak in languages they had not known before, to prophesy, and to perform miraculous healings. According to Acts, the number of believers grew rapidly, for "many wonders and signs were being done by the apostles" (Acts 2:43). Acts also reports that the first Christians spent "much time together in the temple" (Acts 2:46), reminding us that they were Jews who continued to live and worship as Jews. It did not occur to them that their belief that Jesus was the Messiah had given them a new religious identity outside of Judaism.

The Teachings of Jesus

The gospels describe Jesus as a great teacher who astounded the crowds who gathered to hear him, "for he taught them as one having authority" (Matthew 7:29). Though he engaged in debate with learned Pharisees and Sadducees, Jesus also took great interest in ordinary people. He often taught them in **parables**, stories that employed vivid images from everyday life to illustrate spiritual truths.

The central theme in Jesus's teaching was the kingdom of God (in Matthew, the kingdom of heaven). For Jesus, the kingdom of God was not an ordinary realm but the state of affairs that exists when human beings recognize God's sovereignty over the world and respond in love and obedience to God's will. To put it another way, the kingdom of God means the world as it ought to be, a world in which God's love and righteous rule are fully realized. In the gospels, Jesus sometimes speaks of the kingdom as a future event to be heralded by dramatic signs such as a darkening sun and stars falling from heaven. In the midst of these cataclysmic events, the present age would pass away and the kingdom would be revealed in all its glory. But Jesus also spoke of the kingdom as already present within himself and his followers. Asked when it would come, he replied, "The kingdom of God *is* among you" (Luke 17:21). Though it was still small, Jesus expected the kingdom to grow into something great and wondrous. In one of his parables, he compared it to a tiny mustard seed that "grows up and becomes the greatest of all shrubs, and puts forth large branches, so that the birds of the air can make nests in its shade" (Mark 4:30). Whether speaking of the kingdom of God as present or future, Jesus emphasized its all-surpassing importance. Nothing can compare to the kingdom, he said, and so it is worth any price: "The kingdom of heaven is like treasure hidden in a field, which someone found and hid; then in his joy he goes and sells all that he has and buys that field" (Matthew 13:44).

Jesus taught that the kingdom of God is open to all who repent. By repentance, he meant something more than a mere expression of regret for some wrong one has done. The Greek *metanoia* ("a change of mind") found in the gospels suggests a turning away from anything that might prevent one from doing God's will. Like other Jews, Jesus found God's will expressed in the Torah and its commandments. In his famous Sermon on the Mount (Matthew 5–7), however, he gave the commandments his own interpretation, emphasizing that what God requires is obedience in thought as well as in deed. Thus, true obedience to the commandment against murder goes beyond not killing; it means never harboring anger toward anyone in one's heart. Similarly, the commandment against adultery prohibits not only the act itself but any thought of it (Matthew 5:21–28). For Jesus, it was this absolute obedience to the will of God that constituted the true righteousness of the kingdom of God.

Jesus also taught that true obedience to God's commandments was an expression of love. When pressed by a Pharisee to identify the greatest of the commandments, he cited two (Deuteronomy 6:5 and Leviticus 19:18), explaining that they embody the essence of scripture: "'You shall love the Lord your God with all your heart, and with all your soul, and with all your mind.' This is the greatest and first commandment. And a second is like it: 'You shall love your neighbor as yourself.' On these two commandments hang all the law and the prophets" (Matthew 22:37–40).

The nature of love lies at the heart of Jesus's teachings. Jesus taught that genuine love knows no limits and is offered freely to everyone: "Love your enemies and pray for those who persecute you, so that you may be children of your Father in heaven" (Matthew 5:44–45). Understood in this way, love leaves no room for the condemnation of others: "Do not judge, so that you may not be judged" (Matthew 7:1). Instead, love requires forgiveness: "For if you forgive others their trespasses, your heavenly Father will also forgive you" (Matthew 6:14). These principles are richly illustrated in Jesus's parables. The parable of the Good Samaritan (Luke 10:25–37), for example, demonstrates that even enemies deserve love and compassion. In the parable of the Prodigal Son (Luke 15:11–32), a father greets a dissolute and disrespectful son who has returned home—not with any thought of reproach, but with love and forgiveness gladly given.

The gospels describe Jesus as embodying these principles of repentance, obedience, and love. They also depict Jesus as living in the expectation of his crucifixion. In Mark, he tells his disciples that his death will be "a ransom for many" (Mark 10:45). Jesus spoke of God as Father, sometimes using the Aramaic *abba* ("papa") to suggest a relationship of special intimacy, as well as obedience. He urged his followers to draw close to God as well. They were God's children, he told them. As such, they should approach God in prayer with the words "Our Father" (Matthew 6:9) and with confidence that, like a loving parent, he would provide for their needs (Luke 12:22–31).

As we discuss later in this section, these fundamental teachings of Jesus lie at the heart of what Christians believe about sin, divine love, and salvation. But we first turn our attention to Paul of Tarsus, the first great interpreter of the life and teachings of Jesus, to see how Christian beliefs began to take shape in the years immediately following Jesus's crucifixion.

Paul and the Mission to the Gentiles

The most famous of the Jewish Christians who took the gospel and its teachings to Gentile lands was **Paul of Tarsus**. A Pharisee devoted to Judaism, Paul had been a persecutor of Christians, but after a dramatic experience of the risen Christ (Acts 9:1–19), he dedicated himself to preaching Christianity in Asia Minor (modern Turkey), Greece, and Macedonia. In his letters to young churches in Corinth, Thessalonica, Rome, and other cities, we can see Paul breaking with traditional Jewish thought in emphasizing God's love for Gentiles and disputing the necessity of observing the commandments in the Torah. Because Paul was the first to describe the role of Jesus in the salvation of humanity from sin, some have described him as the second founder—and even the *true* founder—of Christianity. It was due in part to his influence that Christianity was transformed in the middle of the first century from a Jewish sect into a largely Gentile movement.

At the heart of Paul's teaching was his belief that in Jesus Christ God had acted to bring salvation from sin to the world. Paul saw sin as a condition affecting all humanity: "All have sinned and fall short of the glory of God" (Romans 3:23). Controlling human beings and separating them from God, sin corrupts and ultimately destroys human life (Romans 6:23). For Paul, the good news of the gospel was that God's promise of salvation from sin, anticipated in the Jewish Scriptures, had been fulfilled in Jesus's death on the cross. Though sinless and undeserving of death, Jesus had offered himself as a sacrifice in atonement for all sin. Although Paul's language of "sin," "sacrifice," and "atonement" may sound strange today, it is really quite similar to what we might mean when we say we have done some "wrong" to someone and that we must do something to "make up for it." In Paul's time, Jews and Gentiles alike understood that sacrifice was the means of "making up for" an offense against God, or the gods.

Paul was always emphatic in maintaining that salvation cannot be earned by "works," whether human efforts to obey the commandments in the Torah (Galatians 3:10) or good works in general. Instead, he taught that the salvation made possible by Christ's sacrifice is a gift, the ultimate expression of God's love, or **grace**. Salvation is given to those who respond to God's grace in faith, the conviction that God has acted through Jesus Christ to atone for human sin. Although Paul was very clear in teaching that salvation depends on God's grace and the individual's turning to God in faith, he did not dismiss the importance of works. In Romans 2:5–10, for example, he says that people will be held responsible for the good and evil they do. Paul's letters are not always precise about the relationship between faith and works, but they leave no doubt about the necessity and priority of faith. In his letter to the Galatians (2:16), Paul wrote that individuals are brought into a right relationship with God "not by works of the law but through faith in Jesus Christ."

For Paul, faith does more than bring salvation; it unites the believer with Christ in a "newness of life" (Romans 6:4) so real that Paul could say, "It is no longer I who live, but it is Christ who lives in me" (Galatians 2:20). Like the apostles who had been filled with the Holy Spirit at Pentecost, Paul believed that the Spirit lives in believers and brings them into union with God. To the Christians at Rome he wrote: "You are in the Spirit, since the Spirit of God dwells in you" (Romans 8:9). As a divine presence within, the Spirit encourages the growth of spiritual virtues, the greatest of which is love (1 Corinthians 12:27–14:1). Paul also believed that the Spirit makes all Christians one in the Church, which he often called the "body of Christ" (1 Corinthians 12:12–27).

Like other early Christians, Paul looked forward to a time when Christ would return in glory to bring an end to evil, sin, and suffering (1 Corinthians 15:20–28). But he also believed that the transformation of the world, signaled by the resurrection of Christ, had already begun. Signs of change were especially evident in the lives of believers, who had been renewed, even recreated, through the action of God's grace: "So if anyone is in Christ, there is a new creation; everything old has passed away; see, everything has become new!" (2 Corinthians 5:17).

God, Creation, and Original Humanity

Christian thought about God, the world, and humanity begins with the first verse in the Bible: "In the beginning God created the heavens and the earth" (Genesis 1:1). Here, and in the story of creation that follows, the Bible makes a clear distinction be- tween created things and their Creator. God is transcendent, existing outside space, time, and the other limiting factors that give the world its order and finitude. And yet God is also immanent, or present in the world, sustaining and caring for all things with a loving benevolence that touches even the least of creatures.

Much as a work of art tells us something about the artist, Christians believe that creation tells us something about God. Paul made this point in his letter to the Romans: "Ever since the creation of the world his eternal power and divine nature, invisible though they are, have been understood and seen through the things he has made" (Romans 1:20). For Christians, the goodness, beauty, power, and design evident in the world are all expressions of God's nature. But it is God's goodness, and the consequent goodness of the world itself, that are emphasized in the biblical story of the world's beginnings. At the completion of each stage of creation, it says, "God saw that it was good" (Genesis 1:10, 18, 21, 25, 31). Finally, Christianity teaches that the entire order of existing things, and especially human beings, is the deliberate and purposeful expression of a divine love that a grateful creation should return to God in praise. "Let heaven and earth praise him, the seas and everything that moves in them" (Psalms 69:34).

Christians believe that, despite its original perfection, the world as we know it today falls far short of God's intentions, plagued as it is by suffering, injustice, and death. These evils cannot be attributed to God, however, for they are completely opposed to God's perfection. Instead, Christianity points to creation itself—and, more specifically, to humanity.

The story of creation relates that "God created humankind in his image" (Genesis 1:27). For centuries, Christian thinkers have sought to understand all that is entailed by this assertion. Some have found the image of God in the human capacity for rational thought. Others have said it can be seen in the "dominion" God gave to human beings over all the earth (Genesis 1:26), which resembles God's rule over the entire universe. All Christian thought, however, acknowledges that human beings have a unique ability to relate to God, and to love God, just as God relates to and loves them.

Andrei Rublev's icon of the Holy Trinity (1411) is considered a masterpiece of Orthodox religious art. It depicts (from left to right) God the Father, God the Son, and God the Holy Spirit. On one level, the three figures are the "angels" through whom God appeared to Abraham in the Old Testament. On a higher level, they represent the Trinity in a way that uses color, light, and imagery to give the viewer a glimpse into its unfathomable mystery.

This idea is found in the biblical narrative that describes how God placed Adam and Eve, the first human beings, in a garden-like paradise called Eden. Whether we understand Adam and Eve as literal human beings or as symbols of original humanity—the Hebrew word *adam* means "humankind"—the point of the story remains the same. For as long as human beings related to God in loving obedience, they lived in joyous harmony with their Creator, but their eventual decision to disobey God brought an end to that harmony and, consequently, to the harmony of creation as a whole (Genesis 2:4–3:24). It was through sin that evil in all its forms became a reality in the world. Worst of all, sin separated humanity from God. In the Christian view, the salvation of creation from sin's destructive effects begins with the salvation of human beings. It is only through salvation from sin that they are restored to that original relationship with God in which they find their true place, purpose, and fulfillment. In the words of Augustine, the great fifth-century saint, "You have made us for yourself, and our hearts are restless until they find rest in you."[1]

God as Trinity

Like Judaism, Christianity is a monotheistic religion. But Christianity differs from its parent religion in defining the one God in terms of three aspects of divinity. For Christians, there is a single divine nature that expresses itself eternally in the "persons" of Father, Son, and Holy Spirit.

The doctrine of the Trinity was not put into precise language until 381 at the Council of Constantinople, one of the meetings at which early Christian leaders assembled to establish doctrine. Building on the work of the Council of Nicea (325), the **bishops** at Constantinople produced the **Nicene Creed**, a statement of the doctrine that many Christians continue to recite in public worship:

> We believe in one God, the Father, the Almighty,
>> maker of heaven and earth, of all that is seen and unseen.
> We believe in one Lord, Jesus Christ, the only Son of God,
>> eternally begotten of the Father,
>> God from God, Light from Light, true God from true God,
>> begotten, not made, one in Being with the Father.
>> Through him all things were made.
>> For us and for our salvation he came down from heaven:
>> by the power of the Holy Spirit
>> he was born of the Virgin Mary, and became man.
>> For our sake he was crucified under Pontius Pilate;
>> he suffered, died, and was buried.
>> On the third day he rose again in fulfillment of the scriptures;
>> he ascended into heaven and is seated at the right hand of the Father.
>> He will come again in glory to judge the living and the dead,
>> and his kingdom will have no end.
> We believe in the Holy Spirit, the Lord, the giver of life,
>> who proceeds from the Father [*and from the Son*].
>> He has spoken through the prophets.
>> We believe in one holy catholic ["universal"] and apostolic Church.
>> We acknowledge one baptism for the forgiveness of sins.
>> We look for the resurrection of the dead,
>> and the life of the world to come. Amen.

As you can see, the Creed is divided into three parts corresponding to the three "persons" of the Trinity. It tells us about the relationships among the three persons as well as the functions of each.

How do Christian teachings about God compare with those of the related religions of Judaism and Islam and those of Hinduism and Buddhism?

Adam and Eve Banished from Paradise. In this fresco, the Renaissance painter Tommaso Masaccio (1401–1428) captured both the shame of Adam and Eve and the fear they felt as they were expelled from the Garden of Eden and separated from God.

The opening statement is about God the Father, the omnipotent ("almighty") Creator of all reality, spiritual as well as material, visible as well as invisible. There is one God, upon whom all things depend for their existence.

The second part of the Creed focuses on God the Son, who is "one in Being with the Father"—that is, of the same divine substance or essence as the Father. For the sake of humanity, the Son became fully human as well as fully divine. This is why Jesus, as God incarnate, can say in the Gospel of John: "I and the Father are one" (John 10:30). As a revelation of divinity on earth, the Son enabled those who recognized him as such to come to a greater understanding of God: "If you know me, you will know my Father also" (John 14:7). Beyond revealing the Father, the Son has three other roles. First, recalling the Gospel of John (1:3), the Creed states that "through him all things were made." Second, the suffering and death of the Son have made salvation possible. Third, the Son, as the risen Christ, will one day return to judge the world.

The final part of the Creed affirms that the Holy Spirit "proceeds" from the Father, implying the Spirit's sameness in substance or essence with the Father. The addition of the Latin *filioque* ("and from the Son") by the Western Church, never accepted in the East, underscores the sameness of all three persons of the Trinity. Just as the Father represents God's power in the creation of the world, and just as the Son both reveals the Father and redeems a sinful humanity, the Holy Spirit represents God's continuing presence in the world. Since the beginning, when God breathed the "breath of life" into Adam (Hebrew *ruach* means both "breath" and "spirit"), the Spirit has given life to all of creation. Christians believe that since the descent of the Holy Spirit at Pentecost, it has animated, empowered, and guided the Church. Finally, it is the Spirit within that helps believers as they reach out to God in prayer (Romans 8:26) and that nurtures virtues such as love, patience, kindness, gentleness, and self-control (Galatians 5:22–23).

Sin and Human Nature

Christianity emphasizes the sinfulness of human nature. This may seem a harsh way of thinking about human beings. After all, there are good reasons to believe in their essential *goodness*. Of course, Christians do acknowledge the human capacity to do good things. But they are equally aware of the human capacity for evil and the fact that people are often destructive in their thought and behavior. Christianity teaches that sin is universal; everyone sins. It also insists that the tendency to sin is far more serious than an acquired habit one might overcome through greater self-control or moral effort. The inability of human beings to rise above sin—to be as loving, humble, generous, and righteous as they should be—suggests that something has gone wrong within human nature. In the Christian view, because human beings cannot overcome sin on their own, they stand in need of salvation from its power over them—a power that cuts them off from God, the source of all good things.

Grace and Salvation

For Christianity, sin is the fundamental problem of human existence. But it is a problem solved by the good news of God's grace, the love God gives freely to human beings despite their sin. In the Christian view, it is only through reliance on divine grace that salvation from sin becomes possible.

Christianity explains *how* salvation is made possible by using the language of sacrifice, a common Jewish practice in Jesus's time. In the sacrificial ritual, the sins of the people were ritually placed on animals sacrificed as innocent victims for the transgressions of others. For Christians, Jesus's death on the cross was the fulfillment of this sacrificial practice. It is with his crucifixion that the significance of the Christian teaching that Jesus Christ was both human and divine becomes clear. Jesus's divinity allowed him to do for human beings what they could not do for themselves. As the sinless "lamb of God" (John 1:29), he alone could make the perfect atonement for sin that would allow sinners to be restored to their original relationship with God. As a human being, he could suffer the consequences of sin on behalf of humanity. In doing so, Christians say, Jesus fulfilled the words of the Old Testament prophet Isaiah, who spoke of the "suffering servant" of God: "But he was wounded for our transgressions, crushed for our iniquities; upon him was the punishment that made us whole, and by his bruises we are healed" (Isaiah 53:5). Christians see in Christ's suffering for the salvation of humanity the supreme proof of God's grace:

> God is love. God's love was revealed among us in this way: God sent his only Son into the world so that we might live through him. In this is love, not that we loved God but that he loved us and sent his Son to be the atoning sacrifice for our sins.
>
> —*1 John 4:8*

Grace makes salvation possible, but it requires a human response in the form of faith. For Christians, faith is more than intellectual acceptance of the fact that God has made salvation possible through Jesus Christ. Faith in God involves a wholehearted opening of oneself to God so that God's love replaces sinfulness as the prevailing power in one's life.

For Roman Catholic and Orthodox Christians, as well as for some Protestants, good works are an expression of faith, even a part of faith, as a faith that does not involve action is not faith at all. As the New Testament letter of James (3:23) puts it, "So faith by itself, apart from works, is dead." Most Protestants, on the other hand, make a distinction between faith and good works. Because works, they believe, are not a part of faith, works do not contribute to salvation. In support of this view, Protestants cite New Testament passages such as Paul's letter to the Romans (3:28), "For we hold that a person is justified by faith apart from works. . . ." For those who hold this view, good works are something one does *because* one has faith. The differences here are finely nuanced, but they have profound implications that are partly responsible for the separation of the Roman Catholic, Orthodox, and Protestant traditions.

Christians admit that they are no closer to perfection than anyone else, yet they are confident that faith allows them to "walk in a newness of life" (Romans 6:4) on a path that leads toward rather than away from God.

The Church

Christians do not live the Christian life in isolation. Instead, their faith and baptism unite them with all other believers. In its most basic sense, the Church is the sum of all believers, but most Christians believe that the Church is far more than this. Following Paul, they understand the Church as the "body of Christ," a body whose diverse members are unified by the Holy Spirit: "For just as the body is one and has many members, and all the members of the body, though many, are one body, so it is with Christ. For in the one Spirit we were all baptized into one body—Jews or Greeks, slaves or free—and we were all made to drink of one Spirit" (1 Corinthians 12:13).

VOICES: An Interview with Terrie M. and Father Art

Terrie M. is a member of a Roman Catholic church in Sacramento. Father Art is one of three priests who serve its nearly three thousand members.

How does the Roman Catholic Church stand in relation to other Christian churches?

Terrie: Some people mistakenly make a distinction between "Catholics" and "Christians," so I want to begin by saying that to be a Catholic is to be a Christian. We share with other Christians our belief in Jesus as Lord. Like other Christians, we believe that salvation comes through faith. We Catholics also believe that God's love and compassion are boundless and given to all, and so we cannot say that the Roman Catholic Church is the only path to salvation.

Father Art: We share with other Christians our reverence for Sacred Scripture, the inspired Word of God, but we have equal reverence for Sacred Tradition, the handing on to each new generation of the wider reality of all that the Church is and believes—that is, its doctrine, life, and worship. The Church's teaching authority [*Magisterium*], guided by the Holy Spirit, is both the servant and the authentic interpreter of the Word of God revealed in Sacred Scripture and Sacred

Tradition. This authority, exercised in the name of Jesus Christ, has been entrusted to the bishops in communion with the Bishop of Rome. Catholics grieve that not all Christians share this belief, but I know that all Christian churches recognize some form of tradition and teaching authority, as well as the authority of Sacred Scripture. Our sacred task is to pray and to work for that unity of all Christians desired by Jesus.

What is the great problem of human existence?

Terrie: The great problem we face as human beings is sin, which separates us from God and ultimately results in death. We come into this world, not evil, but certainly with the ability to sin as part of our human condition. Much suffering is caused when we make a choice to live for ourselves. But we are also born with God's grace, an unmerited love that is given freely. Reconciliation is possible for all and there is nothing that cannot be forgiven. Through the love of God through Christ Jesus, even death has been conquered and the original goodness of humanity is restored.

Father Art: Sin not only separates us from God, it prevents us from being all that God intends us to be. We are justified before God thanks to the gratuitous gift of God's grace in Jesus Christ, crucified and risen, given us by the Holy Spirit at baptism. By the gift of God's grace, we are enabled to live lives of faith expressed in love.

Does being a Roman Catholic give you a heightened awareness or a different way of looking at reality?

Terrie: My reality as a Catholic is grounded in Christ's teaching that we must love and live for each other. We do not go it alone. It is this knowledge and awareness that helps me see that the joys and challenges of life are navigated together. It is perhaps in the celebration of the Eucharist that I am most aware of my union with others, for this ritual is not so much about eating as it is about sharing— our stories, all that we are, and all that we have.

Terrie M. and Father Art

Father Art: Yes, Christ is made manifest to us in the liturgy and the sacraments, and especially in the Eucharist. His presence there heightens our sensitivity to his presence throughout the world, in everyday life, in our work, and in our relationships, so that every moment and every situation becomes an opportunity for praise and worship and for sharing our joy with others.

Scripture

When the first Christians spoke of scripture, they meant the Jewish Scriptures. In Greek, these texts were called *ta biblia*, or "the books"—hence, our English "Bible." It was not long, however, before certain Christian writings assumed an importance equal to that of the Jewish Scriptures. By the end of the fourth century, there was general agreement that twenty-seven of these texts had greater authority than all others. These came to be known collectively as the New Testament. Since then, the Christian Bible has consisted of the Old Testament (the Jewish Scriptures) and the New Testament. In Christian interpretation, the Old Testament, which tells of

God's covenant with the Jewish people, anticipates and is fulfilled by the New Testament, which reveals that the Messiah has come and established a new and universal covenant between God and the Church. Roman Catholic and Orthodox versions of the Bible also include several Deuterocanonical ("secondary canon") texts, which they place in the Old Testament. Protestants call these texts the Apocrypha ("hidden texts") and sometimes place them between the Old and New Testaments in their versions of the Bible.

The first four books in the New Testament are the gospels. Although tradition attributes the gospels to specific individuals, some of them disciples of Jesus, none identifies its author by name. Each gospel portrays Jesus in its own way. In the Gospel of Mark, Jesus is a Messiah who resolutely submits to suffering on behalf of humanity. In the Gospel of Matthew, Jesus is a figure reminiscent of Moses who reveals the true meaning of the Torah. The Gospel of Luke focuses on Jesus's compassion for sinners, women, the poor, and the sick. Finally, the Gospel of John emphasizes the divinity of Jesus. In describing him as God's "Word" (Greek **logos**, "word," but also "divine reason") "made flesh," John presents Jesus as a revelation of God in human form.

The gospels are followed by the Acts of the Apostles, which describes the founding of the Church in Jerusalem and tells the story of Paul's missionary journeys. All but one of the texts that follow Acts are letters, many of them written by Paul. These texts describe the organization of the first Christian churches, tell us about early Christian beliefs and practices, and offer insights into the complex relationship between early Christianity and Judaism. The New Testament concludes with Revelation. Written at the end of the first century, when Christians were beginning to suffer persecution, Revelation is an apocalyptic text that employs vivid imagery in describing the coming of the kingdom of God after a climactic battle between good and evil.

Christians have always seen scripture as the revealed word of God. They turn to the Bible for instruction in doctrine, ethics, and higher truths, confident that this collection of divinely inspired texts has an authority that sets it above all others. But what, exactly, does "divinely inspired" mean? More important, does the Bible make the claim of divine inspiration about itself?

As it turns out, one New Testament text speaks of scripture as "God-breathed" (2 Timothy 3:16), which comes very close to "divinely inspired." Of course, the reference here is only to the Jewish Scriptures, or Old Testament, as the New Testament was not recognized as scripture until long after this text was written. Another New Testament passage describes the prophets of the Old Testament as men who "spoke from God as they were carried along by the Holy Spirit" (2 Peter 1:21). Two Old Testament passages say that God himself wrote the Ten Commandments (Exodus 24:12 and Deuteronomy 5:22). There are also several Old and New Testament texts that describe Old Testament figures as taking dictation from God when writing small portions of scripture (e.g., Ezekiel 11:5, Matthew 22:43). Beyond this, the Bible says little about divine inspiration.

Until the Reformation of the sixteenth century, divine inspiration was not an issue of great importance. The Roman Catholic and Orthodox traditions agreed that the biblical texts were *somehow* inspired by God, who chose their authors and worked *with* and *through* them, and that seems to have been enough. But the Protestant reformers advanced the doctrine that scripture is the only authority on which Christians can completely rely. This meant that that the authority of scripture had to be raised to a level at which it was beyond question. In order to do so, Protestant thinkers formulated a variety of theories to explain just how divine inspiration "works." Some claim that God inspired the biblical writers even to the point of determining every word they chose to use. Others say that God has ensured the truth of the message in the biblical texts but without influencing the means by which the biblical authors chose to communicate it.

Today, there is a broad range of opinion on divine inspiration and the Bible. Some Christians credit the authors of the biblical texts for their spiritual insights and leave little or no room for divine influence. Others downplay the human contribution to scripture, some to the point of attributing every word and idea to God.

The issue of divine inspiration is closely tied to that of biblical accuracy. As you might imagine, the more one emphasizes God's involvement in creating the biblical texts, the more necessary it becomes to insist on their inerrancy. After all, since God cannot lie or contradict himself, a Bible whose ultimate author is God cannot possibly contain even a single error. Of course, there do seem to be errors and contradictions in the Bible. In such cases, Christians who support absolute inerrancy use biblical, historical, and linguistic arguments to show that these are only apparent, not real. Those who endorse a limited inerrancy say that the Bible is inerrant in matters essential to faith and doctrine but may contain insignificant errors relating to geography and history. For the most part, conservative Protestants favor absolute inerrancy. Liberal Protestants, Roman Catholics, and Orthodox Christians tend to support limited inerrancy.

Tradition

Tradition has great authority in the lives of most people. We look to the accumulated wisdom of the past in forms such as laws and constitutions, scientific discoveries, masterpieces of art and literature, and folklore for guidance in organizing society and understanding the world and our place in it. In a similar way, Christians have always looked to their past for guidance in matters of belief and practice. For them, tradition is the "handing on" (Latin *traditio*) and continuing interpretation of the gospel message through the centuries. The idea of tradition is found in the Bible. In one of his letters to the Christians of Corinth, Paul wrote: "I handed on to you as of first importance what I in turn had received" (1 Corinthians 15:3). Although different groups define the content of tradition in different ways, in the broadest sense it includes creeds, forms of worship, doctrines, the decisions of church councils, papal decrees, the works of major theologians, and even the illustration of the gospel in art, music, and literature.

All Christians place great value on tradition. For Roman Catholics and Orthodox, its authority is on the same level as scripture. In fact, some point out that because the earliest Christians were "handing on" the faith even before the first New Testament texts were written, scripture can be seen as a *part* of tradition. Protestants set tradition below scripture but still acknowledge its importance. Most Protestants believe that tradition is helpful in understanding scripture and accept the ancient creeds, basic patterns of worship, and a great many other "traditional" features of belief and practice.

"Last Things"

We have seen that Jesus proclaimed the coming of the kingdom of God—God's loving and righteous rule in the world. Jesus taught that the kingdom was already present in him and in his followers but that its full realization lay in the future. In doing so, he made a distinction between the *now* and the *not yet* that is evident throughout the New Testament.

The Letter to the Hebrews, for example, describes Christians as "those who have once been enlightened, and have tasted the heavenly gift, and have shared in the Holy Spirit, and have tasted the goodness of the word of God and the powers of the age to come" (Hebrews 6:4). Similarly, Paul's letters speak of world-transforming events that had already occurred, such as the resurrection of Christ and the descent of the Holy Spirit upon his followers, but they also look forward to events that would take place at the end of the age. Greek-speaking Christians called these events *ta eschata*, "the last things." They include eschatological events such as the Second Coming of Christ, the resurrection of the dead, the Last Judgment, and the glorious consummation of the kingdom of God.

Most early Christians assumed that the end of their age was not far off. As time passed, however, many came to believe that the consummation of the kingdom would occur within a spiritual context rather than in an earthly kingdom. There is a biblical basis for this view in the Gospel of John, whose "realized eschatology" holds that events such as judgment and resurrection into eternal life have already been realized in the interior lives of believers. Both points of view are still very much alive today, and so it is fair to say that Christians hold a very wide range of opinions with respect to the time and nature of the fulfillment of God's purposes in the world.

The Afterlife

Like the adherents of many other religions, Christians believe that human existence extends beyond this life. In the afterlife, the consequences of the choices people make now in relation to God and God's grace will be fully realized. Traditionally, Christians have illustrated these consequences with images of heaven and hell. Some also believe in purgatory, an intermediate state between earthly life and heaven.

Christian beliefs about the afterlife have been influenced by the cultures in which Christianity has developed, as well as by scripture. As a result, they are extremely varied and complex.

Heaven Perhaps it is best to begin with what most Christians believe about heaven. In essence, heaven is perfect and eternal union with God, the fulfillment of the true purpose and deepest desire of human beings. Whether understood as an actual place or a state of being, as physical or spiritual, as earthly or celestial, "heaven" always means the ineffable bliss of everlasting existence in the loving presence of God.

Although the New Testament texts make frequent reference to heaven, they do not describe it in detail. Instead, the New Testament authors provide glimpses of heaven as the city of God, the heavenly Jerusalem, life everlasting, the holy place, and the great reward. In the gospels, Jesus speaks of heaven as "paradise" (Luke 23:43) and as a place he will prepare for his followers (John 14:2–3). Paul's letters describe heaven both as the present dwelling place of God and as the future home of believers. According to Paul, Christians can be certain of heaven because their experience of the Holy Spirit in this life gives them a taste of a future reality in which mortality will be "swallowed up by life" (2 Corinthians 5:12).

For some Christians, heaven is not a place but a spiritual state of being. This view evinces the influence of ancient Greek thought, which held that the true self is an immortal soul that can exist apart from the body and beyond space and time. For other Christians, heaven is the abode of God in the starry firmament above the earth. With roots in both the Old and New Testaments, this conception of heaven as a physical place is associated with the belief that those in heaven will possess physical bodies made perfect and immortal following the resurrection of the dead that will occur when Christ returns to judge the world (1 Corinthians 15; Philippians 3:20). Finally, some Christians understand heaven as an earthly phenomenon. The basis for this view is the vision of "a new heaven and a new earth" in the New Testament book of Revelation (21–22). According to Revelation, the day will come when a "heavenly Jerusalem" will become present on earth. Here, evils such as death and disease will no longer exist, and God himself will live among his people.

Purgatory One of the most striking differences between Christian views of the afterlife concerns **purgatory**. In Roman Catholic thought, purgatory is an intermediate place or state between earthly life and heaven in which the souls of the dead suffer temporal punishment due for sin. Just as a friend might forgive you for some wrong you have done but still expect you to suffer a bit in demonstrating your sorrow, Roman Catholic doctrine holds that sinners must make reparation or satisfaction for sins already forgiven by God. Traditionally imagined as a cleansing fire, purgatory offers the opportunity to complete the work of reparation left undone in earthly life. The scriptural basis for belief in purgatory is found in 2 Maccabees (12:39–45), a deuterocanonical text in which prayer is offered for the dead so that "they might be released from their sin."

Although Orthodox Christianity does not accept the Roman Catholic doctrine of purgatory, most Orthodox Christians believe that after death souls enter a "condition of waiting" in which they can benefit from prayers said on their behalf. Protestant

Christians reject belief in purgatory because they find no basis for it in scripture (most Protestant Bibles do not include 2 Maccabees).

Hell   Hell is not so much God's punishment for sin as the self-imposed consequence of rejecting God's grace. Some Christians understand hell as an actual place, others think of it as a state of being, and still others do not believe in hell at all. In describing why hell must exist, one Orthodox writer has said: "God will not force us to love Him, for love is no longer love if it is not free; how then can God reconcile to Himself those who refuse all reconciliation?"[2]

The word translated as "hell" in English versions of the New Testament is Gehenna, the name of a valley bordering Jerusalem where many Jews in the time of Jesus expected that the worst of sinners would one day suffer torment. Thus Gehenna works well as a way of illustrating the pain of separation from God. Although hell clearly refers to a state of existence, there is little basis in the New Testament for understanding it as an actual place. It was not until the early Middle Ages that hell was transformed in the popular imagination into a subterranean pit of fiery horrors.[3] Although hell has long been understood as a necessary expression of divine justice, many Christian thinkers have found this idea to be inconsistent with God's love. Some have taught that God will ultimately save all people from the consequences of sin.

Christianity and Other Religions

Existing alongside other religions, Christianity has always sought to define itself in relation to them. This is particularly true of Judaism, within which it originated. The bitterness felt by Jewish Christians after their expulsion from synagogues in the first century can be seen in New Testament passages critical of Jewish piety and religious groups (for example, in Matthew 23 and John 5–8). It must also have influenced the gospel accounts of the crucifixion of Jesus, which place greater blame on Jewish authorities than on the Romans, who actually carried out the execution.

Tragically, the presence of anti-Jewish feeling in scripture continued to influence Christian attitudes toward Jews and Judaism long after the first century. Denounced as Christ-killers and enemies of humanity, seventh-century French and Spanish Jews were subjected to forced baptism. In the late Middle Ages, Jews were expelled from England, Spain, France, and Portugal. Anti-Jewish feeling assumed its most virulent form with the rise of fascism in Germany, Italy, and other parts of Europe in the twentieth century. It was not until after the Holocaust, the genocidal murder of six million Jews carried out by Nazi Germany during World War II, that church leaders began working for an end to hostility toward Jews and Judaism. At its inaugural meeting in 1948, the World Council of Churches declared that anti-Semitism is incompatible with the Christian faith and "a sin against God and man." Today, many Christian groups are engaged in efforts to heal the wounds of the past and to encourage a Jewish-Christian dialogue that will foster mutual appreciation and respect.

Historically, most Christians have believed that there is no salvation outside of the Church, a view based on New Testament passages that speak of Jesus as the only way in which God has been fully revealed to humanity. But the cultural pluralism of today's global society has raised interest in other ways of understanding spiritual realities. In fact, some Christians find a scriptural basis for the possibility of salvation in other religions. They point to Paul's letter to the Romans, which says that those who follow the dictates of their consciences will be judged as righteous on the last day (Romans 2:14–16). Similarly, the letter of James defines "pure" religion not in specifically Christian terms but as caring for the needy and keeping oneself "unstained by the world" (James 1:27). Biblical passages like these have encouraged many Christians to value the spiritual insights of other religious traditions and to enter into cooperative relationships with them. The spirit of this new attitude, expressed in formal statements by many Christian groups, is represented in the *Declaration on Non-Christian Religions* issued by the Roman Catholic bishops who assembled for the Second Vatican Council (1962–1965):

> Prudently and lovingly, through dialogue and collaboration with the followers of other religions and in witness of the Christian faith and life, we should acknowledge, preserve and promote the spiritual and moral goods found among these men, as well as the values in their society and culture.[4]

Changes in Christian thought remind us that the history of Christianity is a story about the changing ways in which the Church has existed in the world. We turn to that story now in order to discover how the Church of the earliest Christian centuries became the one, or ones, we know today.

THE HISTORY OF CHRISTIANITY

Christianity in the Roman World

Historians agree that Christianity spread steadily throughout the Roman Empire. As it did, Christians met with criticism and persecution that continued until Rome's emperors became Christians themselves. Also, as the Christian movement grew during these early years, it became necessary to define basic doctrines and to adopt a form of church government capable of uniting Christians and promoting uniformity of belief and practice among them.

The Church and the Roman State   The Roman world was often hostile to Christians. Many suspected them of disloyalty to Rome because they refused to recognize its gods or participate in public events that involved pagan rituals. Localized persecutions began in the first century and expanded into empire-wide assaults in the third. Despite the terrors of mass arrests and executions, however, persecution failed to check the growth of Christianity. A dramatic turning point came in 313, when the Emperor

The first Christian emperor of Rome, Constantine the Great promoted the spread of Christianity throughout the Roman Empire and founded a new capital at Constantinople (modern Istanbul) in 330.

Constantine (r. 306–337) defeated a rival after seeing a vision of a cross in the sky. Convinced that the God of the Christians had given him the victory, Constantine decreed religious freedom for Christians and began to promote Christianity by building churches and extending privileges to church leaders.

When Constantine transferred the imperial capital from Rome to Constantinople (modern Istanbul) in 330, he did so in the hope that it would be a truly Christian city free of paganism. Decades later, Theodosius I (r. 379–395) made Christianity the official state religion of the Roman Empire and began the suppression of other religions and schools of philosophy.

Diversity in the Early Church   During the first five centuries C.E., Christians formulated many important doctrines, thereby establishing a standard of orthodoxy, or "correct belief." However, some early Christian groups challenged the emerging mainstream Church on issues as basic as the nature of God, the humanity of Christ, salvation, and ecclesiastical (Greek *ekklesia*, "church") authority.

Three such groups are especially important. The first is Gnostic Christianity, whose unique writings, discovered in 1945, are still making news in popular magazines and television documentaries, as well as in scholarly publications. Some Gnostic beliefs were strikingly different from those of most Christians. Gnostics believed that Christ's body had been a mere illusion; therefore, he could not have atoned for sin by dying a physical death upon the cross. Salvation came instead from secret knowledge (Greek *gnosis*) that Christ gave only to a select group of *gnostics* ("knowers"), who had passed it down to others. Because Gnostic Christians saw all material reality as evil, they understood salvation as the liberation of souls from human bodies rather than as liberation from sin. Gnostics claimed that the Christianity preached publicly in churches was incomplete, as they alone understood the higher teachings of Christ.

A second group was founded by Marcion (c. 85–160 C.E.), a theologian who had been expelled from the church at Rome for teaching that there are two Gods: the God of the Jewish Scriptures, whom Marcion described as the unjust creator of an evil world, and the supremely good God revealed by Christ. According to Marcion, it was this good God who had sent Christ to rescue human souls. Seeking to cut Christianity off from its Jewish roots, Marcion rejected the Jewish Scriptures and all Christian texts that seemed dependent upon them.

A third form of Christianity, known as Montanism, began with Montanus, a charismatic prophet of the late second century who claimed to be the mouthpiece of the Holy Spirit. Montanus prophesied that Christ would soon return to a "new Jerusalem" that was about to appear in southern Asia Minor. The greatest difficulty posed by Montanus was his claim that he preached a *new* prophecy. This raised two critical questions. First, would Christian teaching require ongoing revision in order to accommodate every new group and its revelations? Second, did claims of prophetic inspiration give charismatic figures like Montanus an authority greater than that of church leaders?

Defining Orthodoxy Resolving questions related to correct belief, scripture, and the authority of the Church was one of the great themes in the early history of the Church. In order to establish its authority and define orthodox belief, the Church created a canon of scripture, formulated creeds, and implemented a system of ecclesiastical government that put authority into the hands of bishops.

We have already seen that a canon of scripture consisting of the Old and New Testaments was in place by the end of the fourth century. Texts widely believed to have been written by the apostles were included, as were writings from the apostolic era that were widely used in public worship. Because the Old and New Testaments were regarded as having a unique authority, they constituted a standard against which the orthodoxy of any new teaching could be judged.

The creeds developed by the early Church were formal and concise statements of essential Christian beliefs. In fact, the word *creed* itself comes from the Latin *credo*, which means "I believe." Creeds such as the Apostles' Creed and the Nicene Creed served two functions. The first is that they proclaimed orthodox doctrine on the incarnation, suffering, and death of Christ, as well as his resurrection and ascension into heaven. The second is that repeated recitation of the creeds by Christians throughout the empire promoted uniformity of belief within the Church.

Finally, the early Church established a form of government that concentrated power in the hands of bishops, who had jurisdiction over large territories called dioceses. According to the doctrine of **apostolic succession**, bishops were the successors of the apostles, who had been commissioned by Christ himself to lead the Church. Claiming to have received both their offices and correct belief through direct lines of transmission, they held an authority that Gnostics, Montanists, and Marcionite Christians found difficult to challenge. Bishops were assisted by priests, who were responsible for individual churches, and every church was served by deacons (Greek *diakonos*, "servant") who assisted priests.

Gradually, the bishops of Rome and Constantinople emerged as the leaders of the churches of the Western and Eastern halves of the empire. Known as "popes" (Latin *papa*, "father"), the bishops of Rome were said to be the successors of the Apostle Peter, the "rock" (Greek *petra*) upon whom Christ had said he would build his Church (Matthew 16:18–19). They claimed the same authority Christ had given to Peter. Other bishops—including the great patriarchs of Constantinople, Alexandria, Antioch, and Jerusalem—acknowledged the bishops of Rome as "first among equals" but without recognizing the right of popes to rule over them.

Early Christian Thought The success of the early Christian movement was due in part to the work of Christian writers who produced carefully reasoned statements of Christian belief. These texts gave Christianity intellectual respectability in a world accustomed to the high standards of Greek philosophy and tended to encourage a search for commonalities linking Christian and pagan culture.

For example, theologians such as Clement of Alexandria (c. 150–215) and Origen (c. 185–254) taught that God had long been at work among the Greeks and Romans, preparing them for the coming of Christ. Just as God had given the Torah to the Jews, said Clement, he had given philosophy to the Greeks as a kind of "schoolmaster" in order to "bring the Greek mind . . . to Christ."[5] Like many thinkers of his time, Clement held that all truth comes from the divine "Word," or **Logos**. Thus, truths found in scripture and philosophy were compatible. However, since the Logos had become incarnate in Jesus Christ (John 1:18), said Clement, it was only in Christ that seekers of truth would find it fully revealed.

Controversies and Councils Beginning in the third century, Christian theologians turned their attention to the concept of the Trinity and to the nature of Christ. Discussion of these issues led to ecumenical councils ("worldwide councils") of bishops at which doctrines were defined.

From the beginning, most Christians believed that God the Father, the Creator of the universe, had become present in the world in Jesus Christ, God the Son. They also believed in the Holy Spirit as the continuing expression of God's loving presence and power in the world. But how could the one God also be three? This question was taken up by early theologians such as Tertullian, who gave Latin theology its Trinitarian vocabulary by speaking of God as *tres personae, una substantia* ("three persons, one substance"). Similarly, Greek-speaking theologians described God as a single divine *ousia* ("substance" or "essence") made manifest in three *hypostases* ("subsistences").

This way of thinking about the Trinity sufficed until the early 300s, when Arius, an Egyptian priest from Alexandria, began teaching that God the Son, or Logos, was of a different substance than God the Father. Going further, Arius claimed that whereas the Father was eternal, the Son was created in time. Arius's views alarmed other theologians, for they seemed to undermine the unity of the Trinity. If the Father and the Son were so different, they asked, how could God be truly one?

Arius's provocative teachings soon had Alexandria buzzing as people in shops and streets argued theology with an enthusiasm we reserve for debates about sports and politics. Fearing that Arianism threatened the unity of the empire, as well as the Church, the Emperor Constantine stepped in and convened an ecumenical council to settle the matter. The Council of Nicea (325) condemned Arius's views, ordered the burning of Arian texts, and formulated a creed affirming that God the Son is *homoousios* ("of the same substance" or "being") with God the Father. An expanded form of this creed, the Nicene Creed (see p. 421), produced by the Council of Constantinople (381), describes God as a Trinity of three distinct yet unified divine "persons."

Even as the Trinitarian controversy was being settled, another debate began over the person of Christ. Christians had long believed that Christ was both human and divine, but they differed in explaining how humanity and divinity coexisted in him. The orthodox position on this issue was determined at yet another ecumenical council at Chalcedon (451): in Christ, two complete and perfect natures, human and divine, were united without separation or fusion in a single person.

Augustine   The drama of the Trinitarian and Christological controversies was played out in the Greek-speaking Eastern half of the Roman world and involved many leading theologians. The Latin West produced just one theological giant. This was Augustine (354–430), a North African bishop who laid the intellectual foundations for much of Western Christianity and Western civilization.

Central to Augustine's theology are his views on sin and human nature. Elaborating on the theology of Paul, Augustine argued that sinfulness is a fundamental flaw in human nature that clouds our moral vision and perverts the will by causing us to desire evil rather than good. In the *Confessions*, his spiritual autobiography, he illustrated this point by recalling the pleasure he and some teenage friends once found in stealing and throwing away pears from a neighbor's tree. According to Augustine, the tendency to sin is so deeply ingrained that we are spiritually helpless and therefore completely dependent upon God for salvation.

But *how* did human nature become so corrupt? Augustine's answer came in his famous doctrine of **Original Sin**. All of humanity, it says, participated in the first sin: the sin of Adam and Eve, the first human beings, described in Genesis (3:1–24). At that time, Adam and Eve *were* humanity, with all future generations present in them. Thus, when they made themselves sinners by choosing to disobey God, this original sin transformed human nature in a way that was bound to affect their descendants. Every human being, said Augustine, is born with the "stain" of original sin in the form of a sinful nature.

Augustine's awareness that some people are saved from sin led him to formulate a theory of predestination. Because all human beings are sinful and therefore incapable of responding on their own to God in faith, he reasoned, God must give some people a grace that inspires faith. Divine grace is irresistible, he said, for a love that could be resisted would be incompatible with God's perfection. Thus those whom God touches with his grace are destined to be saved. Augustine conceded that it is impossible to know *why* God extends a saving grace to some people and not to others, but he insisted that God is neither arbitrary nor unjust. Some are allowed a destiny better than they deserve, but no one receives a destiny worse than he deserves.

As you might imagine, Augustine was never entirely comfortable with his conclusions about original sin and predestination, but his reading of scripture and observation of human behavior made them inescapable. Having seen jealousy in a baby whose brother had taken his place at their mother's breast, he felt he had no choice but to conclude that sin must be something we are born with and not simply a habit everyone happens to pick up. Similarly, though predestination seemed to be the work of an unfair God, Augustine knew that scripture taught that only some would be saved and that God's justice is not always within reach of human understanding.

Augustine's masterpiece was his *City of God*, in which he formulated a Christian philosophy of history. Writing amidst the panic following the sack of Rome by a Germanic tribe in 410, he rejected the pagan claim that Rome's traditional gods allowed the city to fall because they were angry with the Romans for converting to Christianity. Augustine argued that the fall of Rome was part of God's plan for the salvation of the world. God had ordained two "cities": the earthly city, blemished by sin, and the City of God, a spiritual community grounded in love of God. Like all other manifestations of the earthly city, said Augustine, Rome must pass away so that history can move toward the full realization of the City of God on earth. This view of history as progress toward the fulfillment of God's plan for salvation soon became standard in the Christian West.

The Church in the Middle Ages

In the fifth century, Germanic tribes overran the Western half of the Roman Empire. From the resulting chaos a new medieval civilization emerged that combined Christianity with Roman and Germanic culture. The Eastern half of the Roman Empire survived for another thousand years. Known as the Byzantine Empire, it was Greek in its language and outlook. As the gulf between West and East widened, distinctively Western and Eastern traditions within the catholic ("universal") Church began to take shape.

The Church in the West The most powerful of the Germanic tribes were the Franks, who controlled most of Western Europe by the ninth century. The Franks supported the Roman Church and granted rich lands to bishops and monasteries. In return, the Church sanctioned the rule of the Frankish kings, supplied clergy to serve in their government, and sent missionaries to convert pagan peoples in their kingdom.

The Church's involvement in secular affairs continued after the decline of the Franks and often led to conflict between secular and spiritual rulers, and especially the popes. Early medieval popes claimed that their spiritual responsibilities gave them an authority greater than that of secular rulers, but it was not until the eleventh century that the papacy rose to the level they had imagined. The most powerful of popes was Innocent III (r. 1198–1216). Intent on unifying the Christian world under the papal banner, Innocent intervened constantly in secular matters, deposing kings and emperors whenever they displeased him.

Completed c. 1250, the height and soaring towers of the Gothic cathedral at Chartres in France express the medieval yearning for God. For centuries, pilgrims and secular tourists have come to experience its exquisite, light-filled interior and to see its famous relic, the tunic of the Virgin Mary.

A very ugly aspect of medieval Christianity in the West was the **Inquisition**, the Church's inquiry into allegations of heresy that began in the twelfth century. Working in partnership with secular rulers, who feared that religious diversity would undermine their authority, the inquisitors sought to eradicate false teachings they believed would endanger the salvation of those who accepted them. The Inquisition also targeted Jews and Muslims. Despite its use of torture and the execution of heretics by burning, the Inquisition could not stamp out heresy. Nevertheless, it persisted in various forms until its final and cruelest phase, the Spanish Inquisition, was abolished in 1834.

The Church in the East   In the East, the patriarchs of Constantinople governed the Church jointly with the Byzantine emperors. The Byzantine ideal was a *symphonia* ("harmony") of emperor and patriarch based on their shared vision of a holy empire on earth that reflected the glory of the celestial society of heaven. Clashes did occur, but only one threatened the symbiosis of emperor and patriarch. This was the controversy over iconoclasm, or "icon smashing." **Icons**, painted images of Christ and the saints, had long been revered by Byzantine Christians. But some saw this as idolatry. When the Emperor Leo III began removing icons from churches and other public places (726), riots erupted throughout the empire. Leo and his successors responded by deposing uncooperative patriarchs and executing monks, the leading defenders of icons. A formal end to iconoclasm came in 787, when the Second Council of Nicea determined that icons are worthy of veneration but not worship, which must be reserved for God alone.

By the twelfth century, Byzantine missionaries had brought the Slavic peoples of Russia and the Balkans into the Eastern Church. But the position of the Church became increasingly difficult in later years as the Byzantine Empire gradually collapsed under pressure from the expanding Islamic world. The empire fell in 1453 with the capture of Constantinople by the Ottoman Turks. For the next four centuries, most Eastern Christians outside Russia lived in the Ottoman Empire, an Islamic state in which they were tolerated but denied full religious freedom.

The Great Schism   The Great Schism, the split between Western and Eastern Christianity, came after centuries of gradual separation during which the two traditions developed their distinctive forms. Some of their differences were minor: baptism, for example, was performed by a sprinkling of water in the West but by full immersion in the East, and the West urged priests to be celibate whereas the East preferred them to be married. Far more divisive were the attempts of popes to control Eastern bishops and Byzantine lands. In the end, it was the West's addition of the Latin *filioque* ("and from the Son") to the Nicene Creed that brought a final break. The East rejected this move for theological reasons and because the West had acted without sanction by an ecumenical council. In 1054, angry words over the *filioque* combined with tensions over other issues to force a division of the Church into separate Roman Catholic and Orthodox traditions that remain divided even today.

The Interior of the Cathedral of Hagia Sophia. Dedicated to the "holy wisdom" embodied by Christ, this sixth-century church is the supreme achievement of Byzantine architecture. After the capture of Constantinople by the Turks in 1453, the city was renamed Istanbul and the church first became a mosque, then a museum.

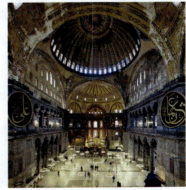

The Crusades Despite their differences, Eastern and Western Christians did share a common concern over the westward advance of Islamic armies. In 1095, Pope Urban II proclaimed a military crusade intended to push the Muslims back and liberate Jerusalem. Crying *"Deus vult!"* ("God wills it!"), armies of knights, peasants, and townspeople set out on the First Crusade. In 1099, they celebrated their capture of Jerusalem with a frenzied slaughter of Muslims and Jews. But the crusaders were unable to defend the lands they had conquered, and subsequent crusades to regain them were often military or moral disasters. Participants in the infamous Fourth Crusade (1204) never made it to the Holy Land, deciding instead to plunder Constantinople. The crusades ended at the close of the thirteenth century, having failed to deliver the Holy Land permanently into Christian hands.

Monasticism and Mysticism One of the most visible features of medieval Christianity was monasticism, a movement that began in the third century when Christians seeking a deeper experience of God withdrew into the deserts of Egypt and Syria. Most early Christian monks and nuns lived solitary lives and practiced a severe asceticism. According to legend, Macarius of Alexandria (d. 395) remained standing for periods as long as forty days, subsisting on a weekly meal of cabbage. The nun Alexandra walled herself up in a tomb for ten years, never seeing another human face.

In the medieval period, monks and nuns were brought together in monasteries governed by "rules" that regularized monastic life and discouraged extreme forms of self-denial. Both the Eastern *Rule* of Basil the Great (330–379) and the Western *Rule* of Benedict of Nursia (480–547) required monks and nuns to take vows of chastity and poverty and to spend their days in communal worship, prayer, and labor. Although the monastic aim of pursuing holiness through the imitation of Christ meant that monks and nuns spent much time in prayer and contemplation, monasteries also served nearby communities, providing them with spiritual guidance, education, shelter for travelers, and care for the poor and sick.

The monastic movement also encouraged mysticism, the direct and intuitive experience of God beyond the limits of mere intellect. Eastern mystics emphasized the absolute "otherness" of God, whom they regarded as so utterly unlike anything else we experience that even concepts as basic as "being" and "nonbeing" are useless in describing divinity. Though remote in his incomprehensibility, they said, God is also near, touching human beings with a love that restores the sinful nature to its original state of perfection in "the image of God" (Genesis 1:26–27). "Love, the divine gift," wrote Maximus the Confessor (c. 580–662), "perfects human nature until it makes it appear in unity and identity with the divine nature."[6] Building on these

In this fresco by Giovanni Sodoma (1477–1549), Benedictine monks of the Monte Oliveto monastery in Italy eat their meal together—just as they worked and worshipped together in accordance with the Rule of St. Benedict. Note that one of the monks reads to the others from the Bible or some other holy book as they eat.

ideas, Eastern monks such as Simeon the New Theologian (949–1022) and Gregory Palamas (c. 1296–1359) practiced Hesychasm, the cultivation of an inner quietude (*hesychia*) that brings an experience of God as divine light.

Western mystics also emphasized the power of divine love. Bernard of Clairvaux (1090–1153) compared Christ to a bridegroom whose love for the soul fills her with a bliss that transcends all earthly feeling. Bonaventure (1217–1274) described how divine love lifts the mind above rational thought, allowing it to unite with God in ecstasy. Many of the great Western mystics were women. Catherine of Siena (1347–1380) described a dialogue between God and a human soul seeking union with the divine in her famous *Dialogue on Divine Providence*. In her *Revelations of Divine Love*, the English recluse Julian of Norwich (1342–1416) spoke of God's love as the only means to abiding joy. "Until I am substantially united to him," she wrote, "I can never have love or rest or true happiness."[7]

On April 29, the feast day of St. Catherine of Siena, four citizens of Siena, Italy, dress in medieval costumes and carry a casket holding the saint's relics in a procession.

Theology In the West, early medieval theology was centered in monasteries, where learned monks and nuns engaged in debates on issues such as predestination, free will, and the sacraments. In seeking to understand how Christ can be truly present in the eucharist, for example, medieval theologians formulated a doctrine of **transubstantiation**. According to this doctrine, the bread and wine consecrated by a priest during the eucharist become the actual body and blood of Christ in substance, though their secondary qualities, such as taste, color, and texture, remain unchanged.

The growth of major universities in the twelfth century created a new setting for theological inquiry. Here, theologians applied the science of logic as developed by Aristotle to grasp the full meaning of truths revealed in the scripture. Known as **scholasticism**, this effort became the chief intellectual enterprise of the West in the Middle Ages. The greatest of the scholastic theologians was Thomas Aquinas (1226–1274), a professor at the University of Paris. In his *Summa Theologica*, Thomas argued that although some truths can be known through reason alone, others can be grasped only through faith. Ultimately, said Thomas, there is a perfect harmony between reason and faith, as both come from God.

The most distinctive feature of Eastern theology was its view that all essential Christian truths had been defined once and for all by seven ecumenical councils that completed their work in the eighth century. After the Second Council of Nicea (787), Orthodox theologians devoted themselves to the analysis and elaboration of the faith as articulated by the seven ecumenical councils.

The Reformation

In the sixteenth century, a religious revolution known as the Reformation rocked Western Christianity. The Reformation's first phase is known as the Protestant Reformation because of the protests of reformers against Roman Catholic doctrines and practices. Its second phase was the Catholic Reformation, which included direct responses to Protestantism, as well as reforms undertaken independently of it. Ultimately, the Reformation left Europe religiously divided, destroying forever the ancient and medieval ideal of a united Christendom.

Background to the Reformation   Throughout the Middle Ages, the Roman Catholic Church engaged in constant self-examination and reform. Despite this, voices calling for change grew louder and more numerous. Some complained of corruption among the clergy. Christians north of the Alps resented taxes imposed by the Church, especially since most revenues were spent in Rome. Many were angered by the luxuries enjoyed by popes. Those who wished to emulate the simple piety of the apostles were discouraged by the example set by church leaders more interested in wealth and power. Calls for reform were also encouraged by the revival of humanism, a deep faith in human beings that inspired the Renaissance, a cultural movement that was flourishing at the time of the Reformation. Humanists such as Desiderius Erasmus (1466–1536) argued that Christians had no need to rely on the Church. Instead, they were capable of taking charge of their spiritual lives based on their own reading and interpretation of the Bible. By the dawn of the sixteenth century, the desire for religious reform was intense and widespread. The situation was volatile. In 1517, a German monk named **Martin Luther** (1483–1546) provided a spark.

Portrait of Martin Luther by Lucas Cranach the Elder (1529). It was Luther who set the Protestant Reformation in motion by posting his Ninety-Five Theses on the door of the All Saints' Church in Wittenberg, Germany.

The Protestant Reformation   Luther had not found peace in monastic life. Despite his efforts to be an ideal monk, he was plagued by a sense of unworthiness and fear of God's judgment that followed him from his monastery to the University of Wittenberg, where he became a professor of theology. It was in Wittenberg that Luther, reading about "the righteousness of God" in Paul's letter to the Romans (1:17), came to believe that God's righteousness did not consist in his desire to condemn the unrighteous but in his eagerness to forgive them. God does not set before sinners the impossible task of *earning* their salvation, Luther concluded. Instead, he asks only that it be accepted, as an expression of divine grace, by faith. For Luther, it was faith alone, and not good works or sacraments, that "justified" sinners before God.

As Luther considered the implications of "justification by faith," he identified practices of the Church that he found objectionable. Among them was the distribution of indulgences. For centuries, popes had claimed the authority to apply the surplus merits of the saints to penitent sinners, thereby releasing them from punishment otherwise due for unconfessed sin in purgatory. By Luther's time, the outright sale of indulgences (certificates of remission of punishment in purgatory) had become an important means of raising funds to finance the papal office.

In 1517 Luther called for public debate on indulgences and other issues by nailing his Ninety-Five Theses, a statement of his theological positions, to the door of the church in Wittenberg. Supporters quickly rallied behind him, and soon Germany teetered on the edge of religious and social chaos. When ecclesiastical and secular leaders ordered Luther to recant his views, he refused, setting the Protestant movement in motion.

Luther now began building a Protestant theology based on three principles. First, salvation is made possible by divine "grace alone." Second, it is "by faith alone" that sinners must respond to grace. Third, "scripture alone," and not papal pronouncements or church councils, is the only authority on which Christians can completely rely. In order to make the scriptures available to the people, Luther translated the Bible into German. Because he found no mandate in the Bible for an ecclesiastical hierarchy, he rejected the authority of bishops and popes, as well as the traditional distinction between clergy and laity. According to Luther's doctrine of the "priesthood of all believers," Christians represent themselves before God and have no need of a special class of priests.

Luther's intention had been only to reform the Roman Catholic Church, not to create a new Christian movement, but his teachings cut too close to the heart of Catholicism to make reconciliation possible. Moreover, the rulers of many German territories saw in Luther a champion who might end the unwelcome influence of the pope and his ally, the Holy Roman Emperor, in their lands. They encouraged a break with Rome. Fighting between Catholics and Protestants broke out. By the time it ended in 1555, Lutheranism had triumphed in northern Germany and Scandinavia.

Luther was soon joined by other reformers who expanded the geographical scope of the Reformation. In his *Institutes of the Christian Religion*, **John Calvin** (1509–1564) articulated Protestant doctrines with a power and clarity that put his life in danger in Catholic France. Welcomed by the Swiss city of Geneva, Calvin accepted the essential features of Luther's thought but gave Protestant theology his own stamp by emphasizing God's sovereignty over the universe and teaching that every honest occupation is a "calling" given by God. Calvinism quickly took root in Switzerland in the Swiss Reformed churches, in the Dutch Netherlands as the Dutch Reformed Church, and in England and Scotland as Presbyterianism.

In Zurich, the Swiss reformer Ulrich Zwingli (1484–1531) denounced all beliefs and practices not described in the Bible. Because the Bible makes no mention of images of Christ and the saints, candles, and incense, he removed these from Zurich's churches. A space without symbolic and decorative distractions, he reasoned, would be more likely to bring worshippers into direct communion with God. In teaching that the bread and wine used in the eucharist were mere symbols, Zwingli went far beyond Luther and Calvin, who joined him in rejecting the doctrine of transubstantiation but retained the belief that Christ was in the sacrament.

The Reformation was brought to England by King Henry VIII, depicted here in a famous portrait by the sixteenth-century painter Hans Holbein the Younger.

Alongside the Lutheran, Calvinist, and Zwinglian movements emerged smaller, more radical groups that make up what some scholars call the Radical Reformation. Anabaptists ("*rebaptizers*") insisted that Christians baptized as infants must be "born again" and baptized again as mature believers. Refusing to recognize the authority of civil governments and their laws, Anabaptists refused to take oaths and were committed to nonviolence. Other radical groups placed such great importance on the inner presence of the Holy Spirit that they saw little value in the Bible or traditional worship. Still others rejected doctrines as basic as the Trinity and the divinity of Christ.

In England, the Reformation began when the pope refused the request of King Henry VIII (r. 1509–1547) for an annulment of his marriage. Taking matters into his own hands, Henry prevailed upon Parliament to pass an Act of Supremacy (1534) that made the king of England, not the pope, the head of the Church in England. This break marked the beginning of the Church of England and of an Anglican tradition that was later exported to England's colonies. In America, the Anglican Church, as it is sometimes called, came to be known as the Episcopal Church.

Although Henry had wanted to effect only political change, the Church of England soon felt the impact of Protestant thought on the Continent. In the end, a kind of compromise was reached that left the Church of England very "Catholic" in its theology and patterns of worship but clearly influenced by elements of Calvinist and Lutheran theology. Although this arrangement satisfied most Anglicans, there were important groups of dissenters. Calvinist Puritans wanted to "purify" the Church of England of every vestige of Catholicism. Presbyterians, also inspired by Calvinism, wanted to replace the episcopal hierarchy with assemblies of presbyters ("elders"). Quakers rejected all formal worship and all forms of church governance.

The Catholic Reformation   The primary response of the Roman Catholic Church to Protestantism was the Council of Trent (1545–1563), which reaffirmed Catholic teachings but took great care to clarify them. Against Protestant belief in the authority of scripture alone, the council held that tradition is equally authoritative. Against the Protestant reduction of the sacraments to baptism and the eucharist, it reaffirmed the seven sacraments. In response to the Protestant doctrine of justification by faith, the council insisted that faith must be expressed by good works and cited the New Testament in support of this view (e.g., Romans 2:6; 2 Corinthians 5:10). The council also upheld transubstantiation, confession, priestly celibacy, monasticism, purgatory, and the intercession of saints in heaven on behalf of the living. Although it gave no ground to Protestantism on doctrinal issues, the Council of Trent did take decisive action to end corruption in the Church, to improve the quality of education received by priests, and

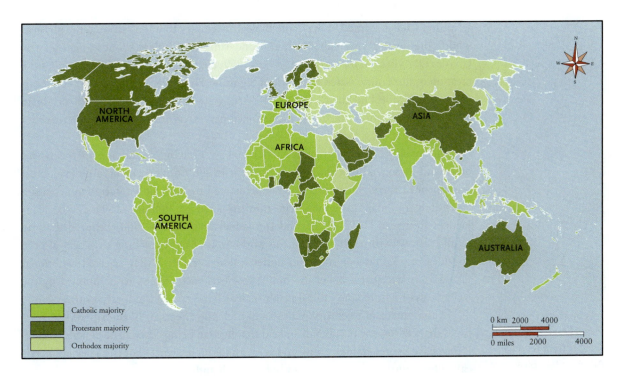

Catholic majority

Protestant majority

Orthodox majority

0 km 2000   4000

0 miles   2000   4000

to ensure that essential doctrines were made clear in the sermons, or homilies, that were a part of the Mass.

Although the Council of Trent left Catholics and Protestants divided, its reforms and clarification of doctrine did reinvigorate the Roman Catholic Church, especially in its efforts to spread the faith. New religious orders such as the Jesuits, founded by Ignatius Loyola (1491–1556), spearheaded the effort to reestablish Catholicism in lands where Protestantism had become popular and to bring Christianity to parts of the world where it had never been known, including China, Japan, India, the Philippines, and Latin America.

Christianity in the Modern World

The Reformation was only the first challenge faced by Christianity in the modern era. Dramatic scientific, social, political, and intellectual developments also required the Church to respond to a changing world.

As early as the Reformation era, a scientific revolution was beginning to transform the traditional understanding of the universe. For centuries, the Church had endorsed the widespread belief that the universe revolves around the earth—and therefore around humanity, the supreme object of God's love. But this view was abandoned after Nicholas Copernicus (1473–1543) and Galileo Galilei (1564–1642) proved that the earth and other planets revolve around the sun. When Isaac Newton (1642–1727) demonstrated that the universe operates according to laws of nature not found in

Distribution of major branches of Christianity throughout the world.

How have reformers and reform movements influenced the development of other religions?

scripture, science seemed to make the Bible unnecessary to understanding the physical world. The new scientific approach also undermined old ideas about human beings. Charles Darwin's *On the Origin of Species* (1859) challenged the biblical account of the creation of humanity. Later, the work of Sigmund Freud (1856–1939) and the French sociologist Émile Durkheim (1858–1917) suggested that religion did not originate with divine revelation but in the maladjusted psyche or out of a need to create order in society.

The scientific revolution was encouraged by growing confidence in the power of human reason. This was especially evident in the Enlightenment, a philosophical movement of the eighteenth century. Encouraged by Newton's description of nature as entirely rational, Enlightenment thinkers such as Voltaire (1694–1778), Jean-Jacques Rousseau (1712–1778), and Immanuel Kant (1724–1804) believed the way to all truth was through study of the world around us. Unwilling to accept as true any idea that could not stand up under rational scrutiny, they rejected traditional Christianity except for belief in God, whose existence seemed to be implied by the orderliness of nature, and ethical ideals such as honesty and kindness to others.

In the nineteenth century, Christianity felt the effects of liberalism and secularism. Nineteenth-century liberalism held that human beings can create an ideal society if they have the freedom to think and act without interference. For this reason, liberals called for limits on the influence of both church and state. Many liberals found it difficult to reconcile Christian beliefs about the sinfulness of human nature and the revelation of truth in scripture with their own views concerning the essential goodness of human beings and the importance of independent thought. Moreover, the progress of democracy across Europe in the nineteenth century brought the implementation of liberal policies that promoted secularism, the belief that religious ideas and institutions should have much less influence in the operation of the state, and especially in public education. The American ideal of the separation of church and state is just one example of this new attitude toward the place of religion in society.

The Missionary Movement Despite the challenges posed by modern thought and culture, the geographical scope of Christianity grew dramatically

This mosaic of the Virgin Mary and Christ Child is from the Annunciation Basilica in Nazareth, Israel. It is a wonderful example of the desire of Christians all over the world to understand Jesus in relation to themselves and their own cultures.

In this wood carving from West Africa, an anonymous twentieth-century artist portrays Jesus as African and manages to capture the sorrow and suffering of the savior, who was about to face crucifixion.

in the modern era as European colonial powers expanded their influence into other continents. Most Westerners brought to foreign lands a confidence in the superiority of their own culture and the conviction that they had a moral obligation to share its benefits, including Christianity, with the peoples they found there. As the British poet Rudyard Kipling (1865–1936) put it, "the white man's burden" was to civilize the world's "lesser breeds." Regrettably, the "civilizing" of non-Christians sometimes involved conversions accomplished through intimidation or outright force by colonizers.

Roman Catholicism in the Modern World The Roman Catholic Church adapted slowly to the new realities of the modern era. Shaken by the Protestant Reformation and intent on resisting modern influences, it maintained the defensive posture adopted at the Council of Trent until the middle of the twentieth century.

Bishops gathered at the Second Vatican Council (1962–1965) in St. Peter's Basilica.

Perhaps the greatest challenge faced by Catholicism was secularization. In France, the Emperor Napoleon (r. 1804–1815) stripped the Church of the authority it had enjoyed for centuries over important aspects of public life. Marriage and divorce became civil procedures, and responsibility for education was assumed by the state, which promoted its own ideals in public schools. In Germany, the state seized vast tracts of land from bishops and monasteries and made priests public employees. Chancellor Otto von Bismarck, outraged by the loyalty of German Catholics to Rome, launched an all-out attack on Catholicism known as the *Kulturkampf* ("struggle for civilization") in the 1870s.

During these difficult years, Catholics turned to Rome for decisive leadership. Intent on providing it, nineteenth-century popes asserted their spiritual authority even as their influence in secular affairs rapidly eroded. This trend culminated under Pius IX, whose *Syllabus of Errors* (1864) urged Catholics to reject modern evils such as civil marriage, separation of church and state, public education, and Marxism. The climax of Pius IX's reign came with the First Vatican Council (1869–1870), which increased the power of the papacy by proclaiming a doctrine of papal infallibility. According to this doctrine, the pope cannot err when defining doctrines relating to faith and morals.

Later popes upheld Pius IX's conception of papal authority but also attempted to address modernity in constructive ways. Leo XIII (r. 1878–1903), for example, decried the social inequities created by capitalism and industrialization and outlined principles by which justice might be achieved.

A major turning point came when John XXIII convened the Second Vatican Council (1962–1965), which called for recognition of the realities of modern culture. Vatican II urged an openness to dialogue with non-Catholic Christians and described

Pope Francis washed the feet of a dozen inmates, including women and Muslims, at a juvenile detention center in a Holy Thursday ritual during the first year of his papacy. Francis's boldly inclusive gesture just two weeks after his election helped define his papacy.

the "high regard" of the Roman Catholic Church for other religions. It also reformed Catholic worship by requiring celebration of the Mass in modern languages instead of Latin and allowing laypeople greater participation in worship. Moving away from the traditional tendency to set the clergy above laypeople, the council emphasized the equality of the faithful. Since Vatican II, the Roman Catholic Church has continued to make its relevance apparent in the modern world while at the same time holding fast to tradition. Thus Pope John Paul II (r. 1978–2005) was a driving force in bringing about the collapse of communism in Eastern Europe at the end of the twentieth century but made no concessions to Catholics who urged a greater role for women in the Church and an end to its stand against birth control.

Pope Francis (r. 2013–) has canonized both John XXIII and John Paul II as saints. A former Archbishop of Buenos Aires, Francis upholds traditional Roman Catholic teachings against abortion, contraception, and gay marriage, but he has also set an extraordinary example in his humility and has called upon all Christians to join him in service to all who are poor and marginalized.

Protestantism in the Modern World From the beginning, Protestantism encouraged Christians to read and interpret the Bible for themselves. It also resisted the creation of any central authority capable of imposing uniformity of belief and practice. As a result, the number of Protestant denominations grew rapidly. Today, the world's 600 million Protestant Christians belong to thousands of groups. In the United States, the largest Protestant denominations are the Methodist, Lutheran, Presbyterian, Baptist, and Reformed churches.

Despite their many differences, most Protestants share basic doctrines that go back to the Reformation. Following Luther, they believe that salvation from sin is based on faith alone. They regard the Bible as the only authoritative source of revealed truth. Finally, Protestantism allows for diverse forms of church government that give great authority to laypeople and individual congregations.

Since the early 1800s, liberalism and liberal theology have had a significant influence on older and larger Protestant denominations. Interpreting Christianity in the light of modern culture, liberal Protestants have questioned the doctrine of original sin, asked whether a loving God would allow even the worst sinners to suffer in hell, and emphasized the human element in the composition of the scriptures. Embracing the liberal idea that the essential goodness of human beings makes progress toward a better world possible, they have advocated social activism based on the teachings of Jesus as a means of making the kingdom of God a reality. Liberal Protestants have played important roles in the civil rights and antiwar movements and struggled to open the Church to greater participation by women, homosexuals, and other groups.

At the other end of the Protestant spectrum are three important conservative movements: fundamentalism, evangelicalism, and Pentecostalism.

Fundamentalism emerged a century ago as a reaction against liberal theology, the theory of evolution, the academic study of the Bible, and other features of modern culture that conservatives found threatening. The movement takes its name from *The Fundamentals*, a series of booklets that identified five doctrines essential to Christianity: (1) the literal inerrancy of the Bible, (2) the divinity and virgin birth of Christ, (3) Christ's atonement for human sin on the cross, (4) the bodily resurrection of Christ, and (5) the imminent Second Coming of Christ. Seeking to defend these doctrines, leaders such as the television evangelist Jerry Falwell made fundamentalism a powerful force in American culture in the 1970s and 1980s. Fundamentalists also fought to defend what they called "traditional values" against feminism, gay rights, legalized abortion, and the elimination of prayer in public schools.

Fundamentalism grew out of **evangelicalism**, a much larger movement with roots in the "Great Awakening," a revival of religious fervor that swept through England and North America in the eighteenth century. As its name suggests, evangelicalism encourages the preaching and sharing of the gospel (Greek *evangelion*). It also emphasizes the need for every Christian to have a conversion experience, often described as being "born again" (John 3:3), that leads to a personal relationship with Jesus Christ. Evangelicals regard the Bible as the sole basis of faith, though they do not always insist on its literal interpretation. Like fundamentalists, many evangelicals believe that the end of the age and Second Coming of Christ will occur in the near future. Evangelicalism is a fast-growing worldwide movement that is making its presence felt both in older Protestant denominations and in new movements. It has become a major force in Africa and Asia and is particularly strong in North America. Evangelicals make up as much as one-fourth of the population of the United States,[8] where they have had considerable success in applying their understanding of biblical principles to politics and public policy.

Pentecostalism takes its name from the holy day of Pentecost, which commemorates the descent of the Holy Spirit upon Jesus's followers after his ascension to heaven. According to Acts 1:1–4, these Spirit-filled believers were empowered to "speak in other tongues," to prophesy, and to perform healings in the name of Christ. Since its beginnings in America in the early twentieth century, the Pentecostal movement has sought to reclaim this feature of earliest Christianity. Its most essential belief is that conversion

Pentecostal worship at the Catedral Evangelica de Chile in Santiago, Chile.

must be followed by a "baptism in the Spirit" made evident by an ability to speak in tongues and at least one of the other "spiritual gifts" described by Paul in 1 Corinthians 12–14. The belief that the ecstatic experience of God belongs at the center of Christian life is unmistakable in Pentecostal churches, where enthusiastic worshippers raise their arms in praise, speak in tongues, and sometimes dance or weep. The phenomenal growth of Pentecostalism during the last century has made it a major force in contemporary Christianity throughout the world. Today, Pentecostalism is the most popular form of Protestantism in Latin America, and it is rapidly gaining converts in Africa and Asia. In America, the most visible Pentecostal denominations include the Assemblies of God, the Church of God, and the Church of the Foursquare Gospel.

Orthodoxy in the Modern World   We saw earlier that the Ottoman Turks completed their conquest of the Byzantine Empire, the home of Orthodox Christianity, with their capture of Constantinople in 1453. The Muslim rulers of the Ottoman state tolerated the Orthodox Church, but they also brought it under government control. When Greeks, Bulgarians, Serbs, and other Orthodox peoples began declaring their independence from the declining Ottoman Empire in the 1800s, they established independent national churches. Today's 225 million Orthodox Christians belong to fifteen autonomous churches, including the Orthodox churches of Greece and Russia and the Orthodox Church in America. The Ecumenical Patriarch of Constantinople retains an honorary primacy among Orthodox bishops but has no real authority over them. Despite this, the Orthodox churches are united by a tradition of shared theology and forms of worship they trace back to the apostles.

Orthodox Christianity resisted the influence of Western rationalism and liberalism in the eighteenth and nineteenth centuries. But Western influence in the form of Marxism had a devastating effect on Orthodoxy after the Bolshevik Revolution in Russia (1917) and the creation of a bloc of communist states in Eastern Europe after World War II. Because these states saw all religion as an obstacle to the achievement of their social and political goals, they took drastic measures to strip the Church of its influence. Priests and monks were imprisoned, seminaries were closed, and church property was seized. The collapse of communism in the early 1990s brought a restoration of religious freedom and the revival of Orthodoxy. Since then, a dramatic rise in church attendance has testified to the commitment of millions of Russians, Ukrainians, Georgians, Bulgarians, Romanians, and Serbs to Orthodox Christianity.

Women in Christianity

The historical development of Christianity has occurred largely in patriarchal cultures. Although women have distinguished themselves as mystics, theologians, saints, members of religious orders, and founders of schools, hospitals, and other service organizations, they have generally been excluded from positions of leadership and authority. But women's roles began to change in the nineteenth and twentieth centuries. This is especially true of the Protestant tradition, in which women are now ordained

Branches of Christianity

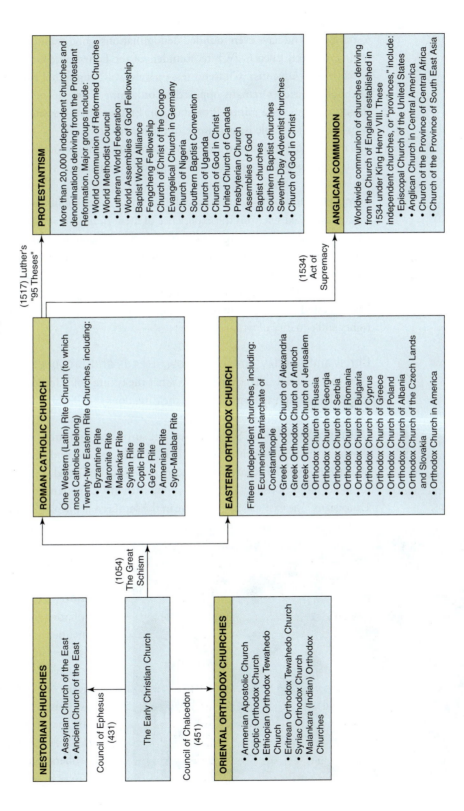

PROTESTANTISM

More than 20,000 independent churches and denominations deriving from the Protestant Reformation. Major groups include:
• World Communion of Reformed Churches
• World Methodist Council
• Lutheran World Federation
• World Assemblies of God Fellowship
• Baptist World Alliance
• Fengcheng Fellowship
• Church of Christ of the Congo
• Evangelical Church in Germany
• Church of Nigeria
• Southern Baptist Convention
• Church of Uganda
• Church of God in Christ
• United Church of Canada
• Presbyterian Church
• Assemblies of God
• Baptist churches
• Southern Baptist churches
• Seventh-Day Adventist churches
• Church of God in Christ

(1517) Luther's "95 Theses"

ANGLICAN COMMUNION

Worldwide communion of churches deriving from the Church of England established in 1534 under King Henry VIII. These independent churches, or "provinces," include:
• Episcopal Church of the United States
• Anglican Church in Central America
• Church of the Province of Central Africa
• Church of the Province of South East Asia

(1534) Act of Supremacy

ROMAN CATHOLIC CHURCH

One Western (Latin) Rite Church (to which most Catholics belong)
Twenty-two Eastern Rite Churches, including:
• Byzantine Rite
• Maronite Rite
• Malankar Rite
• Syrian Rite
• Coptic Rite
• Ge'ez Rite
• Armenian Rite
• Syro-Malabar Rite

EASTERN ORTHODOX CHURCH

Fifteen independent churches, including:
• Ecumenical Patriarchate of Constantinople
• Greek Orthodox Church of Alexandria
• Greek Orthodox Church of Antioch
• Greek Orthodox Church of Jerusalem
• Orthodox Church of Russia
• Orthodox Church of Georgia
• Orthodox Church of Serbia
• Orthodox Church of Romania
• Orthodox Church of Bulgaria
• Orthodox Church of Cyprus
• Orthodox Church of Greece
• Orthodox Church of Poland
• Orthodox Church of Albania
• Orthodox Church of the Czech Lands and Slovakia
• Orthodox Church in America

(1054) The Great Schism

NESTORIAN CHURCHES

• Assyrian Church of the East
• Ancient Church of the East

Council of Ephesus (431)

The Early Christian Church

Council of Chalcedon (451)

ORIENTAL ORTHODOX CHURCHES

• Armenian Apostolic Church
• Coptic Orthodox Church
• Ethiopian Orthodox Tewahedo Church
• Eritrean Orthodox Tewahedo Church
• Syriac Orthodox Church
• Malankara (Indian) Orthodox Churches

to the clergy and have even founded denominations; good examples are Aimee Semple McPherson and Ellen G. White, founders of the Foursquare Gospel Church and the Seventh-day Adventist Church, respectively. Although the Roman Catholic and Orthodox churches remain opposed to ordaining them to the clergy, women from these traditions have joined Protestants in finding other ways to lead and serve. Perhaps the most notable is their work in the academic world. As scholars specializing in biblical studies, ethics, and theology, women are communicating new ideas and insights that are bringing profound change to Christian thought.

Feminist Theology   Feminist theologians have called for liberation from a Christian worldview based solely on the experience of men. In her *Beyond God the Father* (1973), Mary Daly (1928–2010) argued that the Christian habit of thinking of God as Father allows misogyny to masquerade as a spiritual norm, thereby relegating women to a secondary status in the Church. Rosemary Radford Ruether (b. 1936), another influential feminist theologian, urges a new way of thinking about God as "God/ess" and has suggested the creation of churches open only to women and men committed to the rights and equality of women.

Christianity Today and Tomorrow: Trends and Prospects

We live in a rapidly changing world. What the future holds for Christianity is difficult to predict, though there are signs of the directions it is likely to take.

Demographic Shifts   Some of the most surprising indicators are demographic. Just a century ago, 80 percent of Christians lived in Europe and North America. Today, 60 percent live in Africa, Asia, and Latin America. This trend will continue. According to some projections, by 2050 only one-fifth of Christians will be non-Hispanic Caucasians. The vast majority will live in the southern hemisphere. This global shift will bring major changes as African and South American Christians assume greater influence in the Church.

The ordination of women as pastors is becoming increasingly common in Protestant denominations.

Liberation Theology   The beginnings of theological change along these lines became evident in the mid-twentieth century in the form of liberation theology, which grew out of the concern of Latin American priests such as Gustavo Gutiérrez for the plight of the poor. Originating with Gutiérrez's *A Theology of Liberation* (1971), liberation theology calls for radical action to correct the social, political, and economic injustices perpetrated against impoverished Latin Americans by landowners, governments, and the Church itself. It holds that the Church must work to ensure at least the basic necessities of life for all human beings. Moreover, it finds a scriptural basis for its views in the New Testament ideal of the Church as a community of believers committed to caring for each other's material, as well as spiritual, needs.

The principles of liberation theology have been put to work outside Latin America. In addition to their influence on feminist theology, they are central to black liberation theology, a movement originating in the thought of James Cone (b. 1938). Cone's *Black Theology and Black Power* (1969) and *A Black Theology of Liberation* (1970) offered a scathing criticism of white Christianity and society for their indifference to the problems of race and social injustice. Calling for the application of Christian principles to these problems in *this* world, Cone wrote that "the idea of heaven is irrelevant for Black Theology. The Christian cannot waste time contemplating the next world. . . . Jesus' work is essentially one of liberation."[9]

Lay Movements Another recent development has been the increasing number of lay movements within the Church. Traditionally, the ordained clergy have taken responsibility for determining how the mission of the Church should be carried out. The new lay movements turn this model on its head. Founded, directed, and composed mainly of laypeople, they seek to strengthen the spiritual lives of members through service to others in the form of evangelization, charitable work, or social justice advocacy. Among the larger Roman Catholic lay movements are Focolare and the Community of St. Egidio. Founded in Italy in 1943, Focolare (Italian, "hearth") has a presence in 182 countries. It seeks to foster unity among Christians and universal brotherhood among religious and nonreligious people worldwide through education, publications, and other means. The Community of St. Egidio began in 1968 through the initiative of a high school student. Taking its name from a small church in Rome, the Community is active in more than seventy countries. With the aim of alleviating the suffering caused by injustice and war, it has helped to end crises in countries such as Mozambique (1990–1992), Algeria (1994–1995), and Guatemala (1996). One of the most visible Protestant lay movements is the *Evangelische Kirchentag*, or Protestant Church Congress. The *Kirchentag* is a five-day event held every two years in a German city. Nearly 200,000 participants meet to address theological, social, and political issues in speeches, performances, study groups, and other events. Like most lay movements, the *Kirchentag* has made the solidarity and unity of all Christians worldwide one of its highest ideals. Accordingly, the 2003 and 2010 *Kirchentags* were jointly organized by Roman Catholic and Protestant churches.

Ecumenism A final development in contemporary Christianity is ecumenism. Based on the ancient ideal of a single worldwide church, the aim of the ecumenical movement (Greek *oikoumene*, "the inhabited world") is the restoration of Christian unity. It was not until the twentieth century that organizations such as the World Council of Churches began moving deliberately in this direction. In recent decades most larger churches have declared their interest in ecumenism, and many have established cooperative agreements with each other. There have also been extraordinary ways in which Christians from different traditions have come together in pursuit of unity. A good example is the Taizé Community in France, an ecumenical monastic order of men from both Catholic and Protestant backgrounds. Committed to a shared vision of the essence of the gospel message, the community at Taizé has gained a reputation for holiness that draws thousands of pilgrims every year.

CHRISTIANITY AS A WAY OF LIFE

There is much more to Christianity than the beliefs Christians hold inwardly. Like the followers of other religions, Christians express their beliefs outwardly in a variety of ways. Some are public, such as formal worship in church, participation in rituals, and the observance of holy days. Others are more private and personal, such as prayer and meditation. Together, these practices constitute much of what Christians do in living the Christian life.

Worship

Because the first Christians were Jews, they patterned their worship on the Jewish synagogue service, which consisted of readings from scripture, prayer, and a sermon. To this, they added the celebration of the **eucharist**, a commemoration of the Last Supper Jesus shared with his disciples. The result was a **liturgy** (Greek *leitourgia*, "work of the people") consisting of two parts: the liturgy of the word, including readings from scripture, prayer, and a sermon, and the liturgy of the eucharist. The Western custom of referring to the liturgy as the "Mass" can be traced back to *missa*, one of the Latin words used to dismiss the congregation: *Ite, missa est* ("Go, the dismissal is made").

Today's Roman Catholic and Orthodox churches are highly liturgical. In worship, members of these traditions feel themselves caught up in ritual rhythms of praise and adoration that reach back through more than two millennia. In contrast, most Protestant groups have adopted much simpler forms of worship that emphasize readings from scripture and preaching over ritual.

Christians have always made Sunday, the day of Christ's resurrection, a day set apart for communal worship. Typically, worship in Protestant churches begins with a hymn followed by an invocation, or opening prayer. After readings from scripture, congregants might sing another hymn in preparation for the sermon. Informal announcements of interest to the congregation often follow, along with a collection taken up for support of the church and its charitable causes. A recitation of the Lord's Prayer (p. 457) follows the collection. The service concludes with a final prayer and a closing hymn. In Roman Catholic churches, worship begins with a formal procession of the clergy toward the altar (a table used in celebrating the eucharist) accompanied by the singing of an opening hymn. Next, in a penitential rite, those present confess their sins and ask God's forgiveness. The liturgy of the word that follows consists primarily of readings from scripture, a short sermon, or homily, and a recitation of the Nicene Creed. At this point, the liturgy of the eucharist begins with the presentation of bread and wine, which are set on the altar. After the priest blesses these elements, there is a special eucharistic prayer followed by a singing of the *Sanctus*, a short hymn taken from the Old Testament (Isaiah 6:3). The congregation then recites an affirmation of faith and the Lord's Prayer. In a final preparatory act, members of the congregation wish each other "the peace of the Lord." It is at this point that the bread and wine are consecrated, making Christ present upon the altar. The members of the congregation then share in the rite of communion, in which each person receives a bit of the consecrated elements of bread and wine. Many Roman Catholic Christians say that it is in this solemn moment that they are most acutely aware of God's loving presence. The liturgy concludes with a final prayer, a benediction (blessing), and the formal dismissal of the congregation. The liturgy celebrated in Orthodox churches follows this same pattern, though additional processions, prayers, and blessings make it more elaborate.

Sacraments

Like worship, the special rituals known as **sacraments** are central to Christian life. Understood as visible symbols of God's grace, the sacraments infuse believers with spiritual nourishment and impart a sacred character to transitional moments in their lives. The Greek word for sacrament, *musterion* ("mystery"—the term preferred by Orthodox Christians), helps to explain the significance these rituals have for Christians. Making use of ordinary elements such as bread, wine, water, and oil, they bring the individual into an experience of something extraordinary—the mystery of God's love. Roman Catholic and Orthodox Christians celebrate seven sacraments. Protestants acknowledge only two: baptism and the eucharist.

Early Christians used the "sign of the fish" as a secret symbol to identify themselves during times of persecution. Today, many Christians identify themselves as such by mounting the symbol on their cars. The letters of the Greek word for "fish" (ΙΧΘΥΣ) are the first letters in the words that make up the phrase "Jesus Christ, Son of God, and Savior."

The cross has served as a Christian symbol since ancient times and appears in many forms. With its longer vertical and shorter horizontal arms, the Latin cross is the form favored by the Roman Catholic and Protestant churches. This one stands atop Monte Crocione in northern Italy.

Orthodox Christians use many different forms of the cross. The most common is a simple figure formed by four arms of equal length. This one decorates a small convent on the island of Mykonos, Greece.

The Celtic cross. According to legend, the Celtic cross on the left originated with St. Patrick, who brought Christianity to Ireland. This one serves as a grave marker in a cemetery in Dublin, Ireland.

(continued)

A crucifix is a cross with an image of the crucified Christ. It is used extensively in the Roman Catholic, Orthodox, Anglican, and Lutheran traditions. A vivid reminder of Christ's suffering on behalf of humanity, it is usually displayed prominently in church interiors.

The custom of using alpha and omega, the first and last letters of the Greek alphabet, to symbolize the eternality of God is based on a verse from the book of Revelation in the New Testament (1:8): "I am the Alpha and the Omega," says the Lord God, "who is, and who was, and who is to come, the Almighty."

The Chi-Rho is a symbol of Christ. Its name is based on those of the Greek letters chi and rho, the first two letters in the Greek word Christos, or "Christ." According to one legend, the Chi-Rho was revealed in a dream to the Emperor Constantine, who won a great victory against a rival for the imperial throne after marking it on the shields of his soldiers.

Today, the Chi-Rho appears on altars, plaques, priestly vestments, pendants, and other items. The symbol depicted here appears on a Christian stele from Seville in Spain and was created c. 600.

The "sign of the cross" is a ritual hand motion in which the shape of the cross of Christ is traced across the forehead and chest. It is used in both public worship and private prayer. The practice of "signing" one-self as an act of devotion goes back to ancient times. Writing c. 200, the North African theologian Tertullian noted that the Christians of his time "wore out their foreheads" making the sign of the cross.

The first sacrament celebrated in the life of a Christian is baptism, a cleansing of sin that marks the beginning of a new spiritual life in which one is united with Christ and sanctified by the Holy Spirit. Baptism can take the form of complete immersion in water or a sprinkling of water on one's head. However it is performed, the priest or minister always follows the instruction of Christ to baptize "in the name of the Father and of the Son and of the Holy Spirit" (Matthew 28:19).

After baptism, a Christian is entitled to participate in the eucharist, also known as Holy Communion and the Lord's Supper. As we have seen, the eucharist commemorates Christ's Last Supper with his disciples before his crucifixion. On that occasion, he identified the bread and wine they shared with his body and blood:

> While they were eating, he took a loaf of bread, and after blessing it he broke it and gave it to them, and said, "Take; this is my body." Then he took a cup, and after giving thanks he gave it to them, and all of them drank from it. He said to them, "This is my blood of the covenant, which is poured out for many."
> —Mark 14:22–24

Historically, most Christians have taken these words to mean that Christ is truly present in the eucharist. Only with the Reformation of the sixteenth century did some Protestant groups adopt the view that the bread and wine are mere symbols of Christ's presence. Although those who believe in the "real presence" have sought to explain it in various ways, most acknowledge that it is ultimately a mystery. In a sense, it is similar to the gestures we use to communicate inward feelings in everyday life. For example, most of us believe that the love we feel for someone else can be conveyed by a hug or a kiss, but we would find it difficult to

This baptistry basin was built in the sixth century as part of the Basilica of St. Vitalis in what is now Sbeitla, Tunisia. Candidates for baptism were led down the steps and then baptized by full immersion in water.

explain in precise terms how our love is present in the gesture. We can understand the eucharist as a kind of sacred gesture in which God offers grace to human beings. Although they have different ways of explaining how this happens, Christians agree that their participation in the ritual meal of bread and wine brings them into closer union with God and each other.

A third sacrament is confirmation. In the Roman Catholic Church, confirmation is administered to adolescents who have completed formal instruction in the faith. *Because* they understand its teachings, they are recognized as fully responsible members of the Church. In the Orthodox tradition, confirmation usually occurs when an infant is baptized *in order that*, nourished by grace, he or she might grow into a mature understanding of the faith and share in the work of the Church.

The four sacraments that remain are essentially the same in Catholicism and Orthodoxy. Holy matrimony gives a sacred character to marriage. For men who feel called to become priests, the sacrament of holy orders confers a grace that enables them to be effective leaders in the Church. Penance, also known as confession and reconciliation, involves confessing sin to a priest in order to receive his assurances of God's forgiveness and his prescription for the performance of an act of penance or reparation for the sin committed. The final sacrament, anointing of the sick, is meant to strengthen those who are in immediate danger of death.

Church Interiors: Sacred Space

The interior design of a church reflects its theology and liturgical style. Most Protestant churches are quite plain and have rows of seats facing a pulpit in the front as their

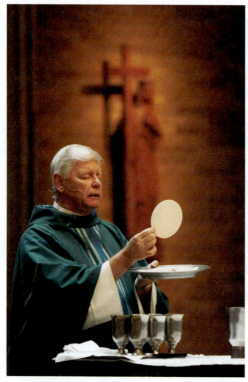

main features. It is from the pulpit, a raised lectern, that the pastor or minister delivers the weekly sermon. Because Protestants emphasize scripture over sacraments, the pulpit generally has a more prominent position than the altar. Protestant churches make sparing use of decorative effects. There may be candles on the altar and a cross displayed on the wall, but little more. The intention behind this simplicity is to create an environment without distractions in which worshippers can meet God in prayer and in the reading and exposition of scripture.

Roman Catholic churches are more elaborate. Because Catholicism emphasizes the sacraments, and the eucharist in particular, it is the altar rather than the pulpit that stands out from the worshipper's perspective. Religious paintings and statues of saints are commonly found, as are crucifixes, or images of Christ on the cross. To the side of some churches is a stand supporting rows of votive candles set in colored glass. When music is added to these physical features of the church, the senses are filled with sights and sounds meant to lift the mind and heart to God.

This approach to creating a sacred space is even more pronounced in Orthodox churches, whose design and decoration

In this celebration of the eucharist, a Roman Catholic priest prays over a wafer of bread and chalices of wine, which are believed to become the body and blood of Christ.

The design and decor of this small Protestant church are simple. The attention of the congregation is directed toward the pulpit, from which the pastor delivers a sermon based on the scriptures.

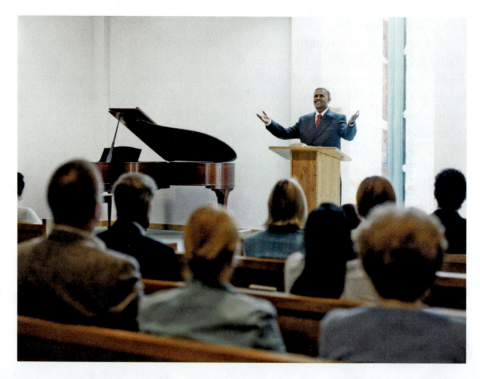

give worshippers a sense of entering into the heavenly presence of God. The main body of the Orthodox church is separated from the sanctuary in the front by a screen, called an iconostasis ("icon stand"), covered with painted images of Christ and the saints. Icons fill the rest of the church as well, reminding worshippers that they belong to a spiritual communion that includes the whole company of heaven. Even the magnificent domes atop Orthodox churches display iconic murals of Christ and the saints. But the main focus of attention is the sanctuary, which can be glimpsed through several doors that provide access to the priest and his assistants. It is in this sacred space that the mystery of the eucharist is celebrated, with chanting and incense that reveal in the material world the realities of the spiritual realm.

Like all Roman Catholic churches, this church in St. Maarten in the Netherlands Antilles gives the most prominent place to the altar, where the eucharist is celebrated. The priest's homily, or sermon, is delivered from a pulpit set to the side. Images of the saints that Catholics venerate can be seen along the walls.

Prayer

For Christians, Jesus provides the ultimate example of the importance of prayer. The gospels describe him as praying frequently, often for hours and with great fervency. On one occasion, he taught his disciples to pray in this way:

> Our Father in heaven,
> hallowed be your name.
> Your kingdom come.
> Your will be done,
> on earth as it is in heaven.
> Give us this day our daily bread.
> And forgive us our debts,
> as we also have forgiven our debtors.
> And do not bring us to the time of trial,
> but deliver us from the evil one.
> —*Matthew 6:9–13*

This prayer, known as the **Lord's Prayer**, is just one of many forms of prayer in Christianity. In the early Christian centuries, additional prayers were created and formally integrated into the liturgy. Of course, from the beginning Christians also prayed privately, informally, and silently. Today, it is customary for Christians to offer a prayer of thanksgiving before meals, on rising in the morning, and before going to bed at night. When the troubles and concerns of daily life arise, they ask God for guidance, forgiveness, and peace. In the face of sickness and death, they find in prayer the assurance of God's loving presence.

The interior of a Greek Orthodox church. Note the iconostasis, or "icon screen" at the far end of the aisle. In Orthodox churches, the altar is always located behind the iconostasis. Worshippers sit under a dome, partially visible here, on which images of Christ and the saints are painted.

What similarities do you see between the aims and practices of Christian contemplative prayer and the Hindu recitation of *mantras*?

Most Christian traditions include specialized forms of prayer practiced by those who wish to deepen their spiritual lives. For example, the interior walls of Roman Catholic churches display fourteen images of the passion, or suffering, of Christ during the final hours of his life. Catholics visit these Stations of the Cross in order, reciting prayers and meditating on each incident as a means of coming to a deeper understanding of Christ's suffering. Another form of Catholic devotion is praying the **rosary**. This involves recitation of a series of prayers counted on a string of beads while meditating on important moments in the lives of Jesus and his mother, Mary.

For instruction in prayer, Orthodox Christians turn to the *Philokalia*, a collection of mystical texts written between the fourth and the fifteenth centuries. Containing the words of Orthodoxy's greatest sages, the *Philokalia* is considered a treasury of wisdom concerning the practice of contemplative prayer. Whereas meditation centers on the intellect, contemplative prayer is a "prayer of the heart" in which it is not just the mind but one's whole being that reaches out to God. Its most common form is the Jesus Prayer: "Lord Jesus Christ, Son of God, have mercy on me." Ideally, the Jesus Prayer is recited continually, whether one is driving to work, standing in line, or attending to any other matter. In time, it embeds itself in one's being, and its repetition becomes as natural and effortless as breathing. According to one Orthodox saint, "even when [the practitioner] is immersed in sleep, the perfumes of prayer will breathe in his heart spontaneously."[10] In recent years, the Jesus Prayer and other forms of Orthodox contemplation have become increasingly popular among Catholics and Protestants, who share with Orthodox Christians a yearning for communion with God not only at certain times but throughout the course of each day.

The Liturgical Year

Just as the life of every Christian is punctuated by the sacraments, each year in the life of the Church is defined by the celebration of holy days and the observance of religious seasons that make up the liturgical year. Built around the two great feasts of **Christmas** and **Easter**, the cycle of the liturgical year draws believers into the experience of Christ, allowing them to relive in a vicarious way the events in his life through which God brought salvation to the world.

The first great season of the liturgical year is Advent, a time of preparation and looking forward to the "coming" (Latin, *adventus*) of God into the world. Advent culminates in Christmas, a celebration of the birth of Christ on December 25, when expectation turns into rejoicing. The Christmas season ends on January 6 with a celebration of **Epiphany** (from the Greek *epiphaneia*, "manifestation"), which recalls the manifestation of Jesus's divinity as an infant (emphasized in the West) and at his baptism (emphasized in the East).

After Epiphany, the liturgical year moves forward to Easter, a springtime celebration of Christ's resurrection. Easter is preceded by the season of Lent, when many Christians practice self-denial as a way of participating vicariously in the suffering of Christ. Awareness of Christ's suffering is heightened during Holy Week, the last week of Lent, when most

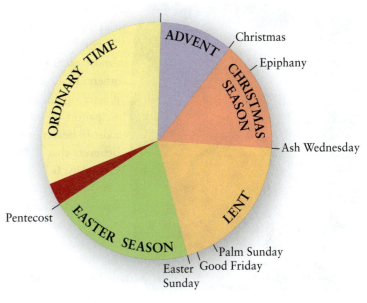

The liturgical year is an annual cycle of holy days and seasons that re-create events and times during the life of Jesus.

days have special significance. Palm Sunday recalls Christ's triumphal entry into Jerusalem, when enthusiastic crowds placed palm branches on the road before him. Maundy Thursday marks Jesus's institution of the eucharist at the Last Supper. Good Friday commemorates the crucifixion of Jesus. Holy Week concludes with Easter, the most important of Christian holidays because it is in Christ's resurrection that Christians see his triumph over death and the promise of eternal life. Easter is a truly joyous holiday, filled with signs and symbols of new life. In Orthodox countries, Easter mornings resound with the cry, "Christ is risen!" and the response, "He is risen indeed!" Rejoicing continues through the following weeks as Christians celebrate the ascension of Christ into heaven and the coming of the Holy Spirit at Pentecost. After Pentecost, the liturgical year moves into six months of "ordinary time" that ends with Advent, when the annual cycle begins again.

Veneration of Saints

Like the members of any group, Christians have always had their heroes. Known as **saints** ("holy ones"), they are spiritual role models who have shown how the Christian life should be lived. Without doubt, the greatest of saints is Mary, the virgin mother of Christ, who is considered the foremost example of what God can do in sanctifying a human life. Those who honor Mary point to her virtues of gentleness, humility, and submission to God's will and recall her expression of joy on learning that she had been chosen to bear the Christ: "Surely, from now on all generations will call me blessed" (Luke 1:48). According to Roman Catholic teaching, Mary was unique in being conceived without sin (the doctrine of the Immaculate Conception) and in being taken up bodily into heaven at her death (the doctrine

This Greek icon depicts Christ holding the scriptures and raising his right hand in a sign of blessing. The Greek letters outside his halo identify him as Jesus Christ. The letters inside the halo identify him as God.

of the Assumption). Orthodox Christians honor Mary with the titles *Theotokos* ("God-bearer") and *Panagia* ("All-holy").

For Protestant Christians, the significance of the saints lies almost exclusively in the inspiring examples they have set for others. In Roman Catholicism and Orthodoxy, the saints have greater significance. These traditions emphasize the eternal participation of the saints in the Church, for though they now exist in heaven, they remain within the mystical communion of believers that is "the body of Christ." Catholic and Orthodox Christians believe that Paul made this point when he wrote that Christians are "citizens with the saints and also members of the household of God" (Ephesians 2:16).

Just as the living pray for the welfare of their fellow Christians, the saints are thought to intercede for them in prayer as well. Belief in the intercession of saints is evident in early Christian literature and in ancient epitaphs found on sarcophagi and grave markers. These implore both saints and departed family members to pray for the living. "Pray for us," says one inscription, "that we may be saved." On the sarcophagus of their little boy, his mother and father wrote: "To our son Philemon, who lived happily for two years with his parents: Pray for us, together with the saints."[11] Belief in the intercession of saints remains an important part of Roman Catholicism and Orthodoxy. Strictly speaking, one does not pray *to* the saints, but *with* them. Saints are not worshipped. Instead, they are venerated with a reverential respect that recognizes their holiness.

The veneration of saints takes a variety of forms. Most Catholic and Orthodox Christians are given a saint's name at baptism, and their churches are usually named after saints. Many believers honor saints on their feast days and wear medals with their likenesses imprinted on them. In addition, the physical remains of saints, known as relics, are objects of veneration. Preserved in special containers known as reliquaries, relics can be found in many churches, where they bring a sense of the sacred to those who pray in their presence. The relics are often brought out for special observances or processions on the saint's feast day (p. 439). If this practice seems a bit strange to you, it might be helpful to consider how you might be affected by a more secular "relic." For example, a photograph or keepsake from a loved one you have lost can provide a sense of that person's presence. In some mysterious way, it seems, something of that person's essence remains within the item itself. So it is with the saints, whose holiness is thought to remain in the relics they have left behind.

Images of saints also produce a heightened awareness of holiness. In Roman Catholicism, images take the forms of paintings and statues whose lifelike quality is meant to underscore the experience of earthly existence that the saints share with all other believers. Meditating on a painting or statue, believers are encouraged in the spiritual life by knowing that the saint it represents once experienced the same challenges they experience. The **icons** of the Orthodox, who make no use of statues, are meant to have just the opposite effect. These highly stylized paintings are not intended to be lifelike. Their purpose is to represent not earthly reality but the reality of transfigured and perfected humanity in heaven. Gazing intently at their observers and communicating through symbolic gestures, the saints depicted in icons offer a glimpse of the higher, spiritual realm that is the ultimate goal of every Christian.

Social and Political Activism

Service to others is an important part of Christian practice. According to the New Testament (Acts 4:32–35), the earliest Christians took seriously the command to love one's neighbor as oneself: the wealthy gave all their money to the church, all property was held in common, and no one experienced great need. In the Middle Ages, the churches of the East and West provided important social services by supporting orphans, widows, and the disabled; seeking the release of prisoners of war; and caring for victims of plagues, earthquakes, and other disasters.

This tradition of social service continues today. Most congregations make significant contributions to support the poor, the sick, and the homeless in their communities. On a larger scale, there are hundreds of national and international Christian charities dedicated to fighting social and political injustice, bringing an end to poverty, and providing food, health services, and education to those in need. They include Habitat for Humanity, Bread for the World, International Orthodox Charities, Catholic Relief Services, the Salvation Army, and World Vision.

Christian activism has often brought important social and political change. American abolitionists such as Theodore Weld (1803–1895) and Harriet Beecher Stowe (1811–1896) played leading roles in the American antislavery movement, whose aims were realized in the Emancipation Proclamation of 1863. In the 1960s, it was a black Baptist minister, Dr. Martin Luther King Jr. (1929–1968), who championed the civil rights movement that succeeded in outlawing discrimination against minorities and women in the Civil Rights Act of 1964. Today's Christian activists are involved in causes ranging from placing water for migrants in the deserts of Arizona to protesting nuclear weapons to fighting HIV/AIDS in Africa.

CONCLUSION

With a history reaching back 2,000 years, Christianity has proven to be a durable religion. Like other religions that have met the test of time, much of its vitality lies in the meaning its message has had for countless adherents through the centuries. History, geography, culture, and other forces have produced many forms of Christianity, but they share basic beliefs that go back to Jesus and to the New Testament texts that expound the meaning of his teachings, life, death, and resurrection: there is a single, transcendent, all-powerful, and personal God who created the universe as an expression of divine love and who seeks loving union with humanity.

In addressing the most basic questions arising from human existence, the Christian message has had an incalculable influence on individual lives. But it has also contributed to the formation of entire civilizations, shaping their political and social institutions, informing their cultural values and ideals, and inspiring some of their greatest achievements in art, architecture, and literature.

It seems that there are two great issues we must consider, however briefly, in concluding our discussion of Christianity. The first is the role Christianity will play in shaping the world of the future. How will Christians respond to the environmental, social, and political problems our world faces? What actions will they take in promoting justice? How will they apply the gospel message in acknowledging and protecting the rights of women, homosexuals, and the poor—both inside and outside the Church? The second issue is how Christianity will be affected by the rapid change we see all around us. Will its traditional forms and institutions remain solidly entrenched? As the world's Christian population becomes increasingly concentrated in Africa, South America, and Asia, how will the religious and cultural traditions of these regions influence a religion with a history that has been played out largely in Europe and North America? Of course, we cannot be certain of the answers to questions like these. We can be certain only that Christianity, the world's largest religion, will remain a major force in the world in which we live.

SEEKING ANSWERS

What Is Ultimate Reality?

Christianity teaches that there is a single, personal, transcendent, and all-powerful God—a God who is one in essence but threefold in his manifestations as Father, Son, and Holy Spirit. God created a perfect world as an expression of divine love, but it has fallen into imperfection due to human sin. Like Jews and Muslims, Christians believe that God wants to be known in and by Creation, and especially by humanity. For Christians, the supreme revelation of the divine nature is found in Jesus Christ, who was the very incarnation of God. They also believe that God has revealed himself in other ways, such as through scripture and through the immensity and beauty of the universe.

How Should We Live in This World?

Christians believe that God has reached out in grace (love) to humanity, making atonement for sin through Jesus Christ. For those who respond to God's love in faith, a new kind of life in Christ becomes possible—a life in which the fundamental ethical principle is love. Jesus spoke of love for God and one's neighbor as the essence of scripture and described it in a radical way. Even enemies must be loved and forgiven. This demanding conception of love

(continued)

SEEKING ANSWERS *(continued)*

is one of the essential ideals in Christianity. It is also one that requires great effort. To achieve it, Christians find inspiration in study and reflection on scripture, through prayer, and in fellowship with other Christians who take love seriously. Christians find good examples of love and other virtues in the lives of the saints, whom they seek to emulate. They also believe that the sacraments offer a spiritual nourishment that is helpful in the cultivation of lives they attempt to live in imitation of Christ.

What Is Our Ultimate Purpose?

For Christians, the ultimate goal of human existence is union with God. As Augustine wrote in the fifth century, "You have made us for yourself, O Lord, and our hearts are restless until they find rest in you." The path to reunion with God is through Jesus Christ, whose sacrificial death, an expression of God's love, atoned for all human sin. When human beings respond in faith to God's love, or grace, they are brought into union with the divine. Christians hope to share in the resurrection of Christ, which leads to eternal blessedness in union with God. But there is also the possibility of eternal separation from God. Because the Bible offers few concrete details about these two possibilities, traditionally understood as heaven and hell, they have been interpreted in many different ways.

REVIEW QUESTIONS

For Review

1. What were the means by which the Christian movement defined orthodox belief and established ecclesiastical authority in late antiquity?

2. How did the Roman Catholic, Orthodox, and Protestant traditions within Christianity emerge from the "catholic" or "universal" Christianity of the first millennium? What were the main factors that contributed to the formation of these traditions?

3. What are the seasons and holy days of the liturgical year? What is their significance for Christians? How are they observed?

4. What is the doctrine of the Trinity? Why is this doctrine central to Christianity?

5. What are the major challenges Christianity has encountered in the modern era? How has it responded to them?

For Further Reflection

1. What are some of the more important ways in which basic Christian beliefs are expressed outwardly in worship, the sacraments, prayer, and other devotional practices?

2. If asked by a friend, how would you describe the essence of Christianity? Are there teachings embraced by all (or, at least, most) forms of Christianity?

3. How do Christian beliefs about God/ ultimate reality, human nature, the world,

and the ultimate goal or purpose of human existence compare with those of the closely related religions of Judaism and Islam?

4. How do Christian beliefs about these same issues compare with those of religions such as Hinduism, Buddhism, Daoism, Confucianism, Sikhism, and Jainism?

5. Do you think the Christian ecumenical movement has a realistic chance of restoring the original unity of the Christian religion?

GLOSSARY

apostle In the New Testament, Jesus's disciples, sent out to preach and baptize, are called apostles (Greek *apostolos*, "one who is sent out"). Paul of Tarsus and some other early Christian leaders also claimed this title. Because of their close association with Jesus, the apostles were accorded a place of honor in the early Church.

apostolic succession According to this Roman Catholic and Orthodox doctrine, the spiritual authority conferred by Jesus on the apostles has been transmitted through an unbroken line of bishops, who are their successors.

baptism Performed by immersion in water or a sprinkling with water, baptism is a sacrament in which an individual is cleansed of sin and admitted into the Church.

bishop Responsible for supervising other priests and their congregations within specific regions known as dioceses, bishops are regarded by Roman Catholic and Orthodox Christians as successors of the apostles.

Calvin, John (1509–1564) One of the leading figures of the Protestant Reformation, Calvin is notable for his *Institutes of the Christian Religion* and his emphasis on the absolute power of God, the absolute depravity of human nature, and the absolute dependence of human beings on divine grace for salvation.

Christmas An annual holiday commemorating the birth of Jesus, Christmas is observed by Western Christians on December 25. Although many Orthodox Christians celebrate Christmas on this date, others observe the holiday on January 7.

church In the broadest sense, "church" refers to the universal community of Christians, but the term can also refer to a particular tradition within Christianity (such as the Roman Catholic Church or the Lutheran Church) or to an individual congregation of Christians.

Easter An annual holiday commemorating the resurrection of Christ, Easter is a "moveable feast" whose date changes from year to year, though it is always celebrated in spring (as early as March 22 and as late as May 8).

Epiphany An annual holiday commemorating the "manifestation" of the divinity of the infant Jesus, Epiphany is celebrated by most Western Christians on January 6. Most Eastern Christians observe it on January 19.

eucharist (*yoó-ka-rist*) Also known as the Lord's Supper and Holy Communion, the eucharist is a sacrament celebrated with consecrated bread and wine in commemoration of Jesus's Last Supper with his disciples.

evangelicalism This Protestant movement stresses the importance of the conversion experience, the Bible as the only reliable authority in matters of faith, and preaching the gospel. In recent decades, evangelicalism has become a major force in North American Christianity.

fundamentalism Originating in the early 1900s, this movement in American Protestantism was dedicated to defending doctrines it identified as fundamental to Christianity against perceived threats posed by modern culture.

(continued)

GLOSSARY *(continued)*

gospel In its most general sense, "gospel" means the "good news" (from Old English *godspel*, which translates the Greek *evangelion*) about Jesus Christ. The New Testament gospels of Matthew, Mark, Luke, and John are proclamations of the good news concerning the life, teachings, death, and resurrection of Jesus Christ.

grace Derived from the Latin *gratia* (a "gift" or "love"), "grace" refers to God's love for humanity, expressed in Jesus Christ and through the sacraments.

icons Painted images of Christ and the saints, icons are used extensively in the Orthodox Church.

Inquisition The investigation and suppression of heresy by the Roman Catholic Church, the Inquisition began in the twelfth century and was formally concluded in the middle of the nineteenth century.

kingdom of God God's rule or dominion over the universe and human affairs. The kingdom of God is one of the primary themes in the teaching of Jesus.

liturgy The liturgy (from Greek, *leitourgia*, "a work of the people" in honor of God) is the basic order of worship in Christian churches. It consists of prescribed prayers, readings, and rituals.

logos In its most basic sense, the Greek *logos* means "word," but it also means "rational principle," "reason," or "divine reason." The Gospel of John uses *logos* in the sense of the "divine reason" through which God created and sustains the universe when it states that "the Word became flesh" in Jesus Christ (John 1:14).

Lord's Prayer A prayer attributed to Jesus, the Lord's Prayer serves as a model of prayer for Christians. Also known as the "Our Father" (since it begins with these words), its most familiar form is found in the Gospel of Matthew (6:9–13).

Luther, Martin (1483–1546) A German monk who criticized Roman Catholic doctrines and practices in his Ninety-Five Theses (1517), Luther was the original leader and one of the seminal thinkers of the Protestant Reformation.

Messiah In the Jewish Scriptures (Old Testament), the Hebrew "messiah" ("anointed one") refers to kings and priests, who were anointed with consecrated oil. In later Jewish literature, the Messiah is sometimes understood as a figure—in some cases, a supernatural figure—who, having been "anointed" by God, rescues the Jewish people and the world from evil. Christianity understands Jesus of Nazareth as the Messiah.

Nicene Creed A profession of faith formulated by the Councils of Nicea (325) and Constantinople (381), the Nicene Creed articulates the Christian doctrine of the Trinity.

original sin Formulated by St. Augustine in the fourth century, the doctrine of original sin states that the sin of Adam and Eve affected all of humanity, so that all human beings are born with a sinful nature.

Orthodox Church Also known as the Eastern Orthodox Church and the Orthodox Catholic Church, the Orthodox Church is the Eastern branch of Christianity that separated from the Western branch (the Roman Catholic Church) in 1054.

parable According to the gospels of Matthew, Mark, and Luke, Jesus made extensive use of parables—short, fictional stories that use the language and imagery of everyday life to illustrate moral and religious truths.

Paul of Tarsus A first-century apostle who founded churches throughout Asia Minor, Macedonia, and Greece. Paul was also the author of many of the letters, or epistles, found in the New Testament.

Pentecost A holiday celebrated by Christians in commemoration of the outpouring of the Holy Spirit on the disciples of Jesus as described in the second chapter of the New Testament book of Acts.

Pentecostalism A movement that emphasizes the importance of spiritual renewal and the experience of God through baptism in the Holy Spirit, Pentecostalism is a primarily Protestant movement that has become extremely popular in recent decades.

(continued)

GLOSSARY *(continued)*

Protestant Christianity One of the three major traditions in Christianity (along with Roman Catholicism and Orthodoxy), Protestantism began in the sixteenth century as a reaction against medieval Roman Catholic doctrines and practices.

purgatory In Roman Catholicism, purgatory is an intermediate state between earthly life and heaven in which the debt for unconfessed sin is expiated.

Roman Catholic Church One of the three major traditions within Christianity (along with Orthodoxy and Protestantism), the Roman Catholic Church, which recognizes the primacy of the bishop of Rome, or pope, has historically been the dominant church in the West.

rosary Taking its name from the Latin *rosarium* ("garland of roses"), the rosary is a traditional form of Roman Catholic devotion in which practitioners make use of a string of beads in reciting prayers.

sacraments The sacraments are rituals in which material elements such as bread, wine, water, and oil serve as visible symbols of an invisible grace conveyed to recipients.

saint A saint is a "holy person" (Latin *sanctus*). Veneration of the saints and belief in their intercession on behalf of the living is an important feature of Roman Catholic and Orthodox Christianity.

scholasticism Represented by figures such as Peter Abelard, Thomas Aquinas, and William of Ockham, scholasticism was the medieval effort to reconcile faith and reason using the philosophy of Aristotle.

sin The violation of God's will in thought or action.

transubstantiation According to this Roman Catholic doctrine, the bread and wine consecrated by a priest in the eucharist become the body and blood of Christ and retain only the appearance, not the substance, of bread and wine.

Trinity According to the Christian doctrine of the Trinity, God is a single divine substance or essence consisting in three "persons."

SUGGESTIONS FOR FURTHER READING

Bowden, John. *Encyclopedia of Christianity*. New York: Oxford University Press, 2005. A one-volume collection of short scholarly articles on hundreds of topics.

Dowell, Graham. *The Heart Has Seasons: Travelling through the Christian Year*. Worthing, UK: Churchman, 1989. A superb introduction to the significance and celebration of the "seasons" of the liturgical year.

Dowley, Tim, and David Wright. *Introduction to the History of Christianity*. Minneapolis, MN: Fortress Press, 1995. Includes hundreds of photos, maps, charts, and articles on topics of special interest.

Ehrman, Bart. *The New Testament: A Historical Introduction to the Early Christian Writings*. New York: Oxford University Press, 2000. An excellent introduction to the New Testament texts and selected Christian texts from the second century.

Marsden, George. *Understanding Fundamentalism and Evangelicalism*. Grand Rapids, MI: William B. Eerdmans, 1991. Describes the essential features of these two movements and their involvement in politics and science.

McGrath, Alister. *Theology: The Basics*. Malden, MA: Blackwell, 2004. Individual chapters focus on specific issues such as God, Jesus, faith, salvation, and heaven. Emphasis on Roman Catholic and Protestant thought.

Ware, Timothy (Kallistos). *The Orthodox Church*. New York: Penguin, 1993. A classic presentation of the history, thought, and practices of the Orthodox tradition by one of its greatest spokespersons.

White, James. *Introduction to Christian Worship*. 3rd ed. Nashville, TN: Abingdon Press, 2001. An ideal book for beginners interested in the history and forms of Christian worship.

ONLINE RESOURCES

"From Jesus to Christ: The First Christians"
pbs.org/wgbh/pages/frontline/shows/religion
From the PBS documentary series *Frontline*, this website features the full documentary, as well as supplemental materials from theologians, historians, and archaeologists.

Virtual Religion Index
virtualreligion.net
An excellent gateway to religion-related sites of all kinds, including collections of texts, religion-specific sites, and academic program sites.

Catholic Online
catholic.org
This online resource provides access to information "on all things Catholic," including saints, holy days, Roman Catholic theology, and announcements from the Vatican.

Orthodox Wiki
orthodoxwiki.org
This online resource includes nearly 4,000 articles on all aspects of Orthodox Christianity. A great place to begin an exploration of Orthodoxy.

Theopedia
theopedia.com
An online "encyclopedia of biblical Christianity" with articles on hundreds of topics written from an evangelical Protestant perspective.

ISLAM

FAINT TRACES OF DAWN light up the tops of tall coconut palms and lush mango trees in a village in Zanzibar, an East African island in the Indian Ocean. Amina, a woman in her early thirties and a devout Muslim, rises from her bed. She was awakened by the sound of the call to prayer from the local mosque. In the open-air courtyard of her house, she begins her morning ablutions to prepare for the first of her daily prayers. She takes cool water from the cistern in the courtyard and carefully washes her face, hands, and feet, and rinses her mouth, nose, and ears. She also wets her head and hair. Before each of the five daily prayers, Amina performs similar ablutions. Although she occasionally wears eye makeup and lipstick, she is careful to avoid nail polish. She explains that all such adornment must be removed to purify herself for each prayer; makeup is easily removed with water, but nail polish is not.

After her ablutions, Amina returns to the house, covers her head and shoulders with a clean cotton wrap, and spreads a colorful woven prayer mat on the floor next to her bed. She removes her sandals, steps onto the mat, and begins the first of the five prescribed daily ritual prayers that are expected of all devout Muslims. The prayers are called *salat*, and consist of the recitation of verses from the **Qur'an**, the sacred text of Islam, accompanied by specific bodily movements. Together, the cycles of prayer and movement are called *raka*. Amina has made her daily prayers since

Pilgrims circumambulate the Ka'ba in Mecca, Saudi Arabia. The pilgrimage to Mecca, known as the hajj, is a once-in-a-lifetime duty for devout Muslims.

Significant sites in the history of Islam.

she was a young girl. As a child, her mother and elder sisters taught her how to pray; eventually, she will do the same for her own children. She begins the prayer standing, then kneels, bows her forehead to the ground, and kneels again in accordance with her recitation. Hand movements accompany the bodily postures. Daily prayer is an essential part of Muslim worship. Through prayer, Amina is acknowledging to herself and her community that she is submitting herself to the will of God—an important tenet of the Islamic faith. In fact, the term Muslim means "one who submits" in Arabic.

Amina prays alone in her modest home, but men in her community typically gather at the local mosque for each of the daily prayers, which are led by a prayer leader called an **imam**. Like women, most Zanzibari men cover their heads when praying, most often with a brimless, embroidered cap. Although in some parts of the Muslim world women regularly pray in mosques, in Zanzibar, particularly in rural areas, it is uncommon for women to do so. However, women often gather together at mosques for other reasons, such as Qur'an study groups and sessions in religious instruction.

When she completes her prayers, Amina rolls up her prayer mat and sets it aside for later. She reads a few verses from the Qur'an in the early morning light, and then begins the first tasks of her day—making tea and sweeping the courtyard. ☀

Amina is one of about 1.6 billion Muslims living in the world today; Islam is second only to Christianity in numbers of adherents. Amina lives in Africa, and most of the world's Muslims live in South and Southeast Asia, not in the Arabic-speaking countries of the Middle East. In fact, Arab Muslims make up less than 20 percent of the total Muslim population worldwide. The country with the largest Muslim population in the world is the Southeast Asian nation of Indonesia, followed closely by Pakistan, India, and Bangladesh. Many countries in Africa also have very large Muslim populations. Today, there are nearly 3 million Muslims in the United States,[1] and the number of Muslims in North America is increasing rapidly, mostly through immigration. Muslims also make up significant minority populations in many parts of Western Europe, especially in France, where they make up nearly 9 percent of the population.[2]

Islam developed in the Arabian Peninsula and rapidly spread through the Middle East, Asia, and Africa. Because of its global presence, Islam is practiced, understood, and interpreted in diverse ways in many different countries, cultures, and communities. However, certain beliefs and practices can be considered universal parts of Muslim religious life. Most important of these is the monotheistic belief in the oneness of **Allah**, which is the Arabic term for God. Secondly, Muslims recognize **Muhammad**, who received the message of the Qur'an from God, as the final prophet in a long line of prophets sent to humanity by God. The Qur'an is believed to be the word of God and is the holy text of Muslims. In addition, Muslims around the world share the observance of the five pillars of worship practice. The term "**Islam**" (Arabic, "submission") reflects Muslim belief in the importance of submitting to God's will.

TIMELINE
Islam

570 C.E.   The birth of Muhammad.

610   The first revelations of the Qur'an to Muhammad.

622   The *hijra* (migration) from Mecca to Medina.

632   The death of Muhammad; issue of succession.

632–661   Period of the Rightly Guided Caliphs.

657   Battle of Siffin.

661   'Ali killed.

661–750   Umayyad period.

680   Battle at Karbala and martyrdom of Husayn.

750–1258   Abbasid period.

1095–1453   Crusades.

1207–1273   Jalalludin Rumi.

1281–1924   Ottoman Empire.

1483–1857   Mughal Empire.

1501–1722   Safavid Empire.

1703–1792   Ibn Abd al-Wahhab.

1849–1905   Muhammad Abduh.

1881–1938   Mustafa Kemal Ataturk.

1923   Huda Sha'rawi unveils at Egyptian train station.

1947   Partition of India and Pakistan.

1979   Iranian Revolution.

2004   France bans wearing of headscarves and other religious identifiers in schools.

2006   Keith Ellison is first Muslim elected to U.S. Congress.

2009   Green Movement, Iran.

2011   "Arab Spring" pro-democracy movements spread across the Middle East.

THE TEACHINGS OF ISLAM

Islam arose in the Arabian Peninsula in the seventh century, when Muslims believe that a man called Muhammad began receiving communication from God. The primary source of Islamic teachings is the Qur'an, which Muslims believe is the word of

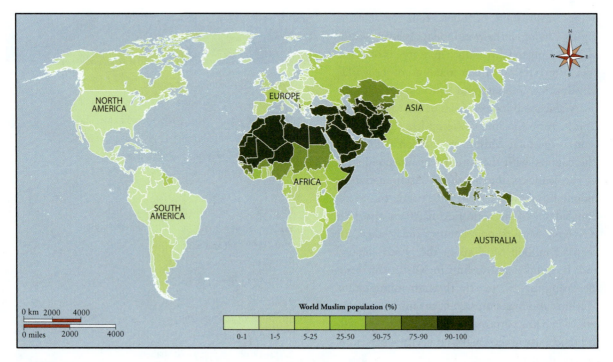

World Muslim population (%)

| 0-1 | 1-5 | 5-25 | 25-50 | 50-75 | 75-90 | 90-100 |

World Muslim population.

God as revealed to Muhammad. According to Muslim belief, Islam was not introduced as a new religion. Rather, the revelations of the Qur'an to Muhammad were a reawakening or reintroduction of the original monotheistic faith of the prophet Abraham, a figure who is also important to Jews (Chapter 11) and Christians (Chapter 12). Islam is considered one of the Abrahamic religions, along with Judaism and Christianity, and the three religions share a great deal. Although many people in pre-Islamic Arabia were polytheists, significant numbers of Jews and Christians also lived in the region. People in Arabia were therefore familiar with biblical stories and characters, and several of these are mentioned in the Qur'an. In the Islamic view, Abraham (or Ibrahim, as Muslims call him) was the original monotheist who received a revelation from God, a revelation that taught him the true religion centering on the oneness of God. Muslims believe that when Muhammad received the revelations of the Qur'an, he was given a reminder for humanity of what God conveyed to Abraham. This section explores what Muslims believe about the revelation of the Qur'an to Muhammad. In a later section, we explore his life, his prophecy, and his leadership roles.

Muhammad and the Revelations

Muslims consider Muhammad (c. 570–632 C.E.) the final messenger in a series of prophets sent by God to humanity. In addition to Abraham, these prophets include many other figures important in the Jewish and Christian traditions, such as Noah, Moses, and Jesus. In Muslim belief, all prophets are solely human—not divine. However, the importance of Muhammad to Muslims should not be underestimated.

In addition to receiving the revelation of the Qur'an, Muhammad is considered an extraordinary man in all respects. He was the religious and political leader of the early Muslim community and, even today—fourteen centuries after his death—his life is considered an example for all Muslims to follow.

Some of what we know about Muhammad and his life comes from the Qur'an. We also know something of his life from biographical writings and from what his close friends, associates, and family (who are known together as his *companions*) observed about him and passed on in reports. In addition, there are many stories and legends about the Prophet. Because most of what we know about Muhammad comes from sources that were compiled by Muslims after he became a prophet, we know very little about his early life. Muslims do not believe that Muhammad was divine, but rather consider him to be *al-insan al-kamil*, the ideal human. And although he was a prophet, in many respects he lived the life of a normal man. He had a family, earned a living, and was active in his community.

Most Muslims believe that Muhammad was a spiritual man and a religious seeker even before he began receiving the revelation of the Qur'an. He was considered a devout monotheist even at a time in which many of his contemporaries were polytheists, and it is said that he often meditated alone on the oneness of God. When he reached the age of forty, in the year 610 C.E., the Angel Gabriel (known in Arabic as Jibril) visited Muhammad while he was praying in an isolated cave outside Mecca. Muhammad heard a voice that told him that he was the messenger of God and commanded him to "Recite!" Muhammad is said to have been awed and bewildered. He is thought to have hesitated three times at Jibril's command, because as an illiterate man he did not feel he was able to recite. Eventually he repeated the words the angel told him to recite, and these are considered to be the first revealed verses of the Qur'an. The rest of the Qur'an was revealed to Muhammad over the next twenty-three years.

Muhammad confided in his wife, **Khadija**, a wealthy and successful businesswoman, about the revelations. She listened carefully and believed his message. Because she was the first to believe the truth of the message received by Muhammad, Khadija is considered to be the first convert to Islam. Other early followers were Muhammad's close friends and family members. Muhammad's young cousin 'Ali, who later became his son-in-law when he married Muhammad's daughter Fatima, was the first male convert to Islam. A friend of Muhammad's called Abu Bakr was also an early convert, and he became Muhammad's father-in-law much later in life when, after Khadija's death, Muhammad married Abu Bakr's daughter.

After the first revelations, Muhammad began a life of preaching in Mecca. The verses of the Qur'an that he received during this time emphasized the oneness of God—the central tenet of the Islamic faith. Muhammad preached this idea to the people of Mecca and also taught about morality, social justice for the poor and downtrodden, and the inevitability of the Day of Judgment.

Muhammad was not the only prophet in the Islamic tradition. The Qur'an mentions several prophets by name and refers to the existence of many others. Muhammad, however, is known as the "seal of the prophets," which means that the door of prophecy was closed—or "sealed"—with him because he was the final prophet. Muslims believe that the revelations to Muhammad came at a time when it was necessary to reawaken understanding of God's message to humanity.

The Holy Qur'an

The Qur'an is the sacred text of Islam, and it is considered the literal word of God. The Arabic word *qur'an* means "recitation," and the book is called such because Muhammad received the Qur'an orally and taught it to his followers in the same way. When the Qur'an was eventually written down, the text was corrected by the oral knowledge of those who had committed it to memory. Even today, printed copies of the Qur'an bear the stamp of approval of a person known as *hafidh* or "keeper of the Qur'an." This is a person who knows the entire Qur'an by heart.

The Qur'an was not revealed all at once to Muhammad, but rather gradually over a period of more than twenty years until his death. The language of the Qur'an is classical Arabic, and stylistically it resembles the beauty of the Arabic poetry of the time in which it was revealed. However, it is important to note that Muslims do not regard the Qur'an as poetry. This is because poetry is a human endeavor, and Muslims view the Qur'an as solely the word of God. Reciting, reading, and studying the Qur'an are an important part of daily life for devout Muslims today, in all parts of the world.

The Qur'an is not a narrative text, which means that it does not tell a story from beginning to end (although there are some stories within the text). The Qur'an consists of 114 chapters, each of which is called a **surah**. Each *surah* consists of several verses. The *surahs* are not organized around specific topics or time periods, and they are not arranged in the order of revelation, as one might expect. Rather, they are arranged roughly from the longest to the shortest, with the exception of the opening *surah*, which is quite short. Some *surahs* are only a few verses long, and the longest has almost 300 verses. Each *surah* has a title. The titles were not revealed to Muhammad but were, rather, based on a distinctive element of the *surah*. For example, the third *surah* is called "The Women" because of the many verses within it that reference the status of women.

At the time of Muhammad's death, the revelations of the Qur'an had not been collected into one book. The primary mode of teaching and learning the Qur'an was oral. During the rule of the caliph 'Uthman, however, the revelations were organized into a written text. For centuries, Muslims have considered this text standard. Today, however, some secular scholars think that a number of versions of the Qur'an originally existed and that the written text of the Qur'an emerged gradually in the seventh and eighth centuries.

The most well-known *surah* is the first one, which is called al-*fatihah*, or the "the opening." The *fatihah* is a common prayer used by

This illuminated Qur'an is from the thirteenth century.

Muslims in many different contexts. It is the first *surah* that Muslims learn when they begin studying the Qur'an as children or as adults. A devout Muslim will recite the *fatihah* several times during the day's many prayers. The *surah* evokes the oneness of God, the all-powerful nature of God, the Day of Judgment, and God's guidance for a righteous life.

THE OPENING/AL-FATIHAH

In the name of Allah, most benevolent, ever-merciful
All praise be to Allah,
Lord of all the worlds,
Most beneficent, ever merciful,
King of the Day of Judgment.
You alone we worship, and to You
alone turn for help.
Guide us (O Lord) to the path that is straight,
The path of those You have blessed,
Not of those who have earned Your anger,
Nor those who have gone astray.[3]

Today, most Muslims consider the Qur'an both inimitable and uncreated. This means that Muslims regard the holy text as unique and eternal. Today and historically, Muslims have believed that the Qur'an's equal cannot be created by human effort, which is considered proof of its divine origins. Most contemporary Muslims also believe that the Qur'an is eternal—that it has always existed. This view has not always dominated, however. The Mutazilites, a rationalist school of Islamic thought that was prominent many centuries ago, argued that the Qur'an was not eternal but was rather created by God. The Mutazilite scholars argued that the idea of an eternal Qur'an compromised the unity of God because God alone was eternal and the creator of all things—including the Qur'an. This view had some support in the tenth century, but eventually the idea of the eternal Qur'an became dominant in the Islamic tradition.[4]

The Teachings of the Qur'an

The major teachings of the Qur'an are found throughout the text. In any number of verses, we can find reference to the nature of God, the reality of the Day of Judgment, and guidelines for moral behavior.

The Oneness of God Like the other Abrahamic religions, Islam is a monotheistic religion, and the most important principle of Islamic belief is the oneness of God. The Qur'an teaches that God, known in Arabic as "Allah," is eternal, uncreated, all-knowing, and all-powerful, and it is God alone who created the universe and humankind. God is also merciful, just, and good. God is transcendent but also present, or immanent, in the lives of believers. A much-quoted verse of the Qur'an refers to God as closer to humanity "than the jugular vein" (50:16). Muslims believe that it is impossible for God to have a partner, consort, or family because no other being shares God's divinity. Muslims believe that God is the same God of the Jews and Christians. However, to Muslims, the Christian doctrine of the Trinity compromises the unity of God. The Qur'an specifically comments on the impossibility of God begetting a son, as in the following verse:

> He to whom belongs the kingdom of the heavens and the earth: who has neither begotten a son, nor has He a partner in kingdom: (who) created every thing, and determined its exact measure (25:2).[5]

The Qur'an also teaches that Muslims should strive to acknowledge the oneness of God through acts of devotion. Because the unity of God is the central tenet of Islamic belief, it follows that denying or compromising this oneness is the greatest sin. This sin of associating anything or anyone else with God is called **shirk**. In the Qur'an, *shirk* is noted as the only unforgivable sin in the eyes of Allah. This is because it denies the existence of God and the true nature of God. For the believing Muslim, the worship of God should be given to God alone, and human beings should worship nothing else. Therefore, nature, idols, images, and human beings must not be worshipped.

In Muslim belief, Allah created the universe, the world, and everything in it, including the sun and the moon, the mountains and oceans, and all living things. The natural world is mentioned throughout the Qur'an, and elements of nature are referred to as *ayat*, or signs of God: "We shall show them Our signs in every region of the earth and in themselves, until it becomes clear to them that this is the truth" (41:53). Muslims view the natural world and the entire cosmos as a type of revelation from God. (The Qur'an itself, remember, is another type of revelation.) Therefore, in Muslim belief, the natural world as a whole is evidence of the existence of God, and human beings should be able to realize this simply by observing nature. Despite this, human beings cannot truly know the ultimate essence of God, God's ultimate purpose, and ultimate reality. Thus Muslims may not be able to understand rationally why bad things happen to good people. However, they should have faith in God's purpose, even though they cannot truly know it (2:216).

Prophecy Prophecy is also an essential component of Islamic belief, and it is mentioned several times in the Qur'an. The belief in prophecy is also important to Judaism and Christianity, and the three Abrahamic faiths share many of the same prophets. In Islam, it is through the messages revealed to prophets that humanity comes to know the desires of God and the divine laws that govern the universe and creation. The belief in revealed scripture goes hand in hand with the belief in prophecy, because Muslims believe that it is through prophets that humanity obtains scripture.

Muslims recognize many prophets since the beginning of creation. Each prophet received special words from God that were appropriate for humanity at the time in which the particular prophet lived. The prophet Abraham is mentioned several times in the Qur'an. The stories of his life resemble those told by Jews and Christians, and they serve as an important basis for the annual pilgrimage to Mecca (discussed in the next section). The Qur'an also names Jesus as an important prophet (and indeed says that Jesus will return to herald the Day of Judgment), and the Gospels are considered part of God's revelation to humanity. Muslims believe that Jesus was born of the Virgin Mary, who is also mentioned in the Qur'an and is held in very high regard by Muslims. However, Muslims do not believe that Jesus was divine or the son of God. Verse 25:2, which you read earlier, reflects this idea.

Muslims believe that all prophets bring communication from God. The Qur'an teaches that prophets fall into different classes based on the nature of that communication. Some are said to bring simply "news" from God. Others, like Muhammad, bring a major message. In addition to Muhammad, prophets such as Moses and Jesus also received major messages. Moses received the Torah as guidance for humankind, and the teachings of Jesus are regarded as a major message from God. All scriptures, including the Torah and the Gospels, are considered by Muslims to be the work of God. Although the Qur'an refers to those peoples to whom scripture was revealed as "Peoples of the Book," the Qur'an also teaches that the earlier messages have been misinterpreted or forgotten by the Christians and the Jews.

According to the Qur'an, Adam and his wife, Hawa (or Eve), are regarded as the first two humans. Adam became the first prophet in the Islamic tradition. Adam and Hawa were created separately by God from a single soul (4:1) and made of dust or clay according to a divine model. Muslims believe that God blew spirit into humanity. Therefore, as in nature, the signs of God are also in humanity. The Qur'an teaches that human beings were created to worship God (51:56) and that the nature of humanity is to obey God and to give thankfulness for God's blessings.

You will recall that the meaning of the term *Muslim* is "one who submits." However, as part of God's creation on earth, Muslims believe that humans should also act as responsible members of society and stewards of the natural world. The Qur'an contains a story that is similar to the one in Genesis, in which the first humans disobeyed God by tasting a forbidden fruit. In the Qur'anic story, Adam and Hawa are both to blame for this disobedience, and they are immediately forgiven for their transgressions by God (71:13–17). Most Muslims believe that, unlike other living creatures, all human beings have free choice and thus must choose to submit to the will of God. Each individual's choices will be evaluated on the Day of Judgment.

The Day of Judgment The coming of the Day of Judgment and the reality of the afterlife is another central teaching of the Qu'ran. Many of the early *surahs* focus on God's judgment and can be read as warnings to humanity to live a righteous life or suffer the consequences when facing God at the end of days. Despite the dire warning of some of these verses, God's justice is strongly emphasized, and the Qur'an gives details about how to live a righteous life. Greed and hypocrisy are criticized, and kindness and generosity are praised. The Qur'an teaches that all believers, men and women alike, will stand alone in front of Allah and will be judged according to their actions in life. The Qur'an teaches that after death, a person resides in the grave in a sleeplike state until the end of days, at which time the judgment will take place. The end of days is described in the Qur'an as a time when the world turns upside down in great calamity. *Surah* 99 dramatically describes Judgment Day:

> When the world is shaken up by its cataclysm
> And earth throws out its burdens,
> And man enquires: "What has come over it?"
> That day it will narrate its annals,
> For your Lord will have commanded it.
> That day people will proceed separately to be shown their deeds.
> Whosoever has done even an atom's weight of good will behold it;
> And whosoever has done even an atom's weight of evil will behold that.[6]

On Judgment Day, each person will have a book that details the deeds of his or her life. The book held in the right hand indicates a righteous life, and the book held in the left hand indicates a sinner. The Qur'an teaches that each individual stands alone before God and that no one can intercede on his or her behalf. However, there is some debate about this issue, and some traditions in Islam suggest that Muhammad will be able to intercede on behalf of believers. Some Muslims believe that the Day of Judgment will be ushered in by a person known as the Mahdi, whose just rule will come to the earth at the end of days. The Mahdi is not mentioned in the Qur'an. Rather, the idea developed in Islamic thought in later centuries.

Those who are judged to be righteous will enter paradise. In the Qur'an, paradise is described in much detail as a lush garden with bountiful blessings of food, drink, and beautiful young men and women. Although some take this description to be literal, other Muslims think that it is instead a metaphor for the beauties of paradise. Those who have led sinful lives will be cast into hell, which is often referred to simply as "the fire." Those who are doomed to hell include nonbelievers and Muslims who have rejected their faith by failing to live up to prescribed duties and moral standards. Some Muslims believe that sinners will eventually be forgiven and taken to paradise.

Angels and *Jinn* The existence of angels is another component of Islamic belief, and angels are mentioned throughout the Qur'an. Angels are part of God's creation, without body or gender. Humans are said to be made of clay, and angels from light. Angels serve as important messengers and assistants to God. The most well known of the angels in Islamic tradition is Gabriel, or Jibril. This angel is mentioned several times in the Qur'an and was instrumental in bringing the revelation of the Qur'an to

Muhammad from God. Islamic tradition also recognizes supernatural beings called *jinn*, which are said to be created from fire. They are also mentioned in several places in the Qur'an. *Jinn* can take various forms, and, like humans, they can be both good and evil and Muslim or non-Muslim. Much folklore has developed surrounding the *jinn*, and they are represented in tales like *One Thousand and One Nights* as both helping and harming humans. The English term "genie" derives from the Arabic word *jinn*.

Commentary on the Qur'an

The text of the Qur'an is ambiguous in some places and repetitive in others. This has resulted in a long tradition of commentary upon and interpretation of the meaning of the verses. The general Arabic term for commentary on the Qur'an is **tafsir**, which is translated in English as "interpretation." Scholars have been engaging in *tafsir* for centuries, and their commentary takes many forms. In the first few generations following Muhammad's death, scholarly commentary on the Qur'an focused primarily on grammar, language, and explanations of inconsistencies in the text. The goal of this type of *tafsir* was to clarify the meaning of the words of the Qur'an.

Muslims have not always agreed on how the Qur'an should be interpreted and understood. Some scholars have argued that the Qur'an must only be interpreted vis-à-vis itself. In other words, verses of the Qur'an should only be explained by using other passages of the text. Other scholars think that Muslims should use their own reason and rationality as believers to interpret the meaning of the verses. This method of *tafsir* is known as speculative *tafsir*.[7] A famous eleventh-century Persian scholar called Abu Hamid al-Ghazali (1058–1111) wrote that, as rational judgment is a gift from God, people should always use it when considering the meaning of the Qur'an. However, some scholars criticized his approach as preferring human reason over the words of God. Ibn Taymiyya (1263–1328), an Arab scholar, argued that using human reason was not necessary because the entire meaning of the Qur'an could be found within the text. As we discuss later in this chapter, Ibn Taymiyya's approach became influential to some Islamic reformist movements in the modern era.

The *Sunnah*: The Example of the Prophet

After the Qur'an, the second most important source of Islamic teachings is in the **Sunnah**, which refers to the "tradition" or way of life of the prophet Muhammad. The *Sunnah* encompasses Muhammad's actions and words. It includes the way he handled disputes in the early community, the way he dealt with his wives, friends, and children, and the way he went about the daily business of life. This extends even to such seemingly mundane matters as how the Prophet cleaned his teeth. To Muslims, Muhammad is considered the ideal human. He is therefore the model of the best way to live. To this day, Muhammad is an inspiration to all Muslims, who strive to follow his example of conduct in their own lives. Muhammad is discussed in more detail in the section on the history of Islam.

The *Hadith* Literature How do Muslims know how Muhammad lived his life, how he treated his family, and how he handled problems facing members of the early Muslim community? Muslims have knowledge of Muhammad's life through a literary tradition known as the **hadith**. *Hadith* is a form of literature that records in brief reports the details of the life of the prophet, including his sayings and his deeds. The *hadith* reports come from the observations of Muhammad's close friends and family, known as his "companions." His companions realized his importance as an example of righteous behavior. They strove to remember his actions and words, and then passed them on through the generations in *hadith* reports.

A *hadith* consists of two parts: the *isnad*, or the chain of transmission of the *hadith*; and the *matn*, the report itself. The *matn* relates Muhammad's words or deeds, and the *isnad* names those people who transmitted the *hadith* from the time of the prophet. The *isnad* always originates with one of Muhammad's close companions or a family member. Muhammad's wife **Aisha** was one of the most important transmitters of *hadith*, as she passed on many reports about Muhammad's life. Muslims do not consider all *hadith* to be equally valid. A complex science of *hadith* developed in the centuries following the death of the Prophet to evaluate their reliability as true reports of Muhammad's life. Scholars ranked *hadith* from "solid" to "weak" based on the likelihood of authenticity. The *hadith* are compiled into collections of several thousand.

Reports known as *hadith qudsi*, or sacred sayings, are also important in the Islamic tradition. Although the name is similar, this is a very different sort of literary tradition from the regular *hadith*. The *hadith qudsi* are not reports of Muhammad's life but are believed to be words of God. Muhammad is believed to have occasionally transmitted direct words of God that were not intended to be part of the Qur'an. Many of the *hadith qudsi* are succinct and beautiful. They focus on God's love for humanity, God's mercy, and the closeness of God to creation. The following *hadith qudsi* illustrates the quality of God's mercy:

> God says: "If my Servant intends a good deed and does not do it, I write it down for him as a good deed. Then if he does it, I write it down for him as ten good deeds, or up to seven hundred times that. And if my servant intends an evil deed and does not do it, I do not write it down against him. And if he does it, I write it down for him as [only one] evil deed."[8]

Explore the concept of scripture in Judaism, Christianity, and Islam. What important elements do these religions share? How do they differ?

The Five Pillars

The essential teachings of Islam are closely related to Muslim worship practice. The five pillars form the basis of practice. These pillars are

1. *Shahadah:* the declaration of faith
2. *Salat:* the daily prayer
3. *Zakat:* almsgiving
4. *Sawm:* fasting during the month of **Ramadan**
5. *Hajj:* pilgrimage to Mecca

Muslims believe that the foundations for the five pillars were set during the lifetime of Muhammad. The five pillars are carefully articulated in the *hadith* literature. All of the pillars are equally important. However, they address different elements of religious practice that must be performed at special times. For example, although prayer is a daily requirement, the Ramadan fast happens once per year, and the **hajj** must be performed only once in a lifetime. The pillars are generally required of all adult Muslims. However, individuals are sometimes excused from performing the pillars. For example, someone who is ill, pregnant, or nursing an infant would not be required to fast. Devout Muslims generally aim to observe all of the pillars, but as with every religious tradition, there are variations in levels of observance. Furthermore, there has been some historical variation across communities and cultures in how much emphasis is placed on the pillars. Some Muslim scholars have even debated the relative necessity of the observance of the pillars, though these scholars have always been in the minority.

The Declaration of Faith   The first pillar is the declaration of faith, called the *shahadah*. This is the statement of belief: "There is no God but God and Muhammad is the messenger of God." The other four pillars all deal directly with religious practice, but the *shahadah* is different in that it is much more a statement of belief than a ritualized religious practice. To become a Muslim, all one must do is utter the *shahadah* with utmost sincerity in the presence of witnesses. Most new Muslims will first declare the *shahadah*, and then begin a lifetime's journey of learning the Qur'an, the *Sunnah*, and other aspects of the faith. Many people in North America and elsewhere who have converted to Islam note the simplicity of the faith as something that attracted them to Islam. This simplicity is illustrated by the succinct nature of the *shahadah*.

Daily Prayer   The *salat*, the mandatory daily prayers, is the second pillar. You encountered the careful preparations for the daily *salat* of Amina at the opening of this chapter. Devout Muslims perform five daily prayers at specific times of the day. Muslims cannot decide to perform all the prayers at once to get them over with for the day, week, or month. Rather, they should do them at the required times. The first prayer should be done at dawn every morning. The next prayer is performed at about noon. The remaining prayers are the late afternoon prayer, the sunset prayer, and the final prayer in the evening. Prayer is mentioned in several places in the Qur'an. However, the number of prayers is established not in the Qur'an but rather in the *hadith*. The *hadith* literature relates that during a miraculous journey to heaven, known as the **miraj**, Muhammad came into the presence of God. God told Muhammad he should instruct people to make fifty daily prayers. However, when Muhammad told the prophet Moses about the prayers, Moses told him to go back to God to ask for a reduction, as fifty would be too many. Eventually, the number was settled at five, although God said that every prayer would count for ten.

The *salat* are not individualized prayers requesting aid from God or giving thanks, although those personal prayers, called *dua*, are also common among Muslims. Rather, the *salat* prayers are formalized. For each prayer, specific verses of the Qur'an are recited, and special body movements accompany the recitation.

Before beginning the prayers, a Muslim must enter a state of ritual purity. As you learned from Amina at the beginning of this chapter, this purification consists of ablutions, called *wudu'*, which involve cleansing the hands, head, face, and feet. The body should be covered for prayer, and most women and men also cover their heads. The prayer begins with the *takbir*, or the declaration *Allahu Akbar*, which means "God is great." Throughout the prayer, the believer faces the direction of Mecca, where an important structure known as the Ka'ba is located (you will learn more about the Ka'ba later in this section). This means that Muslims in America pray facing the east. In prayer, a Muslim stands, kneels, and bows his head to the floor. These cycles of movements, along with the proper recitation, are called *raka* and vary in number according to the prayer. In some parts of the world, such as regions of Indonesia, the prayer opens with a declaration of intent to indicate that the Muslim is in the right frame of mind for performing the prayer.[9] Not all Muslims declare their intent to pray, but most agree that proper intention is necessary. The intention of the believer is what validates and legitimizes the action of prayer. Many Muslims believe that the intention of the prayer is even more important than the prayer itself. After reciting verses of the Qur'an, the prayer closes with a greeting of peace.

Prayers may be done anywhere—even in a park or airport. However, many Muslims perform prayers at a **mosque** (this English word is taken from the Arabic term *masjid*). A mosque is a place that is designated for prayer. Many people imagine elaborate feats of architectural workmanship when they think of mosques, but a mosque

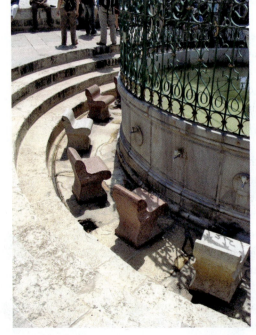

Ablution fountains outside of a mosque.

can be as simple as an unadorned room in a commercial building or even a clearing in the woods. Although mosque architecture and decoration varies from the very simple to the very ornate, mosques tend to share some features. All mosques have a prayer space, and most have a fountain so people can perform the required ablutions. The direction of prayer, known as the *qibla*, is marked inside a mosque by a niche called a *mihrab*, which is sometimes beautifully decorated with botanical designs or Qur'anic verses. The floors of a mosque are often completely covered with colorful rugs or woven mats. Because Muslim prayer requires open space for bodily movement, there are usually no seats or pews. Many mosques, particularly those in the Middle East and North Africa, also have a tower called a *minaret*. The minaret is often used to broadcast the calls to prayer.

In much of the world, visitors of all faiths are welcome to enter mosques. Normally, all those entering a mosque will be asked to leave their shoes outside. Sometimes, shoes are placed in a designated cabinet watched by someone who may receive a tip and even clean the shoes. Leaving shoes outside ensures that no outside dirt will enter the mosque to violate the ritual purity of those who have made the proper ablutions for prayer. The prayer space in a mosque is open and peaceful, and people may use the mosque as a place for contemplation and rest throughout the day. When walking through the hot and dusty streets of busy Cairo, one can see men—and sometimes women—taking a break from the urban noise and bustle by resting in the serene interior of a neighborhood mosque. In many parts of the world, mosques are also used for teaching classes or for other community needs.

Friday is designated as the day for congregational prayer, known as *salat al-jum'a*. It is incumbent upon Muslim men to attend the midday prayer together, and they may also gather at a mosque for other prayers during the day. In some areas, women also attend the communal prayer, though their attendance is not regarded as mandatory. When Muslims pray in a group in a mosque or elsewhere, it is important that one person acts as the imam, or prayer leader. The imam regulates the prayer session and ensures that all believers are praying together. The Friday prayer often features a sermon, which may be delivered by the imam or another preacher. Friday should not be confused with the Christian or Jewish Sabbath. Rather than a day of rest, it is a day for group prayer. In some Muslim countries, Friday is a work day, and businesses are open. In others, businesses are closed.

The five daily prayers are announced in the words of the **adhan**, or the call to prayer. The *adhan* is delivered by a person called a **muezzin**, who calls the faithful to prayer from the door of the mosque or the minaret, sometimes using a loudspeaker. The *adhan* is usually called in a rhythmic, recitational fashion. Hearing the *adhan* several times a day from the wee hours of the morning to evening is very much a part of

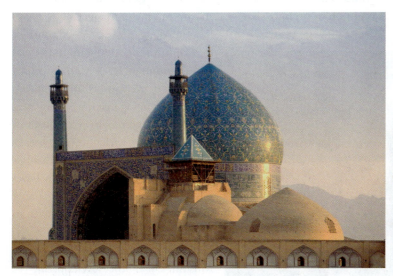

The beautiful Shah Mosque, in Isfahan, Iran, was built in the 1600s during the Safavid period.

This small mosque in rural Zanzibar, Tanzania, is built in an architectural style that is similar to houses in the area.

life in the Muslim world. Many residents and travelers miss it enormously when they move away; non-Muslim travelers often remark that hearing the *adhan* is one of the most memorable experiences of visiting a Muslim country.

ADHAN

God is most great (repeated four times)
I testify that there is no god but God (repeated twice)
I testify that Muhammad is the messenger of God (repeated twice)
Hurry to prayer (repeated twice)
Hurry to success (repeated twice)
Prayer is better than sleep (repeated twice before the morning prayer)
God is most great (repeated twice)
There is no god but God (once)[10]

Like the other pillars, the *salat* is incumbent upon all Muslims, both male and female. In much of the Muslim world, it is more common for men to pray in mosques than women, although this is not always the case. In such places as urban Egypt and Indonesia, women often pray in mosques. Although females may serve as imam for other women, most Muslims believe that they may not do so for men. When women and men both pray in mosques, usually the genders are separated—either in separate prayer halls or with women praying in rows behind the men. Some Muslims reason that this requirement is due to modesty and concentration. They argue that women and men should not be distracted from their prayers by the presence of the opposite sex. Others argue that men's leadership in prayer is prescribed in the Qur'an. However, some Muslim feminist scholars, such as the American professor Amina Wadud, are challenging this tradition by arguing that women can lead men in prayer.

Muslim men pray together at a mosque in Burma.

The daily prayers are important for Muslims on both an individual and a communal level. Many Muslims feel closest to God during prayer. Although praying five times a day may sound very rigorous to non-Muslims, many Muslims welcome the breaks from mundane tasks to focus their attention completely on God. A believer must stop all activity to remember God five times every day. This indicates that submission to God is the most important part of life for a devout Muslim. On another level, praying the same prayers at the same time every day, and often in a group, draws the community of Muslims together in worship of God. Many Muslims report that, in addition to feeling an individual closeness to God during prayer, they also feel at one with the **umma**, the global community of Muslims, in the common purpose of worship.

Almsgiving   The third pillar, *zakat*, refers to required almsgiving, which is part of a believer's devotion to God and the Muslim community. The rules about *zakat* are very specific, and the amount of *zakat* is figured as a percentage (about 2.5 percent) of the value of certain types of property, including cash. *Zakat* is therefore something like a tax. The wealth on which *zakat* has been paid is considered to be pure and clean. Therefore, some Muslims describe *zakat* as a means of purifying their property. The payment of *zakat* also expresses a Muslim's commitment to improving his or her community in a real and concrete way. This is because the proceeds from *zakat* are normally distributed to the poor or are used to maintain public institutions such as mosques and schools. In some countries today, such as Pakistan, the government collects and redistributes *zakat* funds.[11] Elsewhere, it is up to individuals themselves to make the *zakat* payments. All adults should pay *zakat*. However, adults who are mentally ill or unstable are exempt from the requirement.

Fasting during Ramadan   The next pillar is *sawm*, which is the mandatory fast during the month of Ramadan, the ninth month in the Islamic calendar. Ramadan is considered a sacred month by Muslims because it was during Ramadan that the Qur'an was first revealed to Muhammad. During Ramadan, all Muslims are required to fast from dawn to sundown. When fasting, Muslims refrain from eating, drinking, and sexual activity. Muslims also strive to avoid arguing and negative thoughts during the hours of the fast.

All adult and adolescent Muslims are generally expected to fast. However, exceptions are made for those who are traveling, or women who are pregnant, nursing, or menstruating. In Pakistan, curtained food stalls are set up at train stations during Ramadan. The stalls allow travelers to eat in private, where they are respectfully out of view of those who are fasting and do not wish to be tempted by the sight of someone eating. Individuals who miss fasting days or break the fast are expected to make up the days later. However, children, the sick, the mentally ill, and the very elderly are exempt from fasting entirely. Children are usually encouraged to begin fasting when they show interest, but they are only expected to fast when they are comfortable doing so.

The month of Ramadan is a special time. Although the fast can be challenging, many Muslims find Ramadan to be filled with religious meaning, joy, and sociability. In Muslim countries or communities, the rhythm of daily life changes significantly during Ramadan. Daily activity lessens, and streets are quiet during daylight hours. However, the world awakens at sunset, when the fast ends. Many people share the evening meal with family and friends, and streets are filled late into the evening with well-wishers. Many families eat again around midnight and also before dawn to gain the strength to make it through the day.

This open-air market in Sumbawa Besar, Indonesia, is very popular during Ramadan, when people buy special delicacies to break the fast.

Muslims often break the fast with dates before performing the evening prayer. This is because eating dates is *Sunnah*: Muhammad broke the fast with dates, so many Muslims follow his example. In many cultures, special treats are prepared during Ramadan. Indonesian Muslims look forward to breaking the fast with a delectable drink made with coconut milk and tropical fruits. Some Indonesians say that the drink is so sweet because it represents the beauty of a day of focusing solely on God. In Iran and in Persian communities in the United States and Canada, a rice pudding flavored with saffron and rosewater is served during Ramadan.

During Ramadan, Muslims around the world may spend time in the evenings reciting the Qur'an. Many try to achieve the goal of reciting the entire Qur'an during this special month. People may also stay up late into the night visiting friends and enjoying the celebratory and devotional atmosphere of the month. During the last few days of Ramadan, the Night of Power occurs. This is the night when Muslims believe that the Qur'an was originally revealed to Muhammad. Many Muslims believe that a wish may be granted during this special night. The end of Ramadan is marked by an important feast day called *Id al-Fitr*, the feast of fast-breaking, which we discuss later in this chapter.

Like the preceding pillars, *sawm* is important on both personal and community levels. Fasting demonstrates an individual's dependence upon God, who provides for humanity. Also, by refraining from food and drink, Muslims become more sympathetic to the plight of the poor and the hungry and learn to appreciate the food that they have. Like *salat* and *zakat*, fasting together also brings a sense of community to Muslims worldwide. A Muslim observing the fast in Los Angeles, for example, will know that his fellow believers thousands of miles away in Malaysia are keeping the fast. In the United States, many mosques and Muslim organizations view Ramadan as a time of outreach to non-Muslim friends and neighbors and a way of teaching people about Islam. For example, at California State University in Sacramento, the Muslim student organization holds a popular "fast for a day" event every year. Non-Muslims are invited to try fasting for a day and then breaking the fast with a special meal prepared for the entire community. These events often include guest speakers who talk about the meaning of Ramadan and the basics of the Islamic tradition. Guests are also sometimes invited to watch the evening prayer.

Pilgrimage to Mecca   The final pillar is called the *hajj*, which is the holy pilgrimage to Mecca in Saudi Arabia. The Qur'an specifies the pilgrimage as incumbent upon humanity. Every year, millions of Muslims descend upon the city of Mecca in a spectacular display of devotion. The *hajj* is generally understood to be required of all

Muslims who are physically and financially able to make it. A Muslim only needs to perform the *hajj* once in his or her lifetime, but many Muslims who are able to do so repeat it. Pilgrims describe the event as one of unparalleled spiritual significance, and they experience intense feelings of connection to God and humanity during the *hajj*. Muslims who return from the *hajj* often use the title *hajj* (for men) or *hajja* (for women) before their name to indicate that they have made the journey.

The *hajj* must be undertaken at a particular time of year. This is during the second week of the month *Dhu al-Hajj*, which is the final month in the Islamic calendar. A person must be physically and financially able to make the trip, or else it is not valid. One may not borrow money to make the pilgrimage, but it is appropriate to accept financing for the trip as a gift. In addition, the money set aside for the *hajj* must be purified by paying *zakat* on it. As a means of organizing the millions of travelers who come for *hajj*, the government of Saudi Arabia today requires pilgrims to join a travel group to make the *hajj*. Planned excursions depart from every corner of the world, and tour companies arrange everything from air travel to bus transfers to accommodations. In Saudi Arabia, a great deal of planning is involved because of the sheer numbers of Muslims who arrive in Mecca and its environs during the week of *hajj*. Only Muslims may make the journey; curious tourists are not allowed to partake in the experience.

When making the *hajj*, pilgrims must leave behind indicators of their social and economic status to properly enter a state of ritual purity. This state is called *ihram*. All men must wear special clothing, also called *ihram*. This consists of two very simple pieces of white cloth—one is worn above the waist and one is worn below. Women

Muslim pilgrims prepare for prayer at the Haram mosque in Mecca.

may wear what they choose, and most dress in simple clothing and avoid makeup, jewelry, and perfume. Pilgrims should also refrain from sexual activity, arguing, and frivolous conversation while in a state of *ihram*. Ideally, these restrictions are meant to ensure that the pilgrim's mind is solely on God and the *hajj*. The state of *ihram* also emphasizes the equality of all Muslims before God because all status markers, such as expensive jewelry, are removed.

The pilgrimage involves a number of highly specific, ritualized acts. Muhammad determined the sequence of the events of the *hajj* before his death, and some events reenact moments from his life. Many of the rituals also recall the actions of Abraham and his family. In this way, the rituals connect the believer to the distant past and the origins of monotheism with Abraham.

Perhaps the most important focus of the *hajj* is the structure known as the Ka'ba. The Ka'ba was a focus of pilgrimage in Arabia even before the time of Muhammad. It is a cubical building about thirty feet by thirty feet, and Muslims believe it was originally built and dedicated to Allah by Abraham and his son Ishmael. Today, the Ka'ba is covered by a cloth embroidered with gold thread that is replaced every year by the Saudi government. When a pilgrim first arrives in Mecca, he enters the Great Mosque that encircles the Ka'ba while reciting verses of the Qur'an. The pilgrim then circumambulates the Ka'ba seven times in a counterclockwise direction. This is known as the *tawaf*. This ritual is an act of devotion that is believed to be in imitation of the angels circling God's throne. The *tawaf* is performed three times during the course of the pilgrimage.

Another important rite of the *hajj* is called the *sa'y*. This rite commemorates the story of Hagar, mother of Ishmael, who frantically searched for water in the desert by rushing seven times between two hills. During Hagar's search, God made a spring appear, and Hagar and Ishmael were able to quench their thirst. Pilgrims visit this spring to this day, many taking the special waters home as a symbol of Mecca. Today, the route between the two hills is enclosed as part of the Great Mosque.

Another part of the *hajj* involves a journey to the plain of Arafat, where a tent city is established every year to house millions of pilgrims from around the world. It is here that Muslims recollect a story about Abraham that is also prominent in Jewish and Christian traditions. In all three traditions, Abraham is believed to have been commanded by God to sacrifice his son. (Most Muslims believe he intended to sacrifice Ishmael, but Jews and Christians usually regard Isaac as the object of sacrifice; the Qur'an does not mention which son was the intended sacrifice.) As Abraham prepared to make the sacrifice, the Angel Gabriel (Jibril) appeared at the last minute, and a ram was substituted for the son. Abraham's willingness to sacrifice his beloved son is regarded as a model of faith in Islam, and this is a solemn, reflective time of the *hajj*. The pilgrims perform the "standing ceremony," in which they remain standing from noon until sundown in praise of Allah. The *hajj* ends with the most important holiday of the year, the Feast of Sacrifice, which we discuss later in the chapter.

Now that we have covered the major teachings of Islam, let us turn to the history of the religious tradition, beginning with the birth of Muhammad.

THE HISTORY OF ISLAM

Muhammad ibn Abd Allah was born around the year 570 c.e. in the town of **Mecca**, a city in the southern Arabian Peninsula. At the time of his birth, the peninsula was not politically united, and much of the population were nomadic herders, known as Bedouins, who lived in remote desert areas. Despite this lack of political centralization, the region was by no means isolated. The peninsula was situated between the Byzantine Empire to the northwest, the Persian Sassanian Empire to the northeast, and the Christian Abyssinian kingdom across the Red Sea in Ethiopia. In addition, the city of Mecca was a significant trading center and place of religious pilgrimage. Although there were Christians and Jews in Arabia at the time, the majority of the people living in Arabia were polytheists who worshiped several deities. Trade fairs regularly took place in Mecca, and people passing through often left representations of deities at the temple called the Ka'ba, a large cube-shaped building in the center of town; today, this is the site to which all Muslims turn as they pray, and toward which they make a *hajj* at least once in their lives, as you learned in the preceding section. Tradition holds that at the time of Muhammad, more than 300 deities and spirits were represented by idols in the Ka'ba. Muslims call this period before the revelation of the Qur'an the **jahiliyya**, or the "age of ignorance."

Muhammad was born into a tribe called Quraysh, a powerful extended family that was very influential in Mecca. His father died before he was born, and his mother died when he was a young child. After her death, Muhammad went to live with his grandfather, who was his appointed guardian. When his grandfather died, Muhammad was raised by his uncle, a man named Abu Talib. Although he spent most of his early life in the city of Mecca, as a young boy Muhammad was sent out to the desert to live with the Bedouin, who many considered to live the ideal Arab lifestyle. At the time, sending children to the Bedouin was considered an important way to impart Arab values and culture to young city dwellers.

Muhammad is known to have been a hard worker, and he was active in business and trade. Indeed, he met his first wife, Khadija, while he was working for her in a trading caravan. Khadija was a widow about fifteen years older than Muhammad, and she was so taken with the integrity and dignity of the young man that she proposed to him. They married when he was about twenty-five years old and she forty. Their marriage was thought to be one of close companionship and deep love, and they had several children together.

As was discussed earlier, Muhammad began preaching in Mecca after receiving the first revelations. His preaching was not welcomed, however, and was even controversial in some quarters of Mecca. The reason was that he criticized both the polytheistic beliefs held by many Meccans and the disregard that wealthy Meccans showed toward the poor. The controversy led to persecution of the small but growing community of Muslims. Because they held much power in Mecca, Muhammad's own clan, the Quraysh, stood to lose the most with the social change that Muhammad's teachings advocated. The Quraysh were thus particularly active in ridiculing and persecuting Muhammad's followers.

This persecution inspired some Muslims to flee to Abyssinia (Ethiopia), where they were granted refuge by the Christian king. Others tried to resist. One well-known Muslim who resisted persecution was Bilal, an Abyssinian slave who had converted to Islam. The man who owned Bilal forced him to lie in the hot sun with a stone on his chest and told him to renounce his Muslim beliefs by denying the oneness of God. Bilal refused, crying out "One! One!" until he was rescued by Abu Bakr, who purchased him from his tormentor and then freed him from slavery. Bilal is remembered by Muslims to this day for his devotion and is also known as the first *muezzin*—the person who calls the faithful to prayer.

What is the role of prophecy in Islam, Christianity, and Judaism? Consider the figures Abraham, Moses, Jesus, and Muhammad. How are they understood in each tradition?

The *Hijra* and the Growth of the Muslim Community

Because of the troubles in Mecca, Muhammad eventually encouraged his followers to leave and make a new home elsewhere. The people of a little settlement north of Mecca with a small Jewish population welcomed him, and he encouraged his followers to go there. This town became known as **Medina** (from the term *medinat al-nabi*, which means "the city of the prophet"). The Muslims moved from Mecca to Medina in the year 622 C.E., and this migration is called the *hijra*. The *hijra* is a very important event in Islamic history; as you have learned, the Islamic lunar calendar begins not with Muhammad's birth, but with the *hijra*. The reason is that the *hijra* marked the beginning of a distinct Muslim community, or *umma*, with Muhammad as its leader.

Muhammad did not travel with the first group to go to Medina. He and some of his companions waited for a few weeks to make the trip. When they finally left for Medina, angry Meccans from the Quraysh tribe pursued them. A popular story recounts that during Muhammad's journey to Medina he hid from the Quraysh in a cave for three days. When his pursuers reached the cave, they did not look inside because a kindly spider had spun a web to hide the entrance, thus saving Muhammad. Even today, some Muslims will not kill spiders because of their appreciation for the spider's important role in protecting the Prophet from the Meccans. Stories about the *hijra* and the foundational period of Islam are well known and inform the way many Muslims live their lives. Today, Muslims around the world recall the *hijra* as a difficult but very important time.

What happened to the Muslim community with the move to Medina? With the move, the growing Muslim community took on a new political and social form. Additionally, Muhammad's role expanded over the years as he became the leader of the new community. In Mecca, Muhammad had primarily preached and taught the revelations to his followers. In Medina, however, he took on a wide variety of new roles and oversaw political, social, and religious matters. In addition to his role as prophet of God and religious leader, Muhammad became the political head of the community. He continued to receive revelations from God for twenty more years, and reflecting these changes, the verses of the Qur'an that Muslims believe were revealed to Muhammad in Medina concern the regulation of community life.

The migration to Medina did not end the Muslim community's problems with Mecca. Muhammad and the Muslims lived a perilous existence for several years as they suffered economic hardships in Medina and threats from Mecca. With the aim of providing economically for the community, the Muslims had begun to raid trade caravans bound for Mecca, though with limited success. Although it may sound surprising to the modern reader, raiding was a common and even acceptable economic practice in Arabia at that time, especially in times of hardship. Most often, raids did not involve bloodshed.

Conflicts with the Meccans continued, primarily with the Quraysh tribe, who still viewed the Muslims as a threat. Furthermore, the raids caused many economic problems for the Meccans and increased the tension between the two cities. This resulted in one of the most famous clashes in early Muslim history, the Battle of Badr in the year 624 C.E. The Muslims had planned a raid on a Meccan caravan at a place called Badr. The Meccans learned of the plan, and sent a force of more than 900 men to protect the caravan. However, the Muslims, at only 300 strong, soundly defeated the Meccan forces, even though they were outnumbered. The battle is mentioned in the Qur'an, which reports that angels helped the outnumbered Muslims win the battle (8:9). The Qur'an also notes this as a critical moment in the development of the spirit and destiny of the Muslims. After this dramatic battle, Muhammad's reputation as a great leader grew.

A few years later, in 628 C.E., Muhammad attempted to lead the Muslims back to Mecca for a pilgrimage. The people of Arabia had been making pilgrimages to the Ka'ba for centuries. The Meccans, expecting an attack, proposed a negotiation with the now more powerful Muslims. Muhammad agreed, and the pilgrimage was postponed through the signing of a treaty between the Meccans and the Muslims. Two years later, in 630 C.E., the Muslims returned, and the Meccans surrendered when they saw Muhammad's even greater political and military strength. Muhammad accepted the surrender and allowed the Meccan people to go free if they would convert to Islam. Muhammad and the Muslims entered Mecca. They destroyed the polytheistic idols housed at the Ka'ba and rededicated the building to the one and only God and the religion of Abraham.

Muhammad lived for only two more years after his victorious return to Mecca. At the time of his death, he had a large family. Khadija had died several years earlier, and after her death Muhammad married several more wives. Some of his marriages were contracted for political alliances, and others to care for widowed and divorced women who had no one else. The best known of his later wives was a woman called Aisha, who was the daughter of Abu Bakr. She was much younger than Muhammad, which was not unusual in marriages at the time. Aisha was a very important early figure in Islamic history and is thought to be one of Muhammad's most beloved wives. As mentioned earlier, she was the source of much information about Muhammad's life and was often consulted by other Muslims because of her vast knowledge of religious matters. In 632 C.E., Muhammad is believed to have died peacefully in Aisha's arms after returning from a final journey to Mecca. He was buried under her home in Medina, and to this day, some Muslims visit this site as a place of pilgrimage.

By the time of his death, Muhammad was the political and religious leader of much of Arabia. After the move to Medina, Muslim rule had spread rapidly across the Arabian Peninsula through both nonviolent political alliances and military conquests. Many people of Arabia had converted to Islam. Some did so because they believed in the truth of Muhammad's message, and others converted for political reasons, namely to form alliances with Muhammad and the powerful Muslim community.

Not all people living under Muslim rule converted to Islam, however. Significant Christian, Jewish, and other religious minority populations remained. From this early period, Muslims have considered Christians and Jews to be People of the Book, a designation that means that they are a people who have received scripture from God and are thus close to the Muslim community. Later, Hindus and Buddhists were also considered People of the Book, as Muslim rule spread into South Asia. Under Muslim rule, these minority communities were governed by what are termed *dhimmi* laws; the term *dhimmi* refers to their status as protected peoples. These laws allowed non-Muslims in Muslim territories to worship how they chose, provided they paid taxes and submitted to Muslim authority. The *dhimmis* did not enjoy all the privileges of Muslims—they were not allowed to bear arms, for example—but they were entitled to the protection of the Islamic state.

The Crisis of Succession and the Rightly Guided Caliphs

At the time of Muhammad's death, communities throughout Arabia were united under Islam, but it was unclear to Muhammad's followers who should succeed him to lead the Muslims. When he died, most Muslims thought that Muhammad had not designated a successor. The companions of the Prophet thus chose the highly respected Abu Bakr to lead the Muslim community. Recall that Abu Bakr was one of the first converts to Islam and was Muhammad's father-in-law. A minority of Muslims, however, believed that Muhammad had designated his cousin 'Ali to succeed him. 'Ali was also Muhammad's son-in-law because he had married Fatima, Muhammad's daughter by Khadija. Although 'Ali was highly regarded even by those who did not think Muhammad had designated him to be his successor, he was much younger than Abu Bakr. Therefore, many considered him too young to lead the community.

This controversy over leadership of the Muslim community is often known as the crisis of succession, and it led to the development of the two major branches of Islam: the **Sunni** and the **Shi'a**. The majority group became known as the Sunni, which remains the larger of the two major branches. The minority group became known as the Shi'a. The name comes from the term *shi'at 'Ali*, which means the "party of 'Ali." The Shi'a is the smaller of the two major branches of Islam. Later in the chapter, we discuss how this dispute led to other differences between the Sunni and the Shi'a.

The leaders who came after Muhammad were not viewed as prophets. They were known rather as **caliphs**, who ruled as the representatives of God and the prophet and had both religious and political authority. This was a new form of government called a caliphate, and it remained the model for Islamic society for several hundred years. The designation of Abu Bakr as caliph started a historical period that came to be known as the time of the Rightly Guided Caliphs, who were Abu Bakr and his successors: 'Umar, 'Uthman, and finally 'Ali.

As caliph, Abu Bakr sought to strengthen relationships with the communities and tribes of Arabia who had formed alliances with Muhammad. Abu Bakr faced the potential breakdown of Muslim unity because some of these tribes, particularly those in parts of Arabia far from Medina and Mecca, wanted to break their ties to the Muslim community when Muhammad died. After the death of Abu Bakr, which was only two years after he had been appointed caliph, the Muslims chose a man called 'Umar to lead. Like Abu Bakr, 'Umar had been close to Muhammad. Also like Abu Bakr, he was confronted with the problem of some communities wanting to break away from Islamic rule. However, he managed to preserve unity and expand Muslim rule, conquering the lands of Egypt, Syria, and Iraq. When 'Umar died in 644 C.E., another of the Prophet's companions, a man called 'Uthman, was selected as the new caliph.

'Uthman led the Muslims for twelve years, from 644 to 656 C.E. He continued the rapid political expansion that 'Umar had begun, but also faced many problems. Muslim rule now extended from the Mediterranean and North Africa into Central Asia. Because the *umma* now reached beyond Arabic-speaking lands, there was a great deal of cultural and linguistic diversity among the Muslims. This situation made leadership a far more complex undertaking than it had been in the time of Muhammad and Abu Bakr, when nearly all Muslims were Arabs. This eventually led to charges that the caliphs discriminated against non-Arab Muslims. Furthermore, many accused 'Uthman of nepotism when he appointed his nephew Mu'awiya as governor of Syria. He also placed other relatives in key posts, and many of them grew rich as a result. A few years into his rule, 'Uthman faced a number of rebellions in outer provinces of the empire, and in 656 C.E. he was killed by insurgents who had marched on Medina.

After 'Uthman's death, 'Ali was named caliph. During the time of the first three caliphs, 'Ali's supporters grew in numbers. Despite this growing support, 'Ali's time as caliph saw many fractures in the Muslim community. Supporters of 'Uthman were upset that 'Ali had never punished his murderers. This controversy resulted in the Battle of the Camel. This was a traumatic moment in Islamic history because it was the first to pit Muslims against Muslims. In the battle, 'Ali defeated an army led by Aisha and other prominent Meccans. Aisha directed the battle from her mount on a camel, from which the battle took its name. 'Ali's forces took down her camel in order to hinder her leadership, and his forces were victorious. Mu'awiya, 'Uthman's nephew, also challenged 'Ali's authority. This conflict reached a peak in the Battle of Siffin in 657 C.E. When they met on the battlefield in Syria, Mu'awiya asked 'Ali for an arbitration of their dispute, and he accepted. However, some of 'Ali's followers disapproved of the arbitration, which they viewed as a surrender to Mu'awiya. This group formed a splinter group known as the Kharijites, which means "those who seceded." In 661 C.E., 'Ali was murdered by a Kharijite.

The Umayyads and the Abbasids

After 'Ali was killed, Mu'awiya claimed the caliphate. His leadership gave birth to what is known as the **Umayyad** Dynasty. This marked the end of the period of the Rightly Guided Caliphs. The institution of the caliphate survived, but the divisions in the community of believers that had worsened under 'Ali remained.

The Umayyad period lasted over a century, from 661 until 750 C.E. Umayyad leaders ruled from the city of Damascus in Syria. Although they were considered fairly effective leaders who expanded the Muslim Empire farther east to India and farther west to Spain, the reign of the Umayyads was controversial. For example, many Muslims thought that the Umayyads did not truly represent the diversity of the Muslim people, favoring Arab Muslims over non-Arab Muslims. Such criticism arose in part because Mu'awiya had designated his son Yazid as his successor instead of letting the community select a leader. This turned the caliphate into a dynasty.

Many Muslims who were opposed to the Umayyad Dynasty felt that the leadership of the *umma* should come from the line of Muhammad through Fatima and 'Ali. They argued that, therefore, their sons, Hasan and Husayn, should lead the *umma*. With the support of the Shi'a, **Husayn** eventually challenged the Umayyads for authority. However, he was slain in 680 C.E. when Yazid's armies ambushed him on the plains of Karbala in what is now Iraq. This tragic event is referred to as the "martyrdom of Husayn." This is a moment in Shi'a history that is solemnly commemorated to the present day as Husayn's sacrifice for the Muslim people. With the death of Husayn, the number of Muslims who believed the leader of the *umma* should be from the family of the Prophet grew. It was at this point that the Shi'a formally broke away from the Sunnis and established a line of successors to the prophet that remained within Muhammad's family.

In the late seventh and early eighth centuries C.E., many more Muslims began to criticize the Umayyad Dynasty. This group included those who were critical of the Umayyads for their perceived discrimination against non-Arabs and also those who supported the family of 'Ali as rightful leaders of the *umma*. Muslims opposed to the Umayyads became known as the **Abbasids**, taking the name of Muhammad's uncle. In 750 C.E., the Abbasid Revolution succeeded in removing the Umayyads from power.

The first caliph of the Abbasids was a man named Abu al-Abbas, and during his rule the Abbasids moved their capital from Damascus to Baghdad. Baghdad became a cultural capital of the world. Islamic arts and sciences flowered in this time, which became known as the classical period of Islamic civilization. One of the most wellknown pieces of literature from this period is the *One Thousand and One Nights*. These colorful tales celebrate the reign of the most famous Abbasid caliph, Harun al-Rashid, who ruled for twenty-five years in the late eighth century.

Many of these intellectual and artistic developments had an enormous impact on world history and the cultures of Europe and Asia. Islamic scholarship in science, philosophy, and medicine built on earlier knowledge from Greek and Persian sources and was very influential in European schools and universities for many centuries. The time of the Abbasids was also the period during which many Islamic religious doctrines were developed into forms that are still accepted today. For example, it was in this period that the Islamic legal schools of thought, which we discuss later in this chapter, were formalized.

Abbasid rule continued for several centuries, but not all Muslims were united under the Abbasid Caliphate. In 950 C.E., for example, rulers in Cairo and Spain also claimed the title of caliph. Furthermore, the Abbasid period saw the influence of the Crusades in Syria and Palestine, when European Christians sought to win control of the Holy Land. Christian forces captured Jerusalem from Islamic control in 1099. The holy city was later recaptured by Salah ad-Din (also known as Saladin), a famed Muslim military leader, in 1187. The rule of the Abbasids ended in 1258 C.E. when Baghdad was sacked by a Mongol army from the east led by the grandson of Genghis Khan.

By the end of the Abbasid Caliphate and the beginning of the fourteenth century, Islam was the majority religion in a vast region stretching from Spain and the western edge of North Africa all the way to Iran in Central Asia. The religion was also gaining converts in sub-Saharan Africa and South and Southeast Asia. Although military conquest expanded Muslim rule in some areas, it is incorrect to think that the historical spread of Islam around the globe was solely by the sword. In the earliest years of the *umma*, many tribes in Arabia joined the Muslims through political alliance. The growth of Islam throughout much of Asia and sub-Saharan Africa was gradual and peaceful. Often, Islam was introduced largely through traveling preachers, teachers, and traders.

Later Islamic Empires: The Ottomans, the Mughals, and the Safavids

After the fall of the Abbasids, several powerful Islamic empires arose in the next few centuries. These were the Ottoman Empire in the Mediterranean region, the Safavids in Iran, and the Mughal Dynasty in India.

The Ottoman Empire spanned over 600 years, from the fourteenth to the twentieth centuries. The early empire was marked by rapid expansion, and at the height of its power, the Ottomans controlled much of the Middle East and Mediterranean, reaching into southeastern Europe and Africa. The height of the empire was the fifteenth and sixteenth centuries, and in 1453 the Turks took the city of Constantinople, the former capital of the Byzantine Empire. The city, now called Istanbul, became the Ottoman capital and an important seat of Islamic learning and Islamic power. The Ottoman Empire came to an end after World War I.

At the same time that the Ottoman Empire reached its height, another Muslim empire arose thousands of miles away in South Asia. This dynasty, known as the Mughals, ruled much of India from the early sixteenth to the eighteenth centuries, even though the Muslim population was in the minority. The Mughal Dynasty, though not as long-lived as the Ottomans, saw a growth of literary and artistic development in South Asia, and Mughal architecture is considered to

The Sultan Ahmed Mosque in Istanbul, Turkey, was built in the 1600s and is a fine example of Ottoman architecture. It is also known as the Blue Mosque because of blue tiling inside.

have created some of the world's most impressive buildings such as the Taj Mahal in Agra, India. The stunningly beautiful Taj Mahal was built in the 1600s by the Mughal emperor Shah Jahan as a memorial and mausoleum for his beloved wife, Mumtaz Mahal. The Mughal Empire reached its peak in the eighteenth century, and although there was a Mughal ruler until 1857 in India, Mughal power and territory saw a decline with the advent of British occupation of South Asia.

To the west of the Mughals during the same period, the Safavid Empire flourished in Iran. Perhaps the most notable aspect of the Safavid rule was the establishment of Shi'a Islam as the religion of Iran; to the present day, the vast majority of Iran's Muslims are Shi'a. The Safavid period saw significant developments in Shi'a religious and philosophical thought. As with the Mughals, the period saw the development of great works of art and architecture.

Islam and Nationalism

In the twentieth century, the nation-state came to dominate the political organization of the world. Muslim leaders took different positions on the ideal relationship between religion and the nation-state. In many places, religion has served as a means to unify people across ethnic, class, and social boundaries. Some Muslim nationalists and political leaders envisioned a close link between their ideals of new states and Islam. Their vision involved a state government based on the principles of Islam and Islamic law as the basis for the legal system. Other leaders sought to distance nationalist policy from Islam and favored European secular states as political models.

When the Ottoman Empire collapsed at the end of World War I, Turkey moved toward embracing European ideals of secular nationalism. A man called Mustafa Kemal, better known as Ataturk, the founder of modern Turkey, embraced this ideal. He argued that Turkey should follow the path of the Western European nations and separate religion from politics. Ataturk disbanded the powerful religious brotherhoods, which had been very important in Turkey, and embraced a secular legal system that did not incorporate Islamic law at any level. He also required Turkish people to dress in a European style, which meant that women had to abandon headscarves and men had to stop wearing the traditional hat called a fez.

Although these policies were far reaching, they did not eradicate Islam from public life in Turkey. For example, although **Sufi** religious brotherhoods had been made illegal, many Turkish people still followed the mystical path known as Sufism, which we discuss later in this chapter. Though Islamic courts were no longer a part of the official legal system, Muslims still took disputes to Islamic legal authorities, particularly in rural areas. During the late twentieth and early twenty-first centuries, many Turks have reembraced the Islamic heritage of

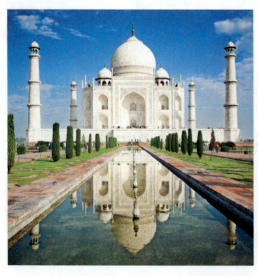

The Taj Mahal, a mausoleum in Agra, India, was built in the 1600s by the Mughal emperor Shah Jahan as a memorial and mausoleum for his beloved wife, Mumtaz Mahal.

Turkey. The Justice and Development Party, which has been supportive of reintroducing Islam into public life, has been the majority party in the governing coalition since the early 2000s.

Other Muslim countries followed a very different path. For example, in the Indian subcontinent, which was colonized by Great Britain, discussions of independence and nationalism early in the twentieth century focused a great deal on religious divisions in the region. With India's independence from Great Britain in 1947, two countries were formed: India and Pakistan. Pakistan was created as a Muslim homeland for the millions of Muslims who lived in South Asia. An important thinker behind the creation of Pakistan, Muhammad Iqbal, argued that Muslims needed a separate country to protect them from the majority Hindus in India. An organization called the Muslim League was instrumental in the early twentieth century in launching the idea of a separate state for the Muslim people of India. That ideal became a reality with independence. At first, Pakistan was divided into East and West Pakistan. In the 1970s, East Pakistan became the country that is now known as Bangladesh. Today, Pakistan and Bangladesh are among the largest Muslim-majority countries in the world, and India has a significant Muslim minority.

Iran is an important case study of Islam and nationalism in the twentieth century. Throughout much of the century, the *shah* (or king) of Iran was Reza Pahlavi. The *shah* embraced the ideals of the Western world and looked to Europe and the United States as models for development. However, Iran's Shi'a religious scholars were critical of the monarchy for marginalizing religious learning and religious authority in Iran. Iranian liberals and Marxists also criticized the *shah* as a corrupt leader who was entranced with the Western world and closely tied to Western governments, particularly the United States. In 1978, a coalition of clerics, intellectuals, and women's groups formed with the goal of removing the *shah* and his family from power. The revolution they staged in 1979 deposed the *shah* and ushered in the leadership of Islamic clerics. Not surprisingly, after the revolution, many of those people who had supported the overthrow of the *shah* felt neglected when the religious clerics took charge and formed an Islamic Republic.

A religious scholar known as Ayatollah Khomeini (1902–1989) headed the new government. The term *ayatollah*, which literally means "sign of God," refers to Shi'a religious scholars who have achieved a very high level of religious learning and scholarship. Khomeini had been one of the most outspoken critics of the *shah* among the religious scholars, and he argued that it was the duty of the religious scholars to build an Islamic state in Iran. This is precisely what happened in the aftermath of the revolution. The new government instituted strict reforms, which they argued reflected Islamic rules of behavior. Women were required to dress in a full-length black garment known as the *chador*. Many Iranians, among them intellectuals and professionals, left the country and made their homes abroad in places such as the United States and Canada.

Today, people in Iran are divided in terms of their views on how much authority religious scholars should have in the government. In 2009, huge numbers of Iranians took to the streets to protest the disputed reelection of President Mahmoud Ahmedi-nejad, and many have interpreted the protests as criticism of the Islamic Republic. The protest has been called the Green Movement, or Green Revolution, after the color adopted by the opposition presidential candidate, Mir-Hossein Mousavi.

Islamic Reform Movements

In the last two centuries, many movements have aimed to reform local Muslim communities and the worldwide *umma*. As we discussed earlier in this chapter, in their early history, the Muslims rapidly grew into an important world power. Various Muslim empires remained powerful for many centuries, through the Abbasid period and into the later Ottoman, Mughal, and Safavid sultanates. European powers were generally eclipsed by the Islamic world during this time. However, in the eighteenth century, European empires began to gain prominence as economic and political world powers. European power continued to grow with the advent of industrialization. Eventually the British, French, and Dutch empires colonized much of the Muslim world. The British and French colonized much of Muslim Africa and the Middle East; the British and the Dutch controlled Muslim lands in South and Southeast Asia.

Wahhabism   During the eighteenth century, several Muslim reform movements developed. These movements were spearheaded by those who were concerned about what they viewed as a decline in Muslim communities and in Muslim power worldwide. One of the most well-known reforms was the Wahhabi movement. This was originated by a scholar named Muhammad Ibn Abd al-Wahhab (d. 1792), and it is still influential today. Ibn Abd al-Wahhab disapproved of Muslim practices that he perceived as falling outside of the Qur'an and *Sunnah* and that had developed after the time of Muhammad. The Wahhabi movement was especially critical of saint veneration and tomb visitation. Al-Wahhab argued that these practices and others were considered innovations and had contributed to the decline of Islam and the Muslim world. As a result, al-Wahhab's followers razed many saints' tombs and shrines, including those of Muhammad, his companions, and Husayn.

In the late eighteenth century, followers of al-Wahhab formed significant ties with the ruling family of Arabia. To this day, the movement remains influential in Saudi Arabia and in other parts of the Muslim world, where it has sent teachers and established schools. Followers of the movement call themselves Muwahiddun, though they are commonly called Wahhabis in the news media.

The Wahhabi movement is often characterized as very conservative and "fundamentalist." However, we must be careful in using the latter term when discussing any religious movement. This is because not all movements called "fundamentalist" are the same. The reason the Wahhabi movement is often termed "fundamentalist" is its emphasis on the primacy of the Qur'an and the *Sunnah* and its criticism of later developments in Muslim thought and practice. The movement thus emphasizes the "fundamentals" of Islam—the Qur'an and the model of the Prophet. Today, the Wahhabi movement is often portrayed very negatively in the Western media. This is due to the influence of the movement on notorious extremists such as Osama bin Laden and the emphasis some Wahhabis place on bringing their version of Islam to other parts of the Muslim world. Although followers of Wahhabi Islam are generally more conservative than other Muslims, not all embrace a political version of Islam.

Resisting Colonialism During the nineteenth century, European powers increasingly dominated Muslim lands. Many Muslim thinkers lamented the loss of a cohesive and powerful *umma* and regretted the decline of several important Muslim empires. The Mughals had dominated much of South Asia for several generations, but the introduction of British rule in the nineteenth century saw the end of the Mughals. The Ottoman Empire, too, had thrived in the eastern Mediterranean and North Africa, but by the early nineteenth century it was threatened by increasing European power.

As a result, reformist movements developed that prioritized revitalizing the *umma*. Some focused on trying to revive the lost glory and power of the *umma*. Other movements directly resisted European imperialism and, later, American expansion and influence. And some reformers tried to deflect the criticism of the Islamic world that was coming from powerful Western governments. European leaders and scholars were often quick to criticize Islam and Muslim cultures as being "backward," and some Muslim reformers made concerted efforts to combat these developing stereotypes.

These movements took several forms. One reformer was Muhammad Ahmed ibn Abdallah (1844–1885), more commonly known as the Sudanese Mahdi. The Sudanese Mahdi organized a powerful military uprising against the Egyptian and British forces that occupied the Sudan in the nineteenth century. Many people have claimed the title of Mahdi over the years, and Abdallah convinced people that he was indeed the Mahdi heralding the end of days. In this way, he was able to recruit a large number of followers. His movement emphasized social equality, and he entirely revamped the five pillars. For example, he incorporated a declaration of himself as Mahdi in the *shahadah*, and he dropped the *hajj* as a requirement. His revamping of the pillars was highly controversial, and many Sudanese Muslims did not support his efforts. However, his aims were more political than religious, and he successfully took the city of Khartoum in 1885 from the British and Egyptian armies.

Jamal al-din al-Afghani (1838–1897) was a reformer who sought to inspire Muslims by convincing them that the roots of revitalization were within their own faith and their own history. Born in Iran, al-Afghani traveled extensively in the Middle East and Central Asia and advocated the idea that all Muslims worldwide should join together with the goal of revitalizing the *umma* and defeating Western imperialism. He called upon his fellow Muslims to unify against Western influence. Al-Afghani is often considered the originator of the anti-imperialist sentiment among many Muslim thinkers of the time. In addition, he argued that Islam was the religion most amenable to scientific knowledge. Al-Afghani was also well known as an activist for the poor and downtrodden, and he called for social reform in Muslim countries to alleviate their plight.

Through calling for unification of the *umma*, al-Afghani is often considered the father of pan-Islamism, and he was a great inspiration to other reformers. Perhaps the best known of his followers is Muhammad Abduh (1849–1905), who was born in Egypt and achieved great renown as an advocate of Egyptian nationalism. Like al-Afghani, Abduh saw no conflict between religion and science, and he asserted that Islam had always embraced scientific methodologies. And like many reformers of his time, Abduh thought that the Qur'an should be interpreted in light of social changes. Abduh argued that although certain Islamic doctrines were absolute and unchangeable, some teachings should change with the times. For example, he is well known for his criticisms of polygamy, discussed in more detail later in this chapter.

A third reformer of the same period was the modernist thinker Sayyid Ahmed Khan (1817–1898). Khan is best known for his educational reforms in South Asia and his support of the British. Unlike reformers such as al-Afghani, Khan admired the West, particularly the British, and attempted to bring Western ways of thought and education to India. Although he did not advocate imperial rule, he believed that the Muslims of South Asia could only move forward through embracing certain Western ways. In light of these views, it is not surprising that he was criticized by other reformers of his time as being too sympathetic with the British. He is also known for advocating interpretation of the Qur'an in a rational way in light of social changes. Like Abduh and Afghani, he embraced developments in science and argued that there was no conflict between Islam and science.

The Muslim Brotherhood The reformist spirit of the nineteenth century carried over into the twentieth. Several important and wide-reaching twentieth-century movements responded to and built on the developments of the nineteenth century. A key goal for many twentieth-century reformers involved finding a path to economic development for Muslim countries that did not follow Western models. More specifically, many thinkers have sought a path that allows Muslim countries and cultures to maintain their Muslim identities and still embrace certain ideas and technologies that originated in the West. Even in the postcolonial world, Europe and the United States are criticized for cultural imperialism because Western cultural models and products are spread throughout the world, particularly through business and media.

One of the most influential contemporary movements has been the Muslim Brotherhood. The Brotherhood has been in existence for several decades. It is based in Egypt, though it has been influential all over the globe. The founder was Hassan al-Banna, who organized the movement in 1928 to revitalize Islam from within by focusing on a return to the Qur'an and the *Sunnah*. Like other reformers of his time, al-Banna was opposed to Western imperialism. He argued that encroaching Western values were contributing to the decline of Islamic societies.

Sayyid Qutb, one of the more influential members of the Brotherhood, was an outspoken critic of Western influence, and he aimed to revitalize the Islamic world solely through Islamic principles. Qutb was executed in 1966 by the Egyptian government after being repeatedly accused of treason, terrorism, and a plot to kill President Gamal Abdel Nasser. Qutb's writings have continued to influence certain Islamic activists and some extremists, including those who are highly critical of Western influence on the Muslim world, such as Osama bin Laden and members of al-Qaeda. However, it is important to note that many members of the Muslim Brotherhood have been very critical of Sayyid Qutb's radical views.

Throughout its existence, the Brotherhood has had a fractured relationship with the Egyptian government. It was banned in the 1950s, after members of the Brotherhood attempted to assassinate Egyptian President Nasser. Despite this, the Brotherhood remained active, and in later years it made attempts to reconcile with the government under President Hosni Mubarak, who was deposed in 2011. In 2012, Muhammad Morsi was the first member of the Brotherhood to be elected president in Egypt. He was ousted in 2013, and the Brotherhood was again banned by the new government.

Varieties of Islam

As you learned earlier in this chapter, Islam has two major branches: the Sunni and the Shi'a. Most of what we discuss in this chapter is applicable to both branches. Although the essential beliefs of the Sunnis and Shi'a are the same—including the oneness of God, the Qur'an as the word of God, and Muhammad as the messenger of God—the two branches have some important differences.

Who Are the Sunni? Sunnis make up the majority of Muslims worldwide, about 80 percent, and the Shi'a make up about 20 percent. As you learned earlier, the Sunni and Shi'a split began over the controversy surrounding leadership of the Muslim community after the death of the Prophet Muhammad. The majority of Muhammad's companions thought that he had not chosen a successor, and they supported Abu Bakr as the next leader. However, Sunnism did not develop into a distinct branch of Islam until about 300 years later. At that point, certain scholars emphasized that Muslims should primarily emphasize following the example of the Prophet Muhammad, the Qur'an, and the opinions of earlier scholars over engaging in rationalist thought like that of the Mutazilites, discussed earlier. The word "sunni" comes from this emphasis on the *Sunnah* of the Prophet.

One of the differences between Sunni and Shi'a Islam concerns the sources of Islamic law, which we discuss in more detail in a later section. In short, both branches agree on the importance of the Qur'an and the Sunnah. In Sunni Islam, however, an additional source is the consensus of the community. This became a source of law because of a *hadith* that reported the Prophet saying, "My community will never agree upon an error." Of course, it is impossible to solicit the opinion of every Muslim on a particular legal question, so Sunnis have generally agreed that the community in question consists of the *ulama*, or legal scholars.

Who Are the Shi'a? Shi'a Muslims are in the majority in Iran and Iraq, and they form significant minorities in other countries, including Pakistan and India. In addition to believing that Muhammad designated 'Ali to be his successor, the Shi'a believe that Muhammad passed on special religious knowledge to his relatives through 'Ali. Therefore, to the Shi'a, only Muhammad's family and their descendants should lead the Muslim community. This belief in a continuing spiritual leadership of the Muslim community through the line of successors is the most significant contrast between Sunni and Shi'a Islam. For the Shi'a, the rightful leaders of the Muslim community are known as imams, the same term used for someone who leads prayer. In Shi'a Islam, the imam is both the political and the religious leader of the community, and he possesses the special religious knowledge that Muhammad passed on to the members of his family. 'Ali is regarded as the first imam. It is important to note that, although the imam has a very prominent role in Shi'a Islam, he is not a prophet.

The authority of the Shi'a imams has a special role in Shi'a law that we do not see in Sunni approaches to Islamic law. The Shi'a schools do not recognize consensus as a source of law but focus instead on the infallibility of the imam. Islamic scholarship is highly important in the Shi'a tradition. Also, although scholarship and learning are valued among Sunni Muslims, there is a more formal religious authority structure in Shi'ism that we do not find in Sunni Islam.

The Shi'a community itself has several branches. They differ in how they trace the line of imams in descent from 'Ali. The largest branch is known as the Twelvers, who make up the majority of Muslims in Iran and Iraq. The Twelvers believe that the line of imams went through several generations until the twelfth imam disappeared in the

World Sunni and Shi'a distribution.

Sunni distribution

Shi'a distribution

ninth century. This twelfth imam is considered to be in "occultation," or hiding. Twelvers believe that he will eventually return. In the meantime, the Islamic scholars are considered responsible for the leadership of the Muslim community. This idea was important in the new government set up in Iran after the 1979 revolution.

Another branch of Shi'ism, known as the *Ismailis*, believes that there has been an unbroken line of imams from 'Ali until the present day. They take their name from the seventh imam, a man named Ismail, whom the Twelvers do not recognize as an imam.

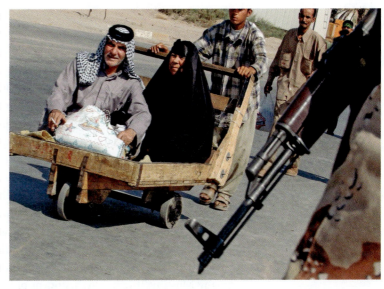

An Iraqi soldier stands guard as Shi'a pilgrims approach the holy city of Karbala.

The month of the Islamic calendar known as Muharram is especially significant to Shi'a Muslims. This is because the martyrdom of Muhammad's grandson Husayn, discussed earlier in this chapter, is recalled on the tenth of the month. This date is called **Ashura**, and the entire month of Muharram is recognized as an important and somber time. At this time of year, the death of Husayn is commemorated in many ways by Shi'a Muslims in places such as Iran and Iraq. Husayn's story is retold through passion plays and street processions, called Ta'ziya, in which Muslims reenact the events of Husayn's death.

For Shi'a Muslims, the tombs of the prophet's family are sites of very important pilgrimages. Making pilgrimages to the tombs is an important way to commemorate and honor the Prophet's family. Karbala, where Husayn was martyred and is said to be buried, is an important pilgrimage site in Iraq.

Muslims in North America

Today, about 2.6 million Muslims live in the United States, and close to 1 million live in Canada. Both populations are growing rapidly, primarily through immigration. American Muslims are making inroads and social contributions in their home communities and in regional and national politics. Many Muslims live in large urban areas, but significant populations also live in smaller towns and more rural areas. The Muslim population in the United States is not limited to one particular city or even one particular region. Muslims live everywhere, from Los Angeles to Salt Lake City to Dearborn, Michigan, the city that has the largest Muslim population in the United States.

The African American Muslim population grew significantly in the twentieth century. Scholars estimate that from 10 to 30 percent of the Africans who were enslaved and brought to the United States from the seventeenth to the nineteenth centuries were Muslims. Once in the United States, however, many slaves were not permitted to freely practice their religion, although some were literate in Arabic and tried to maintain their religious practice. Many slaves were also forced to convert to Christianity or converted by choice.

In the twentieth century, African Americans were attracted to Islam and converted for a variety of reasons. For example, many people regarded Islam as the likely religion of their African ancestors. Thus Muslim religious leaders often stressed these ties to Africa, and some claimed that Islam was a more "authentic" religion for African Americans. The reason was that Islam was not the religion of the European American slave owners. Today, perhaps half of the Muslims in the United States are African Americans.[12] The Nation of Islam has played an important role in the U.S. Muslim community. However, the majority of African American Muslims are not members of the organization. The Nation was founded by a man who was known by several different names, among them Wallace Ford and Wali D. Fard. In the 1930s, Fard established the Temple of Islam in Detroit, Michigan, and he preached that all black people were originally Muslims. Eventually, a student of his named Elijah Muhammad succeeded him as the leader of the Nation of Islam. The Nation differs significantly from mainstream Islam on several key teachings. Most significantly, followers regard Fard as God incarnate, and Elijah is considered his prophet. The Nation of Islam has been controversial in the United States because of teachings that suggest the natural supremacy of black people and encourage the rejection of white society. Despite its controversial nature, the Nation has been active in improving the lives of African Americans.

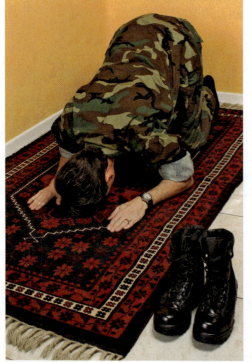

An American Muslim soldier praying.

When Elijah Muhammad died in 1975, the Nation of Islam split. One group, led by his son Warith Deen Muhammad, moved away from the teachings of the Nation toward mainstream Sunni Islam and became known as the American Muslim Mission. This is the largest organized group of African American Muslims today. Louis Farrakhan, a radical preacher who is very controversial for his espousal of black supremacist ideas and politics, has led the other group, which retained the name Nation of Islam, for many years.

Malcolm X, a leader in the black power movement of the 1960s, was perhaps the most famous American Muslim and the most famous member of the Nation of Islam. He was raised a Christian with the name Malcolm Little and converted to Islam while serving a prison sentence. He took the name X as a statement decrying his "slave name" of Little, in reference to the historical practice of slaves being given the surnames of their masters. He eventually took the name Malik al-Shabazz. Malcolm X was affiliated with the Nation of Islam for several years and became an influential public figure. However, after he made the *hajj* to Mecca in the 1960s, he moved toward mainstream Islam and eventually separated himself from the Nation. In his autobiography, he movingly describes the sense of harmony and unity he felt while on *hajj* with Muslims of all colors, ethnicities, and cultural backgrounds.[13]

As noted earlier, most African American Muslims are not members of the Nation but are rather Sunni Muslims whose beliefs and practices are like those of other Sunni Muslims around the world. Many American Muslims today are either immigrants or the descendants of immigrants. Like all immigrants to the United States, Muslims have come in waves from many parts of the world; most are from the Middle East, South Asia, Southeast Asia, and Iran, though others came from Eastern Europe, Africa, and elsewhere. In the late nineteenth century, people migrated from the Middle East, namely Syria, Jordan, and Lebanon, to the Americas for economic reasons. Most of them were uneducated, and most were single men. This resulted in much intermarriage between these Muslim newcomers and people of varied cultural and religious backgrounds.

In the middle of the twentieth century, Muslim immigrants began to come from other areas of the Middle East, the Soviet Union, and Eastern Europe. Many in this wave of immigrants were educated and from wealthy families, and many had a great interest in assimilating to the wider American population. In later years, Muslim peoples came to the United States from South Asia, Iran, and other parts of the world. Many in this most recent wave have had less interest in assimilating to mainstream American culture, instead hoping to preserve their cultural and religious heritage.

As the Muslim population grows in the United States and Canada, Muslims are becoming an increasingly important religious minority. In 2006, the United States saw the election of the first Muslim member of Congress, Representative Keith Ellison of Minnesota. However, as with many immigrant groups before them, immigrants from the Muslim world face challenges when moving to the United States. Not only will they be in a religious and cultural minority, but they also face the added difficulty of an American population that does not know much about Islam except for unflattering stereotypes.

The tragic events of September 11, 2001, brought Islam to the forefront of many Americans' minds. Although the attackers referenced religion to explain their actions, American Muslims have joined other Muslims around the world in denouncing terrorist attacks as antithetical to the teachings of Islam, which prohibit the killing of innocents. Many cite the Qur'anic verse (5:32) that equates the killing of one person to be as sinful as killing all of humanity. It is perhaps best to understand terrorism as acts of political violence that perpetrators have attempted to justify with religion. Understood this way, we can see many parallels in recent and more distant world history when individuals or nations have used various religions to justify warfare, colonization, and other forms of violence.

In the aftermath of September 11, 2001, North American Muslims faced suspicion and hostility from their non-Muslim neighbors. Some non-Muslim Americans mistakenly viewed the terrorist attacks as representative of Islam and Muslims, and in turn targeted Muslim communities, breaking windows in mosques and threatening teachers at Islamic elementary schools. In 2010, a controversy about the building of an Islamic center in lower Manhattan turned especially heated. Many non-Muslim Americans were vehemently opposed to the center because it was a few blocks away from the site of the September 11 attacks on New York.

Despite these difficulties, however, many Americans have expressed increased interest in understanding other faiths and cultures—particularly Islam. Also, many American Muslim individuals and communities have made concerted efforts to educate other Americans about their faith, beliefs, and religious practices and to explain that the vast majority of the world's Muslims regard terrorist acts as distinctly un-Islamic with no basis in the faith. With these efforts at outreach and the efforts of non-Muslim Americans to understand Islam and Muslim peoples and cultures, we can have great hope for meaningful religious diversity in the United States.

ISLAM AS A WAY OF LIFE

What does it mean to be a practicing Muslim? What does one do on a daily basis? Now that we have covered the major teachings and history of the religion, we turn our attention to Islam as a way of life. We discuss worship practice, the Islamic year and important holidays, and Islamic law. We also explore gender roles and family life and the complex concept of *jihad*.

VOICES: An Interview with Tunay Durmaz

Tunay Durmaz is a graduate student in physics at a university in the United States. He was born in Bulgaria in a Turkish family and raised a Sunni Muslim. When he was eleven years old, his family moved to Turkey. After getting his university degree, he moved to the United States to study for a Ph.D. in a scientific field.

In your view, what is the essence of Islam?

The essence of Islam is to guide humanity along the right path and bring them happiness in this world and the hereafter. It is also to teach humanity about their Creator, the purpose of creation, where we came from, and where we are going.

What is humanity's place in the world, and what does it mean to be a practicing Muslim today and also a scientist?

Humanity and all creation are the manifestation of Creator's Art. Humanity is the best of the creation. Humans differ from most of the other creation with the conscience given to them. This brings responsibility. Today, with the technology and knowledge we have it is easy to get distracted and drawn away from spirituality. This presents challenges to Muslims, because in Islam, faith (the spiritual part of religion) and worship (religious practice) go hand in hand. Fortunately, Islam does not contradict with science; in contrast, science and scientific knowledge is embraced in Islam. . . . Science is a human effort to understand Creation. And as humans we can make mistakes—this is part of doing science. If scientific knowledge seems to conflict with religion, we should think about how we have interpreted this knowledge rather than assume it falsifies religion.

How does being a Muslim shape your worldview?

Islam is a very comprehensive religion. It draws our attention to the hereafter. But . . . the rewards in the afterlife will depend on how we live this life. . . . So, everything in this life becomes an opportunity to do good deeds and gain God's good pleasure . . . it becomes important to watch for evil and to abstain from it. Thus, a Muslim lives a cautious life, and it brings him awareness. Islam offers guidance in every aspect of life. Sometimes guidance is in the form of commandment, sometimes encouragement, sometimes a prohibition. So believers have responsibilities towards themselves, their families, relatives, neighbors, friends and all humanity. This is how Islam shapes my worldview. In the big picture, I have permanent and eternal life as a goal, but I can reach that goal through this temporary, short life. Islam offers all the guidance to achieve that goal. This helps me to get through difficulties and hardship I face.

From your perspective, what is it like to be a Muslim in North America today? What opportunities and challenges do you face?

I have had quite a good experience so far. Although we face the problems of maintaining a sense of spirituality in the face of many distractions of modern life, I haven't experienced any difficulties regarding my faith or practice. I can freely and comfortably perform my daily prayers anywhere. When it is time to pray I can do it in my office, I can do it in the airport. When I attend conferences, I ask the organizers for a place that I can use for a few minutes, and I have been helped every time so far. Sometimes, due to the circumstances, I have to perform my prayers outside, and I look for silent and calm spots to pray. In these circumstances, people see me but nobody has confronted me or threatened me or anything like that. On the contrary, I have been invited to classes, and even to church gatherings to talk about my religion and to share my faith. Those were very good experiences. It gives me hope, because I can see that people can work together regardless of their differences in faith, religion, race, or culture. Those differences are not problems. We face other common problems, real problems like poverty and warfare, which we all need to solve together.

The Qur'an in Daily Life

The Qur'an is an important part of the daily life of all Muslims, and the text itself is treated with great reverence and respect. To Muslims, the Qur'an is authentic only in the original Arabic. This means that a translation, such as an English version of the Qur'an, is not the holy book itself but merely an interpretation of the meaning. In many Muslim countries, children are encouraged to attend Qur'an schools, where they are often introduced to religious study through learning to memorize and recite

This building in Zanzibar, Tanzania, houses both Islamic and secular primary courts, as well as government offices.

sections of the Qur'an. In most communities, both boys and girls study the Qur'an, and people will often continue to study the Qur'an throughout adulthood. Indeed, Muhammad encouraged all Muslims to pursue a life of learning.

To Muslims, the true meaning of the Qur'an can only be understood in the original Arabic. The beauty of the language is said to lend itself to the spiritual nature of the words of God. Because of this, Muslims around the world learn to recite the Qur'an in Arabic—even if they do not speak or understand the language. (Often, a teacher will explain the meaning of the text in the local language.) Verses of the Qur'an are recited during the daily prayers, and the Qur'an is also recited at numerous other occasions, including weddings, funerals, birth celebrations, holidays, and political events.

Hearing the Qur'an recited by a talented person can be a moving experience for people of all faiths, even if they do not understand the words. Although people can achieve great fame for their ability to recite beautifully, Muslims do not normally regard recitation as entertainment or singing. In many places, children and adults recite the Qur'an in highly organized competitions that can resemble an American spelling bee. Amina, the woman introduced at the beginning of the chapter, has studied the Qur'an for years and has great skill in recitation. As a teenager, she once won a sewing machine in a recitation contest.

What Is *Jihad*?

The term *jihad* comes from an Arabic verb meaning to "struggle" or "strive" and has historically had complex meanings. The concept of *jihad* is often distorted in contemporary Western media. In general, the term *jihad* means exerting oneself in the name of God. *Jihad* can refer to several types of struggle on both personal and social levels. The term is used only rarely in the Qur'an, and nowhere is it explicitly linked to armed struggle. Rather, it was early in Islamic history that the term became associated with defensive military endeavors against the enemies of the growing Muslim community. There have been some Muslim groups both today and throughout history that have called for a military *jihad* against nonbelievers, even out of the context of defense of the Muslim community. You can see how the term is used in different verses of the Qur'an:

> O Believers, go out in the cause of God, (whether) light or heavy, and strive (*jihad*) in the service of God, wealth and soul. This is better for you if you understand.
>
> —9:41

> And strive (*jihad*) in the way of God with a service worthy of Him. He has chosen you and laid no hardship on you in the way of faith, the faith of your forebear Abraham. He named you Muslim earlier, and in this (Qur'an) in order that the Prophet be witness over you, and you be witness over mankind. So be firm in devotion, pay the *zakat*, and hold on firmly to God. He is your friend: How excellent a friend is He, how excellent a helper!
>
> —22:78

> So do not listen to unbelievers and strive (*jihad*) against them with greater effort.
>
> —25:52

Muslims often refer to the *greater jihad* as one's struggle to become a better person by striving against one's own sinful tendencies and to live in accordance with the will of God. Although we often see the term *jihad* translated into English as "holy war," Muslims regard the military connotations of the term as the *lesser jihad*. The idea of "greater and lesser" *jihad* comes from the *hadith* literature. Muhammad is reported to have said upon returning home from a battle, "We return from the little *jihad* to the greater *jihad*."

Now we turn our attention to other elements of Muslim life and practice.

The Islamic Year and Holidays

The Islamic calendar begins with the *hijra*, which as noted earlier in this chapter was the migration of Muhammad and the early Muslim community from Mecca to Medina in 622 C.E. The Islamic calendar is lunar because the Qur'an stipulates that the moon should be the measure of time. However, in most of the Muslim world, people use both the lunar and solar calendars. The Qur'an also designates the names of the twelve months of the year. Of these, four months are considered sacred.

Several important celebrations and feast days occur throughout the Islamic year, and Muslims around the world celebrate these days in a variety of ways. The Feast of Sacrifice, or *Id al-Adha*, is the primary holiday of the Muslim year. The feast takes place at the end of the *hajj* season, and it is celebrated by all Muslims—not just those who made the pilgrimage that year. The feast commemorates Abraham's willingness to sacrifice his son at God's command. In many countries, offices and shops close for two days, and people spend time with their families and friends. In commemoration of the ram that was sacrificed instead of Ishmael, Muslims are expected to slaughter an animal to mark the holiday. However, because this is not always possible, Muslims may make charitable donations as a substitute.

The second most significant holiday in the Muslim calendar is *Id al-Fitr*, the Feast of Fast-Breaking. This holiday marks the end of the month of Ramadan. This feast is a time of joy and forgiveness and is celebrated in many different ways around the world. Muslims mark the day by attending congregational prayers, visiting friends and family, or celebrating in public festivals and carnivals. Often, Muslims will wear elegant clothing for the holiday, and children are dressed in their finest new clothes. In some places, children are also given special treats, money, or gifts.

The Prophet's birth is also an occasion for celebration in many parts of the Muslim world, such as North Africa, East Africa, and South Asia. This celebration is known as *Mawlid al-Nabi*, and takes place around the twelfth day of the third month of the Islamic calendar. The birth of the prophet may be marked by state-sponsored ceremonies. Elsewhere, the birthday is marked by all-night recitation sessions, at which participants recite the Qur'an and devotional poetry. Some Muslims criticize the celebration of the Prophet's birth. They argue that such celebration of Muhammad risks elevating the prophet to the status of God. Muslims in Saudi Arabia, for example, do not generally celebrate *Mawlid al-Nabi*. As you learned earlier in this chapter, the month of Muharram is particularly important for Shi'a Muslims as a time to commemorate the martyrdom of the Prophet's grandson Husayn.

The *Shari'ah*: Islamic Law

Muslims believe that God, as the creator of the universe and humanity, established a wide-ranging set of guidelines for human beings to follow. These guidelines are known as the **shari'ah**. The literal translation of the Arabic term *shari'ah* is the "road" or "way." In English, it is most often translated as "law." However, the *shari'ah* encompasses a much broader range of law and legal activity than what is normally associated with law in the Western world. The *shari'ah* regulates almost every aspect of daily life for believers. Proper religious practice is included in the *shari'ah*, and so are areas of law that North Americans find more familiar, such as marriage and divorce, inheritance, commerce, and crime. However, very few countries actually apply Islamic law in full, either today or in the past.

In Islamic belief, God is the sole legislator. In theory, this means that while humanity can interpret law, humans cannot legislate or make new laws. The *shari'ah* is drawn from several sources. The Qur'an is the primary legal source. In the early Meccan *surahs*, general legal principles are introduced. These include the importance of generosity, of obeying God's command, and of performing prayer and religious duties with sincerity. In the later Medinan *surahs*, many technical legal matters are presented in great detail. Some of these *surahs* contain very specific laws governing community relations, marriage and family, and inheritance and commerce.

Although the Qur'an is the primary source of law, Islamic scholars throughout history have recognized that it does not address every legal situation. As a result, there are also other sources of Islamic law. Different branches of Islam, such as the Sunni and Shi'a traditions, and different schools of thought within them have recognized different sources as more or less important. For example, in Sunni Islam, many scholars have referenced the *Sunnah* as a very important additional legal source, which is second only to the Qur'an in importance. For centuries and up to the present day,

Islamic jurists have consulted the *Sunnah* for answers to legal questions that are not explicitly addressed by the Qur'an. The *Sunnah* is important because Muhammad is considered the ideal human, the person closest to God, and the recipient of the revelation of the Qur'an. For that reason, his words and actions became an important legal source as a model for human behavior. Furthermore, Muhammad acted as a judge and a mediator of disputes in Medina, and the way he resolved legal conflicts is recorded in the *hadith*.

There are also other sources of Islamic law. In the sections on Sunni and Shi'a Islam, we discussed sources of law that are distinct to each. For example, many Sunni scholars agree that if a legal matter is not addressed by the Qur'an or the *Sunnah*, then it is appropriate to use human reason to find an analogous situation; this reasoning by analogy is known as *qiyas*. In addition, Sunni Muslims recognize the consensus of the Muslim community as a source of law; this is known as *ijma* and is recognized as a source of law because a hadith reports that Muhammad said, "my community will never agree upon an error." Law for Shi'a Muslims is somewhat different. For example, Shi'a legal traditions do not recognize consensus as a source of law but do recognize the imams as a very important source of law, as they are considered infallible.

Because Islamic legal scholars have not always agreed on the merit of sources of law such as reasoning by analogy and consensus, several schools of Islamic law developed in the centuries following the death of Muhammad. Among the Sunni, there are four schools, each named after the legal scholar who founded it. The schools were formalized by the tenth century, and all the schools recognize the validity of the others.

Both historically and today, studying *shari'ah* is an important part of Islamic education. Those who gain expertise in the law may have a special status in the community. The term *ulama* refers to Islamic legal scholars. Among these are legal practitioners known as *qadis*, who are court judges who issue rulings on various matters. A *mufti* is an expert in Islamic law who is qualified to give nonbinding legal opinions, known as *fatwas*.

Today, many Muslim-majority states include Islamic law and courts in the state legal systems. However, in most countries in which Islamic law is applied, Islamic courts handle only matters of family law, and only for Muslims. Family law includes issues such as marriage, divorce, child custody, and inheritance. It is only in a very few countries, such as Iran and Saudi Arabia, that Islamic criminal and commercial law are recognized in the state legal system. One reason for this is that many countries that were colonized by European powers adopted European legal codes for criminal matters. Also, some countries have determined that centuries-old laws are not appropriate for modern contexts.

Many Muslims live in accordance with Islamic law in their personal lives, even if they do not live in a country with Islamic courts. As noted earlier, Islamic law informs the daily life of the believer and regulates how a Muslim worships God. In addition, much like Jewish law, Islamic law

Case files from an Islamic court in East Africa.

regulates what a believer should eat and drink. For example, Muslims are prohibited from consuming pork and alcohol. Much of the legal basis for the prohibition on pork comes from the Qur'an. The prohibition on alcohol, although mentioned in the Qur'an, is more thoroughly developed in the *hadith* literature.

Sufism

Muslims have sometimes described the *shari'ah*, or Islamic law, as the "outer" way to God because it regulates a person's "outer" existence: how he or she should handle relationships with other people, how he or she should live in a community, and how he or she should worship. For many Muslims, however, there is also an "inner" way to God. This is the mystical tradition of Islam, which is known as Sufism. Like traditions of mysticism in other religions, the goal of a follow of Sufism, a **Sufi,** is to draw close to and personally experience God. However, unlike mystics of other religions, Sufis base this spiritual quest on the sources of Islam, namely the Qur'an and the example of Muhammad.

It is likely that Sufism arose in the years after the death of Muhammad as a response to the worldly excesses and materialism of the Umayyad Dynasty. Many early Sufis were ascetics who taught that a simple way of life was in keeping with the way Muhammad lived. One famous eighth-century Sufi was Hasan of Basra (Basra is a city in Iraq). He was known for preaching asceticism and for his constant weeping out of fear of God. A renowned early female Sufi was Rabi'a al-Adawiyya, also of Basra. Rabi'a was known for her almost giddy happiness in the love of God. There are many wonderful stories about Rabi'a. In one, she criticized Hasan of Basra by telling him that his constant weeping and fear of God drew the focus to himself rather than God. This theme is echoed in another story, in which she walks through the streets of Basra carrying a pitcher of water and a flaming torch. When asked why she was doing this, she explained that she wanted to set paradise ablaze and put out the fires of hell so people would love God solely for the sake of God—not out of hope of paradise or fear of hell.

After Rabi'a's time, this ideal of intense love for God became a primary focus for Sufis. Love is often expressed in Sufi poetry, which is one of the premier art forms in Islamic history. The following poem, by the great thirteenth-century Sufi poet Jalalludin Rumi, describes the beauty of submitting to God. Those who love and submit to God are compared to a moth who is drawn to a candle's flame.

> Love whispers in my ear,
> "Better to be a prey than a hunter,
> Make yourself My fool.
> Stop trying to be the sun and become a speck!
> Dwell at My door and be homeless.
> Don't pretend to be a candle, be a moth,
> so you may taste the savor of Life
> and know the power hidden in serving."[14]

Sufis ground their belief and worship practice in the teachings of the Qur'an. Sufi readings of the Qur'an have often searched for the inner, or hidden, meaning. This approach to interpreting the Qur'an often focuses on God's love for creation and God's closeness to humanity. Sufis often emphasize the teachings of the *hadith qudsi*, which focus on these themes.

Like all Muslims, Sufis consider Muhammad the ideal human, and they strive to emulate the way he lived his life. Sufis emphasize the story of the miraculous night when Muhammad journeyed from Mecca to Jerusalem and from there ascended to heaven to meet God. The ascension to heaven is known as the *miraj*. Muslims believe that the Angel Gabriel came to Muhammad one night while he was sleeping and took him to Jerusalem. From there, Muhammad ascended upward through the many levels of heaven. He met earlier prophets like Jesus and Moses. Eventually, Muhammad came into the presence of God. God gave him significant blessings and special spiritual knowledge that he later passed on to his companions, particularly 'Ali. Because Muhammad is believed to have personally experienced the presence of God, Sufis consider him to be the first Sufi and the source of the special spiritual knowledge they seek. In East Africa and the Middle East, Muslims learn of the *miraj* through epic poems, which are recited on special occasions like *mawlid al-nabi*. Because Muhammad ascended to heaven from Jerusalem, it is recognized as a holy city for Muslims, along with Mecca and Medina.

The night journey is mentioned in the Qur'an (17:1) and the *hadith* literature and is considered by many Muslims to be the greatest of all Muhammad's spiritual experiences. Because Muhammad ascended to heaven from Jerusalem, the city holds a special place in Islam, and it is one of the three Muslim holy cities, along with Mecca and Medina. In the year 691 C.E., the beautiful shrine known as the Dome of the Rock was built over the spot from which Muhammad ascended to heaven. The Dome of the Rock is located on the place known as the Temple Mount, where the ancient Jewish temples were located. It is therefore easy to understand why this place in the center of Jerusalem is special to both Muslims and Jews. This is one of the primary reasons that the status of Jerusalem is so central to the Arab-Israeli conflict today: practitioners of both faiths (as well as Christians) consider the city to be holy and long to have unfettered access to it.

Most Sufis agree that an individual needs guidance along the spiritual path to God. As a result, a master-disciple relationship is very important in Sufism. The *shaykh*, or master, directs the spiritual training of the novices. In the early centuries of Islam, respected *shaykhs* would guide several pupils, and as a result a number of Sufi orders, *tariqas*, developed around particular Sufi masters. Each order traces a spiritual lineage of

The Dome of the Rock in Jerusalem.

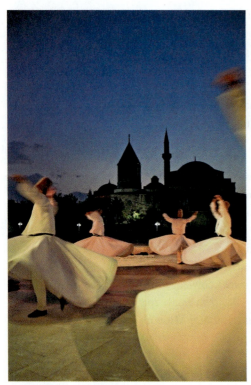

Mevlevi dhikr; Mevlevis are sometimes known as Whirling Dervishes.

learned leaders back to Muhammad and from Muhammad to God. Muhammad is believed to have passed on his special religious knowledge to his companions, who then passed it down through the generations from master to disciple.

Although members of all the orders have the same goal—personally experiencing God—they emphasize different meditation techniques and spiritual practices. Some orders are widespread and have members all over the world. Others are limited to a particular region. The most well-known order in the Western world is perhaps the Mevlevi order, which is based on the teachings of Jalalludin Rumi.

Sufi orders emphasize the necessity of some type of *dhikr*. The term means "recollection" and refers to Sufi meditation in which the believer strives to "recollect" God so completely that he forgets himself. *Dhikr* can take many forms and varies from order to order. Sometimes *dhikr* is as simple as the recitation of the *shahadah*, and sometimes it is much more elaborate. The Mevlevis have an elaborate *dhikr*. In the West, they are often called the "Whirling Dervishes" because their *dhikr* involves controlled whirling. For all Sufis, the goal of *dhikr* is to lose the sense of self entirely in complete remembrance of God.

Not all Sufi practice takes place in the formal context of the orders. In many parts of the world, Muslims may participate in Sufi practice without affiliation to an order. A good example of this is the practice of saint veneration. Many Sufis venerate *shaykhs*, or saints, who were well-known and respected for their religious learning and spirituality. In some areas, such as Pakistan and northern India, the tombs of deceased *shaykhs* become places of pilgrimage. At the tombs, people seek blessings from the saints. Tomb visitation is very common in South Asia, when the celebration of the saints' death date can draw thousands of pilgrims. Many pilgrims are not affiliated with a Sufi order, and some are not even Muslim; people of all faiths may recognize the power of a saint.

Throughout Islamic history, occasional tension has arisen between Sufis and other Muslims. For example, the practice of saint veneration has drawn criticism from some, who argue that the celebration of saints compromises the oneness of God by raising mere mortals to the level of the divine; you read earlier about al-Wahhab's criticism of saint veneration. Of course, those involved in saint veneration do not view saints as divine. Rather, they view saints more as close friends of God, who are filled with blessings that can be transferred to others. Historically, Sufis have sometimes been criticized by other Muslims for neglecting the five pillars in favor of more esoteric religious knowledge and practice. Some early Sufis rejected adherence to the *shari'ah* on the grounds that the technical laws merely served to veil God from the believer, not draw him or her closer. However, this was not a majority opinion among Sufism. Indeed, some Sufis have made a specific effort to reconcile the *shari'ah* and Sufism. The eleventh century scholar al-Ghazali was one of these. In his writings, he established Sufism as a branch of formal learning in the Islamic sciences.

Marriage and Family

Marriage and family life are the cornerstones of Muslim communities. Devout Muslims, who strive to follow the example of the Prophet in their daily lives, consider Muhammad to have set the example of marriage and to have been the ideal husband and father. As a result, marriage is generally regarded as incumbent upon all Muslim men and women when they reach adulthood. Celibacy is not normally encouraged, and sexual pleasure is considered a gift from God to be enjoyed within a marriage.

Pilgrims at the shrine of Hazrat Mu'in ud-Din Chishti in Ajmer (Rajasthan), India.

Much variation exists throughout the Muslim world concerning marriage arrangements, weddings, and the organization of the family life. In some areas, marriages for young people are arranged by their parents, whereas in others, women and men select their own marriage partners. However, in most Muslim communities, dating is not an acceptable practice—even among Muslims living in North America. Furthermore, adult children in many Muslim families live with their parents until they marry, even if they are financially able to live on their own. Regardless of the method of arranging marriages, according to the *shari'ah*, young men and women may reject a marriage partner they deem unsuitable; the consent of both the bride and the groom is necessary for the marriage to take place. However, this legal right does not always coincide with community or cultural norms. In some cultures, a bride's silence about her parents' choice of a marriage partner is considered to indicate acceptance of the proposal.

A Muslim bride signs her marriage contract.

In Islam, a marriage is considered a contractual relationship. For the marriage to be valid, the bride, the groom, and witnesses must sign a marriage contract. The contract designates the *mahr*, which is the gift a bride will receive from the groom and his family. The gift may be cash or other property. The marriage contract may be considered invalid without the *mahr*, though the amount may vary greatly from family to family and culture to culture. The amount depends not only on the family's wealth but also on community norms. For example, urban Muslims in the Middle East might give a *mahr* of thousands of dollars, whereas the normal amount in a small African village might be only fifty dollars.

According to *shari'ah*, the *mahr* is solely the property of the bride. However, in many cultures, a bride's parents may take some of the *mahr*.

On the wedding day, the bride and groom may be separated for most of the festivities. The groom usually signs the marriage contract in a mosque in the company of his male friends and relatives. The marriage official, often an imam, then takes the contract to the bride in her family's home, where she is accompanied by her female relatives and friends. Wedding celebrations are often large affairs, and feasting, Qur'an recitation, and sometimes music and dancing may accompany the signing of the contract. In many communities, men and women celebrate entirely separately. This is because some Muslims do not consider it acceptable for men and women to socialize together. In some cultures, the bride is taken to the groom's home in a big procession at the end of the day. There, the new couple shares a special meal and begins their life together.

According to most interpretations of Islamic law, Muslim men are allowed to marry up to four wives. However, this is only under certain conditions, and only if he can support all his wives and treat them equally. For example, the verses in the Qur'an concerning polygamy suggest that the practice is appropriate in times of warfare when there may be many unmarried women. Furthermore, the Qur'an states, "Marry such women as seem good to you, two, three, four; but if you fear you will not be equitable, then marry only one" (4:3). A later verse says that "You will not be equitable between your wives, even if you try" (4:129). Some thinkers, such as the Egyptian reformer Muhammad Abduh (about whom you read earlier in this chapter), argued that these two verses actually prohibited polygamy because the latter stated that no man could possibly treat multiple wives equitably, which is a necessary condition of polygamy. Abduh also argued that although polygamy may have been necessary in the time of the prophet to protect women who had no one to care for them, it was destructive in the modern context. However, most Muslims have considered polygamy legal, though the occurrence of the practice varies tremendously around the world, and some countries, like Tunisia, have banned it entirely.

Several types of divorce are permitted in Islam. Guidelines for divorce come from both the Qur'an and *hadith* literature. One type is divorce by male unilateral repudiation. In this type of divorce, a man writes or pronounces the formula "I, (the man's name), divorce you, (the wife's name)." In classical Islamic law, this type of divorce does not need the approval of the wife or a legal authority. However, in many countries today, unilateral divorce is no longer permissible, and men and women must both file for divorce in court. According to *shari'ah*, women may seek divorce from Islamic judges on a variety of grounds. Stipulations for divorce are occasionally written into the marriage contract. For example, a woman may specify that she can divorce her husband if he marries another wife. Divorce is common in some Muslim countries and uncommon in others. In some places, a divorced man or woman is dishonored and finds it difficult to remarry, whereas in others there is little or no stigma attached to a divorced man or woman.

Women and Islam

There is much variation in the way in which gender roles are perceived and interpreted throughout Muslim cultures. As in other religious traditions, such as Judaism, Christianity, and Hinduism, patriarchal cultural norms are sometimes justified in terms of religion. When we consider the historical context in which it was revealed, the Qur'an introduced many legal rights and privileges to women that they had not previously enjoyed. For example, women were given the right to divorce their husbands on a variety of grounds; they were allowed to inherit and hold property that remained theirs even in marriage (women in England did not gain this right until the late nineteenth century); and they were given the right to refuse arranged marriages. The Qur'an also prohibited female infanticide.

According to Islamic belief, women and men are viewed as equals in the eyes of God and will be judged on their own accord. In the Qur'an, verse 35 of *surah* 33 addresses this:

> Verily for all men and women who have come to submission,
> Men and women who are believers,
> Men and women who are devout,
> Truthful men and truthful women.
> Men and women with endurance,
> Men and women who are modest,
> Men and women who give alms,
> Men and women who observe fasting,
> Men and women who guard their private parts,
> And those men and women who remember God a great deal,
> For them God has forgiveness and a great reward.[15]

The Qur'an requires all Muslims, women and men, to live a righteous life and to seek education. Women may work outside the home, though this is still uncommon in some areas. According to religious law, all of a woman's earnings remain her property. Thus women are not required to use their earnings to support the family and maintain the home; it is a man's legal duty to provide for his family, even if his wife is wealthier than he. Of course, in practice, many women contribute their earnings to the household.

Despite this, the place of women in Islam has occasionally been interpreted in very strict fashion. One need only consider the case of the Taliban in Afghanistan, who deny women the right to work outside the home, the right to be educated, and even the right to walk freely in the street. However, this strict interpretation of religious texts and traditions is far from mainstream. Most Muslims view the Taliban's orders as radical and even religiously unlawful.

Along these same lines, much cultural variation exists in the practices regarding interaction between Muslim men and women. In some parts of the world, men and women live very separate lives. The seclusion of women is called *purdah* in South Asia

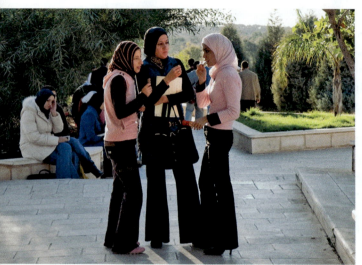

Three young Palestinian students in modest dress.

and is practiced by some Hindus and Sikhs, as well as some Muslims. Elsewhere, as in many parts of Southeast Asia and Africa, Muslim men and women intermingle freely.

The Qur'an encourages both men and women to dress and behave modestly. The verses concerning dress—particularly that of women—are interpreted in many ways. Modest women's dress takes many different cultural forms. In some cultures, modest dress is interpreted as long pants and a modest top. In other contexts, Muslim women wear a type of cloak over their clothing when they leave the home. And some Muslim women choose to cover their heads and hair with a scarf. But this is not solely a Muslim practice: in the Middle East and Mediterranean, women covered their heads long before the time of Muhammad.[16] Covering the head has also been common practice among many Christian, Jewish, Hindu, and Sikh women.

Many Muslim women dress modestly strictly out of religious commitment. For others, wearing modest dress is an important move toward gender equality in the workplace and the public sphere. Such women believe that when they are dressed modestly, they are valued by others on their merit alone, not on their appearance. To others, maintaining modest dress makes a statement of resistance to Western scholars and activists by demonstrating that feminism can be defined in myriad ways in different cultural and religious contexts. Some Muslim women say they pity Western women, who they believe must dress in a way that serves men's pleasure in viewing the female form.

We should not consider the status of women in any religious tradition without also considering historical change, and this is particularly true of Islam because of the many negative stereotypes Muslim women have faced in recent years.

Reform and Women's Status Several important reformers in the nineteenth and twentieth centuries sought to improve women's status in Muslim countries and cultures. Many of these reformers have focused on proper understanding of religious sources and Islamic law concerning women.

In much of the twentieth century, particularly in the first half, Muslim feminists were upper-class women who had the time and leisure to deliberate these issues, not working-class women whose labor was necessary to support their families. One of the most famous of these early Muslim feminists was Huda Sha'rawi (1879–1947), an educated upper-class Egyptian woman who symbolically removed her face veil in an Alexandria train station in 1923. Sha'rawi was president and founder of the Egyptian Feminist Union and did not believe that veiling was an Islamic requirement. When she removed her veil, she had just returned from a women's conference in Rome. She

Compare the role of women in the Islamic tradition with that of women in other religions. How are the roles of women similar or different?

encouraged women to cast off their headscarves in a quest for liberation. Many Egyptian women, particularly educated and elite women, were inspired by her example and ceased wearing face veils and headscarves. Sha'rawi remained an activist and feminist leader throughout her life. She founded schools and medical facilities in Egypt and also advocated for women's rights throughout the Arab world.

In the later years of the twentieth century, many Muslim feminists have sought paths to equality that diverge from Western models. In their view, Islam itself provides the necessary means for women to achieve their rights. Many argue that the Qur'an must be reinterpreted in an attempt to eradicate cultural practices that are detrimental to women but have been justified as appropriate Islamic practice. Some have argued that women's status would be much improved only if Islamic laws were properly followed. As discussed earlier, many women in recent decades have, in a sense, reembraced modest dress as a feminist statement. In Egypt, this idea became prominent in the 1980s, and many mothers and grandmothers who had consciously decided against wearing veils or headscarves were dismayed that their daughters were wearing them, ironically with the same rationale their grandmothers used to discard it.

It is important to note that Muslim feminists differ in their approaches to Islam. Zaynab al-Ghazali (b. 1917) is an Egyptian feminist who advocates increasing women's rights and improving women's status through Islam. Nawal al-Sa'dawi (b. 1931), also Egyptian, is a woman who advocates that women can only achieve equality by rejecting what she views as the patriarchal tendencies of religion. Al-Sa'dawi is both a medical doctor and a writer, and her novels and stories have been both influential and controversial in the Arab world for her focus on feminist issues and problems facing Arab women. Recently, al-Sa'dawi was active in the 2011 Egyptian revolution that overthrew the thirty-year presidency of Hosni Mubarak.

Calligraphy developed as a very important art form in Islam. This is because of a widespread understanding that imagery is prohibited by the sacred sources of Islam. This example is the word Allah. Beautiful calligraphy decorates pages of the Qur'an, mosques, and other items.

Throughout the daily prayer, the believer faces the Ka'ba in Mecca and stands, kneels, and bows his head to the floor. These cycles of movements, along with the proper recitation, are called raka and vary in number according to the prayer.

The direction of prayer, known as the qibla, is marked in a mosque by a niche called a mihrab, which is sometimes highly decorated with designs or Qur'anic verses, like this mihrab at a mosque in Cairo, Egypt.

The Ka'ba, a cubical building in Mecca that measures about thirty feet by thirty feet. Many Muslims believe it was built and dedicated to the one God by Abraham and Ishmael.

CONCLUSION

In this chapter, you have learned about the historical development, the beliefs, and the practices of Islam and Muslims. Islam is truly a global religion and is perhaps the fastest growing religion in the world. Many Muslim-majority counties are experiencing rapid population growth, but numbers are also increasing because of conversions. One of the most marked characteristics of the Muslim world today—its diversity—is unlikely to change. In fact, the ethnic diversity of the Muslim world is likely to increase. Muslims live in nearly every country in the world and on every inhabited continent.

Muslims everywhere, however, are responding to a rapidly changing world and increased globalization. Today, Muslims are facing questions about the role of religion in private and public life, the relationships with other religious communities in plural environments, and what it means to be a person of faith in the modern world. Some of these issues are common to many religions. Others, such as the role of Islamic law in modern governments, are specific to Muslims. How will Muslims address these issues in years to come? One issue that has had much attention in the press lately is the question of Islamic dress in Western Europe. In France in 2004, schoolgirls were prohibited from wearing headscarves because officials argued it violated France's commitment to secularism. (Other religious symbols, like the yarmulke worn by Jewish boys, were also banned.) Many Muslims, however, thought this was a violation of their freedom to practice religion. In Britain, a recent controversy focused on whether or not a Muslim teacher should be allowed to wear a scarf that covered her face while teaching.

A related challenge Muslims face is the negative perceptions some Westerners hold about the nature of Islam and Muslim life. How will Muslims living in religiously plural societies grapple with this sort of challenge? In the United States, some Muslim Americans who have been invited or have volunteered visit churches, synagogues, schools, and community centers with the aim of teaching people about Islam and increasing their familiarity with Muslim ways of life. Muslim communities around the world struggle with competing interpretations of Islam's teachings. Sometimes, young Muslims who go abroad to study in places such as Saudi Arabia, Indonesia, or Egypt come back to their home communities with different ideas about the way in which Islam should be practiced and taught. In many countries, as exemplified recently by some participants in the "Arab Spring" demonstrations of early 2011, Muslims are considering the relationship between Islam and democracy. Although some argue that Islam is inherently compatible with democracy because of examples such as the historical emphasis on consensus, others argue that democracy is a Western concept that is not compatible with an Islamic system of government.

As you have learned, Islam is a unique religious tradition, but it also shares a great deal with Christianity and Judaism. Will these similarities lead to greater communication and cooperation between Muslim and other religious communities? Although it is difficult to predict what the future will bring, it is clear that Islam will remain a dynamic and diverse religious tradition. Throughout history, Muslim thinkers, artists, and practitioners have contributed a great deal to global human culture, and they will continue to do so in the future.

SEEKING ANSWERS

What Is Ultimate Reality?

Muslims believe that God is the creator and sustainer of the universe, the world, and all that is in it. Muslims believe that elements of the beautiful natural world are signs of God. Humans can learn something about ultimate reality through God's revelations, which are communicated to humanity through prophets. The Qur'an is the source of God's teachings about the nature of ultimate reality and the nature of the world.

How Should We Live in This World?

Muslims believe that human beings are part of God's creation. The Islamic tradition offers many guidelines concerning the right way for human beings to live. People should worship God, be generous to the needy, and live righteously. The life of the prophet Muhammad, especially as related in the *Sunnah*, serves as an example for Muslims of how to live. The "five pillars" of Muslim worship practice are the foundation for how Muslims live their faith.

What Is Our Ultimate Purpose?

Muslims believe in an afterlife and a Day of Judgment, when all humans will be judged on their actions and deeds in this life. Those who have lived righteously will enter paradise, and those who have led sinful lives will be cast into the fire. Some Muslims think that human beings have free choice and must choose to submit to the will of God. The choices that individuals make will be evaluated on the Day of Judgment, when God will judge each person independently. Other Muslims do not adhere to an idea of free will. Devout Muslims aim to live righteous lives by submitting to the will of God, adhering to the "five pillars," and following the example of the Prophet Muhammad.

REVIEW QUESTIONS

For Review

1. What are the essential principles of belief in the Islamic religion?
2. What are the key religious practices in Islam? How do beliefs relate to religious practice and expression?
3. What are the most important sources of spirituality for Muslims?
4. What is a prophet in the Islamic tradition? What role does Muhammad play in Islam and in the life of Muslims today? How do Muslims know about the life of Muhammad, and how does he differ from other prophets?
5. What is Sufism, and how is it rooted in the Islamic tradition?

For Further Reflection

1. How do the teachings of Islam inform religious practice? How might the daily life of

Muslims reflect their commitment to Islamic ideals? How do Islamic teachings about God compare with those of other monotheistic traditions?

2. What important challenges do Muslims face in the modern world? Why do you think Islam has been so stereotyped in North America and the West?

GLOSSARY

Abbasids An important Muslim empire from 750 to 1258 C.E.

adhan (a-than; Arabic) The call to prayer.

Aisha A beloved wife of Muhammad who is known for transmitting many *hadith*.

Allah (a-lah; Arabic) The Arabic term for God.

Ashura The tenth day of the month of Muharram, recognized by Shi'a Muslims as the anniversary of the martyrdom of Husayn.

caliph (ka-lif; Arabic) Leader of the Muslim community after the death of Muhammad.

hadith (ha-deeth; Arabic) Literary tradition recording the sayings and deeds of the Prophet Muhammad.

hajj (hahj; Arabic) The annual pilgrimage to Mecca, one of the five pillars of Islam.

hijra (hij-rah; Arabic) The migration of the early Muslim community from Mecca to Medina in 622 C.E.; the Islamic calendar dates from this year.

Husayn Grandson of Muhammad who was killed while challenging the Umayyads.

imam (ee-mam; Arabic) Prayer leader; in the Shi'a tradition, one of the leaders of the Muslim community following the death of the Prophet Muhammad.

Islam (is-lahm; Arabic) Lit. "submission"; specifically, the religious tradition based on the revealed Qur'an as Word of God.

jahiliyya (ja-hil-ee-ah; Arabic) The "age of ignorance," which refers to the time before the revelation of the Qur'an.

jihad (jee-had; Arabic) Lit. "striving"; sometimes, the greater *jihad* is the struggle with one's self to become a better person; the lesser *jihad* is associated with military conflict in defense of the faith.

Khadija Muhammad's beloved first wife.

Mecca The city in which Muhammad was born; place of pilgrimage for Muslims.

Medina The city to which Muhammad and his early followers migrated to escape persecution in Mecca.

miraj (mir-aj; Arabic) Muhammad's Night Journey from Mecca to Jerusalem and from there to heaven, where he met with God.

mosque (mosk) Place of prayer, from the Arabic term "masjid."

muezzin (mu-ez-in; Arabic) The person who calls the *adhan*.

Muhammad The prophet who received the revelation of the Qur'an from God. The final prophet in a long line of prophets sent by God to humanity.

Qur'an (kur-an; Arabic) The holy text of Muslims; the Word of God as revealed to Muhammad.

Ramadan (rah-mah-dan; Arabic) The month in which Muslims must fast daily from dawn until dusk; the fast is one of the five pillars of Islam, the month in which the Qur'an is believed to have been revealed to Muhammad.

salat (sa-laht; Arabic) The daily prayers, which are one of the pillars of Islam.

sawm (som; Arabic) The mandatory fast during the month of Ramadan; one of the pillars of Islam.

shahadah (sha-ha-dah; Arabic) The declaration of faith: "There is no God but God and Muhammad is the Messenger of God"; the first of the five pillars.

shari'ah (sha-ree-ah; Arabic) Lit. "the way to the water hole"; specifically, Islamic law.

Shi'a (shee-ah; Arabic) One of the two major branches of Islam. The Shi'a believed that 'Ali

(continued)

GLOSSARY *(continued)*

should have succeeded as leader of the Muslim community after the death of Muhammad.

shirk (sherk; Arabic) The sin of idolatry, of worshipping anything other than God, the one unforgivable sin in Islam.

Sufi (soof-i) A follower of the mystical tradition of Islam, Sufism, which focuses on the believer's personal experience of God and goal of union with God.

Sunnah (sun-na; Arabic) Lit. "way of life" or "custom"; specifically refers to example of the life of the prophet Muhammad; important religious source for Muslims.

Sunni (soon-e; Arabic) One of the two main branches of Islam. The Sunnis believed that the

Muslim community should decide on a successor to lead after the death of Muhammad.

surah (soor-ah; Arabic) Chapter of the Qur'an; there are 114 surahs in the Qur'an.

tafsir (taf-seer; Arabic) Interpretation of or commentary on the Qur'an. There are several types of *tafsir*, which aim to explain the meaning of the Qur'an.

Umayyad Dynasty Controversial Muslim dynasty from 661 to 750 C.E.

umma (um-mah; Arabic) The worldwide Muslim community.

zakat (za-kaht; Arabic) Regulated almsgiving; one of the five pillars of Islam.

SUGGESTIONS FOR FURTHER READING

Armstrong, Karen. *Muhammad: A Biography of the Prophet*. San Francisco: Harper San Francisco, 1993. A detailed and readable account of Muhammad's life.

Denny, Frederick M. *An Introduction to Islam*. Englewood Cliffs, NJ: Prentice Hall, 2010. A very thorough introduction to Islam aimed at college students.

Ernst, Carl W. *Following Muhammad: Rethinking Islam in the Contemporary World*. Chapel Hill: University of North Carolina Press, 2003. A readable introduction to Islam for the general public, focusing on Islam in the modern world.

Netton, Ian Richard. *A Popular Dictionary of Islam*. Chicago: NTC Publishing Group, 1997. A useful

dictionary of key terms, people, and places in the Islamic tradition.

Renard, John, ed. *Windows on the House of Islam*. Berkeley: University of California Press, 1998. A collection of primary source materials from early Islamic history until the present; includes poetry, essays, philosophical writings, and more.

Schimmel, Annemarie. *Mystical Dimension of Islam*. Chapel Hill: University of North Carolina Press, 1975. A classic and comprehensive overview of Sufism.

Sells, Michael. *Approaching the Qur'an: The Early Revelations*. Ashland, OR: White Cloud Press, 2002. Translation and explanation of the earliest *surahs* of the Qur'an.

ONLINE RESOURCES

Oxford Islamic Studies Online
www.oxfordislamicstudies.com
A very comprehensive source with contributions from top scholars on all topics related to Islam.

Center for Muslim-Jewish Engagement
usc.edu/schools/college/crcc/engagement/resources/texts/muslim
Useful site from the University of Southern California with databases for searching English translations of the Qur'an and *hadith* collections.

NEW RELIGIOUS MOVEMENTS

IT IS THE EVENING of August 1, and Barbara Z. is preparing an altar for the celebration of Lughnassadh, a Fall harvest festival celebrated by practitioners of Wicca. For centuries, European men and women who worshipped the forces of nature, or who believed that they could perform acts of magical power by communing with these forces, were often referred to as "witches," a term contemporary Wiccans often use to describe themselves. Unlike the witches of fairy tales and films, however, Barbara Z. is not gruesome or menacing, nor does she cast evil spells upon unsuspecting princesses; in fact, she does not even own a broomstick (or ride upon one) and has never considered keeping a black cat around her home. In reality, she is a successful businesswoman in her thirties who was raised as an Episcopalian and who had never heard of Wicca until a close friend suggested she read *The Spiral Dance* by Miriam Simos (better known by her Wiccan name of "Starhawk").

Reading that book, and many others that described the beliefs and practices of Wicca, changed Barbara's life. She soon established a personal connection with a local coven, or witches' circle. In their company she discovered a community of like-minded men and women whose worldviews were remarkably similar to her own. For Wiccans, the natural universe is alive with sacred energy, a power that is often represented in Wiccan ritual as the worship of a specific "god," and by paying homage to that

An offering of wine to the earth spirits is a common feature of Wiccan ceremonies.

deity, Wiccans believe they are celebrating the beauty and wonder of Nature itself. **Lughnassadh** (also known as *Lammas*), named for the Celtic god Lugh, is one such festival. Wiccans take a particular interest in pre-Christian European deities, and many of their sacred festivals are dedicated to one or another of these "pagan" gods. Like many of those who have joined a new religious movement, Barbara thinks of Wicca as a break with her Christian upbringing and as an essential part of a journey of spiritual self-discovery.

The celebration of Lughnassadh entails several distinct ritual acts, all of them related symbolically to the Fall harvest. Part of the day was spent baking a loaf of bread, to be used later that evening during the Lughnassadh ceremony. Wiccans customarily share pieces of this bread in celebration of the harvesting of grains, and it is from this practice that the name Lammas—meaning "loaf-mass"—is derived. At dusk, Barbara will create a magic circle of lights, placing her altar at the center of this circle. On that altar Barbara will place a sheaf of wheat and several cornbread figures, representing the god Lugh and his worshippers, and a basket of star-shaped cookies. Each member of the coven will be asked, in turn, what they fear and what they desire most from the coming year, and they will then perform a dance in honor of the dying year that will soon be reborn. Having tossed the cornbread figures into a fire, the participants in this ceremony will then eat the star-shaped cookies in anticipation of a bountiful year to come. Following the conclusion of this ritual, the members of the coven will sit down to a celebratory meal, at which time the witches will address each other by their "craft" names. As a third-degree Wiccan priestess, Barbara will be addressed as Lady Sparrow, combining a title of honor with the name she chose on entering the Wiccan community.

Ritual practices will differ from one Wiccan community to another, the great constant being the underlying conviction that each act performed by the coven brings their community—and every member of that circle—closer to the indestructible source of life that is Nature itself. ❋

WHAT IS "NEW" ABOUT NEW RELIGIOUS MOVEMENTS?

Anyone who has surfed the Web using such key words "cults" and "sects,"[1] or who has ventured into a bookstore in search of works on astrology, witchcraft, or nontraditional methods of healing, must be aware of how diverse the audience for religious information has grown in our time. In fact, social scientists and historians have estimated that, globally, no less than 14,000 new religious communities have come into existence in the course of the twentieth and early twenty-first centuries. While not everyone agrees on what constitutes a "new" religious movement, most students of religion in the modern era are aware of both an exponential growth of new religious communities worldwide and of the often aggressively nontraditional (and even countercultural) character exhibited by many of these new religions. It will be useful, therefore, to begin with some general observations about the larger cultural milieu within which these new religions arose and then to identify what is really innovative in their teachings and practices. However, it should already be evident to readers of this volume that, at some point in history, practically *every* religious movement or philosophy has been perceived as "new" by its contemporaries and oftentimes rejected for that very reason.

Modernization, Globalization, and Secularization

In Chapter 1 we considered several interrelated phenomena that have brought about profound changes in religious thought and behavior, particularly during the last two centuries. The first, and arguably the most important, of these phenomena is the process known as **modernization**, which historians most often identify with the condition of postindustrial Europe and America in the nineteenth and twentieth centuries. Modernized societies, as we noted, exhibit higher levels of literacy and advanced technological capabilities. These societies have witnessed both the growth of scientific knowledge and a greater diffusion of political power, with a corresponding erosion of traditional authority and respect for the past, in politics as well as religion. The long-term effect of modernization, therefore, is not only a loss of influence and credibility on the part of established religious institutions but an even more dramatic increase in the number of new religious movements that have been empowered by the very process of cultural change. This was especially true of nineteenth-century America, where "communities of dissent" (in Stephen Stein's phrase[2]) suddenly began to mushroom after the Civil War and where a culture of religious "liberalism" and experimentation increasingly took root in American soil. Collectively, these new religious leaders (as well as their followers) often referred to themselves as "**seekers**," and their quest for new spiritual insights led many thousands to explore nontraditional beliefs and social ideals. The new technology of mass communications—at first books and newspapers, and much later, the digital media of our own period—ensured that the dissemination of information about any innovative teaching or social organization would be both rapid and widespread.

Globalization is yet another important factor in the growth of new religious movements. Even before the creation of the Internet, the pace of cultural interaction had increased multifold as a direct result of Western imperialism and of colonialist encounters between Western and non-Western peoples. Evidence of such interactions within the religious domain can be seen in the **World's Parliament of Religions**, held in Chicago in 1893 as part of an International Trade Exposition. Representatives of such non-Western religious traditions as Vedanta, Zoroastrianism, Jainism, and Buddhism shared the stage with liberal Protestants, Reform Jews, and spokespersons for various types of Spiritualist and Theosophical belief systems, with the aim of achieving some form of global understanding of human religious diversity. When, in 1993, a second World's Parliament of Religions was held in Chicago, an even larger number of religious communities were represented, and a special effort was made to include those (such as Native Americans) who had been excluded a century earlier.

These gatherings demonstrated, beyond any reasonable doubt, the exponential growth of interest in the West in religious cultures that had earlier been ignored or marginalized (or even demonized) by the West but which were now accorded a much greater measure of respect. This movement toward a multicultural perspective on religion was enhanced significantly in the United States by the repeal of the Asian Exclusion Act in 1965 and the resulting immigration of increasing numbers of non-Western peoples to America over the following decades. But even before this demographic shift occurred, greater numbers of thoughtful, spiritually oriented persons had already come to embrace a pluralistic view of religious diversity: that is, a view of modern society that presupposes multiple forms of religious experience and expression as the *normal* condition of life in the contemporary world.

Along with these changes in outlook and socialization in the modern era, however, one more phenomenon should be discussed, and that is **secularization**. A secular society is one in which the values and methodologies of science are viewed as culturally dominant and in which religious beliefs and worldviews are seen as largely subjective or simply lacking in intellectual authority. This subordination of religion to science is one of the immediate consequences of what historians call the Scientific Revolution, and ongoing disputes between conservative Christians and biologists who support a Darwinian model of species evolution provide ample evidence that the struggle between science and religion that began with Galileo's new astronomy in the sixteenth century is still being waged today with as much emotional intensity as in the past. However, the difference between a Galileo, who challenged the prevailing geocentric view of the solar system, and a contemporary biologist who challenges the biblical portrait of divine creation is profound: the weight of educated opinion in most modern societies is on the side of the scientist, whose cosmology is seen as more credible than that of his fundamentalist adversary. Moreover, the prevalence of materialist values in modern societies and the persistent view that religious belief is a matter of personal choice serves to reinforce the often critical perspective from which all religious ideas and institutions are regarded. It follows, therefore, that if all religious teachings are equally problematic from a radically secular point of view, then any new form of religious belief has as much, or as little, claim to credibility (in the eyes of a skeptical observer) as any more established faith. The secularization of modern societies thereby creates an opportunity for new religious ideas and social directives to develop without fear of overwhelming cultural rejection, and for many new religious communities the need to "reenchant" the world is the most pressing spiritual need of our time.

This need is particularly evident in religious communities that have been linked to **New Age** thought and to counterculture movements growing out of the 1960s and 1970s that embrace a belief in magic and in esoteric wisdom. New Age religious practices include (though are not limited to) the channeling of disembodied spirits, the use of crystals and magnets for healing purposes, and a reliance on astrological calculations to determine one's fate and fortune. All of these practices are commonly viewed by secularists as culturally obsolete and empirically invalid efforts at controlling the natural environment, but New Age advocates argue, in opposition, that science has neglected or suppressed ancient teachings about the human body or the physical universe that cannot be reconciled to any current model of "truth." And although it is impossible to speak of a single, coherent New Age philosophy, many groups that fall under this rubric are clearly in search of an alternative worldview that will allow a "transformation of consciousness," or at the very least a renewed sense of wonder and reverence for those hidden forces of nature, or of the human spirit, that contemporary science refuses to acknowledge.

Theoretical Models and Social Typologies

Over the past three decades, several attempts have been made to categorize the various kinds of new or "alternative" religions (as they are sometimes called) that have developed during the twentieth and early twenty-first centuries. One very popular theoretical model, formulated by J. Gordon Melton,[3] divides these new movements into eight distinctive "families" of religious thought and lifestyle. Each of these groupings exhibits its own peculiar "thought-world," though a certain amount of overlap (of outlook and social organization) can be observed throughout several of these "alternative spiritualities." The obvious advantage of this model is its ability to arrange historical data into fairly precise thematic, as well as regional, patterns of perception. The disadvantage of this schema, however, is that its conceptual boundaries are at times *too* precise—an obvious weakness when one is describing religions whose teachings are frequently eclectic in nature.

Another, much simpler paradigm of cultural differentiation has been proposed by Roy Wallis,[4] who classifies new religious movements in relation to their perception of the world and of human destiny. For Wallis, new religions can be understood as either "world affirming," "world renouncing," or "world accommodating," though once again a certain amount of overlap and ambiguity is inevitable when attempting to situate any particular religious system within any one of these categories. Thus a world-affirming religion is one that attributes positive value to human existence and whose goal is to improve the conditions of life wherever it is possible to do so through human effort. Removing oneself from society or longing for self-annihilation consequently has no value for someone who has embraced this point of view. A world-renouncing religion, on the other hand, takes the very opposite position, proceeding instead from the assumption that human society is irredeemably evil and that life itself is too filled with pain and futility to be worth improving. Adherents of this religious philosophy typically envision an imminent and destructive end to the world we know and even devise strategies for bringing about an end, either to the social order or to one's individual existence. World-accommodating religions, as the term suggests, are prepared to adapt to a world that is manifestly deficient in goodness or grace, while at the same time asserting their belief in a "higher" goal for humankind (which it cannot, at present, attain). The merit of these typologies is that they focus our attention quite specifically on the relationship between a core perception of social reality and a corresponding

MELTON'S EIGHT RELIGIOUS FAMILIES

1. **The Latter-day Saint Family**

   For the past century and a half, more than fifty separate Latter-day Saint communities have come into existence, each claiming some direct connection to the teachings and revelations of Joseph Smith, the chief prophet and founder of the Church of Jesus Christ of Latter-day Saints. Many of these communities have disappeared, but doctrinally they were all committed to a core belief in "restoration" of true, apostolic Christianity through the ministry and writings of Joseph Smith (and most especially the Book of Mormon).

2. **The Communal Family**

   Any religious community that is organized around monastic ideals that entail some form of spiritual and personal discipline can be categorized as a "communal" organization. Communities such as the Shakers and the Hutterites (who migrated from Russia to North America in the 1870s) are committed to principles of collective ownership and individual austerity and tend to view mainstream society as materialistic and corrupt.

3. **The New Thought Metaphysical Family**

   By the late nineteenth century the phrase "New Thought" was applied to a variety of religious and philosophical views that derived from American Transcendentalism and the writings of such figures as Ralph Waldo Emerson. One important line of development in this "family" can be traced through Mary Baker Eddy and the Christian Science movement she founded in the 1870s. Common to all forms of New Thought is the belief that each individual has access to spiritual forces and realities that lie behind the material world and that this knowledge can be used to cure illnesses or end poverty and social conflict.

4. **The Spiritualist/Psychic Family**

   Tracing their descent from the philosophical writings of the Swedish mystic Emanuel Swedenborg (1688–1772), these religious groups share a belief that life after death and communication with the dead are both scientifically valid and experimentally verifiable ideas. Among such "spiritualists" the practices of mediumship and **"channeling"**—that is, contacting the dead and speaking on their behalf—are widespread. One popular variation of this paradigm can be found in **Ufology** (the belief that intelligences from other worlds are attempting to communicate with earth, and have been landing space vehicles or unidentified flying objects [UFOs] on our planet for centuries). Other offshoots of this family of ideas can be found in the renewed interest in astrology, reincarnation, and various forms of meditation in the later twentieth century.

5. **Ancient Wisdom Groups**

   These alternative religious communities trace their beginnings back to some wisdom tradition in the ancient past. Believing in the advent of a "New Age" made possible by the release of spiritual energies that have lain dormant in the human race for many centuries, members of this family argue that they are continuing the work of ancient "masters" whose spiritual wisdom and psychic powers have been repressed by Western rationalism.

(continued)

MELTON'S EIGHT RELIGIOUS FAMILIES (continued)

6. **The Magical Family**

   These groups believe that they are empowered by "paranormal" forces to control both mind and matter, and, like their spiritualist counterparts, they assume they possess powers of healing and transformation. In the late nineteenth century, groups such as the Hermetic Order of the Golden Dawn arose that claimed to have revived ancient occult practices designed to put the participant in contact with the controlling forces of consciousness and of nature. The revival of witchcraft as a form of neopagan nature worship (often focused on the figure of the Goddess) is one expression of this worldview.

7. **The Eastern Family**

   The dissemination of various forms of Eastern religious philosophy, particularly after 1965, has led to exponential growth in the number of alternative communities that have been influenced by some form of Hinduism, Buddhism, or Daoism. Characteristically, these communities form around the personality and teachings of one (often charismatic) leader who claims to have found the secret of spiritual enlightenment. Within these groups, social and ritual practices vary widely, with some communities leading an austere, even monastic lifestyle, whereas others follow a more hedonistic path. In both cases the "guru" or group leader will often attempt to represent his life philosophy as both an experiential process and an ancient wisdom tradition.

8. **The Middle Eastern Family**

   Communities deriving their inspiration from some form of Judaism or Islam fall into this category. Examples of this distinctive alternative spirituality can be found in groups espousing the beliefs and practices of Kabbalah and of Sufism (representing Jewish and Muslim mystical traditions, respectively). Offshoots of these teachings can be found in groups such as the Nation of Islam, whose belief system constitutes a radical departure from normative Muslim teachings.

---

metaphysical view that surrounds it. The basic weakness of Wallis's system, however, is that it tends to oversimplify the often eclectic teachings and social ideals of the religious movements it seeks to categorize.

Yet another theoretical overview is that of Peter Clarke,[5] who emphasizes the theme of "social transformation" that seems to run through nearly all of those religious movements commonly thought of as "new" or "alternative." Many of these new movements, Clarke notes, fix on the inner life as the primary agency of transformation, hoping that through the attainment of a "true" Self, the individual can either begin to change the conditions of life for the better or begin the process of disengagement from life altogether. In either case, the individual who enters a new religious community is more likely than not to be searching for an ideology of change that is not to be found within existing religious cultures. Such individuals, Clarke observes, are inclined to describe themselves as "spiritual" rather than as "religious," with an implicit acknowledgement that the only personally valid religious experience these "seekers" are likely to find acceptable is one that lies outside the framework of established religious institutions or systems of thought.

None of the preceding systems of classification, or several others that have been proposed, can claim to be exhaustive or universally applicable; but taken together, or employed selectively, they at least provide some insight into the social/intellectual dynamic of the innovative religious cultures that we are about to examine. What follows, then, is a series of historical vignettes of contemporary religious movements and philosophies that sociologists of religion such as Melton, Wallis, and Clarke have identified as demonstrably "new" and therefore representative of the latest phase of global religious expression. We have chosen to focus on the new religions of the West, however, partly because these communities are likely to be more familiar to our readers and partly because the sheer number of "alternative" religions worldwide is so large that no single chapter in a book could honestly claim to represent all of them.

ALTERNATIVE CHRISTIANITIES AND THEIR OFFSHOOTS

Some of the most successful new religious movements of the modern era are churches that derive their origins from recognizably Christian sources and the beginnings of which can be traced back to nineteenth-century America. Then, as now, religious culture in the United States was pluralistic, and although most Americans professed some form of Christian belief, no single Christian denomination was dominant. What historians refer to as the "**Second Great Awakening**"—a nationwide evangelical movement that evoked intense religious fervor in many communities—continued to affect Christian thought in the United States up through the mid-1800s. One manifestation of this upsurge in religious enthusiasm can be found in the formation of new Christian churches, some claiming new revelations of divine truth, and many looking forward eagerly to the imminent Second Coming of Christ. The following discussion focuses on those groups whose influence continues to be felt today: the Church of Jesus Christ of Latter-day Saints, Christian Science, Seventh-day Adventists, and Jehovah's Witnesses.

The Church of Jesus Christ of Latter-day Saints

The Church of Jesus Christ of Latter-day Saints was founded by Joseph Smith (1805–1844) in 1830 in Fayette, New York. Although its members are commonly referred to as "Mormons," they prefer to be known as Latter-day Saints. According to Joseph Smith's account, he was just fourteen years old when, in 1820, he withdrew to the woods near his home and asked God which church he should join. While praying for guidance, he was approached by two figures who identified themselves as God the Father and Jesus Christ. They informed Smith that he should not join any existing church but rather establish his own, and that he had been chosen to restore the one true faith of Jesus Christ. Three years later, Smith was visited by the Angel Moroni, who revealed to him the location of two thin golden plates covered with strange writing. His translation of these plates, accomplished "by the gift and power of God," resulted in the writing of the Book of Mormon, one of the principal scriptures of the Church of Latter-day Saints. Although these plates were later taken away by an angel, witnesses testified to having seen and touched them.

Published in 1830, the Book of Mormon tells how the prophet Lehi and his followers fled Jerusalem around the year 600 B.C.E. and migrated to America, where they founded a great civilization. During subsequent centuries, their descendants recorded their history on metal plates. These described how conflict eventually divided the people into two groups, the Nephites and the Lamanites. These plates also included prophecies of the birth and crucifixion of Jesus Christ and described how, after his resurrection, Jesus appeared to the peoples of North America and established his church among them. In 421 C.E., the Lamanites (ancestors of the people we know as Native Americans) annihilated the Nephites, whose memory was preserved only in the history they had written. A surviving Nephite, the prophet Mormon, wrote an abridgment of that history on two golden plates and gave them to his son, the prophet Moroni, who hid them. Fourteen centuries later, Moroni—who by then had become an angel—revealed their location to Joseph Smith. Mormons believe that the Book of Mormon is divinely inspired scripture and recognize it as having an authority equal to that of the Old and New Testaments. They also make extensive use of two other texts: *Doctrines and Covenants* (1835) and *The Pearl of Great Price* (1842), both of which consist of revelations, statements, translations and other writings, many by Joseph Smith.

The discovery of the Book of Mormon soon attracted followers to Joseph Smith and his church. At the same time, conflict with their detractors soon forced the Mormons to leave New York. After settling briefly in Kirtland, Ohio, continued opposition to Smith's teachings forced the Mormons to move on,

The Angel Moroni delivering the plates of the Book of Mormon to Joseph Smith.

The Mormon Temple in Salt Lake City, Utah.

first to Jackson County, Missouri, and then to Nauvoo, Illinois. For a time the Mormons prospered in Nauvoo, but their practice of polygamy (abolished in 1890) aroused the animosity of their neighbors, and on June 24, 1844, Joseph Smith was killed by an angry mob opposed to the Mormon way of life. The leadership of the movement then fell to Brigham Young (1801–1877), who led the Mormons on an epic trek from Nauvoo to the Great Salt Basin of Utah, where they settled and established their church headquarters at a site known today as Salt Lake City.

Mormons accept many familiar Christian doctrines, though often with radical (and, to most Christians, unacceptable) changes. Like mainstream Christians, the Mormons believe in a Trinity, consisting of God, the Heavenly Father; his Son, Jesus Christ; and the Holy Ghost (sometimes referred to as the Holy Spirit). However, Mormons understand these figures to be three separate gods. Moreover, Mormons believe that the Heavenly Father was once a mortal man: descended from human beings who themselves had become gods, the Heavenly Father attained divinity and became the ruler of our region of the universe. Through intercourse with a celestial wife, he produced a Son, Jesus Christ, who also progressed from humanity to divinity, and finally the Holy Ghost. Whereas the Heavenly Father and Jesus Christ possess material bodies (albeit perfect and immortal), the Holy Ghost is pure spirit.

Mormons also believe that all human beings are "spirit children" of the Heavenly Father, who sends us to earth so that we can receive physical bodies and gain both knowledge and experience that are essential for spiritual progress. We are guided in this life by the perfect example of Jesus Christ and by the Holy Ghost that dwells within believers and helps them to grasp eternal truths. Ultimately, we can return to dwell eternally with the Heavenly Father, become gods ourselves, and have spirit children of our own. Sin can prevent us from achieving this goal, but it need not do so, for Jesus Christ atoned for our sins through his suffering and death. We can therefore achieve salvation if we have faith in Christ's atonement, repent our sins, accept baptism, and receive "the gift of the Holy Ghost." The critical factor, for Mormons, in determining who can or cannot be saved from sin is the acceptance of "the Gospel of Jesus Christ in its fullness," and that form of Christian teaching can only be found within the Church of Latter-day Saints. However, it is possible for Mormons to obtain baptism (by proxy) on behalf of deceased family members who were not Latter-day Saints—and therefore ensure their retroactive salvation; this explains the extraordinary interest Mormons take in genealogical research. Finally, Mormons abstain from the consumption of alcohol, tobacco, coffee, tea, caffeinated soft drinks, and illegal drugs, believing that such abstentions are not only conducive to good health but are also part of the revelation given to Joseph Smith in 1833.

Mormons are millennialists who believe that one day Christ will return to judge and rule the world for a thousand years. Though they acknowledge the existence of a hell, where some will suffer temporary punishments, Mormons are convinced that, in the end, all people will be saved. However, the final destiny of every individual will be determined by the extent of his or her obedience to God's commandments. Accordingly, there are two distinct levels of salvation: Mormons who faithfully follow the teachings of their church will attain divinity and eternal life in the presence of the Heavenly Father; non-Mormons will receive lesser rewards and will therefore enter lesser "kingdoms" in eternity. Mormons also believe in continuing divine revelation and, more specifically, that God's will is revealed through the senior leadership of their church. Its president (often referred to as "the prophet"), his two counselors, and the members of the Quorum of the Twelve Apostles are all recognized as having prophetic abilities, and together they possess the same authority as the prophets and apostles described in the Bible. This link with the biblical past underlies the Mormon Church's conception of itself as the *restored* church of Jesus Christ, and because other churches have corrupted the teachings of Christ, the Mormon Church is therefore the only true and living church upon the earth. Needless to say, no other Christian community is prepared to accept this claim.

Christian Science and New Thought

The religious philosophy known as Christian Science has its origins in the life experiences and teachings of Mary Baker Eddy (1821–1910). As a young woman, Eddy suffered from a variety of illnesses and nervous disorders for which the physicians and hypnotists she consulted could offer no lasting relief. In 1866, however, she claimed to have been completely cured while reading an account of one of the miraculous healings effected by Jesus in the New Testament. This led her to discover the Science of Christianity, or "Christian Science," which she later described in her book *Science and Health with Key to the Scriptures* (published in 1875). A skilled organizer, Mrs. Eddy (as church members prefer to call her) established the Church of Christ, Scientist, in 1879 with its headquarters in Boston. Today there are nearly 2,500 Christian Science communities throughout the world, and the newspaper she helped establish, *The Christian Science Monitor*, is a well-known and respected publication.

Like many "offshoot" Christian communities, including the Mormons, Christian Scientists regard their church as a "restored" form of primitive Christianity. Although they acknowledge the Bible as the inspired word of God, they nevertheless maintain that its full meaning can only be grasped through studying *Science and Health*, which they believe was written under divine inspiration. But what truly distinguishes Christian Science is its

Mary Baker Eddy was the founder of the Church of Christ, Scientist (Christian Science).

foundational belief that all reality is spiritual, for it derives from the purely spiritual nature of God. Matter and the body do not really exist, nor do the many evils associated with them, such as disease, deformity, and death. These are nothing more than mental errors created by our limited minds. We experience pain and illness only as long as we *think* we are suffering from these things, and as long as we attribute objective reality to these illusions, we will find ourselves cut off from God. To achieve salvation from this delusional state, we must follow the example of Jesus Christ, the "Way-shower," whose awareness of God and God's goodness allowed him to overcome all forms of suffering and to perform miraculous healings of body and mind.

Because Christian Scientists deny the existence of material reality, they do not accept the traditional Christian doctrine of the Incarnation. Instead, they believe in Christ as the divine idea of "sonship" to God and in Jesus as the one in whom that idea was perfectly expressed. God is the Father-Mother of all, while the Holy Spirit is God's loving relationship with creation. Christian Science teaches that prayer based on a correct understanding of God and reality as spiritual existence is the key to improving human life. Prayer is therefore not so much a matter of asking God for healing as it is a yielding of the individual mind to the Divine Mind and to the truth that whenever God's presence and loving power are recognized, health and healing are sure to follow. As a rule, Christian Scientists trust in God's love rather than in vaccinations for the prevention of diseases; when they do become ill, however, they turn to prayer for healing, often with the assistance of "practitioners," that is, church members who devote themselves full time to teach others how to use "scientific prayer" in gaining access to God's healing love. Nevertheless, church members remain free to obtain help from medical professionals if they so choose, and they have broadened their understanding of the principle of spiritual healing to include the elimination of major social problems.

Christian Science is viewed by historians as just one of the forms taken by a larger American religious movement known as **New Thought**. Though more a philosophical current within late nineteenth-century religious thought than an actual creed, New Thought advocates tended to embrace a transcendentalist belief in the presence of the divine within nature, and especially within the human mind. This thesis was best expressed by Ralph Trine in his book *In Tune with the Infinite* (1897), and from that premise an amazing variety of related religious philosophies soon emerged. In 1914, the International New Thought Alliance was formed, dedicated to the constructive power of the mind and the "freedom of each soul as to choice and as to belief." Within that larger community of optimistic faith in the human spirit various groups took root, particularly the Unity School of Christianity. Founded by Charles Fillmore (1854–1948) and his wife Myrtle (1845–1931) in 1903, Unity was originally based on the concept of "mind cure," or the relief from illness through the exercise of mind over matter. A prime example of this phenomenon occurred in 1886, when Myrtle Fillmore was cured of tuberculosis after repeating inwardly, for two years, "I am a child of God and therefore I do not inherit sickness." Today, Unity practitioners describe themselves as engaged in a positive and practical form of Christianity in which the daily application of the principles exemplified by Jesus Christ promotes health, prosperity, and happiness. Unity teaches that the spirit of God lived in Jesus Christ, just as it lives in everyone. By living as Christ did, we overcome sin—which Unity understands to be separation from God in our consciousness—as well as illness, depression, and doubt. Like many New Thought churches, Unity believes that a heightened awareness of God's presence will bring peace, health, and happiness to the human race.

Adventism

The Adventist movement, based on the belief that Christ would soon return to earth, represents one of the more radical tendencies of nineteenth-century Christian thought. By mid-century a number of Adventist denominations became increasingly prominent in American religious life. The first of these groups gathered around a Baptist minister named William Miller (1782–1849), whose experience at a revival meeting led him to undertake the study of biblical prophecy. In 1835, Miller announced that Christ would return to earth between March 21, 1843, and March 21, 1844, to preside over a final judgment, destroy the world, and inaugurate a new heaven and a new earth. The failure of this Second Coming to materialize prompted recalculations and predictions of new dates, but when these, too, passed without incident, many Millerites gave up their hope of seeing Christ's return. Others, sometimes scorned and ridiculed in their churches, emulated Miller by forming new ones, most of which were organized as part of the Evangelical Adventist Association.

The largest of the Adventist churches to emerge from what the Millerites called "**The Great Disappointment**" was that of the Seventh-day Adventists, founded by Ellen White (1827–1915). White became a follower of Miller in 1842, but after the Great Disappointment of 1844 White taught that the Second Coming of Christ had been delayed by the failure of Christians to obey the Ten Commandments—especially the fourth commandment, which requires observance of the Sabbath on the seventh day of the week (that is, Saturday). In addition, White believed (like her counterparts in Christian Science) that scripture contains rules for physical, as well as spiritual, health: "Disease," she wrote, "is the result of violating God's laws, both natural and spiritual," and would not exist if people lived "in harmony with the Creator's plan." For this reason, and because they consider the body a "temple" of the Holy Spirit, Seventh-day Adventists practice vegetarianism, abstain from alcohol and tobacco, and prefer natural remedies to drugs when ill. It was in hope of creating a health food that would meet the standards White discerned in scripture that Dr. John Kellogg, one of her disciples, invented his famous cornflakes.

Today there are more than ten million Seventh-day Adventists worldwide, the great majority of whom live outside of North America (principally in Africa and Central and South America). Emphasizing the apocalyptic books of Daniel and Revelation in the Bible, they preach that the world must be prepared for the Second Coming, which will occur after the gospel has been spread to all parts of the world. The returning

Christ will raise the faithful from their present state of unconsciousness, make them immortal, and bring them back to heaven for his millennial reign. At the conclusion of the millennium, Satan will be destroyed, along with sinners who indicate they have no wish to live in Christ's presence. The saints will then descend from heaven to live forever on an earth restored to its original perfection.

Most Christian denominations consider the Seventh-day Adventist Church to be a genuine Christian church, although they may not share its preoccupation with Christ's Second Coming or recognize the legitimacy of a Saturday Sabbath worship tradition. However, some groups with roots in Seventh-day Adventism are much further from the Christian mainstream. The Worldwide Church of God, for example, urges its members to observe the dietary laws and many of the other commandments found in the Hebrew Bible. Moreover, its leaders (Herbert Armstrong [1892–1986], and his son Garner Ted Armstrong [1930–2003]) believed that the English-speaking peoples were the literal descendants of the "lost tribes" of ancient Israel. The Davidian Seventh-day Adventists, founded in the 1930s by a Bulgarian immigrant, Victor Houteff, also observe many of the ritual requirements found in the Hebrew Bible; however, they criticize traditional Seventh-day Adventists for claiming that prophecy came to an end with the death of Ellen White. God, the Davidians say, continues to guide their church through the prophets he sends. One particular splinter group, the Branch Davidian Church (founded by Benjamin Roden in the 1960s), achieved tragic notoriety in 1993 when David Koresh (born Vernon Howell in 1959), who had taken control of a Branch Davidian community located in Waco, Texas, in the 1980s, convinced his followers that he was the Messiah and that Armageddon would take place in the United States rather than in Israel. When federal agents raided the Branch Davidian compound on February 28, 1993, a shootout and fifty-one-day siege followed, culminating in an assault and fire that left eighty members of the Waco community (including Koresh himself) dead.

Jehovah's Witnesses

Another millennialist church that succeeded the Millerites was founded in 1881 by the lay preacher Charles Taze Russell (1852–1916). Officially called Zion's Watch Tower Bible and Tract Society, it is more commonly known as the Jehovah's Witnesses. Russell was only twenty years old when his study of the Bible led him to the conclusion that the Second Coming would occur in 1874, when Christ would return invisibly to prepare for the kingdom of God. This event was to be followed by the battle of Armageddon and the end of the world in 1914, after which Christ would begin his millennial reign over the earth. Russell published a more detailed account of his thought in a seven-volume work titled *Studies in Scripture*, and in 1879 he began the publication of a magazine called *The Watchtower*. Russell's followers were at first referred to as Bible Students and Watchtower People, but once Joseph Franklin Rutherford (1869–1942) had succeeded Russell as the head of the Watchtower organization, members of that community were officially known as Jehovah's Witnesses.

Under Rutherford's leadership, centralized control both of the Watchtower organization and of its teachings increased. At the same time, its membership grew, and today there are approximately four million Witnesses in two hundred countries. As the most "world-renouncing" of the Adventist churches of the modern era, the Witnesses continued to predict the end of history as we know it and the imminent rule of Christ and his saints. In 1920, for example, when Rutherford published his *Millions Now Living Will Never Die*, he gave 1925 as the date by which the rule of God would be established on the earth. Rutherford's successor, Nathan Knorr (1905–1977), predicted in the October 8, 1966, issue of the Witnesses magazine *Awake* that the world would end in 1975, only to see that "prophecy" disconfirmed. More recently, however, Witnesses have become wary of fixing dates for the apocalypse and are generally content to proclaim that Christ's return to earth will come sooner than later.

Jehovah's Witnesses take their name from the King James Bible, which (erroneously) vocalized the biblical Hebrew name for God. Although they understand Jesus Christ as God's "Son," they reject the doctrine of the Trinity and insist that the Son is simply the first of God's creations. As for the Holy Spirit, that is understood as "God's active force" within persons of true Christian faith. Witnesses continue to believe that a "great tribulation" is imminent and that, after destroying the present world system, the elect (whose "core" number is fixed at 144,000), will experience full salvation. These elect individuals, who alone have immortal souls, will ultimately be taken up into heaven. All others may be saved through obedience to God and faith in the efficacy of Christ's sacrificial death, but their reward will be eternal life on earth, which will be restored to its original, paradisiacal condition. As for the wicked, they will surely perish in the cataclysmic end-time battle (that is, Armageddon), but only after they have been given fair warning of their fate. The familiar practice of going door-to-door, which brings teams of Witnesses into thousands of neighborhoods every year, is premised on the belief that they have a responsibility to warn their fellow human beings that the world—which they believe to be under the present dominion of Satan—will soon come to an end. Witnesses also refuse military service and will not salute the flag or hold government offices, believing these practices to be a compromise with worldly evil. Their refusal to accept blood transfusions, based on their interpretation of biblical precepts forbidding the consumption of blood (Gen. 9:4), has often placed the Witnesses in opposition to contemporary medical practice and public policy. Finally, since they regard other churches as having fallen into gross error, they have little contact with other Christian denominations and do not join in celebrating holidays such as Christmas and Easter.

The Family (Children of God)

A far less successful, and socially problematic, example of Adventist thought in the later twentieth century can be found in a community known first as the "Children of God" and subsequently as the "Family of Love," or more simply **The Family**. The Children of God was established by David Brandt Berg (1919–1994), an evangelical minister who declared, in 1969, that he had received a revelation concerning a cataclysmic earthquake that would plunge California into the Pacific Ocean. Fearing imminent destruction, Berg led his small band of followers from California to Texas, where they proceeded to live a communal existence. Convinced that disaster loomed for the entire country, Berg moved once again, leaving the United States and ultimately relocating in London, where he established his headquarters in the 1970s.

In the decades that followed, Berg's teachings became increasingly radical, and he urged his followers to abandon their families and to renounce all allegiance to existing social and political structures, believing that the Second Advent of Christ—and all of the violent events that would precede it—was imminent. Like the Witnesses, the Children of God are millennialists who look forward to the beginnings of Christ's 1,000-year reign. Committed to what he termed the "law of love," Father Berg (as he was called) commanded his flock to celebrate the "sacrament" of free sexuality as often, and with as many partners, as possible, and he urged his female followers to prostitute themselves for the purpose of drawing male recruits into his movement. This practice (called "flirty fishing") brought considerable notoriety to Berg's community, and by the 1980s this behavior was discontinued, partly out of fear of the AIDS epidemic. By the 1990s the movement had become somewhat more conservative in lifestyle, and it adopted a written constitution that endowed individual members with a greater measure of religious autonomy. Berg's death in 1994 left the Children of God, now renamed The Family, without a dominating prophetic personality, though he was immediately succeeded by his second wife, Karen Zerby (b. 1946, and known to members of the Family as "Maria"); nevertheless, the emphasis on charismatic gifts and an evangelical style of worship remain constants in this community. "Father David," as he is posthumously known, continues to exert considerable influence upon members of the Family from beyond the grave, however, as his spirit messages are channeled through Maria and her second husband, Steve Kelly (b. 1951; known as Peter Amsterdam).

The Unification Church

At an even greater remove from traditional Christian thought, we encounter the Unification Church, officially known today as "The Family Federation for World Peace and Unification." First established in 1954 by the "Reverend" Sun Myung Moon (1920–2012), the "**Moonies**," as they are popularly called, constitute a particularly aggressive and theologically eclectic Adventist community. Within this community, the Reverend Moon occupies a position of honor and spiritual influence equal to that of Jesus, and it is therefore arguable whether the Unification Church can be considered a historically legitimate form of Christianity. Though often derided during the 1970s as a "cult," the Unification Church has consistently denied charges of brainwashing and exploitation (financial and psychological) of its members. The organization has recently sought mainstream acceptance by devoting considerable sums to the promotion of international peace gatherings and interfaith conferences and through the purchase of major newspapers such as the *Washington Times*. Still, at the heart of this movement we find both the personal presence and teachings of Sun Myung Moon, whose followers consistently think of him as the Messiah of our age.

Moon's spiritual journey began in 1936 in what is now the People's Republic of North Korea, when he received a vision of Jesus at Easter time. In that vision, Jesus informed Moon that he was to take up the mission of world redemption where Jesus had left off, succeeding where the Christian savior had failed. Believing himself, therefore, a successor to Jesus Christ, Moon proceeded to construct a belief system that is largely based on Christian scriptures but that also reveals a mixture of Buddhist, Daoist, and shamanistic elements. Moon's principal publication, entitled *Divine Principle*, lays out the basis for his claim to have "completed" the Testaments and to represent the next stage in the progression of Christian thought. Thus, according to Moon, God can be thought of as an invisible essence, from which all life flows. God's original plans for the biblical Adam and Eve were thwarted, however, when the Serpent (Satan) seduced Eve, inspiring her to have intercourse with Adam "prematurely," thus leading in turn to the fall of the human race. Because the sins of our first parents extend to every generation, the salvation of humankind depends on the appearance of a messiah, who, along with his wife (who serves as a second Eve), will restore the purity of the family and reconcile the world to God's will. Moon's second wife, Hak Ja Han, whom he married in 1960, is referred to by Unificationists as the "True Mother," and, through the thirteen children she bore after that, she has provided a model for the movement of authentic motherhood and spiritual guidance.

The ability to receive new revelations extends beyond the Reverend Moon himself, however, to at least one other member of his family. In 1984, Moon's second son, Heung Jin, was fatally injured in an auto accident, but almost immediately after his funeral, Moon announced that his son had become a "commander in chief" in the spirit world to those who had died unmarried. To insure that Heung Jin would not remain a bachelor through eternity, a postmortem marriage was arranged between the daughter of one of Moon's aides and the spirit of Heung Jin, whereupon members of the Unification Church began receiving revelations from him. Perhaps the most important of these messages are those that confirm the status in heaven of both Moon and his wife, who are spoken of as the "True Parents" before whom even Jesus bows in humility and reverence. Additional testimonials from the spirit realm, celebrating Moon's cosmic preeminence, have come not only from Heung Jin but also from a deceased Unification scholar, Dr. Sang Hun Lee, who informed a Unification receptor that Buddha, Confucius, Muhammad, and Jesus all acknowledge Moon's role as the ultimate redemptive "parent" of humanity. Charles Taze Russell, Mary Baker Eddy, Joseph Smith, and no fewer than thirty-six deceased presidents of the United States have added their voices to this swelling chorus of affirmation. Not surprisingly, critics of the Unification Church have seized upon such statements as proof of a "personality cult" at the heart of Moon's gospel, and it is clear that Moon's redeemer persona is central to the salvific claims made by the Unification Church and its defenders.

The Reverend Sun Myung Moon blessing a mass wedding ceremony in Madison Square Garden, New York.

Rastafarianism

The Rastafarian movement, which can be traced back to the slums of Kingston, Jamaica, during the 1920s and 1930s, exhibits only the most tenuous relationship to either Christianity or the advent movements that grew out of Christian thought in the nineteenth and twentieth centuries. However, like the Unification Church, it shows unmistakable signs of millennarian thought. Combining elements of black nationalist ideology and "liberation theology," Rastafari religious culture attempted to lift up the African Diaspora of the Caribbean out of poverty and despair and to inspire both a pride in African ancestry and a desire for repatriation to an Africa freed from white colonial oppression.

Probably the most important influence on Rastafarian thought in its beginnings can be found in the writings of Marcus Garvey (1887–1940), a militant Jamaican socialist leader who expressed not only indignation over the plight of the island's poor but also disdain for the shallow materialism of the West and its deeply ingrained racist hatred of Africans. Regarding the enslavement of blacks as a form of divine punishment, Garvey concluded that the African Diaspora's period of tribulation was drawing to an end and that a king would emerge in Africa who would lead the disenfranchised black masses back to their homelands and to a life of dignity and prosperity.

The ascension of the Ethiopian prince Ras Tafari Makonnen—better known by his throne name as Haile Selassie (1891–1975)—to the position of emperor of Ethiopia in 1930 seemed to give concrete shape to Garvey's prophecy. Jamaicans who were influenced by the teachings of the mystic Leonard Howell became convinced that the moment of collective liberation from white rule had finally come. For Howell, and others who now began to speak of themselves as followers of Ras Tafari—hence "Rastafarians"—Haile Selassie was more than a mortal ruler: he was either Christ returned to earth or God incarnate.

When Selassie first visited Jamaica in the 1950s and met with Rastafarian leaders, many in the movement concluded that Howell's "Adventist" view of Selassie had been validated and that this visit signaled the final move back to "Ethiopia" (understood as a metaphor for the whole of Africa). However, the few thousand Jamaicans who did emigrate to Ethiopia in the 1960s soon found that their dreams of apocalyptic fulfillment were not to be realized and that the moment of divine deliverance had to be deferred.

The overthrow of Selassie in 1974 and his death a year later shook the Rastafarian movement to its core. Some followers denied that Selassie had really died, and others were convinced that his spirit would return to his earthly body at some point in the future. Today, most Rastafarians speak of "liberation before repatriation"—signifying a demand for social justice within the countries they reside in—and although many still revere Haile Selassie and believe that his spirit lives on in Rastafarian artists and teachers, they are prepared to wait some time for the Day of Final Judgment against "Babylon" (i.e. Anglo-European society) to arrive.

Rastafarians have adopted a number of distinctive religious practices that—to those outside the movement—typify the behavior of all Rastafarians. This is particularly true of the somewhat controversial practice of smoking marijuana (or "ganja"). Although not universal, this practice is encouraged within the Rastafarian community in the belief that it both enhances one's health and opens the mind to greater sources of spiritual influence. Similarly, the practice of wearing one's hair in dreadlocks (particularly among men) is quite common and reflects the Rastafarian belief that they have adopted the behavior of the biblical Nazirites (Samson, for example), whose uncut hair was a sign of strength and devotion to God. In addition, and out of desire to live a "natural" life, many Rastafarians have adopted a vegetarian diet consisting only of organically grown foods. Avoidance of pork and alcohol are also common, once again reflecting the influence of Old Testament mores on Rastafarian thought.

A simple Rastafarian food shop named Lion House in Stony Hill, Jamaica, features paintings of Rasta heroes Marcus Garvey, Haile Selassie, and Bob Marley.

Most Rastafarian festivals revolve around important dates in the life of Haile Selassie, and particularly the date of his accession to the throne of Ethiopia (November 2, 1930). In addition, Rastafarians will gather together for informal discussions called "reasonings" or for celebratory dances connected to formal holidays (known as "nyabinghis"). The smoking of ganja is common to both occasions.

THE REDISCOVERY OF EASTERN RELIGIOUS THOUGHT

As early as the 1890s, liberal intellectuals and religious "seekers" in the United States came under the spell of a charismatic Hindu reformer and writer named Swami Vivekananda (1863–1902), who was one of the more memorable speakers at the World's Parliament of Religions. Vivekananda saw himself as a cultural ambassador for Indian religion generally, and his influence in the West was felt by a number of alternative religious communities, including those attracted to "New Thought." Through his speaking tours and through the formation of the Vedanta Society, Vivekananda popularized knowledge of Hindu metaphysics and encouraged an appreciation for Raja-Yoga and a variety of meditative disciplines. The constant theme, in fact, of his writings and lectures was the urgent need to liberate the spirit from the dead weight of the material world. In the historical vignettes that follow, we focus on some of the more notable religious movements that reflect the encounter between Eastern religious thought and practice and that show Westerners in search of alternative (and culturally disparate) sources of religious enlightenment.

Madame Helena
Blavatsky, founder
of the theosophy
movement.

The Theosophical Society

The Theosophical Society, founded in 1875 by Helena Petrovna Blavatsky (1831–1891) and Henry S. Olcott (1832–1907), was an attempt to combine Hindu and Buddhist ideas in a new approach, which Blavatsky and Olcott termed **"theosophy"** (i.e., "divine wisdom"). The Society sought to popularize these ideas in the West. Blavatsky and Olcott not only wanted to make Eastern spirituality accessible to religious "seekers" of the late nineteenth century but also, more important, to create a bridge between Western and occult and mystical thought. Blavatsky and Olcott claimed to have knowledge of the secret teachings of the "Ascended Masters" of India and Tibet, whom they claimed to have "channeled."

Blavatsky, the dominant figure and principal theorist of the Theosophical Society, became a figure of some notoriety in the United States when she promoted the practice of séances, through which she claimed to contact the spirits of the dead. Her critics dismissed her as a fraud, but for a time her writings—particularly *Isis Unveiled* (1877) and *The Secret Doctrine* (1889)—had considerable influence on "spiritualists" of this period.

Believing that all religions reveal a common source, often referred to as "perennial wisdom," the mission statement of the Theosophical Society reflected its global view of religion, designed to promote a belief in the unity of all peoples and cultures:

1. To form the nucleus of a universal brotherhood of humanity, without distinction of race, creed, sex, caste, or color.
2. [To promote] the study of ancient and modern religions, philosophies, and sciences, and the demonstration of the importance of such study.
3. [To encourage] the investigation of the unexplained laws of nature and the psychical powers latent in man.[6]

Of these three goals, the last was the most important to theosophists. The antimaterialist character of Blavatsky's speculative writings defined the philosophical character of the Theosophical Society for decades to come. Believing that a philosophy based on psychic powers could best be propagated by a Hindu sage, Blavatsky's successors—C. W. Leadbeater and Annie Besant—encouraged their followers to embrace a young Indian mystic named Jiddu Krishnamurti (1895–1986). Krishnamurti was regarded by Leadbeater and Besant as the "Maitreya" (or "World Teacher") who would succeed in bringing together all of the world's religious leaders under the banner of theosophy. This great enterprise failed in the late 1920s when Krishnamurti himself withdrew his support from the Society and renounced all of the titles and claims it had bestowed upon him.

Today, the Society's headquarters are in Pasadena, California, and it still has many adherents in India, as well as the United States. It continues to promote a belief in the "oneness of life," and in such familiar concepts as karma and reincarnation, through its publication *Sunrise*.

ISKCON: The International Society for Krishna Consciousness

Better known in North America as the "Hare Krishna Movement," **ISKCON** derives its religious philosophy from the teachings of A. C. Bhaktivedanta Swami (1896–1977), a follower of the sixteenth-century Hindu reformer and mystic Sri Chaitnaya Mahaprabhu. Chaitnaya's disciples regarded him as a divine avatar, and his particular form of Hinduism stressed devotion to the god Krishna, through whom all peoples, regardless of caste or origin, could achieve spiritual fulfillment. Bhaktivedanta (referred to as Prabhupada by his closest followers) brought this message to the West in 1965 when he sailed to New York in the hopes of establishing a center for the study of Chaitnayan devotional practices. Two years later, Prabhupada was drawn to San Francisco and its emergent counterculture, where he developed a communalistic movement dedicated to both Krishna worship and an austere code of conduct. Since then, Prabhupada's disciples have established ISKCON centers in more than 300 communities worldwide, and the movement appears to have survived the death of its founder in 1977.

At the heart of the ISKCON philosophy is the belief that Krishna is the sole, supreme deity in the universe and that the highest goal of human life is to achieve "Krishna consciousness," through which the soul can return to its Creator. One of the central rituals of the movement, through which the attainment of Krishna consciousness is facilitated, is the repetitive chanting of one particular mantra—*Hare Krishna, Hare Krishna, Krishna, Hare, Hare Rama, Hare Rama, Rama, Hare Hare*—accompanied by the rosary-like counting of prayer beads, sixteen times each day. To serve Krishna, Prabhupada taught, one must adopt a strictly vegetarian diet and abstain from violence, gambling, alcohol, tobacco, and drugs. Sexual relations outside of marriage are forbidden, and even within marriage, sexual relations are intended for procreation alone. During the early stages of the movement, ISKCON members committed themselves to selling translations of Prabhupada's commentaries on the Vedas, and the presence of Hare Krishnas (as they were called) at airports and other public locales became a familiar sight during the 1970s.

Prabhupada's death in 1977 occasioned, at first, a crisis within the movement, as the eleven gurus he had chosen to lead ISKCON proved too inexperienced (or, in some cases, corrupt), and widespread criticism of the institution of the guru was voiced, both within and outside the movement. There are now approximately 100 ISKCON gurus throughout the world, and though their activities are supposed to be monitored by a governing body, it is clear that organizational structure within the movement is still fairly loose. Increasingly, local ISKCON temples are independent of policies established by the main Indian congregation in

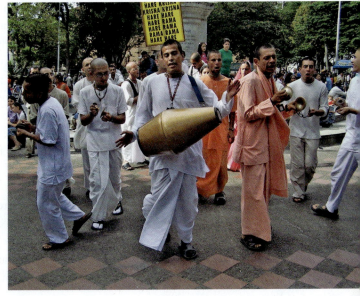

Members of a Hare Krishna community dancing on a London street.

Mayapur (Bengal). Nevertheless, ISKCON continues to maintain a missionary outlook and thinks of itself as an international religious movement with an appropriately global membership.

The Osho Rajneesh Movement

An even more controversial religious movement with Hindu roots that came to prominence in the 1970s bears the name of its founder, Rajneesh Chandra Mohan (1931–1990). In 1981 Rajneesh, an Indian professor of philosophy, moved from India to a ranch in central Oregon, where he and his followers established a religious commune they named Rajneeshpuram. It was there that Rajneesh hoped to establish a "Buddhafield," as he called it—a utopian community committed to his own blend of Hindu and Buddhist values—though, in fact, the outcome of this experiment in communal living was anything but utopian. The numerous critics of Rajneesh and his works regarded this movement as a fairly typical personality cult. Rajneesh changed his name at least twice during his lifetime, with each change representing a different representation of his self-defined spiritual role: in 1971, for example, he began referring to himself as "Bhagwan" Rajneesh, meaning "enlightened one," and in 1989 (after having tried and failed to convince his followers to address him as "Buddha"), he settled on the tile "**Osho**," a name whose precise meaning remains obscure today, but which clearly conveys the idea of spiritual master.[7] Nor was Rajneesh the only one in this movement to alter his name or identity: his disciples (known as *sannyasins*, a Hindu term denoting someone whose life was devoted to spiritual pursuits), upon entering the community, also adopted new names (often those of Hindu gods). Each *sannyasin* was required to wear a saffron robe, the traditional garb of Hindu holy men. More revealingly, members of Rajneeshpuram were also obliged to wear a necklace of prayer beads, with a locket containing Rajneesh's picture attached to it, and to perform at least one meditation every day based on Rajneesh's teachings.

Both Rajneesh and the movement had run afoul of the law by the mid-1980s, in part because of his uncertain immigration status, but mostly because his extravagant lifestyle (including a fleet of ninety-three Rolls-Royces) and political ambitions had put him in direct conflict with his neighbors. After evidence surfaced that Rajneesh's lieutenants had attempted a mass poisoning of the local population, Rajneesh was arrested (while attempting to flee the country) and subsequently deported. Upon returning to India, Rajneesh (or Osho, as he insisted on being called) resumed his career as a teacher of meditation, returning to his ashram in the city of Poona, which he renamed the Osho Commune International. His death in 1990 left the movement without its charismatic leader, but the nearly 500 books (consisting largely of his informal talks and lectures) he left behind still provide his *sannyasins* with a body of teachings that functions very much like a formal doctrine. Nevertheless, Osho International, as the movement is commonly known today, is a largely decentralized network of independent communities that draw inspiration from the variety of meditative and therapeutic ideas Rajneesh articulated during his lifetime.

Rajneesh's philosophy of life was nothing if not eclectic: he drew inspiration from practically everything he read, which included traditional tantric thought, Zen Buddhism, Hasidism, Sufism, Marxism, and the writings of Sigmund Freud. Though sometimes portrayed as an atheist, Rajneesh's ideas about the divine more often resemble a form of pantheism, and he taught his followers to search for truth and ultimate reality within themselves, as well as within nature:

> My trust is total. I trust the outer, I trust the inner—because outer and inner are both together. They cannot be separated. There is no God without this world; there is no world without God. God is the inner-most core of this world. The juice flowing in the trees is God, the blood circulating in your body is God, the consciousness residing in you is God. God and the world are mixed together just like a dancer and his dance; they cannot be separated, they are inseparable. . . .
> I teach the whole man. I am not a materialist or a spiritualist. My approach is wholistic [sic]—and the whole man can only be holy.[8]

With superb inconsistency, Rajneesh taught the necessity of annihilating the ego to achieve final enlightenment while engaging in flamboyant self-promotion (and self-enrichment). It was his aggressive advocacy of sexual freedom, however, that landed him in trouble with religious authorities in his native India, while at the same time attracting young people in the West to his potpourri of religious ideas. Believing, as he once said, that there were "108 paths" (the number of beads in a prayer necklace) to enlightenment, Rajneesh encouraged his *sannyasins* to plot their own journey to self-realization, while encouraging them constantly to "live wakefully." Rajneesh's defenders have long seen his avid pursuit of material goods and pleasures as, paradoxically, a demonstration of the need to reconcile (rather than oppose) spiritual and material desires, and those who still find his influence meaningful continue to heed his admonition to "live in the moment."

Transcendental Meditation

At an even further remove from traditional Hindu thought is a meditative discipline that denies it is actually a religious philosophy at all: Transcendental Meditation. "TM," as it is popularly known, was founded by the Maharishi Mahesh Yogi, a figure surrounded by mystery (which includes uncertainty about his given name or actual date of birth). What is known of his personal history reveals that he was a graduate of Allahabad University (in physics) who spent thirteen years at a monastery in northern India studying under Swami Brahmananda Saraswan, commonly called Guru Dev. After Guru Dev's death in 1953, the Maharishi (a self-appointed title meaning "Great Seer") went into seclusion for a time, but when he emerged he set out to share the techniques of meditation he had learned from Guru Dev with the world. Having first established a meditation center that he named the Spiritual Regeneration Movement in

Madras in 1958, the Maharishi went on to open similar centers in Los Angeles and in London in 1960, which led to the founding of the International Meditation Society in 1961 and (a decade later) the opening of the Maharishi International University in Iowa in 1971. Each of these institutions was designed both to disseminate the Maharishi's teachings and to promote greater understanding among diverse peoples, all of whom, it is asserted, can benefit from the practice of meditation. In the 1990s TM renamed itself the "Maharishi Foundation," and as part of its plan to promote world peace, it sponsored the creation (in Great Britain) of the Natural Law party, whose manifesto calls for bringing existing political systems into line with "the intelligence and infinite organizing power that silently maintains and guides the evolution of everything in the universe."[9]

Those who promote TM as the solution to all human problems define it, variably, as a "technology of consciousness" and as a "Science of Creative Intelligence," though its presumed benefits to both the individual and society have been questioned by skeptical observers who find that TM's claims to enhance physical well-being and conflict resolution are simply not borne out by objective evidence. This is particularly true of the technique known as "**Yogic Flying**," during which the TM practitioner rocks back and forth with legs crossed, hoping to levitate a few inches through the air. The object of this exercise is to maximize mind-body coordination, and TM literature suggests that the key to future spiritual and moral evolution lies in this yogic form of physical transcendence. In addition, TM students are given a special mantra to recite—consisting of a sacred sound rather than a word—with the expectation that reciting this mantra will facilitate a transformation of consciousness leading to greater peace of mind. Those who have benefited from this procedure insist that it has led to significant stress reduction.

The question remains, of course, whether this is merely a therapeutic procedure of possible psychological value or a spiritual discipline of personal growth. Unlike Christian Science and other religious philosophies influenced by New Thought, TM offers its disciples no dogmas, and its view of life is entirely "world affirming."

THE REVIVAL OF ESOTERIC AND NEOPAGAN THOUGHT

The religious philosophies subsumed under this heading combine many of the ideas and behaviors that Melton describes as peculiar to the Wisdom, Magical, and Spiritualist "families." What all of these alternative communities share is the belief that a superior kind of spiritual knowledge—known in antiquity as *gnosis* (Greek, "knowledge")—is available to everyone in the modern world, often due to the presence of enlightened intermediaries in our midst. Once one is possession of such knowledge, the world we presently call "real" appears very different—whether enhanced or diminished— depending on how "world affirming" or "world denying" one's experience of a greater reality turns out to be. The belief that the world of common, everyday perception is only a fragment (or a shadowy reflection) of something much more real is a recurrent insight of most of the world's religions. Nevertheless, the conviction that direct knowledge of that greater reality is a guarded secret that only a few initiates into the mysteries of the universe can possibly grasp is the core presumption behind all forms of esoteric thought in the West.

Although it is certainly possible to trace the origins of this secretive worldview back to the Middle Ages, most new religious communities that engage in some form of metaphysical speculation have been influenced by two visionary figures of the early modern period: Jacob Boehme (1575–1624) and Emmanuel Swedenborg (1688–1772). From Boehme, a German shoemaker-turned-mystic, readers of his first published book (*Aurora*, 1612) learn of the existence of a parallel world, perfect and eternal, into which each human being is destined to be reborn, but only after that individual's spiritual nature has been realized. Readers of Swedenborg, however—and especially those who survey his most often cited work, *On Heaven and Hell* (1758)—learn of the passing of successive ages, with the fifth and final age set aside for the realization of the Second Coming of Christ. With the advent of this new age, Swedenborg taught, it will suddenly be possible to converse with angels and to raise all human relationships to a higher level. Both Boehme and Swedenborg were convinced that we are surrounded by supernal intelligences, and both were equally certain that the coming age would see a lifting of the veil that presently obscures our view of a spiritual reality that lies just beyond the horizon of "normative" experience. Echoes of these beliefs can be found in movements that have been influenced by what we have called New Age thought, and a recurrent motif in such philosophies is the realization that the "horizontal" reality of the material world is constantly intersected by a "vertical" reality of even greater power and knowledge.

Eckankar

Though first established as a distinctive religious community in 1965, Eckankar claims to be the most ancient of all faiths and, therefore, the spiritual "root" from which all later religious traditions have descended. In his book *Eckankar: The Key to Secret Worlds* (1969), Eckankar's founder, Paul Twitchell (1908?–1971), endorses a belief in "**astral voyages**" (the projection of the mind or spirit onto higher levels of experience) and asserts that we can inhabit two very different planes of reality at the same time. Through the exercise of certain ancient meditational techniques, Twitchell taught, it is possible for the soul to travel outside of the body and to free itself from both the prison world of ordinary perception and the cycle of reincarnations. These same spiritual exercises allow one to experience God's Voice as a form of light and sound and thereby draw closer to the Source of all being. Only the *chela*, or student of Eckankar-based wisdom, can make this spiritual ascent, and a lengthy period of initiation is required before the movement of the mind to this astral plane can be accomplished successively.

Because emanative forces flowing out of God course through the consciousness of the living Eck Master, his influence is vital if one is to experience the divine reality, whether waking or dreaming. Twitchell believed himself to be such a Master—the 971st Eck Master, to be precise—which placed him in a very long line of spiritual guides going back to remote antiquity, one that included Jesus and St. Paul. Twitchell believed that they too had been influenced by Eck Masters and that Christianity could therefore be viewed as an offshoot, or further development, of Eck teachings. However, it is important to recognize that any living Eck Master can not only "channel" the thinking of deceased Masters but can also correct any mistaken notions proclaimed by his immediate predecessors. The words of the living Master, therefore, are determinative of whatever doctrines emerge, at any given time, from the Eckankar community—an assumption that has led, as we shall see, to a measure of institutional instability.

Upon Twitchell's death in 1971, leadership of the movement fell to Darwin Gross (1928–2008), who, despite some opposition within the Eckankar community, immediately declared himself to be Living Master No. 972. That claim was later disputed, however, by his successor, Harold Klemp (b. 1942), who, as Living Master No. 973, declared that Gross was no longer an Eck Master. This power struggle within the Eckankar leadership led to a splintering of the community and came at the culminating point of a series of public attacks on Twitchell's claims to credibility. Several critics of the movement have even demonstrated Twitchell's literal indebtedness—often in the form of outright plagiarism—to earlier writers of the Sant Mat tradition (which combines elements of Hindu and Sikh mysticism). Today, Twitchell's followers generally acknowledge similarities between his "revelations" and earlier religious texts and traditions, but insist, nevertheless, that he was merely echoing truths that have been revealed to all great religious teachers. Since the 1980s, the movement has been headquartered in Chanhassen, Minnesota, where the Temple of Eck was constructed in 1990. The number of "Eckists," as members of this community are known, is somewhat difficult to determine today, but one source speculates that the number of active members may be as high as 20,000.

The Findhorn Foundation

Like so many of the movements described herein, the Findhorn community was the product of both the political turmoil and revolutionary expectations of the 1960s. When its founders, Peter and Eileen Caddy, withdrew to a quiet Scottish village named Findhorn in 1962, they hoped to establish there a communitarian way of life that would be open to new forms of religious experience. Their choice of this place was dictated in part by its natural beauty, but also out of a belief that it was inhabited by friendly spirits who would inspire those who lived there. Eileen Caddy had long believed that she was receiving messages from God and that, by gathering like-minded, spiritually oriented people together, she might create a socially and economically viable alternative to modern urban existence.

From its beginnings, Findhorn has encouraged both the study and practice of a number of esoteric forms of religious expression, many of which have been labeled types of New Age belief: for example, the use of crystals for purposes of healing; telepathic contact with internationally renowned mediums; and attempts to contact extraterrestrials.

As the community grew, the thinking of its leaders gradually moved away from a postapocalyptic view of survival amid imminent worldwide destruction to a more adaptive, gradualist view of small-scale social change coupled with a culture of self-realization. This shift in self-understanding and political perspective—corresponding to Wallis's distinction between world-renouncing and world-accommodating ideologies—was accompanied not only by the physical expansion of the Findhorn colony (which presently consists of a Universal Hall, a hotel, a trailer park, a community center, and several smaller buildings) but also by the development of residential educational programs designed to promote "planetary cleansing." In fact, a synthesis of ecological and spiritually therapeutic concerns dominates Findhorn thinking, and its ability to sustain itself financially—Findhorn became a foundation in 1972 and has managed to remain profitable ever since—has given hope to other quasi-utopian experiments in communitarian living. Decision making at Findhorn is arrived at by consensus, though long-term policies and major purchases fall under the purview of a management group.

Visitors to Findhorn, however, see very little of the operational structure of the community. Their encounter with Findhorn begins with a reorientation process, known as "Experience Week," during which they are encouraged to engage in rigorous self-analysis and to open themselves to the spiritual forces that are believed to permeate and sustain our world. Meditation and "sacred dancing" are among the various activities guests are invited to participate in, and everyone must share in common maintenance tasks, such as cleaning up and making beds. Unlike some of the more coercive, cult-like organizations that grew out of the counterculture of the 1960s, Findhorn makes no attempt to control the lives or thought processes of those who pass through its doors. The ideal of the spiritual "seeker" who is searching for enlightenment rather than institutional affiliation is still viewed with respect in the Findhorn community, and the absence of a central authoritarian personality has helped to preserve the open, egalitarian character of this organization.

Members of Findhorn Foundation engaged in Sacred Dance.

The Raelian Movement

Another major expression of esoteric religious thought in the contemporary period can be found in movements committed to a belief in extraterrestrial beings. Popularly dubbed "UFO cults," many of these communities have assumed the concerns—and in some cases the language—of millenarian Christian theology by projecting a visionary future in which believers will be rescued from a dying earth by visitors from outer space, who will then transport only the chosen few to a distant planet, where they will live in bliss.

In addition, one recurrent article of faith among such groups is the belief that human civilization is the result of interaction with beings from another planetary system who have used our world as a laboratory for genetic and cultural experimentation. Within the context of this quasi-religious creed—which sociologists commonly refer to as "Ufology"—spiritual enlightenment consists of the realization that our collective destinies are ultimately in the hands of unearthly beings whose power and intelligence vastly exceeds our own and whose immediate goal is to make contact with those few human beings who are capable of receiving their secret (and ultimately world-redeeming) revelations.

The Raelian movement, which was given its name and its creed by its founder, Claude "Rael" Vorilhon (b. 1946), is one of the better known communities of UFO worshippers, and its belief system should be at once familiar and strange to anyone living within a Judeo-Christian culture. In his book *The Message Given to Me by Extraterrestrials: They Took Me to Their Planet* (1978), Rael revisits the various accounts of divine-human interaction in the Hebrew Bible and identifies the **Elohim**—one of the principal terms used in the Hebrew Bible to identify the Creator-God—as the true creators of our planet and of the human race. However, the Elohim are not supernatural beings, Rael insists, but rather an advanced race of extraterrestrials, somewhat smaller and greener than humans, perhaps, but in no other way different (except for their superior knowledge) from the human species with whom they elected to procreate. It was the Elohim who renamed Vorilhon "Rael," and it was one of the Elohim who impregnated Mary of Nazareth and fathered Jesus centuries ago. Rael believes that he too is the result of human-extraterrestrial mating, which places him among a select group of prophets and teachers that includes, among others, Buddha, Jesus, and Muhammad. Believing himself to be the Messiah of our age, Rael founded the Raelian religion in 1974 (known formally as "The Movement to Welcome the Elohim, Creators of Humanity") as a means of publicizing the presence of the Elohim within our planetary system and as an anticipation of the day when the peoples of the earth will be able to receive the Elohim in peace. Only then will a new world order be possible and the global reign of men and women of superior intelligence really commence.

Rael's flair for publicity is one of the reasons that the Raelians have achieved a larger measure of public recognition than most UFO religions. In 2002, Dr. Brigitte Boisselier (b. 1956) announced that she and her fellow Raelians had successfully cloned a human baby in fulfillment of the Raelian goal of achieving immortality through scientific means. No proof has been offered to date confirming this claim, but it did succeed in drawing international press coverage of her news conference. On a slightly more lurid plane, Rael himself has organized a conference promoting masturbation, arguing that "self-love" would stimulate the growth of new brain cells and thereby make it possible for humans to experience sexual pleasure without guilt. And for whatever reason, Rael has repeatedly sought public confrontations with the Catholic Church, insisting, for example, that his followers address him as "Your Holiness"—a title normally reserved for the Pope. Yet even without such provocations, the Raelian movement has received so much negative publicity in France (and later in Canada, where it is now headquartered) for its promotion of sexual freedom that it could not have escaped notoriety, even if it had wished to.

It should be noted, however, that many of the Raelian teachings that have provoked controversy can be found in other UFO-oriented organizations and in esoteric religious communities generally. Critics of Vorilhon's writings have accused him of having "borrowed" Erich von Daniken's mythic account of the extraterrestrial origins of human civilization (*Chariot of the Gods,* 1968) for his own purposes and have focused on his advocacy of various kinds of sexual "liberation" as proof of the inherently antisocial character of the movement (though a belief in "free love" is hardly unique among alternative religions). But in his own defense, Rael has pointed out that his belief in superior beings from another galaxy, or in spaceships circling the earth, is no stranger than believing in supernatural "guides" who direct the course of human history. From his perspective, all he has done is offer a more "scientific" version of a very ancient belief—a belief that, in one form or another, has been embraced by most of the world's religions. As for the Raelians' promotion of cloning (for pets as well as humans) as a legitimate response to the dilemma of mortality, it was never the desire of the Elohim, they argue, that the human race remain forever limited to a single lifespan, nor that we should suffer helplessly from the ravages of incurable diseases. The Elohim, they teach, remain poised, waiting for the next evolutionary leap in human development to occur, at which time they will share with us the wealth of superior knowledge and technological expertise they have accumulated over eons of time.

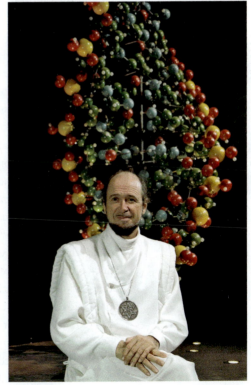

Rael is seated in front of a model of a double helix as he announces the supposed cloning of a human child.

Critics insist that what is particularly disturbing about this movement (and others like it) is the potential for socially destructive behavior that resides within the core beliefs of dedicated UFO communities. Anticult activists point to the collective suicides of the Heaven's Gate community in 1997—whose thirty-nine members took their lives in the belief that, having shed their bodies, their spirits would ascend into the heavens and join the "mother ship"—as proof that Ufology, carried to its extreme conclusion, can generate a pathological form of world renunciation. Still, although it is not possible to assert that the Raelian community will never adopt a radical and apocalyptic view of the human condition, Vorilhon has yet to display any sign of the psychopathology that compelled Marshall Herff Applewhite (1931–1997), the leader of the Heaven's Gate movement, and his followers to take their lives as an act of spiritual liberation.

The Church of Scientology

Of all the new religious movements we have discussed thus far, none has aroused as much opposition, or public curiosity, as the movement founded by Lafayette Ron Hubbard (1911–1986) in 1954. Hubbard's personality, and the extraordinary claims made on his behalf by his followers, have been the focus of much of the criticism directed at the Church of Scientology over the years, but even if Hubbard had not played such a visible role in the formation of Scientology's core belief system, its teachings themselves would have stirred controversy. At its beginnings, Scientology was presented to the public as a new form of mental healing. Hubbard's best-known publication, *Dianetics: The Modern Science of Mental Health* (1950), offered its readers an alternative view of the self and the dynamic forces at work within the subconscious mind. Yet, even at this early stage in the development of his largely esoteric belief system, Hubbard was committed to a view of the "true" self—or **thetan** as it is called in his writings—that stresses the immaterial nature of what most Western religions would call the "soul." Thus, even though the thetan inhabits the body during an individual's life span, and even though it interacts with matter and energy, it possesses an eternal and independent reality and can therefore survive death and pass on to other bodies. To attain enlightenment, Hubbard believed, one must first acknowledge the primary reality of the thetan, or in Hubbard's language, attain "an awareness of awareness," before passing on to higher levels of spiritual understanding.

The critical moment, Scientologists believe, in this search for expanded consciousness comes when the presence of "**engrams**"—traumatic events stored as images in the "reactive" or subconscious mind—is made evident to both the subject of mental analysis and the "auditor" engaged in detecting unsettling memories and deeply irrational feelings. One of the primary purposes, then, of Scientology's form of counseling is to release the troubled individual—referred to as "pre-clear" in Scientological literature—from emotionally crippling past experiences. Indeed, once one is declared "clear" of whatever destructive engrams have accumulated in the mind, one's health (physical and mental) will improve dramatically, Hubbard believed, and those who have benefited from the process of "auditing" have testified to its liberating effects.

However, Scientology is more than the sum of its therapeutic promises and procedures. Before his death, Hubbard had evolved a complex mythology in which the "thetans"—now thought of as a race of super-beings—were seen as creators of our material universe who gradually lost their creative powers and fell victims to the reactive mind, which grew in influence as their powers waned. To recover the energy and imagination once possessed by these primordial thetans has become the mission of Scientology's elite cadres, and at the highest levels of spiritual and intellectual development within the movement, the secrets of continued progressive evolution are revealed. Such emphasis on secrecy and hidden truths, disclosed only to the initiated, is one of the persistent characteristics of esoteric movements generally, and it is only within their movement, Scientologists insist, that one can achieve the status of a spiritually evolved individual (or an "Operating Thetan," in Scientological terminology). Of course, by tightly controlling the means of progressive self-development, Scientology has, ironically, committed itself to the same kind of therapeutic monopoly that Hubbard bitterly denounced in his attacks on modern psychiatry.

Critics of Scientology[10] have attacked the movement on several fronts. The official biography of its founder, they argue, is filled with distortions of fact and outright lies and amounts to little more than a hagiography of an almost mythical figure. In reality, they insist, L. Ron Hubbard was nothing like the hero of the mind portrayed in movement literature but a scheming science-fiction writer whose cravings for power and wealth led him to fabricate a mock religion of mental health. As for the E-meter—used to detect the presence of engrams in the pre-clear mind—it is no more effective, these critics charge, than an ordinary lie detector (which it resembles) in eliminating the reactive mind or in tracing the effects of negative mental energy. Counseling of practically any kind, they point out, can accomplish much of what Scientologists attribute to their methodology, and without the trappings of a science-fiction cult. Scientology's struggles with the Internal Revenue Service to have itself recognized as a legitimate religious organization were at least provisionally resolved in the church's favor by 1993. Still, the testimonies of former Scientologists to the authoritarian nature of its leadership and to the suppression of criticism within the movement seem to indicate a fundamental discrepancy between the aspirations of the church and its actual policies.

In response to such critics, Scientologists point out that apostates from any religious movement often bear tales of deception and mistreatment and just as often misrepresent the very teachings they have come to reject. The ultimate goals of the Church of Scientology, its defenders insist, have not changed in the half-century or so in which the movement has existed; its goals, they claim, clearly reflect the redemptive mission of its founder: to achieve "a civilization without insanity, without criminals and without war, where the able can prosper and honest beings can have rights, and where man is free to rise to greater heights." At present there are well over 100 Scientology churches worldwide, in at least as many countries, and the influence of Scientology's teachings can be seen in a variety of public health and educational programs, most especially Narconon, a drug-treatment organization whose protocol was (according to organization literature) established by Hubbard in the 1970s. The precise number of members still actively affiliated with the church is difficult to determine, but its presence within the contemporary religious landscape appears to be growing.

An E-meter and a display of Hubbard's *Dianetics*.

Wicca

In the popular imagination, and in much of Western folklore, "witches" have been around forever, but the contemporary nature religion known as *Wicca* is a far cry from the various literary incarnations of the archetypal embodiment of evil that Shakespeare, for example, drew upon in *Macbeth*. Contemporary witches, or *Wiccans*, as they prefer to be called, do not cast harmful spells, do not communicate with spirits of the underworld, and most especially do not worship the Devil. They do claim to practice various types of magic, however, and they often worship various pre-Christian deities, particularly those associated with natural forces and phenomena. Contemporary Wiccans prefer to be thought of as pagans, though the ensemble of beliefs and practices that characterizes witchcraft today is often so eclectic that no direct link between Wicca and pre-Christian religious cultures can be said to exist.

The Wiccan movement appears to have been the brainchild of one British enthusiast, Gerald B. Gardner (1884–1964), who, after a lifetime as a civil servant in Southeast Asia, returned to England to pursue an interest in folklore and esoteric religious thought. In concert with Margaret Murray (1863–1963), an anthropologist and Egyptologist (as well as a prominent early feminist) whose book *The Witch Cult in Western Europe* (1921) argued that the witch cults of medieval Europe were survivals of an indigenous fertility religion, Gardner sought to prove that remnants of these ancient pagan rituals could still be found in the modern world. And although professional anthropologists have rejected, decisively, both Murray's research and Gardner's more extravagant claims, the modern form of Wicca seems to have been born out of their collaboration. Following the repeal in 1954 of England's 1735 Witchcraft Act, Gardner set out to revive contemporary interest in "the Craft" by describing ancient pagan beliefs in his landmark book *Witchcraft Today* (1954), which both legitimated the pursuit of once-forbidden practices and opened the door to future development of basic Wiccan principles and ritual acts. Gardner's critics have since cast doubts on the authenticity of his claims to have recovered the secrets of ancient witch cults; nevertheless, his work has inspired a generation of Wiccan writers and practitioners whose varied interpretations of Gardnerian lore have led to the proliferation of distinct schools of Wiccan thought.

At the heart of Wiccan teachings is the belief that divine magic and mystery lie within ourselves and within the natural world. The Wiccan concept of the sacred is almost entirely immanental—that is, dwelling *within* Nature rather than outside or above—and although many Wiccan communities have chosen to worship a variety of pre-Christian deities, these "gods" are generally viewed as personifications of the power and grandeur that resides within Nature and within the human imagination. When Wiccans speak of "the God" or "the Goddess" they are not referring to the transcendent Creator of the Abrahamic faiths but rather to a creative force that lies within all existing things, to which human cultures attribute gender and personality. Wiccans are not content, however, simply to worship the powers that permeate our universe; they also seek to access those powers through ritualized acts of magic (or "magick" as most Wiccans prefer to spell that word). It is this more assertive aspect of Wicca that places it within Melton's "magical" family of new religions. The only constraint that Wiccans acknowledge upon the exercise of such power is embodied in the **Wiccan Rede**—that is, those principles of ethical behavior that virtually all modern witches accept as binding—which teaches: "An it harm none, do what you will."

For Wiccan communities, however, that rule entails the use of "magick" to achieve positive ends, and many Wiccan authors urge their readers to practice deeds that will be of benefit to humanity. In addition, many versions of the Wiccan "Rede" (or "rule" in modern English) teach a belief in some form of karma; thus Wiccans are cautioned to expect that harmful acts will return to afflict the witch who inflicts them on others.

As indicated in the vignette with which this chapter began, Wiccans celebrate the change of seasons, as well as the phases of the moon. Two very common ceremonies within the Wiccan community are the *Esbat* and the *Sabbat,* which are designed, respectively, to pay honor to the Goddess of the Moon and the God of the Sun. Esbats most often occur when the moon is full, though custom varies from community to community. Sabbats, on the other hand, are seasonal and mark the occurrence of

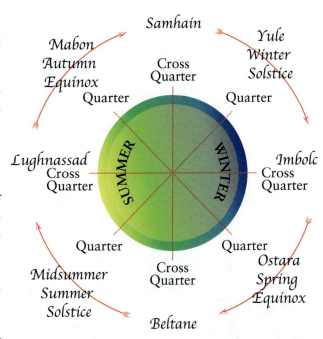

Wiccan wheel of the year.

equinoxes and solstices, or midpoints between them. There are eight Sabbats within the Wiccan calendar, the most familiar of which is Yule (or "Yuletide," as it is known in many Christian cultures). The ceremonies associated with Esbats and Sabbats differ considerably: during an Esbat celebration, for example, some attempt to "draw down the moon" (that is, draw the moon's energy into oneself) is the ritual's focus; on a Sabbat, however, it is customary to light bonfires and to decorate an altar in a way that pays tribute to the character of the particular god who is being honored that season. In each case, Wiccans hope to align themselves with the hidden energies of Nature and to confer blessings on themselves and their loved ones through such acts of natural communion.

A Council of American Witches was held in 1974, and though it succeeded in drawing up a set of basic principles for the Wiccan movement in the United States, the council itself no longer exists, and Wicca remains today one of the most decentralized of new religious communities. Wiccans generally gather in small groups known as **covens**, though some witches prefer to practice their "Craft" in isolation. One of the more influential schools of Wiccan thought is the "Reclaiming" Movement, founded by Miriam Simos (b. 1951; better known in Wiccan circles as "Starhawk") in the 1970s. The Reclaiming philosophy is more openly political than most varieties of Wicca, and in her writings Simos blends an eclectic mix of feminist, anticapitalist, and ecological concerns in an attempt to "reclaim" the earth from political forces that have despoiled the planet and oppressed its population. Most Wiccans, however, prefer not to align their communities with a specific political agenda, though the formation of the Witches' League for Public Awareness in 1986 and other lobbying organizations (such as the Alternative Religious Education Network) have received widespread support in the Wiccan movement. One of the more organized Wiccan communities, the Church and School of Wicca (founded in 1968), estimates the number of its adherents to be around 200,000, and although it is impossible to extrapolate the number of Wiccans worldwide, the movement has clearly benefited greatly from court decisions in the United States that conferred legal status on the practice of witchcraft, allowing individuals to claim Wicca as their legally acknowledged faith.

VOICES: An Interview with Rev. Lucy Bunch

Lucy Bunch

Rev. Lucy Bunch is the Assistant Minister of the Unitarian Universalist Society of Sacramento, California.

You were ordained in 2012. What led you toward the Unitarian Universalist ministry?

The Unitarians and the Universalists both had a strong tradition of promoting gender equality, going back to the nineteenth century, and the combined Unitarian Universalist Society has consistently exhibited particular sensitivity to the LGBT community—an issue that has particular resonance for me. More than that, however, the Unitarian Universalists are deeply committed to the cause of social justice and to the pursuit of social and personal transformation. Prior to entering the ministry I had worked as an academic administrator, but I felt a calling to minister to people who held progressive values as strongly as I did. I was convinced that I could contribute something to the spiritual life of this community.

How would you describe the Unitarian Universalist Society today?

Unitarian Universalists are, as I perceive them, people who are trying to find themselves within the continuum of religious experience and belief—or unbelief—and therefore their spirituality can best be described as "evolving." Ours is an essentially tolerant community, a community of "seekers," and particularly welcoming to those who have become "unchurched," either because they could no longer accept the dogmas of their previous faith communities, or because they had found the social values of those communities unacceptable.

That said, I have found, more recently, a desire on the part of the younger generation of Unitarian Universalists to explore various forms of enhanced spirituality and a corresponding movement away from the more assertive humanist orientation that has characterized this community in decades past. For some, the reclaiming of spiritual connection entails the introduction of more traditional modes of prayer and ritual, whereas for others it takes the form of an awakened interest in various types of mysticism. Our challenge, then, as a community is to find a way of satisfying both those who need to be constantly asking questions and those who are seeking answers.

THE EMERGENCE OF UNIVERSALIST RELIGIOUS THOUGHT

The global presence of both Christianity and Islam ensured that, by the late nineteenth century, emergent religions throughout the world would reflect the influence and prestige of at least these Abrahamic faiths. The most direct manifestation of this influence can be found in their embrace of a monotheistic paradigm, in which the idea of a single and singular "God" becomes a core precept in their offshoot theology. But no less direct an influence can be found in the belief—shared by so many "universalist" religions, and in particular by Baha'i and Unitarianism—that their teachings reach beyond the boundaries of time and geography and therefore speak to the whole of humankind, irrespective of differences in history and culture.

The Baha'i Faith

As the last of the "Abrahamic" religions that traces its origins to the Middle East, Islam presents itself as the final and decisive revelation of divine truth to mankind. This belief has been challenged not only by the two Abrahamic faiths that preceded it, Judaism and Christianity, but by later monotheistic faiths as well. Perhaps the most significant challenge to Islam's belief in the finality of the Qur'an, however (at least within the context of Middle Eastern religious culture), occurred in mid-nineteenth-century Iran, in the person of a merchant-turned-religious-reformer named Sayyid Ali-Muhammad Shirazi (1819–1850), who saw himself as a successor to Muhammad and as the recipient of new revelations from Allah. His followers called him the *Bab*—meaning the "Gate" through which the Twelfth Imam of Shi'ism would enter the world—and before long his teachings were declared heretical by Muslim authorities. His imprisonment and death failed to stifle the messianic movement he had ignited, and in 1853 one of his most devoted followers, Mirza Husayn Ali Nuri (1817–1892)—better known by the title he later bore, *Baha'u'llah*—declared himself to be a "Messenger of God," and therefore the legitimate successor to the Bab. Many of the followers of the Bab subsequently pledged their allegiance to Baha'u'llah and their adherence to his teachings, and thus began the new religious movement known as *Baha'i*.

Baha'i is both a monotheistic and a universalistic faith, based on a belief in one Creator God who is the source of all existence and goodness in the universe and the ultimate object of worship for all peoples. Because this God is a wholly transcendent, eternal, and unknowable Being, "He" cannot be described or comprehended by human minds, but his representatives or chosen "messengers" on earth can at least impart something of his will for mankind. According to Baha'u'llah, there has been a succession of such messengers in history (including Moses, Zoroaster, Buddha, Jesus, and Muhammad), each one serving as a prophet for his respective faith community. Baha'u'llah clearly saw himself as the most recent of these manifestations of divine wisdom, and for his followers no future messenger from God is expected for another thousand years. Because divine revelation for Baha'is is progressive, each of these prophets advances human understanding of the divine one step further, reaching higher and higher levels with each successive revelation. It follows, then, that for

Baha'is the teachings of Baha'u'llah and his successors within the Baha'i movement constitute the most complete understanding of divine thought that human beings have yet attained. As for the writings of Baha'u'llah, they have become for Baha'is a significant part of an unfolding authoritative "scripture," and as a written revelation they have the advantage of having no competing oral tradition (unlike the *hadith* in Islam, for example).

The core truth that Baha'u'llah sought to impart to his followers and to the world was simply this: that because God is one, humanity must also be one. Baha'u'llah believed that all the barriers that separate people from one another (such as differences of race, nationality, gender, wealth, and religious belief) must give way to an awakened sense that the human race has at last "come of age" and that the world is ripe for political structures and cultural values that unite rather than divide our planet's population. World government (and its necessary concomitant, world peace) is finally attainable, he insisted, but only if we are willing to embrace something like the following twelve "principles" of thought and behavior:

1. The oneness of God and the common foundation of all religions
2. The oneness of humanity
3. The equality of men and women
4. The need to eliminate all types of prejudice
5. The need to eliminate all extremes of wealth and poverty
6. A belief in the harmony of science and religion
7. The need for compulsory universal education
8. The need for a common language spoken by all peoples
9. The need for independent inquiries into truth
10. The pursuit of spiritual solutions to political and social problems
11. Obedience to one's government coupled with avoidance of partisan politics
12. The establishment of a world government as the guarantor of world peace

The mission of the Baha'i community, as Baha'u'llah understood it, was to promote these teachings and to become a role model for the world's religious communities, demonstrating in their communal life just how diverse cultures can embrace a vision of universal harmony and mutual understanding.

Over the past century and a half the Baha'i community has evolved a body of scripture, religious practices, and governing structure that have given their faith a distinctive character. Chief among the texts that Baha'is consider holy are the writings of the Bab, Baha'u'llah, Abdul-Baha (1844–1921, Baha'u'llah's eldest son), and Shoghi Effendi (1897–1957, Abdul-Baha's eldest grandson and the last individual leader of the Baha'i community). Baha'is study these writings throughout the year and integrate readings from them in their religious services. Daily prayer is obligatory for Baha'i males over the age of fifteen, and because there are no Baha'i clergy, any member sufficiently familiar with the liturgy can lead these services.

The Baha'i religious calendar is made up of nineteen months, each of which has nineteen days, with an additional four days added to bring it into line with the solar year. The first day of each month is a feast day, consisting of both prayers and social events. Baha'is also celebrate eleven holy days, the most important of which are the birthday of the Bab (October 20) and his martyrdom (July 9) and three days marking the declaration of Baha'u'llah's divine mission in 1863 (April 21 and 29 and May 2). Like Muslims, Baha'is fast once a year (for nineteen days, from March 2 to March 20) and abstain from alcohol. Marriage and family life are important aspects of Baha'i life, and, as in most Middle Eastern societies,

Referred to as the Lotus Temple, this structure borrows its design from Hindu iconography.

parental consent is necessary for any marriage to take place and to be recognized by the community.

There are eight major Baha'i Houses of Worship, the most striking of which is the temple in New Delhi—its shape is that of a lotus flower—and an administrative center in Haifa, Israel. The Universal House of Justice is also located there, and since 1963 its elected members serve as governing body for all members of the Baha'i community. At present there are over five million Baha'is worldwide.

Unitarian Universalism

The Unitarian Universalist Association came into being in 1961 as the result of a merger of two previously independent institutions: the American Unitarian Association (founded in 1825) and the Universalist Church of America (established in 1866). Each of these religious communities represented, within the context of nineteenth-century Christianity, a radical deviation from the more familiar forms of Christian faith: the Unitarians denied the Trinity, and the Universalists denied any belief in eternal damnation. As both groups evolved, they moved closer to what we think of today as a "humanist" worldview, in which the rule of reason and the authority of science displaced religious dogmas as an acceptable basis for understanding the universe, as well as human nature. By the time of their merger, neither the Unitarians nor the Universalists saw themselves as definably (or exclusively) "Christian" any longer, though Unitarian Universalists feel free to adapt specific Christian ideas—such as the Golden Rule or the forgiveness of one's enemies—to their own developing system of ethics.

At the heart of Unitarian Universalist teachings today we find seven "principles and purposes" that constitute the spiritual core of the Association's belief system:

1. A belief in the inherent dignity and worth of every human being.
2. A need for justice, equity, and compassion in all human relationships.

3. Toleration and respect for each other as the basis for spiritual growth.
4. A need for a free and responsible search for truth and meaning.
5. The right of the individual conscience and a commitment to the democratic process.
6. The goal of a world community based on peace, liberty, and justice for all.
7. Recognition of the "web" of all living things and the interdependence of all life forms, human and nonhuman.

None of these teachings amounts to a creed. Instead, they can be viewed as guidelines for moral conduct and social relationships, accompanied by an enduring respect for the "mystery and wonder that all peoples have experienced in the presence of those forces that create and uphold life."

Unitarian Universalists have adopted a variety of rituals to embody these teachings, depending on the cultural and religious backgrounds of any particular congregation. Thus any given Unitarian Universalist community may observe some version of a Passover Seder, a Muslim Iftaar, a Buddhist meditation, or a Christmas Eve celebration (possibly combined with a winter solstice rite). Such eclecticism reflects both the openness of Unitarian Universalist society and a recognition of religious diversity, seen from a global perspective.

THE NEW ATHEISM

Strange though it may seem to conclude a discussion of modern trends and movements in religious thought with a reference to systems of *disbelief*, any analysis of contemporary spirituality would be incomplete without some recognition of a recent groundswell of oppositional voices representing those—particularly in the West—who view any and all religious ideas as delusional and politically dangerous. And although some form of atheism—understood as the denial of belief in any supernatural being or agency—has been a fact of cultural life in both the East and the West since antiquity, the term "atheist" is most commonly applied today to those who reject the idea of a God who is presumed to be the Creator of the universe and of humankind.

Since the Enlightenment of the eighteenth century, Western cultures have seen the rise of philosophical opponents of Christianity who have sought to refute the very basis of Christian faith by denying either the validity or the rationality of any and all theistic beliefs. Baron d'Holbach's (1723–1789) *The System of Nature* (1770) is an example of this type of Enlightenment atheism in its most aggressive form. His argument against religion proceeds from the belief, supported by the science of his day, that the universe consists of nothing but matter and energy. From that premise it follows, d'Holbach insists, that there is neither a soul nor an afterlife, no heaven and no hell, and that all ideas about God are really nothing but human attributes projected onto a cosmos that obeys only the laws of physics. This argument on behalf of a materialistic antitheism has been replicated and elaborated many times since d'Holbach's time, but it remains the essential narrative of atheism today. In the words of the modern

French philosopher Jean-Paul Sartre (1905–1980), atheism has left a "God-shaped hole"[11] in the cultural consciousness of the West, and nothing, he argues, has emerged to fill that void.

That was certainly the position of a number of later twentieth-century theological skeptics—known collectively as the "Death of God" movement—who took up the cry of the nineteenth-century German philosopher Friedrich Nietzsche (1844–1900) that God was "dead," at least in the sense that it was no longer possible, in the modern world, to maintain a belief in a Deity of rewards and punishments, of Creation and of a Judgment Day. In the words of one representative voice of this movement, Thomas J. J. Altizer (b. 1927):

> We shall understand the death of God as an historical event: God has died in *our* time, in *our* history, in *our* existence. The man who chooses to live in our destiny can neither know the reality of God's presence nor understand the world as his creation; or at least he can no longer respond . . . to the classical Christian images of the Creator and the creation.[12]

In contrast to their eighteenth- and nineteenth-century counterparts, these religiously oriented "atheists" hoped that old images of a transcendent, omnipotent, and benevolent deity—which, they argued, are no longer supportable in an age of scientific skepticism and mass murder—will give way to a renewed faith in creative potentialities of the human imagination. This faith-infused humanism is not Christianity, of course, nor is it really compatible with the theistic assumptions that underlie any of the Abrahamic faiths, but to its defenders it represented a response to the nihilism that followed decades of global warfare, as well as an alternative to the numbing fear that, without some form of life-affirming faith, humanity would finally succeed in exterminating itself.

More recently, a new school of polemical atheists (or "positive" atheists as they are sometimes called) have taken up d'Holbach's campaign against religion in the name of both contemporary science and enlightened political values, and unlike their Death of God predecessors, they betray no sorrow over the loss of religious conviction among their secularized contemporaries. Chief among these writers is the biologist Richard Dawkins (b. 1941), whose book *The God Delusion* (2006) offers the following critique of the claim that religious values promote human welfare:

> Religious behavior is a writ-large human equivalent of anting or bower-building. It is time-consuming, energy-consuming, often as extravagantly ornate as the plumage of a bird of paradise. Religion can endanger the life of the pious individual, as well as the lives of others. Thousands of people have been tortured for their loyalty to a religion, persecuted by zealots for what is in many cases a scarcely

distinguishable alternative faith. Religion devours resources, sometimes on a massive scale. . . . Devout people have died for their gods
and killed for them; whipped blood from their backs, sworn themselves to a lifetime of celibacy or to lonely silence, all in the service
of religion. What is it all for? What is the benefit of religion?"[13]

Obviously, for Dawkins, religion has no utility at all: it is merely a divisive social
force, and its very presence in society all but guarantees some form of conflict and,
not infrequently, sectarian violence. For Dawkins, no religion is ultimately a religion
of peace.

But on a very different level of intellectual dissent, Dawkins's objections to religion—
and those of fellow atheists such as Sam Harris (b. 1967) (*The End of Faith*, 2005) and
Daniel Dennett (b. 1942) (*Breaking the Spell*, 2006)—spring from the perception that
a religious worldview, and specifically belief in an Intelligent Designer, is simply untenable, and that science provides a truer understanding of how the universe came into
existence and how humankind evolved from less complex life forms. For centuries,
Dawkins insists, religious authorities have made pronouncements on the nature of
physical reality that have since been disproved and advanced claims of inerrancy on
behalf of their sacred texts that are no longer believable, and in any case mutually con-
tradictory. And although scientists cannot answer every question the human mind can
pose about the nature of reality, Dawkins concedes, they are bound by a self-correcting
process of inquiry that will bring us closer to truth than any dogmatic system of beliefs
that has ever been devised.

Critics of the "New Atheists," as Dawkins and those who echo his arguments have
been dubbed, often observe that the zeal and certitude that this intellectual community displays is remarkably similar to the dogmatic certainty of traditional religionists;
in place of God and revelation, these atheists (their critics say) substitute a materialist
worldview and an empirical process of inquiry, thereby turning science into a kind of
surrogate religion, with its own peculiar dogmas from which no one in the scientific
community is allowed to dissent.[14] To which defenders of the atheist position reply
that scientific theories are always open to disconfirmation, which religious beliefs are
not, and therefore any similarities between the convictions of scientists and those of
religionists are either exaggerated or mistakenly applied. Of course, the future of this
debate, like the future of the global phenomenon we have termed "religion," has yet to
be written.

CONCLUSION

The variety and multiplicity of religions in the modern world suggests that, despite
the influence of secular thought and the challenge of scientific rationalism, religious
cultures continue to be born anew, to survive and even flourish. Whatever needs
religion may be thought to satisfy—the desire to identify oneself with some greater
Being or Power, for example, or an unsatisfied curiosity about humanity's place in the

universe—the teachings and social organization of a multitude of faith communities continue to draw adherents all over the globe. Even those who are reluctant to identify themselves as persons of any particular religious faith or creed can be seen to express an interest in "spirituality" and can be numbered among readers of "New Age" publications. Certainly no one who has lived through the first decade of the twenty-first century can doubt the enduring power of religious ideas and emotions or fail to see how they continue to shape our world.

Whether future generations will see the present time as an Age of Faith or an Era of Disbelief cannot possibly be known, but the sheer diversity of religious expression, accompanied by a persistent and global tendency to reach outside of one's culture for spiritual stimulation, make predictions about the "Death of God" and the demise of religious experience improbable at best. As long as human beings search for a more-than-material existence, recognizably religious ideas and feelings are likely to survive as well.

SEEKING ANSWERS

What Is Ultimate Reality?

Virtually all of the new religious movements we have studied reveal a desire to move beyond the world of common, material existence, and many of them attempt to reach out to some higher plane of reality. The followers of Bhagwan Rajneesh (or "Osho"), for example, see the world as a place in which material and spiritual forces, or God and Nature, converge. We can create a utopian "Buddhafield," they believe, wherever human beings live "wakefully" through meditation and self-realization. Similarly, the followers of Paul Twitchell (the founder of Eckankar) believe that there are two distinct levels of reality and that through techniques of spiritual ascent we can access a higher plane of reality and release the soul from its imprisoned condition in the material world. Followers of Bhaktivedanta Prabhupada, whose teachings have their origin in Hindu mysticism, also believe that the soul can achieve release and return to its Creator—in this case the Hindu god Krishna. The Hare Krishnas, as they are commonly known, engage in devotional and meditative practices designed to raise the individual consciousness to the level of divine awareness and self-transcendence. For Christian communities, however—and especially those influenced by Adventist thought—ultimate reality is to be found in the biblical God and the soul's deepest longing is to be united to Him. That union, for Adventists, will occur once this world has vanished or been destroyed, to be replaced at last by the Kingdom of God.

How Should We Live in This World?

New religious movements emerge in response to a rapidly changing world, in which traditional certainties about society and culture are subject to swift and sometimes brutal

(continued)

challenges. Each of the broad categories of movements we have studied in this chapter has developed tenets by which adherents should live in this world and with each other. Some alternative Christianities, such as Christian Scientists, hold that human life can be made better by first acknowledging that we are spirit beings rather than simply material organisms. Only then can we draw near the Divine Mind and experience God's love in the form of real healing of body and mind. For followers of the Guru Prabhupada (or Hare Krishnas), whose beliefs are based in Eastern thought, the purest life is attained only when one has achieved Krishna consciousness, which entails a strict vegetarian diet and equally strict avoidance of such vices as alcohol, tobacco, drugs, gambling, and sexual immorality. The diversity of neopagan systems reflects the fractured state of contemporary society, with Wiccans emphasizing the need for humans to live in a respectful and harmonious relationship with the natural world, whereas Scientologists believe in the power of the human mind, assisted by specific technologies, to overcome unnecessary repression of the "true" self (or thetan) and recover those creative energies which the "reactive" mind stifles or distorts. Once free from such repression, Scientologists believe, humanity can free itself from insanity, crime, and war. The Baha'i faith looks to the perfection of social and political structures in order to help all of humanity live together peacefully, whereas the New Atheists believe that the triumph of reason over faith would allow humans to coexist peacefully without succumbing to ancient prejudices.

What Is Our Ultimate Purpose?

Virtually all religious communities invest human existence with some ultimate end or purpose, though not all rationalize that belief by appealing to the will of a Higher Power. Scientologists, for example, believe that, as a species, we have the potential to attain enlightenment and to allow the true self (or "thetan") to grow in understanding. Similarly, practitioners of Transcendental Meditation believe that the enhancement of well-being through the meditative unification of body and mind will enable all of humanity to become one with the creative intelligence that lies behind everything in the universe. For members of the Church of Jesus Christ of Latter-day Saints (or Mormons), however, the purpose of human life is defined in more nearly Christian terms: to return to the Heavenly Father after death and to even become divine oneself, by embracing the teachings of the Mormon Church. Ultimately, all people, Mormons believe, will enter one of the eternal kingdoms and enjoy immortality. Members of the Unification Church (or "Moonies"), another alternative form of Christian faith, similarly believe that the goal of life is to advance beyond our present fallen state and to enter a condition of spiritual purity, guided by the teachings of the Reverend Sun Myung Moon, whose messianic role (like that of Jesus) is to lead the world back to God.

REVIEW QUESTIONS

For Review

1. What does the term "neopagan" mean, and why is it applied to movements like Wicca?
2. What are "engrams" and how do Scientologists claim to be rid of them?
3. What is "New Thought," and which religious communities embody its principles?
4. Who are the "Moonies," and whom does the founder of this religious community claim to be?
5. Who was the founder of the Osho Rajneesh Movement, and why did that community attract so much notoriety?
6. What did nineteenth-century Unitarians and Universalists reject in traditional Christian thought?

For Further Reflection

1. How sharply do Adventist churches differ in their outlook from "mainstream" Christianity? Are they more "world renouncing" or simply closer to early Christian thought?

2. If another World Parliament of Religion were held sometime in the near future, which religious communities would you like to see invited to attend? Why?
3. What is the appeal of religious movements that focus on the personality of a powerful and charismatic leader? Are such larger-than-life figures essential to the growth of new religions?
4. Are communities that embrace some form of "Ufology" (that is, a belief in the existence of extraterrestrials) really religious organizations? Is there a difference between communicating with angels, or other spiritual beings, and talking with visitors from outer space?
5. Of all of the religious movements we have studied in this chapter, which one appears to be the most "world accommodating"? What are the advantages in belonging to such a community?

GLOSSARY

astral voyages Any visionary experience of a mind-body projection through space and time.

channeling The ability to receive and transmit messages sent by spiritual beings not of this world.

coven A community of witches.

Elohim One of several terms used in the Hebrew Bible to identify the Creator-God; the name of alien creators responsible for the creation of the human race and culture in Raelian myths.

engrams In Scientology, traumatic events stored as images in the subconscious mind.

The Family The revised name of the Children of God movement, led by David Berg until his death in 1994.

globalization Any movement, within commerce or culture, toward the internationalization of human interchange.

The Great Disappointment Disillusionment and shock following the failure, in 1844, of William Miller's prediction of the Second Advent.

ISKCON The official name of the "Hare Krishna" movement founded by A. C. Bhaktivedanta Swami.

Lughnassadh (LOO-*nus-uh*) A summer harvest festival (August 2) celebrated by Wiccans, honoring the Celtic god Lugh.

modernization Any transformation of postindustrial Western society that leads to the abandonment of traditional religious beliefs and values.

(continued)

GLOSSARY (continued)

Moonies A slang term for members of the Unification Church.

New Age An umbrella term for various religious and quasi-religious practices based on a belief in the transformation of both nature and human consciousness.

New Thought A philosophical school of thought, popular in the late nineteenth century, that stressed the power of the human mind to discover the divine within nature and to control material reality.

Osho Another name for the religious movement established by Rajneesh Chandra Mohan in the 1980s.

Second Great Awakening An evangelical movement popular in the United States from the early nineteenth century to the 1880s.

secularization Any tendency in modern society that devalues religious worldviews or seeks to substitute scientific theories for religious beliefs.

seekers A popular term, current in the late nineteenth century, for individuals who cannot find spiritual satisfaction in "mainstream" religious institutions and who describe themselves as "spiritual" rather than "religious."

thetan A term used by Scientologists to identify the immortal self and source of creativity in the human mind.

theosophy Any religious philosophy that entails communication with deceased "spiritual masters" and emphasizes the superiority of "spirit" to "matter."

Ufology Any systematized belief in extraterrestrials.

yogic flying A meditational practice, similar to levitation, attributed to members of the Transcendental Meditation community.

Wiccan Rede A traditional set of rules and ethical values cherished by Wiccans.

World's Parliament of Religions Two worldwide gatherings of religious leaders, first in Chicago in 1893 and then a larger centennial gathering, also in Chicago, in 1993.

SUGGESTIONS FOR FURTHER READING

Barrett, David V. *The New Believers*. London: Cassell & Co., 2001. A comprehensive (and often polemical) overview of alternative religious movements, with extensive historical and biographical information.

Chevannes, Barry. *Rastafari: Roots and Ideology*. New York: Syracuse University Press, 1994. A historical analysis of the development of Rastafarian culture combined with field research into contemporary Rastafarian self-understanding.

Clarke, Peter B. ed. *Encyclopedia of New Religious Movements*. London: Routledge, 2006. Brief but comprehensive essays on new religious movements, arranged alphabetically.

Clifton, Chas S. *Her Hidden Children: The Rise of Wicca and Paganism in America*. Lanham, MD: AltaMira Press, 2006. A carefully documented, chronologically organized account of paganism in North America.

Hinnells, John R., ed. *A New Handbook of Living Religions*. London: Penguin Books, 1997. A popular resource work, this provides a global view of the religious landscape with essays on all of the world's principal religions, including new religious movements in Western and non-Western cultures.

Klemp, Harold. *Autobiography of a Modern Prophet*. Minneapolis, MN: Eckankar, 2000. The present Eck Master's account of his spiritual journey toward "God-Realization."

Lachman, Gary. *Madame Blavatsky: The Mother of Modern Spirituality*. New York: Penguin Group, 2012. A thoroughly researched account of Mme. Blavatsky's spiritual development and close analysis of her writings.

Lewis, James R. ed. *The Oxford Handbook of New Religious Movements*. New York: Oxford University Press, 2004. A scholarly survey of sociological research on some of the most widely studied new religions.

Lewis, James R., and Jesper A. Petersen, eds. *Controversial New Religions*. New York: Oxford University Press, 2005. A collection of essays focusing on new religions that have exhibited violent and antisocial tendencies.

Palmer, Susan. *Aliens Adored: Rael's UFO Religion*. New Brunswick, N.J.: Rutgers University Press, 2004. Extensive background information on the UFO phenomenon, coupled with a largely sympathetic analysis of the Raelian movement.

Partridge, Christopher, ed. *New Religions: A Guide*. New York: Oxford University Press, 2004. The most extensive collection of brief scholarly vignettes of new religions, combined with lengthier articles of a historical and analytical nature. Cross-referenced and arranged by religious "families."

Roderick, Timothy. *Wicca: A Year and a Day*. Saint-Paul, MN: Llewellyn Publications, 2005. A detailed and reliable portrait of Wiccan beliefs and practices.

Schmidt, Leigh Eric. *Restless Souls: The Making of American Spirituality*. San Francisco: HarperCollins, 2005. In-depth biographical accounts of leading spokespersons for "liberal" religious causes and alternative spiritualities.

Stein, Stephen J. *Communities of Dissent: A History of Alternative Religions in America*. New York: Oxford University Press, 2003. A readable overview of religious nonconformity in nineteenth- and twentieth-century America.

ONLINE RESOURCES

Hartford Institute for Religion Research
http://hirr.hartsem.edu/denom/new_religious_movements.html
A selective website maintained by the Hartford Institute for Religion Research, which provides a wide-ranging list of NRM sites and journals.

Religious Worlds
www.religious worlds.com/new religions.html
An extensive list of websites and scholarly journals that discuss NRMs, with links to diverse textual and bibliographic sources.

NOTES

Chapter 1

1. See especially Tomoko Masuzawa, *The Invention of World Religions: Or, How European Universalism Was Preserved in the Language of Pluralism* (Chicago: University of Chicago Press, 2005).
2. See especially Immanuel Kant, *Religion within the Limits of Reason Alone*, trans. Theodore M. Greene and Hoyt H. Hudson (New York: Harper & Row, 1960).
3. Émile Durkheim, *Elementary Forms of the Religious Life*, trans. J. W. Swain (1912; repr., New York: Free Press, 1965), 62.
4. William James, *The Varieties of Religious Experience* (1902; repr., London: Penguin Books, 1985), 31.
5. Paul Tillich, *Theology of Culture*, ed. Robert C. Kimball (New York: Oxford University Press, 1959), 7–8.
6. Jonathan Z. Smith, ed., *HarperCollins Dictionary of Religion* (New York: HarperCollins, 1995), 893.
7. Bruce Lincoln, *Holy Terrors: Thinking about Religion after September 11* (Chicago: University of Chicago Press, 2003), 5–7.
8. Peter Berger, *The Sacred Canopy* (New York: Doubleday, 1967), 175.
9. Sigmund Freud, *The Future of an Illusion*, trans. James Strachey (1927; repr., New York: W. W. Norton & Company, 1961), 55.
10. Karl Marx, "Contribution to the Critique of Hegel's Philosophy of Right," in *On Religion* (Chico, CA: Scholars Press, 1964), 41–42.
11. The term "transtheistic" is used of Jainism by Heinrich Zimmer, *Philosophies of India,* ed. Joseph Campbell (Princeton, NJ: Princeton University Press, 1951), 182.
12. Mircea Eliade, *The Sacred and the Profane: The Nature of Religion*, trans. Willard Trask (London: Harcourt Brace & Company, 1959), 11.
13. Matthew 7:12.
14. *Tremendum* literally means "causing to tremble." The English term "awesome" conveys this meaning.
15. See especially Smart's *Dimensions of the Sacred: An Anatomy of the World's Beliefs* (Berkeley: University of California Press, 1999) and his earlier and very popular *Worldviews: Crosscultural Explanations of Human Belief* (New York: Scribner's, 1983), which details six of the dimensions (Smart later separated out the material dimension as a seventh).
16. Barna Group, "Number of Female Senior Pastors in Protestant Churches Doubles in Past Decade," September 14, 2009, https://www.barna.org /barna-update/leadership/304-number-of-female-senior-pastors-in-protestant-churches-doubles-in-past-decade.
17. Rice University Office of Public Affairs, "Misconceptions of Science and Religion Found in New Study," news release, February 16, 2004, http://rplp.rice.edu/uploadedFiles/RPLP/Ecklund _MediaRelease_2014_0218.pdf.
18. This analogy is drawn from Wilfred Cantwell Smith, *The Meaning and End of Religion* (San Francisco: Harper & Row, 1964), 7.

Chapter 2

1. Denise Lardner Carmody and John Tully Carmody, *Native American Religions: An Introduction* (New York: Paulist Press, 2003).
2. Dennis Tedlock, trans., *Popol Vuh: The Definitive Edition of the Mayan Book of the Dawn of Life and the Glories of Gods and Kings* (New York: Simon and Schuster, 1985).
3. Sam Gill, *Native American Religions: An Introduction* (Belmont, CA: Wadsworth/Thomson Learning, 2005).
4. Sam Gill, *Sacred Worlds: A Study of Navajo Religion and Prayer* (London: Greenwood Press, 1981), 54–55.
5. John D. Loftin, *Religion and Hopi Life* (Bloomington: Indiana University Press, 2003), 110.
6. Richard Erdoes and Alfonso Ortiz, *American Indian Myths and Legends* (New York: Pantheon Books, 1984), 346.
7. Gill, *Native American Religions*, 64.
8. Ibid., 96.
9. Tedlock, *Popol Vuh*.
10. John Neihardt and Black Elk, *Black Elk Speaks: Being an Account of the Life of a Holy Man of the Oglala Sioux* (Lincoln, NE: University of Nebraska Press, 1972), 1.
11. Erdoes and Ortiz, *American Indian Myths and Legends*, 85.

12. Joseph Epes Brown, *Teaching Spirits: Understanding Native American Religious Tradition* (London: Oxford University Press, 2001), 87.

13. Keith Basso, *Wisdom Sits in Places: Landscape and Language among the Western Apache* (Albuquerque: University of New Mexico Press, 1996).

14. Brown, *Teaching Spirits*, 36.

15. Ibid., 13.

16. Ibid., 15.

17. Ibid., 49.

18. Thomas J. Nevins and M. Eleanor Nevins, "'We Have Always Had the Bible': Christianity and the Composition of White Mountain Apache Heritage," *Heritage Management* 2, no. 1 (2009): 11–34.

19. Ibid.

20. Helen McCarthy, "Assaulting California's Sacred Mountains: Shamans vs. New Age Merchants of Nirvana" in *Beyond Primitivism: Indigenous Religions and Modernity,* ed. Jacob Olopuna (New York: Routledge, 2004), 172–178.

21. Arlene Hirschfelder and Paulette Molin, *An Encyclopedia of Native American Religions* (New York: Facts on File Ltd., 1992), 176.

22. Annemarie Shimony, "Iroquois Religion and Women in Historical Perspective," in *Women, Religion and Social Change,* ed. Y. Haddad and E. Finley (Albany, NY: State University of New York Press, 1985), 412.

23. Hirschfelder and Molin, *Encyclopedia of Native American Religions,* 130, 328.

24. Greg Sarris, *Mabel McKay: Weaving the Dream* (Berkeley: University of California Press, 1997).

25. Gill, *Native American Religions*, 98.

26. Ibid., 72.

27. Brown, *Teaching Spirits*, 17.

28. Carmody and Carmody, *Native American Religions,* 73.

29. Hirschfelder and Molin, *Encyclopedia of Native American Religions*, 287.

30. Loftin, *Religion and Hopi Life*, 37.

31. Gill, *Native American Religions*.

Chapter 3

1. Tepilit Ole Saitoti, *Worlds of a Maasai Warrior: An Autobiography* (Berkeley: University of California Press, 1988), 67.

2. Ibid., 69.

3. Ibid., 71.

4. Bilinda Straight, *Miracles and Extraordinary Experience in Northern Kenya* (Philadelphia: University of Pennsylvania Press, 2009), 56.

5. Marcel Griaule, *Conversations with Ogotemmeli* (London: Oxford University Press, 1965).

6. Rowland Abiodun, "Hidden Power: Osun, the Seventeenth Odu," in *Osun Across the Waters: A Yoruba Goddess in Africa and the Americas*, ed. Joseph M. Murphy and Mei-Mei Sanford (Bloomington: Indiana University Press, 2001), 17–18.

7. E. E. Evans-Pritchard, *Nuer Religion* (London: Oxford University Press, 1971).

8. John S. Mbiti, *African Religions and Philosophy* (New York: Praeger, 1969), 85–86.

9. Ibid., 89–90.

10. Ibid., 84–85.

11. Ibid., 92.

12. Benjamin C. Ray, *African Religions: Symbol, Ritual, and Community* (Upper Saddle River, NJ: Prentice Hall, 2000), 170–171.

13. Ibid., 61.

14. Ibid., 171.

15. Ibid., 184–191.

16. Ibid., 85–88.

17. Ibid., 53.

18. Adeline Masquelier, *Prayer Has Spoiled Everything: Possession, Power and Identity in an Islamic Town of Niger* (Durham, NC: Duke University Press, 2002).

19. Ibid.

20. E. E. Evans-Pritchard, *Witchcraft, Oracles and Magic among the Azande* (London: Oxford University Press, 1976).

21. Ray, *African Religions*, 58–59, citing Edith Turner, *Experiencing Ritual* (Philadelphia: University of Pennsylvania Press, 1992).

22. Mbiti, *African Religions and Philosophy*, 113.

23. Ibid., 114–115.

24. Ibid., 120.

25. Margaret Drewal, *Yoruba Ritual: Performers, Play, Agency* (Bloomington: Indiana University Press, 1992), 53.

26. Jack Goody, *Death, Property and the Ancestors: A Study of the Mortuary Customs of the LoDagaa of West Africa* (Palo Alto, CA: Stanford University Press, 1962), 239.

27. Ray, *African Religions*, 102–103.

28. For example, Marion Kilson, "Women in African Traditional Religions," *Journal of Religion in Africa* 8, no. 2 (1976): 133–143.

29. Paula Girshick Ben-Amos, "The Promise of Greatness: Women and Power in a Benin Spirit Possession Cult," in *Religion in Africa: Experience and Expression*, ed. T. D. Blakely, W. E. A. Van Beek, and D. L. Thomson (London: James Currey, 1994).

30. Cynthia Hoehler-Fatton, "Christianity: Independent and Charismatic Churches in Africa," in

Encyclopedia of Africa, ed. K. A. Appiah and H. L. Gates (New York: Oxford University Press, 2010), 273–274.

31. Brigid M. Sackey, *New Directions in Gender and Religion: The Changing Status of Women in African Independent Churches* (Lanham, MD: Lexington Books, 2006), 30–32.

32. Hoehler-Fatton, "Christianity," 273.

33. Beverly B. Mack and Jean Boyd, *One Woman's Jihad: Nana Asma'u, Scholar and Scribe* (Bloomington: Indiana University Press, 2000).

34. Ellen Gruenbaum, *The Female Circumcision Controversy: An Anthropological Perspective* (Philadelphia: University of Pennsylvania Press, 2000).

35. Ray, *African Religions,* 198.

Chapter 4

1. *Brhadaranyaka Upanishad* 3.9.1–2. In Sarvepalli Radhakrishnan and Charles A. Moore, *A Sourcebook in Indian Philosophy* (Princeton, NJ: Princeton University Press, 1957), 85.

2. Sarvepalli Radhakrishnan and Charles A. Moore, *A Sourcebook in Indian Philosophy* (Princeton, NJ: Princeton University Press, 1957), 77.

3. *Bhagavad Gita* 4:6–8. In Laurie L. Patton, trans., *The Bhagavad Gita* (London: Penguin Books, 2008), 50–51.

4. David M. Knipe, *Hinduism: Experiments in the Sacred* (New York: HarperCollins, 1991), 44–45. The passage appears repeatedly in the *Chandogya Upanishad* 6.9–6.13.

5. *Bhagavad Gita* 2.71. In Radhakrishnan and Moore, *Sourcebook in Indian Philosophy,* 112.

6. *Bhagavad Gita* 5.11–12. In Barbara Stoler Miller, trans., *The Bhagavad-Gita: Krishna's Counsel in Time of War* (New York: Bantam Books, 1986), 60.

7. *Bhagavad Gita* 12.6–8. In Miller, *Bhagavad-Gita,* 110.

8. *Bhagavad Gita* 4.38–39. In Radhakrishnan and Moore, *Sourcebook in Indian Philosophy,* 118–119.

9. *Laws of Manu* II.36. In Radhakrishnan and Moore, *Sourcebook in Indian Philosophy,* 177.

10. An oft-quoted line from Major-General Charles Stuart's (1758–1828) *Vindication of the Hindoos,* which was published in 1808.

11. Diana Eck, *Darsan: Seeing the Divine Image in India* (New York: Columbia University Press, 1998).

12. *Laws of Manu* III.56. In Radhakrishnan and Moore, *Sourcebook in Indian Philosophy,* 189.

Chapter 5

1. "The Global Religious Landscape," December 18, 2012, Pew Research Religion and Public Life Project, www.pewforum.org/2012/12/18/global-religious-landscape-exec/.

2. This term is used of Jainism by Heinrich Zimmer, *Philosophies of India,* ed. Joseph Campbell (Princeton, NJ: Princeton University Press, 1951), 182.

3. Henry Clarke Warren, *Buddhism in Translations* (New York: Atheneum, 1984), 109.

4. Richard H. Robinson and Willard L. Johnson, *The Buddhist Religion: A Historical Introduction,* 3rd ed. (Belmont, CA: Wadsworth, 1982), 40.

5. Juan Mascaró, trans. *The Dhammapada: The Path of Perfection* (London and New York: Penguin Books, 1973), 35.

6. Stephen Beyer, *The Cult of Tara: Magic and Ritual in Tibet* (Berkeley: University of California Press, 1973), 92.

7. "Flash Animated Philosophy from South Park Creators," coldhardflash.com/2007/07/flash-animated-philosophy-from-south.html.

8. Anne Bancroft, *Zen: Direct Pointing to Reality* (New York: Thames and Hudson, 1979), 5.

9. See, for instance, Bernard Faure, "Buddhism and Violence," December 6, 2003, sangam.org/articles/view/?id=118.

Chapter 6

1. *Acarangasutra* 1.4.1.1–2, trans. Hermann Jacobi. In *Sacred Books of the East,* vol. 20, ed. Friedrich Max Müller (Oxford: Oxford University Press, 1884).

2. Yogendra Jain, *Jain Way of Life: A Guide to Compassionate, Healthy, and Happy Living* (Boston: Federation of Jain Associations of North America, 2007), i.

3. *Tattvarthadhigama Sutra,* Chapter II, 22–23, trans. J. L. Jaini. In *A Sourcebook in Indian Philosophy,* ed. Sarvepalli Radhakrishnan and Charles A. Moore (Princeton, NJ: Princeton University Press, 1957), 254.

4. This term is used of Jainism by Heinrich Zimmer, *Philosophies of India,* ed. Joseph Campbell (Princeton, NJ: Princeton University Press, 1951), 182.

5. Paul Dundas, *The Jains* (New York: Routledge, 1992), 47; the text referenced here is the *Sthānānga* 171.

6. *Avashyakasutra* 32; cited in Dundas, *The Jains,* 171.

7. Dundas, *The Jains,* 55–56; the text referenced here is the *Kalpasutra.*

8. Padmanabh S. Jaini, *The Jaina Path of Purification* (Berkeley: University of California Press, 1979), 196–197.

Chapter 7

1. Gurinder Singh Mann, *Sikhism* (Upper Saddle River, NJ: Prentice Hall), 14.
2. Hew McLeod, *Sikhism* (London: Penguin, 1997), 219.
3. Adapted from a quotation in W. Owen Cole and Piara Singh Sambhi, *The Sikhs: Their Religious Beliefs and Practices* (London: Routledge & Kegan Paul, 1978), 9.
4. Quoted in ibid., 10.
5. Quoted in Khushwant Singh, "Sikhism," *Encyclopedia of Religion* (New York: Simon & Schuster Macmillan, 1995), 13:316.
6. Quoted in ibid., 316.
7. From *Puratan Janam-sakhi*, cited in W. H. McLeod, ed. and trans., *Textual Sources for the Study of Sikhism* (Totowa, NJ: Barnes & Noble Books, 1984), 25.
8. Khushwant Singh, "Sikhism," 319.
9. Cited in McLeod, *Sikhism*, 271.
10. Cited in ibid., 272.
11. Ibid., 98.
12. Gopal Singh, *A History of the Sikh People* (New Delhi, India: World Sikh University Press, 1979), 263–264.
13. Teja Singh and Ganda Singh, *A Short History of the Sikhs: Volume One (1469–1765)*, 3rd ed. (Patiala, India: Punjabi University, 1999), 67.
14. Mann, *Sikhism*, 14.
15. Ibid.
16. Cited in W. H. McLeod, *Textual Sources,* 79–80.
17. Cited in Hew McLeod, *Sikhism*, 216.
18. *Āsā ki Vār* 19:2, Adi Granth, 473. Cited in W. H. McLeod, *Textual Sources*, 109.
19. Mann, *Sikhism*, 106.

Chapter 8

1. All Chinese names in this chapter are indicated in the conventional Chinese manner, namely, the family name comes first, followed by the given name. All romanization of Chinese terms and names adheres to the official Chinese pinyin system. Terms and names with an established familiar spelling in the West, such as Taoism (instead of the official pinyin rendition of Daoism) are provided in parentheses at their first occurrence.
2. See Joseph Needham, ed., *Science and Civilization in China* (Cambridge, UK: Cambridge University Press, 1956), 2:55ff.
3. This term is not found in the *Book of Changes* itself but is in fact a later Daoist rendition of the idea of the primordial one.
4. Refer to the highly suggestive article of David N. Keightley, "The Religious Commitment: Shang Theology and the Genesis of Chinese Political Culture," *History of Religions* 17, nos. 3–4 (Feb.–May 1978): 211–225.
5. Also translated as *Book of Songs* or *Book of Poetry*.
6. Also known as the *Book of Documents*.
7. The masculine pronoun is used advisedly throughout the entire discussion of Confucian teachings. Confucius and his intellectual followers after him, like many in the premodern age worldwide, did not seriously entertain the possibility that women could participate meaningfully in the exercise of virtue, pursuit of scholarship, and service in government. The masculine pronoun is adopted not as an endorsement of that view but as a faithful reflection of the Confucian assumption.
8. William Theodore de Bary, *Neo-Confucian Orthodoxy and the Learning of the Mind-and-Heart* (New York: Columbia University Press, 1981), 9.
9. See Tu Wei-ming, "Li as a Process of Humanization," in *Philosophy East and West* 22, no. 2 (April 1972): 187–201.
10. See Herbert Fingarette's *Confucius: The Secular as Sacred* (New York: Harper Torchbooks, 1972), 7.
11. See Xinzhong Yao, *An Introduction to Confucianism* (Cambridge, UK: Cambridge University Press, 2000), 46.
12. See the highly nuanced discussion of the topic by Li-Hsiang Lisa Rosenlee, in her *Confucianism and Women: A Philosophical Interpretation* (Albany: State University of New York Press, 2006). See also Chenyang Li, ed., *The Sage and the Second Sex: Confucianism, Ethics, and Gender* (Chicago: Open Court, 2000). Deborah Achtenberg's "Aristotelian Resources in Feminist Thinking," in *Feminism and Ancient Philosophy*, ed. Julie K. Ward (London: Routledge, 1996), 97, is also very suggestive.
13. Many Chinese books carry the name of their supposed author as their title. To distinguish between the text and its reputed author, the former will be indicated in italics.
14. This discussion of *feng* and *shan* rites is based on Stephen Bokenkamp's "Record of the Feng and Shan Sacrifices," in *Religions of China in Practice*, ed. Donald S. Lopez Jr. (Princeton, NJ: Princeton University Press, 1996), 251–260.
15. Summary based on Patricia Buckley Ebrey, ed., *Chinese Civilization: A Sourcebook*, 2nd ed. (New York: Free Press, 1993), 157–163.
16. This summary of the *jiao* liturgy is based on a composite description of two separate ceremonies conducted, respectively, in 1994 and 2005 in Hong

Kong. A DVD depicting the rites and explaining their religious meaning was produced in 2009 by the Center for the Study of Daoist Culture of the Department of Culture and Religion, Chinese University of Hong Kong.

Chapter 9

1. This "body" is known as the *shintai*, the physical embodiment of the deity, which is believed to contain the spirit and magical power of the deity. It is discussed in greater detail in the section on the teachings of Shinto.
2. Quoted in H. Byron Earhart, *Religion in the Japanese Experience: Sources and Interpretations*, 2nd ed. (Belmont, CA: Wadsworth, 1997), 10.
3. That the Japanese should regard the sun as female is most noteworthy. That this female sun goddess should serve as the primordial ancestor of the imperial line, as is discussed later, is even more significant, for it is incongruent with the later patriarchal orientation of the country.
4. The *Nihongi* has a slightly different version of this episode. It asserts that the three deities are the product of the union between Izanagi and Izanami.
5. Quoted in William Theodore de Bary et al., eds., *Sources of Japanese Tradition* (New York: Columbia University Press, 2001), 1:259.
6. Quoted in de Bary et al., eds., *Sources of Japanese Tradition* (New York: Columbia University Press, 2005), 2:498, 512.
7. See Evan Zuesse, *Ritual Cosmos* (Athens: Ohio University Press, 1979), 402.

Chapter 10

1. This chart is a modification of that presented in Jenny Rose, *Zoroastrianism: An Introduction* (London and New York: I. B. Tauris, 2011), 7.
2. Mary Boyce, ed. and trans., *Textual Sources for the Study of Zoroastrianism* (Manchester, UK: Manchester University Press, 1984), 35.
3. Boyce, *Textual Sources,* 48.

Chapter 11

1. Richard Rubenstein, *The Cunning of History* (New York: Harper and Row), 90–97.
2. Martin Buber, *The Eclipse of God: Studies in the Relation Between Religion and Philosophy* (New York: Harper and Row, 1957), 13–24.
3. See Roger Kamenetz, *Stalking Elijah: Adventures with Today's Jewish Mystical Masters* (San Francisco: HarperSanFrancisco, 1998), for an engaging

first-person perspective on the Renewal Movement in Judaism. A more scholarly approach can be found in George W. Wilkes, "Jewish Renewal," in *Modern Judaism: An Oxford Guide,* ed. Nicholas de Lange and Miri Freud-Kandel (Oxford, UK: Oxford University Press, 2005), 114–125.

4. Stephen Hodge, *The Dead Sea Scrolls Rediscovered* (Berkeley, CA: Ulysses Press, 2003), 158–210.
5. Paula Fredricksen, *From Jesus to Christ: The Origins of the New Testament Images of Jesus* (New Haven, CT: Yale University Press, 1988), 160–176.
6. Wayne A. Meeks and Robert L. Wilken, *Jews and Christians in Antioch: In the First Four Centuries of the Common Era* (Missoula, MT: Scholars Press, 1978), 85–126.
7. Ignaz Maybaum, "The Face of God After Auschwitz," in *Holocaust Theology: A Reader,* ed. Dan Cohn-Sherbok (New York: New York University Press, 2002), 96–98.
8. Richard Rubenstein, *After Auschwitz: History, Theology, and Contemporary Judaism* (Baltimore: Johns Hopkins Press, 1992), 171–174.
9. Eliezer Berkovits, "Free Will and the Hidden God," in *Holocaust Theology*, 153–156.
10. Abraham Joshua Heschel, "No Religion Is an Island," in *Moral Grandeur and Spiritual Audacity,* ed. Susannah Heschel (New York: Farrar, Straus and Giroux, 1997), 235–250.
11. Emil L. Fackenheim, *The Jewish Return into History* (New York: Schocken Books, 1978), 129–143. See also *God's Presence in History* (New York: Harper and Row, 1970), 67–79, for Fackenheim's reflections on the significance of the Shoah as the pivotal event in modern Jewish history.
12. Arthur Hertzberg, ed., *The Zionist Idea* (New York: Atheneum, 1984), 103–114.
13. Theodor Herzl, "The Jewish State," *The Zionist Idea,* 204–230.
14. Theodor Herzl, *The Old New Land,* trans. Lotta Levensohn (Princeton, NJ: Marcus Wiener, 2000).
15. "The Balfour Declaration," in *The Jew in the Modern World,* ed. Paul Mendes-Flohr and Jehuda Reinharz (Oxford, UK: Oxford University Press, 1995), 582. See also, Jonathan Schneer, *The Balfour Declaration* (New York: Random House, 2010).
16. Renee Kogel and Zev Katz, eds., *Judaism in a Secular Age* (New York: KTAV Publishing, 1995), 228–234.
17. Sherwin Wine, "Secular Humanistic Jewish Ideology," in *Judaism in a Secular Age,* 235–250.
18. Rachel Adler, *Engendering Judaism* (Boston: Beacon Press, 1998), 61–103.

Chapter 12

All translations from the New Testament are from the New Revised Standard Version of the Bible.

1. Augustine, *Confessions* 1.1. Author's translation.
2. Timothy (Kallistos) Ware, *The Orthodox Church* (New York: Penguin Books, 1997), 261.
3. This later view was informed by New Testament images of a "furnace of fire" (Matthew 13:42) and "lake of fire" (Revelation 21:8).
4. *Declaration on Non-Christian Religions*, no. 2, quoted in Anthony Wilhelm, *Christ among Us*, 2nd ed. (New York: Paulist Press, 1975), 396.
5. Clement of Alexandria, *Stromata* 1.5.28. Author's translation.
6. Maximus the Confessor, *Book of Ambiguities* 41, quoted in Vladimir Lossky, *The Mystical Theology of the Eastern Church* (London: James Clarke, 1957), 214. The idea that Christians participate in the divine nature is found in the New Testament (for example, in 2 Peter 1:4) and is supported by the doctrine that the Holy Spirit is at work in every believer (e.g., in Romans 8).
7. Julian of Norwich, *Revelations of Divine Love* 4 (short text), in *Julian of Norwich: Showings*, trans. E. Colledge and J. Walsh (New York: Paulist Press, 1978), 131.
8. "The Religious Composition of the United States," Pew Forum on Religion and Public Life/U.S. Religious Landscape Survey, at religions.pewforum.org/pdf/report-religious-landscape-study-chapter-1.pdf.
9. James Cone, *Black Theology and Black Power* (New York: Seabury, 1969), 35.
10. Quoted in Ware, *The Orthodox Church*, 305.
11. See Orazio Marucchi, *Christian Epigraphy*, trans. J. Willis (Chicago: Ares Press, 1974), 153–155.

Chapter 13

All translations from the Qur'an are from Ahmed Ali, trans., *al-Qur'an* (Princeton, NJ: Princeton University Press, 1993).

1. The Association of Religion Data Archives, thearda.com, accessed June 2014.
2. Ibid.
3. Ali, *al-Qur'an*.
4. Frederick Mathewson Denny, *An Introduction to Islam* (New York: Pearson Prentice Hall, 2006), 174–175.
5. Ali, *al-Qur'an*.
6. Ibid.
7. Denny, *An Introduction to Islam*, 110–111.
8. William A. Graham, *Divine Word and Prophetic Word in Early Islam* (The Hague and Paris: Mouton, 1977), 157.
9. John R. Bowen, *Muslims through Discourse* (Princeton, NJ: Princeton University Press, 1993).
10. Denny, *An Introduction to Islam*, 110–111.
11. Abdallah al-Shiekh, "Zakat," in *Oxford Encyclopedia of the Modern Islamic World* (New York: Oxford University Press, 1995), 366–370.
12. Sherman A. Jackson, *Islam and the Black American: Looking Toward the Third Resurrection* (New York: Oxford University Press, 2005).
13. Malcolm X, *The Autobiography of Malcolm X: As Told to Alex Haley* (New York: Ballantine Books, 1965).
14. *Mathnawi* V, 411–414. In *The Rumi Collection*, trans. Kabir Helminski (Boston: Shambala Press, 2005), 165.
15. Ali, *al-Qur'an*.
16. Leila Ahmed, *Women and Gender in Islam* (New Haven, CT: Yale University Press, 1992).

Chapter 14

1. We have deliberately avoided using the terms "cult" and "sect" to describe the various religious communities discussed in this chapter and instead have adopted the more neutral phrases "new religious movements" and "alternative religions," chiefly because of the stigma that has been associated with groups designated as "cults" since the 1970s. As employed by contemporary sociologists, however, the word "sect" commonly describes a subgroup within an established religious community, whereas a "cult" is an innovative religious organization that exists outside of any established structure. Where appropriate, however, we have noted the pejorative use of the word "cult" when it is used in criticism of a particular movement or figure.
2. Stephen Stein, *Communities of Dissent: A History of Alternative Religions in America* (Oxford, UK: Oxford University Press, 2003).
3. J. Gordon Melton, "Modern Alternative Religions in the West," in *A New Handbook of Living Religions*, ed. John R. Hinnells (London: Penguin Books, 1997).
4. Roy Wallis, *The Elementary Forms of Religious Life* (London: Routledge and Kegan Paul, 1984).
5. Peter B. Clarke, ed., *Encyclopedia of New Religious Movements* (London: Routledge, 2006).
6. Gary Lachman, *Madame Blavatsky: The Mother of Modern Spirituality* (New York: Penguin Group, 2012), 134.

7. Various etymologies for this term have been proposed, from William James's neologism "oceanic" (meaning, in this context, "One who embraces all that exists") to the Japanese term for "king" in the game of Go.

8. David V. Barrett, *The New Believers: A Survey of Sects, Cults, and Alternative Religions* (London: Cassell, 2001), 293.

9. Christopher Partridge, ed., *New Religions: A Guide* (Oxford, UK: Oxford University Press, 2004), 184.

10. See Janet Treitman, *Inside Scientology* (Boston: Houghton Mifflin Harcourt, 2011). Treitman's study of the organizational history and dynamics of Scientology is the most complete to date.

11. See Karen Armstrong, *The Battle for God* (New York: Ballantine Books, 2001), 199.

12. Thomas J. J. Altizer and William Hamilton, *Radical Theology and the Death of God* (New York: Bobbs-Merrill, 1966), 95.

13. Richard Dawkins, *The God Delusion* (Boston: Houghton Mifflin, 2006), 164–165.

14. See William A. Stahl, "One-Dimensional Rage: The Social Epistemology of the New Atheism and Fundamentalism," in *Religion and the New Atheism: A Critical Appraisal*, ed. Amarnath Amarasingam (Leiden: Brill, 2010), 97–108.

GLOSSARY

Abbasids An important Muslim empire from 750 to 1258 C.E.

adhan (a-than; Arabic) The call to prayer.

Adi Granth (ah'dee gruhnth; Punjabi, "first book") Sikhism's most important sacred text and, since the death of Guru Gobind Singh in 1708, Sikhism's primary earthly authority; traditionally known as Sri Guru Granth Sahib.

ahimsa (ah-him'suh; Sanskrit, "nonviolence," "not desiring to harm") Both the avoidance of violence toward other life forms and an active sense of compassion toward them; a basic principle of Jainism, Hinduism, and Buddhism.

Ahura Mazda (uh-hoo'rah moz'dah; "Wise Lord") The God of Zoroastrianism; also known as Ohrmazd.

Aisha A beloved wife of Muhammad who is known for transmitting many *hadith*.

ajiva (uh-jee'vuh; Sanskrit, "nonsoul") Nonliving components of the Jain universe: space, time, motion, rest, and all forms of matter.

Allah (a-lah; Arabic) The Arabic term for God.

Amaterasu (ah-mah'-te-rah'-soo) "Deity that shines in the sky," the Sun Goddess in Shinto. Enshrined at Ise, Amaterasu is the *kami* of the imperial family. As the Sun Goddess, she is the most august of all deities. Her descendants are considered the only rightful rulers of Japan.

American Indian Religious Freedom Act 1978 U.S. law to guarantee freedom of religious practice for Native Americans.

Amesha Spentas (ah-mesh'-ah spent'ahs; "Beneficial Immortals") Seven angels—including Spenta Mainyu, the Holy Spirit of Ahura Mazda—who help Ahura Mazda govern creation.

Amma (ah-ma; Dogon) The High God of the Dogon people.

amrit (ahm-reet; Punjabi, "immortalizing fluid") A special drink made from water and sugar crystals, used in the Khalsa initiation ceremony.

anatman (un-aat-mun; Sanskrit) The doctrine that there is no independent, eternal self or soul underlying personal existence.

Angra Mainyu (ang'grah mine'yoo; "Foul Spirit") Evil adversary of Ahura Mazda; also called Ahriman.

apostle In the New Testament, Jesus's disciples, sent out to preach and baptize, are called apostles (Greek *apostolos*, "one who is sent out"). Paul of Tarsus and some other early Christian leaders also claimed this title. Because of their close association with Jesus, the apostles were accorded a place of honor in the early Church.

apostolic succession According to this Roman Catholic and Orthodox doctrine, the spiritual authority conferred by Jesus on the apostles has been transmitted through an unbroken line of bishops, who are their successors.

arati (aah-ra-tee) Worship with light, involving the waving of a lamp in front of the deity.

arhat (ar'hut) In Theravada Buddhism, one who has attained enlightenment.

asha (ah'shah) The true, cosmic order that pervades both the natural and social spheres of reality, encompassing the moral and religious life of individuals; opposed to *druj*.

Ashura The tenth day of the month of Muharram, recognized by Shi'a Muslims as the anniversary of the martyrdom of Husayn.

astral voyages Any visionary experience of a mind/body projection through space and time.

atheism Perspective that denies the existence of God or gods.

atman (aat-mun; Sanskrit) The eternal self or soul that is successively reincarnated until released from *samsara* through *moksha*.

avatar (ah-vah-taahr; from Sanskrit *avatara*) A "descent" of God (usually Vishnu) to earth in a physical form with the specific goal of aiding the world.

Avesta The oldest and most important of Zoroastrian scriptures, consisting of a collection of texts including the *Yasna* and *Gathas*.

axis mundi (ax-is mun-di; Latin) An academic term for the center of the world, which connects the earth with the heavens.

Baal Shem Tov (1698–1760) A charismatic faith-healer, mystic, and teacher (whose given name was Israel ben Eliezer) who is generally regarded as the founder of the Hasidic movement.

baptism Performed by immersion in water or a sprinkling with water, baptism is a sacrament in which an individual is cleansed of sin and admitted into the Church.

Bar/Bat Mitzvah A rite of passage for adolescents in Judaism, the *Bar Mitzvah* (for males age thirteen) and the *Bat Mitzvah* (for females ages twelve to thirteen) signal their coming of age and the beginning of adult religious responsibility.

bhakti marga (bhah-k-tee mar-guh; Sanskrit) The path of devotion.

bishop Responsible for supervising other priests and their congregations within specific regions known as dioceses, bishops are regarded by Roman Catholic and Orthodox Christians as successors of the apostles.

Black Elk Famous Lakota religious leader.

bodhichitta (bow-dhi-chit-ta; Sanskrit, "the awakening mind or heart") In Mahayana Buddhism, the wise and compassionate intention to attain Buddhahood for the sake of all other sentient beings.

bodhisattva (bow-dhi-sut-tva; Sanskrit, "enlightenment being") One who is on the verge of enlightenment. In Mahayana Buddhism, a bodhisattva is one who has taken a "bodhisattva vow" to remain in samsara in order to work for the enlightenment of all sentient beings.

bori (boh-ree; various languages) A term for West African spirits.

Brahman (braah-mun; Sanskrit, "expansive") For monistic Hinduism, the supreme, unitary reality, the ground of all Being; for dualistic Hinduism, *Brahman* can refer to the supreme God (e.g., Vishnu).

brahmin (braah-mun; Sanskrit) A member of the priestly class of the *varna* or caste system.

Buddha (bood-dha; Sanskrit, "the Awakened One") A fully enlightened being.

caliph (ka-lif; Arabic) Leader of the Muslim community after the death of Muhammad.

Calvin, John (1509–1564) One of the leading figures of the Protestant Reformation, Calvin is notable for his *Institutes of the Christian Religion* and his emphasis on the absolute power of God, the absolute depravity of human nature, and the absolute dependence of human beings on divine grace for salvation.

Candomblé New World religion with roots in West Africa—particularly Yoruba culture—which is prominent in Brazil.

Chan/Zen (Chinese/Japanese) Respectively, the Chinese and Japanese names for the "meditation" school of Buddhism that values meditative experience far and above doctrine.

Changing Woman Mythic ancestor of the Navajo people who created the first humans.

channeling The ability to receive and transmit messages sent by spiritual beings not of this world.

chantway The basis of Navajo ceremonial practice; includes chants, prayers, songs, and other ritual practice.

Chinvat Bridge The bridge that needs to be crossed by the soul in order to reach the afterlife, wide and easy to cross for the good, razor-thin and impossible to cross for the evil.

Christmas An annual holiday commemorating the birth of Jesus, Christmas is observed by Western Christians on December 25. Although many Orthodox Christians celebrate Christmas on this date, others observe the holiday on January 7.

church In the broadest sense, "church" refers to the universal community of Christians, but the term can also refer to a particular tradition within Christianity (such as the Roman Catholic Church or the Lutheran Church) or to an individual congregation of Christians.

cosmology Understanding of the nature of the world that typically explains its origin and how it is ordered.

coven A community of witches.

Covenant A biblical concept that describes the relationship between God and the Jews in contractual terms, often thought of as an eternal bond between the Creator and the descendants of the ancient Israelites.

Daena (die'nuh) The feminine being who embodies the individual's ethical quality and who appears to the soul after death.

daevas (die'vuhs) The various demonic powers aligned with Angra Mainyu.

dalit (daah-lit; Sanskrit, "oppressed"; Marathi, "broken") Self-designation of people who had traditionally been classified as untouchables or outcastes.

dama (dah-ma; Dogon) A Dogon rite of passage marking the transition to adulthood and to the afterlife.

dana (dah'nuh; Sanskrit, Pali, "giving") Ritual of giving.

dantian (dahn'-tee'ən) "Fields for the refinement of the immortal pill"; major nodal points in the human body where the "pill" of immortality can be refined through alchemical means.

dao (dow) A fundamental concept in Chinese religion, literally meaning the "path" or the "way." In Confucianism, it specifically refers to the entire ideal human order ordained by the numinous Absolute, *Tian*. In Daoism, it is the primary source of the cosmos, the very ground of all beings.

Daodejing (dow'-duh-jing) Basic Daoist scripture, lit. "The Scripture of the Way and Its Potent Manifestation"; also known as the Book of *Laozi*, the name of its purported author.

Daozang (dow' zahng) Literally "Treasury of the Dao," this is the Daoist Canon that contains the entire corpus of Daoist texts. The most complete version, still in use today, was first published in 1445.

darshan (dur-shaan; Sanskrit, "to see") Worship through simultaneously seeing and being seen by a deity in the presence of its image.

de (duh) Another fundamental concept in Chinese religions, meaning "virtue" or "potency." In Confucianism, it is the charismatic power of the ruler or the man of virtue, while in Daoism it means the concrete manifestation of the *dao*.

Dead Sea Scrolls Religious literature hidden in caves near the shores of the Dead Sea (c. second–first centuries B.C.E.).

dharma/**Dharma** (dhur-mah; Sanskrit) Duty, righteousness, "religion"; basis for living in a way that upholds cosmic and social order. In the Buddhist context, Dharma refers both to Buddhist teaching and Buddhism as a religion.

Diaspora A Greek word in origin, it refers to those Jewish communities that live outside of the historical land of Israel.

Digambara (dig-ahm'buh-ruh; Sanskrit, "those whose garment is the sky") The second largest Jain sect, whose monks go about naked so as to help abolish any ties to society; generally more conservative than the Shvetambara sect.

divination The attempt to learn about events that will happen in the future through supernatural means.

druj (drooj; Avestan, "lie") Cosmic principle of chaos and evil, opposed to *asha*.

dualism In Zoroastrianism, of two types: cosmic dualism of order and chaos (or good and evil); dualism of spirit and matter (or thought and body).

dukkha (doo-kah; Pali, "suffering") Usually translated as "suffering," it can also be understood as the anxiety, unease, and dissatisfaction caused by desire.

Easter An annual holiday commemorating the resurrection of Christ, Easter is a "moveable feast" whose date changes from year to year, though it is always celebrated in spring (as early as March 22 and as late as May 8).

election The belief that the biblical God "chose" the people of Israel to be His "kingdom of priests" and a "holy nation." This biblical concept is logically connected to the idea of the Covenant, and it entails the belief that the Jews' relationship with God obliges them to conform to His laws and fulfill His purposes in the world.

Elohim One of several terms used in the Hebrew Bible to identify the Creator-God; the name of alien creators responsible for the creation of the human race and culture in Raelian myths.

ema (ə-mah') Wooden tablets expressing pleadings to *kami* for success in life.

empathy The capacity for seeing things from another's perspective, and an important methodological approach for studying religions.

engrams In Scientology, traumatic events stored as images in the subconscious mind.

Epiphany An annual holiday commemorating the "manifestation" of the divinity of the infant Jesus, Epiphany is celebrated by most Western Christians on January 6. Most Eastern Christians observe it on January 19.

eschatological Any belief in an "End-Time" of divine judgment and world destruction.

ethical monotheism A core concept of Judaism: it is the belief that the world was created and is governed by only one transcendent Being, whose ethical attributes provide an ideal model for human behavior.

eucharist (*yoó-ka-rist*) Also known as the Lord's Supper and Holy Communion, the eucharist is a sacrament celebrated with consecrated bread and wine in commemoration of Jesus's Last Supper with his disciples.

evangelicalism This Protestant movement stresses the importance of the conversion experience, the Bible as the only reliable authority in matters of faith, and preaching the gospel. In recent decades, evangelicalism has become a major force in North American Christianity.

Exodus The escape (or departure) of Israelite slaves from Egypt as described in the Hebrew Bible (c. 1250 B.C.E.).

Family, The The revised name of the Children of God movement, led by David Berg until his death in 1994.

fangshi (fahng-shər) "Magicians" who allegedly possessed the recipe for immortality.

Five Classics The five canonical works of Confucianism designated in the Han Dynasty. They are *Book of Odes, Book of History, Book of Changes, Record of Rites,* and *Spring and Autumn Annals.*

Four Books The four texts identified by the Neo-Confucian Zhu Xi as fundamental in understanding the Confucian teaching. Between 1313 and 1905, they made up the curriculum for the civil service examination. They are *Analects, Mencius, Great Learning,* and *Doctrine of the Mean.*

Four Noble Truths The four truths that form the basis of the Dharma: Suffering is inherent in human life, suffering is caused by desire, there can be an end to desire, the way to end desire is the Noble Eightfold Path.

fravishis (frah-veesh'ees) Preexisting higher souls and guardian spirits of individual human beings.

fundamentalism Originating in the early 1900s, this movement in American Protestantism was dedicated to defending doctrines it identified as fundamental to Christianity against perceived threats posed by modern culture.

Ghost Dance Religious resistance movements in 1870 and 1890 that originated in Nevada among Paiute peoples.

globalization The linking and intermixing of cultures; any process that moves a society toward an internationalization of religious discourse.

Gospel In its most general sense, "gospel" means the "good news" (from Old English *godspel*, which translates the Greek *evangelion*) about Jesus Christ. The New Testament gospels of Matthew, Mark, Luke, and John are proclamations of the good news concerning the life, teachings, death, and resurrection of Jesus Christ.

grace Derived from the Latin *gratia* (a "gift" or "love"), "grace" refers to God's love for humanity, expressed in Jesus Christ and through the sacraments.

Great Disappointment, The Disillusionment and shock following the failure, in 1844, of William Miller's prediction of the Second Advent.

gui (gwei) Ghosts and demons, malevolent spirits.

gurdwara (goor'dwah-ruh; Punjabi, "doorway of the Guru" or "by means of the Guru's [grace]") A building for Sikh worship that houses a copy of the Adi Granth; the central structure of any Sikh community.

Guru (goo'roo; Sanskrit, "venerable person") A spiritual teacher and revealer of truth, common to Hinduism, Sikhism, and some forms of Buddhism. When the word *Guru* is capitalized, it refers to the ten historical leaders of Sikhism, to the sacred text (Sri Guru Granth Sahib, or Adi Granth), and to God (often as True Guru).

hadith (ha-deeth; Arabic) Literary tradition recording the sayings and deeds of the Prophet Muhammad.

hajj (hahj; Arabic) The annual pilgrimage to Mecca, one of the five pillars of Islam.

halacha An authoritative formulation of traditional Jewish law.

haoma Sacred drink made in ancient times from the sour, milky juice of the soma plant; in modern times from water, pomegranate, ephedra, and goat's milk.

harae (hah-rah'-ə) Shinto purification.

Hasidism A popular movement within eighteenth-century Eastern European Judaism, Hasidism stressed the need for spiritual restoration and deepened individual piety. In the course of the nineteenth and twentieth centuries the Hasidic movement spawned a number of distinctive communities that have physically separated themselves from the rest of the Jewish and non-Jewish worlds and who are often recognized by their attire and their devotion to a dynasty of hereditary spiritual leaders.

haumai (how'may; Punjabi, "self-reliance," "pride," or "egoism") The human inclination toward being self-centered rather than God-centered, which increases the distance between the individual and God.

henotheism The belief that acknowledges a plurality of gods but elevates one of them to special status.

hijra (hij-rah; Arabic) The migration of the early Muslim community from Mecca to Medina in 622 C.E.; the Islamic calendar dates from this year.

hindutva (hin-doot-vah; Sanskrit, "Hindu-ness") A modern term that encompasses the ideology of Hindu nationalism.

hogan (ho-gan; Pueblo) A sacred structure of Pueblo peoples.

Holocaust The genocidal destruction of approximately six million European Jews by the government of Nazi Germany during World War II. This mass slaughter is referred to in Hebrew as the *Shoah*.

Holy People Ancestors to the Navajo people, described in mythic narratives.

Holy Wind Navajo conception of a spiritual force that inhabits every element of creation.

hukam (huh'kahm; Punjabi, "order") The divine order of the universe.

Husayn Grandson of Muhammad who was killed while challenging the Umayyads.

icons Painted images of Christ and the saints, icons are used extensively in the Orthodox Church.

Ifa (ee-fah; Yoruba) The divination system of the Yoruba religion, believed to be revealed to humanity by the gods.

imam (ee-mam; Arabic) Prayer leader; in the Shi'a tradition, one of the leaders of the Muslim community following the death of the Prophet Muhammad.

Immanence The divine attribute of in-dwelling, or God being present to human consciousness.

Impermanence According to the Buddha's doctrine of Impermanence, all phenomena are in a constant state of change.

Inquisition The investigation and suppression of heresy by the Roman Catholic Church, the Inquisition began

in the twelfth century and was formally concluded in the middle of the nineteenth century.

Interdependent Origination (Sanskrit: *pratitya-samutpada*, "arising on the ground of a preceding cause") The doctrine that reality is a complex of interrelated and interdependent phenomena in which nothing exists independently; instead, the origination of all things depends on other things.

ISKCON The official name of the "Hare Krishna" movement founded by A. C. Bhaktivedanta Swami.

Islam (is-lahm; Arabic) Lit. "submission"; specifically, the religious tradition based on the revealed Qur'an as Word of God.

Izanagi (ee-zanah'-gee) The male *kami* who is the pro-creator of the Japanese islands.

Izanami (ee-za-nah'-mee) The female *kami* who is the procreator of the Japanese islands.

jahiliyya (ja-hil-ee-ah; Arabic) The "age of ignorance," which refers to the time before the revelation of the Qur'an.

jati (jaah-tee; Sanskrit, "birth group") One of thousands of endogamous groups or subcastes, each equal in social and ritual status.

jiao (jee'au) Daoist communal sacrificial offerings to signal cosmic renewal and collective cohesion.

jihad (jee-had; Arabic) Lit. "striving"; sometimes, the greater *jihad* is the struggle with one's self to become a better person; the lesser *jihad* is associated with military conflict in defense of the faith.

jina (ji'nuh; Sanskrit, "conqueror") Jain title for one who has "conquered" *samsara;* synonymous with *tirthankara.*

jinja (jin'-ja) Shinto shrine.

jiva (jee'vuh; Sanskrit, "soul") The finite and eternal soul; also the category of living, as opposed to non-living, entities of the universe.

jnana marga (nyah-nah mar-guh; Sanskrit) The path of knowledge.

Jump Dance Renewal dance of Yurok people.

junzi (ju'un zee) The personality ideal in Confucianism; the noble person.

Kabbalah One of the dominant forms of Jewish mysticism, kabbalistic texts begin to appear in Europe during the twelfth and thirteenth centuries. Mystics belonging to this tradition focus on the emanative powers of God—referred to in Hebrew as *Sephirot*—and on their role within the Godhead, as well as within the human personality.

kachina (ka-chee-na; Hopi) Pueblo spiritual beings.

kami (kah-mee) Shinto deity and spirit with awe-inspiring power.

karma (Sanskrit, "action") "Action" and the consequences of action; determines the nature of one's reincarnation; in Jainism, all activity is believed to involve various forms of matter that weigh down the soul (*jiva*) and thus hinder the quest for liberation.

karma marga (kur-mah mar-guh; Sanskrit) The path of ethical and ritual works, or "action."

kevala (kay'vuh-luh; shortened form of Sanskrit *kevala-jnana*, "isolated knowledge" or "absolute knowledge") The perfect and complete knowledge or omniscience that is Jain enlightenment; marks the point at which one is free from the damaging effects of karma and is liberated from *samsara*.

Khadija Muhammad's beloved first wife.

Khalsa (khal'sah; Punjabi, "pure ones") An order within Sikhism to which the majority of Sikhs belong, founded by Guru Gobind Singh in 1699.

Kinaalda (kee-nal-dah) Rite of passage for young Navajo women.

kingdom of God God's rule or dominion over the universe and human affairs. The kingdom of God is one of the primary themes in the teaching of Jesus.

Kinjiketele (kin-jee-ke-te-le) The leader of the Maji Maji rebellion in Tanganyika (today's Tanzania).

Kojiki (koh'-jee-kee) *Record of Ancient Matters*, compiled in the eighth century C.E.

kshatriya (kshut-ree-yuh; Sanskrit) A member of the warrior and administrator class of the *varna* or caste system.

kusti (koo'stee) Sacred cord that is to be worn daily by Zoroastrians who have undergone the initiatory rite of the investiture ceremony.

lama (laah-mah; Tibetan) In Tibet, a teacher of the Dharma.

li (lee) Etiquette and proper manners; rituals and holy rites.

liturgy The liturgy (from Greek, *leitourgia*, "a work of the people" in honor of God) is the basic order of worship in Christian churches. It consists of prescribed prayers, readings, and rituals.

logos In its most basic sense, the Greek *logos* means "word," but it also means "rational principle," "reason," or "divine reason." The Gospel of John uses *logos* in the sense of the "divine reason" through which God created and sustains the universe when it states that "the Word became flesh" in Jesus Christ (John 1:14).

loka (loh'kah; Sanskrit, "world") The Jain universe, often depicted as having the shape of a giant man.

Lord's Prayer A prayer attributed to Jesus, the Lord's Prayer serves as a model of prayer for Christians. Also known as the "Our Father" (since it begins with these words), its most familiar form is found in the Gospel of Matthew (6:9–13).

Lughnassadh (LOO-nus-uh) A summer harvest festival (August 2) celebrated by Wiccans, honoring the Celtic god Lugh.

Luria, Isaac A sixteenth-century mystic who settled in Safed (Israel) and gathered around him a community of disciples. Lurianic mysticism seeks to explain the mystery surrounding both the creation of the world and its redemption from sin.

Luther, Martin (1483–1546) A German monk who criticized Roman Catholic doctrines and practices in his Ninety-Five Theses (1517), Luther was the original leader and one of the seminal thinkers of the Protestant Reformation.

Mahayana (muh-haah-yaah-na; Sanskrit, "great vehicle") Also known as the "Great Vehicle," Mahayana is the form of Buddhism most prominent in China, Japan, Mongolia, Tibet, and Korea.

Maimonides A twelfth-century philosopher and rabbinic scholar whose codification of Jewish beliefs and religious practices set the standard for both in subsequent centuries.

Maji Maji (mah-jee mah-jee; Swahili) A 1905 rebellion against German colonizers in Tanganyika (today's Tanzania).

mandala (muhn-daah-la; Sanskrit "circle") Typically, a circular diagram representing the entire universe. Often used as an aid in meditation.

mantra (mun-trah; Sanskrit) A sacred sound or syllable used as a focus for meditation, as an invocation of a deity, or as a protective spell; a ritual formula recited to produce a spiritual effect.

matsuri (mah-tsu'ree) Shinto religious festival.

maya (my-yah: Sanskrit, "magic" or "illusion") In the *Vedas*, the magical power the gods used to create this world; in *Vedanta* philosophy, illusion that veils the mind.

McKay, Mabel A Pomo woman who was well known as healer and basket weaver.

Mecca The city in which Muhammad was born; place of pilgrimage for Muslims.

Medina The city to which Muhammad and his early followers migrated to escape persecution in Mecca.

medium A person who is possessed by a spirit and thus mediates between the human and spirit worlds.

Messiah In the Jewish Scriptures (Old Testament), the Hebrew "messiah" ("anointed one") refers to kings and priests, who were anointed with consecrated oil. In later Jewish literature, the Messiah is sometimes understood as a figure—in some cases, a supernatural figure—who, having been "anointed" by God, rescues the Jewish people and the world from evil. Christianity understands Jesus of Nazareth as the Messiah.

Middle Way The Buddha's principle of the path between extremes of asceticism and self-indulgence that leads to enlightenment.

miko (mee'-koh) Unmarried female Shinto shrine attendants.

mikoshi (mee-koh'-shee) Portable shrine temporarily housing a Shinto deity.

mikveh A ritual bath in which married Jewish women immerse themselves each month, after the end of their menstrual cycle and before resuming sexual relation with their husbands.

ming (see *Tianming*)

miraj (mir-aj; Arabic) Muhammad's Night Journey from Mecca to Jerusalem and from there to heaven, where he met with God.

misogi (mee-soh'-gee) Shinto ritual of purification with water.

mitzvot Literally translated, the Hebrew word *mitzvot* means "commandments," and it refers to the 613 commandments that the biblical God imparted to the Israelites in the Torah (i.e., the first five books of the Hebrew Bible).

modernization The general process through which societies transform economically, socially, and culturally to become more industrial, urban, and secular; any transformation of societies and cultures that leads to the abandonment of traditional religious values.

moksha (mohk-shah; Sanskrit, "release") Liberation, the final release from *samsara*.

monism The belief that all reality is ultimately one.

monotheism The belief in only one god.

Moonies A slang term for members of the Unification Church.

moran (mor-an; Samburu and Maasai) A young man in Samburu or Maasai culture who has been circumcised and thus has special cultural and religious duties.

Moses The legendary leader and prophet who leads the Israelite slaves out of Egypt, Moses serves as a mediator between the people of Israel and God in the Torah and is later viewed as Israel's greatest prophet. It is to Moses that God imparts the Ten Commandments and the teachings that later became the Torah.

mosque (mosk) Place of prayer, from the Arabic term "masjid."

muezzin (mu-ez-in; Arabic) The person who calls the *adhan*.

Muhammad The prophet who received the revelation of the Qur'an from God. The final prophet in a long line of prophets sent by God to humanity.

mukti (mook'tee; Punjabi, "liberation") Spiritual liberation bringing on the eternal and infinitely blissful state of being in the presence of God; sometimes the Sanskrit term *moksha* is used instead.

Mul Mantra The summary of Sikh doctrine that comprises the opening lines of the *Japji*, Guru Nanak's composition that in turn comprises the opening section of the Adi Granth.

multiculturalism The coexistence of different peoples and their cultural ways in one time and place.

mysterium tremendum and *fascinans* The contrasting feelings of awe-inspiring mystery and of overwhelming attraction that are said by Rudolf Otto to characterize the numinous experience.

mystical experience A general category of religious experience characterized in various ways, for example, as the uniting with the divine through inward contemplation or as the dissolution of the sense of individual selfhood.

myth A story or narrative, originally conveyed orally, that sets forth basic truths of a religious tradition; myths often involve events of primordial time that describe the origin of things.

Native American Church A church founded in early twentieth century based on peyote religion.

neidan (nay'-dahn) Daoist "internal" alchemy designed to attain immortality through meditation, breath control, gymnastics, diet, and massage.

neisheng waiwang (nay'-sheng' wī'-wahng) Neo-Confucian ideal of "inner sagely moral perfection and outer political skills."

New Age An umbrella term for various religious and quasi-religious practices based on a belief in the transformation of both nature and human consciousness.

New Thought A philosophical school of thought, popular in the late nineteenth century, that stressed the power of the human mind to discover the divine within nature and to control material reality.

Nicene Creed A profession of faith formulated by the Councils of Nicea (325) and Constantinople (381), the Nicene Creed articulates the Christian doctrine of the Trinity.

Nihon shoki (nee-hohn shoh-kee) *Chronicles of [the Land Where] the Sun Originates.*

nirvana (nihr-vaah-nah; Sanskrit, an "extinguishing" or "blowing out") The ultimate goal of Buddhist practice, nirvana is the extinguishing of desire and the suffering it causes.

Noble Eightfold Path The Buddha's prescription for a way of life that leads to enlightenment. Based on the principle of the Middle Way, it is also defined by eight virtues.

nontheistic Term denoting a religion that does not maintain belief in God or gods.

norito (noh-ree'-toh) Invocational prayer offered by Shinto priests to the *kami*.

No-Self The doctrine that there is no independent, eternal self or soul underlying personal existence. See also *anatman*.

Nowruz (now-rooz') Zoroastrian New Year's Day coinciding with the vernal equinox, the most popularly observed annual holy day; celebrated in varying ways throughout western Asia by people of all religious and ethnic backgrounds.

numinous experience Rudolf Otto's term for describing an encounter with "the Holy"; it is characterized by the powerful and contending forces, *mysterium tremendum* and *fascinans*.

Odu (oh-doo; Yoruba) The original prophets in Yoruba religion.

OM (oh-m; from Sanskrit letters A, U, M) The primordial sound through which the universe is manifested.

omikuji (oh'-mee-koo-jee) Paper fortunes wrapped around tree branches at shrines.

omnipotence The divine attribute of total and eternal power.

omniscience The divine attribute of total and eternal knowledge.

original sin Formulated by St. Augustine in the fourth century, the doctrine of original sin states that the sin of Adam and Eve affected all of humanity, so that all human beings are born with a sinful nature.

orisa (oh-ree-sha; Yoruba) Term for lesser deities in Yoruba religion.

Orthodox Church Also known as the Eastern Orthodox Church and the Orthodox Catholic Church, the Orthodox Church is the Eastern branch of Christianity that separated from the Western branch (the Roman Catholic Church) in 1054.

Osho Another name for the religious movement established by Rajneesh Chandra Mohan in the 1980s.

Oshun (oh-shoon; Yoruba) A Yoruba goddess.

Pali Canon Also known as the *Tripitaka* (Sanskrit, "Three Baskets"), the Pali Canon is the first canon of Buddhist texts. It consists of three "baskets" or sections of sutras.

Panth (puhnth; Punjabi, Hindi, "path") The Sikh community. In lower case, *panth* ("path") is a term applied to any number of Indian (primarily Hindu) religious traditions.

pantheism The belief that the divine reality is identical to nature or the material world.

pantheon A group of deities or spirits.

parable According to the gospels of Matthew, Mark, and Luke, Jesus made extensive use of parables—short, fictional stories that use the language and imagery of everyday life to illustrate moral and religious truths.

parinirvana (pah-ree nihr-vaah-nah; Sanskrit, "supreme release") The full entry into nirvana that occurs at the death of one who has achieved nirvana in his or her lifetime.

Paul of Tarsus A first-century apostle who founded churches throughout Asia Minor, Macedonia, and Greece. Paul was also the author of many of the letters, or epistles, found in the New Testament.

Pentecost A holiday celebrated by Christians in commemoration of the outpouring of the Holy Spirit on the disciples of Jesus as described in the second chapter of the New Testament book of Acts.

Pentecostalism A movement that emphasizes the importance of spiritual renewal and the experience of God through baptism in the Holy Spirit, Pentecostalism is a primarily Protestant movement that has become extremely popular in recent decades.

Pesach An early spring harvest festival that celebrates the liberation of the Israelites from Egypt, Pesach (better known as "Passover" in English) is celebrated for seven days in Israel and eight days in the Diaspora. The first two nights are celebrated within a family setting.

peyote Hallucinogenic cactus used in many Native American religions.

polytheism The belief in many gods.

Popol Vuh (po-pol voo; Quiché Mayan, "council book") The Quiché Mayan book of creation.

Protestant Christianity One of the three major traditions in Christianity (along with Roman Catholicism and Orthodoxy), Protestantism began in the sixteenth century as a reaction against medieval Roman Catholic doctrines and practices.

puja (poo-jah; Sanskrit, "worship") Generally, worship; usually the offering before an image of the deity of fruit, incense, or flowers.

Purana (pooh-raa-nah; Sanskrit, "ancient") A compendium of myth, usually with a sectarian emphasis.

purgatory In Roman Catholicism, purgatory is an intermediate state between earthly life and heaven in which the debt for unconfessed sin is expiated.

qi (chee) Breath, force, power, material energy.

Quanah Parker Comanche man who called for embrace of peyote religion.

Quetzalcoatl (ket-zal-ko-at'-l; Aztec) Aztec God and important culture hero in Mexico.

Qur'an (kur-an; Arabic) The holy text of Muslims; the Word of God as revealed to Muhammad.

Rahit (rah-hit'; Punjabi) The *rahit-nama*, a collection of scripture that specifies ideals of belief and conduct for members of the Khalsa and, by extension, for Sikhism generally; the current authoritative version, the *Sikh Rahit Maryada*, was approved in 1950.

Ramadan (rah-mah-dan; Arabic) The month in which Muslims must fast daily from dawn until dusk; the fast is one of the five pillars of Islam, the month in which the Qur'an is believed to have been revealed to Muhammad.

ren (rən) Human-heartedness, benevolence; the unique moral inclination of humans.

revealed ethics Truth regarding right behavior believed to be divinely established and intentionally made known to human beings.

revelation The expression of the divine will, commonly recorded in sacred texts.

rites of passage Rituals that mark the transition from one life stage or social stage to another.

rites of renewal Rituals that seek to enhance natural processes, like rain or fertility, or enhance the solidarity of a group.

ritual Formal worship practice.

Roman Catholic Church One of the three major traditions within Christianity (along with Orthodoxy and Protestantism), the Roman Catholic Church, which recognizes the primacy of the bishop of Rome, or pope, has historically been the dominant church in the West.

rosary Taking its name from the Latin *rosarium* ("garland of roses"), the rosary is a traditional form of Roman Catholic devotion in which practitioners make use of a string of beads in reciting prayers.

Rosh Hashanah The Jewish New Year, it is celebrated for two days in the fall (on the first day of the month of Tishrai) and accompanied by the blowing of a ram's horn (a *shofar*, in Hebrew). It signals the beginning of the "ten days of repentance" that culminate with Yom Kippur.

ru (rōō) Scribes and ritual performers of the Zhou period; later used exclusively to refer to Confucians.

sacraments The sacraments are rituals in which material elements such as bread, wine, water, and oil serve as visible symbols of an invisible grace conveyed to recipients.

saint A saint is a "holy person" (Latin *sanctus*). Veneration of the saints and belief in their intercession on behalf of the living is an important feature of Roman Catholic and Orthodox Christianity.

saisei-itchi (sai-sei ik'-kee) Unity of the religious and the political realms.

salat (sa-laht; Arabic) The daily prayers, which are one of the pillars of Islam.

samsara (sum-saah-ra; Sanskrit, "continuous flow") The continuing cycle of birth, death, and rebirth; also, the this-worldly realm in which the cycle recurs.

sand painting A painting made with sand used by Navajo healers to treat ailments.

Sangha (suhn-ghaah; Sanskrit, "community") The worldwide community of Buddhists. Alternatively, the order of Buddhist monks or the membership of a particular Buddhist congregation.

sannyasi (sun-nyaah-see; Sanskrit) Renouncer in the fourth stage (*ashrama*) of life.

Santeria (san-teh-ree-a; Spanish) New World religion with roots in West Africa; prominent in Cuba.

sawm (som; Arabic) The mandatory fast during the month of Ramadan; one of the pillars of Islam.

scholasticism Represented by figures such as Peter Abelard, Thomas Aquinas, and William of Ockham, scholasticism was the medieval effort to reconcile faith and reason using the philosophy of Aristotle.

Second Great Awakening An evangelical movement popular in the United States from the early nineteenth century to the 1880s.

secularization The general turning away from traditional religious authority and institutions; any tendency in modern society that devalues religious worldviews or seeks to substitute scientific theories for religious beliefs.

Seder A ritualized meal, observed on the first two nights of Pesach, that recalls the Exodus from Egypt.

seekers A popular term, current in the late nineteenth century, for individuals who cannot find spiritual satisfaction in "mainstream" religious institutions and who describe themselves as "spiritual" rather than "religious."

shahadah (sha-ha-dah; Arabic) The declaration of faith: "There is no God but God and Muhammad is the Messenger of God"; the first of the five pillars.

Shaiva (shay-vah; Sanskrit) A devotee of Shiva.

Shakta (shah-k-tah; Sanskrit) A devotee of the Great Goddess, Devi.

Shangdi (shahng'-dee) The August Lord on High of the Shang period.

shari'ah (sha-ree-ah; Arabic) Lit. "the way to the water hole"; specifically, Islamic law.

Shavuot A later spring harvest festival that is celebrated for two days and is associated with the giving of the Torah at Mt. Sinai. Along with Pesach and Sukkot, it was one of the "pilgrimage" festivals in ancient times.

shen (shən) Gods and deities; benevolent spirits.

shengren (shəng rən) (or **sheng**) The Confucian sage, the epitome of humanity.

shi (shər) Men of service; lower-ranking civil and military officials in the Zhou period.

Shi'a (shee-ah; Arabic) One of the two major branches of Islam. The Shi'a believed that 'Ali should have succeeded as leader of the Muslim community after the death of Muhammad.

shimenawa (shee-mə' nah-wa) Huge rope hung in front of the worship sanctuary of a shrine.

shintai (shin-tai) The "body" of a *kami* housed in a shrine or temporarily in a *mikoshi*.

Shinto (shin-toh) The Way of the Gods. Traditional Japanese religion that acknowledges the power of the *kami*.

shirk (sherk; Arabic) The sin of idolatry, of worshipping anything other than God, the one unforgivable sin in Islam.

shruti (shroo-tee; Sanskrit, "that which is heard") Term denoting the category of Vedic literature, accepted by orthodox Hindus as revealed truth.

shudra (shoo-druh; Sanskrit) A member of the servant class of the *varna* or caste system.

Shvetambara (shvayt-ahm'buh-ruh; Sanskrit, "those whose garment is white") The largest Jain sect, whose monks and nuns wear white robes; generally more liberal than the Digambara sect.

Siddur The prayer book that is used on weekdays and on the Sabbath.

sin The violation of God's will in thought or action.

skandhas (skuhn-dhaah; Sanskrit, "heaps" or "bundles") The five components (body, perceptions, feelings, innate tendencies, and thought) that give rise to a sense of self.

smriti (smree-tee; Sanskrit, "tradition") Term denoting the vast category of Hindu sacred texts that is not *shruti*.

Spenta Mainyu (spen'tah mine'yoo) Ahura Mazda's Holy Spirit; one of the seven *Amesha Spentas*.

stupa (stooh-puh; Sanskrit, "heap") A reliquary mound in which the relics of the Buddha or a Buddhist saint are buried and venerated.

Sufi (soof-i) A follower of the mystical tradition of Islam, **Sufism**, which focuses on the believer's personal experience of God and goal of union with God.

Sukkot A fall harvest festival that is associated with the huts (in Hebrew, *sukkot*) in which the ancient Israelites sought shelter during the Exodus. It is celebrated for seven days in Israel (eight days in the Diaspora). During that time Jews take their meals, and if possible sleep, in huts that are partly open to the sky.

Sun Dance Midsummer ritual common to many Native American religions; details vary across cultures.

Sunnah (sun-na; Arabic) Lit. "way of life" or "custom"; specifically refers to example of the life of the prophet Muhammad; important religious source for Muslims.

Sunni (soon-e; Arabic) One of the two main branches of Islam. The Sunnis believed that the Muslim community should decide on a successor to lead after the death of Muhammad.

surah (soor-ah; Arabic) Chapter of the Qur'an; there are 114 **surahs** in the Qur'an.

sutra (sooh-trah; Sanskrit, "a thread") Verses of text or scripture.

sweat lodge A structure built for ritually cleansing and purifying the body.

synagogue Jewish houses of worship. The focal point of every synagogue is the Ark, a large cabinet where scrolls of the Torah are stored.

tafsir (taf-seer; Arabic) Interpretation of or commentary on the Qur'an. There are several types of *tafsir*, which aim to explain the meaning of the Qur'an.

tallit A prayer shawl that is worn during morning prayers (traditionally by men). The fringes of this shawl represent, symbolically, the 613 *mitzvot* found in the Torah.

Talmud A multivolume work of commentary on the laws of the Torah and on the teachings of the entire Hebrew Bible, composed in two stages: the Mishnah (edited in approximately 200 C.E.) and the Gemara (edited, in its Babylonian version, around 500 C.E.). Traditionally, Jews refer to the Talmud as the "Oral Torah" and regard it as an extension of sacred scripture.

Tanakh An acronym standing for the entire Hebrew Bible: **T**orah (the first five books of the Hebrew Bible); **N**eviim (or "Prophets," which includes works of both prophecy and history); and **Kh**etuvim (or "Writings," a miscellaneous gathering of works in poetry and prose). Taken together, the twenty-four books that make up this collection constitute the core "scriptures" of Judaism.

tefillin Taken from the word for "prayer," the term *tefillin* refers to two small boxes to which leather straps are attached. Traditionally, Jewish males from the age of tefillin wear *tefillin* during weekday morning prayers. Inside each of these boxes is a miniature parchment containing biblical verses; one box is placed on the forehead and the other is placed on the left arm, signifying that the individual's mind and will are devoted to God.

temizuya (te mee' zoo-ya) Purification fountain at a shrine.

theistic Term denoting a religion that maintains belief in God or gods.

theosophy Any religious philosophy that entails communication with deceased "spiritual masters" and emphasizes the superiority of "spirit" to "matter."

Theravada (thair-ah-vaah-duh; Pali, "the Way of the Elders") The form of Buddhism that is most prominent in Sri Lanka, Cambodia, Laos, and Vietnam.

thetan A term used by Scientologists to identify the immortal self and source of creativity in the human mind.

Three Marks of Existence The Buddha's teachings on impermanence, suffering, and the nonexistence of an eternal unchanging self or soul.

Tian (teeən) The transcendent, numinous entity in ancient Chinese religion; the conscious Will that regulates the cosmos and intervenes in human affairs; conventionally translated as "Heaven."

Tianming The mandate or command of *Tian* that confers political legitimacy to the ruler; also understood by Confucians as the calling to morally improve oneself and to transform the world.

Tianshi (tee'ən shər) "Celestial Master"; reference to a Daoist salvational figure, as well as an organized movement.

tipi A typical conical structure of the tribes of the Great Plains which is often constructed with a sacred blueprint.

tirthankaras (teert-hahn'kuhr-uhs; Sanskrit, "makers of the river crossing") The Jain spiritual heroes, such as Parshva and Mahavira, who have shown the way to salvation; synonymous with *jinas*.

Torah Literally, the word *torah* means "teaching," and in its most restrictive sense it refers to the first five books of the Hebrew Bible. Less restrictively, it signifies the totality of God's revelations to the Jewish people, which includes not only the remaining books of the Hebrew Bible but also the writings contained in the Talmud.

torii (toh- ree' ee) Cross-bar gateway leading up to the Shinto shrine.

transcendence The divine attribute of being above and beyond anything human beings can know or imagine.

transtheistic Term denoting a theological perspective that acknowledges the existence of gods while denying that the gods are vital with regard to the most crucial religious issues, such as the quest for salvation.

transubstantiation According to this Roman Catholic doctrine, the bread and wine consecrated by a priest in the eucharist become the body and blood of Christ and retain only the appearance, not the substance, of bread and wine.

trickster A common figure in North American mythologies; trickster tales often teach important moral lessons.

Trinity According to the Christian doctrine of the Trinity, God is a single divine substance or essence consisting in three "persons."

Tripitaka (see Pali Canon)

two-spirit An additional gender identity in many Native North American cultures; often thought to have special spiritual powers.

Ufology Any systematized belief in extraterrestrials.

Umayyad Dynasty Controversial Muslim dynasty from 661 to 750 C.E.

umma (um-mah; Arabic) The worldwide Muslim community.

Upanishad (ooh-pah-nee-shud; Sanskrit, "sitting down near [a teacher]") A philosophical text from the later period of Vedic literature, also called *Vedanta* ("end of the *Vedas*").

upaya (ooh-paah-ya; Sanskrit, "expedient means") "Skillful Means" was developed into a form of Buddhist practice that encourages imaginatively applying wisdom to whatever circumstances one is in to assist in easing suffering or cultivating insight.

urbanization The shift of population centers from rural, agricultural settings to cities.

Vaishnava (vie-sh-na-vah; Sanskrit) A devotee of Vishnu and his *avatars*.

vaishya (vie-sh-yuh; Sanskrit) A member of the producer (farmer and merchant) class of the *varna* or caste system.

Vajrayana (vaah-jiraah-yaah-nah; Sanskrit, "Diamond Vehicle" or "Thunderbolt Vehicle") Often described as a form of *Mahayana*, *Vajrayana* is the most prominent form of Buddhism in Tibet and Nepal. It incorporates both Mahayana and tantric ideas and practices.

varna (vaar-nah; Sanskrit, "color") Caste or class; the four main classes form the basis of the traditional hierarchical organization of Hindu society.

Vedanta (veh-daan-tah; Sanskrit, "end of the *Vedas*") Synonym for *Upanishads*; prominent Hindu philosophical school.

Vedas (veh-duhs; from Sanskrit *veda*, "knowledge") Broadly, all Vedic literature; narrowly, four ancient collections (*samhitas*) of hymns and other religious material.

vision quest A ritual attempt by an individual to communicate with the spirit world.

Vodou (voo-doo; Fon and French) New World religion with roots in West Africa; prominent in Haiti and the Haitian Diaspora.

waidan (wī dahn) Daoist "external" alchemy involving refining of "pills" with herbs and minerals for ingestion so that immortality can be attained.

Wiccan Rede A traditional set of rules and ethical values cherished by Wiccans.

witchcraft A term used by Western scholars to describe the use of supernatural powers to harm others.

World's Parliament of Religions Two worldwide gatherings of religious leaders, first in Chicago in 1893, and then a larger centennial gathering, also in Chicago, in 1993.

Wovoka A Paiute man whose visions started the Ghost Dance of 1890.

wuwei (wōō way) Daoist notion of action without intention; actionless action.

wuxing (wōō shing) The five elemental phases of metal, wood, water, fire, and soil that mutually support and overcome one another.

xian (shee'ən) Daoist immortals and perfected individuals.

xiao (shee'au) Filial piety; respect and care for parents and ancestors.

xinzhai (shin jī) "Fasting of the Mind" in the *Zhuangzi*.

yang (young) Lit. the south-facing side of a mountain, representing the energy that is bright, warm, dry, and masculine.

yangsheng (young shəng) Daoist techniques of nourishing life and attaining immortality.

Yasna Seventy-two-chapter section of the *Avesta* containing material recited by priests in rituals; includes the *Gathas*. The Yasna liturgy, an important ritual, is the sacrifice of the sacred drink *haoma* before a fire.

yazatas (yah-zah'tahs; Avestan, "ones worthy of worship") A large number, eventually fixed at thirty, of deities on the side of Ahura Mazda and order/good.

YHWH These four consonants constitute the most sacred of names associated with the biblical God. The exact pronunciation of this name, according to ancient Jewish tradition, was known only to the High Priest, but after the destruction of the Second Temple the precise vocalization of these letters was lost—only to be recovered in the days of the Messiah.

yin Lit. the north-facing side of a mountain, representing the energy that is dark, cold, wet, and feminine.

yoga (yoh-gah; Sanskrit, "yoking" or "uniting") Generally, uniting of the self with God; sometimes used as an alternative to *marga* when referring to the three main paths to liberation; also (normally capitalized: Yoga) one of the six philosophical schools, focusing on moral, physical, and spiritual practices leading to liberation.

yogic flying A meditational practice, similar to levitation, attributed to members of the Transcendental Meditation community.

Yom Kippur Referred to as the "Day of Atonement," it is the most solemn of all of the fast days in the Jewish religious calendar.

zakat (za-kaht; Arabic) Regulated almsgiving; one of the five pillars of Islam.

zar (zahr; various languages) A term for spirits in East Africa.

Zarathustra (zare'ah-thoos'trah) Called Zoroaster by the ancient Greeks; ancient Iranian prophet and poet, founder of the Zoroastrian religion; dates uncertain (between 1300 and 550 B.C.E.).

Zen (see Chan/Zen)

zhai (jī) Daoist "fasts" designed to seek redemption of transgressions by the gods.

Zionism A modern political philosophy that asserts a belief in Jewish national identity and in the necessity of resuming national life within the historic land of Israel.

ziran (zee'-rahn) Daoist notion of natural spontaneity.

Zohar A kabbalistic *midrash* based on the biblical Book of Genesis (c. 1280 C.E.).

zuowang (zoh'-wahng) "Sitting and Forgetting" in the *Zhuangzi*.

CREDITS

pgs. 2–3: © Shutterstock.com/Ryan Rodrick Beiler

pg. 5: © Pictorial Press Ltd/Alamy

pg. 11: © Shutterstock.com/Hung Chung Chih

pg. 13: © Ancient Art & Architecture Collection Ltd/Alamy

pg. 14: © Shutterstock.com/AHMAD FAIZAL YAHYA

pg. 15: © Shutterstock.com/Giovanni Benintende

pg. 16: Triptych of the Creation, Adam and Eve, Creation of Eve, Expulsion from Paradise (oil on panel) (see also 346195, 346197), German School, (16th century)/Museo de San Carlos, Mexico/Bridgeman Images

pg. 18: Moses & the burning bush, 1990 (charcoal & pastel on paper), Feibusch, Hans (1898–1998)/ Private Collection/© The Estate of Hans Feibusch/Bridgeman Images

pg. 19: Meditating Buddha, Davaravati Period (stone), Thai School/Wat Phra Mahathat, Chaiya, Thailand/ Photo © Luca Tettoni/Bridgeman Images

pg. 20: © iStockphoto.com/Mike Norton

pg. 22: © Christian Kober/Robert Harding World Imagery/Corbis

pg. 25: © Heritage Images/Corbis

pgs. 30–31: 1910 by Edward S. Curtis © 2006–2008 www.old-picture.com

pg. 37: Mueso Popol Vuh, Guatemala

pg. 39: © Shutterstock.com/perlphoto

pg. 41: © iStockphoto.com/ericfoltz

pg. 42: © Shutterstock.com/Namurt

pg. 43: Photo courtesy of Lin Estes

pg. 45: © iStockphoto.com/PacoRomero

pg. 47: National Anthropological Archives, Smithsonian Institution [1659-A]

pg. 50: © Danny Lehman/Corbis

pg. 52, top: bpk, Berlin/Ethnologisches Museum, Staatliche Museen/Art Resource, NY

pg. 52, middle: © Shutterstock.com/ Jeffrey M. Frank

pg. 52, bottom: © iStockphoto.com/ ewg3D

pg. 53: Werner Forman/Art Resource, NY

pgs. 58–59: © Shutterstock.com/Steffen Foerster

pg. 65: Photo courtesy of Sammy Letoole

pg. 66: Photo courtesy of Festus Ogunbitan

pg. 68: E. E. Evans-Prtichard Morton, Chris. "Nuer homestead" Southern Sudan Project (in development). 03 Jan. 2006. Pitt Rivers Museum, southernsuddan.prm.ox.ac.uk/ details/1998.355.143.2

pg. 74: Photo courtesy of Brian Brazeal

pg. 76, top: Image copyright © The Metropolitan Museum of Art. Image source: Art Resource, NY

pg. 76, middle: Yale University Art Gallery/Art Resource, NY

pg. 76, bottom: Werner Forman/Art Resource, NY

pg. 77: SSPL/Science Museum/Art Resource, NY

pg. 78: Photo courtesy of Brian Brazeal

pg. 80: © iStockphoto.com/guenterguni

pg. 81: © Shutterstock.com/Villiers Steyn

pg. 82: © iStockphoto.com/handed

pgs. 88–89: Neale & Indra Neelameggham

pg. 91: Royal Geographical Society/ MovingHere.org

pg. 94: Image copyright © The Metropolitan Museum of Art. Image source: Art Resource, NY

pg. 95: AP Photo/Rajesh Kumar Singh

pg. 98: © Shutterstock.com/O'SHI

pg. 103: Hemis.fr/Hemis.fr

pg. 106: Photo courtesy of Jayashree Venkatesan

pg. 108: © Shutterstock.com/CHEN WS

pg. 109: Image copyright © The Metropolitan Museum of Art. Image source: Art Resource, NY

pg. 110: Nordicphotos/Alamy

pg. 112: age fotostock/SuperStock

pg. 113: age fotostock/age fotostock

pg. 115: Wikimedia Commons, http:// commons.wikimedia.org/wiki/ File:Shiva_Pashupati.jpg

pg. 116: Borromeo/Art Resource, NY

pg. 117: © Shutterstock.com/neelsky

pg. 122: AP Photo/Frank Polich

pg. 126, top: © iStockphoto.com/ VikramRaghuvanshi

pg. 126, 2nd from top: © Shutterstock .com/Igor Shikov

pg. 126, middle: © Shutterstock.com/ Mahesh Patil

pg. 126, 2nd from bottom: © Shutterstock .com/wong yu liang

pg. 126, bottom: © Shutterstock.com/ AJP

pg. 127, top: © Shutterstock.com/ Dhoxax

pg. 127, bottom: © Shutterstock.com/ Snowbelle

pg. 128, left: © Shutterstock.com/AJP

pg. 128, right: © Shutterstock.com/ Aleksandar Todorovic

pg. 130: © Shutterstock.com/ ivanovskyy

pg. 135: Philippe Michel/age fotostock

pg. 136: ZUMA Press, Inc./Alamy

pgs. 142–143: © Shutterstock.com/steve estvanik

pg. 146: Steve Vidler/Steve Vidler

pg. 147: Steve Vidler/Steve Vidler

pg. 148: Robert Harding Picture Library/Robert Harding Picture Library

pg. 154: Photo courtesy of Katherine Sei

pg. 157: © The Trustees of the British Museum/Art Resource, NY

pg. 160, left: © DeA Picture Library/Art Resource, NY

pg. 160, right: Robert Harding Picture Library/Robert Harding Picture Library

INDEX

Page numbers in *italics* indicate photographs/illustrations.

A